Abraham Lincoln

ABRAHAM LINCOLN

COMPLETE WORKS

COMPRISING HIS SPEECHES, LETTERS, STATE
PAPERS, AND MISCELLANEOUS WRITINGS

EDITED BY

JOHN G. NICOLAY
AND JOHN HAY

VOLUME ONE

NEW YORK
THE CENTURY CO.
1894

THE DE VINNE PRESS.

PREFACE

"May 30, 1893.

"*My dear Nicolay:* As you and Colonel Hay have now brought your great work to a most successful conclusion by the publication of your life of my father, I hope and request that you and he will supplement it by collecting, editing, and publishing the speeches, letters, state papers, and miscellaneous writings of my father. You and Colonel Hay have my consent and authority to obtain for yourselves such protection by copyright, or otherwise, in respect to the whole or any part of such a collection, as I might for any reason be entitled to have.   Believe me, very sincerely yours,

"ROBERT T. LINCOLN.

" JOHN G. NICOLAY."

Both in fulfilment of the request contained in the foregoing letter, and in execution of a long-cherished design, we present to the public this edition of the Complete Works of Abraham Lincoln, hoping and trusting that it will be received as a welcome addition to American historical literature.

JOHN G. NICOLAY.
JOHN HAY.

COMPLETE WORKS OF
ABRAHAM LINCOLN

VOLUME ONE

ADDRESSES AND LETTERS OF ABRAHAM LINCOLN

March 9, 1832.—ADDRESS TO THE PEOPLE OF SANGAMON COUNTY.

Fellow-citizens : Having become a candidate for the honorable office of one of your Representatives in the next General Assembly of this State, in accordance with an established custom and the principles of true Republicanism it becomes my duty to make known to you, the people whom I propose to represent, my sentiments with regard to local affairs.

Time and experience have verified to a demonstration the public utility of internal improvements. That the poorest and most thinly populated countries would be greatly benefited by the opening of good roads, and in the clearing of navigable streams within their limits, is what no person will deny. Yet it is folly to undertake works of this or any other kind without first knowing that we are able to finish them,—as half-finished work generally proves to be labor lost. There cannot justly be any objection to having railroads and canals, any more than to other good things, provided they cost nothing. The only objection is to paying for them; and the objection arises from the want of ability to pay.

With respect to the County of Sangamon, some more easy means of communication than it now possesses, for the purpose of facilitating the task of exporting the surplus products of its fertile soil, and importing necessary articles from abroad, are indispensably necessary. A meeting has been held of the citizens of Jacksonville and the adjacent country, for the purpose of deliberating and inquiring into the expediency of constructing a railroad from some eligible point on the Illinois River, through the town of Jacksonville, in Morgan County, to the town of Springfield, in Sangamon County. This is, indeed, a very desirable object. No other improvement that reason will justify us in hoping for can equal in utility the railroad. It is a never-failing source of communication between places of business remotely situated from each other. Upon the railroad the regular progress of commercial intercourse is not interrupted by either high or low water, or freezing weather, which are the principal difficulties that render our future hopes of water communication precarious and uncertain.

Yet, however desirable an object the construction of a railroad through our country may be; however high our imaginations may

VOL. I.—1.

be heated at thoughts of it,—there is always a heart-appalling shock accompanying the amount of its cost, which forces us to shrink from our pleasing anticipations.   The probable cost of this contemplated railroad is estimated at $290,000; the bare statement of which, in my opinion, is sufficient to justify the belief that the improvement of the Sangamon River is an object much better suited to our infant resources.

Respecting this view, I think I may say, without the fear of being contradicted, that its navigation may be rendered completely practicable as high as the mouth of the South Fork, or probably higher, to vessels of from twenty-five to thirty tons burden, for at least one half of all common years, and to vessels of much greater burden a part of the time.   From my peculiar circumstances, it is probable that for the last twelve months I have given as particular attention to the stage of the water in this river as any other person in the country.   In the month of March, 1831, in company with others, I commenced the building of a flatboat on the Sangamon, and finished and took her out in the course of the spring.   Since that time I have been concerned in the mill at New Salem.   These circumstances are sufficient evidence that I have not been very inattentive to the stages of the water.   The time at which we crossed the mill-dam being in the last days of April, the water was lower than it had been since the breaking of winter in February, or than it was for several weeks after.   The principal difficulties we encountered in descending the river were from the drifted timber, which obstructions all know are not difficult to be removed.   Knowing almost precisely the height of water at that time, I believe I am safe in saying that it has as often been higher as lower since.

From this view of the subject it appears that my calculations with regard to the navigation of the Sangamon cannot but be founded in reason; but, whatever may be its natural advantages, certain it is that it never can be practically useful to any great extent without being greatly improved by art.   The drifted timber, as I have before mentioned, is the most formidable barrier to this object.   Of all parts of this river, none will require so much labor in proportion to make it navigable as the last thirty or thirty-five miles; and going with the meanderings of the channel, when we are this distance above its mouth we are only between twelve and eighteen miles above Beardstown in something near a straight direction; and this route is upon such low ground as to retain water in many places during the season, and in all parts such as to draw two thirds or three fourths of the river water at all high stages.

This route is on prairie-land the whole distance, so that it appears to me, by removing the turf a sufficient width, and damming up the old channel, the whole river in a short time would wash its way through, thereby curtailing the distance and increasing the velocity of the current very considerably, while there would be no timber on the banks to obstruct its navigation in future; and being nearly straight, the timber which might float in at the head would be apt to go clear through.   There are also many places above this where the river, in its zigzag course, forms such complete peninsulas as to be easier to cut at the necks than to remove the obstructions from the bends, which, if done, would also lessen the distance.

What the cost of this work would be, I am unable to say. It is probable, however, that it would not be greater than is common to streams of the same length. Finally, I believe the improvement of the Sangamon River to be vastly important and highly desirable to the people of the county; and, if elected, any measure in the legislature having this for its object, which may appear judicious, will meet my approbation and receive my support.

It appears that the practice of loaning money at exorbitant rates of interest has already been opened as a field for discussion; so I suppose I may enter upon it without claiming the honor, or risking the danger which may await its first explorer. It seems as though we are never to have an end to this baneful and corroding system, acting almost as prejudicially to the general interests of the community as a direct tax of several thousand dollars annually laid on each county for the benefit of a few individuals only, unless there be a law made fixing the limits of usury. A law for this purpose, I am of opinion, may be made without materially injuring any class of people. In cases of extreme necessity, there could always be means found to cheat the law; while in all other cases it would have its intended effect. I would favor the passage of a law on this subject which might not be very easily evaded. Let it be such that the labor and difficulty of evading it could only be justified in cases of greatest necessity.

Upon the subject of education, not presuming to dictate any plan or system respecting it, I can only say that I view it as the most important subject which we as a people can be engaged in. That every man may receive at least a moderate education, and thereby be enabled to read the histories of his own and other countries, by which he may duly appreciate the value of our free institutions, appears to be an object of vital importance, even on this account alone, to say nothing of the advantages and satisfaction to be derived from all being able to read the Scriptures, and other works both of a religious and moral nature, for themselves.

For my part, I desire to see the time when education—and by its means, morality, sobriety, enterprise, and industry—shall become much more general than at present, and should be gratified to have it in my power to contribute something to the advancement of any measure which might have a tendency to accelerate that happy period.

With regard to existing laws, some alterations are thought to be necessary. Many respectable men have suggested that our estray laws, the law respecting the issuing of executions, the road law, and some others, are deficient in their present form, and require alterations. But, considering the great probability that the framers of those laws were wiser than myself, I should prefer not meddling with them, unless they were first attacked by others; in which case I should feel it both a privilege and a duty to take that stand which, in my view, might tend most to the advancement of justice.

But, fellow-citizens, I shall conclude. Considering the great de-

gree of modesty which should always attend youth, it is probable
I have already been more presuming than becomes me. However,
upon the subjects of which I have treated, I have spoken as I have
thought. I may be wrong in regard to any or all of them; but,
holding it a sound maxim that it is better only sometimes to be
right than at all times to be wrong, so soon as I discover my opinions to be erroneous, I shall be ready to renounce them.

Every man is said to have his peculiar ambition. Whether it be
true or not, I can say, for one, that I have no other so great as that
of being truly esteemed of my fellow-men, by rendering myself
worthy of their esteem. How far I shall succeed in gratifying this
ambition is yet to be developed. I am young, and unknown to
many of you. I was born, and have ever remained, in the most
humble walks of life. I have no wealthy or popular relations or
friends to recommend me. My case is thrown exclusively upon the
independent voters of the country; and, if elected, they will have
conferred a favor upon me for which I shall be unremitting in my
labors to compensate. But, if the good people in their wisdom
shall see fit to keep me in the background, I have been too familiar
with disappointments to be very much chagrined.

Your friend and fellow-citizen,   A. LINCOLN.

NEW SALEM, March 9, 1832.

April 28, 1832.—RECEIPT FOR ARMS.

Special Order (No.—).   BEARDSTOWN, April 28, 1832.

The Brigade Inspector, having inspected Captain Abraham Lincoln's Company and mustered them into service, reports that thirty
guns are wanting to arm the Company completely. Quartermaster-
General Edwards will furnish the Captain with that number of
arms, if to be had in his department.

JOHN J. HARDIN, Brig. Major.

By order of BRIGADIER-GENERAL SAMUEL WHITESIDE.
Commanding B. M. V. Illinois.

Received April 28, 1832, for the use of the Sangamon County
company under my command, thirty muskets, bayonets, screws, and
wipers, which I oblige myself to return upon demand.

A. LINCOLN, Captain.

Guns.		Bayonets.		Screws.		Wipers.
19	..	15	..	9	..	21
3	..	2	..	1	..	1
1	..	1	..	4	..	1
1	..	1	..	..	..	..
1	..	1	..	..	..	..
1	..	..	..	..	..	..
—		—		—		—
26		20		14		23

I CERTIFY, That *Lewis M House* volunteered and served in the Company of Mounted Volunteers under my command, in the Regiment commanded by Col. SAMUEL M. THOMPSON, in the Brigade under the command of Generals S. WHITESIDE and H. ATKINSON, called into the service of the United States by the Commander-in-Chief of the Militia of the State, for the protection of the North Western Frontier against an Invasion of the British Band of Sac and other tribes of Indians,—that he was enrolled on the *21st* day of *April* 1832, and was HONORABLY DISCHARGED on the *7 day of June* thereafter, having served *48 days*

Given under my hand, this *21st* day of *September* 1832.

A Lincoln *(sig)*

This discharge is the property of George Carpenter of Springfield Ill. being found among the papers of his father Col. John Carpenter formerly of the army

To the county commissioners court for the county of Sangamon at 15 June term 1834.

We the undersigned being appointed to view and locate a road. Beginning at Musick's ferry on Salt creek (Via) New Salem to the County line in the direction to Jacksonville. respectfully report that we have performed the duty, of view and location as required by law, And that we have made the location on ground, and believe the establishment of the ground to be necessary whose gives the courses and distances as required by law

Michael Killion
Hugh Armstrong
A. Lincoln

(Indorsement in pencil on the foregoing.)

A. Lincoln—5 days at $3.00	$15.00
John A. Kelsoe, chain bearer for 5 days at 75 cts	3.75
Robert Lloyd, 5 days at 75 cts	3.75
Hugh Armstrong, for services as axeman, 5 days at 75 cts .	3.75
A. Lincoln, for making plat and report	2.50

June 13, 1836.—ANNOUNCEMENT OF POLITICAL VIEWS.

NEW SALEM, June 13, 1836.

To the Editor of the "Journal": In your paper of last Saturday I see a communication, over the signature of "Many Voters," in which the candidates who are announced in the "Journal" are called upon to "show their hands." Agreed. Here's mine.

I go for all sharing the privileges of the government who assist in bearing its burdens. Consequently, I go for admitting all whites to the right of suffrage who pay taxes or bear arms (by no means excluding females).

If elected, I shall consider the whole people of Sangamon my constituents, as well those that oppose as those that support me.

While acting as their representative, I shall be governed by their will on all subjects upon which I have the means of knowing what their will is; and upon all others I shall do what my own judgment teaches me will best advance their interests. Whether elected or not, I go for distributing the proceeds of the sales of the public lands to the several States, to enable our State, in common with others, to dig canals and construct railroads without borrowing money and paying the interest on it.

If alive on the first Monday in November, I shall vote for Hugh L. White for President. Very respectfully,

A. LINCOLN.

June 21, 1836.—LETTER TO ROBERT ALLEN.

NEW SALEM, June 21, 1836.

Dear Colonel: I am told that during my absence last week you passed through this place, and stated publicly that you were in possession of a fact or facts which, if known to the public, would entirely destroy the prospects of N. W. Edwards and myself at the ensuing election; but that, through favor to us, you should forbear to divulge them. No one has needed favors more than I, and, generally, few have been less unwilling to accept them; but in this case favor to me would be injustice to the public, and therefore I must beg your pardon for declining it. That I once had the confidence of the people of Sangamon, is sufficiently evident; and if I have since done anything, either by design or misadventure, which if known would subject me to a forfeiture of that confidence, he that knows of that thing, and conceals it, is a traitor to his country's interest.

I find myself wholly unable to form any conjecture of what fact or facts, real or supposed, you spoke; but my opinion of your veracity will not permit me for a moment to doubt that you at least believed what you said. I am flattered with the personal regard you manifested for me; but I do hope that, on more mature reflection, you will view the public interest as a paramount consideration, and therefore determine to let the worst come. I here assure you that the candid statement of facts on your part, however low it may sink me, shall never break the tie of personal friendship between us. I wish an answer to this, and you are at liberty to publish both, if you choose. Very respectfully,

COL. ROBERT ALLEN.   A. LINCOLN.

December 13, 1836.—LETTER TO MISS MARY OWENS.

VANDALIA, December 13, 1836.

Mary : I have been sick ever since my arrival, or I should have written sooner. It is but little difference, however, as I have very little even yet to write. And more, the longer I can avoid the mortification of looking in the post-office for your letter and not finding it, the better. You see I am mad about that old letter yet. I don't like very well to risk you again. I'll try you once more, anyhow.

The new State House is not yet finished, and consequently the legislature is doing little or nothing. The governor delivered an inflammatory political message, and it is expected there will be some sparring between the parties about it as soon as the two Houses get to business. Taylor delivered up his petition for the new county to one of our members this morning. I am told he despairs of its success, on account of all the members from Morgan County opposing it. There are names enough on the petition, I think, to justify the members from our county in going for it; but if the members from Morgan oppose it, which they say they will, the chance will be bad.

Our chance to take the seat of government to Springfield is better than I expected. An internal-improvement convention was held here since we met, which recommended a loan of several millions of dollars, on the faith of the State, to construct railroads. Some of the legislature are for it, and some against it; which has the majority I cannot tell. There is great strife and struggling for the office of the United States Senator here at this time. It is probable we shall ease their pains in a few days. The opposition men have no candidate of their own, and consequently they will smile as complacently at the angry snarl of the contending Van Buren candidates and their respective friends as the Christian does at Satan's rage. You recollect that I mentioned at the outset of this letter that I had been unwell. That is the fact, though I believe I am about well now; but that, with other things I cannot account for, have conspired, and have gotten my spirits so low that I feel that I would rather be any place in the world than here. I really cannot endure the thought of staying here ten weeks. Write back as soon as you get this, and, if possible, say something that will please me, for really I have not been pleased since I left you. This letter is so dry and stupid that I am ashamed to send it, but with my present feelings I cannot do any better.

Give my best respects to Mr. and Mrs. Able and family.

Your friend,   LINCOLN.

January 27, 1837.— ADDRESS BEFORE THE YOUNG MEN'S LYCEUM
OF SPRINGFIELD, ILLINOIS.

As a subject for the remarks of the evening, "The perpetuation of
our political institutions" is selected.

In the great journal of things happening under the sun, we, the
American people, find our account running under date of the nine-
teenth century of the Christian era. We find ourselves in the peaceful possession of the fairest portion of the earth as regards extent
of territory, fertility of soil, and salubrity of climate. We find ourselves under the government of a system of political institutions
conducing more essentially to the ends of civil and religious liberty
than any of which the history of former times tells us. We, when
mounting the stage of existence, found ourselves the legal inheri-
tors of these fundamental blessings. We toiled not in the acquirement or establishment of them; they are a legacy bequeathed us by
a once hardy, brave, and patriotic, but now lamented and departed,
race of ancestors. Theirs was the task (and nobly they performed
it) to possess themselves, and through themselves us, of this goodly
land, and to uprear upon its hills and its valleys a political edifice
of liberty and equal rights; 't is ours only to transmit these—
the former unprofaned by the foot of an invader, the latter unde-
cayed by the lapse of time and untorn by usurpation—to the latest
generation that fate shall permit the world to know. This task,
gratitude to our fathers, justice to ourselves, duty to posterity, and
love for our species in general, all imperatively require us faithfully to perform.

How then shall we perform it? At what point shall we expect
the approach of danger? By what means shall we fortify against it?
Shall we expect some transatlantic military giant to step the ocean
and crush us at a blow? Never! All the armies of Europe, Asia,
and Africa combined, with all the treasure of the earth (our own
excepted) in their military chest, with a Bonaparte for a commander, could not by force take a drink from the Ohio or make a
track on the Blue Ridge in a trial of a thousand years.

At what point then is the approach of danger to be expected? I
answer, If it ever reach us it must spring up amongst us; it cannot
come from abroad. If destruction be our lot we must ourselves
be its author and finisher. As a nation of freemen we must live
through all time, or die by suicide.

I hope I am over wary; but if I am not, there is even now something of ill omen amongst us. I mean the increasing disregard
for law which pervades the country—the growing disposition to
substitute the wild and furious passions in lieu of the sober
judgment of courts, and the worse than savage mobs for the executive ministers of justice. This disposition is awfully fearful in any
community; and that it now exists in ours, though grating to our
feelings to admit, it would be a violation of truth and an insult to
our intelligence to deny. Accounts of outrages committed by mobs
form the every-day news of the times. They have pervaded the

country from New England to Louisiana; they are neither peculiar
to the eternal snows of the former nor the burning suns of the latter; they are not the creature of climate, neither are they confined
to the slaveholding or the non-slaveholding States. Alike they
spring up among the pleasure-hunting masters of Southern slaves,
and the order-loving citizens of the land of steady habits. Whatever then their cause may be, it is common to the whole country.

It would be tedious as well as useless to recount the horrors of all
of them. Those happening in the State of Mississippi and at St.
Louis are perhaps the most dangerous in example and revolting to
humanity. In the Mississippi case they first commenced by hanging
the regular gamblers—a set of men certainly not following for a
livelihood a very useful or very honest occupation, but one which,
so far from being forbidden by the laws, was actually licensed by
an act of the legislature passed but a single year before. Next,
negroes suspected of conspiring to raise an insurrection were
caught up and hanged in all parts of the State; then, white men
supposed to be leagued with the negroes; and finally, strangers
from neighboring States, going thither on business, were in many
instances subjected to the same fate. Thus went on this process of
hanging, from gamblers to negroes, from negroes to white citizens,
and from these to strangers, till dead men were seen literally dang-
ling from the boughs of trees upon every roadside, and in numbers
almost sufficient to rival the native Spanish moss of the country as
a drapery of the forest.

Turn then to that horror-striking scene at St. Louis. A single
victim only was sacrificed there. This story is very short, and is
perhaps the most highly tragic of anything of its length that has
ever been witnessed in real life. A mulatto man by the name of
McIntosh was seized in the street, dragged to the suburbs of the
city, chained to a tree, and actually burned to death; and all within
a single hour from the time he had been a freeman attending to his
own business and at peace with the world.

Such are the effects of mob law, and such are the scenes becoming
more and more frequent in this land so lately famed for love of law
and order, and the stories of which have even now grown too familiar to attract anything more than an idle remark.

But you are perhaps ready to ask, "What has this to do with the
perpetuation of our political institutions?" I answer, "It has much
to do with it." Its direct consequences are, comparatively speaking,
but a small evil, and much of its danger consists in the proneness
of our minds to regard its direct as its only consequences. Ab-
stractly considered, the hanging of the gamblers at Vicksburg was
of but little consequence. They constitute a portion of population
that is worse than useless in any community; and their death, if no
pernicious example be set by it, is never matter of reasonable regret
with any one. If they were annually swept from the stage of existence by the plague or smallpox, honest men would perhaps be
much profited by the operation. Similar too is the correct reasoning in regard to the burning of the negro at St. Louis. He had
forfeited his life by the perpetration of an outrageous murder upon

one of the most worthy and respectable citizens of the city, and had he not died as he did, he must have died by the sentence of the law in a very short time afterward. As to him alone, it was as well the way it was as it could otherwise have been. But the example in either case was fearful. When men take it in their heads to-day to hang gamblers or burn murderers, they should recollect that in the confusion usually attending such transactions they will be as likely to hang or burn some one who is neither a gambler nor a murderer as one who is, and that, acting upon the example they set, the mob of to-morrow may, and probably will, hang or burn some of them by the very same mistake. And not only so; the innocent, those who have ever set their faces against violations of law in every shape, alike with the guilty fall victims to the ravages of mob law; and thus it goes on, step by step, till all the walls erected for the defense of the persons and property of individuals are trodden down and disregarded. But all this, even, is not the full extent of the evil. By such examples, by instances of the perpetrators of such acts going unpunished, the lawless in spirit are encouraged to become lawless in practice; and having been used to no restraint but dread of punishment, they thus become absolutely unrestrained. Having ever regarded government as their deadliest bane, they make a jubilee of the suspension of its operations, and pray for nothing so much as its total annihilation. While, on the other hand, good men, men who love tranquillity, who desire to abide by the laws and enjoy their benefits, who would gladly spill their blood in the defense of their country, seeing their property destroyed, their families insulted, and their lives endangered, their persons injured, and seeing nothing in prospect that forebodes a change for the better, become tired of and disgusted with a government that offers them no protection, and are not much averse to a change in which they imagine they have nothing to lose. Thus, then, by the operation of this mobocratic spirit which all must admit is now abroad in the land, the strongest bulwark of any government, and particularly of those constituted like ours, may effectually be broken down and destroyed—I mean the attachment of the people. Whenever this effect shall be produced among us; whenever the vicious portion of population shall be permitted to gather in bands of hundreds and thousands, and burn churches, ravage and rob provision-stores, throw printing-presses into rivers, shoot editors, and hang and burn obnoxious persons at pleasure and with impunity, depend on it, this government cannot last. By such things the feelings of the best citizens will become more or less alienated from it, and thus it will be left without friends, or with too few, and those few too weak to make their friendship effectual. At such a time, and under such circumstances, men of sufficient talent and ambition will not be wanting to seize the opportunity, strike the blow, and overturn that fair fabric which for the last half century has been the fondest hope of the lovers of freedom throughout the world.

I know the American people are much attached to their government; I know they would suffer much for its sake; I know they would endure evils long and patiently before they would ever think of exchanging it for another,—yet, notwithstanding all this, if the laws be continually despised and disregarded, if their rights to be secure in their persons and property are held by no better tenure than the caprice of a mob, the alienation of their affections from the government is the natural consequence; and to that, sooner or later, it must come.

Here, then, is one point at which danger may be expected. The question recurs, "How shall we fortify against it?" The answer is simple. Let every American, every lover of liberty, every well-wisher to his posterity swear by the blood of the Revolution never to violate in the least particular the laws of the country, and never to tolerate their violation by others. As the patriots of seventy-six did to the support of the Declaration of Independence, so to the support of the Constitution and laws let every American pledge his life, his property, and his sacred honor — let every man remember that to violate the law is to trample on the blood of his father, and to tear the charter of his own and his children's liberty. Let reverence for the laws be breathed by every American mother to the lisping babe that prattles on her lap; let it be taught in schools, in seminaries, and in colleges; let it be written in primers, spelling-books, and in almanacs; let it be preached from the pulpit, proclaimed in legislative halls, and enforced in courts of justice. And, in short, let it become the political religion of the nation; and let the old and the young, the rich and the poor, the grave and the gay of all sexes and tongues and colors and conditions, sacrifice unceasingly upon its altars.

While ever a state of feeling such as this shall universally or even very generally prevail throughout the nation, vain will be every effort, and fruitless every attempt, to subvert our national freedom.

When I so pressingly urge a strict observance of all the laws, let me not be understood as saying there are no bad laws, or that grievances may not arise for the redress of which no legal provisions have been made. I mean to say no such thing. But I do mean to say that although bad laws, if they exist, should be repealed as soon as possible, still, while they continue in force, for the sake of example they should be religiously observed. So also in unprovided cases. If such arise, let proper legal provisions be made for them with the least possible delay, but till then let them, if not too intolerable, be borne with.

There is no grievance that is a fit object of redress by mob law. In any case that may arise, as, for instance, the promulgation of abolitionism, one of two positions is necessarily true — that is, the thing is right within itself, and therefore deserves the protection of all law and all good citizens, or it is wrong, and therefore proper to be prohibited by legal enactments; and in neither case is the interposition of mob law either necessary, justifiable, or excusable.

But it may be asked, "Why suppose danger to our political institutions? Have we not preserved them for more than fifty years? And why may we not for fifty times as long?"

We hope there is no sufficient reason. We hope all danger may be overcome; but to conclude that no danger may ever arise would itself be extremely dangerous. There are now, and will hereafter be, many causes, dangerous in their tendency, which have not existed heretofore, and which are not too insignificant to merit attention. That our government should have been maintained in its original form, from its establishment until now, is not much to be wondered at. It had many props to support it through that period, which now are decayed and crumbled away. Through that period it was felt by all to be an undecided experiment; now it is understood to be a successful one. Then, all that sought celebrity and fame and distinction expected to find them in the success of that experiment. Their all was staked upon it; their destiny was inseparably linked with it. Their ambition aspired to display before an admiring world a practical demonstration of the truth of a proposition which had hitherto been considered at best no better than problematical — namely, the capability of a people to govern themselves. If they succeeded they were to be immortalized; their names were to be transferred to counties, and cities, and rivers, and mountains; and to be revered and sung, toasted through all time. If they failed, they were to be called knaves, and fools, and fanatics for a fleeting hour; then to sink and be forgotten. They succeeded. The experiment is successful, and thousands have won their deathless names in making it so. But the game is caught; and I believe it is true that with the catching end the pleasures of the chase. This field of glory is harvested, and the crop is already appropriated. But new reapers will arise, and they too will seek a field. It is to deny what the history of the world tells us is true, to suppose that men of ambition and talents will not continue to spring up amongst us. And when they do, they will as naturally seek the gratification of their ruling passion as others have done before them. The question then is, Can that gratification be found in supporting and maintaining an edifice that has been erected by others? Most certainly it cannot. Many great and good men, sufficiently qualified for any task they should undertake, may ever be found whose ambition would aspire to nothing beyond a seat in Congress, a gubernatorial or a presidential chair; but such belong not to the family of the lion, or the tribe of the eagle. What! think you these places would satisfy an Alexander, a Cæsar, or a Napoleon? Never! Towering genius disdains a beaten path. It seeks regions hitherto unexplored. It sees no distinction in adding story to story upon the monuments of fame erected to the memory of others. It denies that it is glory enough to serve under any chief. It scorns to tread in the footsteps of any predecessor, however illustrious. It thirsts and burns for distinction; and if possible, it will have it, whether at the expense of emancipating slaves or enslaving freemen. Is it unreasonable, then, to expect that some man possessed of the loftiest genius, coupled with ambition sufficient to push it to its utmost stretch, will at some time spring up among us? And when such an one does, it will require the people to be united with each other, attached to the government and laws, and generally intelligent, to successfully frustrate his designs.

Distinction will be his paramount object, and although he would as willingly, perhaps more so, acquire it by doing good as harm, yet, that opportunity being past, and nothing left to be done in the way of building up, he would set boldly to the task of pulling down.

Here then is a probable case, highly dangerous, and such an one as could not have well existed heretofore.

Another reason which once was, but which, to the same extent, is now no more, has done much in maintaining our institutions thus far. I mean the powerful influence which the interesting scenes of the Revolution had upon the passions of the people as distinguished from their judgment. By this influence, the jealousy, envy, and avarice incident to our nature, and so common to a state of peace, prosperity, and conscious strength, were for the time in a great measure smothered and rendered inactive, while the deep-rooted principles of hate, and the powerful motive of revenge, instead of being turned against each other, were directed exclusively against the British nation. And thus, from the force of circumstances, the basest principles of our nature were either made to lie dormant, or to become the active agents in the advancement of the noblest of causes — that of establishing and maintaining civil and religious liberty.

But this state of feeling must fade, is fading, has faded, with the circumstances that produced it.

I do not mean to say that the scenes of the Revolution are now or ever will be entirely forgotten, but that, like everything else, they must fade upon the memory of the world, and grow more and more dim by the lapse of time. In history, we hope, they will be read of, and recounted, so long as the Bible shall be read; but even granting that they will, their influence cannot be what it heretofore has been. Even then they cannot be so universally known nor so vividly felt as they were by the generation just gone to rest. At the close of that struggle, nearly every adult male had been a participator in some of its scenes. The consequence was that of those scenes, in the form of a husband, a father, a son, or a brother, a living history was to be found in every family — a history bearing the indubitable testimonies of its own authenticity, in the limbs mangled, in the scars of wounds received, in the midst of the very scenes related — a history, too, that could be read and understood alike by all, the wise and the ignorant, the learned and the unlearned. But those histories are gone. They can be read no more forever. They were a fortress of strength; but what invading foeman could never do, the silent artillery of time has done — the leveling of its walls. They are gone. They were a forest of giant oaks; but the all-restless hurricane has swept over them, and left only here and there a lonely trunk, despoiled of its verdure, shorn of its foliage, unshading and unshaded, to murmur in a few more gentle breezes, and to combat with its mutilated limbs a few more ruder storms, then to sink and be no more.

They were pillars of the temple of liberty; and now that they have crumbled away that temple must fall unless we, their descendants, supply their places with other pillars, hewn from the solid quarry of sober reason. Passion has helped us, but can do so no more. It will in future be our enemy. Reason—cold, calculating, unimpassioned reason—must furnish all the materials for our future support and defense. Let those materials be molded into general intelligence, sound morality, and, in particular, a reverence for the Constitution and laws ;/and that we improved to the last, that we remained free to the last, that we revered his name to the last, that during his long sleep we permitted no hostile foot to pass over or desecrate his resting-place, shall be that which to learn the last trump shall awaken our Washington.

Upon these let the proud fabric of freedom rest, as the rock of its basis; and as truly as has been said of the only greater institution, " the gates of hell shall not prevail against it."

March 3, 1837.—PROTEST IN THE ILLINOIS LEGISLATURE ON THE SUBJECT OF SLAVERY.

MARCH 3, 1837.

The following protest was presented to the House, which was read and ordered to be spread on the journals, to wit:

Resolutions upon the subject of domestic slavery having passed both branches of the General Assembly at its present session, the undersigned hereby protest against the passage of the same.

They believe that the institution of slavery is founded on both injustice and bad policy, but that the promulgation of abolition doctrines tends rather to increase than abate its evils.

They believe that the Congress of the United States has no power under the Constitution to interfere with the institution of slavery in the different States.

They believe that the Congress of the United States has the power, under the Constitution, to abolish slavery in the District of Columbia, but that the power ought not to be exercised, unless at the request of the people of the District.

The difference between these opinions and those contained in the said resolutions is their reason for entering this protest.

DAN STONE,
A. LINCOLN,
Representatives from the County of Sangamon.

May 7, 1837.— LETTER TO MISS MARY OWENS.

SPRINGFIELD, May 7, 1837.

MISS MARY S. OWENS.

Friend Mary: I have commenced two letters to send you before this, both of which displeased me before I got half done, and so I tore them up. The first I thought was not serious enough, and the second was on the other extreme. I shall send this, turn out as it may.

This thing of living in Springfield is rather a dull business, after all; at least it is so to me. I am quite as lonesome here as I ever was anywhere in my life. I have been spoken to by but one woman since I have been here, and should not have been by her if she could have avoided it. I've never been to church yet, and probably shall not be soon. I stay away because I am conscious I should not know how to behave myself.

I am often thinking of what we said about your coming to live at Springfield. I am afraid you would not be satisfied. There is a great deal of flourishing about in carriages here, which it would be your doom to see without sharing it. You would have to be poor, without the means of hiding your poverty. Do you believe you could bear that patiently? Whatever woman may cast her lot with mine, should any ever do so, it is my intention to do all in my power to make her happy and contented; and there is nothing I can imagine that would make me more unhappy than to fail in the effort. I know I should be much happier with you than the way I am, provided I saw no signs of discontent in you. What you have said to me may have been in the way of jest, or I may have misunderstood it. If so, then let it be forgotten; if otherwise, I much wish you would think seriously before you decide. What I have said I will most positively abide by, provided you wish it. My opinion is that you had better not do it. You have not been accustomed to hardship, and it may be more severe than you now imagine. I know you are capable of thinking correctly on any subject, and if you deliberate maturely upon this before you decide, then I am willing to abide your decision.

You must write me a good long letter after you get this. You have nothing else to do, and though it might not seem interesting to you after you had written it, it would be a good deal of company to me in this "busy wilderness." Tell your sister I don't want to hear any more about selling out and moving. That gives me the "hypo" whenever I think of it. Yours, etc.,

LINCOLN.

August 16, 1837.—LETTER TO MISS MARY OWENS.

SPRINGFIELD, August 16, 1837.

Friend Mary: You will no doubt think it rather strange that I should write you a letter on the same day on which we parted, and I can only account for it by supposing that seeing you lately makes me think of you more than usual; while at our late meeting we had but few expressions of thoughts. You must know that I cannot see you or think of you with entire indifference; and yet it may be that you are mistaken in regard to what my real feelings toward you are. If I knew you were not, I should not trouble you with this letter. Perhaps any other man would know enough without further information; but I consider it my peculiar right to plead ignorance, and your bounden duty to allow the plea. I want in all cases to do right, and most particularly so in all cases with women. I want at this particular time, more than anything else, to do right with you; and if I knew it would be doing right, as I rather suspect it would, to let you alone, I would do it. And for the purpose of making the matter as plain as possible, I now say that you can now drop the subject, dismiss your thoughts (if you ever had any) from me forever, and leave this letter unanswered, without calling forth one accusing murmur from me.   And I will even go further, and say that if it will add anything to your comfort or peace of mind to do so, it is my sincere wish that you should.   Do not understand by this that I wish to cut your acquaintance.   I mean no such thing.   What I do wish is that our further acquaintance shall depend upon yourself.   If such further acquaintance would contribute nothing to your happiness, I am sure it would not to mine.   If you feel yourself in any degree bound to me, I am now willing to release you, provided you wish it; while, on the other hand, I am willing and even anxious to bind you faster, if I can be convinced that it will, in any considerable degree, add to your happiness. This, indeed, is the whole question with me.   Nothing would make me more miserable than to believe you miserable — nothing more happy than to know you were so.

In what I have now said, I think I cannot be misunderstood, and to make myself understood is the only object of this letter.

If it suits you best to not answer this, farewell.   A long life and a merry one attend you.   But if you conclude to write back, speak as plainly as I do.   There can be neither harm nor danger in saying to me anything you think, just in the manner you think it.

My respects to your sister.   Your friend,

LINCOLN.

April 1, 1838.—LETTER TO MRS. O. H. BROWNING.

SPRINGFIELD, April 1, 1838.

Dear Madam : Without apologizing for being egotistical, I shall make the history of so much of my life as has elapsed since I saw you the subject of this letter.   And, by the way, I now discover that in order to give a full and intelligible account of the things I have done and suffered since I saw you, I shall necessarily have to relate some that happened before.

It was, then, in the autumn of 1836 that a married lady of my acquaintance, and who was a great friend of mine, being about to pay a visit to her father and other relatives residing in Kentucky, proposed to me that on her return she would bring a sister of hers with her on condition that I would engage to become her brother-in-law with all convenient despatch.   I, of course, accepted the proposal, for you know I could not have done otherwise had I really been averse to it; but privately, between you and me, I was most confoundedly well pleased with the project.   I had seen the said sister some three years before, thought her intelligent and agreeable, and saw no good objection to plodding life through hand in hand with her.   Time passed on, the lady took her journey and in due time returned, sister in company, sure enough.   This astonished me a little, for it appeared to me that her coming so readily showed that she was a trifle too willing, but on reflection it occurred to me that

VOL. I.—2.

a basis to is withdrawn, which would be in a sound state at least one hundred millions. When one hundred millions, or more, of the circulation we now have shall be withdrawn, who can contemplate without terror the distress, ruin, bankruptcy, and beggary that must follow. The man who has purchased any article — say a horse — on credit, at one hundred dollars, when there are two hundred millions circulating in the country, if the quantity be reduced to one hundred millions by the arrival of pay-day, will find the horse but sufficient to pay half the debt; and the other half must either be paid out of his other means, and thereby become a clear loss to him, or go unpaid, and thereby become a clear loss to his creditor. What I have here said of a single case of the purchase of a horse will hold good in every case of a debt existing at the time a reduction in the quantity of money occurs, by whomsoever, and for whatsoever, it may have been contracted. It may be said that what the debtor loses the creditor gains by this operation; but on examination this will be found true only to a very limited extent. It is more generally true that all lose by it — the creditor by losing more of his debts than he gains by the increased value of those he collects; the debtor by either parting with more of his property to pay his debts than he received in contracting them, or by entirely breaking up his business, and thereby being thrown upon the world in idleness.

The general distress thus created will, to be sure, be temporary, because whatever change may occur in the quantity of money in any community, time will adjust the derangement produced; but while that adjustment is progressing, all suffer more or less, and very many lose everything that renders life desirable. Why, then, shall we suffer a severe difficulty, even though it be but temporary, unless we receive some equivalent for it ?

What I have been saying as to the effect produced by a reduction of the quantity of money relates to the whole country. I now propose to show that it would produce a peculiar and permanent hardship upon the citizens of those States and Territories in which the public lands lie. The land-offices in those States and Territories, as all know, form the great gulf by which all, or nearly all, the money in them is swallowed up. When the quantity of money shall be reduced, and consequently everything under individual control brought down in proportion, the price of those lands, being fixed by law, will remain as now. Of necessity it will follow that the produce or labor that now raises money sufficient to purchase eighty acres will then raise but sufficient to purchase forty, or perhaps not that much; and this difficulty and hardship will last as long, in some degree, as any portion of these lands shall remain undisposed of. Knowing, as I well do, the difficulty that poor people now encounter in procuring homes, I hesitate not to say that when the price of the public lands shall be doubled or trebled, or, which is the same thing, produce and labor cut down to one half or one third of their present prices, it will be little less than impossible for them to procure those homes at all.

In answer to what I have said as to the effect the subtreasury would have upon the currency, it is often urged that the money collected for revenue purposes will not lie idle in the vaults of the treasury; and, farther, that a national bank produces greater derangement in the currency, by a system of contractions and expansions, than the subtreasury would produce in any way. In reply, I need only show that experience proves the contrary of both these propositions. It is an undisputed fact that the late Bank of the United States paid the government $75,000 annually for the privilege of using the public money between the times of its collection and disbursement. Can any man suppose that the bank would have paid this sum annually for twenty years, and then offered to renew its obligations to do so, if in reality there was no time intervening between the collection and disbursement of the revenue, and consequently no privilege of using the money extended to it? Again, as to the contractions and expansions of a national bank, I need only point to the period intervening between the time that the late bank got into successful operation and that at which the government commenced war upon it, to show that during that period no such contractions or expansions took place. If, before or after that period, derangement occurred in the currency, it proves nothing. The bank could not be expected to regulate the currency, either before it got into successful operation, or after it was crippled and thrown into death convulsions, by the removal of the deposits from it, and other hostile measures of the government against it. We do not pretend that a national bank can establish and maintain a sound and uniform state of currency in the country, in spite of the National Government; but we do say that it has established and maintained such a currency, and can do so again, by the aid of that government; and we further say that no duty is more imperative on that government than the duty it owes the people of furnishing them a sound and uniform currency.

I now leave the proposition as to the effect of the subtreasury upon the currency of the country, and pass to that relative to the additional expense which must be incurred by it over that incurred by a national bank as a fiscal agent of the government. By the late national bank we had the public revenue received, safely kept, transferred, and disbursed, not only without expense, but we actually received of the bank $75,000 annually for its privileges while rendering us those services. By the subtreasury, according to the estimate of the Secretary of the Treasury, who is the warm advocate of the system (and which estimate is the lowest made by any one), the same services are to cost $60,000. Mr. Rives, who, to say the least, is equally talented and honest, estimates that these services, under the subtreasury system, cannot cost less than $600,000. For the sake of liberality, let us suppose that the estimates of the secretary and Mr. Rives are the two extremes, and that their mean is about the true estimate, and we shall then find that when to that sum is added the $75,000 which the bank paid us, the difference between the two systems, in favor of the bank and against the subtreasury, is $405,000 a year. This sum, though small when compared to the many millions annually expended by the General Government, is, when viewed by itself, very large; and much too large, when viewed in any light, to be thrown away once a year for nothing. It is sufficient to pay the pensions of more than four thousand Revolutionary soldiers, or to purchase a forty-acre tract of government land for each one of more than eight thousand poor families.

To the argument against the subtreasury, on the score of additional expense, its friends, so far as I know, attempt no answer. They choose, so far as I can learn, to treat the throwing away of $405,000 once a year as a matter entirely too small to merit their Democratic notice.

I now come to the proposition that it would be less secure than a national bank as a depository of the public money. The experience of the past, I think, proves the truth of this. And here, inasmuch as I rely chiefly upon experience to establish it, let me ask how is it that we know anything—that any event will occur, that any combination of circumstances will produce a certain result—except by the analogies of past experience? What has once happened will invariably happen again when the same circumstances which combined to produce it shall again combine in the same way. We all feel that we know that a blast of wind would extinguish the flame of the candle that stands by me. How do we know it? We have never seen this flame thus extinguished. We know it because we have seen through all our lives that a blast of wind extinguishes the flame of a candle whenever it is thrown fully upon it. Again, we all feel to know that we have to die. How? We have never died yet. We know it because we know, or at least think we know, that of all the beings, just like ourselves, who have been coming into the world for six thousand years, not one is now living who was here two hundred years ago. I repeat, then, that we know nothing of what will happen in future, but by the analogy of experience, and that the fair analogy of past experience fully proves that the subtreasury would be a less safe depository of the public money than a national bank. Examine it. By the subtreasury scheme the public money is to be kept, between the times of its collection and disbursement, by treasurers of the mint, custom-house officers, land officers, and some new officers to be appointed in the same way that those first enumerated are. Has a year passed, since the organization of the government, that numerous defalcations have not occurred among this class of officers? Look at Swartwout with his $1,200,000, Price with his $75,000, Harris with his $109,000, Hawkins with his $100,000, Linn with his $55,000, together with some twenty-five hundred lesser lights. Place the public money again in these same hands, and will it not again go the same way? Most assuredly it will. But turn to the history of the national banks in this country, and we shall there see that those banks performed the fiscal operations of the government through a period of forty years, received, safely kept, transferred, disbursed an aggregate of nearly five hundred millions of dollars; and that, in all this time, and with all that money, not one dollar, nor one cent, did the government lose by them. Place the public money again in a similar depository, and will it not again be safe. But, conclusive as the experience of fifty years is that individuals are unsafe depositories of the public money, and of forty

years that national banks are safe depositories, we are not left to
rely solely upon that experience for the truth of those propositions.
If experience were silent upon the subject, conclusive reasons could
be shown for the truth of them.

It is often urged that to say the public money will be more secure
in a national bank than in the hands of individuals, as proposed in
the subtreasury, is to say that bank directors and bank officers are
more honest than sworn officers of the government. Not so. We
insist on no such thing. We say that public officers, selected with
reference to their capacity and honesty (which, by the way, we deny
is the practice in these days), stand an equal chance, precisely, of
being capable and honest with bank officers selected by the same
rule. We further say that with however much care selections may
be made, there will be some unfaithful and dishonest in both classes.
The experience of the whole world, in all bygone times, proves this
true. The Saviour of the world chose twelve disciples, and even one
of that small number, selected by superhuman wisdom, turned out
a traitor and a devil. And it may not be improper here to add that
Judas carried the bag — was the subtreasurer of the Saviour and his
disciples. We, then, do not say — nor need we say to maintain our
proposition — that bank officers are more honest than government
officers selected by the same rule. What we do say is that the interest of the subtreasurer is against his duty, while the interest of the
bank is on the side of its duty. Take instances: A subtreasurer
has in his hands one hundred thousand dollars of public money;
his duty says, "You ought to pay this money over," but his interest
says, "You ought to run away with this sum, and be a nabob the
balance of your life." And who that knows anything of human
nature doubts that in many instances interest will prevail over duty,
and that the subtreasurer will prefer opulent knavery in a foreign
land to honest poverty at home? But how different is it with a
bank. Besides the government money deposited with it, it is doing
business upon a large capital of its own. If it proves faithful to the
government, it continues its business; if unfaithful, it forfeits its
charter, breaks up its business, and thereby loses more than all it
can make by seizing upon the government funds in its possession.
Its interest, therefore, is on the side of its duty—is to be faithful to
the government, and consequently even the dishonest amongst its
managers have no temptation to be faithless to it. Even if robber-
ies happen in the bank, the losses are borne by the bank, and the
government loses nothing. It is for this reason, then, that we say
a bank is the more secure. It is because of that admirable feature
in the bank system which places the interest and the duty of the
depository both on one side; whereas that feature can never enter
into the subtreasury system. By the latter the interest of the individuals keeping the public money will wage an eternal war with
their duty, and in very many instances must be victorious. In answer to the argument drawn from the fact that individual depositories of public money have always proved unsafe, it is urged that,
even if we had a national bank, the money has to pass through the
same individual hands that it will under the subtreasury. This is

only partially true in fact, and wholly fallacious in argument. It is only partially true in fact, because by the subtreasury bill four receivers-general are to be appointed by the President and Senate. These are new officers, and consequently it cannot be true that the money, or any portion of it, has heretofore passed through their hands. These four new officers are to be located at New York, Boston, Charleston, and St. Louis, and consequently are to be depositories of all the money collected at or near those points; so that more than three fourths of the public money will fall into the keeping of these four new officers, who did not exist as officers under the national-bank system. It is only partially true, then, that the money passes through the same hands, under a national bank, as it would do under the subtreasury. It is true that under either system individuals must be employed as collectors of the customs, receivers at the land-offices, etc., but the difference is that under the bank system the receivers of all sorts receive the money and pay it over to the bank once a week when the collections are large, and once a month when they are small; whereas by the subtreasury system individuals are not only to collect the money, but they are to keep it also, or pay it over to other individuals equally unsafe as themselves, to be by them kept until it is wanted for disbursement. It is during the time that it is thus lying idle in their hands that opportunity is afforded and temptation held out to them to embezzle and escape with it. By the bank system each collector or receiver is to deposit in bank all the money in his hands at the end of each month at most, and to send the bank certificates of deposit to the Secretary of the Treasury. Whenever that certificate of deposit fails to arrive at the proper time, the secretary knows that the officer thus failing is acting the knave; and, if he is himself disposed to do his duty, he has him immediately removed from office, and thereby cuts him off from the possibility of embezzling but little more than the receipts of a single month. But by the subtreasury system the money is to lie month after month in the hands of individuals; larger amounts are to accumulate in the hands of the receivers-general and some others, by perhaps ten to one, than ever accumulated in the hands of individuals before; yet during all this time, in relation to this great stake, the Secretary of the Treasury can comparatively know nothing. Reports, to be sure, he will have; but reports are often false, and always false when made by a knave to cloak his knavery. Long experience has shown that nothing short of an actual demand of the money will expose an adroit peculator. Ask him for reports, and he will give them to your heart's content; send agents to examine and count the money in his hands, and he will borrow of a friend, merely to be counted and then returned, a sufficient sum to make the sum square. Try what you will, it will all fail till you demand the money; then, and not till then, the truth will come.

The sum of the whole matter I take to be this: Under the bank system, while sums of money, by the law, were permitted to lie in the hands of individuals for very short periods only, many and very large defalcations occurred by those individuals. Under the subtreasury system much larger sums are to lie in the hands of individuals for much longer periods, thereby multiplying temptation in proportion as the sums are larger, and multiplying opportunity in proportion as the periods are longer to and for those individuals to embezzle and escape with the public treasure; and therefore, just in the proportion that the temptation and the opportunity are greater under the subtreasury than the bank system, will the peculations and defalcations be greater under the former than they have been under the latter. The truth of this, independent of actual experience, is but little less than self-evident. I therefore leave it.

But it is said, and truly too, that there is to be a penitentiary department to the subtreasury. This, the advocates of the system will have it, will be a "king cure-all." Before I go farther, may I not ask if the penitentiary department is not itself an admission that they expect the public money to be stolen? Why build the cage if they expect to catch no birds? But as to the question how effectual the penitentiary will be in preventing defalcations. How effectual have penitentiaries heretofore been in preventing the crimes they were established to suppress? Has not confinement in them long been the legal penalty of larceny, forgery, robbery, and many other crimes, in almost all the States? And yet are not those crimes committed weekly, daily,—nay, and even hourly,—in every one of those States? Again, the gallows has long been the penalty of murder, and yet we scarcely open a newspaper that does not relate a new case of that crime. If, then, the penitentiary has ever heretofore failed to prevent larceny, forgery, and robbery, and the gallows and halter have likewise failed to prevent murder, by what process of reasoning, I ask, is it that we are to conclude the penitentiary will hereafter prevent the stealing of the public money? But our opponents seem to think they answer the charge that the money will be stolen fully if they can show that they will bring the offenders to punishment. Not so. Will the punishment of the thief bring back the stolen money? No more so than the hanging of a murderer restores his victim to life. What is the object desired? Certainly not the greatest number of thieves we can catch, but that the money may not be stolen. If, then, any plan can be devised for depositing the public treasure where it will never be stolen, never embezzled, is not that the plan to be adopted? Turn, then, to a national bank, and you have that plan, fully and completely successful, as tested by the experience of forty years.

I have now done with the three propositions that the subtreasury would injuriously affect the currency, and would be more expensive and less secure as a depository of the public money than a national bank. How far I have succeeded in establishing their truth, is for others to judge. Omitting, for want of time, what I had intended to say as to the effect of the subtreasury to bring the public money under the more immediate control of the President than it has ever heretofore been, I now ask the audience, when Mr. Calhoun shall answer me, to hold him to the questions. Permit him not to escape them. Require him either to show that the subtreasury would not injuriously affect the currency, or that we should in some way receive an equivalent for that injurious effect. Require him either to show that the subtreasury would not be more expensive as a fiscal agent than a bank, or that we should in some way be compensated for that additional expense. And particularly require him to show that the public money would be as secure in the subtreasury as in a national bank, or that the additional insecurity would be overbalanced by some good result of the proposed change.

No one of them, in my humble judgment, will he be able to do; and I venture the prediction, and ask that it may be especially noted, that he will not attempt to answer the proposition that the subtreasury would be more expensive than a national bank as a fiscal agent of the government.

As a sweeping objection to a national bank, and consequently an argument in favor of the subtreasury as a substitute for it, it often has been urged, and doubtless will be again, that such a bank is unconstitutional. We have often heretofore shown, and therefore need not in detail do so again, that a majority of the Revolutionary patriarchs, who ever acted officially upon the question, commencing with General Washington, and embracing General Jackson, the larger number of the signers of the Declaration, and of the framers of the Constitution, who were in the Congress of 1791, have decided upon their oaths that such a bank is constitutional. We have also shown that the votes of Congress have more often been in favor of than against its constitutionality. In addition to all this, we have shown that the Supreme Court—that tribunal which the Constitution has itself established to decide constitutional questions—has solemnly decided that such a bank is constitutional. Protesting that these authorities ought to settle the question,—ought to be conclusive,—I will not urge them further now. I now propose to take a view of the question which I have not known to be taken by any one before. It is that whatever objection ever has or ever can be made to the constitutionality of a bank, will apply with equal force, in its whole length, breadth, and proportions, to the subtreasury. Our opponents say there is no express authority in the Constitution to establish a bank, and therefore, a bank is unconstitutional; but we with equal truth may say there is no express authority in the Constitution to establish a subtreasury, and therefore a subtreasury is unconstitutional. Who, then, has the advantage of this "express authority" argument? Does it not cut equally both ways? Does it not wound them as deeply and as deadly as it does us? Our position is that both are constitutional. The Constitution enumerates expressly several powers which Congress may exercise, superadded to which is a general authority "to make all laws necessary and proper" for carrying into effect all the powers vested by the Constitution in the Government of the United States. One of the express powers given Congress is "to lay and collect taxes, duties, imports, and excises; to pay the debts and provide for the common defense and general welfare of the United States." Now, Congress is expressly authorized to make all laws necessary and proper for carrying this power into execution. To carry it into execution, it is indispensably necessary to collect, safely keep, transfer, and disburse a revenue. To do this, a bank is "necessary and proper." But, say our opponents, to authorize the making of a bank, the necessity must be so great that the power just recited would be nugatory without it; and that that necessity is expressly negatived by the fact that they have got along ten whole years without such a bank. Immediately we turn on them, and say that that sort of necessity for a subtreasury does not exist, because we have got along forty whole years without one. And this time, it may be observed that we are not merely equal with them in the argument, but we beat them forty to ten, or, which is the same thing, four to one. On examination, it will be found that the absurd rule which prescribes that before we can constitutionally adopt a national bank as a fiscal agent, we must show an indispensable necessity for it, will exclude every sort of fiscal agent that the mind of man can conceive. A bank is not indispensable, because we can take the subtreasury; the subtreasury is not indispensable, because we can take the bank. The rule is too absurd to need further comment. Upon the phrase "necessary and proper" in the Constitution, it seems to me more reasonable to say that some fiscal agent is indispensably necessary; but inasmuch as no particular sort of agent is thus indispensable, because some other sort might be adopted, we are left to choose that sort of agent which may be most "proper" on grounds of expediency. But it is said the Constitution gives no power to Congress to pass acts of incorporation. Indeed! What is the passing an act of incorporation but the making of a law? Is any one wise enough to tell? The Constitution expressly gives Congress power "to pass all laws necessary and proper," etc. If, then, the passing of a bank charter be the "making a law necessary and proper," is it not clearly within the constitutional power of Congress to do so?

I now leave the bank and the subtreasury to try to answer, in a brief way, some of the arguments which on previous evenings here have been urged by Messrs. Lamborn and Douglas. Mr. Lamborn admits that "errors," as he charitably calls them, have occurred under the present and late administrations; but he insists that as great "errors" have occurred under all administrations. This we respectfully deny. We admit that errors may have occurred under all administrations; but we insist that there is no parallel between them and those of the two last. If they can show that their errors are no greater in number and magnitude than those of former times, we call off the dogs. But they can do no such thing. To be brief, I will now attempt a contrast of the "errors" of the two latter with those of former administrations, in relation to the public expenditures only. What I am now about to say as to the expenditures will be, in all cases, exclusive of payments on the national debt. By an examination of authentic public documents, consisting of the regular series of annual reports made by all the secretaries of the treasury from the establishment of the government down to the close of the year 1838, the following contrasts will be presented:

(1) The last ten years under General Jackson and Mr. Van Buren cost more money than the first twenty-seven did (including the heavy

expenses of the late British war) under Washington, Adams, Jefferson, and Madison.

(2) The last year of J. Q. Adams's administration cost, in round numbers, thirteen millions, being about one dollar to each soul in the nation; the last (1838) of Mr. Van Buren's cost forty millions, being about two dollars and fifty cents to each soul, and being larger than the expenditure of Mr. Adams in the proportion of five to two.

(3) The highest annual expenditure during the late British war—being in 1814, and while we had in actual service rising 188,000 militia, together with the whole regular army, swelling the number to greatly over 200,000, and they to be clad, fed, and transported from point to point, with great rapidity and corresponding expense, and to be furnished with arms and ammunition, and they to be transported in like manner, and at like expense—was no more in round numbers than thirty millions; whereas the annual expenditure of 1838, under Mr. Van Buren, and while we were at peace with every government in the world, was forty millions; being over the highest year of the late and very expensive war in the proportion of four to three.

(4) General Washington administered the government eight years for sixteen millions; Mr. Van Buren administered it one year (1838) for forty millions; so that Mr. Van Buren expended twice and a half as much in one year as General Washington did in eight, and being in the proportion of twenty to one; or in other words, had General Washington administered the government twenty years at the same average expense that he did for eight, he would have carried us through the whole twenty for no more money than Mr. Van Buren has expended in getting us through the single one of 1838. Other facts equally astounding might be presented from the same authentic document; but I deem the foregoing abundantly sufficient to establish the proposition that there is no parallel between the "errors" of the present and late administrations and those of former times, and that Mr. Van Buren is wholly out of the line of all precedents.

But Mr. Douglas, seeing that the enormous expenditure of 1838 has no parallel in the olden times, comes in with a long list of excuses for it. This list of excuses I will rapidly examine, and show, as I think, that the few of them which are true prove nothing, and that the majority of them are wholly untrue in fact. He first says that the expenditures of that one year were made under the appropriations of Congress—one branch of which was a Whig body. It is true that those expenditures were made under the appropriations of Congress; but it is untrue that either branch of Congress was a Whig body. The Senate had fallen into the hands of the administration more than a year before, as proven by the passage of the Expunging Resolution; and at the time those appropriations were made there were too few Whigs in that body to make a respectable struggle, in point of numbers, upon any question. This is notorious to all. The House of Representatives that voted those appropriations was the same that first assembled at the called session of September, 1838. Although it refused to pass the Subtreasury Bill, a majority of its members were elected as friends of the administra-

tion, and proved their adherence to it by the election of a Van
Buren speaker, and two Van Buren clerks. It is clear, then, that
both branches of the Congress that passed those appropriations were
in the hands of Mr. Van Buren's friends, so that the Whigs had no
power to arrest them, as Mr. Douglas would insist. And is not the
charge of extravagant expenditures equally well sustained, if shown
to have been made by a Van Buren Congress, as if shown to have
been made in any other way? A Van Buren Congress passed the
bills, and Mr. Van Buren himself approved them, and consequently
the party are wholly responsible for them.

Mr. Douglas next says that a portion of the expenditures of that
year was made for the purchase of public lands from the Indians.
Now it happens that no such purchase was made during that year.
It is true that some money was paid that year in pursuance of Indian treaties; but no more, or rather not as much as had been paid
on the same account in each of several preceding years.

Next he says that the Florida war created many millions of this
year's expenditure. This is true, and it is also true that during that
and every other year that that war has existed, it has cost three or
four times as much as it would have done under an honest and judicious administration of the government. The large sums foolishly,
not to say corruptly, thrown away in that war constitute one of the
just causes of complaint against the administration. Take a single
instance. The agents of the government in connection with that
war needed a certain steamboat; the owner proposed to sell it for
ten thousand dollars; the agents refused to give that sum, but hired
the boat at one hundred dollars per day, and kept it at that hire till
it amounted to ninety-two thousand dollars. This fact is not found
in the public reports, but depends with me, on the verbal statement
of an officer of the navy, who says he knows it to be true. That the
administration ought to be credited for the reasonable expenses of
the Florida war, we have never denied. Those reasonable charges,
we say, could not exceed one or two millions a year. Deduct such
a sum from the forty-million expenditure of 1838, and the remainder
will still be without a parallel as an annual expenditure.

Again, Mr. Douglas says that the removal of the Indians to the
country west of the Mississippi created much of the expenditure of
1838. I have examined the public documents in relation to this
matter, and find that less was paid for the removal of Indians in
that than in some former years. The whole sum expended on that account in that year did not much exceed one quarter of a million. For
this small sum, although we do not think the administration entitled
to credit, because large sums have been expended in the same way in
former years, we consent it may take one and make the most of it.

Next, Mr. Douglas says that five millions of the expenditures of
1838 consisted of the payment of the French indemnity money to
its individual claimants. I have carefully examined the public documents, and thereby find this statement to be wholly untrue. Of
the forty millions of dollars expended in 1838, I am enabled to say
positively that not one dollar consisted of payments on the French
indemnities. So much for that excuse.

Next comes the Post-office. He says that five millions were expended during that year to sustain that department. By a like examination of public documents, I find this also wholly untrue. Of the so often mentioned forty millions, not one dollar went to the Post-office. I am glad, however, that the Post-office has been referred to, because it warrants me in digressing a little to inquire how it is that that department of the government has become a charge upon the treasury, whereas under Mr. Adams and the presidents before him it not only, to use a homely phrase, cut its own fodder, but actually threw a surplus into the treasury. Although nothing of the forty millions was paid on that account in 1838, it is true that five millions are appropriated to be so expended in 1839; showing clearly that the department has become a charge upon the treasury. How has this happened? I account for it in this way. The chief expense of the Post-office Department consists of the payments of contractors for carrying the mail. Contracts for carrying the mails are by law let to the lowest bidders, after advertisement. This plan introduces competition, and insures the transportation of the mails at fair prices, so long as it is faithfully adhered to. It has ever been adhered to until Mr. Barry was made postmaster-general. When he came into office, he formed the purpose of throwing the mail contracts into the hands of his friends, to the exclusion of his opponents. To effect this, the plan of letting to the lowest bidder must be evaded, and it must be done in this way: the favorite bid less by perhaps three or four hundred per cent. than the contract could be performed for, and consequently shutting out all honest competition, became the contractor. The Postmaster-General would immediately add some slight additional duty to the contract, and under the pretense of extra allowance for extra services run the contract to double, triple, and often quadruple what honest and fair bidders had proposed to take it at. In 1834 the finances of the department had become so deranged that total concealment was no longer possible, and consequently a committee of the Senate were directed to make a thorough investigation of its affairs. Their report is found in the Senate Documents of 1833–4, Vol. V, Doc. 422; which documents may be seen at the secretary's office, and I presume elsewhere in the State. The report shows numerous cases of similar import, of one of which I give the substance. The contract for carrying the mail upon a certain route had expired, and of course was to be let again. The old contractor offered to take it for $300 a year, the mail to be transported thereon three times a week, or for $600 transported daily. One James Reeside bid $40 for three times a week, or $99 daily, and of course received the contract. On the examination of the committee, it was discovered that Reeside had received for the service on this route, which he had contracted to render for less than $100, the enormous sum of $1999! This is but a single case. Many similar ones, covering some ten or twenty pages of a large volume, are given in that report. The department was found to be insolvent to the amount of half a million, and to have been so grossly mismanaged, or rather so corruptly managed, in almost every particular, that the best friends of the Postmaster-Gen-

eral made no defense of his administration of it. They admitted
that he was wholly unqualified for that office; but still he was retained in it by the President until he resigned it voluntarily about
a year afterward. And when he resigned it, what do you think became of him? Why, he sunk into obscurity and disgrace, to be
sure, you will say. No such thing. Well, then, what did become
of him? Why, the President immediately expressed his high disapprobation of his almost unequaled incapacity and corruption by
appointing him to a foreign mission, with a salary and outfit of
$18,000 a year! The party now attempt to throw Barry off, and
to avoid the responsibility of his sins. Did not the President indorse those sins when, on the very heel of their commission, he appointed their author to the very highest and most honorable office
in his gift, and which is but a single step behind the very goal of
American political ambition?

I return to another of Mr. Douglas's excuses for the expenditures
of 1838, at the same time announcing the pleasing intelligence that
this is the last one. He says that ten millions of that year's expenditure was a contingent appropriation, to prosecute an anticipated
war with Great Britain on the Maine boundary question. Few
words will settle this. First, that the ten millions appropriated was
not made till 1839, and consequently could not have been expended
in 1838; second, although it was appropriated, it has never been expended at all. Those who heard Mr. Douglas recollect that he indulged himself in a contemptuous expression of pity for me. "Now
he's got me," thought I. But when he went on to say that five millions of the expenditure of 1838 were payments of the French indemnities, which I knew to be untrue; that five millions had been for
the Post-office, which I knew to be untrue; that ten millions had
been for the Maine boundary war, which I not only knew to be untrue, but supremely ridiculous also; and when I saw that he was
stupid enough to hope that I would permit such groundless and au-
dacious assertions to go unexposed,—I readily consented that, on
the score both of veracity and sagacity, the audience should judge
whether he or I were the more deserving of the world's contempt.

Mr. Lamborn insists that the difference between the Van Buren
party and the Whigs is that although the former sometimes err in
practice, they are always correct in principle, whereas the latter are
wrong in principle; and, better to impress this proposition, he uses
a figurative expression in these words: "The Democrats are vulnerable in the heel, but they are sound in the head and the heart." The
first branch of the figure—that is, that the Democrats are vulnerable in the heel—I admit is not merely figuratively, but literally true.
Who that looks but for a moment at their Swartwouts, their Prices,
their Harringtons, and their hundreds of others, scampering away
with the public money to Texas, to Europe, and to every spot of the
earth where a villain may hope to find refuge from justice, can at
all doubt that they are most distressingly affected in their heels with
a species of "running itch." It seems that this malady of their heels
operates on these sound-headed and honest-hearted creatures very
much like the cork leg in the comic song did on its owner: which,

when he had once got started on it, the more he tried to stop it, the more it would run away. At the hazard of wearing this point threadbare, I will relate an anecdote which seems too strikingly in point to be omitted. A witty Irish soldier, who was always boasting of his bravery when no danger was near, but who invariably retreated without orders at the first charge of an engagement, being asked by his captain why he did so, replied : "Captain, I have as brave a heart as Julius Cæsar ever had ; but, somehow or other, whenever danger approaches, my cowardly legs will run away with it." So with Mr. Lamborn's party. They take the public money into their hand for the most laudable purpose that wise heads and honest hearts can dictate ; but before they can possibly get it out again, their rascally "vulnerable heels" will run away with them.

Seriously, this proposition of Mr. Lamborn is nothing more or less than a request that his party may be tried by their professions instead of their practices. Perhaps no position that the party assumes is more liable to or more deserving of exposure than this very modest request ; and nothing but the unwarrantable length to which I have already extended these remarks forbids me now attempting to expose it. For the reason given, I pass it by.

I shall advert to but one more point. Mr. Lamborn refers to the late elections in the States, and from their results confidently predicts that every State in the Union will vote for Mr. Van Buren at the next presidential election. Address that argument to cowards and to knaves ; with the free and the brave it will effect nothing. It may be true ; if it must, let it. Many free countries have lost their liberty, and ours may lose hers ; but if she shall, be it my proudest plume, not that I was the last to desert, but that I never deserted her. I know that the great volcano at Washington, aroused and directed by the evil spirit that reigns there, is belching forth the lava of political corruption in a current broad and deep, which is sweeping with frightful velocity over the whole length and breadth of the land, bidding fair to leave unscathed no green spot or living thing ; while on its bosom are riding, like demons on the waves of hell, the imps of that evil spirit, and fiendishly taunting all those who dare resist its destroying course with the hopelessness of their effort ; and, knowing this, I cannot deny that all may be swept away. Broken by it I, too, may be ; bow to it I never will. The probability that we may fall in the struggle ought not to deter us from the support of a cause we believe to be just ; it shall not deter me. If ever I feel the soul within me elevate and expand to those dimensions not wholly unworthy of its almighty Architect, it is when I contemplate the cause of my country, deserted by all the world beside, and I standing up boldly and alone, and hurling defiance at her victorious oppressors. Here, without contemplating consequences, before high heaven and in the face of the world, I swear eternal fidelity to the just cause, as I deem it, of the land of my life, my liberty, and my love. And who that thinks with me will not fearlessly adopt the oath that I take ? Let none falter who thinks he is right, and we may succeed. But if, after all, we shall fail, be it so. We still shall have the proud consolation of saying to our consciences, and to the departed shade of our country's freedom, that the cause approved of our judgment, and adored of our hearts, in disaster, in chains, in torture, in death, we never faltered in defending.

December 23, 1839.—LETTER TO JOHN T. STUART.

SPRINGFIELD, December 23, 1839.

Dear Stuart: Dr. Henry will write you all the political news. I write this about some little matters of business. You recollect you told me you had drawn the Chicago Massack money, and sent it to the claimants. A—— hawk-billed Yankee is here besetting me at every turn I take, saying that Robert Kinzie never received the eighty dollars to which he was entitled. Can you tell anything about the matter? Again, old Mr. Wright, who lives up South Fork somewhere, is teasing me continually about some deeds which he says he left with you, but which I can find nothing of. Can you tell where they are? The legislature is in session, and has suffered the bank to forfeit its charter without benefit of clergy. There seems to be little disposition to resuscitate it.

Whenever a letter comes from you to Mrs. ——, I carry it to her, and then I see Betty; she is a tolerable nice "fellow" now. Maybe I will write again when I get more time. Your friend, as ever,

A. LINCOLN.

P. S. The Democratic giant is here, but he is not now worth talking about.   A. L.

January 1, 1840.—LETTER TO JOHN T. STUART.

SPRINGFIELD, January 1, 1840.

Dear Stuart: There is considerable disposition, on the part of both parties in the legislature, to reinstate the law bringing on the congressional elections next summer. What motive for this the Locos have, I cannot tell. The Whigs say that the canal and other public works will stop, and consequently we shall then be clear of the foreign votes, whereas by another year they may be brought in again. The Whigs of our district say that everything is in favor of holding the election next summer, except the fact of your absence, and several of them have requested me to ask your opinion on the matter. Write me immediately what you think of it.

On the other side of this sheet I send you a copy of my Land Resolutions, which passed both branches of our legislature last winter. Will you show them to Mr. Calhoun, informing him of the fact of their passage through our legislature? Mr. Calhoun suggested a similar proposition last winter; and perhaps if he finds himself backed by one of the States, he may be induced to take it up again. You will see by the resolutions that you and the others of our delegation in Congress are instructed to go for them.

[Without signature.]

January [1 ?], 1840.—CIRCULAR FROM WHIG COMMITTEE.

Confidential.

To MESSRS. ——.

Gentlemen: In obedience to a resolution of the Whig State Convention, we have appointed you the Central Whig Committee of your county. The trust confided to you will be one of watchfulness and labor; but we hope the glory of having contributed to the overthrow of the corrupt powers that now control our beloved country will be a sufficient reward for the time and labor you will devote to it. Our Whig brethren throughout the Union have met in convention, and after due deliberation and mutual concessions have elected candidates for the presidency and vice-presidency not only worthy of our cause, but worthy of the support of every true patriot who would have our country redeemed, and her institutions honestly and faithfully administered. To overthrow the trained bands that are opposed to us, whose salaried officers are ever on the watch, and whose misguided followers are ever ready to obey their smallest commands, every Whig must not only know his duty, but must firmly resolve, whatever of time and labor it may cost, boldly and faithfully to do it. Our intention is to organize the whole State, so that every Whig can be brought to the polls in the coming presidential contest. We cannot do this, however, without your co-operation; and as we do our duty, so we shall expect you to do yours. After due deliberation, the following is the plan of organization, and the duties required of each county committee:

(1) To divide their county into small districts, and to appoint in each a subcommittee, whose duty it shall be to make a perfect list of all the voters in their respective districts, and to ascertain with certainty for whom they will vote. If they meet with men who are doubtful as to the man they will support, such voters should be designated in separate lines, with the name of the man they will probably support.

(2) It will be the duty of said subcommittee to keep a constant watch on the doubtful voters, and from time to time have them talked to by those in whom they have the most confidence, and also to place in their hands such documents as will enlighten and influence them.

(3) It will also be their duty to report to you, at least once a month, the progress they are making, and on election days see that every Whig is brought to the polls.

(4) The subcommittees should be appointed immediately; and by the last of April, at least, they should make their first report.

(5) On the first of each month hereafter we shall expect to hear from you. After the first report of your subcommittees, unless there should be found a great many doubtful voters, you can tell pretty accurately the manner in which your county will vote. In each of your letters to us, you will state the number of certain votes both for and against us, as well as the number of doubtful votes, with your opinion of the manner in which they will be cast.

(6) When we have heard from all the counties, we shall be able to tell with similar accuracy the political complexion of the State. This information will be forwarded to you as soon as received.

(7) Inclosed is a prospectus for a newspaper to be continued until after the presidential election. It will be superintended by ourselves, and every Whig in the State must take it. It will be published so low that every one can afford it. You must raise a fund and forward us for extra copies,—every county ought to send fifty or one hundred dollars,—and the copies will be forwarded to you for distribution among our political opponents. The paper will be devoted exclusively to the great cause in which we are engaged. Procure subscriptions, and forward them to us immediately.

(8) Immediately after any election in your county, you must inform us of its results; and as early as possible after any general election we will give you the like information.

(9) A senator in Congress is to be elected by our next legislature. Let no local interests divide you; but select candidates that can succeed.

(10) Our plan of operations will of course be concealed from every one except our good friends who of right ought to know them.

Trusting much in our good cause, the strength of our candidates, and the determination of the Whigs everywhere to do their duty, we go to the work of organization in this State confident of success. We have the numbers, and if properly organized and exerted, with the gallant Harrison at our head, we shall meet our foes and conquer them in all parts of the Union.

Address your letters to Dr. A. G. Henry, R. F. Barrett, A. Lincoln, E. D. Baker, J. F. Speed.

January 20, 1840.—LETTER TO JOHN T. STUART.

SPRINGFIELD, January 20, 1840.

Dear Stuart: Yours of the 5th instant is received. It is the first from you for a great while. You wish the news from here. The legislature is in session yet, but has done nothing of importance. The following is my guess as to what will be done. The internal improvement system will be put down in a lump without benefit of clergy. The bank will be resuscitated with some trifling modifications. Whether the canal will go ahead or stop is very doubtful. Whether the State House will go ahead depends upon the laws already in force. A proposition made in the House to-day, to throw off to the Territory of Wisconsin about fourteen of our northern counties, decided: ayes, eleven; noes, seventy. Be sure to send me as many copies of the "Life of Harrison" as you can spare from other uses. Be very sure to procure and send me the "Senate Journal" of New York of September, 1814. I have a newspaper article which says that that document proves that Van Buren voted against raising troops in the last war. And, in general, send me everything you think will be a good "war-club."

The nomination of Harrison takes first-rate. You know I am

never sanguine; but I believe we will carry the State. The chance for doing so appears to me twenty-five per cent. better than it did for you to beat Douglas. A great many of the grocery sort of Van Buren men, as formerly, are out for Harrison. Our Irish blacksmith, Gregory, is for Harrison. I believe I may say that all our friends think the chance of carrying the State very good. You have heard that the Whigs and Locos had a political discussion shortly after the meeting of the legislature. Well, I made a big speech which is in progress of printing in pamphlet form. To enlighten you and the rest of the world, I shall send you a copy when it is finished. I can't think of anything else now.

Your friend, as ever,   A. LINCOLN.

January 21, 1840.—LETTER TO JOHN T. STUART.

SPRINGFIELD, January 21, 1840.

Dear Stuart: A bill bringing on the congressional elections in this State next summer has passed the House of Representatives this minute. As I think it will also pass the Senate, I take the earliest moment to advise you of it. I do not think any one of our political friends wishes to push you off the track. Anticipating the introduction of this bill, I wrote you for your feelings on the subject several weeks since, but have received no answer. It may be that my letter miscarried; if so, will you, on the receipt of this, write me what you think and feel about the matter? Nothing new except I believe I have got our Truett debt secured. I have Truett's note at twelve months, with his brother Myers as security.

Your friend, as ever,   A. LINCOLN.

March 1, 1840.—LETTER TO JOHN T. STUART.

SPRINGFIELD, March 1, 1840.

Dear Stuart: I have never seen the prospects of our party so bright in these parts as they are now. We shall carry this county by a larger majority than we did in 1836, when you ran against May. I do not think my prospects individually are very flattering, for I think it probable I shall not be permitted to be a candidate; but the party ticket will succeed triumphantly. Subscriptions to the "Old Soldier" pour in without abatement. This morning I took from the post-office a letter from Dubois inclosing the names of sixty subscribers; and on carrying it to Francis, I found he had received one hundred and forty more from other quarters by the same day's mail. That is but an average specimen of every day's receipts. Yesterday Douglas, having chosen to consider himself insulted by something in the "Journal," undertook to cane Francis in the street. Francis caught him by the hair and jammed him back against a market-cart, where the matter ended by Francis being pulled away from him. The whole affair was so ludicrous that Francis and everybody else (Douglas excepted) have been laughing about it ever since.

I send you the names of some of the Van Buren men who have come out for Harrison about town, and suggest that you send them some documents: Moses Coffman (he let us appoint him a delegate yesterday), Aaron Coffman, George Gregory, H. M. Briggs, ——Johnson (at Birchall's book-store), Michael Glynn, —— Armstrong (not Hosea, nor Hugh, but a carpenter), Thomas Hunter, Moses Pilcher (he was always a Whig, and deserves attention), Matthew Crowder, Jr., Greenberry Smith, John Fagan, George Fagan, William Fagan (these three fell out with us about Early, and are doubtful now), John Cartmel, Noah Rickard, John Rickard, Walter Marsh (the foregoing should be addressed at Springfield). Also send some to Solomon Miller and John Auth at Saulsbury; also to Charles Harper, Samuel Harper, and B. C. Harper; and T. J. Scroggins, John Scroggins, at Pulaski, Logan County.

Speed says he wrote you what Jo. Smith said about you as he passed here. We will procure the names of some of his people here and send them to you before long. Speed also says you must not fail to send us the New York journal he wrote for some time since. Evan Butler is jealous that you never send your compliments to him. You must not neglect him next time.

Your friend, as ever,　　　A. LINCOLN.

March 26, 1840.—LETTER TO JOHN T. STUART.

SPRINGFIELD, March 26, 1840.

Dear Stuart: In relation to the Kinzie matter, I can say no more than this, that the check was taken from the bank by you, and on the same day you made a note in our memorandum-book stating you had sent it by mail to Kinzie; but there is no memorandum concerning it at Irwin's. Kinzie has ceased writing about it, and consequently I have some hope that he has received it.

We have had a convention for nominating candidates in this county. Baker was put on the track for the Senate, and Bradford, Brown of the Island Grove, Josiah Francis, Darneille, and I for the House. Ninian was very much hurt at not being nominated, but he has become tolerably well reconciled. I was much, very much, wounded myself at his being left out. The fact is, the country delegates made the nominations as they pleased; and they pleased to make them all from the country, except Baker and me, whom they supposed necessary to make stump speeches. Old Colonel Elkin is nominated for sheriff. That's right.

The Locos have no candidates on the track yet except Dick Taylor for the Senate. Last Saturday he made a speech, and May answered him. The way May let the wind out of him was a perfect wonder. The court-room was very full, and neither you nor I ever saw a crowd in this county so near all on one side, and all feeling so good, before. You will see a short account of it in the "Journal."

LINCOLN.

Japh Bell has come out for Harrison. Ain't that a caution?

October 31, 1840.—LETTER TO W. G. ANDERSON.

LAWRENCEVILLE, October 31, 1840.

W. G. ANDERSON.

Dear Sir: Your note of yesterday is received. In the difficulty between us of which you speak, you say you think I was the aggressor. I do not think I was. You say my "words imported insult." I meant them as a fair set-off to your own statements, and not otherwise; and in that light alone I now wish you to understand them. You ask for my present "feelings on the subject." I entertain no unkind feelings to you, and none of any sort upon the subject, except a sincere regret that I permitted myself to get into such an altercation. Yours, etc.,

A. LINCOLN.

November 28, 1840.—RESOLUTION IN THE ILLINOIS LEGISLATURE.

In the Illinois House of Representatives, November 28, 1840, Mr. Lincoln offered the following:

Resolved, That so much of the governor's message as relates to fraudulent voting, and other fraudulent practices at elections, be referred to the Committee on Elections, with instructions to said committee to prepare and report to the House a bill for such an act as may in their judgment afford the greatest possible protection of the elective franchise against all frauds of all sorts whatever.

December 4, 1840.—REMARKS IN THE ILLINOIS LEGISLATURE.

In the House of Representatives, Illinois, December 4, 1840, on presentation of a report respecting petition of H. N. Purple, claiming the seat of Mr. Phelps from Peoria, Mr. Lincoln moved that the House resolve itself into Committee of the Whole on the question, and take it up immediately. Mr. Lincoln considered the question of the highest importance, whether an individual had a right to sit in this House or not. The course he should propose would be to take up the evidence and decide upon the facts *seriatim.*

Mr. Drummond wanted time; they could not decide in the heat of debate, etc.

Mr. Lincoln thought that the question had better be gone into now. In courts of law jurors were required to decide on evidence, without previous study or examination. They were required to know nothing of the subject until the evidence was laid before them for their immediate decision. He thought that the heat of party would be augmented by delay.

The Speaker called Mr. Lincoln to order as being irrelevant; no mention had been made of party heat.

Mr. Drummond said he had only spoken of debate.

Mr. Lincoln asked what caused the heat, if it was not party? Mr. Lincoln concluded by urging that the question would be decided now better than hereafter, and he thought with less heat and excitement.

(Further debate, in which Lincoln participated.)

December 4, 1840.—REMARKS IN THE ILLINOIS LEGISLATURE.

In the Illinois House of Representatives, December 4, 1840,—House in Committee of the Whole on the bill providing for payment of interest on the State debt,—Mr. Lincoln moved to strike out the body and amendments of the bill, and insert in lieu thereof an amendment which in substance was that the governor be authorized to issue bonds for the payment of the interest; that these be called "interest bonds"; that the taxes accruing on Congress lands as they become taxable be irrevocably set aside and devoted as a fund to the payment of the interest bonds. Mr. Lincoln went into the reasons which appeared to him to render this plan preferable to that of hypothecating the State bonds. By this course we could get along till the next meeting of the legislature, which was of great importance. To the objection which might be urged that these interest bonds could not be cashed, he replied that if our other bonds could, much more could these, which offered a perfect security, a fund being irrevocably set aside to provide for their redemption. To another objection that we should be paying compound interest, he would reply that the rapid growth and increase of our resources was in so great a ratio as to outstrip the difficulty; that his object was to do the best that could be done in the present emergency. All agreed that the faith of the State must be preserved; this plan appeared to him preferable to a hypothecation of bonds, which would have to be redeemed and the interest paid. How this was to be done, he could not see; therefore he had, after turning the matter over in every way, devised this measure, which would carry us on till the next legislature.

(Mr. Lincoln spoke at some length, advocating his measure.)

Lincoln advocated his measure, December 11, 1840.

December 12, 1840, he had thought some permanent provision ought to be made for the bonds to be hypothecated, but was satisfied taxation and revenue could not be connected with it now.

December 17, 1840.—LETTER TO JOHN T. STUART.

SPRINGFIELD, December 17, 1840.

Dear Stuart: McRoberts was elected senator yesterday. The vote stood: McRoberts, seventy-seven; Cyrus Edwards, fifty; E. D. Baker, one; absent, three. This affair of appointment to office is very annoying—more so to you than to me, doubtless. I am, as you know, opposed to removals to make places for our friends. Bearing this in mind, I express my preference in a few cases, as follows: For marshal, first, John Dawson; second, Dr. B. F. Edwards. For postmaster here, Dr. Henry; Carlinville, Joseph C. Howell. There is no question of the propriety of removing the postmaster at Carlinville. I have been told by so many different persons as to preclude all doubt of its truth, that he boldly refused to deliver from his office during the canvass all documents franked by Whig members of Congress.

Yours,   LINCOLN.

January 23, 1841.—REMARKS IN THE ILLINOIS LEGISLATURE.

In the Illinois House of Representatives, January 23, 1841, while discussing the continuation of the Illinois and Michigan Canal, Mr. Moore was afraid the holders of the "scrip" would lose.

Mr. Napier thought there was no danger of that; and

Mr. Lincoln said he had not examined to see what amount of scrip would probably be needed. The principal point in his mind was this, that nobody was obliged to take these certificates. It is altogether voluntary on their part, and if they apprehend it will fall on their hands, they will not take it. Further, the loss, if any there be, will fall on the citizens of that section of the country. This scrip is not going to circulate over an extensive range of country, but will be confined chiefly to the vicinity of the canal. Now, we find the representatives of that section of the country are all in favor of the bill. When we propose to protect their interests, they say to us: Leave us to take care of ourselves; we are willing to run the risk. And this is reasonable; we must suppose they are competent to protect their own interests, and it is only fair to let them do it.

January 23, 1841.—LETTER TO JOHN T. STUART.

SPRINGFIELD, ILLINOIS, January 23, 1841.

Dear Stuart: Yours of the 3d instant is received, and I proceed to answer it as well as I can, though from the deplorable state of my mind at this time, I fear I shall give you but little satisfaction. About the matter of the congressional election, I can only tell you that there is a bill now before the Senate adopting the general ticket system; but whether the party have fully determined on its adoption is yet uncertain. There is no sign of opposition to you among our friends, and none that I can learn among our enemies; though of course there will be if the general ticket be adopted. The "Chicago American," "Peoria Register," and "Sangamon Journal" have already hoisted your flag upon their own responsibility, and the other Whig papers of the district are expected to follow immediately. On last evening there was a meeting of our friends at Butler's, and I submitted the question to them, and found them unanimously in favor of having you announced as a candidate. A few of us this morning, however, concluded that as you were already being announced in the papers, we would delay announcing you, as by your own authority, for a week or two. We thought that to appear too keen about it might spur our opponents on about their general ticket project. Upon the whole, I think I may say with certainty that your reëlection is sure, if it be in the power of the Whigs to make it so.

For not giving you a general summary of news, you must pardon me; it is not in my power to do so. I am now the most miserable man living. If what I feel were equally distributed to the whole human family, there would not be one cheerful face on the earth. Whether I shall ever be better, I cannot tell; I awfully forebode I shall not. To remain as I am is impossible; I must die or be better, it appears to me. The matter you speak of on my account you may attend to as you say, unless you shall hear of my condition forbidding it. I say this because I fear I shall be unable to attend to any business here, and a change of scene might help me. If I could be myself, I would rather remain at home with Judge Logan. I can write no more. Your friend, as ever,

A. LINCOLN.

February [8?,] 1841.—CIRCULAR FROM WHIG COMMITTEE.

Appeal to the People of the State of Illinois.

Fellow-citizens: When the General Assembly, now about adjourning, assembled in November last, from the bankrupt state of the public treasury, the pecuniary embarrassments prevailing in every department of society, the dilapidated state of the public works, and the impending danger of the degradation of the State, you had a right to expect that your representatives would lose no time in devising and adopting measures to avert threatened calamities, alleviate the distresses of the people, and allay the fearful apprehensions in regard to the future prosperity of the State. It was not expected by you that the spirit of party would take the lead in the councils of the State, and make every interest bend to its demands. Nor was it expected that any party would assume to itself the entire control of legislation, and convert the means and offices of the State, and the substance of the people, into aliment for party subsistence. Neither could it have been expected by you that party spirit, however strong its desires and unreasonable its demands, would have passed the sanctuary of the Constitution, and entered with its unhallowed and hideous form into the formation of the judiciary system.

At the early period of the session, measures were adopted by the dominant party to take possession of the State, to fill all public offices with party men, and make every measure affecting the interests of the people and the credit of the State operate in furtherance of their party views. The merits of men and measures therefore became the subject of discussion in caucus, instead of the halls of legislation, and decisions there made by a minority of the legislature have been executed and carried into effect by the force of party discipline, without any regard whatever to the rights of the people or the interests of the State. The Supreme Court of the State was organized, and judges appointed, according to the provisions of the Constitution, in 1824. The people have never complained of the organization of that court; no attempt has ever before been made to change that department. Respect for public opinion, and regard for the rights and liberties of the people, have hitherto restrained the spirit of party from attacks upon the independence and integrity of the judiciary. The same judges have continued in office since 1824; their decisions have not been the subject of complaint among the people; the integrity and honesty of the court have not been questioned, and it has never been supposed that the court has ever permitted party prejudice or party considerations to operate upon their decisions. The court was made to consist of four judges, and by the Constitution two form a quorum for the transaction of business. With this tribunal, thus constituted, the people have been satisfied for near sixteen years. The same law which organized the Supreme Court in 1824 also established and organized circuit courts to be held in each county in the State, and five circuit judges were appointed to hold those courts. In 1826 the legislature abolished these circuit courts, repealed the judges out of office, and required the judges of the Supreme Court to hold the circuit courts. The reasons assigned for this change were, first, that the business of the country could be better attended to by the four judges of the Supreme Court than by the two sets of judges; and, second, the state of the public treasury forbade the employment of unnecessary officers. In 1828 a circuit was established north of the Illinois River, in order to meet the wants of the people, and a circuit judge was appointed to hold the courts in that circuit.

In 1834 the circuit-court system was again established throughout the State, circuit judges appointed to hold the courts, and the judges of the Supreme Court were relieved from the performance of circuit-court duties. The change was recommended by the then acting governor of the State, General W. L. D. Ewing, in the following terms:

The augmented population of the State, the multiplied number of organized counties, as well as the increase of business in all, has long since convinced every one conversant with this department of our government of the indispensable necessity of an alteration in our judiciary system, and the subject is therefore recommended to the earnest patriotic consideration of the legislature. The present system has never been exempt from serious and weighty objections. The idea of appealing from the circuit court to the same judges in the Supreme Court is recommended by little hopes of redress to the injured party below. The duties of the circuit, too, it may be added, consume one half of the year, leaving a small and inadequate portion of time (when that required for domestic purposes is deducted) to erect, in the decisions of the Supreme Court, a judicial monument of legal learning and research, which the talent and ability of the court might otherwise be entirely competent to.

With this organization of circuit courts the people have never complained. The only complaints which we have heard have come from circuits which were so large that the judges could not dispose of the business, and the circuits in which Judges Pearson and Ralston lately presided.

Whilst the honor and credit of the State demanded legislation upon the subject of the public debt, the canal, the unfinished public works, and the embarrassments of the people, the judiciary stood upon a basis which required no change—no legislative action. Yet the party in power, neglecting every interest requiring legislative action, and wholly disregarding the rights, wishes, and interests of the people, has, for the unholy purpose of providing places for its partizans and supplying them with large salaries, disorganized that department of the government. Provision is made for the election of five party judges of the Supreme Court, the proscription of four circuit judges, and the appointment of party clerks in more than half the counties of the State. Men professing respect for public opinion, and acknowledged to be leaders of the party, have avowed in the halls of legislation that the change in the judiciary was intended to produce political results favorable to their party and party friends. The immutable principles of justice are to make way for party interests, and the bonds of social order are to be rent in twain, in order that a desperate faction may be sustained at the expense of the people. The change proposed in the judiciary was supported upon grounds so destructive to the institutions of the country, and so entirely at war with the rights and liberties of the people, that the party could not secure entire unanimity in its support,—three Democrats of the Senate and five of the House voting against the measure. They were unwilling to see the temples of justice and the seats of independent judges occupied by the tools of faction. The declarations of the party leaders, the selection of party men for judges, and the total disregard for the public will in the adoption of the measure, prove conclusively that the object has been not reform, but destruction; not the advancement of the highest interests of the State, but the predominance of party.

We cannot in this manner undertake to point out all the objections to this party measure; we present you with those stated by the Council of Revision upon returning the bill, and we ask for them a candid consideration.

Believing that the independence of the judiciary has been destroyed, that hereafter our courts will be independent of the people, and entirely dependent upon the legislature; that our rights of property and liberty of conscience can no longer be regarded as safe from the encroachments of unconstitutional legislation; and knowing of no other remedy which can be adopted consistently with the peace and good order of society, we call upon you to avail yourselves of the opportunity afforded, and, at the next general election, vote for a convention of the people.

S. H. LITTLE,
E. D. BAKER,
J. J. HARDIN,   *Committee on behalf of the*
E. B. WEBB,   *Whig members of the Legislature.*
A. LINCOLN,
J. GILLESPIE,

February 26, 1841.—EXTRACT FROM A PROTEST IN THE ILLINOIS LEGISLATURE AGAINST THE REORGANIZATION OF THE JUDICIARY.

For the reason thus presented, and for others no less apparent, the undersigned cannot assent to the passage of the bill, or permit it to become a law, without this evidence of their disapprobation; and they now protest against the reorganization of the judiciary, because—(1) It violates the great principles of free government by subjecting the judiciary to the legislature. (2) It is a fatal blow at the independence of the judges and the constitutional term of their office. (3) It is a measure not asked for, or wished for, by the people. (4) It will greatly increase the expense of our courts, or else greatly diminish their utility. (5) It will give our courts a political and partizan character, thereby impairing public confidence in their decisions. (6) It will impair our standing with other States and the world. (7) It is a party measure for party purposes, from which no practical good to the people can possibly arise, but which may be the source of immeasurable evils.

The undersigned are well aware that this protest will be altogether unavailing with the majority of this body. The blow has already fallen, and we are compelled to stand by, the mournful spectators of the ruin it will cause.

Signed by 35 members, among whom was Abraham Lincoln.

June 19, 1841.—LETTER TO JOSHUA F. SPEED.

SPRINGFIELD, June 19, 1841.

Dear Speed: We have had the highest state of excitement here for a week past that our community has ever witnessed; and although the public feeling is somewhat allayed, the curious affair which aroused it is very far from being even yet cleared of mystery. It would take a quire of paper to give you anything like a full account of it, and I therefore only propose a brief outline. The chief personages in the drama are Archibald Fisher, supposed to be murdered, and Archibald Trailor, Henry Trailor, and William Trailor, supposed to have murdered him. The three Trailors are brothers: the first, Arch., as you know, lives in town; the second, Henry, in Clary's Grove; and the third, William, in Warren County; and Fisher, the supposed murdered, being without a family, had made his home with William. On Saturday evening, being the 29th of May, Fisher and William came to Henry's in a one-horse dearborn, and there stayed over Sunday; and on Monday all three came to Springfield (Henry on horseback), and joined Archibald at Myers's, the Dutch carpenter. That evening at supper Fisher was missing, and so next morning some ineffectual search was made for him; and on Tuesday, at one o'clock P. M., William and Henry started home without him. In a day or two Henry and one or two of his Clary-Grove neighbors came back for him again, and advertised his disappearance in the papers. The knowledge of the matter thus far had not been general, and here it dropped entirely, till about the 10th instant, when Keys received a letter from the postmaster in Warren County, that William had arrived at home, and was telling a very mysterious and improbable story about the disappearance of Fisher, which induced the community there to suppose he had been disposed of unfairly. Keys made this letter public, which immediately set the whole town and adjoining county agog. And so it has continued until yesterday. The mass of the people commenced a systematic search for the dead body, while Wickersham was despatched to arrest Henry Trailor at the Grove, and Jim Maxcy to Warren to arrest William. On Monday last, Henry was brought in, and showed an evident inclination to insinuate that he knew Fisher to be dead, and that Arch. and William had killed him. He said he guessed the body could be found in Spring Creek, between the Beardstown road and Hickox's mill. Away the people swept like a herd of buffalo, and cut down Hickox's mill-dam *nolens volens*, to draw the water out of the pond, and then went up and down and down and up the creek, fishing and raking, and raking and ducking, and diving for two days, and, after all, no dead body found.

In the mean time a sort of scuffling-ground had been found in the brush in the angle, or point, where the road leading into the woods past the brewery and the one leading in past the brick-yard meet. From the scuffle-ground was the sign of something about the size of a man having been dragged to the edge of the thicket, where it joined the track of some small-wheeled carriage drawn by one horse, as shown by the road-tracks. The carriage-track led off toward Spring Creek. Near this drag-trail Dr. Merryman found two hairs, which, after a long scientific examination, he pronounced to be triangular human hair, which term, he says, includes within it the whiskers, the hair growing under the arms and on other parts of the body; and he judged that these two were of the whiskers, because the ends were cut, showing that they had flourished in the neighborhood of the razor's operations. On Thursday last Jim Maxcy brought in William Trailor from Warren. On the same day Arch. was arrested and put in jail. Yesterday (Friday) William was put upon his examining trial before May and Lovely. Archibald and Henry were both present. Lamborn prosecuted, and Logan, Baker, and your humble servant defended. A great many witnesses were introduced and examined, but I shall only mention those whose testimony seemed most important. The first of these was Captain Ransdell. He swore that when William and Henry left Springfield for home on Tuesday before mentioned, they did not take the direct route,—which, you know, leads by the butcher shop,—but that they followed the street north until they got opposite, or nearly opposite, May's new house, after which he could not see them from where he stood; and it was afterward proved that in about an hour after they started, they came into the street by the butcher shop from toward the brick-yard. Dr. Merryman and others swore to what is stated about the scuffle-ground, drag-trail, whiskers, and carriage-tracks. Henry was then introduced by the prosecution. He swore that when they started for home, they went out north, as Ransdell stated, and turned

VOL. I.—4.

down west by the brick-yard into the woods, and there met Archibald; that they proceeded a small distance farther, when he was placed as a sentinel to watch for and announce the approach of any one that might happen that way; that William and Arch. took the dearborn out of the road a small distance to the edge of the thicket, where they stopped, and he saw them lift the body of a man into it; that they then moved off with the carriage in the direction of Hickox's mill, and he loitered about for something like an hour, when William returned with the carriage, but without Arch., and said they had put him in a safe place; that they went somehow — he did not know exactly how — into the road close to the brewery, and proceeded on to Clary's Grove. He also stated that some time during the day William told him that he and Arch. had killed Fisher the evening before; that the way they did it was by him (William) knocking him down with a club, and Arch. then choking him to death.

An old man from Warren, called Dr. Gilmore, was then introduced on the part of the defense. He swore that he had known Fisher for several years; that Fisher had resided at his house a long time at each of two different spells — once while he built a barn for him, and once while he was doctored for some chronic disease; that two or three years ago Fisher had a serious hurt in his head by the bursting of a gun, since which he had been subject to continued bad health and occasional aberration of mind. He also stated that on last Tuesday, being the same day that Maxcy arrested William Trailor, he (the doctor) was from home in the early part of the day, and on his return, about eleven o'clock, found Fisher at his house in bed, and apparently very unwell; that he asked him how he came from Springfield; that Fisher said he had come by Peoria, and also told of several other places he had been at more in the direction of Peoria, which showed that he at the time of speaking did not know where he had been wandering about in a state of derangement. He further stated that in about two hours he received a note from one of Trailor's friends, advising him of his arrest, and requesting him to go on to Springfield as a witness, to testify as to the state of Fisher's health in former times; that he immediately set off, calling up two of his neighbors as company, and, riding all evening and all night, overtook Maxcy and William at Lewiston in Fulton County; that Maxcy refusing to discharge Trailor upon his statement, his two neighbors returned and he came on to Springfield. Some question being made as to whether the doctor's story was not a fabrication, several acquaintances of his (among whom was the same postmaster who wrote Keys, as before mentioned) were introduced as sort of compurgators, who swore that they knew the doctor to be of good character for truth and veracity, and generally of good character in every way. Here the testimony ended, and the Trailors were discharged, Arch. and William expressing both in word and manner their entire confidence that Fisher would be found alive at the doctor's by Galloway, Mallory, and Myers, who a day before had been despatched for that purpose; while Henry still protested that no power on earth could ever show

Fisher alive. Thus stands this curious affair. When the doctor's story was first made public, it was amusing to scan and contemplate the countenances and hear the remarks of those who had been actively in search for the dead body: some looked quizzical, some melancholy, and some furiously angry. Porter, who had been very active, swore he always knew the man was not dead, and that he had not stirred an inch to hunt for him; Langford, who had taken the lead in cutting down Hickox's mill-dam, and wanted to hang Hickox for objecting, looked most awfully woebegone: he seemed the "victim of unrequited affection," as represented in the comic almanacs we used to laugh over; and Hart, the little drayman that hauled Molly home once, said it was too *damned* bad to have so much trouble, and no hanging after all.

I commenced this letter on yesterday, since which I received yours of the 13th. I stick to my promise to come to Louisville. Nothing new here except what I have written. I have not seen —— since my last trip, and I am going out there as soon as I mail this letter.

Yours forever,   LINCOLN.

June 25, 1841.—STATEMENT ABOUT HARRY WILTON.

It having been charged in some of the public prints that Harry Wilton, late United States marshal for the district of Illinois, had used his office for political effect, in the appointment of deputies for the taking of the census for the year 1840, we, the undersigned, were called upon by Mr. Wilton to examine the papers in his possession relative to these appointments, and to ascertain therefrom the correctness or incorrectness of such charge. We accompanied Mr. Wilton to a room, and examined the matter as fully as we could with the means afforded us. The only sources of information bearing on the subject which were submitted to us, were the letters, etc., recommending and opposing the various appointments made, and Mr. Wilton's verbal statements concerning the same. From these letters, etc., it appears that in some instances appointments were made in accordance with the recommendations of leading Whigs, and in opposition to those of leading Democrats; among which instances the appointments at Scott, Wayne, Madison, and Lawrence are the strongest. According to Mr. Wilton's statement, of the seventy-six appointments we examined, fifty-four were of Democrats, eleven of Whigs, and eleven of unknown politics.

The chief ground of complaint against Mr. Wilton, as we had understood it, was because of his appointment of so many Democratic candidates for the legislature, thus giving them a decided advantage over their Whig opponents; and consequently our attention was directed rather particularly to that point. We found that there were many such appointments, among which were those in Tazewell, McLean, Iroquois, Coles, Menard, Wayne, Washington, Fayette, etc.; and we did not learn that there was one instance in which a Whig candidate for the legislature had been appointed. There was no written evidence before us showing us at what time those appointments were made; but Mr. Wilton stated that they all, with one exception, were made before those appointed became candidates for the legislature, and the letters, etc., recommending them all bear date before, and most of them long before, those appointed were publicly announced candidates.

We give the foregoing naked facts, and draw no conclusions from them.

BENJ. S. EDWARDS,
June 25, 1841.   A. LINCOLN.

September 27, 1841.—LETTER TO MISS MARY SPEED.

BLOOMINGTON, ILL., September 27, 1841.

MISS MARY SPEED, Louisville, Ky.

My Friend: Having resolved to write to some of your mother's family, and not having the express permission of any one of them to do so, I have had some little difficulty in determining on which to inflict the task of reading what I now feel must be a most dull and silly letter; but when I remembered that you and I were something of cronies while I was at Farmington, and that while there I was under the necessity of shutting you up in a room to prevent your committing an assault and battery upon me, I instantly decided that you should be the devoted one. I assume that you have not heard from Joshua and myself since we left, because I think it doubtful whether he has written. You remember there was some uneasiness about Joshua's health when we left. That little indisposition of his turned out to be nothing serious, and it was pretty nearly forgotten when we reached Springfield. We got on board the steamboat *Lebanon* in the locks of the canal, about twelve o'clock M. of the day we left, and reached St. Louis the next Monday at 8 P. M. Nothing of interest happened during the passage, except the vexatious delays occasioned by the sand-bars be thought interesting. By the way, a fine example was presented on board the boat for contemplating the effect of condition upon human happiness. A gentleman had purchased twelve negroes in different parts of Kentucky, and was taking them to a farm in the South. They were chained six and six together. A small iron clevis was around the left wrist of each, and this fastened to the main chain by a shorter one, at a convenient distance from the others, so that the negroes were strung together precisely like so many fish upon a trot-line. In this condition they were being separated forever from the scenes of their childhood, their friends, their fathers and mothers, and brothers and sisters, and many of them from their wives and children, and going into perpetual slavery, where the lash of the master is proverbially more ruthless and unrelenting than any other where; and yet amid all these distressing circumstances, as we would think them, they were the most cheerful and apparently happy creatures on board. One whose offense for which he had been sold was an over-fondness for his wife, played the fiddle almost continually, and the others danced, sang, cracked jokes, and played various games with cards from day to day. How true it is that "God tempers the wind to the shorn lamb," or in other words, that he renders the worst of human conditions tolerable, while he permits the best to be nothing better than tolerable. To return to the narrative. When we reached Springfield, I stayed but one day, when I started on this tedious circuit where I now am. Do you remember my going to the city, while I was in Kentucky, to have a tooth extracted, and making a failure of it? Well, that same old tooth got to paining me so much that about a week since I had it torn out, bringing with it a bit of the jaw-bone, the consequence of which is that my mouth is now so sore that I can neither talk nor eat.

I am literally "subsisting on savory remembrances"—that is, being unable to eat, I am living upon the remembrance of the delicious dishes of peaches and cream we used to have at your house. When we left, Miss Fanny Henning was owing you a visit, as I understood. Has she paid it yet? If she has, are you not convinced that she is one of the sweetest girls in the world? There is but one thing about her, so far as I could perceive, that I would have otherwise than as it is—that is, something of a tendency to melancholy. This, let it be observed, is a misfortune, not a fault.

Give her an assurance of my very highest regard when you see her. Is little Siss Eliza Davis at your house yet? If she is, kiss her "o'er and o'er again" for me.

Tell your mother that I have not got her "present" [an "Oxford" Bible] with me, but I intend to read it regularly when I return home. I doubt not that it is really, as she says, the best cure for the blues, could one but take it according to the truth. Give my respects to all your sisters (including Aunt Emma) and brothers. Tell Mrs. Peay, of whose happy face I shall long retain a pleasant remembrance, that I have been trying to think of a name for her homestead, but as yet cannot satisfy myself with one. I shall be very happy to receive a line from you soon after you receive this, and in case you choose to favor me with one, address it to Charleston, Coles County, Ill., as I shall be there about the time to receive it. Your sincere friend,

A. LINCOLN.

October 20, 1841.—CALL FOR WHIG STATE CONVENTION.

The undersigned, acting, as is believed, in accordance with the wishes of the Whig party, and in compliance with their duties as the Whig Central Committee of this State, appoint the third Monday of December next for the meeting of a Whig State Convention, at Springfield, for the purpose of nominating candidates for the offices of Governor and Lieutenant-Governor of this State for the coming election.

It is recommended that the number of delegates to the convention shall conform to the number of representatives entitled under the new apportionment; but that in all cases every county shall be entitled to one delegate.

We would urge upon our political friends in the different counties to call meetings immediately for the election of delegates.

It is ardently hoped that the counties will be fully represented, in order that the will of the people may be expressed in the selection of candidates.

A. G. HENRY,   J. F. SPEED,   A. LINCOLN,
E. D. BAKER,   WM. L. MAY,

Whig State Central Committee.

SPRINGFIELD, Oct. 20, 1841.

January [3 ?], 1842. — LETTER TO JOSHUA F. SPEED.

My dear Speed: Feeling, as you know I do, the deepest solicitude for the success of the enterprise you are engaged in, I adopt this as the last method I can adopt to aid you, in case (which God forbid!) you shall need any aid. I do not place what I am going to say on paper because I can say it better that way than I could by word of mouth, but, were I to say it orally before we part, most likely you would forget it at the very time when it might do you some good. As I think it reasonable that you will feel very badly some time between this and the final consummation of your purpose, it is intended that you shall read this just at such a time. Why I say it is reasonable that you will feel very badly yet, is because of three special causes added to the general one which I shall mention.

The general cause is, that you are naturally of a nervous temperament; and this I say from what I have seen of you personally, and what you have told me concerning your mother at various times, and concerning your brother William at the time his wife died. The first special cause is your exposure to bad weather on your journey, which my experience clearly proves to be very severe on defective nerves. The second is the absence of all business and conversation of friends, which might divert your mind, give it occasional rest from the intensity of thought which will sometimes wear the sweetest idea threadbare and turn it to the bitterness of death. The third is the rapid and near approach of that crisis on which all your thoughts and feelings concentrate.

If from all these causes you shall escape and go through triumphantly, without another "twinge of the soul," I shall be most happily but most egregiously deceived. If, on the contrary, you shall, as I expect you will at some time, be agonized and distressed, let me, who have some reason to speak with judgment on such a subject, beseech you to ascribe it to the causes I have mentioned, and not to some false and ruinous suggestion of the Devil.

"But," you will say, "do not your causes apply to every one engaged in a like undertaking?" By no means. The particular causes, to a greater or less extent perhaps, do apply in all cases; but the general one,— nervous debility, which is the key and conductor of all the particular ones, and without which they would be utterly harmless,— though it does pertain to you, does not pertain to one in a thousand. It is out of this that the painful difference between you and the mass of the world springs.

I know what the painful point with you is at all times when you are unhappy; it is an apprehension that you do not love her as you should. What nonsense! How came you to court her? Was it because you thought she deserved it, and that you had given her reason to expect it? If it was for that, why did not the same reason make you court Ann Todd, and at least twenty others of whom you can think, and to whom it would apply with greater force than to her? Did you court her for her wealth? Why, you know she had none. But you say you reasoned yourself into it. What do you mean by that? Was it not that you found yourself unable to reason yourself out of it? Did you not think, and partly form the purpose, of courting her the first time you ever saw her or heard of her? What had reason to do with it at that early stage? There was nothing at that time for reason to work upon. Whether she was moral, amiable, sensible, or even of good character, you did not, nor could then know, except, perhaps, you might infer the last from the company you found her in.

All you then did or could know of her was her personal appearance and deportment; and these, if they impress at all, impress the heart, and not the head.

Say candidly, were not those heavenly black eyes the whole basis of all your early reasoning on the subject? After you and I had once been at the residence, did you not go and take me all the way to Lexington and back, for no other purpose but to get to see her again, on our return on that evening to take a trip for that express object? What earthly consideration would you take to find her scouting and despising you, and giving herself up to another? But of this you have no apprehension; and therefore you cannot bring it home to your feelings.

I shall be so anxious about you that I shall want you to write by every mail. Your friend,

LINCOLN.

February 3, 1842.—LETTER TO JOSHUA F. SPEED.

SPRINGFIELD, ILLINOIS, February 3, 1842.

Dear Speed: Your letter of the 25th January came to hand to-day. You well know that I do not feel my own sorrows much more keenly than I do yours, when I know of them; and yet I assure you I was not much hurt by what you wrote me of your excessively bad feeling at the time you wrote. Not that I am less capable of sympathizing with you now than ever, not that I am less your friend than ever, but because I hope and believe that your present anxiety and distress about her health and her life must and will forever banish those horrid doubts which I know you sometimes felt as to the truth of your affection for her. If they can once and forever be removed (and I almost feel a presentiment that the Almighty has sent your present affliction expressly for that object), surely nothing can come in their stead to fill their immeasurable measure of misery. The death-scenes of those we love are surely painful enough; but these we are prepared for and expect to see: they happen to all, and all know they must happen. Painful as they are, they are not an unlooked-for sorrow. Should she, as you fear, be destined to an early grave, it is indeed a great consolation to know that she is so well prepared to meet it. Her religion, which you once disliked so much, I will venture you now prize most highly. But I hope your melancholy bodings as to her early death are not well founded. I even hope that ere this reaches you she will have returned with improved and still improving health, and that you will have met her, and forgotten the sorrows of the past in the enjoyments of the present. I would say more if I could, but it seems that I have said enough. It really appears to me that you yourself ought to rejoice, and not sorrow, at this indubitable evidence of your undying affection for her. Why, Speed, if you did not love her, although you might not wish her death, you would most certainly be resigned to it. Perhaps this point is no longer a question with you, and my pertinacious dwelling upon it is a rude intrusion upon your feelings. If so, you must pardon me. You know the hell I have suffered on that point, and how tender I am upon it. You know I do not mean wrong. I have been quite clear of "hypo" since you left; even better than I was along in the fall. I have seen —— but once. She seemed very cheerful, and so I said nothing to her about what we spoke of.

Old Uncle Billy Herndon is dead, and it is said this evening that Uncle Ben Ferguson will not live. This, I believe, is all the news, and enough at that unless it were better. Write me immediately on the receipt of this. Your friend, as ever,

LINCOLN.

February 13, 1842.— LETTER TO JOSHUA F. SPEED.

SPRINGFIELD, ILLINOIS, February 13, 1842.

Dear Speed: Yours of the 1st instant came to hand three or four days ago. When this shall reach you, you will have been Fanny's husband several days. You know my desire to befriend you is everlasting; that I will never cease while I know how to do anything. But you will always hereafter be on ground that I have never occupied, and consequently, if advice were needed, I might advise wrong. I do fondly hope, however, that you will never again need any comfort from abroad. But should I be mistaken in this, should excessive pleasure still be accompanied with a painful counterpart at times, still let me urge you, as I have ever done, to remember, in the depth and even agony of despondency, that very shortly you are to feel well again. I am now fully convinced that you love her as ardently as you are capable of loving. Your ever being happy in her presence, and your intense anxiety about her health, if there were nothing else, would place this beyond all dispute in my mind. I incline to think it probable that your nerves will fail you occasionally for a while; but once you get them firmly guarded now, that trouble is over forever. I think, if I were you, in case my mind were not exactly right, I would avoid being idle. I would immediately engage in some business, or go to making preparations for it, which would be the same thing. If you went through the ceremony calmly, or even with sufficient composure not to excite alarm in any present, you are safe beyond question, and in two or three months, to say the most, will be the happiest of men.

I would desire you to give my particular respects to Fanny; but perhaps you will not wish her to know you have received this, lest she should desire to see it. Make her write me an answer to my last letter to her; at any rate, I would set great value upon a note or letter from her. Write me whenever you have leisure.

Yours forever,   A. LINCOLN.

P. S. I have been quite a man since you left.

February 22, 1842.—ADDRESS BEFORE THE SPRINGFIELD WASHINGTONIAN TEMPERANCE SOCIETY.

Although the temperance cause has been in progress for near twenty years, it is apparent to all that it is just now being crowned with a degree of success hitherto unparalleled.

The list of its friends is daily swelled by the additions of fifties, of hundreds, and of thousands. The cause itself seems suddenly transformed from a cold abstract theory to a living, breathing, active, and powerful chieftain, going forth "conquering and to conquer." The citadels of his great adversary are daily being stormed and dismantled; his temple and his altars, where the rites of his idolatrous worship have long been performed, and where human sacrifices have long been wont to be made, are daily desecrated and deserted. The triumph of the conqueror's fame is sounding from hill to hill, from sea to sea, and from land to land, and calling millions to his standard at a blast.

For this new and splendid success we heartily rejoice. That that success is so much greater now than heretofore is doubtless owing to rational causes; and if we would have it continue, we shall do well to inquire what those causes are.

The warfare heretofore waged against the demon intemperance has somehow or other been erroneous. Either the champions engaged or the tactics they adopted have not been the most proper. These champions for the most part have been preachers, lawyers, and hired agents. Between these and the mass of mankind there is a want of approachability, if the term be admissible, partially, at least, fatal to their success. They are supposed to have no sympathy of feeling or interest with those very persons whom it is their object to convince and persuade.

And again, it is so common and so easy to ascribe motives to men of these classes other than those they profess to act upon. The preacher, it is said, advocates temperance because he is a fanatic, and desires a union of the church and state; the lawyer from his pride and vanity of hearing himself speak; and the hired agent for his salary. But when one who has long been known as a victim of intemperance bursts the fetters that have bound him, and appears before his neighbors "clothed and in his right mind," a redeemed specimen of long-lost humanity, and stands up, with tears of joy trembling in his eyes, to tell of the miseries once endured, now to be endured no more forever; of his once naked and starving children, now clad and fed comfortably; of a wife long weighed down with woe, weeping, and a broken heart, now restored to health, happiness, and a renewed affection; and how easily it is all done, once it is resolved to be done; how simple his language!—there is a logic and an eloquence in it that few with human feelings can resist. They cannot say that he desires a union of church and state, for he is not a church member; they cannot say he is vain of hearing himself speak, for his whole demeanor shows he would gladly avoid speaking at all; they cannot say he speaks for pay, for he receives none, and asks for none. Nor can his sincerity in any way be doubted, or his sympathy for those he would persuade to imitate his example be denied.

In my judgment, it is to the battles of this new class of champions that our late success is greatly, perhaps chiefly, owing. But, had the old-school champions themselves been of the most wise selecting, was their system of tactics the most judicious? It seems to me it was not. Too much denunciation against dram-sellers and dram-drinkers was indulged in. This I think was both impolitic and unjust. It was impolitic, because it is not much in the nature of man to be driven to anything; still less to be driven about that which is exclusively his own business; and least of all where such driving is to be submitted to at the expense of pecuniary interest or burning appetite. When the dram-seller and drinker were incessantly told—not in accents of entreaty and persuasion, diffidently addressed by erring man to an erring brother, but in the thundering tones of anathema and denunciation with which the lordly judge often groups together all the crimes of the felon's life, and thrusts them in his face just ere he passes sentence of death upon him—that they were the authors of all the vice and misery and crime in the land; that they were the manufacturers and material of all the thieves and robbers and murderers that infest the earth; that their houses were the workshops of the devil; and that their persons should be shunned by all the good and virtuous, as moral pestilences—I say, when they were told all this, and in this way, it is not wonderful that they were slow, very slow, to acknowledge the truth of such denunciations, and to join the ranks of their denouncers in a hue and cry against themselves.

To have expected them to do otherwise than they did—to have expected them not to meet denunciation with denunciation, crimination with crimination, and anathema with anathema—was to expect a reversal of human nature, which is God's decree and can never be reversed.

When the conduct of men is designed to be influenced, persuasion, kind, unassuming persuasion, should ever be adopted. It is an old and a true maxim " that a drop of honey catches more flies than a gallon of gall." So with men. If you would win a man to your cause, first convince him that you are his sincere friend. Therein is a drop of honey that catches his heart, which, say what he will, is the great highroad to his reason, and which, when once gained, you will find but little trouble in convincing his judgment of the justice of your cause, if indeed that cause really be a just one. On the contrary, assume to dictate to his judgment, or to command his action, or to mark him as one to be shunned and despised, and he will retreat within himself, close all the avenues to his head and his heart; and though your cause be naked truth itself, transformed to the heaviest lance, harder than steel, and sharper than steel can be made, and though you throw it with more than herculean force and precision, you shall be no more able to pierce him than to penetrate the hard shell of a tortoise with a rye straw. Such is man, and so must he be understood by those who would lead him, even to his own best interests.

On this point the Washingtonians greatly excel the temperance advocates of former times. Those whom they desire to convince and persuade are their old friends and companions. They know they are not demons, nor even the worst of men; they know that generally they are kind, generous, and charitable, even beyond the example of their more staid and sober neighbors. They are practical philanthropists; and they glow with a generous and brotherly zeal that mere theorizers are incapable of feeling. Benevolence and charity possess their hearts entirely; and out of the abundance of their hearts their tongues give utterance; " Love through all their actions runs, and all their words are mild." In this spirit they speak and act, and in the same they are heard and regarded. And when such is the temper of the advocate, and such of the audience, no good cause can be unsuccessful. But I have said that denunciations against dram-sellers and dram-drinkers are unjust, as well as impolitic. Let us see. I have not inquired at what period of time the use of intoxicating liquors commenced; nor is it important to know. It is sufficient that to all of us who now inhabit the world, the practice of drinking them is just as old as the world itself—that is, we have seen the one just as long as we have seen the other. When all such of us as have now reached the years of maturity first opened our eyes upon the stage of existence, we found intoxicating liquor recognized by everybody, used by everybody, repudiated by nobody. It commonly entered into the first draught of the infant and the last draught of the dying man. From the sideboard of the parson down to the ragged pocket of the houseless loafer, it was constantly found. Physicians prescribed it in this, that, and the other disease; government provided it for soldiers and sailors; and to have a rolling or raising, a husking or " hoedown," anywhere about without it was positively insufferable. So, too, it was everywhere a respectable article of manufacture and merchandise. The making of it was regarded as an honorable livelihood, and he who could make most was the most enterprising and respectable. Large and small manufactories of it were everywhere erected, in which all the earthly goods of their owners were invested. Wagons drew it from town to town; boats bore it from clime to clime, and the winds wafted it from nation to nation; and merchants bought and sold it, by wholesale and retail, with precisely the same feelings on the part of the seller, buyer, and bystander as are felt at the selling and buying of plows, beef, bacon, or any other of the real necessaries of life. Universal public opinion not only tolerated but recognized and adopted its use.

It is true that even then it was known and acknowledged that many were greatly injured by it; but none seemed to think the injury arose from the use of a bad thing, but from the abuse of a very good thing. The victims of it were to be pitied and compassionated, just as are the heirs of consumption and other hereditary diseases. Their failing was treated as a misfortune, and not as a crime, or even as a disgrace. If, then, what I have been saying is true, is it wonderful that some should think and act now as all thought and acted twenty years ago? and is it just to assail, condemn, or despise them for doing so? The universal sense of mankind on any subject is an argument, or at least an influence, not easily overcome. The success of the argument in favor of the existence of an overruling Providence mainly depends upon that sense; and men ought not in justice to be denounced for yielding to it in any case, or giving it up slowly, especially when they are backed by interest, fixed habits, or burning appetites.

Another error, as it seems to me, into which the old reformers fell, was the position that all habitual drunkards were utterly incorrigible, and therefore must be turned adrift and damned without remedy in order that the grace of temperance might abound, to the temperate then, and to all mankind some hundreds of years thereafter. There is in this something so repugnant to humanity, so uncharitable, so cold-blooded and feelingless, that it never did nor ever can enlist the enthusiasm of a popular cause. We could not love the man who taught it—we could not hear him with patience. The heart could not throw open its portals to it, the generous man could not adopt it—it could not mix with his blood. It looked so fiendishly selfish, so like throwing fathers and brothers overboard to lighten the boat for our security, that the noble-minded shrank from the manifest meanness of the thing. And besides this, the benefits of a reformation to be effected by such a system were too remote in point of time to warmly engage many in its behalf. Few can be induced to labor exclusively for posterity; and none will do it enthusiastically. Posterity has done nothing for us; and theorize on it as we may, practically we shall do very little for it, unless we are made to think we are at the same time doing something for ourselves.

What an ignorance of human nature does it exhibit, to ask or expect a whole community to rise up and labor for the temporal happiness of others, after themselves shall be consigned to the dust, a majority of which community take no pains whatever to secure their own eternal welfare at no more distant day? Great distance in either time or space has wonderful power to lull and render quiescent the human mind. Pleasures to be enjoyed, or pains to be endured, after we shall be dead and gone are but little regarded even in our own cases, and much less in the cases of others. Still, in addition to this there is something so ludicrous in promises of good or threats of evil a great way off as to render the whole subject with which they are connected easily turned into ridicule. " Better lay down that spade you are stealing, Paddy; if you don't you 'll pay for it at the day of judgment." " Be the powers, if ye 'll credit me so long I 'll take another jist."

By the Washingtonians this system of consigning the habitual drunkard to hopeless ruin is repudiated. They adopt a more enlarged philanthropy; they go for present as well as future good. They labor for all now living, as well as hereafter to live. They teach hope to all — despair to none. As applying to their cause, they deny the doctrine of unpardonable sin; as in Christianity it is taught, so in this they teach — " While the lamp holds out to burn, The vilest sinner may return." And, what is a matter of more profound congratulation, they, by experiment upon experiment and example upon example, prove the maxim to be no less true in the one case than in the other. On every hand we behold those who but yesterday were the chief of sinners, now the chief apostles of the cause. Drunken devils are cast out by ones, by sevens, by legions; and their unfortunate victims, like the poor possessed who were redeemed from their long and lonely wanderings in the tombs, are publishing to the ends of the earth how great things have been done for them.

To these new champions and this new system of tactics our late success is mainly owing, and to them we must mainly look for the final consummation. The ball is now rolling gloriously on, and none are so able as they to increase its speed and its bulk, to add to its momentum and its magnitude — even though unlearned in letters, for this task none are so well educated. To fit them for this work they have been taught in the true school. They have been in that gulf from which they would teach others the means of escape. They have passed that prison wall, which others have long declared impassable; and who that has not shall dare to weigh opinions with them as to the mode of passing?

But if it be true, as I have insisted, that those who have suffered by intemperance personally, and have reformed, are the most powerful and efficient instruments to push the reformation to ultimate success, it does not follow that those who have not suffered have no part left them to perform. Whether or not the world would be vastly benefited by a total and final banishment from it of all intoxicating drinks seems to me not now an open question. Three fourths of mankind confess the affirmative with their tongues, and, I believe, all the rest acknowledge it in their hearts.

Ought any, then, to refuse their aid in doing what good the good of the whole demands? Shall he who cannot do much be for that reason excused if he do nothing? " But," says one, " what good can I do by signing the pledge? I never drink, even without signing." This question has already been asked and answered more than a million of times. Let it be answered once more. For the man suddenly or in any other way to break off from the use of drams, who has indulged in them for a long course of years, and until his appetite for them has grown ten- or a hundred-fold stronger, and more craving than any natural appetite can be, requires a most powerful moral effort. In such an undertaking he needs every moral support and influence that can possibly be brought to his aid and thrown around him. And not only so, but every moral prop should be taken from whatever argument might rise in his mind to lure him to his backsliding. When he casts his eyes around him, he should be able to see all that he respects, all that he admires, all that he loves, kindly and anxiously pointing him onward, and none beckoning him back to his former miserable "wallowing in the mire."

But it is said by some that men will think and act for themselves; that none will disuse spirits or anything else because his neighbors do; and that moral influence is not that powerful engine contended for. Let us examine this. Let me ask the man who could maintain this position most stiffly, what compensation he will accept to go to church some Sunday and sit during the sermon with his wife's bonnet upon his head? Not a trifle, I 'll venture. And why not? There would be nothing irreligious in it, nothing immoral, nothing uncomfortable—then why not? Is it not because there would be something egregiously unfashionable in it? Then it is the influence of fashion; and what is the influence of fashion but the influence that other people's actions have on our actions—the strong inclination each of us feels to do as we see all our neighbors do? Nor is the influence of fashion confined to any particular thing or class of things; it is just as strong on one subject as another. Let us make it as unfashionable to withhold our names from the temperance cause as for husbands to wear their wives' bonnets to church, and instances will be just as rare in the one case as the other.

"But," say some, "we are no drunkards, and we shall not acknowledge ourselves such by joining a reformed drunkards' society, whatever our influence might be." Surely no Christian will adhere to this objection. If they believe as they profess, that Omnipotence condescended to take on himself the form of sinful man, and as such to die an ignominious death for their sakes, surely they will not refuse submission to the infinitely lesser condescension, for the temporal, and perhaps eternal, salvation of a large, erring, and unfortunate class of their fellow-creatures. Nor is the condescension very great. In my judgment such of us as have never fallen victims have been spared more by the absence of appetite than from any mental or moral superiority over those who have. Indeed, I believe if we take habitual drunkards as a class, their heads and their hearts will bear an advantageous comparison with those of any other class. There seems ever to have been a proneness in the brilliant and warm-blooded to fall into this vice—the demon of intemperance ever seems to have delighted in sucking the blood of genius and of generosity. What one of us but can call to mind some relative, more promising in youth than all his fellows, who has fallen a sacrifice to his rapacity? He ever seems to have gone forth like the Egyptian angel of death, commissioned to slay, if not the first, the fairest born of every family. Shall he now be arrested in his desolating career? In that arrest all can give aid that will; and who shall be excused that can and will not? Far around as human breath has ever blown he keeps our fathers, our brothers, our sons, and our friends prostrate in the chains of moral death. To all the living everywhere we cry, "Come sound the moral trump, that these may rise and stand up an exceeding great army." "Come from the four winds, O breath! and breathe upon these slain that they may live." If the relative grandeur of revolutions shall be estimated by the great amount of human misery they alleviate, and the small amount they inflict, then indeed will this be the grandest the world shall ever have seen.

· Of our political revolution of '76 we are all justly proud. It has given us a degree of political freedom far exceeding that of any other nation of the earth. In it the world has found a solution of the long-mooted problem as to the capability of man to govern himself. In it was the germ which has vegetated, and still is to grow and expand into the universal liberty of mankind. But, with all these glorious results, past, present, and to come, it had its evils too. It breathed forth famine, swam in blood, and rode in fire; and long, long after, the orphan's cry and the widow's wail continued to break the sad silence that ensued. These were the price, the inevitable price, paid for the blessings it bought.

Turn now to the temperance revolution. In it we shall find a stronger bondage broken, a viler slavery manumitted, a greater tyrant deposed; in it, more of want supplied, more disease healed, more sorrow assuaged. By it no orphans starving, no widows weeping. By it, none wounded in feeling, none injured in interest; even the dram-maker and dram-seller will have glided into other occupations so gradually as never to have felt the change, and will stand ready to join all others in the universal song of gladness. And what a noble ally this to the cause of political freedom; with such an aid its march cannot fail to be on and on, till every son of earth shall drink in rich fruition the sorrow-quenching draughts of perfect liberty. Happy day when — all appetites controlled, all poisons subdued, all matter subjected — mind, all conquering mind, shall live and move, the monarch of the world. Glorious consummation! Hail, fall of fury! Reign of reason, all hail!

And when the victory shall be complete,— when there shall be neither a slave nor a drunkard on the earth,— how proud the title of that land which may truly claim to be the birthplace and the cradle of both those revolutions that shall have ended in that victory. How nobly distinguished that people who shall have planted and nurtured to maturity both the political and moral freedom of their species.

This is the one hundred and tenth anniversary of the birthday of Washington; we are met to celebrate this day. Washington is the mightiest name of earth — long since mightiest in the cause of civil liberty, still mightiest in moral reformation. On that name no eulogy is expected. It cannot be. To add brightness to the sun or glory to the name of Washington is alike impossible. Let none attempt it. In solemn awe pronounce the name, and in its naked deathless splendor leave it shining on.

February 25, 1842.—LETTER TO JOSHUA F. SPEED.

SPRINGFIELD, February 25, 1842.

Dear Speed: Yours of the 16th instant, announcing that Miss Fanny and you are "no more twain, but one flesh," reached me this morning. I have no way of telling you how much happiness I wish you both, though I believe you both can conceive it. I feel somewhat jealous of both of you now: you will be so exclusively concerned for one another, that I shall be forgotten entirely. My acquaintance with Miss Fanny (I call her this, lest you should think I am speaking of your mother) was too short for me to reasonably hope to long be remembered by her; and still I am sure I shall not forget her soon. Try if you cannot remind her of that debt she owes me — and be sure you do not interfere to prevent her paying it.

I regret to learn that you have resolved to not return to Illinois. I shall be very lonesome without you. How miserably things seem to be arranged in this world! If we have no friends, we have no pleasure; and if we have them, we are sure to lose them, and be doubly pained by the loss. I did hope she and you would make your home here; but I own I have no right to insist. You owe obligations to her ten thousand times more sacred than you can owe to others, and in that light let them be respected and observed. It is natural that she should desire to remain with her relatives and friends. As to friends, however, she could not need them anywhere: she would have them in abundance here.

Give my kind remembrance to Mr. Williamson and his family, particularly Miss Elizabeth; also to your mother, brother, and sisters. Ask little Eliza Davis if she will ride to town with me if I come there again. And finally, give Fanny a double reciprocation of all the love she sent me. Write me often, and believe me

Yours forever,   LINCOLN.

P. S. Poor Easthouse is gone at last. He died awhile before day this morning. They say he was very loath to die. . . .

L.

February 25, 1842.— LETTER TO JOSHUA F. SPEED.

SPRINGFIELD, February 25, 1842.

Dear Speed: I received yours of the 12th written the day you went down to William's place, some days since, but delayed answering it till I should receive the promised one of the 16th, which came last night. I opened the letter with intense anxiety and trepidation; so much so, that, although it turned out better than I expected, I have hardly yet, at a distance of ten hours, become calm.

I tell you, Speed, our forebodings (for which you and I are peculiar) are all the worst sort of nonsense. I fancied, from the time I received your letter of Saturday, that the one of Wednesday was never to come, and yet it *did* come, and what is more, it is perfectly clear, both from its tone and handwriting, that you were much happier, or, if you think the term preferable, less miserable, when you wrote it than when you wrote the last one before. You had so obviously improved at the very time I so much fancied you would have grown worse. You say that something indescribably horrible and alarming still haunts you. You will not say that three months from now, I will venture. When your nerves once get steady now, the whole trouble will be over forever. Nor should you become impatient at their being even very slow in becoming steady. Again you say, you much fear that that Elysium of which you have dreamed so much is never to be realized. Well, if it shall not, I dare swear it will not be the fault of her who is now your wife. I now have no doubt that it is the peculiar misfortune of both you and me to dream dreams of Elysium far exceeding all that anything earthly can realize. Far short of your dreams as you may be, no woman could do more to realize them than that same black-eyed Fanny. If you could but contemplate her through my imagination, it would appear ridiculous to you that any one should for a moment think of being unhappy with her. My old father used to have a saying that "If you make a bad bargain, hug it all the tighter"; and it occurs to me that if the bargain you have just closed can possibly be called a bad one, it is certainly the most pleasant one for applying that maxim to which my fancy can by any effort picture.

I write another letter, inclosing this, which you can show her, if she desires it. I do this because she would think strangely, perhaps, should you tell her that you received no letters from me, or, telling her you do, refuse to let her see them. I close this, entertaining the confident hope that every successive letter I shall have from you (which I here pray may not be few, nor far between) may show you possessing a more steady hand and cheerful heart than the last preceding it.   As ever, your friend,

LINCOLN.

March 27, 1842.—LETTER TO JOSHUA F. SPEED.

SPRINGFIELD, March 27, 1842.

Dear Speed: Yours of the 10th instant was received three or four days since. You know I am sincere when I tell you the pleasure its contents gave me was, and is, inexpressible. As to your farm matter, I have no sympathy with you. I have no farm, nor ever expect to have, and consequently have not studied the subject enough to be much interested with it. I can only say that I am glad you are satisfied and pleased with it. But on that other subject, to me of the most intense interest whether in joy or sorrow, I never had the power to withhold my sympathy from you. It cannot be told how it now thrills me with joy to hear you say you are "far happier than you ever expected to be." That much I know is enough. I know you too well to suppose your expectations were not, at least, some-

VOL. I.—5.

times extravagant, and if the reality exceeds them all, I say, Enough, dear Lord. I am not going beyond the truth when I tell you that the short space it took me to read your last letter gave me more pleasure than the total sum of all I have enjoyed since the fatal 1st of January, 1841. Since then it seems to me I should have been entirely happy, but for the never-absent idea that there is one still unhappy whom I have contributed to make so. That still kills my soul. I cannot but reproach myself for even wishing to be happy while she is otherwise. She accompanied a large party on the railroad cars to Jacksonville last Monday, and on her return spoke, so that I heard of it, of having enjoyed the trip exceedingly. God be praised for that.

You know with what sleepless vigilance I have watched you ever since the commencement of your affair; and although I am almost confident it is useless, I cannot forbear once more to say that I think it is even yet possible for your spirits to flag down and leave you miserable. If they should, don't fail to remember that they cannot long remain so. One thing I can tell you which I know you will be glad to hear, and that is that I have seen —— and scrutinized her feelings as well as I could, and am fully convinced she is far happier now than she has been for the last fifteen months past.

You will see by the last "Sangamon Journal" that I made a temperance speech on the 22d of February, which I claim that Fanny and you shall read as an act of charity to me; for I cannot learn that anybody else has read it, or is likely to. Fortunately it is not very long, and I shall deem it a sufficient compliance with my request if one of you listens while the other reads it.

As to your Lockridge matter, it is only necessary to say that there has been no court since you left, and that the next commences to-morrow morning, during which I suppose we cannot fail to get a judgment.

I wish you would learn of Everett what he would take, over and above a discharge for all the trouble we have been at, to take his business out of our hands and give it to somebody else. It is impossible to collect money on that or any other claim here now; and although you know I am not a very petulant man, I declare I am almost out of patience with Mr. Everett's importunity. It seems like he not only writes all the letters he can himself, but gets everybody else in Louisville and vicinity to be constantly writing to us about his claim. I have always said that Mr. Everett is a very clever fellow, and I am very sorry he cannot be obliged; but it does seem to me he ought to know we are interested to collect his claim, and therefore would do it if we could.

I am neither joking nor in a pet when I say we would thank him to transfer his business to some other, without any compensation for what we have done, provided he will see the court cost paid, for which we are security.

The sweet violet you inclosed came safely to hand, but it was so dry, and mashed so flat, that it crumbled to dust at the first attempt to handle it. The juice that mashed out of it stained a place in the letter, which I mean to preserve and cherish for the sake of her who procured it to be sent. My renewed good wishes to her in particular, and generally to all such of your relations who know me.

As ever,   LINCOLN.

July 4, 1842.—LETTER TO JOSHUA F. SPEED.

SPRINGFIELD, ILLINOIS, July 4, 1842.

Dear Speed: Yours of the 16th June was received only a day or two since. It was not mailed at Louisville till the 25th. You speak of the great time that has elapsed since I wrote you. Let me explain that. Your letter reached here a day or two after I had started on the circuit. I was gone five or six weeks, so that I got the letters only a few weeks before Butler started to your country. I thought it scarcely worth while to write you the news which he could and would tell you more in detail. On his return he told me you would write me soon, and so I waited for your letter. As to my having been displeased with your advice, surely you know better than that. I know you do, and therefore will not labor to convince you. True, that subject is painful to me; but it is not your silence, or the silence of all the world, that can make me forget it. I acknowledge the correctness of your advice too; but before I resolve to do the one thing or the other, I must gain my confidence in my own ability to keep my resolves when they are made. In that ability you know I once prided myself as the only or chief gem of my character; that gem I lost—how and where you know too well. I have not yet regained it; and until I do, I cannot trust myself in any matter of much importance. I believe now that had you understood my case at the time as well as I understood yours afterward, by the aid you would have given me I should have sailed through clear, but that does not now afford me sufficient confidence to begin that or the like of that again.

You make a kind acknowledgment of your obligations to me for your present happiness. I am pleased with that acknowledgment. But a thousand times more am I pleased to know that you enjoy a degree of happiness worthy of an acknowledgment. The truth is, I am not sure that there was any merit with me in the part I took in your difficulty; I was drawn to it by a fate. If I would I could not have done less than I did. I always was superstitious; I believe God made me one of the instruments of bringing your Fanny and you together, which union I have no doubt he had fore-ordained. Whatever he designs he will do for me yet. "Stand still, and see the salvation of the Lord" is my text just now. If, as you say, you have told Fanny all, I should have no objection to her seeing this letter, but for its reference to our friend here: let her seeing it depend upon whether she has ever known anything of my affairs; and if she has not, do not let her.

I do not think I can come to Kentucky this season. I am so poor and make so little headway in the world, that I drop back in a month of idleness as much as I gain in a year's sowing. I should like to visit you again. I should like to see that "sis" of yours that was absent when I was there, though I suppose she would run away again if she were to hear I was coming.

. . . .

My respects and esteem to all your friends there, and, by your permission, my love to your Fanny. Ever yours,

LINCOLN.

August 29, 1842.—INVITATION TO HENRY CLAY.

SPRINGFIELD, ILLINOIS, August 29, 1842.

HON. HENRY CLAY, Lexington, Kentucky.

Dear Sir: We hear you are to visit Indianapolis, Indiana, on the 5th of October next. If our information in this is correct, we hope you will not deny us the pleasure of seeing you in our State. We are aware of the toil necessarily incident to a journey by one circumstanced as you are; but once you have embarked, as you have already determined to do, the toil would not be greatly augmented by extending the journey to our capital. The season of the year will be most favorable for good roads and pleasant weather; and although we cannot but believe you would be highly gratified with such a visit to the prairie-land, the pleasure it would give us, and thousands such as we, is beyond all question. You have never visited Illinois, or at least this portion of it; and should you now yield to our request, we promise you such a reception as shall be worthy of the man on whom are now turned the fondest hopes of a great and suffering nation.

Please inform us at the earliest convenience whether we may expect you. Very respectfully, your obedient servants,

A. G. HENRY,	A. T. BLEDSOE,
C. BIRCHALL,	A. LINCOLN,
J. M. CABANISS,	ROBT. IRWIN,
P. A. SAUNDERS,	J. M. ALLEN,
J. N. FRANCIS,	*Executive Committee,* "*Clay Club.*"

(Clay's answer, September 6, 1842, declines with thanks.)

September 17, 1842.—CORRESPONDENCE ABOUT THE
LINCOLN-SHIELDS DUEL.

TREMONT, September 17, 1842.

A. Lincoln, Esq.: I regret that my absence on public business compelled me to postpone a matter of private consideration a little longer than I could have desired. It will only be necessary, however, to account for it by informing you that I have been to Quincy on business that would not admit of delay. I will now state briefly the reasons of my troubling you with this communication, the disagreeable nature of which I regret, as I had hoped to avoid any difficulty with any one in Springfield while residing there, by endeavoring to conduct myself in such a way amongst both my political friends and opponents as to escape the necessity of any. Whilst thus abstaining from giving provocation, I have become the object of slander, vituperation, and personal abuse, which, were I capable of submitting to, I would prove myself worthy of the whole of it.

In two or three of the last numbers of "The Sangamon Journal," articles of the most personal nature and calculated to degrade me have made their appearance. On inquiring, I was informed by the editor of that paper, through the medium of my friend General Whitesides, that you are the author of those articles. This information satisfies me that I have become by some means or other the object of your secret hostility. I will not take the trouble of inquiring into the reason of all this; but I will take the liberty of requiring a full, positive, and absolute retraction of all offensive allusions used by you in these communications, in relation to my private character and standing as a man, as an apology for the insults conveyed in them.

This may prevent consequences which no one will regret more than myself.   Your obedient servant,

JAS. SHIELDS.

TREMONT, September 17, 1842.

Jas. Shields, Esq.: Your note of to-day was handed me by General Whitesides. In that note you say you have been informed, through the medium of the editor of "The Journal," that I am the author of certain articles in that paper which you deem personally abusive of you; and without stopping to inquire whether I really am the author, or to point out what is offensive in them, you demand an unqualified retraction of all that is offensive, and then proceed to hint at consequences.

Now, sir, there is in this so much assumption of facts and so much of menace as to consequences, that I cannot submit to answer that note any further than I have, and to add that the consequences to which I suppose you allude would be matter of as great regret to me as it possibly could to you. Respectfully,

A. LINCOLN.

TREMONT, September 17, 1842.

A. Lincoln, Esq.: In reply to my note of this date, you intimate that I assume facts and menace consequences, and that you cannot submit to answer it further. As now, sir, you desire it, I will be a little more particular. The editor of "The Sangamon Journal" gave me to understand that you are the author of an article which appeared, I think, in that paper of the 2d September instant, headed "The Lost Townships," and signed Rebecca or 'Becca. I would therefore take the liberty of asking whether you are the author of said article, or any other over the same signature which has appeared in any of the late numbers of that paper. If so, I repeat my request of an absolute retraction of all offensive allusion contained therein in relation to my private character and standing. If you are not the author of any of these articles, your denial will be sufficient. I will say further, it is not my intention to menace, but to do myself justice.   Your obedient servant,

JAS. SHIELDS.

September 19, 1842.—MEMORANDUM OF INSTRUCTIONS TO E. H. MERRYMAN, LINCOLN'S SECOND.

In case Whitesides shall signify a wish to adjust this affair without further difficulty, let him know that if the present papers be withdrawn, and a note from Mr. Shields asking to know if I am the author of the articles of which he complains, and asking that I shall make him gentlemanly satisfaction if I am the author, and this without menace, or dictation as to what that satisfaction shall be, a pledge is made that the following answer shall be given:

"I did write the 'Lost Townships' letter which appeared in the 'Journal' of the 2d instant, but had no participation in any form in any other article alluding to you. I wrote that wholly for political effect—I had no intention of injuring your personal or private character or standing as a man or a gentleman; and I did not then think, and do not now think, that that article could produce or has produced that effect against you; and had I anticipated such an effect I would have forborne to write it. And I will add that your conduct toward me, so far as I know, had always been gentlemanly; and that I had no personal pique against you, and no cause for any."

If this should be done, I leave it with you to arrange what shall and what shall not be published. If nothing like this is done, the preliminaries of the fight are to be—

First. Weapons: Cavalry broadswords of the largest size, precisely equal in all respects, and such as now used by the cavalry company at Jacksonville.

Second. Position: A plank ten feet long, and from nine to twelve inches broad, to be firmly fixed on edge, on the ground, as the line between us, which neither is to pass his foot over upon forfeit of his life. Next a line drawn on the ground on either side of said plank and parallel with it, each at the distance of the whole length of the sword and three feet additional from the plank; and the passing of his own such line by either party during the fight shall be deemed a surrender of the contest.

Third. Time: On Thursday evening at five o'clock, if you can get it so; but in no case to be at a greater distance of time than Friday evening at five o'clock.

Fourth. Place: Within three miles of Alton, on the opposite side of the river, the particular spot to be agreed on by you.

Any preliminary details coming within the above rules you are at liberty to make at your discretion; but you are in no case to swerve from these rules, or to pass beyond their limits.

October [4?], 1842.—LETTER TO JOSHUA F. SPEED.

SPRINGFIELD, October [4?], 1842.

Dear Speed: You have heard of my duel with Shields, and I have now to inform you that the dueling business still rages in this city. Day before yesterday Shields challenged Butler, who accepted, and proposed fighting next morning at sunrise in Bob Allen's meadow, one hundred yards' distance, with rifles. To this Whitesides, Shields's second, said "No," because of the law. Thus ended duel No. 2. Yesterday Whitesides chose to consider himself insulted by Dr. Merryman, so sent him a kind of quasi-challenge, inviting him to meet him at the Planter's House in St. Louis on the next Friday, to settle their difficulty. Merryman made me his friend, and sent Whitesides a note, inquiring to know if he meant his note as a challenge, and if so, that he would, according to the law in such case made and provided, prescribe the terms of the meeting. Whitesides returned for answer that if Merryman would meet him at the Planter's House as desired, he would challenge him. Merryman replied in a note that he denied Whitesides's right to dictate time and place, but that he (Merryman) would waive the question of time, and meet him at Louisiana, Missouri. Upon my presenting this note to Whitesides and stating verbally its contents, he declined receiving it, saying he had business in St. Louis, and it was as near as Louisiana. Merryman then directed me to notify Whitesides that he should publish the correspondence between them, with such comments as he thought fit. This I did. Thus it stood at bedtime last night. This morning Whitesides, by his friend Shields, is praying for a new trial, on the ground that he was mistaken in Merryman's proposition to meet him at Louisiana, Missouri, thinking it was the State of Louisiana. This Merryman hoots at, and is preparing his publication; while the town is in a ferment, and a street fight somewhat anticipated.

But I began this letter not for what I have been writing, but to say something on that subject which you know to be of such infinite solicitude to me. The immense sufferings you endured from the first days of September till the middle of February you never tried to conceal from me, and I well understood. You have now been the husband of a lovely woman nearly eight months. That you are happier now than the day you married her I well know, for without you could not be living. But I have your word for it, too, and the returning elasticity of spirits which is manifested in your letters. But I want to ask a close question, "Are you now in feeling as well as judgment glad that you are married as you are?" From anybody but me this would be an impudent question, not to be tolerated; but I know you will pardon it in me. Please answer it quickly, as I am impatient to know. I have sent my love to your Fanny so often, I fear she is getting tired of it. However, I venture to tender it again.   Yours forever,

LINCOLN.

March 1, 1843.—RESOLUTIONS AT A WHIG MEETING AT
SPRINGFIELD, ILLINOIS.

The object of the meeting was stated by Mr. Lincoln of Springfield, who offered the following resolutions, which were unanimously
adopted:

Resolved, That a tariff of duties on imported goods, producing sufficient
revenue for the payment of the necessary expenditures of the National Government, and so adjusted as to protect American industry, is indispensably
necessary to the prosperity of the American people.

Resolved, That we are opposed to direct taxation for the support of the
National Government.

Resolved, That a national bank, properly restricted, is highly necessary and
proper to the establishment and maintenance of a sound currency, and for
the cheap and safe collection, keeping, and disbursing of the public revenue.

Resolved, That the distribution of the proceeds of the sales of the public
lands, upon the principles of Mr. Clay's bill, accords with the best interests
of the nation, and particularly with those of the State of Illinois.

Resolved, That we recommend to the Whigs of each congressional district
of the State, to nominate and support at the approaching election a candidate of their own principles, regardless of the chances of success.

Resolved, That we recommend to the Whigs of all portions of the State to
adopt and rigidly adhere to the convention system of nominating candidates.

Resolved, That we recommend to the Whigs of each congressional district
to hold a district convention on or before the first Monday of May next, to be
composed of a number of delegates from each county equal to double the
number of its representatives in the General Assembly, *provided*, each county
shall have at least one delegate. Said delegates to be chosen by primary
meetings of the Whigs, at such times and places as they in their respective
counties may see fit. Said district conventions each to nominate one candidate for Congress, and one delegate to a National Convention for the purpose
of nominating candidates for President and Vice-President of the United
States. The seven delegates so nominated to a national convention to have
power to add two delegates to their own number, and to fill all vacancies.

Resolved, That A. T. Bledsoe, S. T. Logan, and A. Lincoln be appointed a
committee to prepare an address to the people of the State.

Resolved, That N. W. Edwards, A. G. Henry, James H. Matheny, John C.
Doremus, and James C. Conkling be appointed a Whig Central State Committee, with authority to fill any vacancy that may occur in the committee.

March 4, 1843.—CIRCULAR FROM WHIG COMMITTEE.

Address to the People of Illinois.

Fellow-citizens: By a resolution of a meeting of such of the Whigs
of the State as are now at Springfield, we, the undersigned, were appointed to prepare an address to you. The performance of that task
we now undertake.

Several resolutions were adopted by the meeting; and the chief
object of this address is to show briefly the reasons for their adoption.

The first of those resolutions declares a tariff of duties upon for-

eign importations, producing sufficient revenue for the support of
the General Government, and so adjusted as to protect American
industry, to be indispensably necessary to the prosperity of the
American people; and the second declares direct taxation for a national revenue to be improper. Those two resolutions are kindred
in their nature, and therefore proper and convenient to be considered
together. The question of protection is a subject entirely too broad
to be crowded into a few pages only, together with several other
subjects. On that point we therefore content ourselves with giving
the following extracts from the writings of Mr. Jefferson, General
Jackson, and the speech of Mr. Calhoun:

To be independent for the comforts of life, we must fabricate them ourselves. We must now place the manufacturer by the side of the agriculturalist.
The grand inquiry now is, Shall we make our own comforts, or go without
them at the will of a foreign nation ? He, therefore, who is now against domestic manufactures must be for reducing us either to dependence on that
foreign nation, or to be clothed in skins and to live like wild beasts in dens
and caverns. I am not one of those; experience has taught me that manufactures are now as necessary to our independence as to our comfort.—
Letter of Mr. Jefferson to Benjamin Austin.

I ask, What is the real situation of the agriculturalist ? Where has the
American farmer a market for his surplus produce ? Except for cotton, he
has neither a foreign nor a home market. Does not this clearly prove, when
there is no market at home or abroad, that there [is] too much labor employed in agriculture ? Common sense at once points out the remedy. Take
from agriculture six hundred thousand men, women, and children, and you
will at once give a market for more breadstuffs than all Europe now furnishes. In short, we have been too long subject to the policy of British
merchants. It is time we should become a little more Americanized, and
instead of feeding the paupers and laborers of England, feed our own; or
else in a short time, by continuing our present policy, we shall all be rendered paupers ourselves.—*General Jackson's Letter to Dr. Coleman.*

When our manufactures are grown to a certain perfection, as they soon
will be, under the fostering care of government, the farmer will find a ready
market for his surplus produce, and— what is of equal consequence — a certain and cheap supply of all he wants ; his prosperity will diffuse itself to
every class of the community.—*Speech of Hon. J. C. Calhoun on the Tariff.*

The question of revenue we will now briefly consider. For
several years past the revenues of the government have been unequal to its expenditures, and consequently loan after loan, sometimes direct and sometimes indirect in form, has been resorted to.
By this means a new national debt has been created, and is still
growing on us with a rapidity fearful to contemplate — a rapidity
only reasonably to be expected in time of war. This state of things
has been produced by a prevailing unwillingness either to increase
the tariff or resort to direct taxation. But the one or the other
must come. Coming expenditures must be met, and the present
debt must be paid; and money cannot always be borrowed for
these objects. The system of loans is but temporary in its nature,
and must soon explode. It is a system not only ruinous while it
lasts, but one that must soon fail and leave us destitute. As an in-

dividual who undertakes to live by borrowing soon finds his original means devoured by interest, and, next, no one left to borrow from, so must it be with a government.

We repeat, then, that a tariff sufficient for revenue, or a direct tax, must soon be resorted to; and, indeed, we believe this alternative is now denied by no one. But which system shall be adopted? Some of our opponents, in theory, admit the propriety of a tariff sufficient for a revenue; but even they will not in practice vote for such a tariff; while others boldly advocate direct taxation. Inasmuch, therefore, as some of them boldly advocate direct taxation, and all the rest—or so nearly all as to make exceptions needless—refuse to adopt the tariff, we think it is doing them no injustice to class them all as advocates of direct taxation. Indeed, we believe they are only delaying an open avowal of the system till they can assure themselves that the people will tolerate it. Let us, then, briefly compare the two systems. The tariff is the cheaper system, because the duties, being collected in large parcels at a few commercial points, will require comparatively few officers in their collection; while by the direct-tax system the land must be literally covered with assessors and collectors, going forth like swarms of Egyptian locusts, devouring every blade of grass and other green thing. And, again, by the tariff system the whole revenue is paid by the consumers of foreign goods, and those chiefly the luxuries, and not the necessaries, of life. By this system the man who contents himself to live upon the products of his own country pays nothing at all. And surely that country is extensive enough, and its products abundant and varied enough, to answer all the real wants of its people. In short, by this system the burthen of revenue falls almost entirely on the wealthy and luxurious few, while the substantial and laboring many who live at home, and upon home products, go entirely free. By the direct tax system none can escape. However strictly the citizen may exclude from his premises all foreign luxuries,—fine cloths, fine silks, rich wines, golden chains, and diamond rings,—still, for the possession of his house, his barn, and his homespun, he is to be perpetually haunted and harassed by the tax-gatherer. With these views we leave it to be determined whether we or our opponents are the more truly democratic on the subject.

The third resolution declares the necessity and propriety of a national bank. During the last fifty years so much has been said and written both as to the constitutionality and expediency of such an institution, that we could not hope to improve in the least on former discussions of the subject, were we to undertake it. We, therefore, upon the question of constitutionality content ourselves with remarking the facts that the first national bank was established chiefly by the same men who formed the Constitution, at a time when that instrument was but two years old, and receiving the sanction, as president, of the immortal Washington; that the second received the sanction, as president, of Mr. Madison, to whom common consent has awarded the proud title of "Father of the Constitution"; and subsequently the sanction of the Supreme Court, the most enlightened judicial tribunal in the world. Upon the question of expediency, we only ask you to examine the history of the times during the existence of the two banks, and compare those times with the miserable present.

The fourth resolution declares the expediency of Mr. Clay's Land Bill. Much incomprehensible jargon is often used against the constitutionality of this measure. We forbear, in this place, attempting an answer to it, simply because, in our opinion, those who urge it are through party zeal resolved not to see or acknowledge the truth. The question of expediency, at least so far as Illinois is concerned, seems to us the clearest imaginable. By the bill we are to receive annually a large sum of money, no part of which we otherwise receive. The precise annual sum cannot be known in advance; it doubtless will vary in different years. Still it is something to know that in the last year—a year of almost unparalleled pecuniary pressure—it amounted to more than forty thousand dollars. This annual income, in the midst of our almost insupportable difficulties, in the days of our severest necessity, our political opponents are furiously resolving to take and keep from us. And for what? Many silly reasons are given, as is usual in cases where a single good one is not to be found. One is that by giving us the proceeds of the lands, we impoverish the national treasury, and thereby render necessary an increase of the tariff. This may be true; but if so, the amount of it only is that those whose pride, whose abundance of means, prompt them to spurn the manufactures of our country, and to strut in British cloaks and coats and pantaloons, may have to pay a few cents more on the yard for the cloth that makes them. A terrible evil, truly, to the Illinois farmer, who never wore, nor ever expects to wear, a single yard of British goods in his whole life. Another of their reasons is that by the passage and continuance of Mr. Clay's bill, we prevent the passage of a bill which would give us more. This, if it were sound in itself, is waging destructive war with the former position; for if Mr. Clay's bill impoverishes the treasury too much, what shall be said of one that impoverishes it still more? But it is not sound in itself. It is not true that Mr. Clay's bill prevents the passage of one more favorable to us of the new States. Considering the strength and opposite interest of the old States, the wonder is that they ever permitted one to pass so favorable as Mr. Clay's. The last twenty-odd years' efforts to reduce the price of the lands, and to pass graduation bills and cession bills, prove the assertion to be true; and if there were no experience in support of it, the reason itself is plain. The States in which none, or few, of the public lands lie, and those consequently interested against parting with them except for the best price, are the majority; and a moment's reflection will show that they must ever continue the majority, because by the time one of the original new States (Ohio, for example) becomes populous and gets weight in Congress, the public lands in her limits are so nearly sold out that in every point material to this question she becomes an old State. She does not wish the price reduced, because there is none left for her citizens to buy; she does not wish them ceded to the States in which they lie, because they no longer lie in her limits, and she will get nothing by the cession. In the nature of things, the States interested in the reduction of price, in graduation, in cession, and in all similar projects, never can be the majority. Nor is there reason to hope that any of them can ever succeed as a Democratic party measure, because we have heretofore seen that party in full power, year after year, with many of their leaders making loud professions in favor of these projects, and yet doing nothing. What reason, then, is there to believe they will hereafter do better? In every light in which we can view this question, it amounts simply to this: Shall we accept our share of the proceeds under Mr. Clay's bill, or shall we rather reject that and get nothing?

The fifth resolution recommends that a Whig candidate for Congress be run in every district, regardless of the chances of success. We are aware that it is sometimes a temporary gratification, when a friend cannot succeed, to be able to choose between opponents; but we believe that that gratification is the seed-time which never fails to be followed by a most abundant harvest of bitterness. By this policy we entangle ourselves. By voting for our opponents, such of us as do it in some measure estop ourselves to complain of their acts, however glaringly wrong we may believe them to be. By this policy no one portion of our friends can ever be certain as to what course another portion may adopt; and by this want of mutual and perfect understanding our political identity is partially frittered away and lost. And, again, those who are thus elected by our aid ever become our bitterest persecutors. Take a few prominent examples. In 1830 Reynolds was so elected governor; in 1835 we exerted our whole strength to elect Judge Young to the United States Senate, which effort, though failing, gave him the prominence that subsequently elected him; in 1836 General Ewing was so elected to the United States Senate; and yet let us ask what three men have been more perseveringly vindictive in their assaults upon all our men and measures than they? During the last summer the whole State was covered with pamphlet editions of misrepresentations against us, methodized into chapters and verses, written by two of these same men,—Reynolds and Young,—in which they did not stop at charging us with error merely, but roundly denounced us as the designing enemies of human liberty itself. If it be the will of Heaven that such men shall politically live, be it so; but never, never again permit them to draw a particle of their sustenance from us.

The sixth resolution recommends the adoption of the convention system for the nomination of candidates. This we believe to be of the very first importance. Whether the system is right in itself we do not stop to inquire; contenting ourselves with trying to show that while our opponents use it, it is madness in us not to defend ourselves with it. Experience has shown that we cannot successfully defend ourselves without it. For examples, look at the elections of last year. Our candidate for governor, with the approbation of a large portion of the party, took the field without a nomination, and in open opposition to the system. Wherever in the counties the Whigs had held conventions and nominated candidates for the legislature, the aspirants who were not nominated were induced to rebel against the nominations, and to become candidates, as is said, "on their own hook." And, go where you would into a large Whig county, you were sure to find the Whigs not contending shoulder to shoulder against the common enemy, but divided into factions, and fighting furiously with one another. The election came, and what was the result? The governor beaten—the Whig vote being decreased many thousands since 1840, although the Democratic vote had not increased any. Beaten almost everywhere for members of the legislature,—Tazewell, with her four hundred Whig majority, sending a delegation half Democratic; Vermillion, with her five hundred, doing the same; Coles, with her four hundred, sending two out of three; and Morgan, with her two hundred and fifty, sending three out of four,—and this to say nothing of the numerous other less glaring examples; the whole winding up with the aggregate number of twenty-seven Democratic representatives sent from Whig counties. As to the senators, too, the result was of the same character. And it is most worthy to be remembered that of all the Whigs in the State who ran against the regular nominees, a single one only was elected. Although they succeeded in defeating the nominees almost by scores, they too were defeated, and the spoils chucklingly borne off by the common enemy?

We do not mention the fact of many of the Whigs opposing the convention system heretofore for the purpose of censuring them. Far from it. We expressly protest against such a conclusion. We know they were generally, perhaps universally, as good and true Whigs as we ourselves claim to be. We mention it merely to draw attention to the disastrous result it produced, as an example forever hereafter to be avoided. That "union is strength" is a truth that has been known, illustrated, and declared in various ways and forms in all ages of the world. That great fabulist and philosopher, Æsop, illustrated it by his fable of the bundle of sticks; and he whose wisdom surpasses that of all philosophers has declared that "a house divided against itself cannot stand." It is to induce our friends to act upon this important and universally acknowledged truth that we urge the adoption of the convention system. Reflection will prove that there is no other way of practically applying it. In its application we know there will be incidents temporarily painful; but, after all, those incidents will be fewer and less intense with than without the system. If two friends aspire to the same office it is certain that both cannot succeed. Would it not, then, be much less painful to have the question decided by mutual friends some time before, than to snarl and quarrel until the day of election, and then both be beaten by the common enemy?

Before leaving this subject, we think proper to remark that we do not understand the resolution as intended to recommend the application of the convention system to the nomination of candidates for the small offices no way connected with politics; though we must say we do not perceive that such an application of it would be wrong.

The seventh resolution recommends the holding of district con-

ventions in May next, for the purpose of nominating candidates for
Congress. The propriety of this rests upon the same reasons with
that of the sixth, and therefore needs no further discussion.

The eighth and ninth also relate merely to the practical application of the foregoing, and therefore need no discussion.

Before closing, permit us to add a few reflections on the present
condition and future prospects of the Whig party. In almost all
the States we have fallen into the minority, and despondency seems
to prevail universally among us. Is there just cause for this? In
1840 we carried the nation by more than a hundred and forty thousand majority. Our opponents charged that we did it by fraudulent
voting; but whatever they may have believed, we know the charge
to be untrue. Where, now, is that mighty host? Have they gone
over to the enemy? Let the results of the late elections answer.
Every State which has fallen off from the Whig cause since 1840
has done so not by giving more Democratic votes than they did
then, but by giving fewer Whig. Bouck, who was elected Democratic governor of New York last fall by more than 15,000 majority,
had not then as many votes as he had in 1840, when he was beaten
by seven or eight thousand. And so has it been in all the other
States which have fallen away from our cause. From this it is evident that tens of thousands in the late elections have not voted at
all. Who and what are they? is an important question, as respects
the future. They can come forward and give us the victory again.
That all, or nearly all, of them are Whigs is most apparent. Our
opponents, stung to madness by the defeat of 1840, have ever since
rallied with more than their usual unanimity. It has not been they
that have been kept from the polls. These facts show what the result must be, once the people again rally in their entire strength.
Proclaim these facts, and predict this result; and although unthink-
ing opponents may smile at us, the sagacious ones will "believe and
tremble." And why shall the Whigs not all rally again? Are their
principles less dear now than in 1840? Have any of their doctrines
since then been discovered to be untrue? It is true, the victory of
1840 did not produce the happy results anticipated; but it is equally
true, as we believe, that the unfortunate death of General Harrison
was the cause of the failure. It was not the election of General
Harrison that was expected to produce happy effects, but the measures to be adopted by his administration. By means of his death,
and the unexpected course of his successor, those measures were
never adopted. How could the fruits follow? The consequences
we always predicted would follow the failure of those measures have
followed, and are now upon us in all their horrors. By the course
of Mr. Tyler the policy of our opponents has continued in operation,
still leaving them with the advantage of charging all its evils upon
us as the results of a Whig administration. Let none be deceived
by this somewhat plausible, though entirely false charge. If they
ask us for the sufficient and sound currency we promised, let them
be answered that we only promised it through the medium of a national bank, which they, aided by Mr. Tyler, prevented our establishing. And let them be reminded, too, that their own policy in

relation to the currency has all the time been, and still is, in full operation. Let us then again come forth in our might, and by a second victory accomplish that which death only prevented in the first. We can do it. When did the Whigs ever fail if they were fully aroused and united? Even in single States and districts, under such circumstances, defeat seldom overtakes them. Call to mind the contested elections within the last few years, and particularly those of Moore and Letcher from Kentucky, Newland and Graham from North Carolina, and the famous New Jersey case. In all these districts Locofocoism had stalked omnipotent before; but when the whole people were aroused by its enormities on those occasions, they put it down never to rise again.

We declare it to be our solemn conviction, that the Whigs are always a majority of this nation; and that to make them always successful needs but to get them all to the polls and to vote unitedly. This is the great desideratum. Let us make every effort to attain it. At every election, let every Whig act as though he knew the result to depend upon his action. In the great contest of 1840, some more than twenty-one hundred thousand votes were cast, and so surely as there shall be that many, with the ordinary increase added, cast in 1844, that surely will a Whig be elected President of the United States.

A. LINCOLN,
S. T. LOGAN,
A. T. BLEDSOE.

March 4, 1843. .

March 24, 1843.—LETTER TO JOSHUA F. SPEED.

SPRINGFIELD, March 24, 1843.

Dear Speed: . . . We had a meeting of the Whigs of the county here on last Monday to appoint delegates to a district convention; and Baker beat me, and got the delegation instructed to go for him. The meeting, in spite of my attempt to decline it, appointed me one of the delegates; so that in getting Baker the nomination I shall be fixed a good deal like a fellow who is made a groomsman to a man that has cut him out and is marrying his own dear "gal." About the prospects of your having a namesake at our town, can't say exactly yet.

A. LINCOLN.

March 26, 1843.—LETTER TO MARTIN M. MORRIS.

SPRINGFIELD, ILLINOIS, March 26, 1843.

Friend Morris: Your letter of the 23d was received on yesterday morning, and for which (instead of an excuse, which you thought proper to ask) I tender you my sincere thanks. It is truly gratifying to me to learn that while the people of Sangamon have cast me off, my old friends of Menard, who have known me longest and best, stick to me. It would astonish, if not amuse, the older citizens to learn that I (a stranger, friendless, uneducated, penniless boy, working on a flatboat at ten dollars per month) have been put down here as the candidate of pride, wealth, and aristocratic family distinction. Yet so, chiefly, it was. There was, too, the strangest combination of church influence against me. Baker is a Campbellite; and therefore, as I suppose, with few exceptions got all that church. My wife has some relations in the Presbyterian churches, and some with the Episcopal churches; and therefore, wherever it would tell, I was set down as either the one or the other, while it was everywhere contended that no Christian ought to go for me, because I belonged to no church, was suspected of being a deist, and had talked about fighting a duel. With all these things, Baker, of course, had nothing to do. Nor do I complain of them. As to his own church going for him, I think that was right enough, and as to the influences I have spoken of in the other, though they were very strong, it would be grossly untrue and unjust to charge that they acted upon them in a body, or were very near so. I only mean that those influences levied a tax of a considerable per cent. upon my strength throughout the religious controversy. But enough of this.

You say that in choosing a candidate for Congress you have an equal right with Sangamon, and in this you are undoubtedly correct. In agreeing to withdraw if the Whigs of Sangamon should go against me, I did not mean that they alone were worth consulting, but that if she, with her heavy delegation, should be against me, it would be impossible for me to succeed, and therefore I had as well decline. And in relation to Menard having rights, permit me fully to recognize them, and to express the opinion, that if she and Mason act circumspectly, they will in the convention be able so far to enforce their rights as to decide absolutely which one of the candidates shall be successful. Let me show the reason of this. Hardin, or some other Morgan candidate, will get Putnam, Marshall, Woodford, Tazewell, and Logan—making sixteen. Then you and Mason, having three, can give the victory to either side.

You say you shall instruct your delegates for me, unless I object. I certainly shall not object. That would be too pleasant a compliment for me to tread in the dust. And besides, if anything should happen (which, however, is not probable) by which Baker should be thrown out of the fight, I would be at liberty to accept the nomination if I could get it. I do, however, feel myself bound not to hinder him in any way from getting the nomination. I should despise myself were I to attempt it. I think, then, it would be proper for your meeting to appoint three delegates, and to instruct them to go for some one as a first choice, some one else as a second, and perhaps some one as a third; and if in those instructions I were named as the first choice, it would gratify me very much. If you wish to hold the balance of power, it is important for you to attend to and secure the vote of Mason also. You should be sure to have men appointed delegates that you know you can safely confide in. If yourself and James Short were appointed from your county, all would be safe; but whether Jim's woman affair a year ago might not be in the way of his appointment is a question. I don't know whether you know it, but I know him to be as honorable a man as there is in the world. You have my permission, and even request, to show this letter to Short; but to no one else, unless it be a very particular friend, who you know will not speak of it.

Yours as ever,   A. LINCOLN.

P. S. Will you write me again?

To MARTIN M. MORRIS, Petersburg, Illinois.

April 14, 1843.—LETTER TO MARTIN M. MORRIS.

April 14, 1843.

Friend Morris: I have heard it intimated that Baker has been attempting to get you or Miles, or both of you, to violate the instructions of the meeting that appointed you, and to go for him. I have insisted, and still insist, that this cannot be true. Surely Baker would not do the like. As well might Hardin ask me to vote for him in the convention. Again, it is said there will be an attempt to get up instructions in your county requiring you to go for Baker. This is all wrong. Upon the same rule, why might not I fly from the decision against me in Sangamon, and get up instructions to their delegates to go for me? There are at least 1200 Whigs in the county that took no part, and yet I would as soon put my head in the fire as to attempt it. Besides, if any one should get the nomination by such extraordinary means, all harmony in the district would inevitably be lost. Honest Whigs (and very nearly all of them are honest) would not quietly abide such enormities. I repeat, such an attempt on Baker's part cannot be true. Write me at Springfield how the matter is. Don't show or speak of this letter.

A. LINCOLN.

May 18, 1843.—LETTER TO JOSHUA F. SPEED.

SPRINGFIELD, May 18, 1843.

Dear Speed: Yours of the 9th instant is duly received, which I do not meet as a "bore," but as a most welcome visitor. I will answer the business part of it first. . . .

In relation to our Congress matter here, you were right in supposing I would support the nominee. Neither Baker nor I, however, is the man, but Hardin, so far as I can judge from present appearances. We shall have no split or trouble about the matter; all will be harmony. In relation to the "coming events" about which Butler wrote you, I had not heard one word before I got your letter; but I have so much confidence in the judgment of a Butler on such a subject that I incline to think there may be some reality in it. What day does Butler appoint? By the way, how do "events" of

VOL. I.—6.

the same sort come on in your family? Are you possessing houses and lands, and oxen and asses, and men-servants and maid-servants, and begetting sons and daughters? We are not keeping house, but boarding at the Globe Tavern, which is very well kept now by a widow lady of the name of Beck. Our room (the same that Dr. Wallace occupied there) and boarding only costs us four dollars a week. Ann Todd was married something more than a year since to a fellow by the name of Campbell, and who, Mary says, is pretty much of a "dunce," though he has a little money and property. They live in Boonville, Missouri, and have not been heard from lately enough for me to say anything about her health. I reckon it will scarcely be in our power to visit Kentucky this year. Besides poverty and the necessity of attending to business, those "coming events," I suspect, would be somewhat in the way. I most heartily wish you and your Fanny would not fail to come. Just let us know the time, and we will have a room provided for you at our house, and all be merry together for a while. Be sure to give my respects to your mother and family; assure her that if ever I come near her, I will not fail to call and see her. Mary joins in sending love to your Fanny and you.   Yours as ever,

A. LINCOLN.

November 17, 1845.—LETTER TO B. F. JAMES.

SPRINGFIELD, November 17, 1845.

Friend James: The paper at Pekin has nominated Hardin for governor; and, commenting on this, the Alton paper indirectly nominated him for Congress. It would give Hardin a great start, and perhaps use me up, if the Whig papers of the district should nominate him for Congress. If your feelings toward me are the same as when I saw you (which I have no reason to doubt), I wish you would let nothing appear in your paper which may operate against me. You understand. Matters stand just as they did when I saw you. Baker is certainly off the track, and I fear Hardin intends to be on it.

In relation to the business you wrote me of some time since, I suppose the marshal called on you; and we think it can be adjusted at court to the satisfaction of you and friend Thompson.

A. LINCOLN.

November 24, 1845.—LETTER TO B. F. JAMES.

SPRINGFIELD, November 24, 1845.

Friend James: Yours of the 19th was not received till this morning. The error I fell into in relation to the Pekin paper I discovered myself the day after I wrote you. The way I fell into it was that Stuart (John T.) met me in the court, and told me about a nomination having been made in the Pekin paper, and about the comments upon it in the Alton paper; and without seeing either paper myself, I wrote you. In writing to you, I only meant to call your attention to the matter; and that done, I knew all would be right with you. Of course I should not have thought this necessary if at the time I had known that the nomination had been made in your paper. And let me assure you that if there is anything in my letter indicating an opinion that the nomination for governor, which I supposed to have been made in the Pekin paper, was operating or could operate against me, such was not my meaning. Now that I know that nomination was made by you, I say that it may do me good, while I do not see that it can do me harm. But, while the subject is in agitation, should any of the papers in the district nominate the same man for Congress, that would do me harm; and it was that which I wished to guard against. Let me assure you that I do not for a moment suppose that what you have done is illjudged, or that anything that you shall do will be. It was not to object to the course of the Pekin paper (as I thought it), but to guard against any falling into the wake of the Alton paper, that I wrote.

You perhaps have noticed the "Journal's" article of last week upon the same subject. It was written without any consultation with me, but I was told by Francis of its purport before it was published. I chose to let it go as it was, lest it should be suspected that I was attempting to juggle Hardin out of a nomination for Congress by juggling him into one for governor. If you, and the other papers a little more distant from me, choose to take the same course you have, of course I have no objection. After you shall have received this, I think we shall fully understand each other, and that our views as to the effect of these things are not dissimilar. Confidential, of course.   Yours as ever,

                                             A. LINCOLN.

January 14, 1846.—LETTER TO B. F. JAMES.

SPRINGFIELD, January 14, 1846.

Friend James: Yours of the 10th was not received until this morning. I cannot but be pleased with its contents. I saw Henry's communication in your paper, as also your editorial remarks, neither of which, in my opinion, was in any way misjudged,—both quite the thing. I think just as you do concerning the dictation of the course of the Alton paper, and also concerning its utter harmlessness. As to the proposition to hold the convention at Petersburg, I will at once tell you all I know and all I feel. A good friend of ours there—John Bennett—wrote me that he thought it would do good with the Whigs of Menard to see a respectable convention conducted in good style. They are a little disinclined to adopt the convention system; and Bennett thinks some of their prejudices would be done away by their having the convention amongst them. At his request, therefore, I had the little paragraph put in the "Journal." This is all I know. Now as to what I feel. I feel a desire that they of Petersburg should be gratified, if it can be done without a sacrifice of the wishes of others, and without detriment to the cause — nothing more. I can gain nothing in the contest by having it there. I showed your letter to Stuart, and he thinks there is something in your suggestion of holding it at your town. I should be pleased if I could concur with you in the hope that my name would be the only one presented to the convention; but I cannot. Hardin is a man of desperate energy and perseverance, and one that never backs out; and, I fear, to think otherwise is to be deceived in the character of our adversary. I would rejoice to be spared the labor of a contest; but "being in," I shall go it thoroughly, and to the bottom. As to my being able to make a break in the lower counties, I tell you that I can possibly get Cass, but I do not think I will. Morgan and Scott are beyond my reach; Menard is safe to me; Mason, neck and neck; Logan is mine. To make the matter sure, your entire senatorial district must be secured. Of this I suppose Tazewell is safe; and I have much done in both the other counties. In Woodford I have Davenport, Simons, Willard, Bracken, Perry, Travis, Dr. Hazzard, and the Clarks and some others, all specially committed. At Lacon, in Marshall, the very most active friend I have in the district (if I except yourself) is at work. Through him I have procured their names, and written to three or four of the most active Whigs in each precinct of the county. Still I wish you all in Tazewell to keep your eyes continually on Woodford and Marshall. Let no opportunity of making a mark escape. When they shall be safe, all will be safe, I think.

The Beardstown paper is entirely in the hands of my friends. The editor is a Whig, and personally dislikes Hardin. When the Supreme Court shall adjourn (which it is thought will be about the 15th of February), it is my intention to take a quiet trip through the towns and neighborhoods of Logan County, Delevan, Tremont, and on to and through the upper counties. Don't speak of this, or let it relax any of your vigilance. When I shall reach Tremont, we will talk over everything at large. Yours truly,

A. LINCOLN.

January 16, 1846.—LETTER TO B. F. JAMES.

SPRINGFIELD, January 16, 1846.

Dear James: A plan is on foot to change the mode of selecting the candidate for this district. The movement is intended to injure me, and, if effected, most likely would injure me to some extent. I have not time to give particulars now; but I want you to let nothing prevent your getting an article in your paper of this week, taking strong ground for the old system under which Hardin and Baker were nominated, without seeming to know or suspect that any one desires to change it. I have written Dr. Henry more at length, and he will probably call and consult with you on getting up the article; but whether he does or not, don't fail, on any account, to get it in this week.

A. LINCOLN.

January 27, 1846.—LETTER TO B. F. JAMES.

SPRINGFIELD, January 27, 1846.

Dear James: Yours, inclosing the article from the "Whig," is received. In my judgment, you have hit the matter exactly right. I believe it is too late to get the article in the "Journal" of this week; but Dickinson will understand it just as well from your paper, knowing as he does your position toward me. More than all, I wrote him at the same time I did you. As to suggestions for the committee, I would say appoint the convention for the first Monday of May. As to the place, I can hardly make a suggestion, so many points desiring it. I was at Petersburg Saturday and Sunday, and they are very anxious for it there. A friend has also written me desiring it at Beardstown.

I would have the committee leave the mode of choosing delegates to the Whigs of the different counties, as may best suit them respectively. I would have them propose, for the sake of uniformity, that the delegates should all be instructed as to their man, and the delegation of each county should go as a unit. If, without this, some counties should send united delegations and others divided ones, it might make bad work. Also have it proposed that when the convention shall meet, if there shall be any absent delegates, the members present may fill the vacancies with persons to act under the same instructions which may be known to have been given to such absentees. You understand. Other particulars I leave to you. I am sorry to say I am afraid I cannot go to Mason, so as to attend to your business; but if I shall determine to go there, I will write you.

Do you hear anything from Woodford and Marshall? Davenport, ten days ago, passed through here, and told me Woodford is safe; but, though in hope, I am not entirely easy about Marshall. I have so few personal acquaintances in that county that I cannot get at [it] right. Dickinson is doing all that any one man can do; but it seems like it is an overtask for one. I suppose Dr. Henry will be with you on Saturday. I got a letter from him to-day on the same subject as yours, and shall write him before Saturday.

Yours truly,   A. LINCOLN.

April 18, 1846.—LETTER TO —— JOHNSTON.

TREMONT, April 18, 1846.

Friend Johnston: Your letter, written some six weeks since, was received in due course, and also the paper with the parody. It is true, as suggested it might be, that I have never seen Poe's "Raven"; and I very well know that a parody is almost entirely dependent for its interest upon the reader's acquaintance with the original. Still there is enough in the polecat, self-considered, to afford one several hearty laughs. I think four or five of the last stanzas are decidedly funny, particularly where Jeremiah "scrubbed and washed, and prayed and fasted."

I have not your letter now before me; but, from memory, I think you ask me who is the author of the piece I sent you, and that you do so ask as to indicate a slight suspicion that I myself am the author. Beyond all question, I am not the author. I would give all I am worth, and go in debt, to be able to write so fine a piece as I think that is. Neither do I know who is the author. I met it in a straggling form in a newspaper last summer, and I remember to have seen it once before, about fifteen years ago, and this is all I know about it. The piece of poetry of my own which I alluded to, I was led to write under the following circumstances. In the fall of 1844, thinking I might aid some to carry the State of Indiana for Mr. Clay, I went into the neighborhood in that State in which I was raised, where my mother and only sister were buried, and from which I had been absent about fifteen years. That part of the country is, within itself, as unpoetical as any spot of the earth; but still, seeing it and its objects and inhabitants aroused feelings in me which were certainly poetry; though whether my expression of those feelings is poetry is quite another question. When I got to writing, the change of subject divided the thing into four little divisions or cantos, the first only of which I send you now, and may send the others hereafter.   Yours truly,

A. LINCOLN.

> My childhood's home I see again,
>   And sadden with the view;
> And still, as memory crowds my brain,
>   There's pleasure in it too.
>
> O Memory! thou midway world
>   'Twixt earth and paradise,
> Where things decayed and loved ones lost
>   In dreamy shadows rise,
>
> And, freed from all that's earthly vile,
>   Seem hallowed, pure, and bright,
> Like scenes in some enchanted isle
>   All bathed in liquid light.
>
> As dusky mountains please the eye
>   When twilight chases day;
> As bugle-notes that, passing by,
>   In distance die away;
>
> As leaving some grand waterfall,
>   We, lingering, list its roar —
> So memory will hallow all
>   We've known, but know no more.
>
> Near twenty years have passed away
>   Since here I bid farewell
> To woods and fields, and scenes of play,
>   And playmates loved so well.

Where many were, but few remain
  Of old familiar things;
But seeing them, to mind again
  The lost and absent brings.

The friends I left that parting day,
  How changed, as time has sped!
Young childhood grown, strong manhood gray,
  And half of all are dead.

I hear the loved survivors tell
  How nought from death could save,
Till every sound appears a knell,
  And every spot a grave.

I range the fields with pensive tread,
  And pace the hollow rooms,
And feel (companion of the dead)
  I 'm living in the tombs.

September 6, 1846.—LETTER TO —— JOHNSTON.

SPRINGFIELD, September 6, 1846.

Friend Johnston: You remember when I wrote you from Tremont last spring, sending you a little canto of what I called poetry, I promised to bore you with another some time. I now fulfil the promise. The subject of the present one is an insane man; his name is Matthew Gentry. He is three years older than I, and when we were boys we went to school together. He was rather a bright lad, and the son of *the* rich man of a very poor neighborhood. At the age of nineteen he unaccountably became furiously mad, from which condition he gradually settled down into harmless insanity. When, as I told you in my other letter, I visited my old home in the fall of 1844, I found him still lingering in this wretched condition. In my poetizing mood, I could not forget the impression his case made upon me. Here is the result.

But here's an object more of dread
  Than aught the grave contains—
A human form with reason fled,
  While wretched life remains.

When terror spread, and neighbors ran
  Your dangerous strength to bind,
And soon, a howling, crazy man,
  Your limbs were fast confined:

How then you strove and shrieked aloud,
  Your bones and sinews bared;
And fiendish on the gazing crowd
  With burning eyeballs glared;

And begged and swore, and wept and prayed,
  With maniac laughter joined;
How fearful were these signs displayed
  By pangs that killed the mind!

And when at length the drear and long
  Time soothed thy fiercer woes,
How plaintively thy mournful song
  Upon the still night rose!

I've heard it oft as if I dreamed,
  Far distant, sweet and lone,
The funeral dirge it ever seemed
  Of reason dead and gone.

To drink its strains I've stole away,
  All stealthily and still,
Ere yet the rising god of day
  Had streaked the eastern hill.

Air held her breath; trees with the spell
  Seemed sorrowing angels round,
Whose swelling tears in dewdrops fell
  Upon the listening ground.

But this is past, and naught remains
  That raised thee o'er the brute;
Thy piercing shrieks and soothing strain
  Are like, forever mute.

Now fare thee well! More thou the cause
  Than subject now of woe.
All mental pangs by time's kind laws
  Hast lost the power to know.

O death! thou awe-inspiring prince
  That keepst the world in fear,
Why dost thou tear more blest ones hence,
  And leave him lingering here?

If I should ever send another, the subject will be a "Bear-Hunt."
              Yours as ever,   A. LINCOLN.

October 22, 1846.—LETTER TO JOSHUA F. SPEED.

                    SPRINGFIELD, October 22, 1846.

Dear Speed: . . . You, no doubt, assign the suspension of
our correspondence to the true philosophic cause; though it must
be confessed by both of us that this is rather a cold reason for
allowing a friendship such as ours to die out by degrees. I propose

now that, upon receipt of this, you shall be considered in my debt, and under obligations to pay soon, and that neither shall remain long in arrears hereafter. Are you agreed?

Being elected to Congress, though I am very grateful to our friends for having done it, has not pleased me as much as I expected.

We have another boy, born the 10th of March. He is very much such a child as Bob was at his age, rather of a longer order. Bob is "short and low," and I expect always will be. He talks very plainly,—almost as plainly as anybody. He is quite smart enough. I sometimes fear that he is one of the little rare-ripe sort that are smarter at about five than ever after. He has a great deal of that sort of mischief that is the offspring of such animal spirits. Since I began this letter, a messenger came to tell me Bob was lost; but by the time I reached the house his mother had found him and had him whipped, and by now, very likely, he is run away again. Mary has read your letter, and wishes to be remembered to Mrs. Speed and you, in which I most sincerely join her. As ever yours,

A. LINCOLN.

February 25, 1847.—LETTER TO —— JOHNSTON.

SPRINGFIELD, February 25, 1847.

Dear Johnston: Yours of the 2d of December was duly delivered to me by Mr. Williams. To say the least, I am not at all displeased with your proposal to publish the poetry, or doggerel, or whatever else it may be called, which I sent you. I consent that it may be done, together with the third canto, which I now send you. Whether the prefatory remarks in my letter shall be published with the verses, I leave entirely to your discretion; but let names be suppressed by all means. I have not sufficient hope of the verses attracting any favorable notice to tempt me to risk being ridiculed for having written them.

Why not drop into the paper, at the same time, the "half dozen stanzas of your own"? Or if, for any reason, it suit your feelings better, send them to me, and I will take pleasure in putting them in the paper here. Family well, and nothing new. Yours sincerely,

A. LINCOLN.

[December 1, 1847?].—FRAGMENTS OF TARIFF DISCUSSION.

Whether the protective policy shall be finally abandoned is now the question.—Discussion and experience already had, and question now in greater dispute than ever.—Has there not been some great error in the mode of discussion?—Propose a single issue of fact, namely: From 1816 to the present, have protected articles cost us more of labor during the higher than during the lower duties upon them?—Introduce the evidence.—Analyze this issue, and try to show that it embraces the true and the whole question of the protective policy.—Intended as a test of experience.—The period selected is fair, because it is a period of peace—a period sufficiently long [to] furnish a fair average under all other causes operating on prices, a period in which various modifications of higher and lower duties have occurred.—Protected articles only are embraced. Show that these only belong to the question.—The labor price only is embraced. Show this to be correct.

.   .   .   .

I suppose the true effect of duties upon prices to be as follows: If a certain duty be levied upon an article which by nature cannot be produced in this country, as three cents a pound upon coffee, the effect will be that the consumer will pay one cent more per pound than before, the producer will take one cent less, and the merchant one cent less in profits; in other words, the burden of the duty will [be] distributed over consumption, production, and commerce, and not confined to either. But if a duty amounting to full protection be levied upon an article which can be produced here with as little labor as elsewhere,—as iron,—that article will ultimately, and at no distant day, in consequence of such duty, be sold to our people cheaper than before, at least by the amount of the cost of carrying it from abroad.

First. As to useless labor. Before proceeding, however, it may be as well to give a specimen of what I conceive to be useless labor. I say, then, that all carrying, and incidents of carrying, of articles from the place of their production to a distant place for consumption, which articles could be produced of as good quality, in sufficient quantity and with as little labor, at the place of consumption as at the place carried from, is useless labor. Applying this principle to our own country by an example, let us suppose that A and B are a Pennsylvania farmer and a Pennsylvania iron-maker whose lands are adjoining. Under the protective policy A is furnishing B with bread and meat, and vegetables and fruits, and food for horses and oxen, and fresh supplies of horses and oxen themselves occasionally, and receiving in exchange all the iron, iron utensils, tools, and implements he needs. In this process of exchange each receives the whole of that which the other parts with, and the reward of labor between them is perfect — each receiving the product of just so much labor as he has himself bestowed on what he parts with for it. But the change comes. The protective policy is abandoned, and A determines to buy his iron and iron manufactures of C in Europe. This he can only do by a direct or an indirect exchange of the produce of his farm for them. We will suppose the direct exchange is adopted. In this A desires to exchange ten barrels of flour—the precise product of one hundred days' labor—for the largest quantity of iron, etc., that he can get. C also wishes to exchange the precise product, in iron, of one hundred days' labor for the greatest quantity of flour he can get. In intrinsic value the things to be so exchanged are precisely equal. But before this exchange can take place, the flour must be carried from Pennsylvania to England, and the iron from England to Pennsylvania. The flour starts. The wagoner who hauls it to Philadelphia takes a part of it to pay him for his labor; then a merchant there takes a little more for storage and forwarding commission, and another takes a little more for insurance; and then the ship-owner carries it across the water, and takes a little more of it for his trouble. Still, before it reaches C, it is tolled two or three times more for storage, drayage, commission, and so on; so that when C gets it there are but seven and a half barrels of it left. The iron, too, in its transit from England to Pennsylvania, goes through the same process of tolling; so that when it reaches A there are but three quarters of it left. The result of this case is that A and C have each parted with one hundred days' labor, and each received but seventy-five in return. That the carrying in this case was introduced by A ceasing to buy of B and turning [to] C; that it was utterly useless; and that it is ruinous in its effects upon A, are all little less than self-evident. "But," asks one, "if A is now only getting three quarters as much iron from C for ten barrels of flour as he used to get of B, why does he not turn back to B?" The answer is: "B has quit making iron, and so has none to sell." "But why did B quit making?" "Because A quit buying of him, and he had no other customer to sell to." "But surely A did not cease buying of B with the expectation of buying of C on harder terms?" "Certainly not. Let me tell you how that was. When B was making iron as well as C, B had but one customer, this farmer A; C had four customers in Europe."

. . . .

It seems to be an opinion very generally entertained that the condition of a nation is best whenever it can buy cheapest; but this is not necessarily true, because if, at the same time and by the same cause, it is compelled to sell correspondingly cheap, nothing is gained. Then it is said the best condition is when we can buy cheapest and sell dearest; but this again is not necessarily true, because with both these we might have scarcely anything to sell, or, which is the same thing, to buy with. To illustrate this, suppose a man in the present state of things is laboring the year round, at ten dollars per month, which amounts in the year to $120. A change in affairs enables him to buy supplies at half the former price, to get fifty dollars per month for his labor, but at the same time deprives him of employment during all the months of the year but one. In this case, though goods have fallen one half, and labor risen five to one, it is still plain that at the end of the year the laborer is twenty dollars poorer than under the old state of things.

These reflections show that to reason and act correctly on this subject we must look not merely to buying cheap, nor yet to buying cheap and selling dear, but also to having constant employment, so that we may have the largest possible amount of something to sell. This matter of employment can only be secured by an ample, steady, and certain market to sell the products of our labor in.

But let us yield the point, and admit that by abandoning the protective policy our farmers can purchase their supplies of manufactured articles cheaper than by continuing it; and then let us see whether, even at that, they will upon the whole be gainers by the change. To simplify this question, let us suppose the whole agricultural interest of the country to be in the hands of one man, who has one hundred laborers in his employ; the whole manufacturing interest to be in the hands of one other man, who has twenty laborers in his employ. The farmer owns all the plow and pasture land, and the manufacturer all the iron-mines and coal-banks and sites of water-power. Each is pushing on in his own way, and obtaining supplies from the other so far as he needs,—that is, the manufacturer is buying of the farmer all the cotton he can use in his cotton-factory; all the wool he can use in his woolen establishment; all the bread and meat, as well as all the fruits and vegetables, which are necessary for himself and all his hands in all his departments; all the corn and oats and hay which are necessary for all his horses and oxen, as well as fresh supplies of horses and oxen themselves to do all his heavy hauling about his iron-works and generally of every sort. The farmer, in turn, is buying of the manufacturer all the iron, iron tools, wooden tools, cotton goods, woolen goods, etc., that he needs in his business and for his hands. But after a while farmer discovers that were it not for the protective policy he could buy all these supplies cheaper from a European manufacturer, owing to the fact that the price of labor is only one quarter as high there as here. He and his hands are a majority of the whole, and therefore have the legal and moral right to have their interest first consulted. They throw off the protective policy, and farmer ceases buying of home manufacturer. Very soon, however, he discovers that to buy even at the cheaper rate requires something to buy with, and somehow or other he is falling short in this particular.

.   .   .   .

In the early days of our race the Almighty said to the first of our race, "In the sweat of thy face shalt thou eat bread"; and since then, if we except the light and the air of heaven, no good thing has been or can be enjoyed by us without having first cost labor. And inasmuch as most good things are produced by labor, it follows that all such things of right belong to those whose labor has produced them. But it has so happened, in all ages of the world, that some have labored, and others have without labor enjoyed a large proportion of the fruits. This is wrong, and should not continue. To secure to each laborer the whole product of his labor, or as nearly as possible, is a worthy object of any good government.

But then a question arises, How can a government best effect this? In our own country, in its present condition, will the protective principle advance or retard this object? Upon this subject the habits of our whole species fall into three great classes—useful labor, useless labor, and idleness. Of these the first only is meritorious, and to it all the products of labor rightfully belong; but the two latter, while they exist, are heavy pensioners upon the first, robbing it of a large portion of its just rights. The only remedy for this is to, so far as possible, drive useless labor and idleness out of existence. And, first, as to useless labor. Before making war upon this, we must learn to distinguish it from the useful. It appears to me that all labor done directly and indirectly in carrying articles to the place of consumption, which could have been produced in sufficient abundance, with as little labor, at the place of consumption as at the place they were carried from, is useless labor. Let us take a few examples of the application of this principle to our own country. Iron, and everything made of iron, can be produced in sufficient abundance, and with as little labor, in the United States as anywhere else in the world; therefore all labor done in bringing iron and its fabrics from a foreign country to the United States is useless labor. The same precisely may be said of cotton, wool, and of their fabrics respectively, as well as many other articles. While the uselessness of the carrying labor is equally true of all the articles mentioned, and of many others not mentioned, it is perhaps more glaringly obvious in relation to the cotton goods we purchase from abroad. The raw cotton from which they are made itself grows in our own country, is carried by land and by water to England, is there spun, wove, dyed, stamped, etc., and then carried back again and worn in the very country where it grew, and partly by the very persons who grew it. Why should it not be spun, wove, etc., in the very neighborhood where it both grows and is consumed, and the carrying thereby dispensed with? Has nature interposed any obstacle? Are not all the agents—animal-power, water-power, and steam-power—as good and as abundant here as elsewhere? Will not as small an amount of human labor answer here as elsewhere? We may easily see that the cost of this useless labor is very heavy. It includes not only the cost of the actual carriage, but also the insurances of every kind, and the profits of the merchants through whose hands it passes. All these create a heavy burden necessarily falling upon the useful labor connected with such articles, either depressing the price to the producer or advancing it to the consumer, or, what is more probable, doing both in part.

A supposed case will serve to illustrate several points now to the purpose. A, in the interior of South Carolina, has one hundred pounds of cotton, which we suppose to be the precise product of one man's labor for twenty days. B, in Manchester, England, has one hundred yards of cotton cloth, the precise product of the same amount of labor. This lot of cotton and lot of cloth are precisely equal to each other in their intrinsic value. But A wishes to part with his cotton for the largest quantity of cloth he can get. B also wishes to part with his cloth for the greatest quantity of cotton he can get. An exchange is therefore necessary; but before this can be effected, the cotton must be carried to Manchester, and the cloth to South Carolina. The cotton starts to Manchester. The man that hauls it to Charleston in his wagon takes a little of it out to pay him for his trouble; the merchant who stores it a while before the ship is ready to sail takes a little out for his trouble; the ship-owner who carries it across the water takes a little out for his trouble. Still, before it gets to Manchester it is tolled two or three times more for drayage, storage, commission, and so on; so that when it reaches B's hands there are but seventy-five pounds of it left. The cloth, too, in its transit from Manchester to South Carolina, goes through the same process of tolling; so that when it reaches A there are but seventy-five yards of it. Now, in this case, A and B have each parted with twenty days' labor, and each received but fifteen in return. But now let us suppose that B has removed to the side of A's farm in South Carolina, and has there made his lot of cloth. Is it not clear that he and A can then exchange their cloth and cotton, each getting the whole of what the other parts with?

This supposed case shows the utter uselessness of the carrying labor in all similar cases, and also the direct burden it imposes upon useful labor.   And whoever will take up the train of reflection suggested by this case, and run it out to the full extent of its just application, will be astonished at the amount of useless labor he will thus discover to be done in this very way.   I am mistaken if it is not in fact many times over equal to all the real want in the world. This useless labor I would have discontinued, and those engaged in it added to the class of useful laborers.   If I be asked whether I would destroy all commerce, I answer, Certainly not; I would continue it where it is necessary, and discontinue it where it is not. An instance: I would continue commerce so far as it is employed in bringing us coffee, and I would discontinue it so far as it is employed in bringing us cotton goods.

But let us yield the point, and admit that by abandoning the protective policy our farmers can purchase their supplies of manufactured articles cheaper than before; and then let us see whether, even at that, the farmers will upon the whole be gainers by the change.   To simplify this question, let us suppose our whole population to consist of but twenty men.   Under the prevalence of the protective policy, fifteen of these are farmers, one is a miller, one manufactures iron, one implements from iron, one cotton goods, and one woolen goods.   The farmers discover that, owing to labor only costing one quarter as much in Europe as here, they can buy iron, iron implements, cotton goods, and woolen goods cheaper when brought from Europe than when made by their neighbors. They are the majority, and therefore have both the legal and moral right to have their interest first consulted.   They throw off the protective policy, and cease buying these articles of their neighbors. But they soon discover that to buy, and at the cheaper rate, requires something to buy with.   Falling short in this particular, one of these farmers takes a load of wheat to the miller and gets it made into flour, and starts, as had been his custom, to the iron furnace. He approaches the well-known spot, but, strange to say, all is cold and still as death; no smoke rises, no furnace roars, no anvil rings. After some search he finds the owner of the desolate place, and calls out to him, "Come, Vulcan, don't you want to buy a load of flour?" "Why," says Vulcan, "I am hungry enough, to be sure,—have n't tasted bread for a week; but then you see my works are stopped, and I have nothing to give you for your flour." "But, Vulcan, why don't you go to work and get something?" "I am ready to do so.   Will you hire me, farmer?" "Oh, no; I could only set you to raising wheat, and you see I have more of that already than I can get anything for." "But give me employment, and send your flour to Europe for a market." "Why, Vulcan, how silly you talk! Don't you know they raise wheat in Europe as well as here, and that labor is so cheap there as to fix the price of flour there so low as scarcely to pay the long carriage of it from here, leaving nothing whatever to me?" "But, farmer, could n't you pay to raise and prepare garden-stuffs, and fruits, such as radishes, cabbages, Irish and sweet potatoes, cucumbers, watermelons and musk-melons, plums, pears, peaches, apples, and the like? All these are good things, and used to sell well." "So they did use to sell well; but it was to *you* we sold them, and now you tell us you have nothing to buy with. Of course I cannot sell such things to the other farmers, because each of them raises enough for himself, and in fact rather wishes to sell than to buy. Neither can I send them to Europe for a market, because, to say nothing of European markets being stocked with such articles at lower prices than I can afford, they are of such a nature as to rot before they could reach there. The truth is, Vulcan, I am compelled to quit raising these things altogether, except a few for my own use; and this leaves part of my own time idle on my hands, instead of my finding employment for you."

   .   .   .   .   .   .

If at any time all labor should cease, and all existing provisions be equally divided among the people, at the end of a single year there could scarcely be one human being left alive; all would have perished by want of subsistence. So, again, if upon such division all that sort of labor which produces provisions should cease, and each individual should take up so much of his share as he could, and carry it continually around his habitation, although in this carrying the amount of labor going on might be as great as ever so long as it could last, at the end of the year the result would be precisely the same — that is, none would be left living.

The first of these propositions shows that universal idleness would speedily result in universal ruin; and the second shows that useless labor is, in this respect, the same as idleness. I submit, then, whether it does not follow that partial idleness and partial useless labor would, in the proportion of their extent, in like manner result in partial ruin; whether, if all should subsist upon the labor that one half should perform, it would not result in very scanty allowance to the whole.

Believing that these propositions and the conclusions I draw from them cannot be successfully controverted, I for the present assume their correctness, and proceed to try to show that the abandonment of the protective policy by the American government must result in the increase of both useless labor and idleness, and so, in proportion, must produce want and ruin among our people.

(The foregoing scraps about protection were written by Lincoln between his election to Congress in 1846 and taking his seat in December, 1847.)

December 5, 1847.—LETTER TO WILLIAM H. HERNDON.

WASHINGTON, December 5, 1847.

Dear William : You may remember that about a year ago a man by the name of Wilson (James Wilson, I think) paid us twenty dollars as an advance fee to attend to a case in the Supreme Court for him, against a Mr. Campbell, the record of which case was in the hands of Mr. Dixon of St. Louis, who never furnished it to us. When I was at Bloomington last fall, I met a friend of Wilson, who mentioned the subject to me, and induced me to write to Wilson, telling him I would leave the ten dollars with you which had been left with me to pay for making abstracts in the case, so that the case may go on this winter; but I came away, and forgot to do it. What I want now is to send you the money, to be used accordingly, if any one comes on to start the case, or to be retained by you if no one does.

There is nothing of consequence new here. Congress is to organize to-morrow. Last night we held a Whig caucus for the House, and nominated Winthrop of Massachusetts for speaker, Sargent of Pennsylvania for sergeant-at-arms, Homer of New Jersey door-keeper, and McCormick of District of Columbia postmaster. The Whig majority in the House is so small that, together with some little dissatisfaction, [it] leaves it doubtful whether we will elect them all.

This paper is too thick to fold, which is the reason I send only a half-sheet.   Yours as ever,

A. LINCOLN.

December 13, 1847.—LETTER TO WILLIAM H. HERNDON.

WASHINGTON, December 13, 1847.

Dear William: Your letter, advising me of the receipt of our fee in the bank case, is just received, and I don't expect to hear another as good a piece of news from Springfield while I am away. I am under no obligations to the bank; and I therefore wish you to buy bank certificates, and pay my debt there, so as to pay it with the least money possible. I would as soon you should buy them of Mr. Ridgely, or any other person at the bank, as of any one else, provided you can get them as cheaply. I suppose, after the bank debt shall be paid, there will be some money left, out of which I would like to have you pay Lavely and Stout twenty dollars, and Priest and somebody (oil-makers) ten dollars, for materials got for house-painting. If there shall still be any left, keep it till you see or hear from me.

I shall begin sending documents so soon as I can get them. I wrote you yesterday about a "Congressional Globe." As you are all so anxious for me to distinguish myself, I have concluded to do so before long.   Yours truly,

A. LINCOLN.

December 22, 1847.—Resolutions in the United States
House of Representatives.

Whereas, The President of the United States, in his message of
May 11, 1846, has declared that "the Mexican Government not only
refused to receive him [the envoy of the United States], or to listen
to his propositions, but, after a long-continued series of menaces,
has at last invaded our territory and shed the blood of our fellow-
citizens on our own soil."

And again, in his message of December 8, 1846, that "we had
ample cause of war against Mexico long before the breaking out of
hostilities; but even then we forbore to take redress into our own
hands until Mexico herself became the aggressor, by invading our
soil in hostile array, and shedding the blood of our citizens."

And yet again, in his message of December 7, 1847, that "the
Mexican Government refused even to hear the terms of adjustment
which he [our minister of peace] was authorized to propose, and
finally, under wholly unjustifiable pretexts, involved the two countries in war, by invading the territory of the State of Texas, striking the first blow, and shedding the blood of our citizens on our
own soil."

And whereas, This House is desirous to obtain a full knowledge
of all the facts which go to establish whether the particular spot on
which the blood of our citizens was so shed was or was not at that
time our own soil: therefore,

Resolved, By the House of Representatives, that the President of
the United States be respectfully requested to inform this House—

First. Whether the spot on which the blood of our citizens was
shed, as in his message declared, was or was not within the territory of Spain, at least after the treaty of 1819 until the Mexican
revolution.

Second. Whether that spot is or is not within the territory which
was wrested from Spain by the revolutionary Government of Mexico.

Third. Whether that spot is or is not within a settlement of
people, which settlement has existed ever since long before the Texas
revolution, and until its inhabitants fled before the approach of the
United States army.

Fourth. Whether that settlement is or is not isolated from any
and all other settlements by the Gulf and the Rio Grande on the
south and west, and by wide uninhabited regions on the north and east.

Fifth. Whether the people of that settlement, or a majority of
them, or any of them, have ever submitted themselves to the government or laws of Texas or of the United States, by consent or by
compulsion, either by accepting office, or voting at elections, or paying tax, or serving on juries, or having process served upon them,
or in any other way.

Sixth. Whether the people of that settlement did or did not flee
from the approach of the United States army, leaving unprotected
their homes and their growing crops, *before* the blood was shed, as
in the message stated; and whether the first blood, so shed, was or

Vol. I—7.

was not shed within the inclosure of one of the people who had thus fled from it.

Seventh. Whether our citizens, whose blood was shed, as in his message declared, were or were not, at that time, armed officers and soldiers, sent into that settlement by the military order of the President, through the Secretary of War.

Eighth. Whether the military force of the United States was or was not so sent into that settlement after General Taylor had more than once intimated to the War Department that, in his opinion, no such movement was necessary to the defense or protection of Texas.

January 5, 1848.—REMARKS IN THE UNITED STATES HOUSE OF REPRESENTATIVES.

Mr. Lincoln said he had made an effort, some few days since, to obtain the floor in relation to this measure [resolution to direct Postmaster-General to make arrangements with railroad for carrying the mails—in Committee of the Whole], but had failed. One of the objects he had then had in view was now in a great measure superseded by what had fallen from the gentleman from Virginia who had just taken his seat. He begged to assure his friends on the other side of the House that no assault whatever was meant upon the Postmaster-General, and he was glad that what the gentleman had now said modified to a great extent the impression which might have been created by the language he had used on a previous occasion. He wanted to state to gentlemen who might have entertained such impressions, that the Committee on the Post-office was composed of five Whigs and four Democrats, and their report was understood as sustaining, not impugning, the position taken by the Postmaster-General. That report had met with the approbation of all the Whigs, and of all the Democrats also, with the exception of one, and he wanted to go even further than this. [Intimation was informally given Mr. Lincoln that it was not in order to mention on the floor what had taken place in committee.] He then observed that if he had been out of order in what he had said, he took it all back so far as he could. He had no desire, he could assure gentlemen, ever to be out of order—though he never could keep long in order.

Mr. Lincoln went on to observe that he differed in opinion, in the present case, from his honorable friend from Richmond [Mr. Botts]. That gentleman had begun his remarks by saying that if all prepossessions in this matter could be removed out of the way, but little difficulty would be experienced in coming to an agreement. Now, he could assure that gentleman that he had himself begun the examination of the subject with prepossessions all in his favor. He had long and often heard of him, and, from what he had heard, was prepossessed in his favor. Of the Postmaster-General he had also heard, but had no prepossessions in his favor, though certainly none of an opposite kind. He differed, however, with that gentleman in politics, while in this respect he agreed with the gentleman from Virginia [Mr. Botts], whom he wished to oblige whenever it was in his power. That gentleman had referred to the report made to the House by the Postmaster-General, and had intimated an apprehension that gentlemen would be disposed to rely on that report alone, and derive their views of the case from that document alone. Now it so happened that a pamphlet had been slipped into his [Mr Lincoln's] hand before he read the report of the Postmaster-General; so that, even in this, he had begun with prepossessions in favor of the gentleman from Virginia.

As to the report, he had but one remark to make: he had carefully examined it, and he did not understand that there was any dispute as to the facts therein stated—the dispute, if he understood it, was confined altogether to the inferences to be drawn from those facts. It was a difference not about facts, but about conclusions. The facts were not disputed. If he was right in this, he supposed the House might assume the facts to be as they were stated, and thence proceed to draw their own conclusions.

The gentleman had said that the Postmaster-General had got into a personal squabble with the railroad company. Of this Mr. Lincoln knew nothing, nor did he need or desire to know anything, because it had nothing whatever to do with a just conclusion from the premises. But the gentleman had gone on to ask whether so great a grievance as the present detention of the Southern mail ought not to be remedied? Mr. Lincoln would assure the gentleman that if there was a proper way of doing it, no man was more anxious than he that it should be done. The report made by the committee had been intended to yield much for the sake of removing that grievance. That the grievance was very great, there was no dispute in any quarter. He supposed that the statements made by the gentleman from Virginia to show this were all entirely correct in point of fact. He did suppose that the interruptions of regular intercourse, and all the other inconveniences growing out of it, were all as that gentleman had stated them to be; and certainly, if redress could be rendered, it was proper it should be rendered as soon as possible. The gentleman said that in order to effect this, no new legislative action was needed; all that was necessary was that the Postmaster-General should be required to do what the law, as it stood, authorized and required him to do.

We come then, said Mr. Lincoln, to the law. Now the Postmaster-General says he cannot give to this company more than two hundred and thirty-seven dollars and fifty cents per railroad mile of transportation, and twelve and half per cent less for transportation by steamboats. He considers himself as restricted by law to this amount; and he says, further, that he would not give more if he could, because in his apprehension it would not be fair and just.

JANUARY 8, 1848.—LETTER TO WILLIAM H. HERNDON.

WASHINGTON, January 8, 1848.

Dear William: Your letter of December 27 was received a day or two ago. I am much obliged to you for the trouble you have taken, and promise to take in my little business there. As to speech-making, by way of getting the hang of the House I made a little speech two or three days ago on a post-office question of no general interest. I find speaking here and elsewhere about the same thing. I was about as badly scared, and no worse, as I am when I speak in court. I expect to make one within a week or two, in which I hope to succeed well enough to wish you to see it.

It is very pleasant to learn from you that there are some who desire that I should be reëlected. I most heartily thank them for their kind partiality; and I can say, as Mr. Clay said of the annexation of Texas, that "personally I would not object" to a reëlection, although I thought at the time, and still think, it would be quite as well for me to return to the law at the end of a single term. I made the declaration that I would not be a candidate again, more from a wish to deal fairly with others, to keep peace among our friends, and to keep the district from going to the enemy, than for any cause personal to myself; so that, if it should so happen that nobody else wishes to be elected, I could not refuse the people the right of sending me again. But to enter myself as a competitor of others, or to authorize any one so to enter me, is what my word and honor forbid.

I got some letters intimating a probability of so much difficulty amongst our friends as to lose us the district; but I remember such letters were written to Baker when my own case was under consideration, and I trust there is no more ground for such apprehension now than there was then. Remember I am always glad to receive a letter from you. Most truly your friend,

A. LINCOLN.

January 12, 1848.—SPEECH IN THE UNITED STATES HOUSE OF REPRESENTATIVES.

Mr. Chairman: Some if not all the gentlemen on the other side of the House who have addressed the committee within the last two days have spoken rather complainingly, if I have rightly understood them, of the vote given a week or ten days ago declaring that the war with Mexico was unnecessarily and unconstitutionally commenced by the President. I admit that such a vote should not be given in mere party wantonness, and that the one given is justly censurable, if it have no other or better foundation. I am one of those who joined in that vote; and I did so under my best impression of the truth of the case. How I got this impression, and how it may possibly be remedied, I will now try to show. When the war began, it was my opinion that all those who because of knowing too little, or because of knowing too much, could not conscientiously oppose the conduct of the President in the beginning of it should nevertheless, as good citizens and patriots, remain silent on that point, at least till the war should be ended. Some leading Democrats, including ex-President Van Buren, have taken this same view, as I understand them; and I adhered to it and acted upon it, until since I took my seat here; and I think I should still adhere to it were it not that the President and his friends will not allow it to be so. Besides the continual effort of the President to argue every silent vote given for supplies into an indorsement of the justice and wisdom of his conduct; besides that singularly candid paragraph in his late message in which he tells us that Congress with great unanimity had declared that "by the act of the Republic of Mexico, a state of war exists between that Government and the United States," when the same journals that informed him of this also informed him that when that declaration stood disconnected from the question of supplies sixty-seven in the House, and not fourteen merely, voted against it; besides this open attempt to prove by telling the truth what he could not prove by telling the whole truth—demanding of all who will not submit to be misrepresented, in justice to themselves, to speak out,—besides all this, one of my colleagues [Mr. Richardson] at a very early day in the session brought in a set of resolutions expressly indorsing the original justice of the war on the part of the President. Upon these resolutions when they shall be put on their passage I shall be compelled to vote; so that I cannot be silent if I would. Seeing this, I went about preparing myself to give the vote understandingly when it should come. I carefully examined the President's message, to ascertain what he himself had said and proved upon the point. The result of this examination was to make the impression that, taking for true all the President states as facts, he falls far short of proving his justification; and that the President would have gone farther with his proof if it had not been for the small matter that the truth would not permit him. Under the impression thus made I gave the vote before mentioned. I propose now to give concisely the process of the examination I made, and how I reached the conclusion I did. The President, in his first war message of May, 1846, declares that the soil was ours on which hostilities were commenced by Mexico, and he repeats that declaration almost in the same language in each successive annual message, thus showing that he deems that point a highly essential one. In the importance of that point I entirely agree with the President. To my judgment it is the very point upon which he should be justified, or condemned. In his message of December, 1846, it seems to have occurred to him, as is certainly true, that title—ownership—to soil or anything else is not a simple fact, but is a conclusion following on one or more simple facts; and that it was incumbent upon him to present the facts from which he concluded the soil was ours on which the first blood of the war was shed.

Accordingly, a little below the middle of page twelve in the message last referred to he enters upon that task; forming an issue and introducing testimony, extending the whole to a little below the middle of page fourteen. Now, I propose to try to show that the whole of this—issue and evidence—is from beginning to end the sheerest deception. The issue, as he presents it, is in these words: "But there are those who, conceding all this to be true, assume the ground that the true western boundary of Texas is the Nueces, instead of the Rio Grande; and that, therefore, in marching our army to the east bank of the latter river, we passed the Texas line and invaded the territory of Mexico." Now this issue is made up of two affirmatives and no negative. The main deception of it is that it assumes as true that one river or the other is necessarily the boundary; and cheats the superficial thinker entirely out of the idea that possibly the boundary is somewhere between the two, and not actually at either. A further deception is that it will let in evidence which a true issue would exclude. A true issue made by the President would be about as follows: " I say the soil was ours, on which the first blood was shed; there are those who say it was not."

I now proceed to examine the President's evidence as applicable to such an issue. When that evidence is analyzed, it is all included in the following propositions:

(1) That the Rio Grande was the western boundary of Louisiana as we purchased it of France in 1803.

(2) That the Republic of Texas always claimed the Rio Grande as her western boundary.

(3) That by various acts she had claimed it on paper.

(4) That Santa Anna in his treaty with Texas recognized the Rio Grande as her boundary.

(5) That Texas before, and the United States after, annexation had exercised jurisdiction beyond the Nueces—between the two rivers.

(6) That our Congress understood the boundary of Texas to extend beyond the Nueces.

Now for each of these in its turn. His first item is that the Rio Grande was the western boundary of Louisiana, as we purchased it of France in 1803; and seeming to expect this to be disputed, he argues over the amount of nearly a page to prove it true; at the end of which he lets us know that by the treaty of 1819 we sold to Spain the whole country from the Rio Grande eastward to the Sabine. Now, admitting for the present that the Rio Grande was the boundary of Louisiana, what, under heaven, had that to do with the present boundary between us and Mexico? How, Mr. Chairman, the line that once divided your land from mine can still be the boundary between us after I have sold my land to you is to me beyond all comprehension. And how any man, with an honest purpose only of proving the truth, could ever have thought of introducing such a fact to prove such an issue is equally incomprehensible. His next piece of evidence is that "the Republic of Texas always claimed this river (Rio Grande) as her western boundary." That is not true, in fact. Texas has claimed it, but she has not always claimed it. There is at least one distinguished exception. Her State constitution—the republic's most solemn and well-considered act; that which may, without impropriety, be called her last will and testament, revoking all others—makes no such claim. But suppose she had always claimed it. Has not Mexico always claimed the contrary? So that there is but claim against claim, leaving nothing proved until we get back of the claims and find which has the better foundation. Though not in the order in which the President presents his evidence, I now consider that class of his statements which are in substance nothing more than that Texas has, by various acts of her Convention and Congress, claimed the Rio Grande as her boundary, on paper. I mean here what he says about the fixing of the Rio Grande as her boundary in her old constitution (not her State constitution), about forming congressional districts, counties, etc. Now all of this is but naked claim; and what I have already said about claims is strictly applicable to this. If I should claim your land by word of mouth, that certainly would not make it mine; and if I were to claim it by a deed which I had made myself, and with which you had had nothing to do, the claim would be quite the same in substance—or rather, in utter nothingness. I next consider the President's statement that Santa Anna in his treaty with Texas recognized the Rio Grande as the western boundary of Texas. Besides the position so often taken, that Santa Anna while a prisoner of war, a captive, could not bind Mexico by a treaty, which I deem conclusive—besides this, I wish to say something in relation to this treaty, so called by the President, with Santa Anna. If any man would like to be amused by a sight of that little thing which the President calls by that big name, he can have it by turning to "Niles's Register," Vol. L, p. 336. And if any one should suppose that "Niles's Register" is a curious repository of so mighty a document as a solemn treaty between nations, I can only say that I learned to a tolerable degree of certainty, by inquiry at the State Department, that the President himself never saw it anywhere else. By the way, I believe I should not err if I were to declare that during the first ten years of the existence of that document it was never by anybody called a treaty—that it was never so called till the President, in his extremity, attempted by so calling it to wring something from it in justification of himself in connection with the Mexican war. It has none of the distinguishing features of a treaty. It does not call itself a treaty. Santa Anna does not therein assume to bind Mexico; he assumes only to act as the President-Commander-in-Chief of the Mexican army and navy; stipulates that the then present hostilities should cease, and that he would not himself take up arms, nor influence the Mexican people to take up arms, against Texas during the existence of the war of independence. He did not recognize the independence of Texas; he did not assume to put an end to the war, but clearly indicated his expectation of its continuance; he did not say one word about boundary, and, most probably, never thought of it. It is stipulated therein that the Mexican forces should evacuate the territory of Texas, passing to the other side of the Rio Grande; and in another article it is stipulated that, to prevent collisions between the armies, the Texas army should not approach nearer than within five leagues—of what is not said, but clearly, from the object stated, it is of the Rio Grande. Now, if this is a treaty recognizing the Rio Grande as the boundary of Texas, it contains the singular features of stipulating that Texas shall not go within five leagues of her own boundary.

Next comes the evidence of Texas before annexation, and the United States afterward, exercising jurisdiction beyond the Nueces and between the two rivers. This actual exercise of jurisdiction is the very class or quality of evidence we want. It is excellent so far as it goes; but does it go far enough? He tells us it went beyond the Nueces, but he does not tell us it went to the Rio Grande. He tells us jurisdiction was exercised between the two rivers, but he does not tell us it was exercised over all the territory between them. Some simple-minded people think it is possible to cross one river and go beyond it without going all the way to the next, that jurisdiction may be exercised between two rivers without covering all the country between them. I know a man, not very unlike myself, who exercises jurisdiction over a piece of land between the Wabash and the Mississippi; and yet so far is this from being all there is between those rivers that it is just one hundred and fifty-two feet long by fifty feet wide, and no part of it much within a hundred miles of either. He has a neighbor between him and the Mississippi — that is, just across the street, in that direction — whom I am sure he could neither persuade nor force to give up his habitation; but which nevertheless he could certainly annex, if it were to be done by merely standing on his own side of the street and claiming it, or even sitting down and writing a deed for it.

But next the President tells us the Congress of the United States understood the State of Texas they admitted into the Union to extend beyond the Nueces. Well, I suppose they did. I certainly so understood it. But how far beyond? That Congress did not understand it to extend clear to the Rio Grande is quite certain, by the fact of their joint resolutions for admission expressly leaving all questions of boundary to future adjustment. And it may be added that Texas herself is proved to have had the same understanding of it that our Congress had, by the fact of the exact conformity of her new constitution to those resolutions.

I am now through the whole of the President's evidence; and it is a singular fact that if any one should declare the President sent the army into the midst of a settlement of Mexican people who had never submitted, by consent or by force, to the authority of Texas or of the United States, and that there and thereby the first blood of the war was shed, there is not one word in all the President has said which would either admit or deny the declaration. This strange omission it does seem to me could not have occurred but by design. My way of living leads me to be about the courts of justice; and there I have sometimes seen a good lawyer, struggling for his client's neck in a desperate case, employing every artifice to work round, befog, and cover up with many words some point arising in the case which he dared not admit and yet could not deny. Party bias may help to make it appear so, but with all the allowance I can make for such bias, it still does appear to me that just such, and from just such necessity, is the President's struggle in this case.

Some time after my colleague [Mr. Richardson] introduced the resolutions I have mentioned, I introduced a preamble, resolution, and interrogations, intended to draw the President out, if possible, on this hitherto untrodden ground. To show their relevancy, I propose to state my understanding of the true rule for ascertaining the boundary between Texas and Mexico. It is that wherever Texas was exercising jurisdiction was hers; and wherever Mexico was exercising jurisdiction was hers; and that whatever separated the actual exercise of jurisdiction of the one from that of the other was the true boundary between them. If, as is probably true, Texas was exercising jurisdiction along the western bank of the Nueces, and Mexico was exercising it along the eastern bank of the Rio Grande, then neither river was the boundary; but the uninhabited country between the two was. The extent of our territory in that region depended not on any treaty-fixed boundary (for no treaty had attempted it), but on revolution. Any people anywhere being inclined and having the power have the right to rise up and shake off the existing government, and form a new one that suits them better. This is a most valuable, a most sacred right—a right which we hope and believe is to liberate the world. Nor is this right confined to cases in which the whole people of an existing government may choose to exercise it. Any portion of such people that can may revolutionize and make their own of so much of the territory as they inhabit. More than this, a majority of any portion of such people may revolutionize, putting down a minority, intermingled with or near about them, who may oppose this movement. Such minority was precisely the case of the Tories of our own revolution. It is a quality of revolutions not to go by old lines or old laws; but to break up both, and make new ones.

As to the country now in question, we bought it of France in 1803, and sold it to Spain in 1819, according to the President's statements. After this, all Mexico, including Texas, revolutionized against Spain; and still later Texas revolutionized against Mexico. In my view, just so far as she carried her resolution by obtaining the actual, willing or unwilling, submission of the people, so far the country was hers, and no farther. Now, sir, for the purpose of obtaining the very best evidence as to whether Texas had actually carried her revolution to the place where the hostilities of the present war commenced, let the President answer the interrogatories I proposed, as before mentioned, or some other similar ones. Let him answer fully, fairly, and candidly. Let him answer with facts and not with arguments. Let him remember he sits where Washington sat, and so remembering, let him answer as Washington would answer. As a nation should not, and the Almighty will not, be evaded, so let him attempt no evasion—no equivocation. And if, so answering, he can show that the soil was ours where the first blood of the war was shed,—that it was not within an inhabited country, or, if within such, that the inhabitants had submitted themselves to the civil authority of Texas or of the United States, and that the same is true of the site of Fort Brown,—then I am with him for his justification. In that case I shall be most happy to reverse the vote I gave the other day. I have a selfish motive for desiring that the President may do this—I expect to gain some votes, in connection with the war, which, without his so doing, will be of doubtful propriety in my own judgment, but which will be free from the doubt if he does so. But if he can not or will not do this,—if on any pretense or no pretense he shall refuse or omit it—then I shall be fully convinced of what I more than suspect already—that he is deeply conscious of being in the wrong; that he feels the blood of this war, like the blood of Abel, is crying to Heaven against him; that originally having some strong motive—what, I will not stop now to give my opinion concerning—to involve the two countries in a war, and trusting to escape scrutiny by fixing the public gaze upon the exceeding brightness of military glory,—that attractive rainbow that rises in showers of blood—that serpent's eye that charms to destroy,—he plunged into it, and has swept on and on till, disappointed in his calculation of the ease with which Mexico might be subdued, he now finds himself he knows not where. How like the half-insane mumbling of a fever dream is the whole war part of his late message! At one time telling us that Mexico has nothing whatever that we can get but territory; at another showing us how we can support the war by levying contributions on Mexico. At one time urging the national honor, the security of the future, the prevention of foreign interference, and even the good of Mexico herself as among the objects of the war; at another telling us that "to reject indemnity, by refusing to accept a cession of territory, would be to abandon all our just demands, and to wage the war bearing all its expenses, without a purpose or definite object." So then this national honor, security of the future, and everything but territorial indemnity may be considered the no-purposes and indefinite objects of the war! But, having it now settled that territorial indemnity is the only object, we are urged to seize, by legislation here, all that he was content to take a few months ago, and the whole province of Lower California to boot, and to still carry on the war—to take all we are fighting for, and still fight on. Again, the President is resolved under all circumstances to have full territorial indemnity for the expenses of the war; but he forgets to tell us how we are to get the excess after those expenses shall have surpassed the value of the whole of the Mexican territory. So again, he insists that the separate national existence of Mexico shall be maintained; but he does not tell us how this can be done, after we shall have taken all her territory. Lest the questions I have suggested be considered speculative merely, let me be indulged a moment in trying to show they are not. The war has gone on some twenty months; for the expenses of which, together with an inconsiderable old score, the President now claims about one half of the Mexican territory, and that by far the better half, so far as concerns our ability to make anything out of it. It is comparatively uninhabited; so that we could establish land offices in it, and raise some money in that way. But the other half is already inhabited, as I understand it, tolerably densely for the nature of the country, and all its lands, or all that are valuable, already appropriated as private property. How then are we to make anything out of these lands with this encumbrance on them? or how remove the encumbrance? I suppose no one would say we should kill the people, or drive them out, or make slaves of them; or confiscate their property. How, then, can we make much out of this part of the territory? If the prosecution of the war has in expenses already equaled the better half of the country, how long its future prosecution will be in equaling the less valuable half is not a speculative, but a practical, question, pressing closely upon us. And yet it is a question which the President seems never to have thought of. As to the mode of terminating the war and securing peace, the President is equally wandering and indefinite. First, it is to be done by a more vigorous prosecution of the war in the vital parts of the enemy's country; and after apparently talking himself tired on this point, the President drops down into a half-despairing tone, and tells us that " with a people distracted and divided by contending factions, and a government subject to constant changes by successive revolutions, the continued success of our arms may fail to secure a satisfactory peace." Then he suggests the propriety of wheedling the Mexican people to desert the counsels of their own leaders, and, trusting in our protestations, to set up a government from which we can secure a satisfactory peace; telling us that " this may become the only mode of obtaining such a peace." But soon he falls into doubt of this too; and then drops back onto the already half-abandoned ground of "more vigorous prosecution." All this shows that the President is in nowise satisfied with his own positions. First he takes up one, and in attempting to argue us into it he argues himself out of it, then seizes another and goes through the same process, and then, confused at being able to think of nothing new, he snatches up the old one again, which he has some time before cast off. His mind, taxed beyond its power, is running hither and thither, like some tortured creature on a burning surface, finding no position on which it can settle down and be at ease.

Again, it is a singular omission in this message that it nowhere intimates when the President expects the war to terminate. At its beginning, General Scott was by this same President driven into disfavor, if not disgrace, for intimating that peace could not be conquered in less than three or four months. But now, at the end of about twenty months, during which time our arms have given us the most splendid successes, every department and every part, land and water, officers and privates, regulars and volunteers, doing all that men could do, and hundreds of things which it had ever before been thought men could not do—after all this, this same President gives a long message, without showing us that as to the end he himself has even an imaginary conception. As I have before said, he knows not where he is. He is a bewildered, confounded, and miserably perplexed man. God grant he may be able to show there is not something about his conscience more painful than all his mental perplexity.

The following is a copy of the so-called " treaty " referred to in the speech:

Articles of Agreement entered into between his Excellency David G. Burnet, President of the Republic of Texas, of the one part, and his Excellency General Santa Anna, President-General-in-Chief of the Mexican Army, of the other part.

Article I. General Antonio Lopez de Santa Anna agrees that he will not take up arms, nor will he exercise his influence to cause them to be taken up, against the people of Texas during the present war of independence.

Article II.   All hostilities between the Mexican and Texan troops will cease immediately, both by land and water.

Article III.   The Mexican troops will evacuate the territory of Texas, passing to the other side of the Rio Grande Del Norte.

Article IV.   The Mexican army, in its retreat, shall not take the property of any person without his consent and just indemnification, using only such articles as may be necessary for its subsistence, in cases when the owner may not be present, and remitting to the commander of the army of Texas, or to the commissioners to be appointed for the adjustment of such matters, an account of the value of the property consumed, the place where taken, and the name of the owner, if it can be ascertained.

Article V.   That all private property, including cattle, horses, negro slaves, or indentured persons, of whatever denomination, that may have been captured by any portion of the Mexican army, or may have taken refuge in the said army, since the commencement of the late invasion, shall be restored to the commander of the Texan army, or to such other persons as may be appointed by the Government of Texas to receive them.

Article VI.   The troops of both armies will refrain from coming in contact with each other ; and to this end the commander of the army of Texas will be careful not to approach within a shorter distance than five leagues.

Article VII.   The Mexican army shall not make any other delay on its march than that which is necessary to take up their hospitals, baggage, etc., and to cross the rivers ; any delay not necessary to these purposes to be considered an infraction of this agreement.

Article VIII.   By an express, to be immediately despatched, this agreement shall be sent to General Vincente Filisola and to General T. J. Rusk, commander of the Texan army, in order that they may be apprized of its stipulations ; and to this end they will exchange engagements to comply with the same.

Article IX.   That all Texan prisoners now in the possession of the Mexican army, or its authorities, be forthwith released, and furnished with free passports to return to their homes ; in consideration of which a corresponding number of Mexican prisoners, rank and file, now in possession of the Government of Texas shall be immediately released ; the remainder of the Mexican prisoners that continue in the possession of the Government of Texas to be treated with due humanity,—any extraordinary comforts that may be furnished them to be at the charge of the Government of Mexico.

Article X.   General Antonio Lopez de Santa Anna will be sent to Vera Cruz as soon as it shall be deemed proper.

The contracting parties sign this instrument for the above-mentioned purposes, in duplicate, at the port of Velasco, this fourteenth day of May, 1836.

DAVID G. BURNET, *President*,
JAS. COLLINGSWORTH, *Secretary of State*,
ANTONIO LOPEZ DE SANTA ANNA,
B. HARDIMAN, *Secretary of the Treasury*,
P. W. GRAYSON, *Attorney-General*.

January 19, 1848.—REPORT IN THE UNITED STATES HOUSE OF REPRESENTATIVES.

Mr. Lincoln, from the Committee on the Post-Office and Post Roads, made the following report:

The Committee on the Post-Office and Post Roads, to whom was referred the petition of Messrs. Saltmarsh and Fuller, report: That, as proved to their satisfaction, the mail routes from Milledgeville to Athens, and from Warrenton to Decatur, in the State of Georgia (numbered 2366 and 2380), were let to Reeside and Avery at $1300 per annum for the former and $1500 for the latter, for the term of four years, to commence on the first day of January, 1835; that, previous to the time for commencing the service, Reeside sold his interest therein to Avery; that on the 11th of May, 1835, Avery sold the whole to these petitioners, Saltmarsh and Fuller, to take effect from the beginning, January 1, 1835; that, at this time, the Assistant Postmaster-General, being called on for that purpose, consented to the transfer of the contracts from Reeside and Avery to these petitioners, and promised to have proper entries of the transfer made on the books of the department, which, however, was neglected to be done; that the petitioners, supposing all was right, in good faith commenced the transportation of the mail on these routes, and after difficulty arose, still trusting that all would be made right, continued the service till December 1, 1837; that they performed the service to the entire satisfaction of the department, and have never been paid anything for it except $——; that the difficulty occurred as follows: Mr. Barry was Postmaster-General at the times of making the contracts and the attempted transfer of them; Mr. Kendall succeeded Mr. Barry, and finding Reeside apparently in debt to the department, and these contracts still standing in the names of Reeside and Avery, refused to pay for the services under them, otherwise than by credits to Reeside; afterward, however, he divided the compensation, still crediting one half to Reeside, and directing the other to be paid to the order of Avery, who disclaimed all right to it. After discontinuing the service, these petitioners, supposing they might have legal redress against Avery, brought suit against him in New Orleans; in which suit they failed, on the ground that Avery had complied with his contract, having done so much toward the transfer as they had accepted and been satisfied with. Still later the department sued Reeside on his supposed indebtedness, and by a verdict of the jury it was determined that the department was indebted to him in a sum much beyond all the credits given him on the account above stated. Under these circumstances, the committee consider the petitioners clearly entitled to relief, and they report a bill accordingly; lest, however, there should be some mistake as to the amount which they have already received, we so frame it as that, by adjustment at the department, they may be paid so much as remains unpaid for service actually performed by them— not charging them with the credits given to Reeside. The committee think it not improbable that the petitioners purchased the right of Avery to be paid for the service from the 1st of January, till their purchase on May 11, 1835; but the evidence on this point being very vague, they forbear to report in favor of allowing it.

January 19, 1848.—LETTER TO WILLIAM H. HERNDON.

WASHINGTON, January 19, 1848.

Dear William: Inclosed you find a letter of Louis W. Chandler. What is wanted is that you shall ascertain whether the claim upon the note described has received any dividend in the Probate Court of Christian County, where the estate of Mr. Overton Williams has been administered on. If nothing is paid on it, withdraw the note and send it to me, so that Chandler can see the indorser of it. At all events write me all about it, till I can somehow get it off my hands. I have already been bored more than enough about it; not the least of which annoyance is his cursed, unreadable, and ungodly handwriting.

I have made a speech, a copy of which I will send you by next mail.   Yours as ever,

                                        A. LINCOLN.

February 1, 1848.—LETTER TO WILLIAM H. HERNDON.

                                WASHINGTON, February 1, 1848.

Dear William: Your letter of the 19th ultimo was received last night, and for which I am much obliged. The only thing in it that I wish to talk to you at once about is that because of my vote for Ashmun's amendment you fear that you and I disagree about the war. I regret this, not because of any fear we shall remain disagreed after you have read this letter, but because if you misunderstand I fear other good friends may also. That vote affirms that the war was unnecessarily and unconstitutionally commenced by the President; and I will stake my life that if you had been in my place you would have voted just as I did. Would you have voted what you felt and knew to be a lie? I know you would not. Would you have gone out of the House—skulked the vote? I expect not. If you had skulked one vote, you would have had to skulk many more before the end of the session. Richardson's resolutions, introduced before I made any move or gave any vote upon the subject, make the direct question of the justice of the war; so that no man can be silent if he would. You are compelled to speak; and your only alternative is to tell the truth or a lie. I cannot doubt which you would do.

This vote has nothing to do in determining my votes on the questions of supplies. I have always intended, and still intend, to vote supplies; perhaps not in the precise form recommended by the President, but in a better form for all purposes, except Locofoco party purposes. It is in this particular you seem mistaken. The Locos are untiring in their efforts to make the impression that all who vote supplies or take part in the war do of necessity approve the President's conduct in the beginning of it; but the Whigs have from the beginning made and kept the distinction between the two. In the very first act nearly all the Whigs voted against the preamble declaring that war existed by the act of Mexico; and yet nearly all of them voted for the supplies. As to the Whig men who have participated in the war, so far as they have spoken in my hearing they do not hesitate to denounce as unjust the President's conduct in the beginning of the war. They do not suppose that such denunciation is directed by undying hatred to him, as "The Register" would have it believed.   There are two such Whigs on this floor (Colonel Haskell and Major James).   The former fought as a colonel by the side of Colonel Baker at Cerro Gordo, and stands side by side with me in the vote that you seem dissatisfied with.   The latter, the history of whose capture with Cassius Clay you well know, had not arrived here when that vote was given; but, as I understand, he stands ready to give just such a vote whenever an occasion shall present.   Baker, too, who is now here, says the truth is undoubtedly that way; and whenever he shall speak out, he will say so.   Colonel Doniphan, too, the favorite Whig of Missouri, and who overran all Northern Mexico, on his return home in a public speech at St. Louis condemned the administration in relation to the war, if I remember.   G. T. M. Davis, who has been through almost the whole war, declares in favor of Mr. Clay; from which I infer that he adopts the sentiments of Mr. Clay, generally at least.   On the other hand, I have heard of but one Whig who has been to the war attempting to justify the President's conduct.   That one was Captain Bishop, editor of the "Charleston Courier," and a very clever fellow.   I do not mean this letter for the public, but for you. Before it reaches you, you will have seen and read my pamphlet speech, and perhaps been scared anew by it.   After you get over your scare, read it over again, sentence by sentence, and tell me honestly what you think of it.   I condensed all I could for fear of being cut off by the hour rule, and when I got through I had spoken but forty-five minutes.   Yours forever,

A. LINCOLN.

February 2, 1848.— LETTER TO WILLIAM H. HERNDON.

WASHINGTON, Februrary 2, 1848.

Dear William: I just take my pen to say that Mr. Stephens, of Georgia, a little, slim, pale-faced, consumptive man, with a voice like Logan's, has just concluded the very best speech of an hour's length I ever heard.   My old withered dry eyes are full of tears yet.

If he writes it out anything like he delivered it, our people shall see a good many copies of it.   Yours truly,

A. LINCOLN.

To WILLIAM H. HERNDON, Esq.

February 15, 1848.— LETTER TO WILLIAM H. HERNDON.

WASHINGTON, February 15, 1848.

Dear William: Your letter of the 29th January was received last night.   Being exclusively a constitutional argument, I wish to submit some reflections upon it in the same spirit of kindness that I know actuates you.   Let me first state what I understand to be your position.   It is that if it shall become necessary to repel invasion, the President may, without violation of the Constitution, cross the line and invade the territory of another country, and that whether such necessity exists in any given case the President is the sole judge.

Before going further consider well whether this is or is not your position. If it is, it is a position that neither the President himself, nor any friend of his, so far as I know, has ever taken. Their only positions are—first, that the soil was ours when the hostilities commenced; and second, that whether it was rightfully ours or not, Congress had annexed it, and the President for that reason was bound to defend it; both of which are as clearly proved to be false in fact as you can prove that your house is mine. The soil was not ours, and Congress did not annex or attempt to annex it. But to return to your position. Allow the President to invade a neighboring nation whenever he shall deem it necessary to repel an invasion, and you allow him to do so whenever he may choose to say he deems it necessary for such purpose, and you allow him to make war at pleasure. Study to see if you can fix any limit to his power in this respect, after having given him so much as you propose. If to-day he should choose to say he thinks it necessary to invade Canada to prevent the British from invading us, how could you stop him? You may say to him, "I see no probability of the British invading us"; but he will say to you, "Be silent: I see it, if you don't."

The provision of the Constitution giving the war-making power to Congress was dictated, as I understand it, by the following reasons: Kings had always been involving and impoverishing their people in wars, pretending generally, if not always, that the good of the people was the object. This our convention understood to be the most oppressive of all kingly oppressions, and they resolved to so frame the Constitution that no one man should hold the power of bringing this oppression upon us. But your view destroys the whole matter, and places our President where kings have always stood. Write soon again.   Yours truly,

                                         A. LINCOLN.

February 20, 1848.— LETTER TO U. F. LINDER.

WASHINGTON, February 20, 1848.

U. F. Linder: . . . In law, it is good policy to never plead what you need not, lest you oblige yourself to prove what you cannot. Reflect on this well before you proceed. The application I mean to make of this rule is that you should simply go for General Taylor, because you can take some Democrats and lose no Whigs; but if you go also for Mr. Polk, on the origin and mode of prosecuting the war, you will still take some Democrats, but you will lose more Whigs; so that in the sum of the operation, you will be the loser. This is at least my opinion; and if you will look around, I doubt if you do not discover such to be the fact among your own neighbors. Further than this: by justifying Mr. Polk's mode of prosecuting the war, you put yourself in opposition to General Taylor himself, for we all know he has declared for, and in fact originated, the defensive line of policy.

March 9, 1848.— REPORT IN THE UNITED STATES
HOUSE OF REPRESENTATIVES.

Mr. Lincoln, from the Committee on the Post-Office and Post
Roads, made the following report:

The Committee on the Post-Office and Post Roads, to whom was
referred the resolution of the House of Representatives entitled
" An Act authorizing Postmasters at county seats of justice to receive subscriptions for newspapers and periodicals, to be paid
through the agency of the Post-Office Department, and for other
purposes," beg leave to submit the following report:

The committee have reason to believe that a general wish pervades the community at large, that some such facility as the proposed measure should be granted by express law, for subscribing,
through the agency of the Post-Office Department, to newspapers
and periodicals which diffuse daily, weekly, or monthly intelligence
of passing events. Compliance with this general wish is deemed
to be in accordance with our republican institutions, which can
be best sustained by the diffusion of knowledge and the due encouragement of a universal, national spirit of inquiry and discussion of public events through the medium of the public press.
The committee, however, has not been insensible to its duty of
guarding the Post-Office Department against injurious sacrifices
for the accomplishment of this object, whereby its ordinary efficacy
might be impaired or embarrassed. It has therefore been a subject
of much consideration; but it is now confidently hoped that the
bill herewith submitted effectually obviates all objections which
might exist with regard to a less matured proposition.

The committee learned, upon inquiry, that the Post-Office Department, in view of meeting the general wish on this subject, made the
experiment through one of its own internal regulations, when the
new postage system went into operation on the first of July, 1845,
and that it was continued until the thirtieth of September, 1847.
But this experiment, for reasons hereafter stated, proved unsatisfac-
tory, and it was discontinued by order of the Postmaster-General.
As far as the committee can at present ascertain, the following
seem to have been the principal grounds of dissatisfaction in this
experiment:

(1) The legal responsibility of postmasters receiving newspaper
subscriptions, or of their sureties, was not defined.

(2) The authority was open to all postmasters instead of being
limited to those of specific offices.

(3) The consequence of this extension of authority was that, in
innumerable instances, the money, without the previous knowledge
or control of the officers of the department who are responsible for
the good management of its finances, was deposited in offices where
it was improper such funds should be placed; and the repayment
was ordered, not by the financial officers, but by the postmasters,
at points where it was inconvenient to the department so to disburse
its funds.

VOL. I.—8.

(4) The inconvenience of accumulating uncertain and fluctuating sums at small offices was felt seriously in consequent overpayments to contractors on their quarterly collecting orders; and, in case of private mail routes, in litigation concerning the misapplication of such funds to the special service of supplying mails.

(5) The accumulation of such funds on draft offices could not be known to the financial clerks of the department in time to control it, and too often this rendered uncertain all their calculations of funds in hand.

(6) The orders of payment were for the most part issued upon the principal offices, such as New York, Philadelphia, Boston, Baltimore, etc., where the large offices of publishers are located, causing an illimitable and uncontrollable drain of the department funds from those points where it was essential to husband them for its own regular disbursements. In Philadelphia alone this drain averaged $5000 per quarter; and in other cities of the seaboard it was proportionate.

(7) The embarrassment of the department was increased by the illimitable, uncontrollable, and irresponsible scattering of its funds from concentrated points suitable for its distributions, to remote, unsafe, and inconvenient offices, where they could not be again made available till collected by special agents, or were transferred at considerable expense into the principal disbursing offices again.

(8) There was a vast increase of duties thrown upon the limited force before necessary to conduct the business of the department; and from the delay of obtaining vouchers impediments arose to the speedy settlement of accounts with present or retired postmasters, causing postponements which endangered the liability of sureties under the act of limitations, and causing much danger of an increase of such cases.

(9) The most responsible postmasters (at the large offices) were ordered by the least responsible (at small offices) to make payments upon their vouchers, without having the means of ascertaining whether these vouchers were genuine or forged, or if genuine, whether the signers were in or out of office, or solvent or defaulters.

(10) The transaction of this business for subscribers and publishers at the public expense, and the embarrassment, inconvenience, and delay of the department's own business occasioned by it, were not justified by any sufficient remuneration of revenue to sustain the department, as required in every other respect with regard to its agency.

The committee, in view of these objections, has been solicitous to frame a bill which would not be obnoxious to them in principle or in practical effect.

It is confidently believed that by limiting the offices for receiving subscriptions to less than one tenth of the number authorized by the experiment already tried, and designating the county seat in each county for the purpose, the control of the department will be rendered satisfactory; particularly as it will be in the power of the Auditor, who is the officer required by law to check the accounts, to approve or disapprove of the deposits, and to sanction not only the payment, but to point out the place of payment. If these payments should cause a drain on the principal offices of the seaboard, it will be compensated by the accumulation of funds at county seats, where the contractors on those routes can be paid to that extent by the department's drafts, with more local convenience to themselves than by drafts on the seaboard offices.

The legal responsibility for these deposits is defined, and the accumulation of funds at the point of deposit, and the repayment at points drawn upon, being known to and controlled by the Auditor, will not occasion any such embarrassments as were before felt; the record kept by the Auditor on the passing of the certificates through his hands will enable him to settle accounts without the delay occasioned by vouchers being withheld; all doubt or uncertainty as to the genuineness of certificates, or the propriety of their issue, will be removed by the Auditor's examination and approval; and there can be no risk of loss of funds by transmission, as the certificate will not be payable till sanctioned by the Auditor, and after his sanction the payor need not pay it unless it is presented by the publisher or his known clerk or agent.

The main principle of equivalent for the agency of the department is secured by the postage required to be paid upon the transmission of the certificates, augmenting adequately the post-office revenue.

The committee, conceiving that in this report all the difficulties of the subject have been fully and fairly stated, and that these difficulties have been obviated by the plan proposed in the accompanying bill, and believing that the measure will satisfactorily meet the wants and wishes of a very large portion of the community, beg leave to recommend its adoption.

March 9, 1848.— REPORT IN THE UNITED STATES
HOUSE OF REPRESENTATIVES.

Mr. Lincoln, from the Committee on the Post-Office and Post Roads, made the following report:

The Committee on the Post-Office and Post Roads, to whom was referred the petition of H. M. Barney, postmaster at Brimfield, Peoria County, Illinois, report: That they have been satisfied by evidence, that on the 15th of December, 1847, said petitioner had his store, with some fifteen hundred dollars' worth of goods, together with all the papers of the post-office, entirely destroyed by fire; and that the specie funds of the office were melted down, partially lost and partially destroyed; that his large individual loss entirely precludes the idea of embezzlement; that the balances due the department of former quarters had been only about twenty-five dollars; and that owing to the destruction of papers, the exact amount due for the quarter ending December 31, 1847, cannot be ascertained. They therefore report a joint resolution, releasing said petitioner from paying anything for the quarter last mentioned.

March 24, 1848.—LETTER TO DAVID LINCOLN.

WASHINGTON, March 24, 1848.

MR. DAVID LINCOLN.

Dear Sir: Your very worthy representative, Gov. McDowell, has given me your name and address, and as my father was born in Rockingham, from whence his father, Abraham Lincoln, emigrated to Kentucky about the year 1782, I have concluded to address you to ascertain whether we are not of the same family. I shall be much obliged if you will write me, telling me whether you in any way know anything of my grandfather, what relation you are to him, and so on. Also, if you know where your family came from when they settled in Virginia, tracing them back as far as your knowledge extends.   Very respectfully,

A. LINCOLN.

March 29, 1848.—REMARKS IN THE UNITED STATES
HOUSE OF REPRESENTATIVES.

The bill for raising additional military force for limited time, etc., was reported from Committee on Judiciary; similar bills had been reported from Committee on Public Lands and Military Committee.

Mr. Lincoln said if there was a general desire on the part of the House to pass the bill now he should be glad to have it done—concurring, as he did generally, with the gentleman from Arkansas [Mr. Johnson] that the postponement might jeopard the safety of the proposition. If, however, a reference was to be made, he wished to make a very few remarks in relation to the several subjects desired by the gentlemen to be embraced in amendments to the ninth section of the act of the last session of Congress. The first amendment desired by members of this House had for its only object to give bounty lands to such persons as had served for a time as privates, but had never been discharged as such, because promoted to office. That subject, and no other, was embraced in this bill. There were some others who desired, while they were legislating on this subject, that they should also give bounty lands to the volunteers of the War of 1812. His friend from Maryland said there were no such men. He [Mr. L.] did not say there were many, but he was very confident there were some. His friend from Kentucky near him [Mr. Gaines] told him he himself was one.

There was still another proposition touching this matter; that was, that persons entitled to bounty land should by law be entitled to locate these lands in parcels, and not be required to locate them in one body, as was provided by the existing law.

Now he had carefully drawn up a bill embracing these three separate propositions, which he intended to propose as a substitute for all these bills in the House, or in Committee of the Whole on the State of the Union, at some suitable time. If there was a disposition on the part of the House to act at once on this separate proposition, he repeated that, with the gentlemen from Arkansas, he should prefer it lest they should lose all. But if there was to be a reference, he desired to introduce his bill embracing the three propositions, thus enabling the Committee and the House to act at the same time, whether favorably or unfavorably, upon all. He inquired whether an amendment was now in order.

The Speaker replied in the negative.

April 2, 1848.— LETTER TO DAVID LINCOLN.

WASHINGTON, April 2, 1848.

Dear Sir: Last evening I was much gratified by receiving and reading your letter of the 30th of March. There is no longer any doubt that your uncle Abraham and my grandfather was the same man. His family did reside in Washington County, Kentucky, just as you say you found them in 1801 or 1802. The oldest son, Uncle Mordecai, near twenty years ago removed from Kentucky to Hancock County, Illinois, where within a year or two afterward he died, and where his surviving children now live. His two sons there now are Abraham and Mordecai; and their post-office is "La Harpe." Uncle Josiah, farther back than my recollection, went from Kentucky to Blue River in Indiana. I have not heard from him in a great many years, and whether he is still living I cannot say. My recollection of what I have heard is that he has several daughters and only one son, Thomas — their post-office is "Coryden, Harrison County, Indiana." My father, Thomas, is still living, in Coles County, Illinois, being in the seventy-first year of his age — his post-office is "Charleston, Coles County, Illinois" — I am his only child. I am now in my fortieth year; and I live in Springfield, Sangamon County, Illinois. This is the outline of my grandfather's family in the West.

I think my father has told me that grandfather had four brothers — Isaac, Jacob, John, and Thomas. Is that correct? And which of them was your father? Are any of them alive? I am quite sure that Isaac resided on Watauga, near a point where Virginia and Tennessee join; and that he has been dead more than twenty, perhaps thirty, years; also that Thomas removed to Kentucky, near Lexington, where he died a good while ago.

What was your grandfather's Christian name? Was he not a Quaker? About what time did he emigrate from Berks County, Pennsylvania, to Virginia? Do you know anything of your family (or rather I may now say our family), farther back than your grandfather?

If it be not too much trouble to you, I shall be much pleased to hear from you again. Be assured I will call on you, should anything ever bring me near you. I shall give your respects to Governor McDowell as you desire. Very truly yours,

A. LINCOLN.

April 30, 1848.—LETTER TO E. B. WASHBURNE.

WASHINGTON, April 30, 1848.

Dear Washburne: I have this moment received your very short note asking me if old Taylor is to be used up, and who will be the nominee. My hope of Taylor's nomination is as high—a little higher than it was when you left. Still, the case is by no means out of doubt. Mr. Clay's letter has not advanced his interests any here. Several who were against Taylor, but not for anybody particularly, before, are since taking ground, some for Scott and some for McLean. Who will be nominated neither I nor any one else can tell. Now, let me pray to you in turn. My prayer is that you let nothing discourage or baffle you, but that, in spite of every difficulty, you send us a good Taylor delegate from your circuit. Make Baker, who is now with you, I suppose, help about it. He is a good hand to raise a breeze.

General Ashley, in the Senate from Arkansas, died yesterday. Nothing else new beyond what you see in the papers.

Yours truly,   A. LINCOLN.

April 30, 1848.—LETTER TO ARCHIBALD WILLIAMS.

WASHINGTON, April 30, 1848.

Dear Williams: I have not seen in the papers any evidence of a movement to send a delegate from your circuit to the June convention. I wish to say that I think it all-important that a delegate should be sent. Mr. Clay's chance for an election is just no chance at all. He might get New York, and that would have elected in 1844, but it will not now, because he must now, at the least, lose Tennessee, which he had then, and in addition the fifteen new votes of Florida, Texas, Iowa, and Wisconsin. I know our good friend Browning is a great admirer of Mr. Clay, and I therefore fear he is favoring his nomination. If he is, ask him to discard feeling, and try if he can possibly, as a matter of judgment, count the votes necessary to elect him.

In my judgment we can elect nobody but General Taylor; and we cannot elect him without a nomination. Therefore don't fail to send a delegate.   Your friend as ever,

A. LINCOLN.

May 11, 1848.—REMARKS IN THE UNITED STATES
HOUSE OF REPRESENTATIVES.

A bill for the admission of Wisconsin into the Union had been passed.

Mr. Lincoln moved to reconsider the vote by which the bill was passed. He stated to the House that he had made this motion for the purpose of obtaining an opportunity to say a few words in relation to a point raised in the course of the debate on this bill, which he would now proceed to make if in order. The point in the case to which he referred arose on the amendment that was submitted by the gentleman from Vermont [Mr. Collamer] in Committee of the Whole on the state of the Union, and which was afterward renewed in the House, in relation to the question whether the reserved sections, which, by some bills heretofore passed, by which an appropriation of land had been made to Wisconsin, had been enhanced in value, should be reduced to the minimum price of the public lands. The question of the reduction in value of those sections was to him at this time a matter very nearly of indifference. He was inclined to desire that Wisconsin should be obliged by having it reduced. But the gentleman from Indiana [Mr. C. B. Smith], the chairman of the Committee on Territories, yesterday associated that question with the general question, which is now to some extent agitated in Congress, of making appropriations of alternate sections of land to aid the States in making internal improvements, and enhancing the price of the sections reserved; and the gentleman from Indiana took ground against that policy. He did not make any special argument in favor of Wisconsin, but he took ground generally against the policy of giving alternate sections of land, and enhancing the price of the reserved sections. Now he [Mr. Lincoln] did not at this time take the floor for the purpose of attempting to make an argument on the general subject. He rose simply to protest against the doctrine which the gentleman from Indiana had avowed in the course of what he [Mr. Lincoln] could not but consider an unsound argument.

It might, however, be true, for anything he knew, that the gentleman from Indiana might convince him that his argument was sound; but he [Mr. Lincoln] feared that gentleman would not be able to convince a majority in Congress that it was sound. It was true the question appeared in a different aspect to persons in consequence of a difference in the point from which they looked at it. It did not look to persons residing east of the mountains as it did to those who lived among the public lands. But, for his part, he would state that if Congress would make a donation of alternate sections of public land for the purpose of internal improvements in his State, and forbid the reserved sections being sold at $1.25, he should be glad to see the appropriation made; though he should prefer it if the reserved sections were not enhanced in price. He repeated, he should be glad to have such appropriations made, even though the reserved sections should be enhanced in price. He did not wish to be understood as concurring in any intimation that they would refuse to receive such an appropriation of alternate sections of land because a condition enhancing the price of the reserved sections should be attached thereto. He believed his position would now be understood; if not, he feared he should not be able to make himself understood.

But, before he took his seat he would remark that the Senate during the present session had passed a bill making appropriations of land on that principle for the benefit of the State in which he resided — the State of Illinois. The alternate sections were to be given for the purpose of constructing roads, and the reserved sections were to be enhanced in value in consequence. When that bill came here for the action of this House—it had been received, and was now before the Committee on Public Lands—he desired much to see it passed as it was, if it could be put in no more favorable form for the State of Illinois. When it should be before this House, if any member from a section of the Union in which these lands did not lie, whose interest might be less than that which he felt, should propose a reduction of the price of the reserved sections to $1.25, he should be much obliged; but he did not think it would be well for those who came from the section of the Union in which the lands lay to do so. He wished it, then, to be understood that he did not join in the warfare against the principle which had engaged the minds of some members of Congress who were favorable to the improvements in the western country.

There was a good deal of force, he admitted, in what fell from the chairman of the Committee on Territories. It might be that there was no precise justice in raising the price of the reserved sections to $2.50 per acre. It might be proper that the price should be enhanced to some extent, though not to double the usual price; but he should be glad to have such an appropriation with the reserved sections at $2.50; he should be better pleased to have the price of those sections at something less; and he should be still better pleased to have them without any enhancement at all.

There was one portion of the argument of the gentleman from Indiana, the chairman of the Committee on Territories [Mr. Smith], which he wished to take occasion to say that he did not view as unsound. He alluded to the statement that the General Government was interested in these internal improvements being made, inasmuch as they increased the value of the lands that were unsold, and they enabled the government to sell the lands which could not be sold without them. Thus, then, the government gained by internal improvements as well as by the general good which the people derived from them, and it might be, therefore, that the lands should not be sold for more than $1.50 instead of the price being doubled. He, however, merely mentioned this in passing, for he only rose to state, as the principle of giving these lands for the purposes which he had mentioned had been laid hold of and considered favorably, and as there were some gentlemen who had constitutional scruples about giving money for these purchases who would not hesitate to give land, that he was not willing to have it understood that he was one of those who made war against that principle. This was all he desired to say, and having accomplished the object with which he rose, he withdrew his motion to reconsider.

May 21, 1848.—LETTER TO REV. J. M. PECK.

WASHINGTON, May 21, 1848.

REV. J. M. PECK.

Dear Sir: On last evening I received a copy of the " Belleville Advocate," with the appearance of having been sent by a private hand;

and inasmuch as it contained your oration on the occasion of the celebrating of the battle of Buena Vista, and is post-marked at Rock Spring, I cannot doubt that it is to you I am indebted for this courtesy.

I own that finding in the oration a labored justification of the administration on the origin of the Mexican war disappointed me, because it is the first effort of the kind I have known made by one appearing to me to be intelligent, right-minded, and impartial. It is this disappointment that prompts me to address you briefly on the subject. I do not propose any extended review. I do not quarrel with facts—brief exhibition of facts. I presume it is correct so far as it goes; but it is so brief as to exclude some facts quite as material in my judgment to a just conclusion as any it includes. For instance, you say, "Paredes came into power the last of December, 1845, and from that moment all hopes of avoiding war by negotiation vanished." A little further on, referring to this and other preceding statements, you say, "All this transpired three months before General Taylor marched across the desert of Nueces." These two statements are substantially correct; and you evidently intend to have it inferred that General Taylor was sent across the desert in consequence of the destruction of all hopes of peace, in the overthrow of Herara by Paredes. Is not that the inference you intend? If so, the material fact you have excluded is that General Taylor was ordered to cross the desert on the 13th of January, 1846, and before the news of Herara's fall reached Washington—before the administration which gave the order had any knowledge that Herara had fallen. Does not this fact cut up your inference by the roots? Must you not find some other excuse for that order, or give up the case? All that part of the three months you speak of which transpired after the 13th of January, was expended in the orders going from Washington to General Taylor, in his preparations for the march, and in the actual march across the desert, and not in the President's waiting to hear the knell of peace in the fall of Herara, or for any other object. All this is to be found in the very documents you seem to have used.

One other thing. Although you say at one point "I shall briefly exhibit facts, and leave each person to perceive the just application of the principles already laid down to the case in hand," you very soon get to making applications yourself,—in one instance as follows: "In view of all the facts, the conviction to my mind is irresistible that the Government of the United States committed no aggression on Mexico." Not in view of all the facts. There are facts which you have kept out of view. It is a fact that the United States army in marching to the Rio Grande marched into a peaceful Mexican settlement, and frightened the inhabitants away from their homes and their growing crops. It is a fact that Fort Brown, opposite Matamoras, was built by that army within a Mexican cotton-field, on which at the time the army reached it a young cotton crop was growing, and which crop was wholly destroyed and the field itself greatly and permanently injured by ditches, embankments, and the like. It is a fact that when the Mexicans captured

Captain Thornton and his command, they found and captured them within another Mexican field.

Now I wish to bring these facts to your notice, and to ascertain what is the result of your reflections upon them. If you deny that they are facts, I think I can furnish proof which shall convince you that you are mistaken. If you admit that they are facts, then I shall be obliged for a reference to any law of language, law of States, law of nations, law of morals, law of religions, any law, human or divine, in which an authority can be found for saying those facts constitute "no aggression."

Possibly you consider those acts too small for notice. Would you venture to so consider them had they been committed by any nation on earth against the humblest of our people? I know you would not. Then I ask, is the precept "Whatsoever ye would that men should do to you, do ye even so to them" obsolete? of no force? of no application?

I shall be pleased if you can find leisure to write me.

Yours truly,   A. LINCOLN.

June 12, 1848.—LETTER TO ARCHIBALD WILLIAMS.

WASHINGTON, June 12, 1848.

Dear Williams: On my return from Philadelphia, where I had been attending the nomination of "Old Rough," I found your letter in a mass of others which had accumulated in my absence. By many, and often, it had been said they would not abide the nomination of Taylor; but since the deed has been done, they are fast falling in, and in my opinion we shall have a most overwhelming, glorious triumph. One unmistakable sign is that all the odds and ends are with us—Barnburners, Native Americans, Tyler men, disappointed office-seeking Locofocos, and the Lord knows what. This is important, if in nothing else, in showing which way the wind blows. Some of the sanguine men have set down all the States as certain for Taylor but Illinois, and it as doubtful. Cannot something be done even in Illinois? Taylor's nomination takes the Locos on the blind side. It turns the war thunder against them. The war is now to them the gallows of Haman, which they built for us, and on which they are doomed to be hanged themselves.

Excuse this short letter. I have so many to write that I cannot devote much time to any one. Yours, as ever,

A. LINCOLN.

June 20, 1848.—SPEECH IN THE UNITED STATES
HOUSE OF REPRESENTATIVES.

In Committee of the Whole on the State of the Union, on the Civil and Diplomatic Appropriation Bill:

Mr. Chairman: I wish at all times in no way to practise any fraud upon the House or the committee, and I also desire to do nothing which may be very disagreeable to any of the members. I therefore state in advance that my object in taking the floor is to make a speech on the general subject of internal improvements; and if I am out of order in doing so, I give the chair an opportunity of so deciding, and I will take my seat.

The Chair: I will not undertake to anticipate what the gentleman may say on the subject of internal improvements. He will, therefore, proceed in his remarks, and if any question of order shall be made, the chair will then decide it.

Mr. Lincoln: At an early day of this session the President sent us what may properly be called an internal improvement veto message. The late Democratic convention, which sat at Baltimore, and which nominated General Cass for the presidency, adopted a set of resolutions, now called the Democratic platform, among which is one in these words:

That the Constitution does not confer upon the General Government the power to commence and carry on a general system of internal improvements.

General Cass, in his letter accepting the nomination, holds this language: -

I have carefully read the resolutions of the Democratic National Convention, laying down the platform of our political faith, and I adhere to them as firmly as I approve them cordially.

These things, taken together, show that the question of internal improvements is now more distinctly made—has become more intense—than at any former period. The veto message and the Baltimore resolution I understand to be, in substance, the same thing; the latter being the more general statement, of which the former is the amplification—the bill of particulars. While I know there are many Democrats, on this floor and elsewhere, who disapprove that message, I understand that all who shall vote for General Cass will thereafter be counted as having approved it,— as having indorsed all its doctrines. I suppose all, or nearly all, the Democrats will vote for him. Many of them will do so not because they like his position on this question, but because they prefer him, being wrong on this, to another whom they consider farther wrong on other questions. In this way the internal improvement Democrats are to be, by a sort of forced consent, carried over and arrayed against themselves on this measure of policy. General Cass, once elected, will not trouble himself to make a constitutional argument, or perhaps any argument at all, when he shall veto a river or harbor bill; he will consider it a sufficient answer to all Democratic murmurs to point to Mr. Polk's message, and to the "Democratic Platform." This being the case, the question of improvements is verging to a final crisis; and the friends of this policy must now battle, and battle manfully, or surrender all. In this view, humble as I am, I wish to review, and contest as well as I may, the general positions of this veto message. When

I say *general* positions, I mean to exclude from consideration so much as relates to the present embarrassed state of the treasury in consequence of the Mexican War.

Those general positions are: that internal improvements ought not to be made by the General Government—First. Because they would overwhelm the treasury. Second. Because, while their burdens would be general, their benefits would be local and partial, involving an obnoxious inequality; and—Third. Because they would be unconstitutional. Fourth. Because the States may do enough by the levy and collection of tonnage duties; or if not—Fifth. That the Constitution may be amended. "Do nothing at all, lest you do something wrong," is the sum of these positions—is the sum of this message. And this, with the exception of what is said about constitutionality, applying as forcibly to what is said about making improvements by State authority as by the national authority; so that we must abandon the improvements of the country altogether, by any and every authority, or we must resist and repudiate the doctrines of this message. Let us attempt the latter.

The first position is, that a system of internal improvements would overwhelm the treasury. That in such a system there is a tendency to undue expansion, is not to be denied. Such tendency is founded in the nature of the subject. A member of Congress will prefer voting for a bill which contains an appropriation for his district, to voting for one which does not; and when a bill shall be expanded till every district shall be provided for, that it will be too greatly expanded is obvious. But is this any more true in Congress than in a State legislature? If a member of Congress must have an appropriation for his district, so a member of a legislature must have one for his county. And if one will overwhelm the national treasury, so the other will overwhelm the State treasury. Go where we will, the difficulty is the same. Allow it to drive us from the halls of Congress, and it will, just as easily, drive us from the State legislatures. Let us, then, grapple with it, and test its strength. Let us, judging of the future by the past, ascertain whether there may not be, in the discretion of Congress, a sufficient power to limit and restrain this expansive tendency within reasonable and proper bounds. The President himself values the evidence of the past. He tells us that at a certain point of our history more than two hundred millions of dollars had been applied for to make improvements; and this he does to prove that the treasury would be overwhelmed by such a system. Why did he not tell us how much was granted? Would not that have been better evidence? Let us turn to it, and see what it proves. In the message the President tells us that "during the four succeeding years embraced by the administration of President Adams, the power not only to appropriate money, but to apply it, under the direction and authority of the General Government, as well to the construction of roads as to the improvement of harbors and rivers, was fully asserted and exercised."

This, then, was the period of greatest enormity. These, if any, must have been the days of the two hundred millions. And how much do you suppose was really expended for improvements during that four years? Two hundred millions? One hundred? Fifty? Ten? Five? No, sir; less than two millions. As shown by authentic documents, the expenditures on improvements during 1825, 1826, 1827, and 1828 amounted to one million eight hundred and seventy-nine thousand six hundred and twenty-seven dollars one cent. These four years were the period of Mr. Adams's administration, nearly and substantially. This fact shows that when the power to make improvements "was fully asserted and exercised," the Congress did keep within reasonable limits; and what has been done, it seems to me, can be done again.

Now for the second portion of the message—namely, that the burdens of improvements would be general, while their benefits would be local and partial, involving an obnoxious inequality. That there is some degree of truth in this position, I shall not deny. No commercial object of government patronage can be so exclusively general as to not be of some peculiar local advantage. The navy, as I understand it, was established, and is maintained at a great annual expense, partly to be ready for war when war shall come, and partly also, and perhaps chiefly, for the protection of our commerce on the high seas. This latter object is, for all I can see, in principle the same as internal improvements. The driving a pirate from the track of commerce on the broad ocean, and the removing a snag from its more narrow path in the Mississippi River, cannot, I think, be distinguished in principle. Each is done to save life and property, and for nothing else.

The navy, then, is the most general in its benefits of all this class of objects; and yet even the navy is of some peculiar advantage to Charleston, Baltimore, Philadelphia, New York, and Boston, beyond what it is to the interior towns of Illinois. The next most general object I can think of would be improvements on the Mississippi River and its tributaries. They touch thirteen of our States—Pennsylvania, Virginia, Kentucky, Tennessee, Mississippi, Louisiana, Arkansas, Missouri, Illinois, Indiana, Ohio, Wisconsin, and Iowa. Now I suppose it will not be denied that these thirteen States are a little more interested in improvements on that great river than are the remaining seventeen. These instances of the navy and the Mississippi River show clearly that there is something of local advantage in the most general objects. But the converse is also true. Nothing is so local as to not be of some general benefit. Take, for instance, the Illinois and Michigan Canal. Considered apart from its effects, it is perfectly local. Every inch of it is within the State of Illinois. That canal was first opened for business last April. In a very few days we were all gratified to learn, among other things, that sugar had been carried from New Orleans through this canal to Buffalo in New York. This sugar took this route, doubtless, because it was cheaper than the old route. Supposing benefit of the reduction in the cost of carriage to be shared between seller and buyer, the result is that the New Orleans merchant sold his sugar a little dearer, and the people of Buffalo sweetened their coffee a little cheaper, than before,—a benefit resulting from the canal, not to Illinois, where the canal is, but to Louisiana and New York, where it is not. In other transactions Illinois will, of course, have her share, and perhaps the larger share too, of the benefits of the canal; but this instance of the sugar clearly shows that the benefits of an improvement are by no means confined to the particular locality of the improvement itself.

The just conclusion from all this is that if the nation refuse to make improvements of the more general kind because their benefits may be somewhat local, a State may for the same reason refuse to make an improvement of a local kind because its benefits may be somewhat general. A State may well say to the nation, " If you will do nothing for me, I will do nothing for you." Thus it is seen that if this argument of " inequality " is sufficient anywhere, it is sufficient everywhere, and puts an end to improvements altogether. I hope and believe that if both the nation and the States would, in good faith, in their respective spheres do what they could in the way of improvements, what of inequality might be produced in one place might be compensated in another, and the sum of the whole might not be very unequal.

But suppose, after all, there should be some degree of inequality. Inequality is certainly never to be embraced for its own sake; but is every good thing to be discarded which may be inseparably connected with some degree of it? If so, we must discard all government. This Capitol is built at the public expense, for the public benefit; but does any one doubt that it is of some peculiar local advantage to the property-holders and business people of Washington? Shall we remove it for this reason? And if so, where shall we set it down, and be free from the difficulty? To make sure of our object, shall we locate it nowhere, and have Congress hereafter to hold its sessions, as the loafer lodged, " in spots about"? I make no allusion to the present President when I say there are few stronger cases in this world of " burden to the many and benefit to the few," of " inequality," than the presidency itself is by some thought to be. An honest laborer digs coal at about seventy cents a day, while the President digs abstractions at about seventy dollars a day. The coal is clearly worth more than the abstractions, and yet what a monstrous inequality in the prices! Does the President, for this reason, propose to abolish the presidency? He does not, and he ought not. The true rule, in determining to embrace or reject anything, is not whether it have any evil in it, but whether it have more of evil than of good. There are few things wholly evil or wholly good. Almost everything, especially of government policy, is an inseparable compound of the two; so that our best judgment of the preponderance between them is continually demanded. On this principle the President, his friends, and the world generally act on most subjects. Why not apply it, then, upon this question? Why, as to improvements, magnify the evil, and stoutly refuse to see any good in them?

Mr. Chairman, on the third position of the message — the constitutional question — I have not much to say. Being the man I am, and speaking where I do, I feel that in any attempt at an original constitutional argument, I should not be, and ought not to be, listened to patiently. The ablest and the best of men have gone over the whole ground long ago. I shall attempt but little more than a brief notice of what some of them have said. In relation to Mr. Jefferson's views, I read from Mr. Polk's veto message:

President Jefferson, in his message to Congress in 1806, recommended an amendment of the Constitution, with a view to apply an anticipated surplus in the Treasury " to the great purposes of the public education, roads, rivers, canals, and such other objects of public improvements as it may be thought proper to add to the constitutional enumeration of the federal powers"; and he adds: "I suppose an amendment to the Constitution, by consent of the States, necessary, because the objects now recommended are not among those enumerated in the Constitution, and to which it permits the public moneys to be applied." In 1825, he repeated in his published letters the opinion that no such power has been conferred upon Congress.

I introduce this not to controvert just now the constitutional opinion, but to show that, on the question of expediency, Mr. Jefferson's opinion was against the present President — that this opinion of Mr. Jefferson, in one branch at least, is in the hands of Mr. Polk like McFingal's gun — "bears wide and kicks the owner over."

But to the constitutional question. In 1826 Chancellor Kent first published his "Commentaries" on American law. He devoted a portion of one of the lectures to the question of the authority of Congress to appropriate public moneys for internal improvements. He mentions that the subject had never been brought under judicial consideration, and proceeds to give a brief summary of the discussion it had undergone between the legislative and executive branches of the government. He shows that the legislative branch had usually been for, and the executive against, the power, till the period of Mr. J. Q. Adams's administration, at which point he considers the executive influence as withdrawn from opposition, and added to the support of the power. In 1844 the chancellor published a new edition of his "Commentaries," in which he adds some notes of what had transpired on the question since 1826. I have not time to read the original text on the notes; but the whole may be found on page 267, and the two or three following pages, of the first volume of the edition of 1844. As to what Chancellor Kent seems to consider the sum of the whole, I read from one of the notes:

Mr. Justice Story, in his commentaries on the Constitution of the United States, Vol. II., pp. 429–440, and again pp. 519–538, has stated at large the arguments for and against the proposition that Congress have a constitutional authority to lay taxes, and to apply the power to regulate commerce as a means directly to encourage and protect domestic manufactures; and without giving any opinion of his own on the contested doctrine, he has left the reader to draw his own conclusions. I should think, however, from the arguments as stated, that every mind which has taken no part in the discussion, and felt no prejudice or territorial bias on either side of the question, would deem the arguments in favor of the Congressional power vastly superior.

It will be seen that in this extract the power to make improvements is not directly mentioned; but by examining the context, both of Kent and Story, it will be seen that the power mentioned in the extract, and the power to make improvements, are regarded as identical. It is not to be denied that many great and good men have been against the power; but it is insisted that quite as many, as great and as good, have been for it; and it is shown that, on a full survey of the whole, Chancellor Kent was of opinion that the arguments of the latter were vastly superior. This is but the opinion of a man; but who was that man? He was one of the ablest and most learned lawyers of his age, or of any age. It is no disparagement to Mr. Polk, nor indeed to any one who devotes much time to politics, to be placed far behind Chancellor Kent as a lawyer. His attitude was most favorable to correct conclusions. He wrote coolly, and in retirement. He was struggling to rear a durable monument of fame; and he well knew that truth and thoroughly sound reasoning were the only sure foundations. Can the party opinion of a party President on a law question, as this purely is, be at all compared or set in opposition to that of such a man, in such an attitude, as Chancellor Kent? This constitutional question will probably never be better settled than it is, until it shall pass under judicial consideration; but I do think no man who is clear on the questions of expediency need feel his conscience much pricked upon this.

Mr. Chairman, the President seems to think that enough may be done, in the way of improvements, by means of tonnage duties under State authority, with the consent of the General Government. Now I suppose this matter of tonnage duties is well enough in its own sphere. I suppose it may be efficient, and perhaps sufficient, to make slight improvements and repairs in harbors already in use and not much out of repair. But if I have any correct general idea of it, it must be wholly inefficient for any general beneficent purposes of improvement. I know very little, or rather nothing at all, of the practical matter of levying and collecting tonnage duties; but I suppose one of its principles must be to lay a duty for the improvement of any particular harbor upon the tonnage coming into that harbor; to do otherwise—to collect money in one harbor, to be expended on improvements in another—would be an extremely aggravated form of that inequality which the President so much deprecates. If I be right in this, how could we make any entirely new improvement by means of tonnage duties? How make a road, a canal, or clear a greatly obstructed river? The idea that we could involves the same absurdity as the Irish bull about the new boots. "I shall niver git 'em on," says Patrick, "till I wear 'em a day or two, and stretch 'em a little." We shall never make a canal by tonnage duties until it shall already have been made awhile, so the tonnage can get into it.

After all, the President concludes that possibly there may be some great objects of improvement which cannot be effected by tonnage duties, and which it therefore may be expedient for the General Government to take in hand. Accordingly he suggests, in case any such be discovered, the propriety of amending the Constitution. Amend it for what? If, like Mr. Jefferson, the President thought improvements expedient, but not constitutional, it would be natural enough for him to recommend such an amendment. But hear what he says in this very message:

In view of these portentous consequences, I cannot but think that this course of legislation should be arrested, even were there nothing to forbid it in the fundamental laws of our Union.

For what, then, would he have the Constitution amended? With him it is a proposition to remove one impediment merely to be met by others which, in his opinion, cannot be removed,—to enable Congress to do what, in his opinion, they ought not to do if they could.

Here Mr. Meade of Virginia inquired if Mr. Lincoln understood the President to be opposed, on grounds of expediency, to any and every improvement.

Mr. Lincoln answered: In the very part of his message of which I am speaking, I understand him as giving some vague expression in favor of some possible objects of improvement; but in doing so I understand him to be directly on the teeth of his own arguments in other parts of it. Neither the President nor any one can possibly specify an improvement which shall not be clearly liable to one or another of the objections he has urged on the score of expediency. I have shown, and might show again, that no work—no object— can be so general as to dispense its benefits with precise equality; and this inequality is chief among the "portentous consequences" for which he declares that improvements should be arrested. No, sir. When the President intimates that something in the way of improvements may properly be done by the General Government, he is shrinking from the conclusions to which his own arguments would force him. He feels that the improvements of this broad and goodly land are a mighty interest; and he is unwilling to confess to the people, or perhaps to himself, that he has built an argument which, when pressed to its conclusions, entirely annihilates this interest.

I have already said that no one who is satisfied of the expediency of making improvements needs be much uneasy in his conscience about its constitutionality. I wish now to submit a few remarks on the general proposition of amending the Constitution. As a general rule, I think we would much better let it alone. No slight occasion should tempt us to touch it. Better not take the first step, which may lead to a habit of altering it. Better, rather, habituate ourselves to think of it as unalterable. It can scarcely be made better than it is. New provisions would introduce new difficulties, and thus create and increase appetite for further change. No, sir; let it stand as it is. New hands have never touched it. The men who made it have done their work, and have passed away. Who shall improve on what *they* did?

Mr. Chairman, for the purpose of reviewing this message in the least possible time, as well as for the sake of distinctness, I have analyzed its arguments as well as I could, and reduced them to the propositions I have stated. I have now examined them in detail. I wish to detain the committee only a little while longer

VOL. I.—9.

with some general remarks upon the subject of improvements. That the subject is a difficult one, cannot be denied. Still it is no more difficult in Congress than in the State legislatures, in the counties, or in the smallest municipal districts which anywhere exist. All can recur to instances of this difficulty in the case of county roads, bridges, and the like. One man is offended because a road passes over his land, and another is offended because it does not pass over his; one is dissatisfied because the bridge for which he is taxed crosses the river on a different road from that which leads from his house to town; another cannot bear that the county should be got in debt for these same roads and bridges; while not a few struggle hard to have roads located over their lands, and then stoutly refuse to let them be opened until they are first paid the damages. Even between the different wards and streets of towns and cities we find this same wrangling and difficulty. Now these are no other than the very difficulties against which, and out of which, the President constructs his objections of "inequality," "speculation," and "crushing the treasury." There is but a single alternative about them: they are sufficient, or they are not. If sufficient, they are sufficient out of Congress as well as in it, and there is the end. We must reject them as insufficient, or lie down and do nothing by any authority. Then, difficulty though there be, let us meet and encounter it. "Attempt the end, and never stand to doubt; nothing so hard, but search will find it out." Determine that the thing can and shall be done, and then we shall find the way. The tendency to undue expansion is unquestionably the chief difficulty.

How to do something, and still not do too much, is the desideratum. Let each contribute his mite in the way of suggestion. The late Silas Wright, in a letter to the Chicago convention, contributed his, which was worth something; and I now contribute mine, which may be worth nothing. At all events, it will mislead nobody, and therefore will do no harm. I would not borrow money. I am against an overwhelming, crushing system. Suppose that, at each session, Congress shall first determine how much money can, for that year, be spared for improvements; then apportion that sum to the most important objects. So far all is easy; but how shall we determine which are the most important? On this question comes the collision of interests. I shall be slow to acknowledge that your harbor or your river is more important than mine, and vice versa. To clear this difficulty, let us have that same statistical information which the gentleman from Ohio [Mr. Vinton] suggested at the beginning of this session. In that information we shall have a stern, unbending basis of facts—a basis in no wise subject to whim, caprice, or local interest. The pre-limited amount of means will save us from doing too much, and the statistics will save us from doing what we do in wrong places. Adopt and adhere to this course, and, it seems to me, the difficulty is cleared.

One of the gentlemen from South Carolina [Mr. Rhett] very much deprecates these statistics. He particularly objects, as I understand him, to counting all the pigs and chickens in the land. I do not perceive much force in the objection. It is true that if everything be enumerated, a portion of such statistics may not be very useful to this object. Such products of the country as are to be consumed where they are produced need no roads or rivers, no means of transportation, and have no very proper connection with this subject. The surplus — that which is produced in one place to be consumed in another; the capacity of each locality for producing a greater surplus; the natural means of transportation, and their susceptibility of improvement; the hindrances, delays, and losses of life and property during transportation, and the causes of each, would be among the most valuable statistics in this connection. From these it would readily appear where a given amount of expenditure would do the most good. These statistics might be equally accessible, as they would be equally useful, to both the nation and the States. In this way, and by these means, let the nation take hold of the larger works, and the States the smaller ones; and thus, working in a meeting direction, discreetly, but steadily and firmly, what is made unequal in one place may be equalized in another, extravagance avoided, and the whole country put on that career of prosperity which shall correspond with its extent of territory, its natural resources, and the intelligence and enterprise of its people.

June 22, 1848.— LETTER TO WILLIAM H. HERNDON.

WASHINGTON, June 22, 1848.

Dear William: Last night I was attending a sort of caucus of the Whig members, held in relation to the coming presidential election. The whole field of the nation was scanned, and all is high hope and confidence. Illinois is expected to better her condition in this race. Under these circumstances, judge how heartrending it was to come to my room and find and read your discouraging letter of the 15th. We have made no gains, but have lost " H. R. Robinson, Turner, Campbell, and four or five more." Tell Arney to reconsider, if he would be saved. Baker and I used to do something, but I think you attach more importance to our absence than is just. There is another cause. In 1840, for instance, we had two senators and five representatives in Sangamon; now we have part of one senator and two representatives. With quite one third more people than we had then, we have only half the sort of offices which are sought by men of the speaking sort of talent. This, I think, is the chief cause. Now, as to the young men. You must not wait to be brought forward by the older men. For instance, do you suppose that I should ever have got into notice if I had waited to be hunted up and pushed forward by older men ? You young men get together and form a "Rough and Ready Club," and have regular meetings and speeches. Take in everybody you can get. Harrison Grimsley, L. A. Enos, Lee Kimball, and C. W. Matheny will do to begin the thing ; but as you go along gather up all the shrewd, wild boys about town, whether just of age or a little under age,— Chris. Logan, Reddick Ridgely, Lewis Zwizler, and hundreds such. Let every one play the part he can play best,— some speak, some sing, and all "holler." Your meetings will be of evenings; the older men, and the women, will go to hear you; so that it will not only contribute to the election of " Old Zach," but will be an interesting pastime, and improving to the intellectual faculties of all engaged. Don't fail to do this.

You ask me to send you all the speeches made about " Old Zach," the war, etc. Now this makes me a little impatient. I have regularly sent you the " Congressional Globe" and "Appendix," and you cannot have examined them, or you would have discovered that they contain every speech made by every man in both houses of Congress, on every subject, during the session. Can I send any more? Can I send speeches that nobody has made? Thinking it would be most natural that the newspapers would feel interested to give at least some of the speeches to their readers, I at the beginning of the session made arrangements to have one copy of the " Globe " and "Appendix" regularly sent to each Whig paper of the district. And yet, with the exception of my own little speech, which was published in two only of the then five, now four, Whig papers, I do not remember having seen a single speech, or even extract from one, in any single one of those papers. With equal and full means on both sides, I will venture that the " State Register" has thrown before its readers more of Locofoco speeches in a month than all the Whig papers of the district have done of Whig speeches during the session.

If you wish a full understanding of the war, I repeat what I believe I said to you in a letter once before, that the whole, or nearly so, is to be found in the speech of Dixon of Connecticut. This I sent you in pamphlet as well as in the "Globe." Examine and study every sentence of that speech thoroughly, and you will understand the whole subject. You ask how Congress came to declare that war had existed by the act of Mexico. Is it possible you don't understand that yet? You have at least twenty speeches in your possession that fully explain it. I will, however, try it once more. The news reached Washington of the commencement of hostilities on the Rio Grande, and of the great peril of General Taylor's army. Everybody, Whigs and Democrats, was for sending them aid, in men and money. It was necessary to pass a bill for this. The Locos had a majority in both houses, and they brought in a bill with a preamble saying: *Whereas,* War exists by the act of Mexico, therefore we send General Taylor money. The Whigs moved to strike out the preamble, so that they could vote to send the men and money, without saying anything about how the war commenced; but being in the minority, they were voted down, and the preamble was retained. Then, on the passage of the bill, the question came upon them, Shall we vote for preamble and bill together, or against both together? They did not want to vote against sending help to General Taylor, and therefore they voted for both together. Is there any difficulty in understanding this? Even my little speech shows how this was; and if you will go to the library, you may get the "Journal" of 1845-46, in which you will find the whole for yourself.

We have nothing published yet with special reference to the Taylor race; but we soon will have, and then I will send them to everybody. I made an internal-improvement speech day before yesterday, which I shall send home as soon as I can get it written out and printed,—and which I suppose nobody will read.

Your friend as ever,   A. LINCOLN.

June 27, 1848.—LETTER TO HORACE GREELEY.

WASHINGTON, June 27, 1848.

Friend Greeley: In the "Tribune" of yesterday I discovered a little editorial paragraph in relation to Colonel Wentworth of Illinois, in which, in relation to the boundary of Texas, you say: "All Whigs and many Democrats having ever contended it stopped at the Nueces." Now this is a mistake which I dislike to see go uncorrected in a leading Whig paper. Since I have been here, I know a large majority of such Whigs of the House of Representatives as have spoken on the question have not taken that position. Their position, and in my opinion the true position, is that the boundary of Texas extended just so far as American settlements taking part in her revolution extended; and that as a matter of fact those settlements did extend, at one or two points, beyond the Nueces, but not anywhere near the Rio Grande at any point. The "stupendous desert" between the valleys of those two rivers, and not either river, has been insisted on by the Whigs as the true boundary.

Will you look at this? By putting us in the position of insisting on the line of the Nueces, you put us in a position which, in my opinion, we cannot maintain, and which therefore gives the Democrats an advantage of us. If the degree of arrogance is not too great, may I ask you to examine what I said on this very point in the printed speech I send you.   Yours truly,

A. LINCOLN.

June 28, 1848.— REMARKS IN THE UNITED STATES HOUSE OF REPRESENTATIVES.

Discussion as to salary of judge of western Virginia.—Wishing to increase it from $1800 to $2500.

Mr. Lincoln said he felt unwilling to be either unjust or ungenerous, and he wanted to understand the real case of this judicial officer. The gentleman from Virginia had stated that he had to hold eleven courts. Now everybody knew that it was not the habit of the district judges of the United States in other States to hold anything like that number of courts; and he therefore took it for granted that this must happen under a peculiar law which required that large number of courts to be holden every year; and these laws, he further supposed, were passed at the request of the people of that judicial district. It came, then, to this: that the people in the western district of Virginia had got eleven courts to be held among them in one year, for their own accommodation; and being thus better accommodated than their neighbors elsewhere, they wanted their judge to be a little better paid. In Illinois there had been, until the present season, but one district court held in the year. There were now to be two. Could it be that the western district of Virginia furnished more business for a judge than the whole State of Illinois?

[July 1?] 1848.—FRAGMENT.

The following paper was written by Lincoln in 1848 as being what he thought General Taylor ought to say:

The question of a national bank is at rest. Were I President, I should not urge its reagitation upon Congress; but should Congress see fit to pass an act to establish such an institution, I should not arrest it by the veto, unless I should consider it subject to some constitutional objection from which I believe the two former banks to have been free.

It appears to me that the national debt created by the war renders a modification of the existing tariff indispensable; and when it shall be modified I should be pleased to see it adjusted with a due reference to the protection of our home industry. The particulars, it appears to me, must and should be left to the untrammeled discretion of Congress.

As to the Mexican war, I still think the defensive line policy the best to terminate it. In a final treaty of peace, we shall probably be under a sort of necessity of taking some territory; but it is my desire that we shall not acquire any extending so far south as to enlarge and aggravate the distracting question of slavery. Should I come into the presidency before these questions shall be settled, I should act in relation to them in accordance with the views here expressed.

Finally, were I President, I should desire the legislation of the country to rest with Congress, uninfluenced by the executive in its origin or progress, and undisturbed by the veto unless in very special and clear cases.

July 10, 1848.—LETTER TO WILLIAM H. HERNDON.

WASHINGTON, July 10, 1848.

Dear William: Your letter covering the newspaper slips was received last night. The subject of that letter is exceedingly painful to me; and I cannot but think there is some mistake in your impression of the motives of the old men. I suppose I am now one of the old men; and I declare, on my veracity, which I think is good with you, that nothing could afford me more satisfaction than to learn that you and others of my young friends at home are doing battle in the contest, and endearing themselves to the people, and taking a stand far above any I have ever been able to reach in their admiration. I cannot conceive that other old men feel differently. Of course I cannot demonstrate what I say; but I was young once, and I am sure I was never ungenerously thrust back. I hardly know what to say. The way for a young man to rise is to improve himself every way he can, never suspecting that anybody wishes to hinder him. Allow me to assure you that suspicion and jealousy never did help any man in any situation. There may sometimes be ungenerous attempts to keep a young man down; and they will succeed, too, if he allows his mind to be diverted from its true channel to brood over the attempted injury. Cast about, and see if this feeling has not injured every person you have ever known to fall into it.

Now, in what I have said, I am sure you will suspect nothing but sincere friendship. I would save you from a fatal error. You have been a laborious, studious young man. You are far better informed on almost all subjects than I have ever been. You cannot fail in any laudable object, unless you allow your mind to be improperly directed. I have somewhat the advantage of you in the world's experience, merely by being older; and it is this that induces me to advise. You still seem to be a little mistaken about the "Congressional Globe" and "Appendix." They contain all of the speeches that are published in any way. My speech and Dayton's speech, which you say you got in pamphlet form, are both, word for word, in the "Appendix." I repeat again, all are there.

Your friend, as ever,   A. LINCOLN.

July 27, 1848.—SPEECH IN THE UNITED STATES HOUSE OF REPRESENTATIVES.

General Taylor and the Veto.

Mr. Speaker, our Democratic friends seem to be in great distress because they think our candidate for the presidency don't suit us. Most of them cannot find out that General Taylor has any principles at all; some, however, have discovered that he has one, but that one is entirely wrong. This one principle is his position on the veto power. The gentleman from Tennessee [Mr. Stanton] who has just taken his seat, indeed, has said there is very little, if any, difference on this question between General Taylor and all the presidents; and he seems to think it sufficient detraction from General Taylor's position on it that it has nothing new in it. But all others whom I have heard speak assail it furiously. A new member from Kentucky [Mr. Clark], of very considerable ability, was in particular concerned about it. He thought it altogether novel and unprecedented for a president or a presidential candidate to think of approving bills whose constitutionality may not be entirely clear to his own mind. He thinks the ark of our safety is gone unless presidents shall always veto such bills as in their judgment may be of doubtful constitutionality. However clear Congress may be on their authority to pass any particular act, the gentleman from Kentucky thinks the President must veto it if he has doubts about it. Now I have neither time nor inclination to argue with the gentleman on the veto power as an original question; but I wish to show that General

Taylor, and not he, agrees with the earlier statesmen on this question. When the bill chartering the first Bank of the United States passed Congress, its constitutionality was questioned. Mr. Madison, then in the House of Representatives, as well as others, had opposed it on that ground. General Washington, as President, was called on to approve or reject it. He sought and obtained on the constitutionality question the separate written opinions of Jefferson, Hamilton, and Edmund Randolph,—they then being respectively Secretary of State, Secretary of the Treasury, and Attorney-General. Hamilton's opinion was for the power; while Randolph's and Jefferson's were both against it. Mr. Jefferson, after giving his opinion deciding only against the constitutionality of the bill, closes his letter with the paragraph which I now read:

It must be admitted, however, that unless the President's mind, on a view of everything which is urged for and against this bill, is tolerably clear that it is unauthorized by the Constitution,—if the *pro* and *con.* hang so even as to balance his judgment,—a just respect for the wisdom of the legislature would naturally decide the balance in favor of their opinion. It is chiefly for cases where they are clearly misled by error, ambition, or interest, that the Constitution has placed a check in the negative of the President.

February 15, 1791.   THOMAS JEFFERSON.

General Taylor's opinion, as expressed in his Allison letter, is as I now read:

The power given by the veto is a high conservative power; but, in my opinion, should never be exercised except in cases of clear violation of the Constitution, or manifest haste and want of consideration by Congress.

It is here seen that, in Mr. Jefferson's opinion, if on the constitutionality of any given bill the President doubts, he is not to veto it, as the gentleman from Kentucky would have him do, but is to defer to Congress and approve it. And if we compare the opinion of Jefferson and Taylor, as expressed in these paragraphs, we shall find them more exactly alike than we can often find any two expressions having any literal difference. None but interested faultfinders, I think, can discover any substantial variation.

Taylor on Measures of Policy.

But gentlemen on the other side are unanimously agreed that General Taylor has no other principles. They are in utter darkness as to his opinions on any of the questions of policy which occupy the public attention. But is there any doubt as to what he will do on the prominent questions if elected? Not the least. It is not possible to know what he will or would do in every imaginable case, because many questions have passed away, and others doubtless will arise which none of us have yet thought of; but on the prominent questions of currency, tariff, internal improvements, and Wilmot proviso, General Taylor's course is at least as well defined as is General Cass's. Why, in their eagerness to get at General Taylor, several Democratic members here have desired to know whether, in case of his election, a bankrupt law is to be established. Can they tell us General Cass's opinion on this question? [Some member answered, "He is against it."] Aye, how do you know he is? There is nothing about it in the platform, nor elsewhere, that I have seen. If the gentleman knows of anything which I do not, he can show it. But to return. General Taylor, in his Allison letter, says:

Upon the subject of the tariff, the currency, the improvement of our great highways, rivers, lakes, and harbors, the will of the people, as expressed through their representatives in Congress, ought to be respected and carried out by the executive.

Now this is the whole matter. In substance, it is this. The people say to General Taylor, "If you are elected, shall we have a national bank?" He answers, "Your will, gentlemen, not mine." "What about the tariff?" "Say yourselves." "Shall our rivers and harbors be improved?" "Just as you please. If you desire a bank, an alteration of the tariff, internal improvements, any or all, I will not hinder you. If you do not desire them, I will not attempt to force them on you. Send up your members of Congress from the various districts, with opinions according to your own, and if they are for these measures, or any of them, I shall have nothing to oppose; if they are not for them, I shall not, by any appliances whatever, attempt to dragoon them into their adoption." Now can there be any difficulty in understanding this? To you Democrats it may not seem like principle; but surely you cannot fail to perceive the position plainly enough. The distinction between it and the position of your candidate is broad and obvious; and I admit you have a clear right to show it is wrong if you can; but you have no right to pretend you cannot see it at all. We see it, and to us it appears like principle, and the best sort of principle at that — the principle of allowing the people to do as they please with their own business. My friend from Indiana [C. B. Smith] has aptly asked, "Are you willing to trust the people?" Some of you answered substantially, "We are willing to trust the people; but the President is as much the representative of the people as Congress." In a certain sense, and to a certain extent, he is the representative of the people. He is elected by them, as well as Congress is; but can he, in the nature of things, know the wants of the people as well as three hundred other men, coming from all the various localities of the nation? If so, where is the propriety of having a Congress? That the Constitution gives the President a negative on legislation, all know; but that this negative should be so combined with platforms and other appliances as to enable him, and in fact almost compel him, to take the whole of legislation into his own hands, is what we object to, is what General Taylor objects to, and is what constitutes the broad distinction between you and us. To thus transfer legislation is clearly to take it from those who understand with minuteness the interests of the people, and give it to one who does not and cannot so well understand it. I understand your idea that if a presidential candidate avow his opinion upon a given question, or rather upon all questions, and the people, with full knowledge of this, elect him, they thereby distinctly approve all those opinions. By means of it, measures are adopted or rejected contrary to the wishes of the whole of one party, and often nearly half of the other. Three, four, or half a dozen questions are prominent at a given time; the party selects its candidate, and he takes his position on each of these questions. On all but one his positions have already been indorsed at former elections, and his party fully committed to them; but that one is new, and a large portion of them are against it. But what are they to do? The whole was strung together; and they must take all, or reject all. They cannot take what they like, and leave the rest. What they are already committed to being the majority, they shut their eyes, and gulp the whole. Next election, still another is introduced in the same way. If we run our eyes along the line of the past, we shall see that almost if not quite all the articles of the present Democratic creed have been at first forced upon the party in this very way. And just now, and just so, opposition to internal improvements is to be established if General Cass shall be elected. Almost half the Democrats here are for improvements; but they will vote for Cass, and if he succeeds, their vote will have aided in closing the doors against improvements. Now this is a process which we think is wrong. We prefer a candidate who, like General Taylor, will allow the people to have their own way, regardless of his private opinions; and I should think the internal-improvement Democrats, at least, ought to prefer such a candidate. He would force nothing on them which they don't want, and he would allow them to have improvements which their own candidate, if elected, will not.

Mr. Speaker, I have said General Taylor's position is as well defined as is that of General Cass. In saying this, I admit I do not certainly know what he would do on the Wilmot proviso. I am a Northern man, or rather a Western free-State man, with a constituency I believe to be, and with personal feelings I know to be, against the extension of slavery. As such, and with what information I have, I hope and believe General Taylor, if elected, would not veto the proviso. But I do not know it. Yet if I knew he would, I still would vote for him. I should do so because, in my judgment, his election alone can defeat General Cass; and because, should slavery thereby go to the territory we now have, just so much will certainly happen by the election of Cass, and, in addition a course of policy leading to new wars, new acquisitions of territory and still further extensions of slavery. One of the two is to be President. Which is preferable?

But there is as much doubt of Cass on improvements as there is of Taylor on the proviso. I have no doubt myself of General Cass on this question; but I know the Democrats differ among themselves as to his position. My internal-improvement colleague [Mr. Wentworth] stated on this floor the other day that he was satisfied Cass was for improvements, because he had voted for all the bills that he [Mr. Wentworth] had. So far so good. But Mr. Polk vetoed some of these very bills. The Baltimore convention passed a set of resolutions, among other things, approving these vetoes, and General Cass declares, in his letter accepting the nomination, that he has carefully read these resolutions, and that he adheres to them as firmly as he approves them cordially. In other words, General Cass voted for the bills, and thinks the President did right to veto them; and his friends here are amiable enough to consider him as being on one side or the other, just as one or the other may correspond with their own respective inclinations. My colleague admits that the platform declares against the constitutionality of a general system of improvements; and that General Cass indorses the platform; but he still thinks General Cass is in favor of some sort of improvements. Well, what are they? As he is against general objects, those he is for must be particular and local. Now this is taking the subject precisely by the wrong end. Particularity—expending the money of the whole people for an object which will benefit only a portion of them—is the greatest real objection to improvements, and has been so held by General Jackson, Mr. Polk, and all others, I believe, till now. But now, behold, the objects most general—nearest free from this objection—are to be rejected, while those most liable to it are to be embraced. To return: I cannot help believing that General Cass, when he wrote his letter of acceptance, well understood he was to be claimed by the advocates of both sides of this question, and that he then closed the door against all further expressions of opinion purposely to retain the benefits of that double position. His subsequent equivocation at Cleveland, to my mind, proves such to have been the case.

One word more, and I shall have done with this branch of the subject. You Democrats, and your candidate, in the main are in favor of laying down in advance a platform—a set of party positions—as a unit, and then of forcing the people, by every sort of appliance, to ratify them, however unpalatable some of them may be. We and our candidate are in favor of making presidential elections, and the legislation of the country distinct matters; so that the people can elect whom they please, and afterward legislate just as they please, without any hindrance, save only so much as may guard against infractions of the Constitution, undue haste, and want of consideration. The difference between us is clear as noonday. That we are right we cannot doubt. We hold the true Republican position. In leaving the people's business in their hands, we cannot be wrong. We are willing, and even anxious, to go to the people on this issue.

Old Horses and Military Coat-tails.

But I suppose I cannot reasonably hope to convince you that we have any principles. The most I can expect is to assure you that we think we have, and are quite contented with them. The other day one of the gentlemen from Georgia [Mr. Iverson], an eloquent man, and a man of learning, so far as I can judge, not being learned myself, came down upon us astonishingly. He spoke in what the "Baltimore American" calls the "scathing and withering style." At the end of his second severe flash I was struck blind, and found myself feeling with my fingers for an assurance of my continued existence. A little of the bone was left, and I gradually revived. He eulogized Mr. Clay in high and beautiful terms, and then declared that we had deserted all our principles, and had turned Henry Clay out, like an old horse, to root. This is terribly severe. It cannot be answered by argument—at least I cannot so answer it. I merely wish to ask the gentleman if the Whigs are the only party he can think of who sometimes turn old horses out to root. Is not a certain Martin Van Buren an old horse which your own party have turned out to root? and is he not rooting a little to your discomfort about now? But in not nominating Mr. Clay we deserted our principles, you say. Ah! In what? Tell us, ye men of principle, what principle we violated. We say you did violate principle in discarding Van Buren, and we can tell you how. You violated the primary, the cardinal, the one great living principle of all democratic representative government—the principle that the representative is bound to carry out the known will of his constituents. A large majority of the Baltimore convention of 1844 were, by their constituents, instructed to procure Van Buren's nomination if they could. In violation—in utter glaring contempt—of this, you rejected him—rejected him, as the gentleman from New-York [Mr. Birdsall] the other day expressly admitted, for availability—that same "general availability" which you charge upon us, and daily chew over here, as something exceedingly odious and unprincipled. But the gentleman from Georgia [Mr. Iverson] gave us a second speech yesterday, all well considered and put down in writing, in which Van Buren was scathed and withered a "few" for his present position and movements. I cannot remember the gentleman's precise language; but I do remember he put Van Buren down, down, till he got him where he was finally to "stink" and "rot."

Mr. Speaker, it is no business or inclination of mine to defend Martin Van Buren in the war of extermination now waging between him and his old admirers. I say, "Devil take the hindmost"—and the foremost. But there is no mistaking the origin of the breach; and if the curse of "stinking" and "rotting" is to fall on the first and greatest violators of principle in the matter, I disinterestedly suggest that the gentleman from Georgia and his present co-workers are bound to take it upon themselves. But the gentleman from Georgia further says we have deserted all our principles, and taken shelter under General Taylor's military coat-tail, and he seems to think this is exceedingly degrading. Well, as his faith is, so be it unto him. But can he remember no other military coat-tail under which a certain other party have been sheltering for near a quarter of a century? Has he no acquaintance with the ample military coat-tail of General Jackson? Does he not know that his own party have run the five last presidential races under that coat-tail? And that they are now running the sixth under the same cover? Yes, sir, that coat-tail was used not only for General Jackson himself, but has been clung to, with the grip of death, by every Democratic candidate since. You have never ventured, and dare not now venture, from under it. Your campaign papers have constantly been "Old Hickories," with rude likenesses of the old general upon them; hickory poles and hickory brooms your never-ending emblems; Mr. Polk himself was "Young Hickory," "Little Hickory," or something so; and even now your campaign paper here is proclaiming that Cass and Butler are of the true "Hickory stripe." Now, sir, you dare not give it up. Like a horde of hungry ticks you have stuck to the tail of the Hermitage lion to the end of his life; and you are still sticking to it, and drawing a loathsome sustenance from it, after he is dead. A fellow once advertised that he had made a discovery by which he could make a new man out of an old one, and have enough of the stuff left to make a little yellow dog. Just such a discovery has General Jackson's popularity been to you. You not only twice made President of him out of it, but you have had enough of the stuff left to make Presidents of several comparatively small men since; and it is your chief reliance now to make still another.

Mr. Speaker, old horses and military coat-tails, or tails of any sort, are not figures of speech such as I would be the first to introduce into discussions here; but as the gentleman from Georgia has thought fit to introduce them, he and you are welcome to all you have made, or can make by them. If you have any more old horses, trot them out; any more tails, just cock them and come at us. I repeat, I would not introduce this mode of discussion here; but I wish gentlemen on the other side to understand that the use of degrading figures is a game at which they may not find themselves able to take all the winnings. ["We give it up!"] Aye, you give it up, and well you may; but for a very different reason from that which you would have us understand. The point—the power to hurt—of all figures consists in the truthfulness of their application; and, understanding this, you may well give it up. They are weapons which hit you, but miss us.

Military Tail of the Great Michigander.

But in my hurry I was very near closing this subject of military tails before I was done with it. There is one entire article of the sort I have not discussed yet,—I mean the military tail you Democrats are now engaged in dovetailing into the great Michigander. Yes, sir; all his biographies (and they are legion) have him in hand, tying him to a military tail, like so many mischievous boys tying a dog to a bladder of beans. True the material they have is very limited, but they drive at it might and main. He *in*vaded Canada without resistance, and he *out*vaded it without pursuit. As he did both under orders, I suppose there was to him neither credit nor discredit in them; but they constitute a large part of the tail. He was not at Hull's surrender, but he was close by; he was volunteer aid to General Harrison on the day of the battle of the Thames; and as you said in 1840 Harrison was picking huckleberries two miles off while the battle was fought, I suppose it is a just conclusion with you to say Cass was aiding Harrison to pick huckleberries. This is about all, except the mooted question of the broken sword. Some authors say he broke it, some say he threw it away, and some others, who ought to know, say nothing about it. Perhaps it would be a fair historical compromise to say, if he did not break it, he did not do anything else with it.

By the way, Mr. Speaker, did you know I am a military hero? Yes, sir; in the days of the Black Hawk war I fought, bled, and came away. Speaking of General Cass's career reminds me of my own. I was not at Stillman's defeat, but I was about as near it as Cass was to Hull's surrender; and, like him, I saw the place very soon afterward. It is quite certain I did not break my sword, for I had none to break; but I bent a musket pretty badly on one occasion. If Cass broke his sword, the idea is he broke it in desperation; I bent the musket by accident. If General Cass went in advance of me in picking huckleberries, I guess I surpassed him in charges upon the wild onions. If he saw any live, fighting Indians, it was more than I did; but I had a good many bloody struggles with the mosquitoes, and although I never fainted from the loss of blood, I can truly say I was often very hungry. Mr. Speaker, if I should ever conclude to doff whatever our Democratic friends may suppose there is of black-cockade federalism about me, and therefore they shall take me up as their candidate for the presidency, I protest they shall not make fun of me, as they have of General Cass, by attempting to write me into a military hero.

Cass on the Wilmot Proviso.

While I have General Cass in hand, I wish to say a word about his political principles. As a specimen, I take the record of his progress in the Wilmot proviso. In the Washington "Union" of March 2, 1847, there is a report of a speech of General Cass, made the day before in the Senate, on the Wilmot proviso, during the delivery of which Mr. Miller of New Jersey is reported to have interrupted him as follows, to wit:

Mr. Miller expressed his great surprise at the change in the sentiments of the senator from Michigan, who had been regarded as the great champion of freedom in the Northwest, of which he was a distinguished ornament. Last year the senator from Michigan was understood to be decidedly in favor of the Wilmot proviso; and as no reason had been stated for the change, he [Mr. Miller] could not refrain from the expression of his extreme surprise.

To this General Cass is reported to have replied as follows, to wit:

Mr. Cass said that the course of the senator from New Jersey was most extraordinary. Last year he [Mr. Cass] should have voted for the proposition, had it come up. But circumstances had altogether changed. The honorable senator then read several passages from the remarks, as given above, which he had committed to writing, in order to refute such a charge as that of the senator from New Jersey.

In the "remarks above reduced to writing" is one numbered four, as follows, to wit:

Fourth. Legislation now would be wholly inoperative, because no territory hereafter to be acquired can be governed without an act of Congress providing for its government; and such an act, on its passage, would open the whole subject, and leave the Congress called on to pass it free to exercise its own discretion, entirely uncontrolled by any declaration found on the statute-book.

In "Niles's Register," Vol. LXXIII., p. 293, there is a letter of General Cass to —— Nicholson, of Nashville, Tennessee, dated December 24, 1847, from which the following are correct extracts:

The Wilmot proviso has been before the country some time. It has been repeatedly discussed in Congress and by the public press. I am strongly impressed with the opinion that a great change has been going on in the public mind upon this subject,—in my own as well as others',—and that doubts are resolving themselves into convictions that the principle it involves should be kept out of the national legislature, and left to the people of the confederacy in their respective local governments. . . . Briefly, then, I am opposed to the exercise of any jurisdiction by Congress over this matter; and I am in favor of leaving the people of any territory which may be hereafter acquired the right to regulate it themselves, under the general principles of the Constitution. Because—

First. I do not see in the Constitution any grant of the requisite power to Congress; and I am not disposed to extend a doubtful precedent beyond its necessity,—the establishment of territorial governments when needed,—leaving to the inhabitants all the right compatible with the relations they bear to the confederation.

These extracts show that in 1846 General Cass was for the proviso at once; that in March, 1847, he was still for it, but not just then; and that in December, 1847, he was against it altogether. This is a true index to the whole man. When the question was raised in 1846, he was in a blustering hurry to take ground for it. He sought to be in advance, and to avoid the uninteresting position of a mere follower; but soon he began to see glimpses of the great Democratic ox-goad waving in his face, and to hear indistinctly a voice saying, "Back! Back, sir! Back a little!" He shakes his head, and bats his eyes, and blunders back to his position of March, 1847; but still the goad waves, and the voice grows more distinct and sharper still, "Back, sir! Back, I say! Further back!"— and back he goes to the position of December, 1847, at which the goad is still, and the voice soothingly says, "So! Stand at that!"

Have no fears, gentlemen, of your candidate. He exactly suits you, and we congratulate you upon it. However much you may be distressed about our candidate, you have all cause to be contented and happy with your own. If elected, he may not maintain all, or even any of his positions previously taken; but he will be sure to do whatever the party exigency for the time being may require; and that is precisely what you want. He and Van Buren are the same "manner of men"; and, like Van Buren, he will never desert you till you first desert him.

Cass on Working and Eating.

Mr. Speaker, I adopt the suggestion of a friend, that General Cass is a general of splendidly successful charges—charges to be sure, not upon the public enemy, but upon the public treasury. He was Governor of Michigan Territory, and ex-officio Superintendent of Indian Affairs, from the 9th of October, 1813, till the 31st of July, 1831 — a period of seventeen years, nine months, and twenty-two days. During this period he received from the United States treasury, for personal services and personal expenses, the aggregate sum of ninety-six thousand and twenty-eight dollars, being an average of fourteen dollars and seventy-nine cents per day for every day of the time. This large sum was reached by assuming that he was doing service at several different places, and in several different capacities in the same place, all at the same time. By a correct analysis of his accounts during that period, the following propositions may be deduced:

First. He was paid in three different capacities during the whole of the time; that is to say — (1) As governor's salary at the rate per year of $2000. (2) As estimated for office rent, clerk hire, fuel, etc., in superintendence of Indian affairs *in* Michigan, at the rate per year of $1500. (3) As compensation and expenses for various miscellaneous items of Indian service *out* of Michigan, an average per year of $625.

Second. During part of the time—that is, from the 9th of October, 1813, to the 29th of May, 1822—he was paid in four different capacities; that is to say, the three as above, and, in addition thereto, the commutation of ten rations per day, amounting per year to $730.

Third. During another part of the time—that is, from the beginning of 1822 to the 31st of July, 1831—he was also paid in four different capacities; that is to say, the first three, as above (the rations being dropped after the 29th of May, 1822), and, in addition thereto, for superintending Indian Agencies at Piqua, Ohio; Fort Wayne, Indiana; and Chicago, Illinois, at the rate per year of $1500. It should be observed here that the last item, commencing at the beginning of 1822, and the item of rations, ending on the 29th of May, 1822, lap on each other during so much of the time as lies between those two dates.

Fourth. Still another part of the time—that is, from the 31st of October, 1821, to the 29th of May, 1822—he was paid in six different capacities; that is to say, the three first, as above; the item of rations, as above; and, in addition thereto, another item of ten rations per day while at Washington settling his accounts, being at the rate per year of $730; and also an allowance for expenses traveling to and from Washington, and while there, of $1022, being at the rate per year of $1793.

Fifth. And yet during the little portion of the time which lies between the 1st of January, 1822, and the 29th of May, 1822, he was paid in seven different capacities; that is to say, the six last mentioned, and also, at the rate of $1500 per year, for the Piqua, Fort Wayne, and Chicago service, as mentioned above.

These accounts have already been discussed some here; but when we are amongst them, as when we are in the Patent Office, we must peep about a good deal before we can see all the curiosities. I shall not be tedious with them. As to the large item of $1500 per year—

amounting in the aggregate to $26,715—for office rent, clerk hire, fuel, etc., I barely wish to remark that so far as I can discover in the public documents, there is no evidence, by word or inference, either from any disinterested witness or of General Cass himself, that he ever rented or kept a separate office, ever hired or kept a clerk, or even used any extra amount of fuel, etc., in consequence of his Indian services. Indeed, General Cass's entire silence in regard to these items, in his two long letters urging his claims upon the government, is, to my mind, almost conclusive that no such claims had any real existence.

But I have introduced General Cass's accounts here chiefly to show the wonderful physical capacities of the man. They show that he not only did the labor of several men at the same time, but that he often did it at several places, many hundreds of miles apart, at the same time. And at eating, too, his capacities are shown to be quite as wonderful. From October, 1821, to May, 1822, he eat ten rations a day in Michigan, ten rations a day here in Washington, and near five dollars' worth a day on the road between the two places! And then there is an important discovery in his example—the art of being paid for what one eats, instead of having to pay for it. Hereafter if any nice young man should owe a bill which he cannot pay in any other way, he can just board it out. Mr. Speaker, we have all heard of the animal standing in doubt between two stacks of hay and starving to death. The like of that would never happen to General Cass. Place the stacks a thousand miles apart, he would stand stock-still midway between them, and eat them both at once, and the green grass along the line would be apt to suffer some, too, at the same time. By all means make him President, gentlemen. He will feed you bounteously—if—if there is any left after he shall have helped himself.

The Whigs and the War.

But, as General Taylor is, *par excellence*, the hero of the Mexican War, and as you Democrats say we Whigs have always opposed the war, you think it must be very awkward and embarrassing for us to go for General Taylor. The declaration that we have always opposed the war is true or false, according as one may understand the term "oppose the war." If to say "the war was unnecessarily and unconstitutionally commenced by the President" be opposing the war, then the Whigs have very generally opposed it. Whenever they have spoken at all, they have said this; and they have said it on what has appeared good reason to them. The marching an army into the midst of a peaceful Mexican settlement, frightening the inhabitants away, leaving their growing crops and other property to destruction, to you may appear a perfectly amiable, peaceful, unprovoking procedure; but it does not appear so to us. So to call such an act, to us appears no other than a naked, impudent absurdity, and we speak of it accordingly. But if, when the war had begun, and had become the cause of the country, the giving of our money and our blood, in common with yours, was support of the war, then it is not true that we have always opposed the war. With few

VOL. I.—10.

individual exceptions, you have constantly had our votes here for all the necessary supplies. And, more than this, you have had the services, the blood, and the lives of our political brethren in every trial and on every field. The beardless boy and the mature man, the humble and the distinguished—you have had them. Through suffering and death, by disease and in battle, they have endured and fought and fell with you. Clay and Webster each gave a son, never to be returned. From the State of my own residence, besides other worthy but less known Whig names, we sent Marshall, Morrison, Baker, and Hardin; they all fought, and one fell, and in the fall of that one we lost our best Whig man. Nor were the Whigs few in number, or laggard in the day of danger. In that fearful, bloody, breathless struggle at Buena Vista, where each man's hard task was to beat back five foes or die himself, of the five high officers who perished, four were Whigs.

In speaking of this, I mean no odious comparison between the lion-hearted Whigs and the Democrats who fought there. On other occasions, and among the lower officers and privates on that occasion, I doubt not the proportion was different. I wish to do justice to all. I think of all those brave men as Americans, in whose proud fame, as an American, I too have a share. Many of them, Whigs and Democrats, are my constituents and personal friends; and I thank them,—more than thank them,—one and all, for the high imperishable honor they have conferred on our common State.

But the distinction between the cause of the President in beginning the war, and the cause of the country after it was begun, is a distinction which you cannot perceive. To you the President and the country seem to be all one. You are interested to see no distinction between them; and I venture to suggest that probably your interest blinds you a little. We see the distinction, as we think, clearly enough; and our friends who have fought in the war have no difficulty in seeing it also. What those who have fallen would say, were they alive and here, of course we can never know; but with those who have returned there is no difficulty. Colonel Haskell and Major Gaines, members here, both fought in the war, and one of them underwent extraordinary perils and hardships; still they, like all other Whigs here, vote, on the record, that the war was unnecessarily and unconstitutionally commenced by the President. And even General Taylor himself, the noblest Roman of them all, has declared that as a citizen, and particularly as a soldier, it is sufficient for him to know that his country is at war with a foreign nation, to do all in his power to bring it to a speedy and honorable termination by the most vigorous and energetic operations, without inquiry about its justice, or anything else connected with it.

Mr. Speaker, let our Democratic friends be comforted with the assurance that we are content with our position, content with our company, and content with our candidate; and that although they, in their generous sympathy, think we ought to be miserable, we really are not, and that they may dismiss the great anxiety they have on our account.

Mr. Speaker, I see I have but three minutes left, and this forces me to throw out one whole branch of my subject. A single word on still another. The Democrats are keen enough to frequently remind us that we have some dissensions in our ranks. Our good friend from Baltimore immediately before me [Mr. McLane] expressed some doubt the other day as to which branch of our party General Taylor would ultimately fall into the hands of. That was a new idea to me. I knew we had dissenters, but I did not know they were trying to get our candidate away from us. I would like to say a word to our dissenters, but I have not the time. Some such we certainly have; have you none, gentlemen Democrats? Is it all union and harmony in your ranks? no bickerings? no divisions? If there be doubt as to which of our divisions will get our candidate, is there no doubt as to which of your candidates will get your party?

Divided Gangs of Hogs!

I have heard some things from New York; and if they are true, one might well say of your party there, as a drunken fellow once said when he heard the reading of an indictment for hog-stealing. The clerk read on till he got to and through the words, "did steal, take, and carry away ten boars, ten sows, ten shoats, and ten pigs," at which he exclaimed, "Well, by golly, that is the most equally divided gang of hogs I ever did hear of!" If there is any other gang of hogs more equally divided than the Democrats of New York are about this time, I have not heard of it.

December 24, 1848.—Letter to Thomas Lincoln.

WASHINGTON, December 24, 1848.

My dear Father: Your letter of the 7th was received night before last. I very cheerfully send you the twenty dollars, which sum you say is necessary to save your land from sale. It is singular that you should have forgotten a judgment against you; and it is more singular that the plaintiff should have let you forget it so long, particularly as I suppose you always had property enough to satisfy a judgment of that amount. Before you pay it, it would be well to be sure you have not paid it, or at least that you cannot prove that you have paid it.

Give my love to mother and all the connections. Affectionately your son,   A. LINCOLN.

January 16, 1849.— Bill to Abolish Slavery in the District of Columbia.

On January 16, 1849, Mr. Lincoln moved the following amendment in the House of Representatives in Congress, instructing the proper committee to report a bill for the abolition of slavery in the District of Columbia, with the consent of the voters of the District, and with compensation to owners:

Resolved, That the Committee on the District of Columbia be instructed to report a bill in substance as follows:

Sec. 1. Be it enacted by the Senate and House of Representatives of the United States, in Congress assembled, That no person not now within the District of Columbia, nor now owned by any person or persons now resident within it, nor hereafter born within it, shall ever be held in slavery within said District.

Sec. 2. That no person now within said District, or now owned by any person or persons now resident within the same, or hereafter born within it, shall ever be held in slavery without the limits of said District: Provided, That officers of the Government of the United States, being citizens of the slaveholding States, coming into said District on public business, and remaining only so long as may be reasonably necessary for that object, may be attended into and out of said District, and while there, by the necessary servants of themselves and their families, without their right to hold such servants in service being thereby impaired.

Sec. 3. That all children born of slave mothers within said District, on or after the first day of January, in the year of our Lord eighteen hundred and fifty, shall be free; but shall be reasonably supported and educated by the respective owners of their mothers, or by their heirs or representatives, and shall owe reasonable service as apprentices to such owners, heirs, or representatives, until they respectively arrive at the age of —— years, when they shall be entirely free; and the municipal authorities of Washington and Georgetown, within their respective jurisdictional limits, are hereby empowered and required to make all suitable and necessary provision for enforcing obedience to this section, on the part of both masters and apprentices.

Sec. 4. That all persons now within this District, lawfully held as slaves, or now owned by any person or persons now resident within said District, shall remain such at the will of their respective owners, their heirs, and legal representatives: Provided, That such owner, or his legal representative, may at any time receive from the Treasury of the United States the full value of his or her slave, of the class in this section mentioned, upon which such slave shall be forthwith and forever free: And provided further, That the President of the United States, the Secretary of State, and the Secretary of the Treasury shall be a board for determining the value of such slaves as their owners may desire to emancipate under this section, and whose duty it shall be to hold a session for the purpose on the first Monday of each calendar month, to receive all applications, and, on satisfactory evidence in each case that the person presented for valuation is a slave, and of the class in this section mentioned, and is owned by the applicant, shall value such slave at his or her full cash value, and give to the applicant an order on the Treasury for the amount, and also to such slave a certificate of freedom.

Sec. 5. That the municipal authorities of Washington and Georgetown, within their respective jurisdictional limits, are hereby empowered and required to provide active and efficient means to arrest and deliver up to their owners all fugitive slaves escaping into said District.

Sec. 6. That the election officers within said District of Columbia are hereby empowered and required to open polls, at all the usual places of holding elections, on the first Monday of April next, and receive the vote of every free white male citizen above the age of twenty-one years, having resided within said District for the period of one year or more next preceding the time of such voting for or against this act, to proceed in taking said votes, in all respects not herein specified, as at elections under the municipal laws, and with as little delay as possible to transmit correct statements of the votes so cast to the President of the United States; and it shall be the duty of the President to canvass said votes immediately, and if a majority of them be found to be for this act, to forthwith issue his proclamation giving notice of the fact; and this act shall only be in full force and effect on and after the day of such proclamation.

Sec. 7. That involuntary servitude for the punishment of crime, whereof the party shall have been duly convicted, shall in no wise be prohibited by this act.

Sec. 8. That for all the purposes of this act, the jurisdictional limits of Washington are extended to all parts of the District of Columbia not now included within the present limits of Georgetown.

February 2, 1849.—LETTER TO —— SCHOOLER.

WASHINGTON, February 2, 1849.

Friend Schooler: In these days of Cabinet making, we out West are awake as well as others. The accompanying article is from the "Illinois Journal," our leading Whig paper; and while it expresses what all the Whigs of the legislatures of Illinois, Iowa, and Wisconsin have expressed,—a preference for Colonel Baker,—I think it is fair and magnanimous to the other Western aspirants; and, on the whole, shows by sound argument that the West is not only entitled to, but is in need of, one member of the Cabinet. Desiring to turn public attention in some measure to this point, I shall be obliged if you will give the article a place in your paper, with or without comments, according to your own sense of propriety.

Our acquaintance, though short, has been very cordial, and I therefore venture to hope you will not consider my request presumptuous, whether you shall or shall not think proper to grant it. This I intend as private and confidential.   Yours truly,

A. LINCOLN.

February 13, 1849.—REMARKS IN THE UNITED STATES
HOUSE OF REPRESENTATIVES.

On the Bill Granting Lands to the States to Make Railroads and Canals.

Mr. Lincoln said he had not risen for the purpose of making a speech, but only for the purpose of meeting some of the objections to the bill. If he understood those objections, the first was that if the bill were to become a law, it would be used to lock large portions of the public lands from sale, without at last effecting the ostensible object of the bill—the construction of railroads in the new States; and secondly, that Congress would be forced to the abandonment of large portions of the public lands to the States for which they might be reserved, without their paying for them. This he understood to be the substance of the objections of the gentleman from Ohio to the passage of the bill.

If he could get the attention of the House for a few minutes, he would ask gentlemen to tell us what motive could induce any State legislature, or individual, or company of individuals, of the new States, to expend money in surveying roads which they might know they could not make? [A voice: They are not required to make the road.]

Mr. Lincoln continued: That was not the case he was making. What motive would tempt any set of men to go into an extensive survey of a railroad which they did not intend to make? What good would it do? Did men act without motive? Did business men commonly go into an expenditure of money which could be of no account to them? He generally found that men who have money were disposed to hold on to it, unless they could see something to be made by its investment. He could not see what motive of advantage to the new States could be subserved by merely keeping the public lands out of market, and preventing their settlement. As far as he could see, the new States were wholly without any motive to do such a thing. This, then, he took to be a good answer to the first objection.

In relation to the fact assumed, that after a while, the new States having got hold of the public lands to a certain extent, they would turn round and compel Congress to relinquish all claim to them, he had a word to say, by way of recurring to the history of the past. When was the time to come (he asked) when the States in which the public lands were situated would compose a majority of the representation in Congress, or anything like it? A majority of Representatives would very soon reside west of the mountains, he admitted; but would they all come from States in which the public lands were situated? They certainly would not; for, as these Western States grew strong in Congress, the public lands passed away from them, and they got on the other side of the question; and the gentleman from Ohio [Mr. Vinton] was an example attesting that fact.

Mr. Vinton interrupted here to say that he had stood on this question just where he was now, for five and twenty years.

Mr. Lincoln was not making an argument for the purpose of convicting the gentleman of any impropriety at all. He was speaking of a fact in history, of which his State was an example. He was referring to a plain principle in the nature of things. The State of Ohio had now grown to be a giant. She had a large delegation on that floor; but was she now in favor of granting lands to the new States, as she used to be? The New England States, New York, and the Old Thirteen were all rather quiet upon the subject; and it was seen just now that a member from one of the new States was the first man to rise up in opposition. And so it would be with the history of this question for the future. There never would come a time when the people residing in the States embracing the public lands would have the entire control of this subject; and so it was a matter of certainty that Congress would never do more in this respect than what would be dictated by a just liberality. The apprehension, therefore, that the public lands were in danger of being wrested from the General Government by the strength of the delegation in Congress from the new States, was utterly futile. There never could be such a thing. If we take these lands (said he) it will not be without your consent. We can never outnumber you. The result is that all fear of the new States turning against the right of Congress to the public domain must be effectually quelled, as those who are opposed to that interest must always hold a vast majority here, and they will never surrender the whole or any part of the public lands unless they themselves choose to do so. That was all he desired to say.

February 20, 1849.—LETTER TO JOSHUA F. SPEED.

February 20, 1849.

My dear Speed: . . . I am flattered to learn that Mr. Crittenden has any recollection of me which is not unfavorable; and for the manifestation of your kindness toward me I sincerely thank you. Still there is nothing about me to authorize me to think of a first-class office, and a second-class one would not compensate my being sneered at by others who want it for themselves. I believe that, so far as the Whigs in Congress are concerned, I could have the General Land Office almost by common consent; but then Sweet and Don Morrison and Browning and Cyrus Edwards all want it, and what is worse, while I think I could easily take it myself, I fear I shall have trouble to get it for any other man in Illinois. The reason is that McGaughey, an Indiana ex-member of Congress, is here after it, and being personally known, he will be hard to beat by any one who is not. . . .

March 9, 1849.— LETTER TO THE SECRETARY OF THE TREASURY.

WASHINGTON, March 9, 1849.

HON. SECRETARY OF THE TREASURY.

Dear Sir: Colonel E. D. Baker and myself are the only Whig members of Congress from Illinois—I of the Thirtieth, and he of the Thirty-first. We have reason to think the Whigs of that State hold us responsible, to some extent, for the appointments which may be made of our citizens. We do not know you personally; and our efforts to see you have, so far, been unavailing. I therefore hope I am not obtrusive in saying in this way, for him and myself, that when a citizen of Illinois is to be appointed in your department, to an office either in or out of the State, we most respectfully ask to be heard. Your obedient servant,

A. LINCOLN.

March 10, 1849.—LETTER TO THE SECRETARY OF STATE.

WASHINGTON, March 10, 1849.

HON. SECRETARY OF STATE.

Sir: There are several applicants for the office of United States Marshal for the District of Illinois, among the most prominent of whom are Benjamin Bond, Esq., of Carlyle, and —— Thomas, Esq., of Galena. Mr. Bond I know to be personally every way worthy of the office; and he is very numerously and most respectably recommended. His papers I send to you; and I solicit for his claims a full and fair consideration.

Having said this much, I add that in my individual judgment the appointment of Mr. Thomas would be the better.

Your obedient servant,   A. LINCOLN.

(Indorsed on Mr. Bond's papers.)

In this and the accompanying envelop are the recommendations of about two hundred good citizens of all parts of Illinois, that Benjamin Bond be appointed marshal for that district. They include the names of nearly all our Whigs who now are, or have ever been, members of the State legislature, besides forty-six of the Democratic members of the present legislature, and many other good citizens. I add that from personal knowledge I consider Mr. Bond every way worthy of the office, and qualified to fill it. Holding the individual opinion that the appointment of a different gentleman would be better, I ask especial attention and consideration for his claims, and for the opinions expressed in his favor by those over whom I can claim no superiority.

A. LINCOLN.

April 7, 1849.—LETTER TO THE SECRETARY OF THE INTERIOR.

SPRINGFIELD, ILLINOIS, April 7, 1849.

HON. SECRETARY OF THE HOME DEPARTMENT.

Dear Sir: I recommend that Walter Davis be appointed Receiver of the Land Office at this place, whenever there shall be a vacancy. I cannot say that Mr. Herndon, the present incumbent, has failed in the proper discharge of any of the duties of the office. He is a very warm partizan, and openly and actively opposed to the election of General Taylor. I also understand that since General Taylor's election, he has received a reappointment from Mr. Polk, his old commission not having expired. Whether this is true the records of the department will show. I may add that the Whigs here almost universally desire his removal.

I give no opinion of my own, but state the facts, and express the hope that the department will act in this as in all other cases on some proper general rule. Your obedient servant,

A. LINCOLN.

P. S. The land district to which this office belongs is very nearly if not entirely within my district; so that Colonel Baker, the other Whig representative, claims no voice in the appointment.

A. L.

April 7, 1849.—LETTER TO THE SECRETARY OF THE INTERIOR.

SPRINGFIELD, ILLINOIS, April 7, 1849.

HON. SECRETARY OF THE HOME DEPARTMENT.

Dear Sir: I recommend that Turner R. King, now of Pekin, Illinois, be appointed Register of the Land Office at this place whenever there shall be a vacancy.

I do not know that Mr. Barret, the present incumbent, has failed in the proper discharge of any of his duties in the office. He is a decided partizan, and openly and actively opposed the election of General Taylor. I understand, too, that since the election of General Taylor, Mr. Barret has received a reappointment from Mr. Polk, his old commission not having expired. Whether this be true, the records of the Department will show.

Whether he should be removed I give no opinion, but merely express the wish that the Department may act upon some proper general rule, and that Mr. Barret's case may not be made an exception to it.   Your obedient servant,

A. LINCOLN.

P. S. The land district to which this office belongs is very nearly if not entirely within my district; so that Colonel Baker, the other Whig representative, claims no voice in the appointment.

A. L.

April 7, 1849.—LETTER TO THE POSTMASTER-GENERAL.

SPRINGFIELD, ILLINOIS, April 7, 1849.

HON. POSTMASTER-GENERAL.

Dear Sir: I recommend that Abner Y. Ellis be appointed postmaster at this place, whenever there shall be a vacancy. J. R. Diller, the present incumbent, I cannot say has failed in the proper discharge of any of the duties of the office. He, however, has been an active partizan in opposition to us.

Located at the seat of government of the State, he has been, for part if not the whole of the time he has held the office, a member of the Democratic State Central Committee, signing his name to their addresses and manifestos; and has been, as I understand, reappointed by Mr. Polk since General Taylor's election. These are the facts of the case as I understand them, and I give no opinion of mine as to whether he should or should not be removed. My wish is that the Department may adopt some proper general rule for such cases, and that Mr. Diller may not be made an exception to it, one way or the other.   Your obedient servant,

A. LINCOLN.

P. S. This office, with its delivery, is entirely within my district; so that Colonel Baker, the other Whig representative, claims no voice in the appointment.

L.

April 7, 1849.—LETTER TO W. B. WARREN AND OTHERS.

SPRINGFIELD, ILLINOIS, April 7, 1849.

Gentlemen: In answer to your note concerning the General Land Office I have to say that, if the office could be secured to Illinois by my consent to accept it, and not otherwise, I give that consent. Some months since I gave my word to secure the appointment to that office of Mr. Cyrus Edwards, if in my power, in case of a vacancy;

and more recently I stipulated with Colonel Baker that if Mr. Edwards and Colonel J. L. D. Morrison could arrange with each other for one of them to withdraw, we would jointly recommend the other. In relation to these pledges, I must not only be chaste, but above suspicion. If the office shall be tendered to me, I must be permitted to say: "Give it to Mr. Edwards or, if so agreed by them, to Colonel Morrison, and I decline it; if not, I accept." With this understanding you are at liberty to procure me the offer of the appointment if you can; and I shall feel complimented by your effort, and still more by its success. It should not be overlooked that Colonel Baker's position entitles him to a large share of control in this matter; however, one of your number, Colonel Warren, knows that Baker has at all times been ready to recommend me, if I would consent. It must also be understood that if at any time previous to an appointment being made I shall learn that Mr. Edwards and Colonel Morrison have agreed, I shall at once carry out my stipulation with Colonel Baker as above stated.   Yours truly,

A. LINCOLN.

April 7, 1849.—LETTER TO THE SECRETARY OF THE INTERIOR.

SPRINGFIELD, ILLINOIS, April 7, 1849.

HON. SECRETARY OF THE HOME DEPARTMENT,

Dear Sir: I recommend that William Butler be appointed Pension Agent for the Illinois agency, when the place shall be vacant. Mr. Hurst, the present incumbent, I believe has performed the duties very well. He is a decided partizan, and, I believe, expects to be removed. Whether he shall, I submit to the Department. This office is not confined to my district, but pertains to the whole State; so that Colonel Baker has an equal right with myself to be heard concerning it.

However, the office is located here; and I think it is not probable that any one would desire to remove from a distance to take it.

Your obedient servant,   A. LINCOLN.

April 25, 1849.—LETTER TO —— THOMPSON.

SPRINGFIELD, April 25, 1849.

Dear Thompson: A tirade is still kept up against me here for recommending T. R. King. This morning it is openly avowed that my supposed influence at Washington shall be broken down generally, and King's prospects defeated in particular. Now, what I have done in this matter I have done at the request of you and some other friends in Tazewell; and I therefore ask you to either admit it is wrong, or come forward and sustain me. If the truth will permit, I propose that you sustain me in the following manner: copy the inclosed scrap in your own handwriting, and get everybody (not three or four, but three or four hundred) to sign it, and then send it to me. Also have six, eight, or ten of our best-known Whig friends there to write to me individual letters, stating the truth in this matter as they understand it. Don't neglect or delay in the matter. I understand information of an indictment having been found against him about three years ago, for gaming or keeping a gaming-house, has been sent to the Department. I shall try to take care of it at the Department till your action can be had and forwarded on.   Yours, as ever,

                                                    A. LINCOLN.

April 25, 1849.—LETTER TO J. M. LUCAS.

SPRINGFIELD, ILLINOIS, April 25, 1849.

J. M. LUCAS, Esq.

Dear Sir: Your letter of the 15th is just received. Like you, I fear the Land Office is not going as it should; but I know nothing I can do. In my letter written three days ago, I told you the Department understands my wishes. As to Butterfield, he is my personal friend, and is qualified to do the duties of the office; but of the quite one hundred Illinoisans equally well qualified, I do not know one with less claims to it. In the first place, what you say about Lisle Smith is the first intimation I have had of any one man in Illinois desiring Butterfield to have any office. Now, I think if anything be given the State, it should be so given as to gratify our friends, and to stimulate them to future exertions. As to Mr. Clay having recommended him, that is *quid pro quo.* He fought for Mr. Clay against General Taylor to the bitter end, as I understand; and I do not believe I misunderstand. Lisle Smith, too, was a Clay delegate at Philadelphia, and against my most earnest entreaties took the lead in filling two vacancies from my own district with Clay men. It will now mortify me deeply if General Taylor's administration shall trample all my wishes in the dust merely to gratify these men.   Yours, as ever,

                                                    A. LINCOLN.

May [1 ?], 1849.—INDORSEMENT CONCERNING ORVILLE PADDOCK.

I have already recommended W. S. Wallace for Pension Agent at this place. It is, however, due the truth to say that Orville Paddock, above recommended, is every way qualified for the office, and that the persons recommending him are of our business men and best Whig citizens.

May 10, 1849.—LETTER TO THE SECRETARY OF THE INTERIOR.

SPRINGFIELD, ILLINOIS, May 10, 1849.

HON. SECRETARY OF THE INTERIOR.

Dear Sir: I regret troubling you so often in relation to the land offices here, but I hope you will perceive the necessity of it, and excuse me. On the 7th of April I wrote you recommending Turner R. King for Register, and Walter Davis for Receiver. Subsequently

I wrote you that, for a private reason, I had concluded to transpose them. That private reason was the request of an old personal friend who himself desired to be Receiver, but whom I felt it my duty to refuse a recommendation. He said if I would transpose King and Davis he would be satisfied. I thought it a whim, but, anxious to oblige him, I consented. Immediately he commenced an assault upon King's character, intending, as I suppose, to defeat his appointment, and thereby secure another chance for himself. This double offense of bad faith to me and slander upon a good man is so totally outrageous that I now ask to have King and Davis placed as I originally recommended,— that is, King for Register and Davis for Receiver.

An effort is being made now to have Mr. Barret, the present Register, retained. I have already said he has done the duties of the office well, and I now add he is a gentleman in the true sense. Still, he submits to be the instrument of his party to injure us. His high character enables him to do it more effectually. Last year he presided at the convention which nominated the Democratic candidate for Congress in this district, and afterward ran for the State Senate himself, not desiring the seat, but avowedly to aid and strengthen his party. He made speech after speech with a degree of fierceness and coarseness against General Taylor not quite consistent with his habitually gentlemanly deportment. At least one (and I think more) of those who are now trying to have him retained was himself an applicant for this very office, and, failing to get my recommendation, now takes this turn.

In writing you a third time in relation to these offices, I stated that I supposed charges had been forwarded to you against King, and that I would inquire into the truth of them. I now send you herewith what I suppose will be an ample defense against any such charges. I ask attention to all the papers, but particularly to the letters of Mr. David Mack, and the paper with the long list of names. There is no mistake about King's being a good man. After the unjust assault upon him, and considering the just claims of Tazewell County, as indicated in the letters I inclose you, it would in my opinion be injustice, and withal a blunder, not to appoint him, at least as soon as any one is appointed to either of the offices here.

Your obedient servant,   A. LINCOLN.

May 18, 1849.—LETTER TO DUFF GREEN.

SPRINGFIELD, ILLINOIS, May 18, 1849.

Dear General: I learn from Washington that a man by the name of Butterfield will probably be appointed Commissioner of the General Land Office. This ought not to be. That is about the only crumb of patronage which Illinois expects; and I am sure the mass of General Taylor's friends here would quite as lief see it go east of the Alleghanies, or west of the Rocky Mountains, as into that man's hands. They are already sore on the subject of his getting office. In the great contest of 1840 he was not seen or heard of; but when the victory came, three or four old drones, including him, got all the valuable offices, through what influence no one has yet been able to tell. I believe the only time he has been very active was last spring a year ago, in opposition to General Taylor's nomination.

Now, cannot you get the ear of General Taylor? Ewing is for Butterfield, and therefore he must be avoided. Preston, I think, will favor you. Mr. Edwards has written me offering to decline, but I advised him not to do so. Some kind friends think I ought to be an applicant, but I am for Mr. Edwards. Try to defeat Butterfield, and in doing so use Mr. Edwards, J. L. D. Morrison, or myself, whichever you can to best advantage. Write me, and let this be confidential.

Yours truly,   A. LINCOLN.

May 25, 1849.—LETTER TO E. EMBREE.

Confidential.

SPRINGFIELD, ILLINOIS, May 25, 1849.

HON. E. EMBREE.

Dear Sir : I am about to ask a favor of you,—one which I hope will not cost you much. I understand the General Land Office is about to be given to Illinois, and that Mr. Ewing desires Justin Butterfield, of Chicago, to be the man. I give you my word, the appointment of Mr. Butterfield will be an egregious political blunder. It will give offense to the whole Whig party here, and be worse than a dead loss to the administration of so much of its patronage. Now, if you can conscientiously do so, I wish you to write General Taylor at once, saying that either I, or the man I recommend, should in your opinion be appointed to that office, if any one from Illinois shall be. I restrict my request to Illinois because you may have a man from your own State, and I do not ask to interfere with that.

Your friend as ever,   A. LINCOLN.

June 5, 1849.—LETTER TO WILLIAM H. HERNDON.

SPRINGFIELD, June 5, 1849.

Dear William : Your two letters were received last night. I have a great many letters to write, and so cannot write very long ones. There must be some mistake about Walter Davis saying I promised him the post-office. I did not so promise him. I did tell him that if the distribution of the offices should fall into my hands, he should have something; and if I shall be convinced he has said any more than this, I shall be disappointed. I said this much to him because, as I understand, he is of good character, is one of the *young* men, is of the mechanics, and always faithful and never troublesome; a Whig, and is poor, with the support of a widow mother thrown almost exclusively on him by the death of his brother. If these are wrong reasons, then I have been wrong; but I have certainly not been selfish in it, because in my greatest need of friends he was against me, and for Baker. Yours as ever,

A. LINCOLN.

P. S. Let the above be confidential.

June 5, 1849.—LETTER ASKING A RECOMMENDATION.

NOTE.—In the files are a considerable number of replies transmitting indorsements, and reporting information on the progress of the contest between Mr. Lincoln and Mr. Justin Butterfield for this appointment.

SPRINGFIELD, ILLINOIS, June 5, 1849.

Dear Sir : Would you as soon I should have the General Land Office as any other Illinoisan ? If you would, write me to that effect at Washington, where I shall be soon. No time to lose.

Yours in haste, A. LINCOLN.

June 8, 1849.— LETTER TO NATHANIEL POPE.

SPRINGFIELD, June 8, 1849.

HON. N. POPE.

Dear Sir : I do not know that it would, but I can well enough conceive it might, embarrass you to now give a letter recommending me for the General Land Office. Could you not, however, without embarrassment or any impropriety, so far vindicate the truth of history as to briefly state to me, in a letter, what you did say to me last spring, on my arrival here from Washington, in relation to my becoming an applicant for that office ? Having at last concluded to be an applicant, I have thought it is perhaps due me to be enabled to show the influences which brought me to the conclusion, and of which influences the wishes and opinions you expressed were not the least. Your obedient servant,

A. LINCOLN.

September [12 ?], 1849.— RESOLUTIONS OF SYMPATHY WITH THE CAUSE OF HUNGARIAN FREEDOM.

At a meeting to express sympathy with the cause of Hungarian Freedom, Dr. Todd, Thos. Lewis, Hon. A. Lincoln, and Wm. Carpenter were appointed a committee to present appropriate resolutions, which reported through Hon. A. Lincoln the following :

Resolved, That in their present glorious struggle for liberty, the Hungarians command our highest admiration and have our warmest sympathy.

Resolved, That they have our most ardent prayers for their speedy triumph and final success.

Resolved, That the Government of the United States should acknowledge the independence of Hungary as a nation of freemen at the very earliest moment consistent with our amicable relations with the government against which they are contending.

Resolved, That in the opinion of this meeting, the immediate acknowledgment of the independence of Hungary by our government is due from American freemen to their struggling brethren, to the general cause of republican liberty, and not violative of the just rights of any nation or people.

September 27, 1849.—LETTER TO JOHN ADDISON.

SPRINGFIELD, ILLINOIS, September 27, 1849.

JOHN ADDISON, Esq.

My dear Sir : Your letter is received. I cannot but be grateful to you and all other friends who have interested themselves in having the governorship of Oregon offered to me; but on as much reflection as I have had time to give the subject, I cannot consent to accept it. I have an ever abiding wish to serve you; but as to the secretaryship, I have already recommended our friend Simeon Francis, of the "Journal." Please present my respects to G. T. M. Davis generally, and my thanks especially for his kindness in the Oregon matter.   Yours as ever,

A. LINCOLN.

November 21, 1849.—LETTER TO THE EDITOR OF THE "CHICAGO JOURNAL."

SPRINGFIELD, November 21, 1849.

EDITOR OF THE " CHICAGO JOURNAL."

Dear Sir : Some person, probably yourself, has sent me the number of your paper containing an extract of a supposed speech of Mr. Linder, together with your editorial comments. As my name is mentioned both in the speech and in the comments, and as my attention is directed to the article by a special mark in the paper sent me, it is perhaps expected that I should take some notice of it. I have to say, then, that I was absent from before the commencement till after the close of the late session of the legislature, and that the fact of such a speech having been delivered never came to my knowledge till I saw a notice of your article in the " Illinois Journal," one day before your paper reached me. Had the intention of any Whig to deliver such a speech been known to me, I should, to the utmost of my ability, have endeavored to prevent it. When Mr. Butterfield was appointed Commissioner of the Land Office, I expected him to be an able and faithful officer, and nothing has since come to my knowledge disappointing that expectation. As to Mr. Ewing, his position has been one of great difficulty. I believe him, too, to be an able and faithful officer. A more intimate acquaintance with him would probably change the views of most of those who have complained of him.   Your obedient servant,

A. LINCOLN.

In the Illinois legislature, Mr. Linder said:

. . . He should speak not as a disappointed politician, but as an independent working Whig, who had never applied for an office in his life; and the individual of whom he desired to speak was the Hon. Thomas Ewing, of Ohio, minister of the Home Department,—a man who was unsuited to wield the immense patronage placed in his hands, from the fact that he was hostile to all that was popular, having no sympathies with the people, and the people no sympathies with him; the man who disposed of the offices and honors at his disposal more like a prince than the minister and servant of a republican people. I speak plainly, sir, for I want what I say to be published, that it may reach the individual for whom it is intended,—the man who could disregard the almost unanimous wish of the people—the Whig people of Illinois,—and overlook the claims of such men as Lincoln, Edwards, and Morrison, and appoint a man known as an anti-war federalist of 1812, and one who avails himself of every opportunity to express his contempt of the people—a man who could not, as against any one of his competitors, have obtained one twentieth of the votes of Illinois. (I refer, sir, to Justin Butterfield, Commissioner of the General Land Office.) Such a man as Ewing has no right to rule the cabinet of a republican president. He is universally odious, and stinks in the nostrils of the nation. He is as a lump of ice, an unfeeling, unsympathizing aristocrat, a rough, imperious, uncouth, and unamiable man. Such a minister, in a four years' administration, would ruin the popularity of forty presidents and as many heroes. Sir, is it wonderful that the popular elections are turning against us? I am not at all surprised at it. If General Taylor retains him two years longer in his cabinet, he will find himself without a corporal's guard in the popular branch of our national legislature.

DECEMBER 15, 1849.—LETTER TO ———.

SPRINGFIELD, December 15, 1849.

———, Esq.

Dear Sir: On my return from Kentucky, I found your letter of the 7th of November, and have delayed answering it till now, for the reason I now briefly state. From the beginning of our acquaintance I have felt the greatest kindness for you, and had supposed it was reciprocated on your part. Last summer, under circumstances which I mentioned to you, I was painfully constrained to withhold a recommendation which you desired, and shortly afterward I learned, in such a way as to believe it, that you were indulging in open abuse of me. Of course my feelings were wounded. On receiving your last letter, the question occurred whether you were attempting to use me at the same time you would injure me, or whether you might not have been misrepresented to me. If the former, I ought not to answer you; if the latter, I ought; and so I have remained in suspense. I now inclose you the letter, which you may use if you see fit.

Yours, etc.,   A. LINCOLN.

FEBRUARY 23, 1850.—LETTER TO JOHN D. JOHNSTON.

SPRINGFIELD, February 23, 1850.

Dear Brother: Your letter about a mail contract was received yesterday. I have made out a bid for you at $120, guaranteed it myself, got our P. M. here to certify it, and send it on. Your former letter, concerning some man's claim for a pension, was also received. I had the claim examined by those who are practised in such matters, and they decide he cannot get a pension.

As you make no mention of it, I suppose you had not learned that we lost our little boy. He was sick fifteen days, and died in the morning of the first day of this month. It was not our first, but our second child. We miss him very much. Your brother, in haste,

A. LINCOLN.

To JOHN D. JOHNSTON.

June 3, 1850.—RESOLUTIONS ON THE DEATH OF JUDGE NATHANIEL POPE.

Circuit and District Court of the U. S. in and for the State and District of Illinois. Monday, June 3, 1850.

. . . On the opening of the Court this morning, the Hon. A. Lincoln, a member of the Bar of this Court, suggested the death of the Hon. Nathaniel Pope, late a judge of this Court, since the adjournment of the last term; whereupon, in token of respect for the memory of the deceased, it is ordered that the Court do now adjourn until to-morrow morning at ten o'clock. . . .

The Hon. Stephen T. Logan, the Hon. Norman H. Purple, the Hon. David L. Gregg, the Hon. A. Lincoln, and George W. Meeker, Esq., were appointed a Committee to prepare resolutions. . . . Whereupon, the Hon. Stephen T. Logan, in behalf of the Committee, presented the following preamble and resolutions:

Whereas the Hon. Nathaniel Pope, District Judge of the United States Court for the District of Illinois, having departed this life during the last vacation of said Court, and the members of the bar of said Court entertaining the highest veneration for his memory, a profound respect for his ability, great experience, and learning as a Judge, and cherishing for his many virtues, public and private, his earnest simplicity of character and unostentatious deportment both in his public and private relations, the most lively and affectionate recollections, have

Resolved, That as a manifestation of their deep sense of the loss which has been sustained in his death, they will wear the usual badge of mourning during the residue of the term.

Resolved, That the Chairman communicate to the family of the deceased a copy of these proceedings, with an assurance of our sincere condolence on account of their heavy bereavement.

Resolved, That the Hon. A. Williams, District Attorney of this Court, be requested in behalf of the meeting to present these proceedings to the Circuit Court, and respectfully to ask that they may be entered on the records.

E. N. POWELL, *Sec'y*.   SAMUEL H. TREAT, *Ch'n*.

[July 1, 1850?].—FRAGMENT. NOTES FOR A LECTURE.

Niagara Falls! By what mysterious power is it that millions and millions are drawn from all parts of the world to gaze upon Niagara Falls? There is no mystery about the thing itself. Every effect is just as any intelligent man, knowing the causes, would anticipate without seeing it. If the water moving onward in a great river reaches a point where there is a perpendicular jog of a hundred feet in descent in the bottom of the river, it is plain the water will have a violent and continuous plunge at that point. It is also plain, the water, thus plunging, will foam and roar, and send up a mist continuously, in which last, during sunshine, there will be perpetual rainbows. The mere physical of Niagara Falls is only this. Yet this is really a very small part of that world's wonder. Its power to excite reflection and emotion is its great charm. The geologist will demonstrate that the plunge, or fall, was once at Lake Ontario, and has worn its way back to its present position; he will ascertain how fast it is wearing now, and so get a basis for determining how long it has been wearing back from Lake Ontario, and finally demonstrate by it that this world is at least fourteen thousand years old. A philosopher of a slightly different turn will say, "Niagara Falls is only the lip of the basin out of which pours all the surplus water which rains down on two or three hundred thousand square miles of the earth's surface." He will estimate with approximate accuracy that five hundred thousand tons of water fall with their full weight a distance of a hundred feet each minute—thus exerting a force equal to the lifting of the same weight, through the same space, in the same time. And then the further reflection comes that this vast amount of water, constantly pounding down, is supplied by an equal amount constantly lifted up, by the sun; and still he says, "If this much is lifted up for this one space of two or three hundred thousand square miles, an equal amount must be lifted up for every other equal space"; and he is overwhelmed in the contemplation of the vast power the sun is constantly exerting in the quiet noiseless operation of lifting water up to be rained down again.

But still there is more. It calls up the indefinite past. When Columbus first sought this continent—when Christ suffered on the cross—when Moses led Israel through the Red Sea—nay, even when Adam first came from the hand of his Maker: then, as now, Niagara was roaring here. The eyes of that species of extinct giants whose bones fill the mounds of America have gazed on Niagara, as ours do now. Contemporary with the first race of men, and older than the first man, Niagara is strong and fresh to-day as ten thousand years ago. The Mammoth and Mastodon, so long dead that fragments of their monstrous bones alone testify that they ever lived, have gazed on Niagara—in that long, long time never still for a single moment [never dried], never froze, never slept, never rested.

[July 1, 1850?]—FRAGMENT. NOTES FOR LAW LECTURE.

I am not an accomplished lawyer. I find quite as much material for a lecture in those points wherein I have failed, as in those wherein I have been moderately successful. The leading rule for the lawyer, as for the man of every other calling, is diligence. Leave nothing for to-morrow which can be done to-day. Never let your correspondence fall behind. Whatever piece of business you have in hand, before stopping, do all the labor pertaining to it which can then be done. When you bring a common-law suit, if you have the facts for doing so, write the declaration at once. If a law point be involved, examine the books, and note the authority you rely on upon the declaration itself, where you are sure to find it when wanted. The same of defenses and pleas. In business not likely to be litigated,—ordinary collection cases, foreclosures, partitions, and the like,—make all examinations of titles, and note them, and even draft orders and decrees in advance. This course has a triple advantage; it avoids omissions and neglect, saves your labor when once done, performs the labor out of court when you have leisure, rather than in court when you have not. Extemporaneous speaking should be practised and cultivated. It is the lawyer's avenue to the public. However able and faithful he may be in other respects, people are slow to bring him business if he cannot make a speech. And yet there is not a more fatal error to young lawyers than relying too much on speech-making. If any one, upon his rare powers of speaking, shall claim an exemption from the drudgery of the law, his case is a failure in advance.

Discourage litigation. Persuade your neighbors to compromise whenever you can. Point out to them how the nominal winner is often a real loser—in fees, expenses, and waste of time. As a peacemaker the lawyer has a superior opportunity of being a good man. There will still be business enough.

Never stir up litigation. A worse man can scarcely be found than one who does this. Who can be more nearly a fiend than he who habitually overhauls the register of deeds in search of defects in titles, whereon to stir up strife, and put money in his pocket? A moral tone ought to be infused into the profession which should drive such men out of it.

The matter of fees is important, far beyond the mere question of bread and butter involved. Properly attended to, fuller justice is done to both lawyer and client. An exorbitant fee should never be claimed. As a general rule never take your whole fee in advance, nor any more than a small retainer. When fully paid beforehand, you are more than a common mortal if you can feel the same interest in the case, as if something was still in prospect for you, as well as for your client. And when you lack interest in the case the job will very likely lack skill and diligence in the performance. Settle the amount of fee and take a note in advance. Then you will feel that you are working for something, and you are sure to do your work faithfully and well. Never sell a fee note—at least not before the consideration service is performed. It leads to negligence and dishonesty—negligence by losing interest in the case, and dishonesty in refusing to refund when you have allowed the consideration to fail.

There is a vague popular belief that lawyers are necessarily dishonest. I say vague, because when we consider to what extent confidence and honors are reposed in and conferred upon lawyers by the people, it appears improbable that their impression of dishonesty is very distinct and vivid. Yet the impression is common, almost universal. Let no young man choosing the law for a calling for a moment yield to the popular belief—resolve to be honest at all events; and if in your own judgment you cannot be an honest lawyer, resolve to be honest without being a lawyer. Choose some other occupation, rather than one in the choosing of which you do, in advance, consent to be a knave.

January [2?], 1851.—LETTER TO JOHN D. JOHNSTON.

January 2, 1851.

Dear Johnston: Your request for eighty dollars I do not think it best to comply with now. At the various times when I have helped you a little you have said to me, "We can get along very well now"; but in a very short time I find you in the same difficulty again. Now, this can only happen by some defect in your conduct. What that defect is, I think I know. You are not lazy, and still you are an idler. I doubt whether, since I saw you, you have done a good whole day's work in any one day. You do not very much dislike to work, and still you do not work much, merely because it does not seem to you that you could get much for it. This habit of uselessly wasting time is the whole difficulty; it is vastly important to you, and still more so to your children, that you should break the habit. It is more important to them, because they have longer to live, and can keep out of an idle habit before they are in it, easier than they can get out after they are in.

You are now in need of some money; and what I propose is, that you shall go to work, "tooth and nail," for somebody who will give you money for it. Let father and your boys take charge of your things at home, prepare for a crop, and make the crop, and you go to work for the best money wages, or in discharge of any debt you owe, that you can get; and, to secure you a fair reward for your labor, I now promise you, that for every dollar you will, between this and the first of May, get for your own labor, either in money or as your own indebtedness, I will then give you one other dollar. By this, if you hire yourself at ten dollars a month, from me you will get ten more, making twenty dollars a month for your work. In this I do not mean you shall go off to St. Louis, or the lead mines, or the gold mines in California, but I mean for you to go at it for the best wages you can get close to home in Coles County. Now, if you will do this, you will be soon out of debt, and, what is better, you will have a habit that will keep you from getting in debt again. But, if I should now clear you out of debt, next year you would be just as deep in as ever. You say you would almost give your place in heaven for seventy or eighty dollars. Then you value your place in heaven very cheap, for I am sure you can, with the offer I make, get the seventy or eighty dollars for four or five months' work. You say if I will furnish you the money you will deed me the land, and, if you don't pay the money back, you will deliver possession.

Nonsense! If you can't now live with the land, how will you then live without it? You have always been kind to me, and I do not mean to be unkind to you. On the contrary, if you will but follow my advice, you will find it worth more than eighty times eighty dollars to you.   Affectionately your brother,

A. LINCOLN.

January 12, 1851.—LETTER TO JOHN D. JOHNSTON.

SPRINGFIELD, January 12, 1851.

Dear Brother: On the day before yesterday I received a letter from Harriet, written at Greenup. She says she has just returned from your house, and that father is very low and will hardly recover. She also says you have written me two letters, and that although you do not expect me to come now, you wonder that I do not write.

I received both your letters, and although I have not answered them, it is not because I have forgotten them, or been uninterested about them, but because it appeared to me that I could write nothing which would do any good. You already know I desire that neither father nor mother shall be in want of any comfort, either in health or sickness, while they live; and I feel sure you have not failed to use my name, if necessary, to procure a doctor, or anything else for father in his present sickness. My business is such that I could hardly leave home now, if it was not as it is, that my own wife is sick-a-bed. (It is a case of baby-sickness, and I suppose is not dangerous.) I sincerely hope father may recover his health, but at all events, tell him to remember to call upon and confide in our great and good and merciful Maker, who will not turn away from him in any extremity. He notes the fall of a sparrow, and numbers the hairs of our heads, and He will not forget the dying man who puts his trust in Him. Say to him that if we could meet now it is doubtful whether it would not be more painful than pleasant, but that if it be his lot to go now, he will soon have a joyous meeting with many loved ones gone before, and where the rest of us, through the help of God, hope ere long to join them.

Write to me again when you receive this. Affectionately,

A. LINCOLN.

August 31, 1851.—LETTER TO JOHN D. JOHNSTON.

SPRINGFIELD, August 31, 1851.

Dear Brother: Inclosed is the deed for the land. We are all well, and have nothing in the way of news. We have had no cholera here for about two weeks. Give my love to all, and especially to mother.

Yours, as ever,
A. LINCOLN.

November 4, 1851.—LETTER TO JOHN D. JOHNSTON.

SHELBYVILLE, November 4, 1851.

Dear Brother: When I came into Charleston day before yesterday, I learned that you are anxious to sell the land where you live and move to Missouri. I have been thinking of this ever since, and cannot but think such a notion is utterly foolish. What can you do in Missouri better than here? Is the land any richer? Can you there, any more than here, raise corn and wheat and oats without work? Will anybody there, any more than here, do your work for you? If you intend to go to work, there is no better place than right where you are; if you do not intend to go to work, you cannot get along anywhere. Squirming and crawling about from place to place can do no good. You have raised no crop this year; and what you really want is to sell the land, get the money, and spend it. Part with the land you have, and, my life upon it, you will never after own a spot big enough to bury you in. Half you will get for the land you will spend in moving to Missouri, and the other half you will eat, drink, and wear out, and no foot of land will be bought. Now, I feel it my duty to have no hand in such a piece of foolery. I feel that it is so even on your own account, and particularly on mother's account. The eastern forty acres I intend to keep for mother while she lives; if you will not cultivate it, it will rent for enough to support her—at least, it will rent for something. Her dower in the other two forties she can let you have, and no thanks to me. Now, do not misunderstand this letter; I do not write it in any unkindness. I write it in order, if possible, to get you to face the truth, which truth is, you are destitute because you have idled away all your time. Your thousand pretenses for not getting along better are all nonsense; they deceive nobody but yourself. Go to work is the only cure for your case.

A word to mother. Chapman tells me he wants you to go and live with him. If I were you I would try it awhile. If you get tired of it (as I think you will not), you can return to your own home. Chapman feels very kindly to you, and I have no doubt he will make your situation very pleasant. Sincerely your son,

A. LINCOLN.

November 9, 1851.—LETTER TO JOHN D. JOHNSTON.

SHELBYVILLE, November 9, 1851.

Dear Brother: When I wrote you before, I had not received your letter. I still think as I did, but if the land can be sold so that I get three hundred dollars to put to interest for mother, I will not object, if she does not. But before I will make a deed, the money must be had, or secured beyond all doubt, at ten per cent.

As to Abram, I do not want him, on my own account; but I understand he wants to live with me, so that he can go to school and get a fair start in the world, which I very much wish him to have.

When I reach home, if I can make it convenient to take, I will take him, provided there is no mistake between us as to the object and terms of my taking him. In haste, as ever,

A. LINCOLN.

December [4?], 1851.—CALL FOR WHIG CONVENTION.

To the Whigs of Illinois.

The Whigs of the State of Illinois are respectfully requested to meet in convention at Springfield, on the fourth Monday of December next, to take into consideration such action as upon consultation and deliberation may be deemed necessary, proper, and effective for the best interests of the party, and to secure a more thorough organization of the Whig party at an early day.

(Signed)

ABRAHAM LINCOLN,	ISAAC HARDY,	O. H. BROWNING,
J. T. STUART,	HORACE MILLER,	C. W. CRAIG,
J. C. CONKLING,	E. B. WASHBURNE,	J. L. WILSON,
H. O. MERRIMAN,	HENRY WATTERMAN,	B. G. WHEELER,
GEO. W. MEEKER,	EZRA GRIFFITH,	H. D. RISLEY,
J. O. NORTON,	SAMUEL HALLER,	LEVI DAVIS,
CHURCHILL COFFING,	JOSEPH T. ECCLES,	B. S. EDWARDS,
JOSEPH GILLESPIE,	JAS. W. SINGLETON,	And many others.

July 16, 1852.—EULOGY ON HENRY CLAY DELIVERED IN THE STATE HOUSE AT SPRINGFIELD, ILLINOIS.

On the fourth day of July, 1776, the people of a few feeble and oppressed colonies of Great Britain, inhabiting a portion of the Atlantic coast of North America, publicly declared their national independence, and made their appeal to the justice of their cause and to the God of battles for the maintenance of that declaration. That people were few in number and without resources, save only their wise heads and stout hearts. Within the first year of that declared independence, and while its maintenance was yet problematical,—while the bloody struggle between those resolute rebels and their haughty would-be masters was still waging,—of undistinguished parents and in an obscure district of one of those colonies Henry Clay was born. The infant nation and the infant child began the race of life together. For three quarters of a century they have traveled hand in hand. They have been companions ever. The nation has passed its perils, and it is free, prosperous, and powerful. The child has reached his manhood, his middle age, his old age, and is dead. In all that has concerned the nation the man ever sympathized; and now the nation mourns the man.

The day after his death one of the public journals, opposed to him politically, held the following pathetic and beautiful language, which I adopt partly because such high and exclusive eulogy, originating with a political friend, might offend good taste, but

you speak, I formed quite an intimate acquaintance, for a short one, while at Washington; and when you meet him again I will thank you to present him my respects. Your present governor, Andrew Johnson, was also at Washington while I was; and he told me of there being people of the name of Lincoln in Carter County, I think. I can no longer claim to be a young man myself; but I infer that, as you are of the same generation as my father, you are some older. I shall be very glad to hear from you again.

Very truly your relative,   A. LINCOLN.

[July 1, 1854?].—FRAGMENT. ON GOVERNMENT.

Government is a combination of the people of a country to effect certain objects by joint effort. The best framed and best administered governments are necessarily expensive; while by errors in frame and maladministration most of them are more onerous than they need be, and some of them very oppressive. Why, then, should we have government? Why not each individual take to himself the whole fruit of his labor, without having any of it taxed away, in services, corn, or money? Why not take just so much land as he can cultivate with his own hands, without buying it of any one?

The legitimate object of government is "to do for the people what needs to be done, but which they can not, by individual effort, do at all, or do so well, for themselves." There are many such things—some of them exist independently of the injustice in the world. Making and maintaining roads, bridges, and the like; providing for the helpless young and afflicted; common schools; and disposing of deceased men's property, are instances.

But a far larger class of objects springs from the injustice of men. If one people will make war upon another, it is a necessity with that other to unite and coöperate for defense. Hence the military department. If some men will kill, or beat, or constrain others, or despoil them of property, by force, fraud, or noncompliance with contracts, it is a common object with peaceful and just men to prevent it. Hence the criminal and civil departments.

[July 1, 1854?].—FRAGMENT. ON SLAVERY.

The ant who has toiled and dragged a crumb to his nest will furiously defend the fruit of his labor against whatever robber assails him. So plain that the most dumb and stupid slave that ever toiled for a master does constantly know that he is wronged. So plain that no one, high or low, ever does mistake it, except in a plainly selfish way; for although volume upon volume is written to prove slavery a very good thing, we never hear of the man who wishes to take the good of it by being a slave himself.

Most governments have been based, practically, on the denial of the equal rights of men, as I have, in part, stated them; ours began by affirming those rights. They said, some men are too ignorant and vicious to share in government. Possibly so, said we; and, by your system, you would always keep them ignorant and vicious. We proposed to give all a chance; and we expected the weak to grow stronger, the ignorant wiser, and all better and happier together.

We made the experiment, and the fruit is before us. Look at it, think of it. Look at it in its aggregate grandeur, of extent of country, and numbers of population—of ship, and steamboat, and railroad.

[July 1, 1854?].—FRAGMENT. ON SLAVERY.

Equality in society alike beats inequality, whether the latter be of the British aristocratic sort or of the domestic slavery sort. We know Southern men declare that their slaves are better off than hired laborers amongst us. How little they know whereof they speak! There is no permanent class of hired laborers amongst us. Twenty-five years ago I was a hired laborer. The hired laborer of yesterday labors on his own account to-day, and will hire others to labor for him to-morrow. Advancement—improvement in condition—is the order of things in a society of equals. As labor is the common burden of our race, so the effort of some to shift their share of the burden onto the shoulders of others is the great durable curse of the race. Originally a curse for transgression upon the whole race, when, as by slavery, it is concentrated on a part only, it becomes the double-refined curse of God upon his creatures.

Free labor has the inspiration of hope; pure slavery has no hope. The power of hope upon human exertion and happiness is wonderful. The slave-master himself has a conception of it, and hence the system of tasks among slaves. The slave whom you cannot drive with the lash to break seventy-five pounds of hemp in a day, if you will task him to break a hundred, and promise him pay for all he does over, he will break you a hundred and fifty. You have substituted hope for the rod. And yet perhaps it does not occur to you that to the extent of your gain in the case, you have given up the slave system and adopted the free system of labor.

[July 1, 1854?].—FRAGMENT. ON SLAVERY.

If A can prove, however conclusively, that he may of right enslave B, why may not B snatch the same argument and prove equally that he may enslave A? You say A is white and B is black. It is color, then; the lighter having the right to enslave the darker? Take care. By this rule you are to be slave to the first man you meet with a fairer skin than your own. You do not mean color exactly? You mean the whites are intellectually the superiors of the blacks, and therefore have the right to enslave them? Take care again. By this rule you are to be slave to the first man you meet with an intellect superior to your own. But, say you, it is a question of interest, and if you make it your interest you have the right to enslave another. Very well. And if he can make it his interest he has the right to enslave you.

[July 1, 1854?].—FRAGMENT. ON GOVERNMENT.

The legitimate object of government is to do for a community of people whatever they need to have done, but cannot do at all, or cannot so well do, for themselves, in their separate and individual capacities. In all that the people can individually do as well for themselves, government ought not to interfere. The desirable things which the individuals of a people cannot do, or cannot well do, for themselves, fall into two classes: those which have relation to wrongs, and those which have not. Each of these branch off into an infinite variety of subdivisions.

The first—that in relation to wrongs—embraces all crimes, misdemeanors, and non-performance of contracts. The other embraces all which, in its nature, and without wrong, requires combined action, as public roads and highways, public schools, charities, pauperism, orphanage, estates of the deceased, and the machinery of government itself.

From this it appears that if all men were just, there still would be some, though not so much, need of government.

October 16, 1854.—SPEECH AT PEORIA, ILLINOIS, IN REPLY TO SENATOR DOUGLAS.

On Monday, October 16, Senator Douglas, by appointment, addressed a large audience at Peoria. When he closed he was greeted with six hearty cheers, and the band in attendance played a stirring air. The crowd then began to call for Lincoln, who, as Judge Douglas had announced, was by agreement to answer him. Mr. Lincoln took the stand and said:

I do not rise to speak now, if I can stipulate with the audience to meet me here at half-past six or at seven o'clock. It is now several minutes past five, and Judge Douglas has spoken over three hours. If you hear me at all, I wish you to hear me through. It will take me as long as it has taken him. That will carry us beyond eight o'clock at night. Now, every one of you who can remain that long can just as well get his supper, meet me at seven, and remain an hour or two later. The judge has already informed you that he is to have an hour to reply to me. I doubt not but you have been a little surprised to learn that I have consented to give one of his high reputation and known ability this advantage of me. Indeed, my consenting to it, though reluctant, was not wholly unselfish, for I suspected, if it were understood that the judge was entirely done, you Democrats would leave and not hear me; but by giving him the close, I felt confident you would stay for the fun of hearing him skin me.

The audience signified their assent to the arrangement, and adjourned to seven o'clock P. M., at which time they reassembled, and Mr. Lincoln spoke substantially as follows:

The repeal of the Missouri Compromise, and the propriety of its restoration, constitute the subject of what I am about to say. As I desire to present my own connected view of this subject, my remarks will not be specifically an answer to Judge Douglas; yet, as I proceed, the main points he has presented will arise, and will receive such respectful attention as I may be able to give them. I wish further to say that I do not propose to question the patriotism or to assail the motives of any man or class of men, but rather to confine myself strictly to the naked merits of the question. I also wish to be no less than national in all the positions I may take, and whenever I take ground which others have thought, or may think, narrow, sectional, and dangerous to the Union, I hope to give a reason which will appear sufficient, at least to some, why I think differently.

And as this subject is no other than part and parcel of the larger general question of domestic slavery, I wish to make and to keep the distinction between the existing institution and the extension of it, so broad and so clear that no honest man can misunderstand me, and no dishonest one successfully misrepresent me.

In order to a clear understanding of what the Missouri Compromise is, a short history of the preceding kindred subjects will perhaps be proper.

When we established our independence, we did not own or claim the country to which this compromise applies. Indeed, strictly speaking, the Confederacy then owned no country at all; the States respectively owned the country within their limits, and some of them owned territory beyond their strict State limits. Virginia thus owned the Northwestern Territory—the country out of which the principal part of Ohio, all Indiana, all Illinois, all Michigan, and all Wisconsin have since been formed. She also owned (perhaps within her then limits) what has since been formed into the State of Kentucky. North Carolina thus owned what is now the State of Tennessee; and South Carolina and Georgia owned, in separate parts, what are now Mississippi and Alabama. Connecticut, I think, owned the little remaining part of Ohio, being the same where they now send Giddings to Congress, and beat all creation in making cheese.

These territories, together with the States themselves, constitute all the country over which the Confederacy then claimed any sort of jurisdiction. We were then living under the Articles of Confederation, which were superseded by the Constitution several years afterward. The question of ceding the territories to the General Government was set on foot. Mr. Jefferson, the author of the Declaration of Independence, and otherwise a chief actor in the Revolution; then a delegate in Congress; afterward, twice President; who was, is, and perhaps will continue to be, the most distinguished politician of our history; a Virginian by birth and continued residence, and withal a slaveholder,—conceived the idea of taking that occasion to prevent slavery ever going into the Northwestern Territory. He prevailed on the Virginia legislature to adopt his views, and to cede the Territory, making the prohibition of slavery therein a condition of the deed.[1] Congress accepted the cession with the condition; and the first ordinance (which the acts of Congress were then called) for the government of the Territory provided that slavery should never be permitted therein. This is the famed "Ordinance of '87," so often spoken of.

Thenceforward for sixty-one years, and until, in 1848, the last scrap of this Territory came into the Union as the State of Wisconsin, all parties acted in quiet obedience to this ordinance. It is now what Jefferson foresaw and intended—the happy home of teeming millions of free, white, prosperous people, and no slave among them.

Thus, with the author of the Declaration of Independence, the policy of prohibiting slavery in new territory originated. Thus, away back to the Constitution, in the pure, fresh, free breath of the Revolution, the State of Virginia and the National Congress put that policy into practice. Thus, through more than sixty of the best years of the republic, did that policy steadily work to its great and beneficent end. And thus, in those five States, and in five millions of free, enterprising people, we have before us the rich fruits of this policy.

But now new light breaks upon us. Now Congress declares this ought never to have been, and the like of it must never be again. The sacred right of self-government is grossly violated by it. We even find some men who drew their first breath—and every other breath of their lives—under this very restriction, now live in dread of absolute suffocation if they should be restricted in the "sacred right" of taking slaves to Nebraska. That perfect liberty they sigh for—the liberty of making slaves of other people—Jefferson never thought of, their own fathers never thought of, they never thought of themselves, a year ago. How fortunate for them they did not sooner become sensible of their great misery! Oh, how difficult it is to treat with respect such assaults upon all we have ever really held sacred!

But to return to history. In 1803 we purchased what was then called Louisiana, of France. It included the present States of Louisiana, Arkansas, Missouri, and Iowa; also the Territory of Minnesota, and the present bone of contention, Kansas and Nebraska. Slavery already existed among the French at New Orleans, and to some extent at St. Louis. In 1812 Louisiana came into the Union as a slave State, without controversy. In 1818 or '19, Missouri showed signs of a wish to come in with slavery. This was resisted by Northern members of Congress; and thus began the first great slavery agitation in the nation. This controversy lasted several months, and became very angry and exciting,—the House of Representatives voting steadily for the prohibition of slavery in Missouri, and the Senate voting as steadily against it. Threats of the breaking up of the Union were freely made, and the ablest public men of the day became seriously alarmed. At length a compromise was made, in which, as in all compromises, both sides yielded something.

[1] Mr. Lincoln afterward authorized the correction of the error into which the report here falls, with regard to the prohibition being made a condition of the deed. It was not a condition.

It was a law, passed on the 6th of March, 1820, providing that Missouri might come into the Union with slavery, but that in all the remaining part of the territory purchased of France, which lies north of thirty-six degrees and thirty minutes north latitude, slavery should never be permitted. This provision of law is the "Missouri Compromise." In excluding slavery north of the line, the same language is employed as in the ordinance of 1787. It directly applied to Iowa, Minnesota, and to the present bone of contention, Kansas and Nebraska. Whether there should or should not be slavery south of that line, nothing was said in the law. But Arkansas constituted the principal remaining part south of the line; and it has since been admitted as a slave State, without serious controversy. More recently, Iowa, north of the line, came in as a free State without controversy. Still later, Minnesota, north of the line, had a territorial organization without controversy. Texas, principally south of the line, and west of Arkansas, though originally within the purchase from France, had, in 1819, been traded off to Spain in our treaty for the acquisition of Florida. It had thus become a part of Mexico. Mexico revolutionized and became independent of Spain. American citizens began settling rapidly with their slaves in the southern part of Texas. Soon they revolutionized against Mexico, and established an independent government of their own, adopting a constitution with slavery, strongly resembling the constitutions of our slave States. By still another rapid move, Texas, claiming a boundary much further west than when we parted with her in 1819, was brought back to the United States, and admitted into the Union as a slave State. Then there was little or no settlement in the northern part of Texas, a considerable portion of which lay north of the Missouri line; and in the resolutions admitting her into the Union, the Missouri restriction was expressly extended westward across her territory. This was in 1845, only nine years ago.

Thus originated the Missouri Compromise; and thus has it been respected down to 1845. And even four years later, in 1849, our distinguished senator, in a public address, held the following language in relation to it:

The Missouri Compromise has been in practical operation for about a quarter of a century, and has received the sanction and approbation of men of all parties in every section of the Union. It has allayed all sectional jealousies and irritations growing out of this vexed question, and harmonized and tranquilized the whole country. It has given to Henry Clay, as its prominent champion, the proud sobriquet of the "Great Pacificator," and by that title, and for that service, his political friends had repeatedly appealed to the people to rally under his standard as a presidential candidate, as the man who had exhibited the patriotism and power to suppress an unholy and treasonable agitation, and preserve the Union. He was not aware that any man or any party, from any section of the Union, had ever urged as an objection to Mr. Clay that he was the great champion of the Missouri Compromise. On the contrary, the effort was made by the opponents of Mr. Clay to prove that he was not entitled to the exclusive merit of that great patriotic measure; and that the honor was equally due to others, as well as to him, for securing its adoption — that it had its origin in the hearts of all patriotic men, who desired to preserve and perpetuate the blessings of our glorious Union — an origin akin to that of the Constitution of the United States, conceived in the same spirit of fraternal affection, and calculated to remove forever the only danger which seemed to threaten, at some distant day, to sever the social bond of union. All the evidences of public opinion at that day seemed to indicate that this Compromise had been canonized in the hearts of the American people, as a sacred thing which no ruthless hand would ever be reckless enough to disturb.

I do not read this extract to involve Judge Douglas in an inconsistency. If he afterward thought he had been wrong, it was right for him to change. I bring this forward merely to show the high estimate placed on the Missouri Compromise by all parties up to so late as the year 1849.

But going back a little in point of time. Our war with Mexico broke out in 1846. When Congress was about adjourning that session, President Polk asked them to place two millions of dollars under his control, to be used by him in the recess, if found practicable and expedient, in negotiating a treaty of peace with Mexico, and acquiring some part of her territory. A bill was duly gotten up for the purpose, and was progressing swimmingly in the House of Representatives, when a member by the name of David Wilmot, a Democrat from Pennsylvania, moved as an amendment, "Provided, that in any territory thus acquired there shall never be slavery."

This is the origin of the far-famed Wilmot proviso. It created a great flutter; but it stuck like wax, was voted into the bill, and the bill passed with it through the House. The Senate, however, adjourned without final action on it, and so both appropriation and proviso were lost for the time. The war continued, and at the next session the President renewed his request for the appropriation, enlarging the amount, I think, to three millions. Again came the proviso, and defeated the measure. Congress adjourned again, and the war went on. In December, 1847, the new Congress assembled. I was in the lower House that term. The Wilmot proviso, or the principle of it, was constantly coming up in some shape or other, and I think I may venture to say I voted for it at least forty times during the short time I was there. The Senate, however, held it in check, and it never became a law. In the spring of 1848 a treaty of peace was made with Mexico, by which we obtained that portion of her country which now constitutes the Territories of New Mexico and Utah, and the present State of California. By this treaty the Wilmot proviso was defeated, in so far as it was intended to be a condition of the acquisition of territory. Its friends, however, were still determined to find some way to restrain slavery from getting into the new country. This new acquisition lay directly west of our old purchase from France, and extended west to the Pacific Ocean, and was so situated that if the Missouri line should be extended straight west, the new country would be divided by such extended line, leaving some north and some south of it. On Judge Douglas's motion, a bill, or provision of a bill, passed the Senate to so extend the Missouri line. The proviso men in the House, including myself, voted it down, because, by implication, it gave up the southern part to slavery, while we were bent on having it all free.

In the fall of 1848 the gold-mines were discovered in California. This attracted people to it with unprecedented rapidity, so that on, or soon after, the meeting of the new Congress in December, 1849, she already had a population of nearly a hundred thousand, had called a convention, formed a State Constitution excluding slavery, and was knocking for admission into the Union. The proviso men, of course, were for letting her in, but the Senate, always true to the other side, would not consent to her admission, and there California stood, kept out of the Union because she would not let slavery into her borders. Under all the circumstances, perhaps, this was not wrong. There were other points of dispute connected with the general question of slavery, which equally needed adjustment. The South clamored for a more efficient fugitive-slave law. The North clamored for the abolition of a peculiar species of slave-trade in the District of Columbia, in connection with which, in view from the windows of the Capitol, a sort of negro livery-stable, where droves of negroes were collected, temporarily kept, and finally taken to Southern markets, precisely like droves of horses, had been openly maintained for fifty years. Utah and New Mexico needed territorial governments; and whether slavery should or should not be prohibited within them was another question. The indefinite western boundary of Texas was to be settled. She was a slave State, and consequently the farther west the slavery men could push her boundary, the more slave country they secured; and the farther east the slavery opponents could thrust the boundary back, the less slave ground was secured. Thus this was just as clearly a slavery question as any of the others.

These points all needed adjustment, and they were held up, perhaps wisely, to make them help adjust one another. The Union now, as in 1820, was thought to be in danger, and devotion to the Union rightfully inclined men to yield somewhat in points, where nothing else could have so inclined them. A compromise was finally effected. The South got their new fugitive-slave law, and the North got California (by far the best part of our acquisition from Mexico) as a free State. The South got a provision that New Mexico and Utah, when admitted as States, may come in with or without slavery as they may then choose; and the North got the slave-trade abolished in the District of Columbia. The North got the western boundary of Texas thrown farther back eastward than the South desired; but, in turn, they gave Texas ten millions of dollars with which to pay her old debts. This is the compromise of 1850.

Preceding the presidential election of 1852, each of the great political parties, Democrats and Whigs, met in convention and adopted resolutions indorsing the compromise of '50, as a "finality," a final settlement, so far as these parties could make it so, of all slavery agitation. Previous to this, in 1851, the Illinois legislature had indorsed it.

During this long period of time, Nebraska had remained substantially an uninhabited country, but now emigration to and settlement within it began to take place. It is about one third as large as the present United States, and its importance, so long overlooked, begins to come into view. The restriction of slavery by the Missouri Compromise directly applies to it—in fact was first made, and has since been maintained, expressly for it. In 1853, a bill to give it a territorial government passed the House of Representatives, and, in the hands of Judge Douglas, failed of passing only for want of time. This bill contained no repeal of the Missouri Compromise. Indeed, when it was assailed because it did not contain such repeal, Judge Douglas defended it in its existing form. On January 4, 1854, Judge Douglas introduces a new bill to give Nebraska territorial government. He accompanies this bill with a report, in which last he expressly recommends that the Missouri Compromise shall neither be affirmed nor repealed. Before long the bill is so modified as to make two territories instead of one, calling the southern one Kansas.

Also, about a month after the introduction of the bill, on the judge's own motion it is so amended as to declare the Missouri Compromise inoperative and void; and, substantially, that the people who go and settle there may establish slavery, or exclude it, as they may see fit. In this shape the bill passed both branches of Congress and became a law.

This is the repeal of the Missouri Compromise. The foregoing history may not be precisely accurate in every particular, but I am sure it is sufficiently so for all the use I shall attempt to make of it, and in it we have before us the chief material enabling us to judge correctly whether the repeal of the Missouri Compromise is right or wrong. I think, and shall try to show, that it is wrong—wrong in its direct effect, letting slavery into Kansas and Nebraska, and wrong in its prospective principle, allowing it to spread to every other part of the wide world where men can be found inclined to take it.

This declared indifference, but, as I must think, covert real zeal, for the spread of slavery, I cannot but hate. I hate it because of the monstrous injustice of slavery itself. I hate it because it deprives our republican example of its just influence in the world; enables the enemies of free institutions with plausibility to taunt us as hypocrites; causes the real friends of freedom to doubt our sincerity; and especially because it forces so many good men among ourselves into an open war with the very fundamental principles of civil liberty, criticizing the Declaration of Independence, and insisting that there is no right principle of action but self-interest.

Before proceeding let me say that I think I have no prejudice against the Southern people. They are just what we would be in their situation. If slavery did not now exist among them, they would not introduce it. If it did now exist among us, we should not instantly give it up. This I believe of the masses North and South. Doubtless there are individuals on both sides who would not hold slaves under any circumstances, and others who would gladly introduce slavery anew if it were out of existence. We know that some Southern men do free their slaves, go North and become tip-top Abolitionists, while some Northern ones go South and become most cruel slave-masters.

When Southern people tell us they are no more responsible for the origin of slavery than we are, I acknowledge the fact. When it is said that the institution exists, and that it is very difficult to get rid of it in any satisfactory way, I can understand and appreciate the saying. I surely will not blame them for not doing what I should not know how to do myself. [If all earthly power were given me, I should not know what to do as to the existing institution. My first impulse would be to free all the slaves, and send them to Liberia, to their own native land. But a moment's reflection would convince me that whatever of high hope (as I think there is) there may be in this in the long run, its sudden execution is impossible. If they were all landed there in a day, they would all perish in the next ten days; and there are not surplus shipping and surplus money enough to carry them there in many times ten days. What then? Free them all, and keep them among us as underlings? Is it quite certain that this betters their condition? I think I would not hold one in slavery at any rate, yet the point is not clear enough for me to denounce people upon. What next? Free them, and make them politically and socially our equals. My own feelings will not admit of this, and if mine would, we well know that those of the great mass of whites will not. Whether this feeling accords with justice and sound judgment is not the sole question, if indeed it is any part of it. A universal feeling, whether well or ill founded, cannot be safely disregarded. We cannot then make them equals. It does seem to me that systems of gradual emancipation might be adopted, but for their tardiness in this I will not undertake to judge our brethren of the South.

When they remind us of their constitutional rights, I acknowledge them — not grudgingly, but fully and fairly; and I would give them any legislation for the reclaiming of their fugitives which should not in its stringency be more likely to carry a free man into slavery than our ordinary criminal laws are to hang an innocent one.

But all this, to my judgment, furnishes no more excuse for permitting slavery to go into our own free territory than it would for reviving the African slave-trade by law. The law which forbids the bringing of slaves from Africa, and that which has so long forbidden the taking of them into Nebraska, can hardly be distinguished on any moral principle, and the repeal of the former could find quite as plausible excuses as that of the latter.

The arguments by which the repeal of the Missouri Compromise is sought to be justified are these: First. That the Nebraska country needed a territorial government. Second. That in various ways the public had repudiated that compromise and demanded the repeal, and therefore should not now complain of it. And, lastly, That the repeal establishes a principle which is intrinsically right.

I will attempt an answer to each of them in its turn. First, then. If that country was in need of a territorial organization, could it not have had it as well without as with a repeal? Iowa and Minnesota, to both of which the Missouri restriction applied, had, without its repeal, each in succession, territorial organizations. And even the year before, a bill for Nebraska itself was within an ace of passing without the repealing clause, and this in the hands of the same men who are now the champions of repeal. Why no necessity then for repeal? But still later, when this very bill was first brought in, it contained no repeal. But, say they, because the people had demanded, or rather commanded, the repeal, the repeal was to accompany the organization whenever that should occur.

Now, I deny that the public ever demanded any such thing—ever repudiated the Missouri Compromise, ever commanded its repeal. I deny it, and call for the proof. It is not contended, I believe, that any such command has ever been given in express terms. It is only said that it was done in principle. The support of the Wilmot proviso is the first fact mentioned to prove that the Missouri restriction was repudiated in principle, and the second is the refusal to extend the Missouri line over the country acquired from Mexico. These are near enough alike to be treated together. The one was to exclude the chances of slavery from the whole new acquisition by the lump, and the other was to reject a division of it, by which one half was to be given up to those chances. Now, whether this was a repudiation of the Missouri line in principle depends upon whether the Missouri law contained any principle requiring the line to be extended over the country acquired from Mexico. I contend it did not. I insist that it contained no general principle, but that it was, in every sense, specific. That its terms limit it to the country purchased from France is undenied and undeniable. It could have no principle beyond the intention of those who made it. They did not intend to extend the line to country which they did not own. If they intended to extend it in the event of acquiring additional territory, why did they not say so? It was just as easy to say that "in all the country west of the Mississippi which we now own, or may hereafter acquire, there shall never be slavery," as to say what they did say; and they would have said it if they had meant it. An intention to extend the law is not only not mentioned in the law, but is not mentioned in any contemporaneous history. Both the law itself, and the history of the times, are a blank as to any principle of extension; and by neither the known rules of construing statutes and contracts, nor by common sense, can any such principle be inferred.

Another fact showing the specific character of the Missouri law—showing that it intended no more than it expressed, showing that the line was not intended as a universal dividing line between free and slave territory, present and prospective, north of which slavery could never go—is the fact that by that very law Missouri came in as a slave State, north of the line. If that law contained any prospective principle, the whole law must be looked to in order to ascertain what the principle was. And by this rule the South could fairly contend that inasmuch as they got one slave State north of the line at the inception of the law, they have the right to have another given them north of it occasionally, now and then, in the indefinite westward extension of the line. This demonstrates the absurdity of attempting to deduce a prospective principle from the Missouri Compromise line.

When we voted for the Wilmot proviso we were voting to keep slavery out of the whole Mexican acquisition, and little did we think we were thereby voting to let it into Nebraska, lying several hundred miles distant. When we voted against extending the Missouri line, little did we think we were voting to destroy the old line, then of near thirty years' standing.

To argue that we thus repudiated the Missouri Compromise is no less absurd than it would be to argue that because we have so far forborne to acquire Cuba, we have thereby, in principle, repudiated our former acquisitions and determined to throw them out of the Union. No less absurd than it would be to say that because I may have refused to build an addition to my house, I thereby have decided to destroy the existing house! And if I catch you setting fire to my house, you will turn upon me and say I instructed you to do it!

The most conclusive argument, however, that while for the Wilmot proviso, and while voting against the extension of the Missouri line, we never thought of disturbing the original Missouri Compromise, is found in the fact that there was then, and still is, an unorganized tract of fine country, nearly as large as the State of Missouri, lying immediately west of Arkansas and south of the Missouri Compromise line, and that we never attempted to prohibit slavery as to it. I wish particular attention to this. It adjoins the original Missouri Compromise line by its northern boundary, and consequently is part of the country into which by implication slavery was permitted to go by that compromise. There it has lain open ever since, and there it still lies, and yet no effort has been made at any time to wrest it from the South. In all our struggles to prohibit slavery within our Mexican acquisitions, we never so much as lifted a finger to prohibit it as to this tract. Is not this entirely conclusive that at all times we have held the Missouri Compromise as a sacred thing, even when against ourselves as well as when for us?

Senator Douglas sometimes says the Missouri line itself was in principle only an extension of the line of the ordinance of '87 — that is to say, an extension of the Ohio River. I think this is weak enough on its face. I will remark, however, that, as a glance at the map will show, the Missouri line is a long way farther south than the Ohio, and that if our senator in proposing his extension had stuck to the principle of jogging southward, perhaps it might not have been voted down so readily.

But next it is said that the compromises of '50, and the ratification of them by both political parties in '52, established a new principle which required the repeal of the Missouri Compromise. This again I deny. I deny it, and demand the proof. I have already stated fully what the compromises of '50 are. That particular part of those measures from which the virtual repeal of the Missouri Compromise is sought to be inferred (for it is admitted they contain nothing about it in express terms) is the provision in the Utah and New Mexico laws which permits them when they seek admission into the Union as States to come in with or without slavery, as they shall then see fit. Now I insist this provision was made for Utah and New Mexico, and for no other place whatever. It had no more direct reference to Nebraska than it had to the territories of the moon. But, say they, it had reference to Nebraska in principle. Let us see. The North consented to this provision, not because they considered it right in itself, but because they were compensated — paid for it.

They at the same time got California into the Union as a free State. This was far the best part of all they had struggled for by the Wilmot proviso. They also got the area of slavery somewhat narrowed in the settlement of the boundary of Texas. Also they got the slave-trade abolished in the District of Columbia.

For all these desirable objects the North could afford to yield something; and they did yield to the South the Utah and New Mexico provision. I do not mean that the whole North, or even a majority, yielded, when the law passed; but enough yielded, when added to the vote of the South, to carry the measure. Nor can it be pretended that the principle of this arrangement requires us to permit the same provision to be applied to Nebraska, without any equivalent at all. Give us another free State; press the boundary of Texas still further back; give us another step toward the destruction of slavery in the District, and you present us a similar case. But ask us not to repeat, for nothing, what you paid for in the first instance. If you wish the thing again, pay again. That is the principle of the compromises of '50, if, indeed, they had any principles beyond their specific terms — it was the system of equivalents.

Again, if Congress, at that time, intended that all future Territories should, when admitted as States, come in with or without slavery, at their own option, why did it not say so? With such a universal provision, all know the bills could not have passed. Did they, then — could they — establish a principle contrary to their own intention? Still further, if they intended to establish the principle that, whenever Congress had control, it should be left to the people to do as they thought fit with slavery, why did they not authorize the people of the District of Columbia, at their option, to abolish slavery within their limits?

I personally know that this has not been left undone because it was unthought of. It was frequently spoken of by members of Congress, and by citizens of Washington, six years ago; and I heard no one express a doubt that a system of gradual emancipation, with compensation to owners, would meet the approbation of a large majority of the white people of the District. But without the action of Congress they could say nothing; and Congress said "No." In the measures of 1850, Congress had the subject of slavery in the District expressly on hand. If they were then establishing the principle of allowing the people to do as they please with slavery, why did they not apply the principle to that people?

Again, it is claimed that by the resolutions of the Illinois legislature, passed in 1851, the repeal of the Missouri Compromise was demanded. This I deny also. Whatever may be worked out by a criticism of the language of those resolutions, the people have never understood them as being any more than an indorsement of the compromises of 1850, and a release of our senators from voting for the Wilmot proviso. The whole people are living witnesses that this only was their view. Finally, it is asked, "If we did not mean to apply the Utah and New Mexico provision to all future territories, what did we mean when we, in 1852, indorsed the compromises of 1850?"

For myself I can answer this question most easily. I meant not to ask a repeal or modification of the fugitive-slave law. I meant not to ask for the abolition of slavery in the District of Columbia. I meant not to resist the admission of Utah and New Mexico, even should they ask to come in as slave States. I meant nothing about additional Territories, because, as I understood, we then had no Territory whose character as to slavery was not already settled. As to Nebraska, I regarded its character as being fixed by the Missouri Compromise for thirty years — as unalterably fixed as that of my own home in Illinois. As to new acquisitions, I said, "Sufficient unto the day is the evil thereof." When we make new acquisitions, we will, as heretofore, try to manage them somehow. That is my answer; that is what I meant and said; and I appeal to the people to say each for himself, whether that is not also the universal meaning of the free States.

And now, in turn, let me ask a few questions. If, by any or all these matters, the repeal of the Missouri Compromise was commanded, why was not the command sooner obeyed? Why was the repeal omitted in the Nebraska bill of 1853? Why was it omitted in the original bill of 1854? Why in the accompanying report was such a repeal characterized as a departure from the course pursued in 1850? and its continued omission recommended?

I am aware Judge Douglas now argues that the subsequent express repeal is no substantial alteration of the bill. This argument seems wonderful to me. It is as if one should argue that white and black are not different. He admits, however, that there is a literal change in the bill, and that he made the change in deference to other senators who would not support the bill without. This proves that those other senators thought the change a substantial one, and that the judge thought their opinions worth deferring to. His own opinions, therefore, seem not to rest on a very firm basis, even in his own mind; and I suppose the world believes, and will continue to believe, that precisely on the substance of that change this whole agitation has arisen.

I conclude, then, that the public never demanded the repeal of the Missouri Compromise.

I now come to consider whether the appeal, with its avowed principles, is intrinsically right. I insist that it is not. Take the particular case. A controversy had arisen between the advocates and opponents of slavery, in relation to its establishment within the country we had purchased of France. The southern, and then best, part of the purchase was already in as a slave State. The controversy was settled by also letting Missouri in as a slave State; but with the agreement that within all the remaining part of the purchase, north of a certain line, there should never be slavery. As to what was to be done with the remaining part south of the line, nothing was said; but perhaps the fair implication was, it should come in with slavery if it should so choose. The southern part, except a portion heretofore mentioned, afterward did come in with slavery, as the State of Arkansas. All these many years, since 1820, the northern part had remained a wilderness. At length settlements began in it also. In due course Iowa came in as a free State, and Minnesota was given a territorial government, without removing the slavery restriction. Finally, the sole remaining part north of the line—Kansas and Nebraska—was to be organized; and it is proposed, and carried, to blot out the old dividing line of thirty-four years' standing, and to open the whole of that country to the introduction of slavery. Now this, to my mind, is manifestly unjust. After an angry and dangerous controversy, the parties made friends by dividing the bone of contention. The one party first appropriates her own share, beyond all power to be disturbed in the possession of it, and then seizes the share of the other party. It is as if two starving men had divided their only loaf; the one had hastily swallowed his half, and then grabbed the other's half just as he was putting it to his mouth.

Let me here drop the main argument, to notice what I consider rather an inferior matter. It is argued that slavery will not go to Kansas and Nebraska, in any event. This is a palliation, a lullaby. I have some hope that it will not; but let us not be too confident. As to climate, a glance at the map shows that there are five slave States—Delaware, Maryland, Virginia, Kentucky, and Missouri, and also the District of Columbia, all north of the Missouri Compromise line. The census returns of 1850 show that within these there are eight hundred and sixty-seven thousand two hundred and seventy-six slaves, being more than one fourth of all the slaves in the nation.

It is not climate then, that will keep slavery out of these Territories. Is there anything in the peculiar nature of the country? Missouri adjoins these Territories by her entire western boundary, and slavery is already within every one of her western counties. I have even heard it said that there are more slaves in proportion to whites in the northwestern county of Missouri, than within any other county in the State. Slavery pressed entirely up to the old western boundary of the State, and when rather recently a part of that boundary at the northwest was moved out a little farther west, slavery followed on quite up to the new line. Now when the restriction is removed, what is to prevent it from going still farther? Climate will not, no peculiarity of the country will, nothing in nature will. Will the disposition of the people prevent it? Those nearest the scene are all in favor of the extension. The Yankees who are opposed to it may be most numerous; but, in military phrase, the battle-field is too far from their base of operations.

But it is said, there now is no law in Nebraska on the subject of slavery, and that, in such case, taking a slave there operates his freedom. That is good book-law, but is not the rule of actual practice. Wherever slavery is it has been first introduced without law. The oldest laws we find concerning it are not laws introducing it, but regulating it as an already existing thing. A white man takes his slave to Nebraska now. Who will inform the negro that he is free? Who will take him before court to test the question of his freedom? In ignorance of his legal emancipation he is kept chopping, splitting, and plowing. Others are brought, and move on in the same track. At last, if ever the time for voting comes on the question of slavery, the institution already, in fact, exists in the country, and cannot well be removed. The fact of its presence, and the difficulty of its removal, will carry the vote in its favor. Keep it out until a vote is taken, and a vote in favor of it cannot be got in any population of forty thousand on earth, who have been drawn together by the ordinary motives of emigration and settlement. To get slaves into the Territory simultaneously with the whites in the incipient stages of settlement is the precise stake played for and won in this Nebraska measure.

The question is asked us: "If slaves will go in notwithstanding the general principle of law liberates them, why would they not equally go in against positive statute law—go in, even if the Missouri restriction were maintained!" I answer, because it takes a much bolder man to venture in with his property in the latter case than in the former; because the positive congressional enactment is known to and respected by all, or nearly all, whereas the negative principle that no law is free law is not much known except among lawyers. We have some experience of this practical difference. In spite of the ordinance of '87, a few negroes were brought into Illinois, and held in a state of quasi-slavery, not enough, however, to carry a vote of the people in favor of the institution when they came to form a constitution. But into the adjoining Missouri country, where there was no ordinance of '87—was no restriction, they were carried ten times, nay, a hundred times, as fast, and actually made a slave State. This is fact—naked fact.

Another lullaby argument is that taking slaves to new countries does not increase their number, does not make any one slave who would otherwise be free. There is some truth in this, and I am glad of it; but it is not wholly true. The African slave-trade is not yet effectually suppressed; and if we make a reasonable deduction for the white people among us who are foreigners and the descendants of foreigners arriving here since 1808, we shall find the increase of the black population outrunning that of the white to an extent unaccountable, except by supposing that some of them, too, have been coming from Africa. If this be so, the opening of new countries to the institution increases the demand for and augments the price of slaves, and so does, in fact, make slaves of freemen, by causing them to be brought from Africa and sold into bondage.

But however this may be, we know the opening of new countries to slavery tends to the perpetuation of the institution, and so does keep men in slavery who would otherwise be free. This result we do not feel like favoring, and we are under no legal obligation to suppress our feelings in this respect.

Equal justice to the South, it is said, requires us to consent to the extension of slavery to new countries. That is to say, inasmuch

VOL. I.—13.

as you do not object to my taking my hog to Nebraska, therefore I must not object to you taking your slave. Now, I admit that this is perfectly logical, if there is no difference between hogs and negroes. But while you thus require me to deny the humanity of the negro, I wish to ask whether you of the South, yourselves, have ever been willing to do as much? It is kindly provided that of all those who come into the world only a small percentage are natural tyrants. That percentage is no larger in the slave States than in the free. The great majority South, as well as North, have human sympathies, of which they can no more divest themselves than they can of their sensibility to physical pain. These sympathies in the bosoms of the Southern people manifest, in many ways, their sense of the wrong of slavery, and their consciousness that, after all, there is humanity in the negro. If they deny this, let me address them a few plain questions. In 1820 you joined the North, almost unanimously, in declaring the African slave-trade piracy, and in annexing to it the punishment of death. Why did you do this? If you did not feel that it was wrong, why did you join in providing that men should be hung for it? The practice was no more than bringing wild negroes from Africa to such as would buy them. But you never thought of hanging men for catching and selling wild horses, wild buffaloes, or wild bears.

Again, you have among you a sneaking individual of the class of native tyrants known as the "Slave-Dealer." He watches your necessities, and crawls up to buy your slave, at a speculating price. If you cannot help it, you sell to him; but if you can help it, you drive him from your door. You despise him utterly. You do not recognize him as a friend, or even as an honest man. Your children must not play with his; they may rollick freely with the little negroes, but not with the slave-dealer's children. If you are obliged to deal with him, you try to get through the job without so much as touching him. It is common with you to join hands with the men you meet, but with the slave-dealer you avoid the ceremony— instinctively shrinking from the snaky contact. If he grows rich and retires from business, you still remember him, and still keep up the ban of non-intercourse upon him and his family. Now why is this? You do not so treat the man who deals in corn, cotton, or tobacco.

And yet again. There are in the United States and Territories, including the District of Columbia, 433,643 free blacks. At five hundred dollars per head they are worth over two hundred millions of dollars. How comes this vast amount of property to be running about without owners? We do not see free horses or free cattle running at large. How is this? All these free blacks are the descendants of slaves, or have been slaves themselves; and they would be slaves now but for something which has operated on their white owners, inducing them at vast pecuniary sacrifice to liberate them. What is that something? Is there any mistaking it? In all these cases it is your sense of justice and human sympathy continually telling you that the poor negro has some natural right to himself—that those who deny it and make mere merchandise of him deserve kickings, contempt, and death.

And now why will you ask us to deny the humanity of the slave, and estimate him as only the equal of the hog? Why ask us to do what you will not do yourselves? Why ask us to do for nothing what two hundred millions of dollars could not induce you to do?

But one great argument in support of the repeal of the Missouri Compromise is still to come. That argument is "the sacred right of self-government." It seems our distinguished senator has found great difficulty in getting his antagonists, even in the Senate, to meet him fairly on this argument. Some poet has said:

Fools rush in where angels fear to tread.

At the hazard of being thought one of the fools of this quotation, I meet that argument — I rush in — I take that bull by the horns. I trust I understand and truly estimate the right of self-government. My faith in the proposition that each man should do precisely as he pleases with all which is exclusively his own lies at the foundation of the sense of justice there is in me. I extend the principle to communities of men as well as to individuals. I so extend it because it is politically wise, as well as naturally just: politically wise in saving us from broils about matters which do not concern us. Here, or at Washington, I would not trouble myself with the oyster laws of Virginia, or the cranberry laws of Indiana. The doctrine of self-government is right,—absolutely and eternally right,—but it has no just application as here attempted. Or perhaps I should rather say that whether it has such application depends upon whether a negro is not or is a man. If he is not a man, in that case he who is a man may as a matter of self-government do just what he pleases with him. But if the negro is a man, is it not to that extent a total destruction of self-government to say that he too shall not govern himself? When the white man governs himself, that is self-government; but when he governs himself and also governs another man, that is more than self-government — that is despotism. If the negro is a man, why then my ancient faith teaches me that "all men are created equal," and that there can be no moral right in connection with one man's making a slave of another.

Judge Douglas frequently, with bitter irony and sarcasm, paraphrases our argument by saying: "The white people of Nebraska are good enough to govern themselves, but they are not good enough to govern a few miserable negroes!"

Well! I doubt not that the people of Nebraska are and will continue to be as good as the average of people elsewhere. I do not say the contrary. What I do say is that no man is good enough to govern another man without that other's consent. I say this is the leading principle, the sheet-anchor of American republicanism. Our Declaration of Independence says:

We hold these truths to be self-evident: That all men are created equal; that they are endowed by their Creator with certain inalienable rights; that among these are life, liberty, and the pursuit of happiness. That to secure these rights, governments are instituted among men, DERIVING THEIR JUST POWERS FROM THE CONSENT OF THE GOVERNED.

I have quoted so much at this time merely to show that, according to our ancient faith, the just powers of governments are derived from the consent of the governed. Now the relation of master and slave is *pro tanto* a total violation of this principle. The master not only governs the slave without his consent, but he governs him by a set of rules altogether different from those which he prescribes for himself. Allow all the governed an equal voice in the government, and that, and that only, is self-government.

) Let it not be said I am contending for the establishment of political and social equality between the whites and blacks. I have already said the contrary. I am not combating the argument of necessity, arising from the fact that the blacks are already among us; but I am combating what is set up as moral argument for allowing them to be taken where they have never yet been—arguing against the extension of a bad thing, which, where it already exists, we must of necessity manage as we best can.

In support of his application of the doctrine of self-government, Senator Douglas has sought to bring to his aid the opinions and examples of our Revolutionary fathers. I am glad he has done this. I love the sentiments of those old-time men, and shall be most happy to abide by their opinions. He shows us that when it was in contemplation for the colonies to break off from Great Britain, and set up a new government for themselves, several of the States instructed their delegates to go for the measure, provided each State should be allowed to regulate its domestic concerns in its own way. I do not quote; but this in substance. This was right; I see nothing objectionable in it. I also think it probable that it had some reference to the existence of slavery among them. I will not deny that it had. But had it any reference to the carrying of slavery into new countries? That is the question, and we will let the fathers themselves answer it.

This same generation of men, and mostly the same individuals of the generation who declared this principle, who declared independence, who fought the war of the Revolution through, who afterward made the Constitution under which we still live—these same men passed the ordinance of '87, declaring that slavery should never go to the Northwest Territory. I have no doubt Judge Douglas thinks they were very inconsistent in this. It is a question of discrimination between them and him. But there is not an inch of ground left for his claiming that their opinions, their example, their authority, are on his side in the controversy.

Again, is not Nebraska, while a Territory, a part of us? Do we not own the country? And if we surrender the control of it, do we not surrender the right of self-government? It is part of ourselves. If you say we shall not control it, because it is only part, the same is true of every other part; and when all the parts are gone, what has become of the whole? What is then left of us? What use for the General Government, when there is nothing left for it to govern?

But you say this question should be left to the people of Nebraska, because they are more particularly interested. If this be the rule, you must leave it to each individual to say for himself whether he will have slaves. What better moral right have thirty-one citizens of Nebraska to say that the thirty-second shall not hold slaves than the people of the thirty-one States have to say that slavery shall not go into the thirty-second State at all?

But if it is a sacred right for the people of Nebraska to take and hold slaves there, it is equally their sacred right to buy them where they can buy them cheapest; and that, undoubtedly, will be on the coast of Africa, provided you will consent not to hang them for going there to buy them. You must remove this restriction, too, from the sacred right of self-government. I am aware, you say, that taking slaves from the States to Nebraska does not make slaves of freemen; but the African slave-trader can say just as much. He does not catch free negroes and bring them here. He finds them already slaves in the hands of their black captors, and he honestly buys them at the rate of a red cotton handkerchief a head. This is very cheap, and it is a great abridgment of the sacred right of self-government to hang men for engaging in this profitable trade.

Another important objection to this application of the right of self-government is that it enables the first few to deprive the succeeding many of a free exercise of the right of self-government. The first few may get slavery in, and the subsequent many cannot easily get it out. How common is the remark now in the slave States, "If we were only clear of our slaves, how much better it would be for us." They are actually deprived of the privilege of governing themselves as they would, by the action of a very few in the beginning. The same thing was true of the whole nation at the time our Constitution was formed.

Whether slavery shall go into Nebraska, or other new Territories, is not a matter of exclusive concern to the people who may go there. The whole nation is interested that the best use shall be made of these Territories. We want them for homes of free white people. This they cannot be, to any considerable extent, if slavery shall be planted within them. Slave States are places for poor white people to remove from, not to remove to. New free States are the places for poor people to go to, and better their condition. For this use the nation needs these Territories.

Still further: there are constitutional relations between the slave and free States which are degrading to the latter. We are under legal obligations to catch and return their runaway slaves to them: a sort of dirty, disagreeable job, which, I believe, as a general rule, the slaveholders will not perform for one another. Then again, in the control of the government—the management of the partnership affairs—they have greatly the advantage of us. By the Constitution each State has two senators, each has a number of representatives in proportion to the number of its people, and each has a number of presidential electors equal to the whole number of its senators and representatives together. But in ascertaining the number of the people for this purpose, five slaves are counted as being equal to three whites. The slaves do not vote; they are only counted and so used as to swell the influence of the white people's votes.

The practical effect of this is more aptly shown by a comparison of the States of South Carolina and Maine. South Carolina has six representatives, and so has Maine; South Carolina has eight presidential electors, and so has Maine. This is precise equality so far; and of course they are equal in senators, each having two. Thus in the control of the government the two States are equals precisely. But how are they in the number of their white people? Maine has 581,813, while South Carolina has 274,567; Maine has twice as many as South Carolina, and 32,679 over. Thus, each white man in South Carolina is more than the double of any man in Maine. This is all because South Carolina, besides her free people, has 384,984 slaves. The South Carolinian has precisely the same advantage over the white man in every other free State as well as in Maine. He is more than the double of any one of us in this crowd. The same advantage, but not to the same extent, is held by all the citizens of the slave States over those of the free; and it is an absolute truth, without an exception, that there is no voter in any slave State, but who has more legal power in the government than any voter in any free State. There is no instance of exact equality; and the disadvantage is against us the whole chapter through. This principle, in the aggregate, gives the slave States in the present Congress twenty additional representatives, being seven more than the whole majority by which they passed the Nebraska bill.

Now all this is manifestly unfair; yet I do not mention it to complain of it, in so far as it is already settled. It is in the Constitution, and I do not for that cause, or any other cause, propose to destroy, or alter, or disregard the Constitution. I stand to it, fairly, fully, and firmly.

But when I am told I must leave it altogether to other people to say whether new partners are to be bred up and brought into the firm, on the same degrading terms against me, I respectfully demur. I insist that whether I shall be a whole man, or only the half of one, in comparison with others, is a question in which I am somewhat concerned, and one which no other man can have a sacred right of deciding for me. If I am wrong in this — if it really be a sacred right of self-government in the man who shall go to Nebraska to decide whether he will be the equal of me or the double of me, then, after he shall have exercised that right, and thereby shall have reduced me to a still smaller fraction of a man than I already am, I should like for some gentleman, deeply skilled in the mysteries of sacred rights, to provide himself with a microscope, and peep about, and find out, if he can, what has become of my sacred rights. They will surely be too small for detection with the naked eye.

Finally, I insist that if there is anything which it is the duty of the whole people to never intrust to any hands but their own, that thing is the preservation and perpetuity of their own liberties and institutions. And if they shall think, as I do, that the extension of slavery endangers them more than any or all other causes, how recreant to themselves if they submit the question, and with it the fate of their country, to a mere handful of men bent only on self-interest. If this question of slavery extension were an insignificant one — one having no power to do harm—it might be shuffled aside in this way; and being, as it is, the great Behemoth of danger, shall the strong grip of the nation be loosened upon him, to intrust him to the hands of such feeble keepers?

I have done with this mighty argument of self-government. Go, sacred thing! Go in peace.

But Nebraska is urged as a great Union-saving measure. Well, I too go for saving the Union. [Much as I hate slavery, I would consent to the extension of it rather than see the Union dissolved, just as I would consent to any great evil to avoid a greater one. But when I go to Union-saving, I must believe, at least, that the means I employ have some adaptation to the end.] To my mind, Nebraska has no such adaptation.

It hath no relish of salvation in it.

It is an aggravation, rather, of the only one thing which ever endangers the Union. When it came upon us, all was peace and quiet. The nation was looking to the forming of new bonds of union, and a long course of peace and prosperity seemed to lie before us. In the whole range of possibility, there scarcely appears to me to have been anything out of which the slavery agitation could have been revived, except the very project of repealing the Missouri Compromise. Every inch of territory we owned already had a definite settlement of the slavery question, by which all parties were pledged to abide. Indeed, there was no uninhabited country on the continent which we could acquire, if we except some extreme northern regions which are wholly out of the question.

In this state of affairs the Genius of Discord himself could scarcely have invented a way of again setting us by the ears but by turning back and destroying the peace measures of the past. The counsels of that Genius seem to have prevailed. The Missouri Compromise was repealed; and here we are in the midst of a new slavery agitation, such, I think, as we have never seen before. Who is responsible for this? Is it those who resist the measure, or those who causelessly brought it forward and pressed it through, having reason to know, and in fact knowing, it must and would be so resisted? It could not but be expected by its author that it would be looked upon as a measure for the extension of slavery, aggravated by a gross breach of faith.

Argue as you will and long as you will, this is the naked front and aspect of the measure. And in this aspect it could not but produce agitation. Slavery is founded in the selfishness of man's nature—opposition to it in his love of justice. These principles are an eternal antagonism, and when brought into collision so fiercely as slavery extension brings them, shocks and throes and convulsions must ceaselessly follow. Repeal the Missouri Compromise, repeal all compromises, repeal the Declaration of Independence, repeal all past history, you still cannot repeal human nature. It still will be the abundance of man's heart that slavery extension is wrong, and out of the abundance of his heart his mouth will continue to speak.

The structure, too, of the Nebraska bill is very peculiar. The people are to decide the question of slavery for themselves; but when they are to decide, or how they are to decide, or whether, when the question is once decided, it is to remain so or is to be subject to an indefinite succession of new trials, the law does not say. Is it to be decided by the first dozen settlers who arrive there, or is it to await the arrival of a hundred? Is it to be decided by a vote of the people or a vote of the legislature, or, indeed, by a vote of any sort? To these questions the law gives no answer. There is a mystery about this; for when a member proposed to give the legislature express authority to exclude slavery, it was hooted down by the friends of the bill. This fact is worth remembering. Some Yankees in the East are sending emigrants to Nebraska to exclude slavery from it; and, so far as I can judge, they expect the question to be decided by voting in some way or other. But the Missourians are awake, too. They are within a stone's-throw of the contested ground. They hold meetings and pass resolutions, in which not the slightest allusion to voting is made. They resolve that slavery already exists in the Territory; that more shall go there; that they, remaining in Missouri, will protect it, and that Abolitionists shall be hung or driven away. Through all this bowie-knives and six-shooters are seen plainly enough, but never a glimpse of the ballot-box.

And, really, what is the result of all this? Each party within having numerous and determined backers without, is it not probable that the contest will come to blows and bloodshed? Could there be a more apt invention to bring about collision and violence on the slavery question than this Nebraska project is? I do not charge or believe that such was intended by Congress; but if they had literally formed a ring and placed champions within it to fight out the controversy, the fight could be no more likely to come off than it is. And if this fight should begin, is it likely to take a very peaceful, Union-saving turn? Will not the first drop of blood so shed be the real knell of the Union?

The Missouri Compromise ought to be restored. For the sake of the Union, it ought to be restored. We ought to elect a House of Representatives which will vote its restoration. If by any means we omit to do this, what follows? Slavery may or may not be established in Nebraska. But whether it be or not, we shall have repudiated—discarded from the councils of the nation—the spirit of compromise; for who, after this, will ever trust in a national compromise? The spirit of mutual concession—that spirit which first gave us the Constitution, and which has thrice saved the Union—we shall have strangled and cast from us forever. And what shall we have in lieu of it? The South flushed with triumph and tempted to excess; the North, betrayed as they believe, brooding on wrong and burning for revenge. One side will provoke, the other resent. The one will taunt, the other defy; one aggresses, the other retaliates. Already a few in the North defy all constitutional restraints, resist the execution of the fugitive-slave law, and even menace the institution of slavery in the States where it exists. Already a few in the South claim the constitutional right to take and to hold slaves in the free States—demand the revival of the slave-trade—and demand a treaty with Great Britain by which fugitive slaves may be reclaimed from Canada. As yet they are but few on either side. It is a grave question for lovers of the Union, whether the final destruction of the Missouri Compromise, and with it the spirit of all compromise, will or will not embolden and embitter each of these, and fatally increase the number of both.

But restore the compromise, and what then? We thereby restore the national faith, the national confidence, the national feeling of brotherhood. We thereby reinstate the spirit of concession and compromise, that spirit which has never failed us in past perils, and which may be safely trusted for all the future. The South ought to join in doing this. The peace of the nation is as dear to them as to us. In memories of the past and hopes of the future, they share as largely as we. It would be on their part a great act—great in its spirit, and great in its effect. It would be worth to the nation a hundred years' purchase of peace and prosperity. And what of sacrifice would they make? They only surrender to us what they gave us for a consideration long, long ago; what they have not now asked for, struggled or cared for; what has been thrust upon them, not less to their astonishment than to ours.

But it is said we cannot restore it; that though we elect every member of the lower House, the Senate is still against us. It is quite true that of the senators who passed the Nebraska bill, a majority of the whole Senate will retain their seats in spite of the elections of this and the next year. But if at these elections their several constituencies shall clearly express their will against Nebraska, will these senators disregard their will? Will they neither obey nor make room for those who will?

But even if we fail to technically restore the compromise, it is still a great point to carry a popular vote in favor of the restoration. The moral weight of such a vote cannot be estimated too highly. The authors of Nebraska are not at all satisfied with the destruction of the compromise—an indorsement of this principle they proclaim to be the great object. With them, Nebraska alone is a small matter—to establish a principle for future use is what they particularly desire.

The future use is to be the planting of slavery wherever in the wide world local and unorganized opposition cannot prevent it. Now, if you wish to give them this indorsement, if you wish to establish this principle, do so. I shall regret it, but it is your right. On the contrary, if you are opposed to the principle,—intend to give it no such indorsement,—let no wheedling, no sophistry, divert you from throwing a direct vote against it.

Some men, mostly Whigs, who condemn the repeal of the Missouri Compromise, nevertheless hesitate to go for its restoration, lest they be thrown in company with the Abolitionists. Will they allow me, as an old Whig, to tell them, good-humoredly, that I think this is very silly? Stand with anybody that stands right. Stand with him while he is right, and part with him when he goes wrong.

Stand with the Abolitionist in restoring the Missouri Compromise, and stand against him when he attempts to repeal the fugitive-slave law. In the latter case you stand with the Southern disunionist. What of that? you are still right. In both cases you are right. In both cases you expose the dangerous extremes. In both you stand on middle ground, and hold the ship level and steady. In both you are national, and nothing less than national. This is the good old Whig ground. To desert such ground because of any company, is to be less than a Whig—less than a man—less than an American.

I particularly object to the new position which the avowed principle of this Nebraska law gives to slavery in the body politic. I object to it because it assumes that there can be moral right in the enslaving of one man by another. I object to it as a dangerous dalliance for a free people—a sad evidence that, feeling prosperity, we forget right; that liberty, as a principle, we have ceased to revere. I object to it because the fathers of the republic eschewed and rejected it. The argument of "necessity" was the only argument they ever admitted in favor of slavery; and so far, and so far only, as it carried them did they ever go. They found the institution existing among us, which they could not help and they cast blame upon the British king for having permitted its introduction. Before the Constitution they prohibited its introduction into the Northwestern Territory, the only country we owned then free from it. At the framing and adoption of the Constitution, they forbore to so much as mention the word "slave" or "slavery" in the whole instrument. In the provision for the recovery of fugitives, the slave is spoken of as a "person held to service or labor." In that prohibiting the abolition of the African slave-trade for twenty years, that trade is spoken of as "the migration or importation of such persons as any of the States now existing shall think proper to admit," etc. These are the only provisions alluding to slavery. Thus the thing is hid away in the Constitution, just as an afflicted man hides away a wen or cancer which he dares not cut out at once, lest he bleed to death,—with the promise, nevertheless, that the cutting may begin at a certain time. Less than this our fathers could not do, and more they would not do. Necessity drove them so far, and further they would not go. But this is not all. The earliest Congress under the Constitution took the same view of slavery. They hedged and hemmed it in to the narrowest limits of necessity.

In 1794 they prohibited an outgoing slave-trade—that is, the taking of slaves from the United States to sell. In 1798 they prohibited the bringing of slaves from Africa into the Mississippi Territory, this Territory then comprising what are now the States of Mississippi and Alabama. This was ten years before they had the authority to do the same thing as to the States existing at the adoption of the Constitution. In 1800 they prohibited American citizens from trading in slaves between foreign countries, as, for instance, from Africa to Brazil. In 1803 they passed a law in aid of one or two slave-State laws, in restraint of the internal slave-trade. In 1807, in apparent hot haste, they passed the law, nearly a year in advance,—to take effect the first day of 1808, the very first day the Constitution would permit,—prohibiting the African slave-trade by heavy pecuniary and corporal penalties. In 1820, finding these provisions ineffectual, they declared the slave-trade piracy, and annexed to it the extreme penalty of death. While all this was passing in the General Government, five or six of the original slave States had adopted systems of gradual emancipation, by which the institution was rapidly becoming extinct within their limits. Thus we see that the plain, unmistakable spirit of that age toward slavery was hostility to the principle and toleration only by necessity.

But now it is to be transformed into a "sacred right." Nebraska brings it forth, places it on the highroad to extension and perpetuity, and with a pat on its back says to it, " Go, and God speed you." Henceforth it is to be the chief jewel of the nation—the very figurehead of the ship of state. Little by little, but steadily as man's march to the grave, we have been giving up the old for the new faith. Near eighty years ago we began by declaring that all men are created equal; but now from that beginning we have run down to the other declaration, that for some men to enslave others is a " sacred right of self-government." These principles cannot stand together. They are as opposite as God and Mammon; and who ever holds to the one must despise the other. When Pettit, in connection with his support of the Nebraska bill, called the Declaration of Independence " a self-evident lie," he only did what consistency and candor require all other Nebraska men to do. Of the forty-odd Nebraska senators who sat present and heard him, no one rebuked him. Nor am I apprised that any Nebraska newspaper, or any Nebraska orator, in the whole nation has ever yet rebuked him. If this had been said among Marion's men, Southerners though they were, what would have become of the man who said it? If this had been said to the men who captured André, the man who said it would probably have been hung sooner than André was. If it had been said in old Independence Hall seventy-eight years ago, the very doorkeeper would have throttled the man and thrust him into the street. Let no one be deceived. The spirit of seventy-six and the spirit of Nebraska are utter antagonisms; and the former is being rapidly displaced by the latter.

Fellow-countrymen, Americans, South as well as North, shall we make no effort to arrest this? Already the liberal party throughout the world express the apprehension "that the one retrograde institution in America is undermining the principles of progress, and fatally violating the noblest political system the world ever saw." This is not the taunt of enemies, but the warning of friends. Is it quite safe to disregard it—to despise it? Is there no danger to liberty itself in discarding the earliest practice and first precept of our ancient faith? In our greedy chase to make profit of the negro, let us beware lest we "cancel and tear in pieces" even the white man's charter of freedom.

Our republican robe is soiled and trailed in the dust. Let us repurify it. Let us turn and wash it white in the spirit, if not the blood, of the Revolution. Let us turn slavery from its claims of " moral right" back upon its existing legal rights and its arguments of " necessity." Let us return it to the position our fathers gave it, and there let it rest in peace. Let us readopt the Declaration of Independence, and with it the practices and policy which harmonize with it. Let North and South—let all Americans—let all lovers of liberty everywhere join in the great and good work. If we do this, we shall not only have saved the Union, but we shall have so saved it as to make and to keep it forever worthy of the saving. We shall have so saved it that the succeeding millions of free happy people, the world over, shall rise up and call us blessed to the latest generations.

At Springfield, twelve days ago, where I had spoken substantially as I have here, Judge Douglas replied to me; and as he is to reply to me here, I shall attempt to anticipate him by noticing some of the points he made there. He commenced by stating I had assumed all the way through that the principle of the Nebraska bill would have the effect of extending slavery. He denied that this was intended, or that this effect would follow.

I will not reopen the argument upon this point. That such was the intention the world believed at the start, and will continue to believe. This was the countenance of the thing, and both friends and enemies instantly recognized it as such. That countenance cannot now be changed by argument. You can as easily argue the color out of the negro's skin. Like the "bloody hand," you may wash it and wash it, the red witness of guilt still sticks and stares horribly at you.

Next he says that congressional intervention never prevented slavery anywhere; that it did not prevent it in the Northwestern Territory, nor in Illinois; that, in fact, Illinois came into the Union as a slave State; that the principle of the Nebraska bill expelled it from Illinois, from several old States, from everywhere.

Now this is mere quibbling all the way through. If the ordinance of '87 did not keep slavery out of the Northwest Territory, how happens it that the northwest shore of the Ohio River is entirely free from it, while the southeast shore, less than a mile distant, along nearly the whole length of the river, is entirely covered with it?

If that ordinance did not keep it out of Illinois, what was it that made the difference between Illinois and Missouri? They lie side by side, the Mississippi River only dividing them while their early settlements were within the same latitude. Between 1810 and 1820, the number of slaves in Missouri increased 7211, while in Illinois in the same ten years they decreased 51. This appears by the census returns. During nearly all of that ten years both were Territories, not States. During this time the ordinance forbade slavery to go into Illinois, and nothing forbade it to go into Missouri. It did go into Missouri, and did not go into Illinois. That is the fact. Can any one doubt as to the reason of it? But he says Illinois came into the Union as a slave State. Silence, perhaps, would be the best answer to this flat contradiction of the known history of the country. What are the facts upon which this bold assertion is based? When we first acquired the country, as far back as 1787, there were some slaves within it held by the French inhabitants of Kaskaskia. The territorial legislation admitted a few negroes from the slave States as indentured servants. One year after the adoption of the first State constitution, the whole number of them was—what do you think? Just one hundred and seventeen, while the aggregate free population was 55,094,—about four hundred and seventy to one. Upon this state of facts the people framed their constitution prohibiting the further introduction of slavery, with a sort of guarantee to the owners of the few indentured servants, giving freedom to their children to be born thereafter, and making no mention whatever of any supposed slave for life. Out of this small matter the judge manufactures his argument that Illinois came into the Union as a slave State. Let the facts be the answer to the argument.

The principles of the Nebraska bill, he says, expelled slavery from Illinois. The principle of that bill first planted it here—that is, it first came because there was no law to prevent it, first came before we owned the country; and finding it here, and having the ordinance of '87 to prevent its increasing, our people struggled along, and finally got rid of it as best they could.

But the principle of the Nebraska bill abolished slavery in several of the old States. Well, it is true that several of the old States, in the last quarter of the last century, did adopt systems of gradual emancipation by which the institution has finally become extinct within their limits; but it may or may not be true that the principle of the Nebraska bill was the cause that led to the adoption of these measures. It is now more than fifty years since the last of these States adopted its system of emancipation.

If the Nebraska bill is the real author of the benevolent works, it is rather deplorable that it has for so long a time ceased working altogether. Is there not some reason to suspect that it was the principle of the Revolution, and not the principle of the Nebraska bill, that led to emancipation in these old States? Leave it to the people of these old emancipating States, and I am quite certain they will decide that neither that nor any other good thing ever did or ever will come of the Nebraska bill.

In the course of my main argument, Judge Douglas interrupted me to say that the principle of the Nebraska bill was very old; that it originated when God made man, and placed good and evil before him, allowing him to choose for himself, being responsible for the choice he should make. At the time I thought this was merely playful, and I answered it accordingly. But in his reply to me he renewed it as a serious argument. In seriousness, then, the facts of this proposition are not true as stated. God did not place good and evil before man, telling him to make his choice. On the contrary, he did tell him there was one tree of the fruit of which he should not eat, upon pain of certain death. I should scarcely wish so strong a prohibition against slavery in Nebraska.

But this argument strikes me as not a little remarkable in another particular—in its strong resemblance to the old argument for the "divine right of kings." By the latter, the king is to do just as he pleases with his white subjects, being responsible to God alone. By the former, the white man is to do just as he pleases with his black slaves, being responsible to God alone. The two things are precisely alike, and it is but natural that they should find similar arguments to sustain them.

I had argued that the application of the principle of self-government, as contended for, would require the revival of the African slave-trade; that no argument could be made in favor of a man's right to take slaves to Nebraska, which could not be equally well made in favor of his right to bring them from the coast of Africa. The judge replied that the Constitution requires the suppression of the foreign slave-trade, but does not require the prohibition of slavery in the Territories. That is a mistake in point of fact. The Constitution does not require the action of Congress in either case, and it does authorize it in both. And so there is still no difference between the cases.

In regard to what I have said of the advantage the slave States have over the free in the matter of representation, the judge replied that we in the free States count five free negroes as five white people, while in the slave States they count five slaves as three whites only; and that the advantage, at last, was on the side of the free States.

Now, in the slave States they count free negroes just as we do; and it so happens that, besides their slaves, they have as many free negroes as we have, and thirty thousand over. Thus, their free negroes more than balance ours; and their advantage over us, in consequence of their slaves, still remains as I stated it.

In reply to my argument that the compromise measures of 1850 were a system of equivalents, and that the provisions of no one of them could fairly be carried to other subjects without its corresponding equivalent being carried with it, the judge denied outright that these measures had any connection with or dependence upon each other. This is mere desperation. If they had no connection, why are they always spoken of in connection? Why has he so spoken of them a thousand times? Why has he constantly called them a series of measures? Why does everybody call them a compromise? Why was California kept out of the Union six or seven months, if it was not because of its connection with the other measures? Webster's leading definition of the verb "to compromise" is "to adjust and settle a difference, by mutual agreement, with concessions of claims by the parties." This conveys precisely the popular understanding of the word "compromise."

We knew, before the judge told us, that these measures passed separately, and in distinct bills, and that no two of them were passed by the votes of precisely the same members. But we also know, and so does he know, that no one of them could have passed both branches of Congress but for the understanding that the others were to pass also. Upon this understanding, each got votes which it could have got in no other way. It is this fact which gives to the measures their true character; and it is the universal knowledge of this fact that has given them the name of "compromises," so expressive of that true character.

I had asked "if, in carrying the Utah and New Mexico laws to Nebraska, you could clear away other objection, how could you leave

Nebraska 'perfectly free' to introduce slavery before she forms a constitution during her territorial government, while the Utah and New Mexico laws only authorize it when they form constitutions and are admitted into the Union ?" To this Judge Douglas answered that the Utah and New Mexico laws also authorized it before; and to prove this he read from one of their laws, as follows : " That the legislative power of said territory shall extend to all rightful subjects of legislation, consistent with the Constitution of the United States and the provisions of this act."

Now it is perceived from the reading of this that there is nothing express upon the subject, but that the authority is sought to be implied merely for the general provision of "all rightful subjects of legislation." In reply to this I insist, as a legal rule of construction, as well as the plain, popular view of the matter, that the express provision for Utah and New Mexico coming in with slavery, if they choose, when they shall form constitutions, is an exclusion of all implied authority on the same subject; that Congress, having the subject distinctly in their minds when they made the express provision, they therein expressed their whole meaning on that subject.

The judge rather insinuated that I had found it convenient to forget the Washington territorial law passed in 1853. This was a division of Oregon organizing the northern part as the Territory of Washington. He asserted that by this act the ordinance of '87, theretofore existing in Oregon, was repealed; that nearly all the members of Congress voted for it, beginning in the House of Representatives with Charles Allen of Massachusetts, and ending with Richard Yates of Illinois; and that he could not understand how those who now oppose the Nebraska bill so voted there, unless it was because it was then too soon after both the great political parties had ratified the compromises of 1850, and the ratification therefore was too fresh to be then repudiated.

Now I had seen the Washington act before, and I have carefully examined it since; and I aver that there is no repeal of the ordinance of '87, or of any prohibition of slavery, in it. In express terms, there is absolutely nothing in the whole law upon the subject—in fact, nothing to lead a reader to think of the subject. To my judgment it is equally free from everything from which repeal can be legally implied; but however this may be, are men now to be entrapped by a legal implication, extracted from covert language, introduced perhaps for the very purpose of entrapping them ? I sincerely wish every man could read this law quite through, carefully watching every sentence and every line for a repeal of the ordinance of '87, or anything equivalent to it.

Another point on the Washington act. If it was intended to be modeled after the Utah and New Mexico acts, as Judge Douglas insists, why was it not inserted in it, as in them, that Washington was to come in with or without slavery as she may choose at the adoption of her constitution ? It has no such provision in it; and I defy the ingenuity of man to give a reason for the omission, other than that it was not intended to follow the Utah and New Mexico laws in regard to the question of slavery.

The Washington act not only differs vitally from the Utah and New Mexico acts, but the Nebraska act differs vitally from both. By the latter act the people are left "perfectly free" to regulate their own domestic concerns, etc.; but in all the former, all their laws are to be submitted to Congress, and if disapproved are to be null. The Washington act goes even further; it absolutely prohibits the territorial legislature, by very strong and guarded language, from establishing banks or borrowing money on the faith of the Territory. Is this the sacred right of self-government we hear vaunted so much? No, sir; the Nebraska bill finds no model in the acts of '50 or the Washington act. It finds no model in any law from Adam till to-day. As Phillips says of Napoleon, the Nebraska act is grand, gloomy and peculiar, wrapped in the solitude of its own originality, without a model and without a shadow upon the earth.

In the course of his reply Senator Douglas remarked in substance that he had always considered this government was made for the white people and not for the negroes. Why, in point of mere fact, I think so too. But in this remark of the judge there is a significance which I think is the key to the great mistake (if there is any such mistake) which he has made in this Nebraska measure. It shows that the judge has no very vivid impression that the negro is human, and consequently has no idea that there can be any moral question in legislating about him. In his view the question of whether a new country shall be slave or free, is a matter of as utter indifference as it is whether his neighbor shall plant his farm with tobacco or stock it with horned cattle. Now, whether this view is right or wrong, it is very certain that the great mass of mankind take a totally different view. They consider slavery a great moral wrong, and their feeling against it is not evanescent, but eternal. It lies at the very foundation of their sense of justice, and it cannot be trifled with. It is a great and durable element of popular action, and I think no statesman can safely disregard it.

Our senator also objects that those who oppose him in this matter do not entirely agree with one another. He reminds me that in my firm adherence to the constitutional rights of the slave States, I differ widely from others who are coöperating with me in opposing the Nebraska bill, and he says it is not quite fair to oppose him in this variety of ways. He should remember that he took us by surprise—astounded us by this measure. We were thunderstruck and stunned, and we reeled and fell in utter confusion. But we rose, each fighting, grasping whatever he could first reach—a scythe, a pitchfork, a chopping-ax, or a butcher's cleaver. We struck in the direction of the sound, and we were rapidly closing in upon him. He must not think to divert us from our purpose by showing us that our drill, our dress, and our weapons are not entirely perfect and uniform. When the storm shall be past he shall find us still Americans, no less devoted to the continued union and prosperity of the country than heretofore.

Finally, the judge invokes against me the memory of Clay and Webster. They were great men, and men of great deeds. But where have I assailed them? For what is it that their life-long enemy shall now make profit by assuming to defend them against me, their life-long friend? I go against the repeal of the Missouri Compromise; did they ever go for it? They went for the compromise of 1850; did I ever go against them? They were greatly devoted to the Union; to the small measure of my ability was I ever less so? Clay and Webster were dead before this question arose; by what authority shall our senator say they would espouse his side of it if alive? Mr. Clay was the leading spirit in making the Missouri Compromise; is it very credible that if now alive he would take the lead in the breaking of it? The truth is that some support from Whigs is now a necessity with the judge, and for this it is that the names of Clay and Webster are invoked. His old friends have deserted him in such numbers as to leave too few to live by. He came to his own, and his own received him not; and lo! he turns unto the Gentiles.

A word now as to the judge's desperate assumption that the compromises of 1850 had no connection with one another; that Illinois came into the Union as a slave State, and some other similar ones. This is no other than a bold denial of the history of the country. If we do not know that the compromises of 1850 were dependent on each other; if we do not know that Illinois came into the Union as a free State,—we do not know anything. If we do not know these things, we do not know that we ever had a Revolutionary war or such a chief as Washington. To deny these things is to deny our national axioms,—or dogmas, at least,—and it puts an end to all argument. If a man will stand up and assert, and repeat and reassert, that two and two do not make four, I know nothing in the power of argument that can stop him. I think I can answer the judge so long as he sticks to the premises; but when he flies from them, I cannot work any argument into the consistency of a mental gag and actually close his mouth with it. In such a case I can only commend him to the seventy thousand answers just in from Pennsylvania, Ohio, and Indiana.

November 27, 1854.—LETTER TO T. J. HENDERSON.

SPRINGFIELD, November 27, 1854.

T. J. HENDERSON, Esq.

My dear Sir: It has come round that a Whig may, by possibility, be elected to the United States Senate; and I want the chance of being the man. You are a member of the legislature, and have a vote to give. Think it over, and see whether you can do better than go for me. Write me at all events, and let this be confidential.

Yours truly,   A. LINCOLN.

November 27, 1854.—LETTER TO I. CODDING.

SPRINGFIELD, November 27, 1854.

I. CODDING, Esq.

Dear Sir: Your note of the 13th requesting my attendance on the Republican State Central Committee, on the 17th instant at Chicago,

VOL. I.—14.

was, owing to my absence from home, received on the evening of that day (17th) only. While I have pen in hand allow me to say I have been perplexed some to understand why my name was placed on that committee. I was not consulted on the subject, nor was I apprised of the appointment until I discovered it by accident two or three weeks afterward. I suppose my opposition to the principle of slavery is as strong as that of any member of the Republican party; but I have also supposed that the extent to which I feel authorized to carry that opposition, practically, was not at all satisfactory to that party. The leading men who organized that party were present on the 4th of October at the discussion between Douglas and myself at Springfield, and had full opportunity to not misunderstand my position. Do I misunderstand them? Please write and inform me. Yours truly,

A. LINCOLN.

December 6, 1854.—LETTER TO JUSTICE JOHN McLEAN.

SPRINGFIELD, ILLINOIS, December 6, 1854.

HON. JUSTICE McLEAN.

Sir: I understand it is in contemplation to displace the present clerk, and appoint a new one, for the Circuit and District Courts of Illinois. I am very friendly to the present incumbent, and both for his own sake and that of his family, I wish him to be retained so long as it is possible for the court to do so. In the contingency of his removal, however, I have recommended William Butler as his successor, and I do not wish what I write now to be taken as any abatement of that recommendation.

William J. Black is also an applicant for the appointment, and I write this at the solicitation of his friends to say that he is every way worthy of the office, and that I doubt not the conferring it upon him will give great satisfaction. Your obedient servant,

A. LINCOLN.

December 11, 1854.—LETTER TO E. B. WASHBURNE.

SPRINGFIELD, ILLINOIS, December 11, 1854.

HON. E. B. WASHBURNE.

My dear Sir: Your note of the 5th is just received. It is too true that by the official returns Allen beats Colonel Archer one vote. There is a report to-day that there is a mistake in the returns from Clay County, giving Allen sixty votes more than he really has; but this, I fear, is itself a mistake. I have just examined the returns from that county at the secretary's office, and find that the aggregate vote for sheriff only falls short by three votes of the aggregate, as reported, of Allen and Archer's vote. Our friends, however, are hot on the track, and will probe the matter to the bottom. As to my own matter, things continue to look reasonably well. I wrote your friend, George Gage; and three days ago had an answer from him, in which he talks out plainly, as your letter taught me to expect. To-day I had a letter from Turner. He says he is not committed, and will not be until he sees how most effectually to oppose slavery extension.

I have not ventured to write all the members in your district, lest some of them should be offended by the indelicacy of the thing — that is, coming from a total stranger. Could you not drop some of them a line? Very truly your friend,

A. LINCOLN.

December 14, 1854.—LETTER TO E. B. WASHBURNE.

SPRINGFIELD, December 14, 1854.

HON. E. B. WASHBURNE.

My dear Sir: So far as I am concerned, there must be something wrong about United States senator at Chicago. My most intimate friends there do not answer my letters, and I cannot get a word from them. Wentworth has a knack of knowing things better than most men. I wish you would pump him, and write me what you get from him. Please do this as soon as you can, as the time is growing short. Don't let any one know I have written you this; for there may be those opposed to me nearer about you than you think.

Very truly yours, etc.,   A. LINCOLN.

December 15, 1854.—LETTER TO T. J. HENDERSON.

SPRINGFIELD, December 15, 1854.

HON. T. J. HENDERSON.

Dear Sir: Yours of the 11th was received last night, and for which I thank you. Of course, I prefer myself to all others; yet it is neither in my heart nor my conscience to say I am any better man than Mr. Williams. We shall have a terrible struggle with our adversaries. They are desperate, and bent on desperate deeds. I accidentally learned of one of the leaders here writing to a member south of here, in about the following language:

We are beaten. They have a clear majority of at least nine on joint ballot. They outnumber us, but we must outmanage them. Douglas must be sustained. We must elect the Speaker; and we must elect a Nebraska United States senator, or elect none at all.

Similar letters, no doubt, are written to every Nebraska member. Be considering how we can best meet, and foil, and beat them.

I send you by this mail a copy of my Peoria speech. You may have seen it before, or you may not think it worth seeing now. Do not speak of the Nebraska letter mentioned above; I do not wish it to become public that I receive such information.

Yours truly,   A. LINCOLN.

December 19, 1854.—LETTER TO E. B. WASHBURNE.

SPRINGFIELD, December 19, 1854.

HON. E. B. WASHBURNE.

My dear Sir: Yours of the 12th just received. The objection of your friend at Winnebago rather astonishes me. For a senator to be the impartial representative of his whole State is so plain a duty that I pledge myself to the observance of it without hesitation, but not without some mortification that any one should suspect me of an inclination to the contrary. I was eight years a representative of Sangamon County in the legislature; and although in a conflict of interests between that and other counties it perhaps would have been my duty to stick to old Sangamon, yet it is not within my recollection that the northern members ever wanted my vote for any interest of theirs without getting it. My distinct recollection is that the northern members and Sangamon members were always on good terms, and always coöperating on measures of policy. The canal was then the great northern measure, and it from first to last had our votes as readily as the votes of the north itself. Indeed, I shall be surprised if it can be pointed out that in any instance the north sought our aid and failed to get it.

Again, I was a member of Congress one term—the term when Mr. Turner was the legal member and you were a lobby member from your then district. Now I think I might appeal to Mr. Turner and yourself, whether you did not always have my feeble service for the asking. In the case of conflict, I might without blame have preferred my own district. As a senator I should claim no right, as I should feel no inclination, to give the central portion of the State any preference over the north, or any other portion of it.

Very truly your friend,   A. LINCOLN.

January 6, 1855.—LETTER TO E. B. WASHBURNE.

Confidential.

SPRINGFIELD, January 6, 1855.

HON. E. B. WASHBURNE.

My dear Sir: I telegraphed you as to the organization of the two houses. T. J. Turner elected Speaker, 40 to 24; House not full; Dr. Richmond of Schuyler was his opponent; Anti-Nebraska also elected all the other officers of the House of Representatives. In the Senate Anti-Nebraska elected George T. Brown, of the "Alton Courier," secretary; and Dr. Ray, of the "Galena Jeffersonian," one of the clerks. In fact they elected all the officers, but some of them were Nebraska men elected over the regular Nebraska nominees. It is said that by this they get one or two Nebraska senators to go for bringing on the senatorial election. I cannot vouch for this. As to the senatorial election, I think very little more is known than was before the meeting of the legislature. Besides the ten or a dozen on our side who are willing to be known as candidates, I think there are fifty secretly watching for a chance. I do not know that it is much advantage to have the largest number of votes at the start. If I did know this to be an advantage, I should feel better, for I cannot doubt but I have more committals than any other man. Your district comes up tolerably well for me, but not unanimously by any means. George Gage is for me, as you know. J. H. Adams is not committed to me, but I think will be for me. Mr. Talcott will not be for me as a first choice. Dr. Little and Mr. Sargent are openly for me. Professor Pinckney is for me, but wishes to be quiet. Dr. Whitney writes me that Rev. Mr. Lawrence will be for me, and his manner to me so indicates, but he has not spoken it out. Mr. Swan I have some slight hopes of. Turner says he is not committed, and I shall get him whenever I can make it appear to be his interest to go for me. Dr. Lyman and old Mr. Diggins will never go for me as a first choice. M. P. Sweet is here as a candidate, and I understand he claims that he has twenty-two members committed to him. I think some part of his estimate must be based on insufficient evidence, as I cannot well see where they are to be found, and as I can learn the name of one only—Day of La Salle. Still it may be so. There are more than twenty-two Anti-Nebraska members who are not committed to me. Tell Norton that Mr. Strunk and Mr. Wheeler come out plump for me, and for which I thank him. Judge Parks I have decided hopes of, but he says he is not committed. I understand myself as having twenty-six committals, and I do not think any other one man has ten. May be mistaken, though. The whole legislature stands:

Senate	A. N. 13	N. 12
House of Representatives	" 44	" 31
	57	43
	43	
	14 majority.	

All here, but Kinney of St. Clair.

Our special election here is plain enough when understood. Our adversaries pretended to be running no candidate, secretly notified all their men to be on hand, and, favored by a very rainy day, got a complete snap judgment on us. In November Sangamon gave Yates 2166 votes. On the rainy day she gave our man only 984, leaving him 82 votes behind. After all, the result is not of the least consequence. The Locos kept up a great chattering over it till the organization of the House of Representatives, since which they all seem to have forgotten it. G.'s letter to L., I think has not been received. Ask him if he sent it. Yours as ever,

A. LINCOLN.

February 9, 1855.—LETTER TO E. B. WASHBURNE.

SPRINGFIELD, February 9, 1855.

HON. E. B. WASHBURNE.

My dear Sir: The agony is over at last, and the result you doubtless know. I write this only to give you some particulars to explain what might appear difficult of understanding. I began with 44 votes, Shields 41, and Trumbull 5,—yet Trumbull was elected. In fact, 47 different members voted for me,—getting three new ones on the second ballot, and losing four old ones. How came my 47 to yield to Trumbull's 5? It was Governor Matteson's work. He has been secretly a candidate ever since (before, even) the fall election. All the members round about the canal were Anti-Nebraska, but were nevertheless nearly all Democrats and old personal friends of his. His plan was to privately impress them with the belief that he was as good Anti-Nebraska as any one else,— at least could be secured to be so by instructions, which could be easily passed. In this way he got from four to six of that sort of men to really prefer his election to that of any other man—all *sub rosa*, of course. One notable instance of this sort was with Mr. Strunk of Kankakee. At the beginning of the session he came a volunteer to tell me he was for me and would walk a hundred miles to elect me; but lo! it was not long before he leaked it out that he was going for me the first few ballots and then for Governor Matteson.

The Nebraska men, of course, were not for Matteson; but when they found they could elect no avowed Nebraska man, they tardily determined to let him get whomever of our men he could, by whatever means he could, and ask him no questions. In the mean time Osgood, Don Morrison, and Trapp of St. Clair had openly gone over from us. With the united Nebraska force and their recruits, open and covert, it gave Matteson more than enough to elect him. We saw into it plainly ten days ago, but with every possible effort could not head it off. All that remained of the Anti-Nebraska force, excepting Judd, Cook, Palmer, Baker and Allen of Madison, and two or three of the secret Matteson men, would go into caucus, and I could get the nomination of that caucus. But the three senators and one of the two representatives above named "could never vote for a Whig," and this incensed some twenty Whigs to "think" they would never vote for the man of the five. So we stood, and so we went into the fight yesterday,— the Nebraska men very confident of the election of Matteson, though denying that he was a candidate, and we very much believing also that they would elect him. But they wanted first to make a show of good faith to Shields by voting for him a few times, and our secret Matteson men also wanted to make a show of good faith by voting with us a few times. So we led off. On the seventh ballot, I think, the signal was given to the Nebraska men to turn to Matteson, which they acted on to a man, with one exception, my old friend Strunk going with them, giving him 44 votes. Next ballot the remaining Nebraska man and one pretended Anti went over to him, giving him 46. The next still another, giving him 47, wanting only three of an election. In the mean time our friends, with a view of detaining our expected bolters, had been turning from me to Trumbull till he had risen to 35 and I had been reduced to 15. These would never desert me except by my direction; but I became satisfied that if we could prevent Matteson's election one or two ballots more, we could not possibly do so a single ballot after my friends should begin to return to me from Trumbull.

So I determined to strike at once, and accordingly advised my remaining friends to go for him, which they did and elected him on the tenth ballot.

Such is the way the thing was done. I think you would have done the same under the circumstances; though Judge Davis, who came down this morning, declares he never would have consented to the forty-seven men being controlled by the five. I regret my defeat moderately, but I am not nervous about it. I could have headed off every combination and been elected, had it not been for Matteson's double game — and his defeat now gives me more pleasure than my own gives me pain. On the whole, it is perhaps as well for our general cause that Trumbull is elected. The Nebraska men confess that they hate it worse than anything that could have happened. It is a great consolation to see them worse whipped than I am. I tell them it is their own fault — that they had abundant opportunity to choose between him and me, which they declined, and instead forced it on me to decide between him and Matteson.

With my grateful acknowledgments for the kind, active, and continued interest you have taken for me in this matter, allow me to subscribe myself   Yours forever,

A. LINCOLN.

August 15, 1855.— LETTER TO GEORGE ROBERTSON.

SPRINGFIELD, ILLINOIS, August 15, 1855.

HON. GEORGE ROBERTSON, Lexington, Kentucky.

My dear Sir: The volume you left for me has been received. I am really grateful for the honor of your kind remembrance, as well as for the book. The partial reading I have already given it has afforded me much of both pleasure and instruction. It was new to me that the exact question which led to the Missouri Compromise had arisen before it arose in regard to Missouri, and that you had taken so prominent a part in it. Your short but able and patriotic speech upon that occasion has not been improved upon since by those holding the same views, and, with all the lights you then had, the views you took appear to me as very reasonable.

You are not a friend to slavery in the abstract. In that speech you spoke of "the peaceful extinction of slavery," and used other expressions indicating your belief that the thing was at some time to have an end. Since then we have had thirty-six years of experience; and this experience has demonstrated, I think, that there is no peaceful extinction of slavery in prospect for us. The signal failure of Henry Clay and other good and great men, in 1849, to effect anything in favor of gradual emancipation in Kentucky, together with a thousand other signs, extinguished that hope utterly. On the question of liberty as a principle, we are not what we have been. When we were the political slaves of King George, and wanted to be free, we called the maxim that "all men are created equal" a self-evident truth, but now when we have grown fat, and have lost all dread of being slaves ourselves, we have become so greedy to be masters that we call the same maxim "a self-evident lie." The Fourth of July has not quite dwindled away; it is still a great day—for burning fire-crackers!!!

That spirit which desired the peaceful extinction of slavery has itself become extinct with the occasion and the men of the Revolution. Under the impulse of that occasion, nearly half the States adopted systems of emancipation at once, and it is a significant fact that not a single State has done the like since. So far as peaceful voluntary emancipation is concerned, the condition of the negro slave in America, scarcely less terrible to the contemplation of a free mind, is now as fixed and hopeless of change for the better, as that of the lost souls of the finally impenitent. The Autocrat of all the Russias will resign his crown and proclaim his subjects free republicans sooner than will our American masters voluntarily give up their slaves.

Our political problem now is, "Can we as a nation continue together permanently—forever—half slave and half free?" The problem is too mighty for me — may God, in his mercy, superintend the solution. Your much obliged friend and humble servant,

A. LINCOLN.

August 24, 1855.—LETTER TO JOSHUA F. SPEED.

SPRINGFIELD, August 24, 1855.

Dear Speed: You know what a poor correspondent I am. Ever since I received your very agreeable letter of the 22d of May I have been intending to write you an answer to it. You suggest that in political action, now, you and I would differ. I suppose we would; not quite as much, however, as you may think. You know I dislike slavery, and you fully admit the abstract wrong of it. So far there is no cause of difference. But you say that sooner than yield your legal right to the slave, especially at the bidding of those who are not themselves interested, you would see the Union dissolved. I am not aware that any one is bidding you yield that right; very certainly I am not. I leave that matter entirely to yourself. I also acknowledge your rights and my obligations under the Constitution in regard to your slaves. I confess I hate to see the poor creatures hunted down and caught and carried back to their stripes and unrequited toil; but I bite my lips and keep quiet. In 1841 you and I had together a tedious low-water trip on a steamboat from Louisville to St. Louis. You may remember, as I well do, that from Louisville to the mouth of the Ohio there were on board ten or a dozen slaves shackled together with irons. That sight was a continued torment to me, and I see something like it every time I touch the Ohio or any other slave border. It is not fair for you to assume that I have no interest in a thing which has, and continually exercises, the power of making me miserable. You ought rather to appreciate how much the great body of the Northern people do crucify their feelings, in order to maintain their loyalty to the Constitution and the Union. I do oppose the extension of slavery because

my judgment and feeling so prompt me, and I am under no obligations to the contrary. If for this you and I must differ, differ we
must.   You say, if you were President, you would send an army
and hang the leaders of the Missouri outrages upon the Kansas
elections; still, if Kansas fairly votes herself a slave State she must
be admitted, or the Union must be dissolved.   But how if she votes
herself a slave State unfairly, that is, by the very means for which you
say you would hang men?   Must she still be admitted, or the Union
dissolved?   That will be the phase of the question when it first becomes a practical one.   In your assumption that there may be
a fair decision of the slavery question in Kansas, I plainly see
you and I would differ about the Nebraska law.   I look upon that
enactment not as a law, but as a violence from the beginning.   It
was conceived in violence, is maintained in violence, and is being
executed in violence.   I say it was conceived in violence, because the
destruction of the Missouri Compromise, under the circumstances,
was nothing less than violence.   It was passed in violence, because
it could not have passed at all but for the votes of many members
in violence of the known will of their constituents.   It is maintained
in violence, because the elections since clearly demand its repeal;
and the demand is openly disregarded.

You say men ought to be hung for the way they are executing
the law; I say the way it is being executed is quite as good as any
of its antecedents.   It is being executed in the precise way which
was intended from the first, else why does no Nebraska man express
astonishment or condemnation?   Poor Reeder is the only public
man who has been silly enough to believe that anything like fairness was ever intended, and he has been bravely undeceived.

That Kansas will form a slave constitution, and with it will ask to
be admitted into the Union, I take to be already a settled question,
and so settled by the very means you so pointedly condemn.   By
every principle of law ever held by any court North or South,
every negro taken to Kansas is free; yet, in utter disregard of
this,—in the spirit of violence merely,—that beautiful legislature
gravely passes a law to hang any man who shall venture to inform
a negro of his legal rights.   This is the subject and real object of
the law.   If, like Haman, they should hang upon the gallows of
their own building, I shall not be among the mourners for their
fate.   In my humble sphere, I shall advocate the restoration of the
Missouri Compromise so long as Kansas remains a Territory, and
when, by all these foul means, it seeks to come into the Union as a
slave State, I shall oppose it.   I am very loath in any case to withhold my assent to the enjoyment of property acquired or located
in good faith; but I do not admit that good faith in taking a negro
to Kansas to be held in slavery is a probability with any man.
Any man who has sense enough to be the controller of his own
property has too much sense to misunderstand the outrageous character of the whole Nebraska business.   But I digress.   In my
opposition to the admission of Kansas I shall have some company,
but we may be beaten.   If we are, I shall not on that account
attempt to dissolve the Union.   I think it probable, however, we

shall be beaten. Standing as a unit among yourselves, you can, directly and indirectly, bribe enough of our men to carry the day, as you could on the open proposition to establish a monarchy. Get hold of some man in the North whose position and ability is such that he can make the support of your measure, whatever it may be, a Democratic party necessity, and the thing is done. Apropos of this, let me tell you an anecdote. Douglas introduced the Nebraska bill in January. In February afterward there was a called session of the Illinois legislature. Of the one hundred members composing the two branches of that body, about seventy were Democrats. These latter held a caucus, in which the Nebraska bill was talked of, if not formally discussed. It was thereby discovered that just three, and no more, were in favor of the measure. In a day or two Douglas's orders came on to have resolutions passed approving the bill; and they were passed by large majorities!!! The truth of this is vouched for by a bolting Democratic member. The masses, too, Democratic as well as Whig, were even nearer unanimous against it; but, as soon as the party necessity of supporting it became apparent, the way the Democrats began to see the wisdom and justice of it was perfectly astonishing.

You say that if Kansas fairly votes herself a free State, as a Christian you will rejoice at it. All decent slaveholders talk that way, and I do not doubt their candor. But they never vote that way. Although in a private letter or conversation you will express your preference that Kansas shall be free, you would vote for no man for Congress who would say the same thing publicly. No such man could be elected from any district in a slave State. You think Stringfellow and company ought to be hung; and yet at the next presidential election you will vote for the exact type and representative of Stringfellow. The slave-breeders and slave-traders are a small, odious, and detested class among you; and yet in politics they dictate the course of all of you, and are as completely your masters as you are the master of your own negroes. You inquire where I now stand. That is a disputed point. I think I am a Whig; but others say there are no Whigs, and that I am an Abolitionist. When I was at Washington, I voted for the Wilmot proviso as good as forty times; and I never heard of any one attempting to unwhig me for that. I now do no more than oppose the extension of slavery. I am not a Know-nothing; that is certain. How could I be? How can any one who abhors the oppression of negroes be in favor of degrading classes of white people? Our progress in degeneracy appears to me to be pretty rapid. As a nation we began by declaring that " all men are created equal." We now practically read it " all men are created equal, except negroes." When the Know-nothings get control, it will read " all men are created equal, except negroes and foreigners and Catholics." When it comes to this, I shall prefer emigrating to some country where they make no pretense of loving liberty,— to Russia, for instance, where despotism can be taken pure, and without the base alloy of hypocrisy.

Mary will probably pass a day or two in Louisville in October.

My kindest regards to Mrs. Speed. On the leading subject of this letter, I have more of her sympathy than I have of yours; and yet let me say I am   Your friend forever,

A. LINCOLN.

December [15?], 1855.—BILL FOR SERVICES RENDERED THE ILLINOIS CENTRAL RAILROAD COMPANY.

THE ILLINOIS CENTRAL RAILROAD COMPANY,
          To A. LINCOLN *Dr.*

To professional services in the case of the Illinois Central Railroad Company against the County of McLean, argued in the Supreme Court of the State of Illinois at December term, 1855 . . . .$5000.00

We, the undersigned members of the Illinois Bar, understanding that the above entitled cause was twice argued in the Supreme Court, and that the judgment therein decided the question of the claim of counties and other minor municipal corporations to tax the property of said railroad company, and settled said question against said claim and in favor of said railroad company, are of opinion the sum above charged as a fee is not unreasonable.

GRANT GOODRICH,   N. H. PURPLE,
N. B. JUDD,   O. H. BROWNING,
ARCHIBALD WILLIAMS,   R. S. BLACKWELL.

June 27, 1856.—LETTER TO JOHN VAN DYKE.

SPRINGFIELD, ILLINOIS, June 27, 1856.
HON. JOHN VAN DYKE.

My dear Sir: Allow·me to thank you for your kind notice of me in the Philadelphia Convention.

When you meet Judge Dayton present my respects, and tell him I think him a far better man than I for the position he is in, and that I shall support both him and Colonel Frémont most cordially. Present my best respects to Mrs. Van Dyke, and believe me

Yours truly,   A. LINCOLN.

July 9, 1856.—LETTER TO —— WHITNEY.

SPRINGFIELD, July 9, 1856.
Dear Whitney: I now expect to go to Chicago on the 15th, and I probably shall remain there or thereabouts for about two weeks.

It turned me blind when I first heard Swett was beaten and Lovejoy nominated; but, after much reflection, I really believe it is best to let it stand. This, of course, I wish to be confidential.

Lamon did get your deeds. I went with him to the office, got them, and put them in his hands myself. Yours very truly,

A. LINCOLN.

August [1?], 1856.—FRAGMENT OF SPEECH AT GALENA, ILLINOIS, IN THE FRÉMONT CAMPAIGN.

You further charge us with being disunionists. If you mean that it is our aim to dissolve the Union, I for myself answer that it is untrue; for those who act with me I answer that it is untrue. Have you heard us assert that as our aim? Do you really believe that such is our aim? Do you find it in our platform, our speeches, our conventions, or anywhere? If not, withdraw the charge.

But you may say that though it is not our aim, it will be the result if we succeed, and that we are therefore disunionists in fact. This is a grave charge you make against us, and we certainly have a right to demand that you specify in what way we are to dissolve the Union. How are we to effect this?

The only specification offered is volunteered by Mr. Fillmore in his Albany speech. His charge is that if we elect a President and Vice-President both from the free States, it will dissolve the Union. This is open folly. The Constitution provides that the President and Vice-President of the United States shall be of different States; but says nothing as to the latitude and longitude of those States. In 1828 Andrew Jackson, of Tennessee, and John C. Calhoun, of South Carolina, were elected President and Vice-President, both from slave States; but no one thought of dissolving the Union then on that account. In 1840 Harrison, of Ohio, and Tyler, of Virginia, were elected. In 1841 Harrison died and John Tyler succeeded to the presidency, and William R. King, of Alabama, was elected acting Vice-President by the Senate; but no one supposed that the Union was in danger. In fact, at the very time Mr. Fillmore uttered this idle charge, the state of things in the United States disproved it. Mr. Pierce, of New Hampshire, and Mr. Bright, of Indiana, both from free States, are President and Vice-President, and the Union stands and will stand. You do not pretend that it ought to dissolve the Union, and the facts show that it won't; therefore the charge may be dismissed without further consideration.

No other specification is made, and the only one that could be made is that the restoration of the restriction of 1820, making the United States territory free territory, would dissolve the Union. Gentlemen, it will require a decided majority to pass such an act. We, the majority, being able constitutionally to do all that we purpose, would have no desire to dissolve the Union. Do you say that such restriction of slavery would be unconstitutional, and that some of the States would not submit to its enforcement? I grant you that an unconstitutional act is not a law; but I do not ask and will not take your construction of the Constitution. The Supreme Court of the United States is the tribunal to decide such a question, and we will submit to its decisions; and if you do also, there will be an end of the matter. Will you? If not, who are the disunionists—you or we? We, the majority, would not strive to dissolve the Union; and if any attempt is made, it must be by you, who so loudly stigmatize us as disunionists. But the Union, in any event, will not be dissolved. We don't want to dissolve it, and if you attempt it we won't let you. With the purse and sword, the army and navy and treasury, in our hands and at our command, you could not do it. This government would be very weak indeed if a majority with a disciplined army and navy and a well-filled treasury could not preserve itself when attacked by an unarmed, undisciplined, unorganized minority. All this talk about the dissolution of the Union is humbug, nothing but folly. We do not want to dissolve the Union; you shall not.

September 8, 1856.—LETTER TO HARRISON MALTBY.

Confidential.

SPRINGFIELD, September 8, 1856.

HARRISON MALTBY, Esq.

Dear Sir: I understand you are a Fillmore man. Let me prove to you that every vote withheld from Frémont and given to Fillmore in this State actually lessens Fillmore's chance of being President. Suppose Buchanan gets all the slave States and Pennsylvania, and any other one State besides; then he is elected, no matter who gets all the rest. But suppose Fillmore gets the two slave States of Maryland and Kentucky; then Buchanan is not elected; Fillmore goes into the House of Representatives, and may be made President by a compromise. But suppose, again, Fillmore's friends throw away a few thousand votes on him in Indiana and Illinois; it will inevitably give these States to Buchanan, which will more than compensate him for the loss of Maryland and Kentucky, will elect him, and leave Fillmore no chance in the House of Representatives or out of it.

This is as plain as adding up the weight of three small hogs. As Mr. Fillmore has no possible chance to carry Illinois for himself, it is plainly to his interest to let Frémont take it, and thus keep it out of the hands of Buchanan. Be not deceived. Buchanan is the hard horse to beat in this race. Let him have Illinois, and nothing can beat him; and he will get Illinois if men persist in throwing away votes upon Mr. Fillmore. Does some one persuade you that Mr. Fillmore can carry Illinois? Nonsense! There are over seventy newspapers in Illinois opposing Buchanan, only three or four of which support Mr. Fillmore, all the rest going for Frémont. Are not these newspapers a fair index of the proportion of the votes? If not, tell me why.

Again, of these three or four Fillmore newspapers, two, at least, are supported in part by the Buchanan men, as I understand. Do not they know where the shoe pinches? They know the Fillmore movement helps them, and therefore they help it. Do think these things over, and then act according to your judgment.

Yours very truly,   A. LINCOLN.

October 1, 1856.—FRAGMENT ON SECTIONALISM.

It is constantly objected to Frémont and Dayton, that they are supported by a sectional party, who by their sectionalism endanger the national union. This objection, more than all others, causes men really opposed to slavery extension to hesitate. Practically, it is the most difficult objection we have to meet. For this reason I now propose to examine it a little more carefully than I have heretofore done, or seen it done by others. First, then, what is the question between the parties respectively represented by Buchanan and Frémont? Simply this, " Shall slavery be allowed to extend into United States territories now legally free?" Buchanan says it shall, and Frémont says it shall not.

That is the naked issue, and the whole of it. Lay the respective platforms side by side, and the difference between them will be found to amount to precisely that. True, each party charges upon the other designs much beyond what is involved in the issue as stated; but as these charges cannot be fully proved either way, it is probably better to reject them on both sides, and stick to the naked issue as it is clearly made up on the record.

And now to restate the question, "Shall slavery be allowed to extend into United States territories now legally free?" I beg to know how one side of that question is more sectional than the other? Of course I expect to effect nothing with the man who makes the charge of sectionalism without caring whether it is just or not. But of the candid, fair man who has been puzzled with this charge, I do ask how is one side of this question more sectional than the other? I beg of him to consider well, and answer calmly.

If one side be as sectional as the other, nothing is gained, as to sectionalism, by changing sides; so that each must choose sides of the question on some other ground, as I should think, according as the one side or the other shall appear nearest right. If he shall really think slavery ought to be extended, let him go to Buchanan; if he think it ought not, let him go to Frémont.

But Frémont and Dayton are both residents of the free States, and this fact has been vaunted in high places as excessive sectionalism. While interested individuals become indignant and excited against this manifestation of sectionalism, I am very happy to know that the Constitution remains calm — keeps cool — upon the subject. It does say that President and Vice-President shall be residents of different States, but it does not say that one must live in a slave and the other in a free State.

It has been a custom to take one from a slave and the other from a free State; but the custom has not at all been uniform. In 1828 General Jackson and Mr. Calhoun, both from slave States, were placed on the same ticket; and Mr. Adams and Dr. Rush, both from free States, were pitted against them. General Jackson and Mr. Calhoun were elected, and qualified and served under the election, yet the whole thing never suggested the idea of sectionalism. In 1841 the President, General Harrison, died, by which Mr. Tyler, the Vice-President and a slave-State man, became President. Mr. Mangum, another slave-State man, was placed in the vice-presidential chair, served out the term, and no fuss about it, no sectionalism thought of. In 1853 the present President came into office. He is a free-State man. Mr. King, the new Vice-President elect, was a slave-State man; but he died without entering on the duties of his office. At first his vacancy was filled by Atchison, another slave-State man; but he soon resigned, and the place was supplied by Bright, a free-State man. So that right now, and for the half year last past, our President and Vice-President are both actually free-State men. But it is said the friends of Frémont avow the purpose of electing him exclusively by free-State votes, and that this is unendurable sectionalism.

This statement of fact is not exactly true. With the friends of Frémont it is an expected necessity, but it is not an " avowed purpose," to elect him, if at all, principally by free-State votes; but it is with equal intensity true that Buchanan's friends expect to elect him, if at all, chiefly by slave-State votes. Here, again, the sectionalism is just as much on one side as the other.

The thing which gives most color to the charge of sectionalism, made against those who oppose the spread of slavery into free territory, is the fact that they can get no votes in the slave States, while their opponents get all, or nearly so, in the slave States, and also a large number in the free States. To state it in another way, the extensionists can get votes all over the nation, while the restrictionists can get them only in the free States.

This being the fact, why is it so? It is not because one side of the question dividing them is more sectional than the other, nor because of any difference in the mental or moral structure of the people North and South. It is because in that question the people of the South have an immediate palpable and immensely great pecuniary interest, while with the people of the North it is merely an abstract question of moral right, with only slight and remote pecuniary interest added.

The slaves of the South, at a moderate estimate, are worth a thousand millions of dollars. Let it be permanently settled that this property may extend to new territory without restraint, and it greatly enhances, perhaps quite doubles, its value at once. This immense palpable pecuniary interest on the question of extending slavery unites the Southern people as one man. But it cannot be demonstrated that the North will gain a dollar by restricting it. Moral principle is all, or nearly all, that unites us of the North. Pity 't is, it is so, but this is a looser bond than pecuniary interest. Right here is the plain cause of their perfect union and our want of it. And see how it works. If a Southern man aspires to be President, they choke him down instantly, in order that the glittering prize of the presidency may be held up on Southern terms to the greedy eyes of Northern ambition. With this they tempt us and break in upon us.

The Democratic party in 1844 elected a Southern president. Since then they have neither had a Southern candidate for election nor nomination. Their conventions of 1848, 1852 and 1856 have been struggles exclusively among Northern men, each vying to outbid the other for the Southern vote; the South standing calmly by to finally cry " Going, going, gone" to the highest bidder, and at the same time to make its power more distinctly seen, and thereby to secure a still higher bid at the next succeeding struggle.

"Actions speak louder than words" is the maxim, and if true the South now distinctly says to the North, "Give us the measures and you take the men." The total withdrawal of Southern aspirants for the presidency multiplies the number of Northern ones. These last, in competing with each other, commit themselves to the utmost verge that, through their own greediness, they have the least hope their Northern supporters will bear. Having got committed in a race of competition, necessity drives them into union to sustain themselves. Each at first secures all he can on personal attachments to him and through hopes resting on him personally. Next they unite with one another and with the perfectly banded South, to make the offensive position they have got into "a party measure." This done, large additional numbers are secured.

When the repeal of the Missouri Compromise was first proposed, at the North there was literally "nobody" in favor of it. In February, 1854, our legislature met in called, or extra, session. From them Douglas sought an indorsement of his then pending measure of repeal. In our legislature were about seventy Democrats to thirty Whigs. The former held a caucus, in which it was resolved to give Douglas the desired indorsement. Some of the members of the caucus bolted,—would not stand it,—and they now divulge the secrets. They say that the caucus fairly confessed that the repeal was wrong, and they pleaded the determination to indorse it solely on the ground that it was necessary to sustain Douglas. Here we have the direct evidence of how the Nebraska bill obtained its strength in Illinois. It was given, not in a sense of right, but in the teeth of a sense of wrong, to sustain Douglas. So Illinois was divided. So New England for Pierce, Michigan for Cass, Pennsylvania for Buchanan, and all for the Democratic party.

And when by such means they have got a large portion of the Northern people into a position contrary to their own honest impulses and sense of right, they have the impudence to turn upon those who do stand firm, and call them sectional. Were it not too serious a matter, this cool impudence would be laughable, to say the least. Recurring to the question, "Shall slavery be allowed to extend into United States territory now legally free?" This is a sectional question—that is to say, it is a question in its nature calculated to divide the American people geographically. Who is to blame for that? Who can help it? Either side can help it; but how? Simply by yielding to the other side; there is no other way; in the whole range of possibility there is no other way. Then, which side shall yield? To this, again, there can be but one answer,—the side which is in the wrong. True, we differ as to which side is wrong, and we boldly say, let all who really think slavery ought to be spread into free territory, openly go over against us; there is where they rightfully belong. But why should any go who really think slavery ought not to spread? Do they really think the right ought to yield to the wrong? Are they afraid to stand by the right? Do they fear that the Constitution is too weak to sustain them in the right? Do they really think that by right surrendering to wrong the hopes of our Constitution, our Union, and our liberties can possibly be bettered?

December 10, 1856.—FRAGMENT OF SPEECH AT A REPUBLICAN
BANQUET IN CHICAGO.

We have another annual presidential message. Like a rejected
lover making merry at the wedding of his rival, the President felicitates himself hugely over the late presidential election. He considers the result a signal triumph of good principles and good men,
and a very pointed rebuke of bad ones. He says the people did it.
He forgets that the "people," as he complacently calls only those
who voted for Buchanan, are in a minority of the whole people by
about four hundred thousand votes—one full tenth of all the votes.
Remembering this, he might perceive that the "rebuke" may not be
quite as durable as he seems to think—that the majority may not
choose to remain permanently rebuked by that minority.

The President thinks the great body of us Frémonters, being
ardently attached to liberty, in the abstract, were duped by a few
wicked and designing men. There is a slight difference of opinion
on this. We think he, being ardently attached to the hope of a
second term, in the concrete, was duped by men who had liberty
every way. He is the cat's-paw. By much dragging of chestnuts
from the fire for others to eat, his claws are burnt off to the gristle,
and he is thrown aside as unfit for further use. As the fool said of
King Lear, when his daughters had turned him out of doors, "He's
a shelled peascod" ["That's a sheal'd peascod"].

So far as the President charges us "with a desire to change
the domestic institutions of existing States," and of "doing everything in our power to deprive the Constitution and the laws of
moral authority," for the whole party on belief, and for myself on
knowledge, I pronounce the charge an unmixed and unmitigated
falsehood.

Our government rests in public opinion. Whoever can change
public opinion can change the government practically just so much.
Public opinion, on any subject, always has a "central idea," from
which all its minor thoughts radiate. That "central idea" in our
political public opinion at the beginning was, and until recently has
continued to be, "the equality of men." And although it has always submitted patiently to whatever of inequality there seemed to
be as matter of actual necessity, its constant working has been a
steady progress toward the practical equality of all men. The late
presidential election was a struggle by one party to discard that
central idea and to substitute for it the opposite idea that slavery is
right in the abstract, the workings of which as a central idea may
be the perpetuity of human slavery and its extension to all countries
and colors. Less than a year ago the Richmond "Enquirer," an
avowed advocate of slavery, regardless of color, in order to favor
his views, invented the phrase "State equality," and now the President, in his message, adopts the "Enquirer's" catch-phrase, telling
us the people "have asserted the constitutional equality of each and
all of the States of the Union as States." The President flatters
himself that the new central idea is completely inaugurated; and so

indeed it is, so far as the mere fact of a presidential election can inaugurate it. To us it is left to know that the majority of the people have not yet declared for it, and to hope that they never will. All of us who did not vote for Mr. Buchanan, taken together, are a majority of four hundred thousand. But in the late contest we were divided between Frémont and Fillmore. Can we not come together for the future? Let every one who really believes, and is resolved, that free society is not and shall not be a failure, and who can conscientiously declare that in the past contest he has done only what he thought best—let every such one have charity to believe that every other one can say as much. Thus let bygones be bygones; let past differences as nothing be; and with steady eye on the real issue, let us reinaugurate the good old "central ideas" of the republic. We can do it. The human heart is with us; God is with us. We shall again be able not to declare that "all States as States are equal," nor yet that "all citizens as citizens are equal," but to renew the broader, better declaration, including both these and much more, that "all men are created equal."

June 26, 1857.—Speech in Springfield, Illinois.

Fellow-citizens : I am here to-night, partly by the invitation of some of you, and partly by my own inclination. Two weeks ago Judge Douglas spoke here on the several subjects of Kansas, the Dred Scott decision, and Utah. I listened to the speech at the time, and have the report of it since. It was intended to controvert opinions which I think just, and to assail (politically, not personally) those men who, in common with me, entertain those opinions. For this reason I wished then, and still wish, to make some answer to it, which I now take the opportunity of doing.

I begin with Utah. If it prove to be true, as is probable, that the people of Utah are in open rebellion to the United States, then Judge Douglas is in favor of repealing their territorial organization, and attaching them to the adjoining States for judicial purposes. I say, too, if they are in rebellion, they ought to be somehow coerced to obedience; and I am not now prepared to admit or deny that the judge's mode of coercing them is not as good as any. The Republicans can fall in with it without taking back anything they have ever said. To be sure, it would be a considerable backing down by Judge Douglas from his much-vaunted doctrine of ᵊrnment for the Territories; but this is only additional ᵗhat was very plain from the beginning, that that doctrine ᵥ deceitful pretense for the benefit of slavery. Those ᵗt see that much in the Nebraska act itself, which forced ᵤd secretaries, and judges on the people of the Territ ᵗt their choice or consent, could not be made to see, ᵤould rise from the dead.
ᵗhis, it is very plain the judge evades the only question ᵃns have ever pressed upon the Democracy in regard ᵤat question the judge well knew to be this: "If the ᴶtah shall peacefully form a State constitution tolerating

polygamy, will the Democracy admit them into the Union?" There is nothing in the United States Constitution or law against polygamy; and why is it not a part of the judge's "sacred right of self-government" for the people to have it, or rather to keep it, if they choose? These questions, so far as I know, the judge never answers. It might involve the Democracy to answer them either way, and they go unanswered.

As to Kansas. The substance of the judge's speech on Kansas is an effort to put the free-State men in the wrong for not voting at the election of delegates to the constitutional convention. He says: "There is every reason to hope and believe that the law will be fairly interpreted and impartially executed, so as to insure to every *bona fide* inhabitant the free and quiet exercise of the elective franchise."

It appears extraordinary that Judge Douglas should make such a statement. He knows that, by the law, no one can vote who has not been registered; and he knows that the free-State men place their refusal to vote on the ground that but few of them have been registered. It is possible that this is not true, but Judge Douglas knows it is asserted to be true in letters, newspapers, and public speeches, and borne by every mail and blown by every breeze to the eyes and ears of the world. He knows it is boldly declared that the people of many whole counties, and many whole neighborhoods in others, are left unregistered; yet he does not venture to contradict the declaration, or to point out how they can vote without being registered; but he just slips along, not seeming to know there is any such question of fact, and complacently declares: "There is every reason to hope and believe that the law will be fairly and impartially executed, so as to insure to every *bona fide* inhabitant the free and quiet exercise of the elective franchise."

I readily agree that if all had a chance to vote, they ought to have voted. If, on the contrary, as they allege, and Judge Douglas ventures not to particularly contradict, few only of the free-State men had a chance to vote, they were perfectly right in staying from the polls in a body.

By the way, since the judge spoke, the Kansas election has come off. The judge expressed his confidence that all the Democrats in Kansas would do their duty—including "free-State Democrats," of course. The returns received here as yet are very incomplete; but so far as they go, they indicate that only about one sixth of the registered voters have really voted; and this, too, when not more, perhaps, than one half of the rightful voters have been registered, thus showing the thing to have been altogether the most exquisite farce ever enacted. I am watching with considerable interest to ascertain what figure "the free-State Democrats" cut in the concern. Of course they voted,—all Democrats do their duty,—and of course they did not vote for slave-State candidates. We soon shall know how many delegates they elected, how many candidates they had pledged to a free State, and how many votes were cast for them.

Allow me to barely whisper my suspicion that there were no such things in Kansas as "free-State Democrats"—that they were altogether mythical, good only to figure in newspapers and speeches in the free States. If there should prove to be one real living free-State Democrat in Kansas, I suggest that it might be well to catch him, and stuff and preserve his skin as an interesting specimen of that soon-to-be-extinct variety of the genus Democrat.

And now as to the Dred Scott decision. That decision declares two propositions—first, that a negro cannot sue in the United States courts; and secondly, that Congress cannot prohibit slavery in the Territories. It was made by a divided court—dividing differently on the different points. Judge Douglas does not discuss the merits of the decision, and in that respect I shall follow his example, believing I could no more improve on McLean and Curtis than he could on Taney.

He denounces all who question the correctness of that decision, as offering violent resistance to it. But who resists it? Who has, in spite of the decision, declared Dred Scott free, and resisted the authority of his master over him?

Judicial decisions have two uses—first, to absolutely determine the case decided; and secondly, to indicate to the public how other similar cases will be decided when they arise. For the latter use, they are called "precedents" and "authorities."

We believe as much as Judge Douglas (perhaps more) in obedience to, and respect for, the judicial department of government. We think its decisions on constitutional questions, when fully settled, should control not only the particular cases decided, but the general policy of the country, subject to be disturbed only by amendments of the Constitution as provided in that instrument itself. More than this would be revolution. But we think the Dred Scott decision is erroneous. We know the court that made it has often overruled its own decisions, and we shall do what we can to have it to overrule this. We offer no resistance to it.

Judicial decisions are of greater or less authority as precedents according to circumstances. That this should be so accords both with common sense and the customary understanding of the legal profession.

If this important decision had been made by the unanimous concurrence of the judges, and without any apparent partizan bias, and in accordance with legal public expectation and with the steady practice of the departments throughout our history, and had been in no part based on assumed historical facts which are not really true; or, if wanting in some of these, it had been before the court more than once, and had there been affirmed and reaffirmed through a course of years, it then might be, perhaps would be, factious, nay, even revolutionary, not to acquiesce in it as a precedent.

But when, as is true, we find it wanting in all these claims to the public confidence, it is not resistance, it is not factious, it is not even disrespectful, to treat it as not having yet quite established a settled doctrine for the country. But Judge Douglas considers this view awful. Hear him:

The courts are the tribunals prescribed by the Constitution and created by the authority of the people to determine, expound, and enforce the law. Hence, whoever resists the final decision of the highest judicial tribunal aims a deadly blow at our whole republican system of government—a blow which, if successful, would place all our rights and liberties at the mercy of passion, anarchy, and violence. I repeat, therefore, that if resistance to the decisions of the Supreme Court of the United States, in a matter like the points decided in the Dred Scott case, clearly within their jurisdiction as defined by the Constitution, shall be forced upon the country as a political issue, it will become a distinct and naked issue between the friends and enemies of the Constitution—the friends and the enemies of the supremacy of the laws.

Why, this same Supreme Court once decided a national bank to be constitutional; but General Jackson, as President of the United States, disregarded the decision, and vetoed a bill for a recharter, partly on constitutional ground declaring that each public functionary must support the Constitution, "as he understands it." But hear the general's own words. Here they are, taken from his veto message:

It is maintained by the advocates of the bank, that its constitutionality, in all its features, ought to be considered as settled by precedent, and by the decision of the Supreme Court. To this conclusion I cannot assent. Mere precedent is a dangerous source of authority, and should not be regarded as deciding questions of constitutional power, except where the acquiescence of the people and the States can be considered as well settled. So far from this being the case on this subject, an argument against the bank might be based on precedent. One Congress, in 1791, decided in favor of a bank; another, in 1811, decided against it. One Congress, in 1815, decided against a bank; another, in 1816, decided in its favor. Prior to the present Congress, therefore, the precedents drawn from that source were equal. If we resort to the States, the expressions of legislative, judicial, and executive opinions against the bank have been probably to those in its favor as four to one. There is nothing in precedent, therefore, which, if its authority were admitted, ought to weigh in favor of the act before me.

I drop the quotations merely to remark that all there ever was in the way of precedent up to the Dred Scott decision, on the points therein decided, had been against that decision. But hear General Jackson further:

If the opinion of the Supreme Court covered the whole ground of this act, it ought not to control the coördinate authorities of this government. The Congress, the executive, and the court must, each for itself, be guided by its own opinion of the Constitution. Each public officer who takes an oath to support the Constitution swears that he will support it as he understands it, and not as it is understood by others.

Again and again have I heard Judge Douglas denounce that bank decision and applaud General Jackson for disregarding it. It would be interesting for him to look over his recent speech, and see how exactly his fierce philippics against us for resisting Supreme Court decisions fall upon his own head. It will call to mind a long and fierce political war in this country, upon an issue which, in his own language, and, of course, in his own changeless estimation, was "a distinct issue between the friends and the enemies of the Constitution," and in which war he fought in the ranks of the enemies of the Constitution.

I have said, in substance, that the Dred Scott decision was in part based on assumed historical facts which were not really true, and I ought not to leave the subject without giving some reasons for saying this; I therefore give an instance or two, which I think fully sustain me. Chief Justice Taney, in delivering the opinion of the majority of the court, insists at great length that negroes were no part of the people who made, or for whom was made, the Declaration of Independence, or the Constitution of the United States.

On the contrary, Judge Curtis, in his dissenting opinion, shows that in five of the then thirteen States—to wit, New Hampshire, Massachusetts, New York, New Jersey, and North Carolina—free negroes were voters, and in proportion to their numbers had the same part in making the Constitution that the white people had. He shows this with so much particularity as to leave no doubt of its truth; and as a sort of conclusion on that point, holds the following language:

The Constitution was ordained and established by the people of the United States, through the action, in each State, of those persons who were qualified by its laws to act thereon in behalf of themselves and all other citizens of the State.   In some of the States, as we have seen, colored persons were among those qualified by law to act on the subject.   These colored persons were not only included in the body of "the people of the United States" by whom the Constitution was ordained and established; but in at least five of the States they had the power to act, and doubtless did act, by their suffrages, upon the question of its adoption.

Again, Chief Justice Taney says:

It is difficult at this day to realize the state of public opinion, in relation to that unfortunate race, which prevailed in the civilized and enlightened portions of the world at the time of the Declaration of Independence, and when the Constitution of the United States was framed and adopted.

And again, after quoting from the Declaration, he says:

The general words above quoted would seem to include the whole human family, and if they were used in a similar instrument at this day, would be so understood.

In these the Chief Justice does not directly assert, but plainly assumes, as a fact, that the public estimate of the black man is more favorable now than it was in the days of the Revolution. This assumption is a mistake. In some trifling particulars the condition of that race has been ameliorated; but as a whole, in this country, the change between then and now is decidedly the other way; and their ultimate destiny has never appeared so hopeless as in the last three or four years. In two of the five States—New Jersey and North Carolina—that then gave the free negro the right of voting, the right has since been taken away, and in a third—New York—it has been greatly abridged; while it has not been extended, so far as I know, to a single additional State, though the number of the States has more than doubled. In those days, as I understand, masters could, at their own pleasure, emancipate their slaves; but since then such legal restraints have been made upon emancipation as to amount almost to prohibition. In those days legislatures held the unquestioned power to abolish slavery in their respective States, but now it is becoming quite fashionable for State constitutions to withhold that power from the legislatures. In those days, by common consent, the spread of the black man's bondage to the new countries was prohibited, but now Congress decides that it will not continue the prohibition, and the Supreme Court decides that it could not if it would. In those days our Declaration of Independence was held sacred by all, and thought to include all; but now, to aid in making the bondage of the negro universal and eternal, it is assailed and sneered at and construed, and hawked at and torn, till, if its framers could rise from their graves, they could not at all recognize it. All the powers of earth seem rapidly combining against him. Mammon is after him, ambition follows, philosophy follows, and the theology of the day is fast joining the cry. They have him in his prison-house; they have searched his person, and left no prying instrument with him. One after another they have closed the heavy iron doors upon him; and now they have him, as it were, bolted in with a lock of a hundred keys, which can never be unlocked without the concurrence of every key — the keys in the hands of a hundred different men, and they scattered to a hundred different and distant places; and they stand musing as to what invention, in all the dominions of mind and matter, can be produced to make the impossibility of his escape more complete than it is.

It is grossly incorrect to say or assume that the public estimate of the negro is more favorable now than it was at the origin of the government.

Three years and a half ago, Judge Douglas brought forward his famous Nebraska bill. The country was at once in a blaze. He scorned all opposition, and carried it through Congress. Since then he has seen himself superseded in a presidential nomination by one indorsing the general doctrine of his measure, but at the same time standing clear of the odium of its untimely agitation and its gross breach of national faith; and he has seen that successful rival constitutionally elected, not by the strength of friends, but by the division of adversaries, being in a popular minority of nearly four hundred thousand votes. He has seen his chief aids in his own State, Shields and Richardson, politically speaking, successively tried, convicted, and executed for an offense not their own, but his. And now he sees his own case standing next on the docket for trial.

There is a natural disgust in the minds of nearly all white people at the idea of an indiscriminate amalgamation of the white and black races; and Judge Douglas evidently is basing his chief hope upon the chances of his being able to appropriate the benefit of this disgust to himself. If he can, by much drumming and repeating, fasten the odium of that idea upon his adversaries, he thinks he can struggle through the storm. He therefore clings to this hope, as a drowning man to the last plank. He makes an occasion for lugging it in from the opposition to the Dred Scott decision. He finds the Republicans insisting that the Declaration of Independence includes *all* men, black as well as white, and forthwith he boldly denies that it includes negroes at all, and proceeds to argue gravely that all who contend it does, do so only because they want to vote, and eat, and sleep, and marry with negroes! He will have it that they cannot be consistent else. Now I protest against the counterfeit logic which concludes that, because I do not want a black woman for a slave I must necessarily want her for a wife. I need not have her for either. I can just leave her alone. In some respects she certainly is not my equal; but in her natural right to eat the bread she earns with her own hands without asking leave of any one else, she is my equal, and the equal of all others.

Chief Justice Taney, in his opinion in the Dred Scott case, admits that the language of the Declaration is broad enough to include the whole human family, but he and Judge Douglas argue that the authors of that instrument did not intend to include negroes, by the fact that they did not at once actually place them on an equality with the whites. Now this grave argument comes to just nothing at all, by the other fact that they did not at once, or ever afterward, actually place all white people on an equality with one another. And this is the staple argument of both the chief justice and the senator for doing this obvious violence to the plain, unmistakable language of the Declaration.

I think the authors of that notable instrument intended to include *all* men, but they did not intend to declare all men equal *in all respects*. They did not mean to say all were equal in color, size, intellect, moral developments, or social capacity. They defined with tolerable distinctness in what respects they did consider all men created equal—equal with "certain inalienable rights, among which are life, liberty, and the pursuit of happiness." This they said, and this they meant. They did not mean to assert the obvious untruth that all were then actually enjoying that equality, nor yet that they were about to confer it immediately upon them. In fact, they had no power to confer such a boon. They meant simply to declare the right, so that enforcement of it might follow as fast as circumstances should permit.

They meant to set up a standard maxim for free society, which should be familiar to all, and revered by all; constantly looked to, constantly labored for, and even though never perfectly attained, constantly approximated, and thereby constantly spreading and deepening its influence and augmenting the happiness and value of life to all people of all colors everywhere. The assertion that "all men are created equal" was of no practical use in effecting our separation from Great Britain; and it was placed in the Declaration not for that, but for future use. Its authors meant it to be—as, thank God, it is now proving itself—a stumbling-block to all those who in after times might seek to turn a free people back into the hateful paths of despotism. They knew the proneness of prosperity to breed tyrants, and they meant when such should reappear in this fair land and commence their vocation, they should find left for them at least one hard nut to crack.

I have now briefly expressed my view of the meaning and object of that part of the Declaration of Independence which declares that "all men are created equal."

Now let us hear Judge Douglas's view of the same subject, as I find it in the printed report of his late speech. Here it is:

No man can vindicate the character, motives, and conduct of the signers of the Declaration of Independence, except upon the hypothesis that they referred to the white race alone, and not to the African, when they declared all men to have been created equal; that they were speaking of British subjects on this continent being equal to British subjects born and residing in Great Britain; that they were entitled to the same inalienable rights, and among them were enumerated life, liberty, and the pursuit of happiness. The Declaration was adopted for the purpose of justifying the colonists in the eyes of the civilized world in withdrawing their allegiance from the British crown, and dissolving their connection with the mother country.

My good friends, read that carefully over some leisure hour, and ponder well upon it; see what a mere wreck—mangled ruin—it makes of our once glorious Declaration.

"They were speaking of British subjects on this continent being equal to British subjects born and residing in Great Britain!" Why, according to this, not only negroes but white people outside of Great Britain and America were not spoken of in that instrument. The English, Irish, and Scotch, along with white Americans, were included, to be sure, but the French, Germans, and other white people of the world are all gone to pot along with the judge's inferior races!

I had thought the Declaration promised something better than the condition of British subjects; but no, it only meant that we should be equal to them in their own oppressed and unequal condition. According to that, it gave no promise that, having kicked off the king and lords of Great Britain, we should not at once be saddled with a king and lords of our own.

I had thought the Declaration contemplated the progressive improvement in the condition of all men everywhere; but no, it merely "was adopted for the purpose of justifying the colonists in the eyes of the civilized world in withdrawing their allegiance from the British crown, and dissolving their connection with the mother country." Why, that object having been effected some eighty years ago, the Declaration is of no practical use now—mere rubbish—old wadding left to rot on the battle-field after the victory is won.

I understand you are preparing to celebrate the "Fourth," to-morrow week. What for? The doings of that day had no reference to the present; and quite half of you are not even descendants of those who were referred to at that day. But I suppose you will celebrate, and will even go so far as to read the Declaration. Suppose, after you read it once in the old-fashioned way, you read it once more with Judge Douglas's version. It will then run thus: "We hold these truths to be self-evident, that all British subjects who were on this continent eighty-one years ago, were created equal to all British subjects born and then residing in Great Britain."

And now I appeal to all—to Democrats as well as others—are you really willing that the Declaration shall thus be frittered away?—

thus left no more, at most, than an interesting memorial of the dead past?—thus shorn of its vitality and practical value, and left without the germ or even the suggestion of the individual rights of man in it?

But Judge Douglas is especially horrified at the thought of the mixing of blood by the white and black races. Agreed for once — a thousand times agreed. There are white men enough to marry all the white women, and black men enough to marry all the black women; and so let them be married. On this point we fully agree with the judge, and when he shall show that his policy is better adapted to prevent amalgamation than ours, we shall drop ours and adopt his. Let us see. In 1850 there were in the United States 405,751 mulattos. Very few of these are the offspring of whites and free blacks; nearly all have sprung from black slaves and white masters. A separation of the races is the only perfect preventive of amalgamation; but as an immediate separation is impossible, the next best thing is to keep them apart where they are not already together. If white and black people never get together in Kansas, they will never mix blood in Kansas. That is at least one self-evident truth. A few free colored persons may get into the free States, in any event; but their number is too insignificant to amount to much in the way of mixing blood. In 1850 there were in the free States 56,649 mulattos; but for the most part they were not born there— they came from the slave States, ready made up. In the same year the slave States had 348,874 mulattos, all of home production. The proportion of free mulattos to free blacks—the only colored classes in the free States—is much greater in the slave than in the free States. It is worthy of note, too, that among the free States those which make the colored man the nearest equal to the white have proportionably the fewest mulattos, the least of amalgamation. In New Hampshire, the State which goes farthest toward equality between the races, there are just 184 mulattos, while there are in Virginia—how many do you think?—79,775, being 23,126 more than in all the free States together.

These statistics show that slavery is the greatest source of amalgamation, and next to it, not the elevation, but the degradation of the free blacks. Yet Judge Douglas dreads the slightest restraints on the spread of slavery, and the slightest human recognition of the negro, as tending horribly to amalgamation.

The very Dred Scott case affords a strong test as to which party most favors amalgamation, the Republicans or the dear Union-saving Democracy. Dred Scott, his wife, and two daughters were all involved in the suit. We desired the court to have held that they were citizens so far at least as to entitle them to a hearing as to whether they were free or not; and then, also, that they were in fact and in law really free. Could we have had our way, the chances of these black girls ever mixing their blood with that of white people would have been diminished at least to the extent that it could not have been without their consent. But Judge Douglas is delighted to have them decided to be slaves, and not human enough to have a hearing, even if they were free, and thus left subject to the forced concubinage of their masters, and liable to become the mothers of mulattos in spite of themselves: the very state of case that produces nine tenths of all the mulattos—all the mixing of blood in the nation.

Of course, I state this case as an illustration only, not meaning to say or intimate that the master of Dred Scott and his family, or any more than a percentage of masters generally, are inclined to exercise this particular power which they hold over their female slaves.

I have said that the separation of the races is the only perfect preventive of amalgamation. I have no right to say all the members of the Republican party are in favor of this, nor to say that as a party they are in favor of it. There is nothing in their platform directly on the subject. But I can say a very large proportion of its members are for it, and that the chief plank in their platform —opposition to the spread of slavery—is most favorable to that separation.

Such separation, if ever effected at all, must be effected by colonization; and no political party, as such, is now doing anything directly for colonization. Party operations at present only favor or retard colonization incidentally. The enterprise is a difficult one; but "where there is a will there is a way," and what colonization needs most is a hearty will. Will springs from the two elements of moral sense and self-interest. Let us be brought to believe it is morally right, and at the same time favorable to, or at least not against, our interest to transfer the African to his native clime, and we shall find a way to do it, however great the task may be. The children of Israel, to such numbers as to include four hundred thousand fighting men, went out of Egyptian bondage in a body.

How differently the respective courses of the Democratic and Republican parties incidentally bear on the question of forming a will —a public sentiment—for colonization, is easy to see. The Republicans inculcate, with whatever of ability they can, that the negro is a man, that his bondage is cruelly wrong, and that the field of his oppression ought not to be enlarged. The Democrats deny his manhood; deny, or dwarf to insignificance, the wrong of his bondage; so far as possible, crush all sympathy for him, and cultivate and excite hatred and disgust against him; compliment themselves as Union-savers for doing so; and call the indefinite outspreading of his bondage " a sacred right of self-government."

The plainest print cannot be read through a gold eagle; and it will be ever hard to find many men who will send a slave to Liberia, and pay his passage, while they can send him to a new country— Kansas, for instance — and sell him for fifteen hundred dollars, and the rise.

April 26, 1858.—LETTER TO E. B. WASHBURNE.

URBANA, ILLINOIS, April 26, 1858.

HON. E. B. WASHBURNE.

My dear Sir : I am rather a poor correspondent, but I think perhaps I ought to write you a letter just now. I am here at this time, but I was at home during the sitting of the two Democratic conventions. The day before those conventions I received a letter from Chicago, having among other things on other subjects the following in it:

A reliable Republican, but an old-line Whig lawyer, in this city told me to-day that he himself had seen a letter from one of our Republican congressmen, advising us all to go for the reëlection of Judge Douglas. He said he was enjoined to keep the author a secret, and he was going to do so. From him I learned that he was not an old-line Democrat or Abolitionist. This narrows the contest down to the congressmen from the Galena and Fulton districts.

The above is a literal copy of all the letter contained on that subject. The morning of the conventions, Mr. Herndon showed me your letter of the 15th to him, which convinced me that the story in the letter from Chicago was based upon some mistake, misconstruction of language, or the like. Several of our friends were down from Chicago, and they had something of the same story amongst them, some half suspecting that you were inclined to favor Douglas, and others thinking there was an effort to wrong you.

I thought neither was exactly the case; that the whole had originated in some misconstruction coupled with a high degree of sensitiveness on the point, and that the whole matter was not worth another moment's consideration.

Such is my opinion now, and I hope you will have no concern about it. I have written this because Charley Wilson told me he was writing you, and because I expect Dr. Ray (who was a little excited about the matter) has also written you; and because I think I, perhaps, have taken a calmer view of the thing than they may have done. I am satisfied you have done no wrong, and nobody has intended any wrong to you.

A word about the conventions. The Democracy parted in not a very encouraged state of mind. On the contrary, our friends, a good many of whom were present, parted in high spirits. They think if we do not triumph, the fault will be our own, and so I really think.

Your friend as ever,   A. LINCOLN.

May 10, 1858.— LETTER TO J. M. LUCAS.

SPRINGFIELD, May 10, 1858.

J. M. LUCAS, Esq.

My dear Sir: Your long and kind letter was received to-day. It came upon me as an agreeable old acquaintance. Politically speaking, there is a curious state of things here. The impulse of almost every Democrat is to stick to Douglas; but it horrifies them to have to follow him out of the Democratic party. A good many are annoyed that he did not go for the English contrivance, and thus heal the breach. They begin to think there is a "negro in the fence,"— that Douglas really wants to have a fuss with the President;—that sticks in their throats. Yours truly,

A. LINCOLN.

May 10, 1858.—LETTER TO E. B. WASHBURNE.

SPRINGFIELD, ILLINOIS, May 10, 1858.

HON. E. B. WASHBURNE.

My dear Sir: I have just reached home from the circuit, and found your letter of the 2d, for which I thank you. My other letter to you was meant for nothing but to hedge against bad feeling being gotten up between those who ought to be friends, out of the incident mentioned in that letter. I sent you an extract from the Chicago letter in order to let you see that the writer did not profess to know anything himself; and I now add that his informant told me that he did tell him exactly what he wrote me—at least I distinctly so understood him. The informant is an exceedingly clever fellow; and I think he, having had a hasty glance at your letter to Charley Wilson, misconstrued it, and consequently misreported it to the writer of the letter to me. I must repeat that I think the thing did not originate in malice to you, or to any one, and that the best way all round is to now forget it entirely. Will you not adjourn in time to be here at our State convention in June?

Your friend as ever,   A. LINCOLN.

May 15, 1858.—LETTER TO E. B. WASHBURNE.

SPRINGFIELD, May 15, 1858.

HON. E. B. WASHBURNE.

My dear Sir: Yours of the 6th, accompanied by yours of April 12th to C. L. Wilson, was received day before yesterday. There certainly is nothing in the letter to Wilson which I in particular, or Republicans in general, could complain of. Of that I was quite satisfied before I saw the letter. I believe there has been no malicious intent to misrepresent you; I hope there is no longer any misunderstanding, and that the matter may drop.

Eight or ten days ago I wrote Kellogg from Beardstown. Get him to show you the letter. It gave my view of the field as it appeared then. Nothing has occurred since, except that it grows more and more quiet since the passage of the English contrivance.

The "State Register" here is evidently laboring to bring its old friends into what the doctors call the "comatose state,"—that is, a sort of drowsy, dreamy condition, in which they may not perceive or remember that there has ever been, or is, any difference between Douglas and the President. This could be done if the Buchanan men would allow it—which, however, the latter seem determined not to do.

I think our prospects gradually and steadily grow better, though we are not yet clear out of the woods by a great deal. There is still some effort to make trouble out of "Americanism." If that were out of the way, for all the rest, I believe we should be "out of the woods." Yours very truly,

A. LINCOLN.

May 27, 1858.—LETTER TO E. B. WASHBURNE.

SPRINGFIELD, May 27, 1858.

HON. E. B. WASHBURNE.

My dear Sir: Yours requesting me to return you the now some-what noted "Charley Wilson letter," is received, and I herewith return that letter. Political matters just now bear a very mixed and incongruous aspect. For several days the signs have been that Douglas and the President have probably buried the hatchet,—Douglas's friends at Washington going over to the President's side, and his friends here and South of here talking as if there never had been any serious difficulty, while the President himself does nothing for his own peculiar friends here. But this morning my partner, Mr. Herndon, receives a letter from Mr. Medill of the "Chicago Tribune," showing the writer to be in great alarm at the prospect North of Republicans going over to Douglas, on the idea that Douglas is going to assume steep Free-soil ground, and furiously assail the administration on the stump when he comes home. There certainly is a double game being played somehow. Possibly—even probably—Douglas is temporarily deceiving the President in order to crush out the 8th of June convention here. Unless he plays his double game more successfully than we have often seen done, he cannot carry many Republicans North, without at the same time losing a larger number of his old friends South. Let this be confidential. Yours as ever,

A. LINCOLN.

June 1, 1858.—LETTER TO CHARLES L. WILSON.

SPRINGFIELD, June 1, 1858.

CHARLES L. WILSON, Esq.

My dear Sir: Yours of yesterday, with the inclosed newspaper slip, is received. I have never said or thought more, as to the inclination of some of our Eastern Republican friends to favor Douglas, than I expressed in your hearing on the evening of the 21st of April, at the State library in this place. I have believed—I do believe now—that Greeley, for instance, would be rather pleased to see Douglas reëlected over me or any other Republican; and yet I do not believe it is so because of any secret arrangement with Douglas. It is because he thinks Douglas's superior position, reputation, experience, ability, if you please, would more than compensate for his lack of a pure Republican position, and therefore his reëlection do the general cause of Republicanism more good than would the election of any one of our better undistinguished pure Republicans. I do not know how you estimate Greeley, but I consider him incapable of corruption or falsehood. He denies that he directly is taking part in favor of Douglas, and I believe him. Still his feeling constantly manifests itself in his paper, which, being so extensively read in Illinois, is, and will continue to be, a drag upon us. I have also

thought that Governor Seward, too, feels about as Greeley does, but
not being a newspaper editor, his feeling in this respect is not much
manifested. I have no idea that he is, by conversation or by letter,
urging Illinois Republicans to vote for Douglas.

As to myself, let me pledge you my word that neither I, nor any
friend so far as I know, has been setting stake against Governor
Seward. No combination has been made with me, or proposed to
me, in relation to the next presidential candidate. The same thing
is true in regard to the next governor of our State. I am not
directly or indirectly committed to any one, nor has any one made
any advance to me upon the subject. I have had many free con-
versations with John Wentworth; but he never dropped a remark
that led me to suspect that he wishes to be governor. Indeed, it is
due to truth to say that while he has uniformly expressed himself
for me, he has never hinted at any condition.

The signs are that we shall have a good convention on the 16th
and I think our prospects generally are improving some every
day. I believe we need nothing so much as to get rid of unjust
suspicions of one another. Yours very truly,

A. LINCOLN.

June 15, 1858.—NOTES OF ARGUMENT IN LAW CASE.

Legislation and adjudication must follow and conform to the
progress of society. The progress of society now begins to produce
cases of the transfer for debts of the entire property of railroad corporations; and to enable transferees to use and enjoy the transferred property, legislation and adjudication begin to be necessary.
Shall this class of legislation just now beginning with us be general
or special? Section ten of our Constitution requires that it should
be general, if possible. [Read the section.] Special legislation always trenches upon the judicial department, and in so far violates
section two of the Constitution. [Read it.]

Just reasoning—policy—is in favor of general legislation, else
the legislature will be loaded down with the investigation of smaller
cases—a work which the courts ought to perform, and can perform
much more perfectly. How can the legislature rightly decide the
facts between P. and B. and S. C. and Co.

It is said that under a general law, whenever a railroad company
gets tired of its debts it may transfer fraudulently to get rid of
them. So they may—so may individuals; and which, the legislature or the courts, is best suited to try the question of fraud in
either case?

It is said, if a purchaser have acquired legal rights, let him not be
robbed of them; but if he needs legislation, let him submit to just
terms to obtain it.

Let him, say we, have general law in advance (guarded in every
possible way against fraud), so that when he acquires a legal right
he will have no occasion to wait for additional legislation; and if
he has practised fraud, let the courts so decide.

June [15 ?], 1858.— BRIEF AUTOBIOGRAPHY.

The compiler of the "Dictionary of Congress" states that while preparing that work for publication, in 1858, he sent to Mr. Lincoln the usual request for a sketch of his life, and received the following reply:

Born, February 12, 1809, in Hardin County, Kentucky.
Education defective.
Profession, a lawyer.
Have been a captain of volunteers in Black Hawk war.
Postmaster at a very small office.
Four times a member of the Illinois legislature, and was a member of the lower house of Congress. Yours, etc.,

A. LINCOLN.

June 16, 1858.— SPEECH DELIVERED AT SPRINGFIELD, ILLINOIS, AT THE CLOSE OF THE REPUBLICAN STATE CONVENTION BY WHICH MR. LINCOLN HAD BEEN NAMED AS THEIR CANDIDATE FOR UNITED STATES SENATOR.

Mr. President and Gentlemen of the Convention: If we could first know where we are, and whither we are tending, we could better judge what to do, and how to do it. We are now far into the fifth year since a policy was initiated with the avowed object and confident promise of putting an end to slavery agitation. Under the operation of that policy, that agitation has not only not ceased, but has constantly augmented. In my opinion, it will not cease until a crisis shall have been reached and passed. "A house divided against itself cannot stand." I believe this government cannot endure permanently half slave and half free. I do not expect the Union to be dissolved—I do not expect the house to fall—but I do expect it will cease to be divided. It will become all one thing, or all the other. Either the opponents of slavery will arrest the further spread of it, and place it where the public mind shall rest in the belief that it is in the course of ultimate extinction; or its advocates will push it forward till it shall become alike lawful in all the States, old as well as new, North as well as South.

Have we no tendency to the latter condition?

Let any one who doubts carefully contemplate that now almost complete legal combination—piece of machinery, so to speak—compounded of the Nebraska doctrine and the Dred Scott decision. Let him consider not only what work the machinery is adapted to do, and how well adapted; but also let him study the history of its construction, and trace, if he can, or rather fail, if he can, to trace the evidences of design and concert of action among its chief architects, from the beginning.

The new year of 1854 found slavery excluded from more than half the States by State constitutions, and from most of the national territory by congressional prohibition. Four days later commenced the struggle which ended in repealing that congressional prohibition. This opened all the national territory to slavery, and was the first point gained.

But, so far, Congress only had acted; and an indorsement by the people, real or apparent, was indispensable to save the point already gained and give chance for more.

This necessity had not been overlooked, but had been provided for, as well as might be, in the notable argument of "squatter sovereignty," otherwise called "sacred right of self-government," which latter phrase, though expressive of the only rightful basis of any government, was so perverted in this attempted use of it as to amount to just this: That if any one man choose to enslave another, no third man shall be allowed to object. That argument was incorporated into the Nebraska bill itself, in the language which follows: "It being the true intent and meaning of this act not to legislate slavery into any Territory or State, nor to exclude it therefrom; but to leave the people thereof perfectly free to form and regulate their domestic institutions in their own way, subject only to the Constitution of the United States." Then opened the roar of loose declamation in favor of "squatter sovereignty" and "sacred right of self-government." "But," said opposition members, "let us amend the bill so as to expressly declare that the people of the Territory may exclude slavery." "Not we," said the friends of the measure; and down they voted the amendment.

While the Nebraska bill was passing through Congress, a law case involving the question of a negro's freedom, by reason of his owner having voluntarily taken him first into a free State and then into a Territory covered by the congressional prohibition, and held him as a slave for a long time in each, was passing through the United States Circuit Court for the District of Missouri; and both Nebraska bill and lawsuit were brought to a decision in the same month of May, 1854. The negro's name was Dred Scott, which name now designates the decision finally made in the case. Before the then next presidential election, the law case came to and was argued in the Supreme Court of the United States; but the decision of it was deferred until after the election. Still, before the election, Senator Trumbull, on the floor of the Senate, requested the leading advocate of the Nebraska bill to state his opinion whether the people of a Territory can constitutionally exclude slavery from their limits; and the latter answered: "That is a question for the Supreme Court."

The election came. Mr. Buchanan was elected, and the indorsement, such as it was, secured. That was the second point gained. The indorsement, however, fell short of a clear popular majority by nearly four hundred thousand votes, and so, perhaps, was not overwhelmingly reliable and satisfactory. The outgoing President, in his last annual message, as impressively as possible echoed back upon the people the weight and authority of the indorsement. The Supreme Court met again; did not announce their decision, but ordered a reargument. The presidential inauguration came, and still no decision of the court; but the incoming President in his inaugural address fervently exhorted the people to abide by the forthcoming decision, whatever it might be. Then, in a few days, came the decision.

The reputed author of the Nebraska bill finds an early occasion to make a speech at this capital indorsing the Dred Scott decision, and vehemently denouncing all opposition to it. The new President, too, seizes the early occasion of the Silliman letter to indorse and strongly construe that decision, and to express his astonishment that any different view had ever been entertained!

At length a squabble springs up between the President and the author of the Nebraska bill, on the mere question of fact, whether the Lecompton constitution was or was not, in any just sense, made by the people of Kansas; and in that quarrel the latter declares that all he wants is a fair vote for the people, and that he cares not whether slavery be voted down or voted up. I do not understand his declaration that he cares not whether slavery be voted down or voted up to be intended by him other than as an apt definition of the policy he would impress upon the public mind—the principle for which he declares he has suffered so much, and is ready to suffer to the end. And well may he cling to that principle. If he has any parental feeling, well may he cling to it. That principle is the only shred left of his original Nebraska doctrine. Under the Dred Scott decision "squatter sovereignty" squatted out of existence, tumbled down like temporary scaffolding,—like the mold at the foundry, served through one blast and fell back into loose sand,—helped to carry an election, and then was kicked to the winds. His late joint struggle with the Republicans against the Lecompton constitution involves nothing of the original Nebraska doctrine. That struggle was made on a point—the right of a people to make their own constitution—upon which he and the Republicans have never differed.

The several points of the Dred Scott decision, in connection with Senator Douglas's "care not" policy, constitute the piece of machinery in its present state of advancement. This was the third point gained. The working points of that machinery are:

(1) That no negro slave, imported as such from Africa, and no descendant of such slave, can ever be a citizen of any State, in the sense of that term as used in the Constitution of the United States. This point for made in order to deprive the negro in every possible event of the benefit of that provision of the United States Constitution which declares that "the citizens of each State shall be entitled to all the privileges and immunities of citizens in the several States."

(2) That, "subject to the Constitution of the United States," neither Congress nor a territorial legislature can exclude slavery from any United States Territory. This point is made in order that individual men may fill up the Territories with slaves, without danger of losing them as property, and thus enhance the chances of permanency to the institution through all the future.

(3) That whether the holding a negro in actual slavery in a free State makes him free as against the holder, the United States courts will not decide, but will leave to be decided by the courts of

any slave State the negro may be forced into by the master. This point is made not to be pressed immediately, but, if acquiesced in for a while, and apparently indorsed by the people at an election, then to sustain the logical conclusion that what Dred Scott's master might lawfully do with Dred Scott in the free State of Illinois, every other master may lawfully do with any other one or one thousand slaves in Illinois or in any other free State.

Auxiliary to all this, and working hand in hand with it, the Nebraska doctrine, or what is left of it, is to educate and mold public opinion, at least Northern public opinion, not to care whether slavery is voted down or voted up. This shows exactly where we now are, and partially, also, whither we are tending.

It will throw additional light on the latter, to go back and run the mind over the string of historical facts already stated. Several things will now appear less dark and mysterious than they did when they were transpiring. The people were to be left "perfectly free," "subject only to the Constitution." What the Constitution had to do with it outsiders could not then see. Plainly enough now, it was an exactly fitted niche for the Dred Scott decision to afterward come in, and declare the perfect freedom of the people to be just no freedom at all. Why was the amendment expressly declaring the right of the people voted down? Plainly enough now, the adoption of it would have spoiled the niche for the Dred Scott decision. Why was the court decision held up? Why even a senator's individual opinion withheld till after the presidential election? Plainly enough now, the speaking out then would have damaged the "perfectly free" argument upon which the election was to be carried. Why the outgoing President's felicitation on the indorsement? Why the delay of a reargument? Why the incoming President's advance exhortation in favor of the decision? These things look like the cautious patting and petting of a spirited horse preparatory to mounting him, when it is dreaded that he may give the rider a fall. And why the hasty after-indorsement of the decision by the President and others?

We cannot absolutely know that all these exact adaptations are the result of preconcert. But when we see a lot of framed timbers, different portions of which we know have been gotten out at different times and places and by different workmen,—Stephen, Franklin, Roger, and James, for instance,—and we see these timbers joined together, and see they exactly make the frame of a house or a mill, all the tenons and mortises exactly fitting, and all the lengths and proportions of the different pieces exactly adapted to their respective places, and not a piece too many or too few, not omitting even scaffolding—or, if a single piece be lacking, we see the place in the frame exactly fitted and prepared yet to bring such piece in— in such a case we find it impossible not to believe that Stephen and Franklin and Roger and James all understood one another from the beginning, and all worked upon a common plan or draft drawn up before the first blow was struck.

It should not be overlooked that, by the Nebraska bill, the people of a State as well as Territory were to be left "perfectly free," "subject only to the Constitution." Why mention a State? They were legislating for Territories, and not for or about States. Certainly the people of a State are and ought to be subject to the Constitution of the United States; but why is mention of this lugged into this merely territorial law? Why are the people of a Territory and the people of a State therein lumped together, and their relation to the Constitution therein treated as being precisely the same? While the opinion of the court, by Chief Justice Taney, in the Dred Scott case, and the separate opinions of all the concurring judges, expressly declare that the Constitution of the United States neither permits Congress nor a territorial legislature to exclude slavery from any United States Territory, they all omit to declare whether or not the same Constitution permits a State, or the people of a State, to exclude it. Possibly, this is a mere omission; but who can be quite sure, if McLean or Curtis had sought to get into the opinion a declaration of unlimited power in the people of a State to exclude slavery from their limits, just as Chase and Mace sought to get such declaration, in behalf of the people of a Territory, into the Nebraska bill—I ask, who can be quite sure that it would not have been voted down in the one case as it had been in the other? The nearest approach to the point of declaring the power of a State over slavery is made by Judge Nelson. He approaches it more than once, using the precise idea, and almost the language too, of the Nebraska act. On one occasion his exact language is: "Except in cases where the power is restrained by the Constitution of the United States, the law of the State is supreme over the subject of slavery within its jurisdiction." In what cases the power of the States is so restrained by the United States Constitution is left an open question, precisely as the same question as to the restraint on the power of the Territories was left open in the Nebraska act. Put this and that together, and we have another nice little niche, which we may, ere long, see filled with another Supreme Court decision declaring that the Constitution of the United States does not permit a State to exclude slavery from its limits. And this may especially be expected if the doctrine of "care not whether slavery be voted down or voted up" shall gain upon the public mind sufficiently to give promise that such a decision can be maintained when made.

Such a decision is all that slavery now lacks of being alike lawful in all the States. Welcome, or unwelcome, such decision is probably coming, and will soon be upon us, unless the power of the present political dynasty shall be met and overthrown. We shall lie down pleasantly dreaming that the people of Missouri are on the verge of making their State free, and we shall awake to the reality instead that the Supreme Court has made Illinois a slave State. To meet and overthrow the power of that dynasty is the work now before all those who would prevent that consummation. That is what we have to do. How can we best do it?

There are those who denounce us openly to their own friends, and yet whisper us softly that Senator Douglas is the aptest instrument there is with which to effect that object. They wish us to infer all from the fact that he now has a little quarrel with the present head of the dynasty; and that he has regularly voted with us on a single point upon which he and we have never differed. They remind us that he is a great man, and that the largest of us are very small ones. Let this be granted. But " a living dog is better than a dead lion." Judge Douglas, if not a dead lion for this work, is at least a caged and toothless one. How can he oppose the advances of slavery? He don't care anything about it. His avowed mission is impressing the " public heart " to care nothing about it. A leading Douglas Democratic newspaper thinks Douglas's superior talent will be needed to resist the revival of the African slave-trade. Does Douglas believe an effort to revive that trade is approaching? He has not said so. Does he really think so? But if it is, how can he resist it? For years he has labored to prove it a sacred right of white men to take negro slaves into the new Territories. Can he possibly show that it is less a sacred right to buy them where they can be bought cheapest? And unquestionably they can be bought cheaper in Africa than in Virginia. He has done all in his power to reduce the whole question of slavery to one of a mere right of property; and as such, how can he oppose the foreign slave-trade. How can he refuse that trade in that "property" shall be "perfectly free," unless he does it as a protection to the home production? And as the home producers will probably not ask the protection, he will be wholly without a ground of opposition.

Senator Douglas holds, we know, that a man may rightfully be wiser to-day than he was yesterday—that he may rightfully change when he finds himself wrong. But can we, for that reason, run ahead, and infer that he will make any particular change of which he, himself, has given no intimation? Can we safely base our action upon any such vague inference? Now, as ever, I wish not to misrepresent Judge Douglas's position, question his motives, or do aught that can be personally offensive to him. Whenever, if ever, he and we can come together on principle so that our great cause may have assistance from his great ability, I hope to have interposed no adventitious obstacle. But clearly, he is not now with us—he does not pretend to be—he does not promise ever to be.

Our cause, then, must be intrusted to, and conducted by, its own undoubted friends—those whose hands are free, whose hearts are in the work, who do care for the result. Two years ago the Republicans of the nation mustered over thirteen hundred thousand strong. We did this under the single impulse of · esistance to a common danger, with every external circumstance against us. Of strange, discordant, and even hostile elements, we gathered from the four winds, and formed and fought the battle through, under the constant hot fire of a disciplined, proud, and pampered enemy. Did we brave all then to falter now?—now, when that same enemy is wavering, dissevered, and belligerent? The result is not doubtful. We shall not fail—if we stand firm, we shall not fail. Wise counsels may accelerate or mistakes delay it, but, sooner or later, the victory is sure to come.

June 25, 1858.—LETTER TO J. W. SOMERS.

SPRINGFIELD, June 25, 1858.

JAMES W. SOMERS, Esq.

My dear Sir : Yours of the 22d, inclosing a draft of two hundred dollars, was duly received. I have paid it on the judgment, and herewith you have the receipt. I do not wish to say anything as to who shall be the Republican candidate for the legislature in your district, further than that I have full confidence in Dr. Hull. Have you ever got in the way of consulting with McKinley in political matters? He is true as steel, and his judgment is very good. The last I heard from him, he rather thought Weldon, of De Witt, was our best timber for representative, all things considered. But you there must settle it among yourselves. It may well puzzle older heads than yours to understand how, as the Dred Scott decision holds, Congress can authorize a territorial legislature to do everything else, and cannot authorize them to prohibit slavery. That is one of the things the court can decide, but can never give an intelligible reason for.

Yours very truly,   A. LINCOLN.

June 25, 1858.— LETTER TO A. CAMPBELL.

SPRINGFIELD, June 25, 1858.

A. CAMPBELL, Esq.

My dear Sir : In 1856 you gave me authority to draw on you for any sum not exceeding five hundred dollars. I see clearly that such a privilege would be more available now than it was then. I am aware that times are tighter now than they were then. Please write me, at all events; and whether you can now do anything or not, I shall continue grateful for the past. Yours very truly,

A. LINCOLN.

July 7, 1858.—LETTER TO J. J. CRITTENDEN.

SPRINGFIELD, July 7, 1858.

TO THE HONORABLE J. J. CRITTENDEN.

Dear Sir : I beg you will pardon me for the liberty in addressing you upon only so limited an acquaintance, and that acquaintance so long past. I am prompted to do so by a story being whispered about here that you are anxious for the reëlection of Mr. Douglas to the United States Senate, and also of Harris, of our district, to the House of Representatives, and that you are pledged to write letters to that effect to your friends here in Illinois, if requested. I do not believe the story, but still it gives me some uneasiness. If such was your inclination, I do not believe you would so express yourself. It is not in character with you as I have always estimated you.

You have no warmer friends than here in Illinois, and I assure you nine tenths—I believe ninety-nine hundredths—of them would be mortified exceedingly by anything of the sort from you. When I tell you this, make such allowance as you think just for my position, which, I doubt not, you understand.   Nor am I fishing for a letter on the other side.   Even if such could be had, my judgment is that you would better be hands off !

Please drop me a line; and if your purposes are as I hope they are not, please let me know. The confirmation would pain me much, but I should still continue your friend and admirer.

Your obedient servant,   A. LINCOLN.

P. S. I purposely fold this sheet within itself instead of an envelop.

July 10, 1858.— SPEECH AT CHICAGO, ILLINOIS.

My Fellow-citizens : On yesterday evening, upon the occasion of the reception given to Senator Douglas, I was furnished with a seat very convenient for hearing him, and was otherwise very courteously treated by him and his friends, and for which I thank him and them.   During the course of his remarks my name was mentioned in such a way as, I suppose, renders it at least not improper that I should make some sort of reply to him.   I shall not attempt to follow him in the precise order in which he addressed the assembled multitude upon that occasion, though I shall perhaps do so in the main.

There was one question to which he asked the attention of the crowd, which I deem of somewhat less importance — at least of propriety for me to dwell upon — than the others, which he brought in near the close of his speech, and which I think it would not be entirely proper for me to omit attending to; and yet if I were not to give some attention to it now, I should probably forget it altogether. While I am upon this subject, allow me to say that I do not intend to indulge in that inconvenient mode sometimes adopted in public speaking, of reading from documents; but I shall depart from that rule so far as to read a little scrap from his speech, which notices this first topic of which I shall speak — that is, provided I can find it in the paper.

I have made up my mind to appeal to the people against the combination that has been made against me.   The Republican leaders have formed an alliance, an unholy and unnatural alliance, with a portion of unscrupulous federal office-holders.   I intend to fight that allied army wherever I meet them.   I know they deny the alliance, but yet these men who are trying to divide the Democratic party for the purpose of electing a Republican senator in my place, are just so much the agents and tools of the supporters of Mr. Lincoln.   Hence I shall deal with this allied army just as the Russians dealt with the allies at Sebastopol — that is, the Russians did not stop to inquire, when they fired a broadside, whether it hit an Englishman, a Frenchman, or a Turk.   Nor will I stop to inquire, nor shall I hesitate, whether my blows shall hit these Republican leaders or their allies, who are holding the federal offices and yet acting in concert with them.

Well, now, gentlemen, is not that very alarming ?   Just to think of it ! right at the outset of his canvass, I, a poor, kind, amiable,

intelligent gentleman—I am to be slain in this way. Why, my friend
the judge is not only, as it turns out, not a dead lion, nor even a
living one—he is the rugged Russian bear.

But if they will have it—for he says that we deny it—that there
is any such alliance, as he says there is,—and I don't propose hanging very much upon this question of veracity,—but if he will have it
that there is such an alliance, that the administration men and
we are allied, and we stand in the attitude of English, French, and
Turk, he occupying the position of the Russian,—in that case I beg
he will indulge us while we barely suggest to him that these allies
took Sebastopol.

Gentlemen, only a few more words as to this alliance. For my
part, I have to say that whether there be such an alliance depends,
so far as I know, upon what may be a right definition of the term
alliance. If for the Republican party to see the other great party to
which they are opposed divided among themselves and not try to
stop the division, and rather be glad of it,—if that is an alliance, I
confess I am in; but if it is meant to be said that the Republicans
had formed an alliance going beyond that, by which there is con-
tribution of money or sacrifice of principle on the one side or the
other, so far as the Republican party is concerned, if there be any
such thing, I protest that I neither know anything of it nor do I
believe it. I will, however, say—as I think this branch of the
argument is lugged in—I would before I leave it state, for the
benefit of those concerned, that one of those same Buchanan men
did once tell me of an argument that he made for his opposition to
Judge Douglas. He said that a friend of our Senator Douglas had
been talking to him, and had among other things said to him: "Why,
you don't want to beat Douglas?" "Yes," said he, "I do want to
beat him, and I will tell you why. I believe his original Nebraska
bill was right in the abstract, but it was wrong in the time that it was
brought forward. It was wrong in the application to a Territory
in regard to which the question had been settled; it was brought
forward at a time when nobody asked him; it was tendered to the
South when the South had not asked for it, but when they could not
well refuse it; and for this same reason he forced that question upon
our party. It has sunk the best men all over the nation, everywhere;
and now when our President, struggling with the difficulties of this
man's getting up, has reached the very hardest point to turn in the
case, he deserts him, and I am for putting him where he will trouble
us no more."

Now, gentlemen, that is not my argument—that is not my argument at all. I have only been stating to you the argument of a
Buchanan man. You will judge if there is any force in it.

Popular sovereignty! everlasting popular sovereignty! Let us
for a moment inquire into this vast matter of popular sovereignty.
What is popular sovereignty? We recollect that at an early period
in the history of this struggle, there was another name for the same
thing—squatter sovereignty. It was not exactly popular sovereignty, but squatter sovereignty. What did those terms mean?
What do those terms mean when used now? And vast credit is

taken by our friend the judge in regard to his support of it, when he declares the last years of his life have been, and all the future years of his life shall be, devoted to this matter of popular sovereignty. What is it? Why, it is the sovereignty of the people! What was squatter sovereignty? I suppose if it had any significance at all, it was the right of the people to govern themselves, to be sovereign in their own affairs while they were squatted down in a country not their own, while they had squatted on a Territory that did not belong to them, in the sense that a State belongs to the people who inhabit it — when it belonged to the nation — such right to govern themselves was called "squatter sovereignty."

Now I wish you to mark what has become of that squatter sovereignty. What has become of it? Can you get anybody to tell you now that the people of a Territory have any authority to govern themselves, in regard to this mooted question of slavery, before they form a State constitution? No such thing at all, although there is a general running fire, and although there has been a hurrah made in every speech on that side, assuming that policy had given the people of a Territory the right to govern themselves upon this question; yet the point is dodged. To-day it has been decided — no more than a year ago it was decided by the Supreme Court of the United States, and is insisted upon to-day — that the people of a Territory have no right to exclude slavery from a Territory; that if any one man chooses to take slaves into a Territory, all the rest of the people have no right to keep them out. This being so, and this decision being made one of the points that the judge approved, and one in the approval of which he says he means to keep me down — put me down I should not say, for I have never been up; he says he is in favor of it, and sticks to it, and expects to win his battle on that decision, which says that there is no such thing as squatter sovereignty, but that any one man may take slaves into a Territory, and all the other men in the Territory may be opposed to it, and yet by reason of the Constitution they cannot prohibit it. When that is so, how much is left of this vast matter of squatter sovereignty, I should like to know?

When we get back, we get to the point of the right of the people to make a constitution. Kansas was settled, for example, in 1854. It was a Territory yet, without having formed a constitution, in a very regular way, for three years. All this time negro slavery could be taken in by any few individuals, and by that decision of the Supreme Court, which the judge approves, all the rest of the people cannot keep it out; but when they come to make a constitution they may say they will not have slavery. But it is there; they are obliged to tolerate it some way, and all experience shows it will be so — for they will not take the negro slaves and absolutely deprive the owners of them. All experience shows this to be so. All that space of time that runs from the beginning of the settlement of the Territory until there is sufficiency of people to make a State constitution — all that portion of time popular sovereignty is given up. The seal is absolutely put down upon it by the court decision, and Judge Douglas puts his own upon the top of that; yet he is appealing to the people to give him vast credit for his devotion to popular sovereignty.

Again, when we get to the question of the right of the people to form a State constitution as they please, to form it with slavery or without slavery—if that is anything new, I confess I don't know it. Has there ever been a time when anybody said that any other than the people of a Territory itself should form a constitution? What is now in it that Judge Douglas should have fought several years of his life, and pledge himself to fight all the remaining years of his life, for? Can Judge Douglas find anybody on earth that said that anybody else should form a constitution for a people? [A voice: "Yes."] Well, I should like you to name him; I should like to know who he was. [Same voice: "John Calhoun."] No, sir; I never heard of even John Calhoun saying such a thing. He insisted on the same principle as Judge Douglas; but his mode of applying it, in fact, was wrong. It is enough for my purpose to ask this crowd whenever a Republican said anything against it? They never said anything against it, but they have constantly spoken for it; and whosoever will undertake to examine the platform and the speeches of responsible men of the party, and of irresponsible men, too, if you please, will be unable to find one word from anybody in the Republican ranks opposed to that popular sovereignty which Judge Douglas thinks he has invented. I suppose that Judge Douglas will claim in a little while that he is the inventor of the idea that the people should govern themselves; that nobody ever thought of such a thing until he brought it forward. We do not remember that in that old Declaration of Independence it is said that "We hold these truths to be self-evident, that all men are created equal; that they are endowed by their Creator with certain inalienable rights; that among these are life, liberty, and the pursuit of happiness; that to secure these rights, governments are instituted among men, deriving their just powers from the consent of the governed." There is the origin of popular sovereignty. Who, then, shall come in at this day and claim that he invented it?

The Lecompton constitution connects itself with this question, for it is in this matter of the Lecompton constitution that our friend Judge Douglas claims such vast credit. I agree that in opposing the Lecompton constitution, so far as I can perceive, he was right. I do not deny that at all; and, gentlemen, you will readily see why I could not deny it, even if I wanted to. But I do not wish to; for all the Republicans in the nation opposed it, and they would have opposed it just as much without Judge Douglas's aid as with it. They had all taken ground against it long before he did. Why, the reason that he urges against that constitution I urged against him a year before. I have the printed speech in my hand. The argument that he makes why that constitution should not be adopted, that the people were not fairly represented nor allowed to vote, I pointed out in a speech a year ago, which I hold in my hand now, that no fair chance was to be given to the people. ["Read it; read it."] I shall not waste your time by trying to read it. ["Read it; read it."] Gentlemen, reading from speeches is a very tedious business, particularly for an old man who has to put on spectacles, and more so if the man be so tall that he has to bend over to the light.

A little more now as to this matter of popular sovereignty and the Lecompton constitution. The Lecompton constitution, as the judge tells us, was defeated. The defeat of it was a good thing, or it was not. He thinks the defeat of it was a good thing, and so do I, and we agree in that. Who defeated it? [A voice: "Judge Douglas."] Yes, he furnished himself, and if you suppose he controlled the other Democrats that went with him, he furnished three votes, while the Republicans furnished twenty.

That is what he did to defeat it. In the House of Representatives he and his friends furnished some twenty votes, and the Republicans furnished ninety odd. Now, who was it that did the work? [A voice: "Douglas."] Why, yes, Douglas did it! To be sure he did.

Let us, however, put that proposition another way. The Republicans could not have done it without Judge Douglas. Could he have done it without them? Which could have come the nearest to doing it without the other? [A voice: "Who killed the bill?" Another voice: "Douglas."] Ground was taken against it by the Republicans long before Douglas did it. The proportion of opposition to that measure is about five to one. [A voice: "Why don't they come out on it?"] You don't know what you are talking about, my friend. I am quite willing to answer any gentleman in the crowd who asks an intelligent question.

Now, who, in all this country, has ever found any of our friends of Judge Douglas's way of thinking, and who have acted upon this main question, that have ever thought of uttering a word in behalf of Judge Trumbull? [A voice: "We have."] I defy you to show a printed resolution passed in a Democratic meeting. I take it upon myself to defy any man to show a printed resolution of a Democratic meeting, large or small, in favor of Judge Trumbull, or any of the five to one Republicans who beat that bill. Everything must be for the Democrats! They did everything, and the five to the one that really did the thing they snub over, and they do not seem to remember that they have an existence upon the face of the earth.

Gentlemen, I fear that I shall become tedious. I leave this branch of the subject to take hold of another. I take up that part of Judge Douglas's speech in which he respectfully attended to me.

Judge Douglas made two points upon my recent speech at Springfield. He says they are to be the issues of this campaign. The first one of these points he bases upon the language in a speech which I delivered at Springfield, which I believe I can quote correctly from memory. I said there that " we are now far into the fifth year since a policy was instituted for the avowed object and with the confident promise of putting an end to slavery agitation; under the operation of that policy, that agitation has not only not ceased, but has constantly augmented. I believe it will not cease until a crisis shall have been reached and passed. 'A house divided against itself cannot stand.' I believe this government cannot endure permanently half slave and half free. I do not expect the Union to be dissolved "— I am quoting from my speech—"I do not expect the house to fall, but I do expect it will cease to be divided. It will become all one thing or all the other. Either the opponents of slavery will arrest the further spread of it, and place it where the public mind shall rest in the belief that it is in the course of ultimate extinction, or its advocates will push it forward until it shall become alike lawful in all the States, old as well as new, North as well as South."

That is the paragraph! In this paragraph which I have quoted in your hearing, and to which I ask the attention of all, Judge Douglas thinks he discovers great political heresy. I want your attention particularly to what he has inferred from it. He says I am in favor of making all the States of this Union uniform in all their internal regulations; that in all their domestic concerns I am in favor of making them entirely uniform. He draws this inference from the language I have quoted to you. He says that I am in favor of making war by the North upon the South for the extinction of slavery; that I am also in favor of inviting (as he expresses it) the South to a war upon the North, for the purpose of nationalizing slavery. Now, it is singular enough, if you will carefully read that passage over, that I did not say that I was in favor of anything in it. I only said what I expected would take place. I made a prediction only—it may have been a foolish one, perhaps. I did not even say that I desired that slavery should be put in course of ultimate extinction. I do say so now, however, so there need be no longer any difficulty about that. It may be written down in the great speech.

Gentlemen, Judge Douglas informed you that this speech of mine was probably carefully prepared. I admit that it was. I am not master of language; I have not a fine education; I am not capable of entering into a disquisition upon dialectics, as I believe you call it; but I do not believe the language I employed bears any such construction as Judge Douglas puts upon it. But I don't care about a quibble in regard to words. I know what I meant, and I will not leave this crowd in doubt, if I can explain it to them, what I really meant in the use of that paragraph.

I am not, in the first place, unaware that this government has endured eighty-two years half slave and half free. I know that. I am tolerably well acquainted with the history of the country, and I know that it has endured eighty-two years half slave and half free. I believe—and that is what I meant to allude to there—I believe it has endured because during all that time, until the introduction of the Nebraska bill, the public mind did rest all the time in the belief that slavery was in course of ultimate extinction. That was what gave us the rest that we had through that period of eighty-two years; at least, so I believe. [I have always hated slavery, I think, as much as any Abolitionist—I have been an old-line Whig—I have always hated it, but I have always been quiet about it until this new era of the introduction of the Nebraska bill began. I always believed that everybody was against it, and that it was in course of ultimate extinction. [Pointing to Mr. Browning, who stood near by.] Browning thought so; the great mass of the nation have rested in the belief that slavery was in course of ultimate extinction. They had reason so to believe.

The adoption of the Constitution and its attendant history led the people to believe so, and that such was the belief of the framers of the Constitution itself. Why did those old men, about the time of the adoption of the Constitution, decree that slavery should not go into the new Territory, where it had not already gone? Why declare that within twenty years the African slave-trade, by which slaves are supplied, might be cut off by Congress? Why were all these acts? I might enumerate more of these acts—but enough. What were they but a clear indication that the framers of the Constitution intended and expected the ultimate extinction of that institution? And now, when I say,—as I said in my speech that Judge Douglas has quoted from,—when I say that I think the opponents of slavery will resist the farther spread of it, and place it where the public mind shall rest in the belief that it is in course of ultimate extinction, I only mean to say that they will place it where the founders of this government originally placed it.

I have said a hundred times, and I have now no inclination to take it back, that I believe there is no right and ought to be no inclination in the people of the free States to enter into the slave States and interfere with the question of slavery at all. I have said that always; Judge Douglas has heard me say it—if not quite a hundred times, at least as good as a hundred times; and when it is said that I am in favor of interfering with slavery where it exists, I know it is unwarranted by anything I have ever intended, and, as I believe, by anything I have ever said. If by any means I have ever used language which could fairly be so construed (as, however, I believe I never have), I now correct it.

So much, then, for the inference that Judge Douglas draws, that I am in favor of setting the sections at war with one another. I know that I never meant any such thing, and I believe that no fair mind can infer any such thing from anything I have ever said.

Now in relation to his inference that I am in favor of a general consolidation of all the local institutions of the various States. I will attend to that for a little while, and try to inquire, if I can, how on earth it could be that any man could draw such an inference from anything I said. I have said very many times in Judge Douglas's hearing that no man believed more than I in the principle of self-government; that it lies at the bottom of all my ideas of just government from beginning to end. I have denied that his use of that term applies properly. But for the thing itself I deny that any man has ever gone ahead of me in his devotion to the principle, whatever he may have done in efficiency in advocating it. I think that I have said it in your hearing—that I believe each individual is naturally entitled to do as he pleases with himself and the fruit of his labor, so far as it in no wise interferes with any other man's rights; that each community, as a State, has a right to do exactly as it pleases with all the concerns within that State that interfere with the right of no other State; and that the General Government, upon principle, has no right to interfere with anything other than that general class of things that does concern the whole. I have said that at all times. I have said as illustrations that I do not believe in the right of Illinois to interfere with the cranberry laws of Indiana, the oyster laws of Virginia, or the liquor laws of Maine. I have said these things over and over again, and I repeat them here as my sentiments.

How is it, then, that Judge Douglas infers, because I hope to see slavery put where the public mind shall rest in the belief that it is in the course of ultimate extinction, that I am in favor of Illinois going over and interfering with the cranberry laws of Indiana? What can authorize him to draw any such inference? I suppose there might be one thing that at least enabled him to draw such an inference that would not be true with me or many others; that is, because he looks upon all this matter of slavery as an exceedingly little thing—this matter of keeping one sixth of the population of the whole nation in a state of oppression and tyranny unequaled in the world. He looks upon it as being an exceedingly little thing, only equal to the question of the cranberry laws of Indiana—as something having no moral question in it—as something on a par with the question of whether a man shall pasture his land with cattle or plant it with tobacco—so little and so small a thing that he concludes, if I could desire that anything should be done to bring about the ultimate extinction of that little thing, I must be in favor of bringing about an amalgamation of all the other little things in the Union. Now, it so happens—and there, I presume, is the foundation of this mistake—that the judge thinks thus; and it so happens that there is a vast portion of the American people that do not look upon that matter as being this very little thing. They look upon it as a vast moral evil; they can prove it as such by the writings of those who gave us the blessings of liberty which we enjoy, and that they so looked upon it, and not as an evil merely confining itself to the States where it is situated; and while we agree that, by the Constitution we assented to, in the States where it exists we have no right to interfere with it, because it is in the Constitution, we are by both duty and inclination to stick by that Constitution in all its letter and spirit from beginning to end.

So much, then, as to my disposition—my wish—to have all the State legislatures blotted out, and to have one consolidated government, and a uniformity of domestic regulations in all the States; by which I suppose it is meant, if we raise corn here, we must make sugarcane grow here too, and we must make those which grow North grow in the South. All this I suppose he understands I am in favor of doing. Now, so much for all this nonsense—for I must call it so. The judge can have no issue with me on a question of establishing uniformity in the domestic regulations of the States.

A little now on the other point—the Dred Scott decision. Another of the issues he says that is to be made with me, is upon his devotion to the Dred Scott decision, and my opposition to it.

I have expressed heretofore, and I now repeat, my opposition to the Dred Scott decision; but I should be allowed to state the nature of that opposition, and I ask your indulgence while I do so. What is fairly implied by the term Judge Douglas has used, "resistance to the decision"? I do not resist it. If I wanted to take Dred Scott from his master, I would be interfering with property, and that terrible difficulty that Judge Douglas speaks of, of interfering with property, would arise. But I am doing no such thing as that; all that I am doing is refusing to obey it as a political rule. If I were in Congress, and a vote should come up on a question whether slavery should be prohibited in a new Territory, in spite of the Dred Scott decision, I would vote that it should.

That is what I would do. Judge Douglas said last night that before the decision he might advance his opinion, and it might be contrary to the decision when it was made; but after it was made he would abide by it until it was reversed. Just so! We let this property abide by the decision, but we will try to reverse that decision. We will try to put it where Judge Douglas would not object, for he says he will obey it until it is reversed. Somebody has to reverse that decision, since it is made; and we mean to reverse it, and we mean to do it peaceably.

What are the uses of decisions of courts? They have two uses. As rules of property they have two uses. First — they decide the question before the court. They decide in this case that Dred Scott is a slave. Nobody resists that. Not only that, but they say to everybody else that persons standing just as Dred Scott stands are as he is. That is, they say that when a question comes up upon another person, it will be so decided again, unless the court decides in another way, unless the court overrules its decision. Well, we mean to do what we can to have the court decide the other way. That is one thing we mean to try to do.

The sacredness that Judge Douglas throws around this decision is a degree of sacredness that has never been before thrown around any other decision. I have never heard of such a thing. Why, decisions apparently contrary to that decision, or that good lawyers thought were contrary to that decision, have been made by that very court before. It is the first of its kind; it is an astonisher in legal history. It is a new wonder of the world. It is based upon falsehood in the main as to the facts,—allegations of facts upon which it stands are not facts at all in many instances,—and no decision made on any question — the first instance of a decision made under so many unfavorable circumstances — thus placed, has ever been held by the profession as law, and it has always needed confirmation before the lawyers regarded it as settled law. But Judge Douglas will have it that all hands must take this extraordinary decision, made under these extraordinary circumstances, and give their vote in Congress in accordance with it, yield to it and obey it in every possible sense. Circumstances alter cases. Do not gentlemen here remember the case of that same Supreme Court, some twenty-five or thirty years ago, deciding that a national bank was constitutional? I ask if somebody does not remember that a national bank was declared to be constitutional? Such is the truth, whether it be remembered or not. The bank charter ran out, and a recharter was granted by Congress. That recharter was laid before General Jackson. It was urged upon him, when he denied the constitutionality of the bank, that the Supreme Court had decided that it was constitutional; and General

Jackson then said that the Supreme Court had no right to lay down a rule to govern a coördinate branch of the government, the members of which had sworn to support the Constitution—that each member had sworn to support that Constitution as he understood it. I will venture here to say that I have heard Judge Douglas say that he approved of General Jackson for that act. What has now become of all his tirade against "resistance to the Supreme Court"?

My fellow-citizens, getting back a little, for I pass from these points, when Judge Douglas makes his threat of annihilation upon the "alliance," he is cautious to say that that warfare of his is to fall upon the leaders of the Republican party. Almost every word he utters, and every distinction he makes, has its significance. He means for the Republicans who do not count themselves as leaders to be his friends; he makes no fuss over them; it is the leaders that he is making war upon. He wants it understood that the mass of the Republican party are really his friends. It is only the leaders that are doing something, that are intolerant, and require extermination at his hands. As this is clearly and unquestionably the light in which he presents that matter, I want to ask your attention, addressing myself to Republicans here, that I may ask you some questions as to where you, as the Republican party, would be placed if you sustained Judge Douglas in his present position by a reëlection? I do not claim, gentlemen, to be unselfish; I do not pretend that I would not like to go to the United States Senate; I make no such hypocritical pretense, but I do say to you that in this mighty issue, it is nothing to you—nothing to the mass of the people of the nation—whether or not Judge Douglas or myself shall ever be heard of after this night; it may be a trifle to either of us, but in connection with this mighty question, upon which hang the destinies of the nation, perhaps, it is absolutely nothing. But where will you be placed if you reindorse Judge Douglas? Don't you know how apt he is—how exceedingly anxious he is at all times to seize upon anything and everything to persuade you that something he has done you did yourselves? Why, he tried to persuade you last night that our Illinois legislature instructed him to introduce the Nebraska bill. There was nobody in that legislature ever thought of such a thing; and when he first introduced the bill, he never thought of it; but still he fights furiously for the proposition, and that he did it because there was a standing instruction to our senators to be always introducing Nebraska bills. He tells you he is for the Cincinnati platform; he tells you he is for the Dred Scott decision. He tells you, not in his speech last night, but substantially in a former speech, that he cares not if slavery is voted up or down; he tells you the struggle on Lecompton is past—it may come up again or not, and if it does he stands where he stood when in spite of him and his opposition you built up the Republican party. If you indorse him, you tell him you do not care whether slavery be voted up or down, and he will close, or try to close, your mouths with his declaration, repeated by the day, the week, the month, and the year. I think, in the position in which Judge Douglas stood in opposing the Lecompton constitution, he was right; he does not know that it will return, but if it does we may know where to find him, and if it does not we may know where to look for him, and that is on the Cincinnati platform. Now I could ask the Republican party, after all the hard names Judge Douglas has called them by, all his repeated charges of their inclination to marry with and hug negroes, all his declarations of Black Republicanism,— by the way, we are improving, the black has got rubbed off,— but with all that, if he be indorsed by Republican votes, where do you stand? Plainly, you stand ready saddled, bridled, and harnessed, and waiting to be driven over to the slavery extension camp of the nation,— just ready to be driven over, tied together in a lot,— to be driven over, every man with a rope around his neck, that halter being held by Judge Douglas. That is the question. If Republican men have been in earnest in what they have done, I think they had better not do it; but I think the Republican party is made up of those who, as far as they can peaceably, will oppose the extension of slavery, and who will hope for its ultimate extinction. If they believe it is wrong in grasping up the new lands of the continent, and keeping them from the settlement of free white laborers, who want the land to bring up their families upon; if they are in earnest, although they may make a mistake, they will grow restless, and the time will come when they will come back again and reorganize, if not by the same name, at least upon the same principles as their party now has. It is better, then, to save the work while it is begun. You have done the labor; maintain it, keep it. If men choose to serve you, go with them; but as you have made up your organization upon principle, stand by it; for, as surely as God reigns over you, and has inspired your mind, and given you a sense of propriety, and continues to give you hope, so surely will you still cling to these ideas, and you will at last come back again after your wanderings, merely to do your work over again.

We were often—more than once at least—in the course of Judge Douglas's speech last night reminded that this government was made for white men—that he believed it was made for white men. Well, that is putting it into a shape in which no one wants to deny it; but the judge then goes into his passion for drawing inferences that are not warranted. I protest, now and forever, against that counterfeit logic which presumes that because I do not want a negro woman for a slave, I do necessarily want her for a wife. My understanding is that I need not have her for either; but, as God made us separate, we can leave one another alone, and do one another much good thereby. There are white men enough to marry all the white women, and enough black men to marry all the black women, and in God's name let them be so married. The judge regales us with the terrible enormities that take place by the mixture of races; that the inferior race bears the superior down. Why, judge, if we do not let them get together in the Territories, they won't mix there. [A voice: "Three cheers for Lincoln!" The cheers were given with a hearty good will.] I should say at least that that is a self-evident truth.

Now, it happens that we meet together once every year, somewhere
VOL. I.—17.

about the 4th of July, for some reason or other. These 4th of July
gatherings I suppose have their uses. If you will indulge me, I will
state what I suppose to be some of them.

We are now a mighty nation: we are thirty, or about thirty, millions of people, and we own and inhabit about one fifteenth part of
the dry land of the whole earth. We run our memory back over
the pages of history for about eighty-two years, and we discover
that we were then a very small people, in point of numbers vastly
inferior to what we are now, with a vastly less extent of country,
with vastly less of everything we deem desirable among men. We
look upon the change as exceedingly advantageous to us and to our
posterity, and we fix upon something that happened away back as
in some way or other being connected with this rise of prosperity.
We find a race of men living in that day whom we claim as our
fathers and grandfathers; they were iron men; they fought for the
principle that they were contending for; and we understood that by
what they then did it has followed that the degree of prosperity
which we now enjoy has come to us. We hold this annual celebra-
tion to remind ourselves of all the good done in this process of
time, of how it was done and who did it, and how we are historically
connected with it; and we go from these meetings in better humor
with ourselves — we feel more attached the one to the other, and
more firmly bound to the country we inhabit. In every way we are
better men, in the age, and race, and country in which we live, for
these celebrations. But after we have done all this, we have not yet
reached the whole. There is something else connected with it. We
have, besides these men — descended by blood from our ancestors —
among us, perhaps half our people who are not descendants at all
of these men; they are men who have come from Europe,— German,
Irish, French, and Scandinavian,— men that have come from Europe
themselves, or whose ancestors have come hither and settled here,
finding themselves our equal in all things. If they look back through
this history to trace their connection with those days by blood, they
find they have none; they cannot carry themselves back into that
glorious epoch and make themselves feel that they are part of us;
but when they look through that old Declaration of Independence,
they find that those old men say that "We hold these truths to be
self-evident, that all men are created equal," and then they feel that
that moral sentiment taught in that day evidences their relation to
those men, that it is the father of all moral principle in them, and
that they have a right to claim it as though they were blood of the
blood, and flesh of the flesh, of the men who wrote that Declaration,
and so they are. That is the electric cord in that Declaration that
links the hearts of patriotic and liberty-loving men together, that
will link those patriotic hearts as long as the love of freedom exists
in the minds of men throughout the world.

Now, sirs, for the purpose of squaring things with this idea of
"don't care if slavery is voted up or voted down," for sustaining
the Dred Scott decision, for holding that the Declaration of Independence did not mean anything at all, we have Judge Douglas
giving his exposition of what the Declaration of Independence

means, and we have him saying that the people of America are equal to the people of England. According to his construction, you Germans are not connected with it. Now I ask you, in all soberness, if all these things, if indulged in, if ratified, if confirmed and indorsed, if taught to our children, and repeated to them, do not tend to rub out the sentiment of liberty in the country, and to transform this government into a government of some other form? Those arguments that are made, that the inferior race are to be treated with as much allowance as they are capable of enjoying; that as much is to be done for them as their condition will allow—what are these arguments? They are the arguments that kings have made for enslaving the people in all ages of the world. You will find that all the arguments in favor of kingcraft were of this class; they always bestrode the necks of the people—not that they wanted to do it, but because the people were better off for being ridden. That is their argument, and this argument of the judge is the same old serpent that says, You work and I eat, you toil and I will enjoy the fruits of it. Turn in whatever way you will—whether it come from the mouth of a king, an excuse for enslaving the people of his country, or from the mouth of men of one race as a reason for enslaving the men of another race, it is all the same old serpent, and I hold if that course of argumentation that is made for the purpose of convincing the public mind that we should not care about this should be granted, it does not stop with the negro. I should like to know —taking this old Declaration of Independence, which declares that all men are equal upon principle, and making exceptions to it,—where will it stop? If one man says it does not mean a negro, why not another say it does not mean some other man? If that Declaration is not the truth, let us get the statute-book in which we find it, and tear it out! Who is so bold as to do it? If it is not true, let us tear it out [cries of "No, no"]. Let us stick to it, then; let us stand firmly by it, then.

It may be argued that there are certain conditions that make necessities and impose them upon us, and to the extent that a necessity is imposed upon a man, he must submit to it. I think that was the condition in which we found ourselves when we established this government. We had slaves among us; we could not get our Constitution unless we permitted them to remain in slavery; we could not secure the good we did secure if we grasped for more; but having by necessity submitted to that much, it does not destroy the principle that is the charter of our liberties. Let that charter stand as our standard.

My friend has said to me that I am a poor hand to quote Scripture. I will try it again, however. It is said in one of the admonitions of our Lord, "Be ye [therefore] perfect even as your Father which is in heaven is perfect." The Saviour, I suppose, did not expect that any human creature could be perfect as the Father in heaven; but he said, "As your Father in heaven is perfect, be ye also perfect." He set that up as a standard, and he who did most toward reaching that standard attained the highest degree of moral perfection. So I say in relation to the principle that all men are created equal, let it be as nearly reached as we can. If we cannot give freedom to every creature, let us do nothing that will impose slavery upon any other creature. Let us then turn this government back into the channel in which the framers of the Constitution originally placed it. Let us stand firmly by each other. If we do not do so, we are tending in the contrary direction that our friend Judge Douglas proposes — not intentionally — working in the traces that tend to make this one universal slave nation. He is one that runs in that direction, and as such I resist him.

My friends, I have detained you about as long as I desired to do, and I have only to say, let us discard all this quibbling about this man and the other man, this race and that race and the other race being inferior, and therefore they must be placed in an inferior position. Let us discard all these things, and unite as one people throughout this land, until we shall once more stand up declaring that all men are created equal.

My friends, I could not, without launching off upon some new topic, which would detain you too long, continue to-night. I thank you for this most extensive audience that you have furnished me to-night. I leave you, hoping that the lamp of liberty will burn in your bosoms until there shall no longer be a doubt that all men are created free and equal.

July 17, 1858.— SPEECH AT SPRINGFIELD, ILLINOIS.

Fellow-citizens: Another election, which is deemed an important one, is approaching; and, as I suppose, the Republican party will without much difficulty elect their State ticket. But in regard to the legislature, we, the Republicans, labor under some disadvantages. In the first place, we have a legislature to elect upon an apportionment of the representation made several years ago, when the proportion of the population was far greater in the South (as compared with the North) than it now is; and inasmuch as our opponents hold almost entire sway in the South, and we a correspondingly large majority in the North, the fact that we are now to be represented as we were years ago, when the population was different, is to us a very great disadvantage. We had in the year 1855, according to law, a census or enumeration of the inhabitants taken for the purpose of a new apportionment of representation. We know what a fair apportionment of representation upon that census would give us. We know that it could not, if fairly made, fail to give the Republican party from six to ten more members of the legislature than they can probably get as the law now stands. It so happened at the last session of the legislature, that our opponents, holding the control of both branches of the legislature, steadily refused to give us such an apportionment as we were rightly entitled to have upon the census already taken. The legislature steadily refused to give us such an apportionment as we were rightfully entitled to have upon the census taken of the population of the State. The legislature would pass no bill upon that subject, except such as was at least as unfair to us as the old one, and in which, in some instances, two men in the Democratic regions were allowed to go as far toward sending a member to the legislature as three were in the Republican regions. Comparison was made at the time as to representative and senatorial districts, which completely demonstrated that such was the fact. Such a bill was passed and tendered to the Republican governor for his signature; but, principally for the reasons I have stated, he withheld his approval, and the bill fell without becoming a law.

Another disadvantage under which we labor is that there are one or two Democratic senators who will be members of the next legislature, and will vote for the election of senator, who are holding over in districts in which we could, on all reasonable calculation, elect men of our own, if we only had the chance of an election. When we consider that there are but twenty-five senators in the Senate, taking two from the side where they rightfully belong, and adding them to the other, is to us a disadvantage not to be lightly regarded. Still, so it is; we have this to contend with. Perhaps there is no ground of complaint on our part. In attending to the many things involved in the last general election for president, governor, auditor, treasurer, superintendent of public instruction, members of congress, of the legislature, county officers, and so on, we allowed these things to happen by want of sufficient attention, and we have no cause to complain of our adversaries, so far as this matter is concerned. But we have some cause to complain of the refusal to give us a fair apportionment.

There is still another disadvantage under which we labor, and to which I will ask your attention. It arises out of the relative positions of the two persons who stand before the State as candidates for the Senate. Senator Douglas is of world-wide renown. All the anxious politicians of his party, or who have been of his party for years past, have been looking upon him as certainly, at no distant day, to be the President of the United States. They have seen in his round, jolly, fruitful face, post-offices, land-offices, marshalships and cabinet appointments, chargéships and foreign missions, bursting and sprouting out in wonderful exuberance, ready to be laid hold of by their greedy hands. And as they have been gazing upon this attractive picture so long, they cannot, in the little distraction that has taken place in the party, bring themselves to give up the charming hope; but with greedier anxiety they rush about him, sustain him, and give him marches, triumphal entries, and receptions beyond what even in the days of his highest prosperity they could have brought about in his favor. On the contrary, nobody has ever expected me to be President. In my poor, lean, lank face nobody has ever seen that any cabbages were sprouting out. These are disadvantages all, taken together, that the Republicans labor under. We have to fight this battle upon principle, and upon principle alone. I am, in a certain sense, made the standard-bearer in behalf of the Republicans. I was made so merely because there had to be some one so placed, I being in no wise preferable to any other one of the twenty-five, perhaps a hundred, we have in the Republican ranks. Then I say I wish it to be distinctly understood and borne in mind, that we have to fight this battle without many — perhaps without any — of the external aids which are brought to bear against us. So I hope those with whom I am surrounded have principle enough to nerve themselves for the task, and leave nothing undone that can be fairly done to bring about the right result.

After Senator Douglas left Washington, as his movements were made known by the public prints, he tarried a considerable time in the city of New York; and it was heralded that, like another Napoleon, he was lying by and framing the plan of his campaign. It was telegraphed to Washington City, and published in the "Union," that he was framing his plan for the purpose of going to Illinois to pounce upon and annihilate the treasonable and disunion speech which Lincoln had made here on the 16th of June. Now, I do suppose that the judge really spent some time in New York maturing the plan of the campaign, as his friends heralded for him. I have been able, by noting his movements since his arrival in Illinois, to discover evidences confirmatory of that allegation. I think I have been able to see what are the material points of that plan. I will, for a little while, ask your attention to some of them. What I shall point out, though not showing the whole plan, are nevertheless the main points, as I suppose.

They are not very numerous. The first is popular sovereignty. The second and third are attacks upon my speech made on the 16th of June. Out of these three points — drawing within the range of popular sovereignty the question of the Lecompton constitution — he makes his principal assault. Upon these his successive speeches are substantially one and the same. On this matter of popular sovereignty I wish to be a little careful. Auxiliary to these main points, to be sure, are their thunderings of cannon, their marching and music, their fizzle-gigs and fireworks; but I will not waste time with them. They are but the little trappings of the campaign.

Coming to the substance, the first point, "popular sovereignty." It is to be labeled upon the cars in which he travels; put upon the hacks he rides in; to be flaunted upon the arches he passes under, and the banners which wave over him. It is to be dished up in as many varieties as a French cook can produce soups from potatoes. Now, as this is so great a staple of the plan of the campaign, it is worth while to examine it carefully; and if we examine only a very little, and do not allow ourselves to be misled, we shall be able to see that the whole thing is the most arrant quixotism that was ever enacted before a community. What is the matter of popular sovereignty? The first thing, in order to understand it, is to get a good definition of what it is, and after that to see how it is applied.

I suppose almost every one knows that, in this controversy, whatever has been said has had reference to the question of negro slavery. We have not been in a controversy about the right of the people to govern themselves in the ordinary matters of domestic concern in the States and Territories. Mr. Buchanan, in one of his late messages (I think when he sent up the Lecompton constitution), urged that the main point of public attention was not in regard to the great variety of small domestic matters, but was directed to the question of negro slavery; and he asserts that if the people had had a fair chance to vote on that question, there was no reasonable ground of objection in regard to minor questions. Now, while I think that the people had not had given, or offered them, a fair chance upon that slavery question, still, if there had been a fair submission to a vote upon that main question, the President's proposition would have been true to the uttermost. Hence, when hereafter I speak of popular sovereignty, I wish to be understood as applying what I say to the question of slavery only, not to other minor domestic matters of a Territory or a State.

Does Judge Douglas, when he says that several of the past years of his life have been devoted to the question of "popular sovereignty," and that all the remainder of his life shall be devoted to it, does he mean to say that he has been devoting his life to securing to the people of the Territories the right to exclude slavery from the Territories? If he means so to say, he means to deceive; because he and every one knows that the decision of the Supreme Court, which he approves and makes especial ground of attack upon me for disapproving, forbids the people of a Territory to exclude slavery. This covers the whole ground, from the settlement of a Territory till it reaches the degree of maturity entitling it to form a State constitution. So far as all that ground is concerned, the judge is not sustaining popular sovereignty, but absolutely opposing it. He sustains the decision which declares that the popular will of the Territories has no constitutional power to exclude slavery during their territorial existence. This being so, the period of time from the first settlement of a Territory till it reaches the point of forming a State constitution is not the thing that the judge has fought for, or is fighting for; but on the contrary, he has fought for, and is fighting for the thing that annihilates and crushes out that same popular sovereignty.

Well, so much being disposed of, what is left? Why, he is contending for the right of the people, when they come to make a State constitution, to make it for themselves, and precisely as best suits themselves. I say again, that is quixotic. I defy contradiction when I declare that the judge can find no one to oppose him on that proposition. I repeat, there is nobody opposing that proposition on principle. Let me not be misunderstood. I know that, with reference to the Lecompton constitution, I may be misunderstood; but when you understand me correctly, my proposition will be true and accurate. Nobody is opposing, or has opposed, the right of the people, when they form a constitution, to form it for themselves. Mr. Buchanan and his friends have not done it; they, too, as well as the Republicans and the Anti-Lecompton Democrats, have not done it; but, on the contrary, they together have insisted on the right of the people to form a constitution for themselves. The difference between the Buchanan men on the one hand, and the Douglas men and the Republicans on the other, has not been on a question of principle, but on a question of fact.

The dispute was upon the question of fact, whether the Lecompton constitution had been fairly formed by the people or not. Mr.

Buchanan and his friends have not contended for the contrary principle any more than the Douglas men or the Republicans. They have insisted that whatever of small irregularities existed in getting up the Lecompton constitution were such as happen in the settlement of all new Territories. The question was, was it a fair emanation of the people? It was a question of fact and not of principle. As to the principle, all were agreed. Judge Douglas voted with the Republicans upon that matter of fact.

He and they, by their voices and votes, denied that it was a fair emanation of the people. The administration affirmed that it was. With respect to the evidence bearing upon that question of fact, I readily agree that Judge Douglas and the Republicans had the right on their side, and that the administration was wrong. But I state again that, as a matter of principle, there is no dispute upon the right of a people in a Territory merging into a State to form a constitution for themselves without outside interference from any quarter. This being so, what is Judge Douglas going to spend his life for? Does he expect to stand up in majestic dignity, and go through his *apotheosis* and become a god, in the maintaining of a principle which neither man nor mouse in all God's creation is opposing? Now something in regard to the Lecompton constitution more specially; for I pass from this other question of popular sovereignty as the most arrant humbug that has ever been attempted on an intelligent community.

As to the Lecompton constitution, I have already said that on the question of fact as to whether it was a fair emanation of the people or not, Judge Douglas with the Republicans and some "Americans" had greatly the argument against the administration; and while I repeat this, I wish to know what there is in the opposition of Judge Douglas to the Lecompton constitution that entitles him to be considered the only opponent to it — as being *par excellence* the very quintessence of that opposition. I agree to the rightfulness of his opposition. He in the Senate, and his class of men there, formed the number three and no more. In the House of Representatives his class of men — the Anti-Lecompton Democrats — formed a number of about twenty. It took one hundred and twenty to defeat the measure, against one hundred and twelve. Of the votes of that one hundred and twenty, Judge Douglas's friends furnished twenty, to add to which there were six Americans and ninety-four Republicans. I do not say that I am precisely accurate in their numbers, but I am sufficiently so for any use I am making of it.

Why is it that twenty shall be entitled to all the credit of doing that work, and the hundred none of it? Why, if, as Judge Douglas says, the honor is to be divided and due credit is to be given to other parties, why is just so much given as is consonant with the wishes, the interests, and advancement of the twenty? My understanding is, when a common job is done, or a common enterprise prosecuted, if I put in five dollars to your one, I have a right to take out five dollars to your one. But he does not so understand it. He declares the dividend of credit for defeating Lecompton upon a basis which seems unprecedented and incomprehensible.

Let us see. Lecompton in the raw was defeated. It afterward took a sort of cooked-up shape, and was passed in the English bill. It is said by the judge that the defeat was a good and proper thing. If it was a good thing, why is he entitled to more credit than others for the performance of that good act, unless there was something in the antecedents of the Republicans that might induce every one to expect them to join in that good work, and at the same time something leading them to doubt that he would? Does he place his superior claim to credit on the ground that he performed a good act which was never expected of him? He says I have a proneness for quoting scripture. If I should do so now, it occurs that perhaps he places himself somewhat upon the ground of the parable of the lost sheep which went astray upon the mountains, and when the owner of the hundred sheep found the one that was lost, and threw it upon his shoulders, and came home rejoicing, it was said that there was more rejoicing over the one sheep that was lost and had been found, than over the ninety and nine in the fold. The application is made by the Saviour in this parable, thus: "Verily, I say unto you, there is more rejoicing in heaven over one sinner that repenteth, than over ninety and nine just persons that need no repentance."

And now, if the judge claims the benefit of this parable, let him repent. Let him not come up here and say: "I am the only just person; and you are the ninety-nine sinners!" Repentance before forgiveness is a provision of the Christian system, and on that condition alone will the Republicans grant him forgiveness.

How will he prove that we have ever occupied a different position in regard to the Lecompton constitution or any principle in it? He says he did not make his opposition on the ground as to whether it was a free or slave constitution, and he would have you understand that the Republicans made their opposition because it ultimately became a slave constitution. To make proof in favor of himself on this point, he reminds us that he opposed Lecompton before the vote was taken declaring whether the State was to be free or slave. But he forgets to say that our Republican senator, Trumbull, made a speech against Lecompton even before he did.

Why did he oppose it? Partly, as he declares, because the members of the convention who framed it were not fairly elected by the people; that the people were not allowed to vote unless they had been registered; and that the people of whole counties, in some instances, were not registered. For these reasons he declares the constitution was not an emanation, in any true sense, from the people. He also has an additional objection as to the mode of submitting the constitution back to the people. But bearing on the question of whether the delegates were fairly elected, a speech of his, made something more than twelve months ago from this stand, becomes important. It was made a little while before the election of the delegates who made Lecompton. In that speech he declared there was every reason to hope and believe the election would be fair, and if any one failed to vote it would be his own culpable fault.

I, a few days after, made a sort of answer to that speech. In that answer I made substantially the very argument with which he combated his Lecompton adversaries in the Senate last winter. I pointed to the facts that the people could not vote without being registered, and that the time for registering had gone by. I commented on it as wonderful that Judge Douglas could be ignorant of these facts, which every one else in the nation so well knew.

I now pass from popular sovereignty and Lecompton. I may have occasion to refer to one or both.

When he was preparing his plan of campaign, Napoleon-like, in New York, as appears by two speeches I have heard him deliver since his arrival in Illinois, he gave special attention to a speech of mine delivered here on the 16th of June last. He says that he carefully read that speech. He told us that at Chicago a week ago last night, and he repeated it at Bloomington last night. Doubtless he repeated it again to-day, though I did not hear him. In the two first places— Chicago and Bloomington— I heard him; to-day I did not. He said he had carefully examined that speech; when, he did not say; but there is no reasonable doubt it was when he was in New York preparing his plan of campaign. I am glad he did read it carefully. He says it was evidently prepared with great care. I freely admit it was prepared with care. I claim not to be more free from errors than others— perhaps scarcely so much; but I was very careful not to put anything in that speech as a matter of fact, or make any inferences which did not appear to me to be true and fully warrantable. If I had made any mistake I was willing to be corrected; if I had drawn any inference in regard to Judge Douglas, or any one else, which was not warranted, I was fully prepared to modify it as soon as discovered. I planted myself upon the truth and the truth only, so far as I knew it, or could be brought to know it.

Having made that speech with the most kindly feelings toward Judge Douglas, as manifested therein, I was gratified when I found that he had carefully examined it, and had detected no error of fact, nor any inference against him, nor any misrepresentations, of which he thought fit to complain. In neither of the two speeches I have mentioned, did he make any such complaint. I will thank any one who will inform me that he, in his speech to-day, pointed out anything I had stated, respecting him, as being erroneous. I presume there is no such thing. I have reason to be gratified that the care and caution used in that speech left it so that he, most of all others interested in discovering error, has not been able to point out one thing against him which he could say was wrong. He seizes upon the doctrines he supposes to be included in that speech, and declares that upon them will turn the issues of the campaign. He then quotes, or attempts to quote, from my speech. I will not say that he wilfully misquotes, but he does fail to quote accurately. His attempt at quoting is from a passage which I believe I can quote accurately from memory. I shall make the quotation now, with some comments upon it, as I have already said, in order that the judge shall be left entirely without excuse for misrepresenting me. I do so now, as I hope, for the last time. I do this in great caution, in order that if he repeats his misrepresentation, it shall be plain to all that he does so wilfully. If, after all, he still persists, I shall be compelled to reconstruct the course I have marked out for myself, and draw upon such humble resources as I have for a new course, better suited to the real exigencies of the case. I set out, in this campaign, with the intention of conducting it strictly as a gentleman, in substance at least, if not in the outside polish. The latter I shall never be, but that which constitutes the inside of a gentleman I hope I understand, and am not less inclined to practise than others. It was my purpose and expectation that this canvass would be conducted upon principle, and with fairness on both sides, and it shall not be my fault if this purpose and expectation shall be given up.

He charges, in substance, that I invite a war of sections; that I propose all local institutions of the different States shall become consolidated and uniform. What is there in the language of that speech which expresses such purpose or bears such construction? I have again and again said that I would not enter into any of the States to disturb the institution of slavery. Judge Douglas said, at Bloomington, that I used language most able and ingenious for concealing what I really meant; and that while I had protested against entering into the slave States, I nevertheless did mean to go on the banks of the Ohio and throw missiles into Kentucky, to disturb them in their domestic institutions.

I said in that speech, and I meant no more, that the institution of slavery ought to be placed in the very attitude where the framers of this government placed it and left it. I do not understand that the framers of our Constitution left the people in the free States in the attitude of firing bombs or shells into the slave States. I was not using that passage for the purpose for which he infers I did use it. I said:

We are now far advanced into the fifth year since a policy was created for the avowed object and with the confident promise of putting an end to slavery agitation. Under the operation of that policy that agitation has not only ceased, but has constantly augmented. In my opinion it will not cease till a crisis shall have been reached and passed. "A house divided against itself cannot stand." I believe that this government cannot endure permanently half slave and half free. It will become all one thing or all the other. Either the opponents of slavery will arrest the further spread of it, and place it where the public mind shall rest in the belief that it is in the course of ultimate extinction, or its advocates will push it forward till it shall become alike lawful in all the States, old as well as new, North as well as South.

Now you all see, from that quotation, I did not express my wish on anything. In that passage I indicated no wish or purpose of my own; I simply expressed my expectation. Cannot the judge perceive a distinction between a purpose and an expectation? I have often expressed an expectation to die, but I have never expressed a wish to die. I said at Chicago, and now repeat, that I am quite aware this government has endured half slave and half free for eighty-two years. I understand that little bit of history. I expressed the opinion I did, because I perceived — or thought I perceived — a new set of causes introduced. I did say at Chicago, in my speech there, that I do wish to see the spread of slavery arrested, and to see it placed where the public mind shall rest in the belief that it is in the course of ultimate extinction. I said that because I supposed, when the public mind shall rest in that belief, we shall have peace on the slavery question. I have believed—and now believe—the public mind did rest in that belief up to the introduction of the Nebraska bill.

Although I have ever been opposed to slavery, so far I rested in the hope and belief that it was in the course of ultimate extinction. For that reason, it had been a minor question with me. I might have been mistaken; but I had believed, and now believe, that the whole public mind, that is, the mind of the great majority, had rested in that belief up to the repeal of the Missouri Compromise. But upon that event, I became convinced that either I had been resting in a delusion, or the institution was being placed on a new basis—a basis for making it perpetual, national, and universal. Subsequent events have greatly confirmed me in that belief. I believe that bill to be the beginning of a conspiracy for that purpose. So believing, I have since then considered that question a paramount one. So believing, I think the public mind will never rest till the power of Congress to restrict the spread of it shall again be acknowledged and exercised on the one hand, or, on the other, all resistance be entirely crushed out. I have expressed that opinion, and I entertain it to-night. It is denied that there is any tendency to the nationalization of slavery in these States.

Mr. Brooks, of South Carolina, in one of his speeches, when they were presenting him canes, silver plate, gold pitchers and the like, for assaulting Senator Sumner, distinctly affirmed his opinion that when this Constitution was formed, it was the belief of no man that slavery would last to the present day.

He said, what I think, that the framers of our Constitution placed the institution of slavery where the public mind rested in the hope that it was in the course of ultimate extinction. But he went on to say that the men of the present age, by their experience, have become wiser than the framers of the Constitution; and the invention of the cotton-gin had made the perpetuity of slavery a necessity in this country.

As another piece of evidence tending to this same point. Quite recently in Virginia, a man—the owner of slaves—made a will providing that after his death certain of his slaves should have their freedom if they should so choose, and go to Liberia, rather than remain in slavery. They chose to be liberated. But the persons to whom they would descend as property claimed them as slaves. A suit was instituted, which finally came to the Supreme Court of Virginia, and was therein decided against the slaves, upon the ground that a negro cannot make a choice—that they had no legal power to choose—could not perform the condition upon which their freedom depended.

I do not mention this with any purpose of criticizing it, but to connect it with the arguments as affording additional evidence of the change of sentiment upon this question of slavery in the direction of making it perpetual and national. I argue now as I did before, that there is such a tendency, and I am backed not merely by the facts, but by the open confession in the slave States.

And now, as to the judge's inference, that because I wish to see slavery placed in the course of ultimate extinction — placed where our fathers originally placed it — I wish to annihilate the State legislatures — to force cotton to grow upon the tops of the Green Mountains — to freeze ice in Florida — to cut lumber on the broad Illinois prairies — that I am in favor of all these ridiculous and impossible things.

It seems to me it is a complete answer to all this to ask, if, when Congress did have the fashion of restricting slavery from free territory, when courts did have the fashion of deciding that taking a slave into a free country made him free — I say it is a sufficient answer to ask, if any of this ridiculous nonsense about consolidation and uniformity did actually follow? Who heard of any such thing, because of the ordinance of '87? because of the Missouri Restriction? because of the numerous court decisions of that character?

Now, as to the Dred Scott decision; for upon that he makes his last point at me. He boldly takes ground in favor of that decision. This is one half the onslaught, and one third of the entire plan of the campaign. I am opposed to that decision in a certain sense, but not in the sense which he puts on it. I say that in so far as it decided in favor of Dred Scott's master, and against Dred Scott and his family, I do not propose to disturb or resist the decision.

I never have proposed to do any such thing. I think that in respect for judicial authority, my humble history would not suffer in comparison with that of Judge Douglas. He would have the citizen conform his vote to that decision; the member of Congress, his; the President, his use of the veto power. He would make it a rule of political action for the people and all the departments of the government. I would not. By resisting it as a political rule, I disturb no right of property, create no disorder, excite no mobs.

When he spoke at Chicago, on Friday evening of last week, he made this same point upon me. On Saturday evening I replied, and reminded him of a Supreme Court decision which he opposed for at least several years. Last night, at Bloomington, he took some notice of that reply, but entirely forgot to remember that part of it.

He renews his onslaught upon me, forgetting to remember that I have turned the tables against himself on that very point. I renew the effort to draw his attention to it. I wish to stand erect before the country, as well as Judge Douglas, on this question of judicial authority, and therefore I add something to the authority in favor of my own position. I wish to show that I am sustained by authority, in addition to that heretofore presented. I do not expect to convince the judge. It is part of the plan of his campaign, and he will cling to it with a desperate grip. Even turn it upon him — the sharp point against him, and gaff him through — he will still cling to it till he can invent some new dodge to take the place of it.

In public speaking it is tedious reading from documents, but I must beg to indulge the practice to a limited extent. I shall read from a letter written by Mr. Jefferson in 1820, and now to be found in the seventh volume of his correspondence, at page 177. It seems he had been presented by a gentleman of the name of Jarvis with a book, or essay, or periodical, called the "Republican," and he was writing in acknowledgment of the present, and noting some of its contents. After expressing the hope that the work will produce a favorable effect upon the minds of the young, he proceeds to say:

That it will have this tendency may be expected, and for that reason I feel an urgency to note what I deem an error in it, the more requiring notice as your opinion is strengthened by that of many others. You seem, in pages 84 and 148, to consider the judges as the ultimate arbiters of all constitutional questions — a very dangerous doctrine indeed, and one which would place us under the despotism of an oligarchy. Our judges are as honest as other men, and not more so. They have, with others, the same passions for party, for power, and the privilege of their corps. Their maxim is, "*Boni judicis est ampliare jurisdictionem*"; and their power is the more dangerous as they are in office for life, and not responsible, as the other functionaries are, to the elective control. The Constitution has erected no such single tribunal, knowing that, to whatever hands confided, with the corruptions of time and party, its members would become despots. It has more wisely made all the departments co-equal and co-sovereign within themselves.

Thus we see the power claimed for the Supreme Court by Judge Douglas, Mr. Jefferson holds, would reduce us to the despotism of an oligarchy.

Now, I have said no more than this—in fact, never quite so much as this—at least I am sustained by Mr. Jefferson.

Let us go a little further. You remember we once had a national bank. Some one owed the bank a debt; he was sued and sought to avoid payment, on the ground that the bank was unconstitutional. The case went to the Supreme Court, and therein it was decided that the bank was constitutional. The whole Democratic party revolted against that decision. General Jackson himself asserted that he, as President, would not be bound to hold a national bank to be constitutional, even though the court had decided it to be so. He fell in precisely with the view of Mr. Jefferson, and acted upon it under his official oath, in vetoing a charter for a national bank. The declaration that Congress does not possess this constitutional power to charter a bank, has gone into the Democratic platform, at their national conventions, and was brought forward and reaffirmed in their last convention at Cincinnati. They have contended for that declaration, in the very teeth of the Supreme Court, for more than a quarter of a century. In fact, they have reduced the decision to an absolute nullity. That decision, I repeat, is repudiated in the Cincinnati platform; and still, as if to show that effrontery can go no farther, Judge Douglas vaunts, in the very speeches in which he denounces me for opposing the Dred Scott decision, that he stands on the Cincinnati platform.

Now, I wish to know what the judge can charge upon me, with respect to decisions of the Supreme Court, which does not lie in all its length, breadth, and proportions at his own door. The plain truth is simply this: Judge Douglas is for Supreme Court decisions when he likes, and against them when he does not like them. He is for the Dred Scott decision because it tends to nationalize slavery — because it is part of the original combination for that object. It so happens, singularly enough, that I never stood opposed to a decision of the Supreme Court till this. On the contrary, I have no recollection that he was ever particularly in favor of one till this. He never was in favor of any, nor opposed to any, till the present one, which helps to nationalize slavery.

Free men of Sangamon, free men of Illinois, free men everywhere, judge ye between him and me upon this issue.

He says this Dred Scott case is a very small matter at most; that it has no practical effect; that at best, or rather, I suppose, at worst, it is but an abstraction. I submit that the proposition that the thing which determines whether a man is free or a slave is rather concrete than abstract. I think you would conclude that it was if your liberty depended upon it, and so would Judge Douglas if his liberty depended upon it. But suppose it was on the question of spreading slavery over the new Territories that he considers it as being merely an abstract matter, and one of no practical importance. How has the planting of slavery in new countries always been effected? It has now been decided that slavery cannot be kept out of our new Territories by any legal means. In what do our new Territories now differ in this respect from the old colonies when slavery was first planted within them? It was planted as Mr. Clay once declared, and as history proves true, by individual men in spite of the wishes of the people; the mother government refusing to prohibit it, and withholding from the people of the colonies the authority to prohibit it for themselves. Mr. Clay says this was one of the great and just causes of complaint against Great Britain by the colonies, and the best apology we can now make for having the institution amongst us. In that precise condition our Nebraska politicians have at last succeeded in placing our own new Territories; the government will not prohibit slavery within them, nor allow the people to prohibit it.

I defy any man to find any difference between the policy which originally planted slavery in these colonies and that policy which now prevails in our new Territories. If it does not go into them, it is only because no individual wishes it to go. The judge indulged himself doubtless, to-day, with the question as to what I am going to do with or about the Dred Scott decision. Well, judge, will you please tell me what you did about the bank decision? Will you not graciously allow us to do with the Dred Scott decision precisely as you did with the bank decision? You succeeded in breaking down the moral effect of that decision; did you find it necessary to amend the Constitution? or to set up a court of negroes in order to do it?

There is one other point. Judge Douglas has a very affectionate leaning toward the Americans and Old Whigs. Last evening, in a sort of weeping tone, he described to us a death-bed scene. He had been called to the side of Mr. Clay, in his last moments, in order that the genius of "popular sovereignty" might duly descend from the dying man and settle upon him, the living and most worthy successor. He could do no less than promise that he would devote the remainder of his life to "popular sovereignty"; and then the great statesman departs in peace. By this part of the "plan of the campaign," the judge has evidently promised himself that tears shall be drawn down the cheeks of all Old Whigs, as large as half-grown apples.

Mr. Webster, too, was mentioned; but it did not quite come to a death-bed scene, as to him. It would be amusing, if it were not disgusting, to see how quick these compromise-breakers administer on the political effects of their dead adversaries, trumping up claims never before heard of, and dividing the assets among themselves. If I should be found dead to-morrow morning, nothing but my insignificance could prevent a speech being made on my authority, before the end of next week. It so happens that in that "popular sovereignty" with which Mr. Clay was identified, the Missouri Compromise was expressly reserved; and it was a little singular if Mr. Clay cast his mantle upon Judge Douglas on purpose to have that compromise repealed.

Again, the judge did not keep faith with Mr. Clay when he first brought in his Nebraska bill. He left the Missouri Compromise unrepealed, and in his report accompanying the bill, he told the world he did it on purpose. The manes of Mr. Clay must have been in great agony, till thirty days later, when "popular sovereignty" stood forth in all its glory.

One more thing. Last night Judge Douglas tormented himself with horrors about my disposition to make negroes perfectly equal with white men in social and political relations. He did not stop to show that I have said any such thing, or that it legitimately follows from anything I have said, but he rushes on with his assertions. I adhere to the Declaration of Independence. If Judge Douglas and his friends are not willing to stand by it, let them come up and amend it. Let them make it read that all men are created equal, except negroes. Let us have it decided whether the Declaration of Independence, in this blessed year of 1858, shall be thus amended. In his construction of the Declaration last year, he said it only meant that Americans in America were equal to Englishmen in England. Then, when I pointed out to him that by that rule he excludes the Germans, the Irish, the Portuguese, and all the other people who have come amongst us since the Revolution, he reconstructs his construction. In his last speech he tells us it meant Europeans.

I press him a little further, and ask if it meant to include the Russians in Asia? or does he mean to exclude that vast population from the principles of our Declaration of Independence? I expect ere long he will introduce another amendment to his definition. He is not at all particular. He is satisfied with anything which does not endanger the nationalizing of negro slavery. It may draw white men down, but it must not lift negroes up. Who shall say, "I am the superior, and you are the inferior?"

My declarations upon this subject of negro slavery may be misrepresented, but cannot be misunderstood. I have said that I do not understand the Declaration to mean that all men were created equal in all respects. They are not our equal in color; but I suppose that it does mean to declare that all men are equal in some respects; they are equal in their right to "life, liberty, and the pursuit of happiness." Certainly the negro is not our equal in color—

perhaps not in many other respects; still, in the right to put into his mouth the bread that his own hands have earned, he is the equal of every other man, white or black. In pointing out that more has been given you, you cannot be justified in taking away the little which has been given him. All I ask for the negro is that if you do not like him, let him alone. If God gave him but little, that little let him enjoy.

When our government was established, we had the institution of slavery among us. We were in a certain sense compelled to tolerate its existence. It was a sort of necessity. We had gone through our struggle, and secured our own independence. The framers of the Constitution found the institution of slavery amongst their other institutions at the time. They found that by an effort to eradicate it, they might lose much of what they had already gained. They were obliged to bow to the necessity. They gave power to Congress to abolish the slave-trade at the end of twenty years. They also prohibited slavery in the Territories where it did not exist. They did what they could and yielded to necessity for the rest. I also yield to all which follows from that necessity. What I would most desire would be the separation of the white and black races.

One more point on this Springfield speech which Judge Douglas says he has read so carefully. I expressed my belief in the existence of a conspiracy to perpetuate and nationalize slavery. I did not profess to know it, nor do I now. I showed the part Judge Douglas had played in the string of facts, constituting to my mind the proof of that conspiracy. I showed the parts played by others.

I charged that the people had been deceived into carrying the last presidential election, by the impression that the people of the Territories might exclude slavery if they chose, when it was known in advance by the conspirators, that the court was to decide that neither Congress nor the people could so exclude slavery. These charges are more distinctly made than anything else in the speech.

Judge Douglas has carefully read and re-read that speech. He has not, so far as I know, contradicted those charges. In the two speeches which I heard he certainly did not. On his own tacit admission I renew that charge. I charge him with having been a party to that conspiracy, and to that deception, for the sole purpose of nationalizing slavery.

July 24 to July 31, 1858.—CHALLENGE TO THE JOINT DEBATES.

Mr. Lincoln to Mr. Douglas.

CHICAGO, ILLINOIS, July 24, 1858.

HON. S. A. DOUGLAS.

My dear Sir: Will it be agreeable to you to make an arrangement for you and myself to divide time, and address the same audiences the present canvass? Mr. Judd, who will hand you this, is authorized to receive your answer; and, if agreeable to you, to enter into the terms of such arrangement. Your obedient servant,

A. LINCOLN.

VOL. I.—18.

Mr. Douglas to Mr. Lincoln.

CHICAGO, July 24, 1858.

HON. A. LINCOLN.

Dear Sir : Your note of this date, in which you inquire if it would be agreeable to me to make an arrangement to divide the time and address the same audiences during the present canvass, was handed me by Mr. Judd. Recent events have interposed difficulties in the way of such an arrangement.

I went to Springfield last week for the purpose of conferring with the Democratic State Central Committee upon the mode of conducting the canvass, and with them, and under their advice, made a list of appointments covering the entire period until late in October. The people of the several localities have been notified of the times and places of the meetings. Those appointments have all been made for Democratic meetings, and arrangements have been made by which the Democratic candidates for Congress, for the legislature, and other offices will be present and address the people. It is evident, therefore, that these various candidates, in connection with myself, will occupy the whole time of the day and evening, and leave no opportunity for other speeches.

Besides, there is another consideration which should be kept in mind. It has been suggested recently that an arrangement had been made to bring out a third candidate for the United States Senate, who, with yourself, should canvass the State in opposition to me, with no other purpose than to insure my defeat, by dividing the Democratic party for your benefit. If I should make this arrangement with you, it is more than probable that this other candidate, who has a common object with you, would desire to become a party to it, and claim the right to speak from the same stand; so that he and you in concert might be able to take the opening and closing speech in every case.

I cannot refrain from expressing my surprise, if it was your original intention to invite such an arrangement, that you should have waited until after I had made my appointments, inasmuch as we were both here in Chicago together for several days after my arrival, and again at Bloomington, Atlanta, Lincoln, and Springfield, where it was well known I went for the purpose of consulting with the State Central Committee, and agreeing upon the plan of the campaign.

While under these circumstances I do not feel at liberty to make any arrangements which would deprive the Democratic candidates for Congress, State offices, and the legislature, from participating in the discussion at the various meetings designated by the Democratic State Central Committee, I will, in order to accommodate you as far as it is in my power to do so, take the responsibility of making an arrangement with you for a discussion between us at one prominent point in each congressional district in the State, except the second and sixth districts, where we have both spoken, and in each of which cases you had the concluding speech. If agreeable to you, I will indicate the following places as those most suitable in the several congressional districts at which we should speak, to wit: Freeport, Ottawa, Galesburg, Quincy, Alton, Jonesboro, and Charleston. I will confer with you at the earliest convenient opportunity in regard to the mode of conducting the debate, the times of meeting at the several places, subject to the condition that where appointments have already been made by the Democratic State Central Committee at any of those places, I must insist upon you meeting me at the time specified. Very respectfully, your most obedient servant,

S. A. DOUGLAS.

Mr. Lincoln to Mr. Douglas.

SPRINGFIELD, July 29, 1858.

HON. S. A. DOUGLAS.

Dear Sir : Yours of the 24th in relation to an arrangement to divide time and address the same audiences is received; and in apology for not sooner replying, allow me to say that when I sat by you at dinner yesterday I was not aware that you had answered my note, nor certainly that my own note had been presented to you. An hour after I saw a copy of your answer in the Chicago "Times," and reaching home, I found the original awaiting me. Protesting that your insinuations of attempted unfairness on my part are unjust, and with the hope that you did not very considerately make them, I proceed to reply. To your statement that " It has been suggested recently that an arrangement had been made to bring out a third candidate for the United States Senate, who, with yourself, should canvass the State in opposition to me," etc., I can only say that such suggestion must have been made by yourself, for certainly none such has been made by or to me, or otherwise, to my knowledge. Surely you did not deliberately conclude, as you insinuate, that I was expecting to draw you into an arrangement of terms, to be agreed on by yourself, by which a third candidate and myself " in concert might be able to take the opening and closing speech in every case."

As to your surprise that I did not sooner make the proposal to divide time with you, I can only say I made it as soon as I resolved to make it. I did not know but that such proposal would come from you; I waited respectfully to see. It may have been well known to you that you went to Springfield for the purpose of agreeing on the plan of campaign; but it was not so known to me. When your appointments were announced in the papers, extending only to the 21st of August, I for the first time considered it certain that you would make no proposal to me, and then resolved that, if my friends concurred, I would make one to you. As soon thereafter as I could see and consult with friends satisfactorily, I did make the proposal. It did not occur to me that the proposed arrangement could derange your plans after the latest of your appointments already made. After that, there was before the election largely over two months of clear time.

For you to say that we have already spoken at Chicago and Springfield, and that on both occasions I had the concluding speech, is hardly a fair statement. The truth rather is this: At Chicago, July 9, you made a carefully prepared conclusion on my speech of June 16. Twenty-four hours after, I made a hasty conclusion on yours of the 9th. You had six days to prepare, and concluded on me again at Bloomington on the 16th. Twenty-four hours after, I concluded again on you at Springfield. In the mean time, you had made another conclusion on me at Springfield which I did not hear, and of the contents of which I knew nothing when I spoke; so that your speech made in daylight, and mine at night, of the 17th, at Springfield, were both made in perfect independence of each other. The dates of making all these speeches will show, I think, that in the matter of time for preparation the advantage has all been on your side, and that none of the external circumstances have stood to my advantage.

I agree to an arrangement for us to speak at the seven places you have named, and at your own times, provided you name the times at once, so that I, as well as you, can have to myself the time not covered by the arrangement. As to the other details, I wish perfect reciprocity, and no more. I wish as much time as you, and that conclusions shall alternate. That is all. Your obedient servant,

A. LINCOLN.

P. S. As matters now stand, I shall be at no more of your exclusive meetings; and for about a week from to-day a letter from you will reach me at Springfield.

A. L.

Mr. Douglas to Mr. Lincoln.

BEMENT, PIATT CO., ILL., July 30, 1858.

Dear Sir : Your letter dated yesterday, accepting my proposition for a joint discussion at one prominent point in each congressional district, as stated in my previous letter, was received this morning. The times and places designated are as follows:

Ottawa, La Salle County.....................August	21,	1858.
Freeport, Stephenson County................. "	27,	"
Jonesboro, Union County....................September	15,	"
Charleston, Coles County .... "	18,	"
Galesburg, Knox County....................October	7,	"
Quincy, Adams County....................... "	13,	"
Alton, Madison County .... "	15,	"

I agree to your suggestion that we shall alternately open and close the discussion. I will speak at Ottawa one hour; you can reply, occupying an hour and a half, and I will then follow for half an hour. At Freeport, you shall open the discussion and speak one hour; I will follow for an hour and a half, and you can then reply for half an hour. We will alternate in like manner in each successive place. Very respectfully, your obedient servant,

S. A. DOUGLAS.

HON. A. LINCOLN, Springfield, Ill.

Mr. Lincoln to Mr. Douglas.

SPRINGFIELD, July 31, 1858.

HON. S. A. DOUGLAS.

Dear Sir: Yours of yesterday, naming places, times, and terms for joint discussions between us, was received this morning. Although by the terms, as you propose, you take four openings and closes to my three, I accede, and thus close the arrangement. I direct this to you at Hillsboro, and shall try to have both your letter and this appear in the " Journal" and " Register" of Monday morning.   Your obedient servant,

A. LINCOLN.

July 31, 1858.— LETTER TO H. ASBURY.

SPRINGFIELD, July 31, 1858.

HENRY ASBURY, Esq.

My dear Sir: Yours of the 28th is received. The points you propose to press upon Douglas he will be very hard to get up to, but I think you labor under a mistake when you say no one cares how he answers. This implies that it is equal with him whether he is injured here or at the South. That is a mistake. He cares nothing for the South; he knows he is already dead there. He only leans Southward more to keep the Buchanan party from growing in Illinois. You shall have hard work to get him directly to the point whether a territorial legislature has or has not the power to exclude slavery. But if you succeed in bringing him to it— though he will be compelled to say it possesses no such power — he will instantly take ground that slavery cannot actually exist in the Territories unless the people desire it, and so give it protection by territorial legislation. If this offends the South, he will let it offend them, as at all events he means to hold on to his chances in Illinois. You will soon learn by the papers that both the judge and myself are to be in Quincy on the 13th of October, when and where I expect the pleasure of seeing you. Yours very truly,

A. LINCOLN.

August 21, 1858.— FIRST JOINT DEBATE, AT OTTAWA, ILLINOIS.

Mr. Douglas's Opening Speech.

Ladies and Gentlemen: I appear before you to-day for the purpose of discussing the leading political topics which now agitate the public mind. By an arrangement between Mr. Lincoln and myself, we are present here to-day for the purpose of having a joint discussion, as the representatives of the two great political parties of the State and Union, upon the principles in issue between those parties; and this vast concourse of people shows the deep feeling which pervades the public mind in regard to the questions dividing us.

Prior to 1854 this country was divided into two great political parties, known as the Whig and Democratic parties. Both were national and patriotic, advocating principles that were universal in their application. An old-line Whig could proclaim his principles in Louisiana and Massachusetts alike. Whig principles had no boundary sectional line — they were not limited by the Ohio River, nor by the Potomac, nor by the line of the free and slave States, but applied and were proclaimed wherever the Constitution ruled or the American flag waved over the American soil. So it was, and so it is with the great Democratic party, which, from the days of Jefferson until this period, has proven itself to be the historic party of this nation. While the Whig and Democratic parties differed in regard to a bank, the tariff, distribution, the specie circular, and the subtreasury, they agreed on the great slavery question which now agitates the Union. I say that the Whig party and the Democratic party agreed on the slavery question, while they differed on those matters of expediency to which I have referred. The Whig party and the Democratic party jointly adopted the compromise measures of 1850 as the basis of a proper and just solution of the slavery question in all its forms. Clay was the great leader, with Webster on his right and Cass on his left, and sustained by the patriots in the Whig and Democratic ranks who had devised and enacted the compromise measures of 1850.

In 1851 the Whig party and the Democratic party united in Illinois in adopting resolutions indorsing and approving the principles of the compromise measures of 1850, as the proper adjustment of that question. In 1852, when the Whig party assembled in convention at Baltimore for the purpose of nominating a candidate for the presidency, the first thing it did was to declare the compromise measures of 1850, in substance and in principle, a suitable adjustment of that question. [Here the speaker was interrupted by loud and long-continued applause.] My friends, silence will be more acceptable to me in the discussion of these questions than applause. I desire to address myself to your judgment, your understanding, and your consciences, and not to your passions or your enthusiasm. When the Democratic convention assembled in Baltimore in the same year, for the purpose of nominating a Democratic candidate for the presidency, it also adopted the compromise measures of 1850 as the basis of Democratic action. Thus you see that up to 1853–54, the Whig party and the Democratic party both stood on the same platform with regard to the slavery question. That platform was the right of the people of each State and each Territory to decide their local and domestic institutions for themselves, subject only to the Federal Constitution.

During the session of Congress of 1853–54, I introduced into the Senate of the United States a bill to organize the Territories of Kansas and Nebraska on that principle which had been adopted in the compromise measures of 1850, approved by the Whig party and the Democratic party in Illinois in 1851, and indorsed by the Whig party and the Democratic party in national convention in 1852. In order that there might be no misunderstanding in relation to the

principle involved in the Kansas and Nebraska bill, I put forth the
true intent and meaning of the act in these words: "It is the true
intent and meaning of this act not to legislate slavery into any State
or Territory, or to exclude it therefrom, but to leave the people thereof
perfectly free to form and regulate their domestic institutions in their
own way, subject only to the Federal Constitution." Thus you see
that up to 1854, when the Kansas and Nebraska bill was brought into
Congress for the purpose of carrying out the principles which both
parties had up to that time indorsed and approved, there had been no
division in this country in regard to that principle except the opposition of the Abolitionists. In the House of Representatives of the Illinois legislature, upon a resolution asserting that principle, every Whig
and every Democrat in the House voted in the affirmative, and only
four men voted against it, and those four were old-line Abolitionists.

In 1854 Mr. Abraham Lincoln and Mr. Lyman Trumbull entered
into an arrangement, one with the other, and each with his respective
friends, to dissolve the Old Whig party on the one hand, and to dissolve the old Democratic party on the other, and to connect the
members of both into an Abolition party, under the name and dis-
guise of a Republican party. The terms of that arrangement between
Lincoln and Trumbull have been published by Lincoln's special
friend, James H. Matheny, Esq., and they were that Lincoln should
have General Shields's place in the United States Senate, which was
then about to become vacant, and that Trumbull should have my
seat when my term expired. Lincoln went to work to Abolitionize
the Old Whig party all over the State, pretending that he was then as
good a Whig as ever; and Trumbull went to work in his part of the
State preaching Abolitionism in its milder and lighter form, and trying to Abolitionize the Democratic party, and bring old Democrats
handcuffed and bound hand and foot into the Abolition camp. In
pursuance of the arrangement, the parties met at Springfield in October, 1854, and proclaimed their new platform. Lincoln was to
bring into the Abolition camp the old-line Whigs, and transfer them
over to Giddings, Chase, Fred Douglass, and Parson Lovejoy, who
were ready to receive them and christen them in their new faith.
They laid down on that occasion a platform for their new Republican
party, which was thus to be constructed. I have the resolutions of
the State convention then held, which was the first mass State convention ever held in Illinois by the Black Republican party, and I now
hold them in my hands and will read a part of them, and cause the
others to be printed. Here are the most important and material resolutions of this Abolition platform:

1. *Resolved*, That we believe this truth to be self-evident, that when parties become subversive of the ends for which they are established, or incapable of restoring the government to the true principles of the Constitution, it is the right and duty of the people to dissolve the political bands
by which they may have been connected therewith, and to organize new parties upon such principles and with such views as the circumstances and
the exigencies of the nation may demand.

2. *Resolved*, That the times imperatively demand the reorganization of
parties, and, repudiating all previous party attachments, names and predi-

lections, we unite ourselves together in defense of the liberty and Constitution of the country, and will hereafter coöperate as the Republican party, pledged to the accomplishment of the following purposes: To bring the administration of the government back to the control of first principles; to restore Nebraska and Kansas to the position of free Territories; that, as the Constitution of the United States vests in the States, and not in Congress, the power to legislate for the extradition of fugitives from labor, to repeal and entirely abrogate the fugitive-slave law; to restrict slavery to those States in which it exists; to prohibit the admission of any more slave States into the Union; to abolish slavery in the District of Columbia; to exclude slavery from all the Territories over which the general government has exclusive jurisdiction; and to resist the acquirement of any more Territories unless the practice of slavery therein forever shall have been prohibited.

3. *Resolved*, That in furtherance of these principles we will use such constitutional and lawful means as shall seem best adapted to their accomplishment, and that we will support no man for office, under the general or State government, who is not positively and fully committed to the support of these principles, and whose personal character and conduct is not a guaranty that he is reliable, and who shall not have abjured old party allegiance and ties.

Now, gentlemen, your Black Republicans have cheered every one of those propositions, and yet I venture to say that you cannot get Mr. Lincoln to come out and say that he is now in favor of each one of them. That these propositions, one and all, constitute the platform of the Black Republican party of this day, I have no doubt; and when you were not aware for what purpose I was reading them, your Black Republicans cheered them as good Black Republican doctrines. My object in reading these resolutions was to put the question to Abraham Lincoln this day, whether he now stands and will stand by each article in that creed, and carry it out. I desire to know whether Mr. Lincoln to-day stands as he did in 1854, in favor of the unconditional repeal of the fugitive-slave law. I desire him to answer whether he stands pledged to-day, as he did in 1854, against the admission of any more slave States into the Union, even if the people want them. I want to know whether he stands pledged against the admission of a new State into the Union with such a constitution as the people of that State may see fit to make. I want to know whether he stands to-day pledged to the abolition of slavery in the District of Columbia. I desire him to answer whether he stands pledged to the prohibition of the slave-trade between the different States. I desire to know whether he stands pledged to prohibit slavery in all the Territories of the United States, North as well as South of the Missouri Compromise line. I desire him to answer whether he is opposed to the acquisition of any more territory unless slavery is prohibited therein. I want his answer to these questions. Your affirmative cheers in favor of this Abolition platform are not satisfactory. I ask Abraham Lincoln to answer these questions, in order that when I trot him down to lower Egypt, I may put the same questions to him. My principles are the same everywhere. I can proclaim them alike in the North, the South, the East, and the West. My principles will apply wherever the

Constitution prevails and the American flag waves. I desire to know whether Mr. Lincoln's principles will bear transplanting from Ottawa to Jonesboro? I put these questions to him to-day distinctly, and ask an answer. I have a right to an answer, for I quote from the platform of the Republican party, made by himself and others at the time that party was formed, and the bargain made by Lincoln to dissolve and kill the Old Whig party, and transfer its members, bound hand and foot, to the Abolition party, under the direction of Giddings and Fred Douglass. In the remarks I have made on this platform, and the position of Mr. Lincoln upon it, I mean nothing personally disrespectful or unkind to that gentleman. I have known him for nearly twenty-five years. There were many points of sympathy between us when we first got acquainted. We were both comparatively boys, and both struggling with poverty in a strange land. I was a school-teacher in the town of Winchester, and he a flourishing grocery-keeper in the town of Salem. He was more successful in his occupation than I was in mine, and hence more fortunate in this world's goods. Lincoln is one of those peculiar men who perform with admirable skill everything which they undertake. I made as good a school-teacher as I could, and when a cabinet-maker I made a good bedstead and tables, although my old boss said I succeeded better with bureaus and secretaries than with anything else; but I believe that Lincoln was always more successful in business than I, for his business enabled him to get into the legislature. I met him there, however, and had sympathy with him, because of the up-hill struggle we both had in life. He was then just as good at telling an anecdote as now. He could beat any of the boys wrestling, or running a foot-race, in pitching quoits or tossing a copper; could ruin more liquor than all the boys of the town together, and the dignity and impartiality with which he presided at a horse-race or fist-fight excited the admiration and won the praise of everybody that was present and participated. I sympathized with him because he was struggling with difficulties, and so was I. Mr. Lincoln served with me in the legislature in 1836, when we both retired, and he subsided, or became submerged, and he was lost sight of as a public man for some years. In 1846, when Wilmot introduced his celebrated proviso, and the Abolition tornado swept over the country, Lincoln again turned up as a member of Congress from the Sangamon district. I was then in the Senate of the United States, and was glad to welcome my old friend and companion. Whilst in Congress, he distinguished himself by his opposition to the Mexican war, taking the side of the common enemy against his own country; and when he returned home he found that the indignation of the people followed him everywhere, and he was again submerged or obliged to retire into private life, forgotten by his former friends. He came up again in 1854, just in time to make this Abolition or Black Republican platform, in company with Giddings, Lovejoy, Chase, and Fred Douglass, for the Republican party to stand upon. Trumbull, too, was one of our own contemporaries. He was born and raised in old Connecticut, was bred a Federalist, but removing to Georgia, turned Nullifier when nullification was popular, and as soon as he disposed of his clocks and wound up his business, migrated to Illinois, turned politician and lawyer here, and made his appearance in 1841 as a member of the legislature. He became noted as the author of the scheme to repudiate a large portion of the State debt of Illinois, which, if successful, would have brought infamy and disgrace upon the fair escutcheon of our glorious State. The odium attached to that measure consigned him to oblivion for a time. I helped to do it. I walked into a public meeting in the hall of the House of Representatives, and replied to his repudiating speeches, and resolutions were carried over his head denouncing repudiation, and asserting the moral and legal obligation of Illinois to pay every dollar of the debt she owed and every bond that bore her seal. Trumbull's malignity has followed me since I thus defeated his infamous scheme.

These two men having formed this combination to Abolitionize the Old Whig party and the old Democratic party, and put themselves into the Senate of the United States, in pursuance of their bargain, are now carrying out that arrangement. Matheny states that Trumbull broke faith; that the bargain was that Lincoln should be the senator in Shields's place, and Trumbull was to wait for mine; and the story goes that Trumbull cheated Lincoln, having control of four or five Abolitionized Democrats who were holding over in the Senate; he would not let them vote for Lincoln, which obliged the rest of the Abolitionists to support him in order to secure an Abolition senator. There are a number of authorities for the truth of this besides Matheny, and I suppose that even Mr. Lincoln will not deny it.

Mr. Lincoln demands that he shall have the place intended for Trumbull, as Trumbull cheated him and got his, and Trumbull is stumping the State traducing me for the purpose of securing the position for Lincoln, in order to quiet him. It was in consequence of this arrangement that the Republican convention was impaneled to instruct for Lincoln and nobody else, and it was on this account that they passed resolutions that he was their first, their last, and their only choice. Archy Williams was nowhere, Browning was nobody, Wentworth was not to be considered; they had no man in the Republican party for the place except Lincoln, for the reason that he demanded that they should carry out the arrangement.

Having formed this new party for the benefit of deserters from Whiggery and deserters from Democracy, and having laid down the Abolition platform which I have read, Lincoln now takes his stand and proclaims his Abolition doctrines. Let me read a part of them. In his speech at Springfield to the convention which nominated him for the Senate, he said:

In my opinion it will not cease until a crisis shall have been reached and passed. "A house divided against itself cannot stand." I believe this government cannot endure permanently half slave and half free. I do not expect the Union to be dissolved — I do not expect the house to fall — but I do expect it will cease to be divided. It will become all one thing, or all the other. Either the opponents of slavery will arrest the further spread of it, and place it where the public mind shall rest in the belief that it is in the course of ultimate extinction, or its advocates will push it forward till it shall become alike lawful in all the States — old as well as new, North as well as South.   [" Good," " good," and cheers.]

I am delighted to hear you Black Republicans say " good." I have no doubt that doctrine expresses your sentiments, and I will prove to you now, if you will listen to me, that it is revolutionary and destructive of the existence of this government. Mr. Lincoln, in the extract from which I have read, says that this government cannot endure permanently in the same condition in which it was made by its framers — divided into free and slave States. He says that it has existed for about seventy years thus divided, and yet he tells you that it cannot endure permanently on the same principles and in the same relative condition in which our fathers made it. Why can it not exist divided into free and slave States ? Washington, Jefferson, Franklin, Madison, Hamilton, Jay, and the great men of that day made this government divided into free States and slave States, and left each State perfectly free to do as it pleased on the subject of slavery. Why can it not exist on the same principles on which our fathers made it ? They knew when they framed the Constitution that in a country as wide and broad as this, with such a variety of climate, production, and interest, the people necessarily required different laws and institutions in different localities. They knew that the laws and regulations which would suit the granite hills of New Hampshire would be unsuited to the rice-plantations of South Carolina, and they therefore provided that each State should retain its own legislature and its own sovereignty, with the full and complete power to do as it pleased within its own limits, in all that was local and not national. One of the reserved rights of the States was the right to regulate the relations between master and servant, on the slavery question. At the time the Constitution was framed, there were thirteen States in the Union, twelve of which were slaveholding States and one a free State. Suppose this doctrine of uniformity preached by Mr. Lincoln, that the States should all be free or all be slave, had prevailed, and what would have been the result ? Of course, the twelve slaveholding States would have overruled the one free State, and slavery would have been fastened by a constitutional provision on every inch of the American republic, instead of being left, as our fathers wisely left it, to each State to decide for itself. Here I assert that uniformity in the local laws and institutions of the different States is neither possible nor desirable. If uniformity had been adopted when the government was established, it must inevitably have been the uniformity of slavery everywhere, or else the uniformity of negro citizenship and negro equality everywhere.

We are told by Lincoln that he is utterly opposed to the Dred Scott decision, and will not submit to it, for the reason that he says it deprives the negro of the rights and privileges of citizenship. That is the first and main reason which he assigns for his warfare on the Supreme Court of the United States and its decision. I ask you, are you in favor of conferring upon the negro the rights and privileges of citizenship? Do you desire to strike out of our State constitution that clause which keeps slaves and free negroes out of the State, and allow the free negroes to flow in, and cover your prairies with black settlements? Do you desire to turn this beautiful State into a free negro colony, in order that when Missouri abolishes slavery she can send one hundred thousand emancipated slaves into Illinois, to become citizens and voters, on an equality with yourselves? If you desire negro citizenship, if you desire to allow them to come into the State and settle with the white man, if you desire them to vote on an equality with yourselves, and to make them eligible to office, to serve on juries, and to adjudge your rights, then support Mr. Lincoln and the Black Republican party, who are in favor of the citizenship of the negro. For one, I am opposed to negro citizenship in any and every form. I believe this government was made on the white basis. I believe it was made by white men, for the benefit of white men and their posterity forever, and I am in favor of confining citizenship to white men, men of European birth and descent, instead of conferring it upon negroes, Indians, and other inferior races.

Mr. Lincoln, following the example and lead of all the little Abolition orators who go around and lecture in the basements of schools and churches, reads from the Declaration of Independence that all men were created equal, and then asks how can you deprive a negro of that equality which God and the Declaration of Independence award to him? He and they maintain that negro equality is guaranteed by the laws of God, and that it is asserted in the Declaration of Independence. If they think so, of course they have a right to say so, and so vote. I do not question Mr. Lincoln's conscientious belief that the negro was made his equal, and hence is his brother; but for my own part, I do not regard the negro as my equal, and positively deny that he is my brother or any kin to me whatever. Lincoln has evidently learned by heart Parson Lovejoy's catechism. He can repeat it as well as Farnsworth, and he is worthy of a medal from Father Giddings and Fred Douglass for his Abolitionism. He holds that the negro was born his equal and yours, and that he was endowed with equality by the Almighty, and that no human law can deprive him of these rights which were guaranteed to him by the Supreme Ruler of the universe. Now, I do not believe that the Almighty ever intended the negro to be the equal of the white man. If he did, he has been a long time demonstrating the fact. For thousands of years the negro has been a race upon the earth, and during all that time, in all latitudes and climates, wherever he has wandered or been taken, he has been inferior to the race which he has there met. He belongs to an inferior race, and must always occupy an inferior position. I do not hold that because the negro is our inferior therefore he ought to be a slave. By no means can such a conclusion be drawn from what I have said. On the contrary, I hold that humanity and Christianity both require that the negro shall have and enjoy every right, every privilege, and every immunity consistent with the safety of the society in which he lives. On that point, I presume, there can be no diversity of opinion. You and I are bound to extend to our inferior and dependent beings every right, every privilege, every facility and immunity consistent with the public good. The question then arises, what rights and privileges are consistent with the public good? This is a question which each State and each Territory must decide for itself — Illinois has decided it for herself. We have provided that the negro shall not be a slave, and we have also provided that he shall not be a citizen, but protect him in his civil rights, in his life, his person and his property, only depriving him of all political rights whatsoever, and refusing to put him on an equality with the white man. That policy of Illinois is satisfactory to the Democratic party and to me, and if it were to the Republicans, there would then be no question upon the subject; but the Republicans say that he ought to be made a citizen, and when he becomes a citizen he becomes your equal, with all your rights and privileges. They assert the Dred Scott decision to be monstrous because it denies that the negro is or can be a citizen under the Constitution.

Now, I hold that Illinois had a right to abolish and prohibit slavery as she did, and I hold that Kentucky has the same right to continue and protect slavery that Illinois had to abolish it. I hold that New York had as much right to abolish slavery as Virginia has to continue it, and that each and every State of this Union is a sovereign power, with the right to do as it pleases upon this question of slavery, and upon all its domestic institutions. Slavery is not the only question which comes up in this controversy. There is a far more important one to you, and that is, what shall be done with the free negro? We have settled the slavery question as far as we are concerned; we have prohibited it in Illinois forever, and in doing so, I think we have done wisely, and there is no man in the State who would be more strenuous in his opposition to the introduction of slavery than I would; but when we settled it for ourselves, we exhausted all our power over that subject. We have done our whole duty, and can do no more. We must leave each and every other State to decide for itself the same question. In relation to the policy to be pursued toward the free negroes, we have said that they shall not vote; whilst Maine, on the other hand, has said that they shall vote. Maine is a sovereign State, and has the power to regulate the qualifications of voters within her limits. I would never consent to confer the right of voting and of citizenship upon a negro, but still I am not going to quarrel with Maine for differing from me in opinion. Let Maine take care of her own negroes, and fix the qualifications of her own voters to suit herself, without interfering with Illinois, and Illinois will not interfere with Maine. So with the State of New York. She allows the negro to vote provided he owns two hundred and fifty dollars' worth of property, but not otherwise. While I would not make any distinction whatever between a negro who held property and one who did not, yet if the sovereign State of New York chooses to make that distinction it is her business and not mine, and I will not quarrel with her for it. She can do as she pleases on this question if she minds her own business, and we will do the same thing. Now, my friends, if we will only act conscientiously and rigidly upon this great principle of popular sovereignty, which guarantees to each State and Territory the right to do so as it pleases on all things, local and domestic, instead of Congress interfering, we will continue at peace one with another. Why should Illinois be at war with Missouri, or Kentucky with Ohio, or Virginia with New York, merely because their institutions differ? Our fathers intended that our institutions should differ. They knew that the North and the South, having different climates, productions, and interests, required different institutions. This doctrine of Mr. Lincoln, of uniformity among the institutions of the different States, is a new doctrine, never dreamed of by Washington, Madison, or the framers of this government. Mr. Lincoln and the Republican party set themselves up as wiser than these men who made this government, which has flourished for seventy years under the principle of popular sovereignty, recognizing the right of each State to do as it pleased. Under that principle, we have grown from a nation of three or four millions to a nation of about thirty millions of people; we have crossed the Allegheny mountains and filled up the whole Northwest, turning the prairie into a garden, and building up churches and schools, thus spreading civilization and Christianity where before there was nothing but savage barbarism. Under that principle we have become, from a feeble nation, the most powerful on the face of the earth, and if we only adhere to that principle, we can go forward increasing in territory, in power, in strength, and in glory until the Republic of America shall be the north star that shall guide the friends of freedom throughout the civilized world. And why can we not adhere to the great principle of self-government upon which our institutions were originally based? I believe that this new doctrine preached by Mr. Lincoln and his party will dissolve the Union if it succeeds. They are trying to array all the Northern States in one body against the South, to excite a sectional war between the free States and the slave States, in order that the one or the other may be driven to the wall.

I am told that my time is out. Mr. Lincoln will now address you for an hour and a half, and I will then occupy a half hour in replying to him.

Mr. Lincoln's Reply in the Ottawa Joint Debate.

My Fellow-citizens: When a man hears himself somewhat misrepresented, it provokes him — at least, I find it so with myself; but when misrepresentation becomes very gross and palpable, it is more apt to amuse him. The first thing I see fit to notice is the fact that Judge Douglas alleges, after running through the history of the old Democratic and the old Whig parties, that Judge Trumbull and myself made an arrangement in 1854 by which I was to have the place of General Shields in the United States Senate, and Judge Trumbull was to have the place of Judge Douglas. Now all I have to say upon that subject is that I think no man — not even Judge Douglas — can prove it, because it is not true. I have no doubt he is "conscientious" in saying it. As to those resolutions that he took such a length of time to read, as being the platform of the Republican party in 1854, I say I never had anything to do with them, and I think Trumbull never had. Judge Douglas cannot show that either of us ever did have anything to do with them. I believe this is true about those resolutions. There was a call for a convention to form a Republican party at Springfield, and I think that my friend Mr. Lovejoy, who is here upon this stand, had a hand in it. I think this is true, and I think if he will remember accurately he will be able to recollect that he tried to get me into it, and I would not go in. I believe it is also true that I went away from Springfield, when the convention was in session, to attend court in Tazewell County. It is true they did place my name, though without authority, upon the committee, and afterward wrote me to attend the meeting of the committee, but I refused to do so, and I never had anything to do with that organization. This is the plain truth about all that matter of the resolutions.

Now, about this story that Judge Douglas tells of Trumbull bargaining to sell out the old Democratic party, and Lincoln agreeing to sell out the Old Whig party, I have the means of knowing about that; Judge Douglas cannot have; and I know there is no substance to it whatever. Yet I have no doubt he is "conscientious" about it. I know that after Mr. Lovejoy got into the legislature that winter, he complained of me that I had told all the Old Whigs of his district that the Old Whig party was good enough for them, and some of them voted against him because I told them so. Now, I have no means of totally disproving such charges as this which the judge makes. A man cannot prove a negative, but he has a right to claim that when a man makes an affirmative charge, he must offer some proof to show the truth of what he says. I certainly cannot introduce testimony to show the negative about things, but I have a right to claim that if a man says he knows a thing, then he must show how he knows it. I always have a right to claim this, and it is not satisfactory to me that he may be "conscientious" on the subject.

Now, gentlemen, I hate to waste my time on such things, but in regard to that general Abolition tilt that Judge Douglas makes, when he says that I was engaged at that time in selling out and Abolitionizing the Old Whig party, I hope you will permit me to read a part of a printed speech that I made then at Peoria, which will show altogether a different view of the position I took in that contest of 1854. [Voice: "Put on your specs."] Yes, sir, I am obliged to do so. I am no longer a young man.

This is the repeal of the Missouri Compromise. The foregoing history may not be precisely accurate in every particular; but I am sure it is sufficiently so for all the uses I shall attempt to make of it, and in it we have before us the chief materials enabling us to correctly judge whether the repeal of the Missouri Compromise is right or wrong.

I think, and shall try to show, that it is wrong; wrong in its direct effect, letting slavery into Kansas and Nebraska — and wrong in its prospective principle, allowing it to spread to every other part of the wide world where men can be found inclined to take it.

This declared indifference, but, as I must think, covert real zeal for the spread of slavery, I cannot but hate. I hate it because of the monstrous injustice of slavery itself. I hate it because it deprives our republican example of its just influence in the world; enables the enemies of free institutions, with plausibility, to taunt us as hypocrites; causes the real friends of freedom to doubt our sincerity, and especially because it forces so many really good men amongst ourselves into an open war with the very fundamental principles of civil liberty — criticizing the Declaration of Independence, and insisting that there is no right principle of action but self-interest.

Before proceeding, let me say I think I have no prejudice against the Southern people. They are just what we would be in their situation. If slavery did not now exist among them, they would not introduce it. If it did now exist among us, we should not instantly give it up. This I believe of the masses North and South. Doubtless there are individuals on both sides who would not hold slaves under any circumstances; and others who would gladly introduce slavery anew, if it were out of existence. We know that some Southern men do free their slaves, go North, and become tip-top Abolitionists; while some Northern ones go South, and become most cruel slave-masters.

When Southern people tell us they are no more responsible for the origin of slavery than we, I acknowledge the fact. When it is said that the institution exists, and that it is very difficult to get rid of it in any satisfactory way, I can understand and appreciate the saying. I surely will not blame them for not doing what I should not know how to do myself. If all earthly power were given me, I should not know what to do as to the existing institution. My first impulse would be to free all the slaves, and send them to Liberia — to their own native land. But a moment's reflection would convince me that whatever of high hope (as I think there is) there may be in this in the long run, its sudden execution is impossible. If they were all landed there in a day, they would all perish in the next ten days; and there are not surplus shipping and surplus money enough in the world to carry them there in many times ten days. What then? Free them all, and keep them among us as underlings? Is it quite certain that this betters their condition? I think I would not hold one in slavery at any rate; yet the point is not clear enough to me to denounce people upon. What next? Free them, and make them politically and socially our equals? My own feelings will not admit of this; and if mine would, we well know that those of the great mass of white people will not. Whether this feeling accords with justice and sound judgment is not the sole question, if, indeed, it is any part of it. A universal feeling, whether well or ill-founded, cannot be safely disregarded. We cannot make them equals. It does seem to me that systems of gradual emancipation might be adopted; but for their tardiness in this, I will not undertake to judge our brethren of the South.

When they remind us of their constitutional rights, I acknowledge them, not grudgingly, but fully and fairly; and I would give them any legislation for the reclaiming of their fugitives, which should not, in its stringency, be more likely to carry a free man into slavery, than our ordinary criminal laws are to hang an innocent one.

But all this, to my judgment, furnishes no more excuse for permitting slavery to go into our own free territory, than it would for reviving the African slave-trade by law. The law which forbids the bringing of slaves from Africa, and that which has so long forbidden the taking of them to Nebraska, can hardly be distinguished on any moral principle; and the repeal of the former could find quite as plausible excuses as that of the latter.

I have reason to know that Judge Douglas knows that I said this. I think he has the answer here to one of the questions he put to me. I do not mean to allow him to catechize me unless he pays back for it in kind. I will not answer questions one after another, unless he reciprocates; but as he has made this inquiry, and I have answered it before, he has got it without my getting anything in return. He has got my answer on the fugitive-slave law.

Now, gentlemen, I don't want to read at any great length, but this is the true complexion of all I have ever said in regard to the institution of slavery and the black race. This is the whole of it, and anything that argues me into his idea of perfect social and political equality with the negro is but a specious and fantastic arrangement of words, by which a man can prove a horse-chestnut to be a chestnut horse. I will say here, while upon this subject, that I have no purpose, either directly or indirectly, to interfere with the institution of slavery in the States where it exists. I believe I have no lawful right to do so, and I have no inclination to do so. I have no purpose to introduce political and social equality between the white and the black races. There is a physical difference between the two, which, in my judgment, will probably forever forbid their living together upon the footing of perfect equality; and inasmuch as it becomes a necessity that there must be a difference, I, as well as Judge Douglas, am in favor of the race to which I belong having the superior position. I have never said anything to the contrary, but I hold that, notwithstanding all this, there is no reason in the world why the negro is not entitled to all the natural rights enumerated in the Declaration of Independence — the right to life, liberty, and the pursuit of happiness. I hold that he is as much entitled to these as the white man. I agree with Judge Douglas he is not my equal in many respects — certainly not in color, perhaps not in moral or intellectual endowment. But in the right to eat the bread, without the leave of anybody else, which his own hand earns, he is my equal and the equal of Judge Douglas, and the equal of every living man.

Now I pass on to consider one or two more of these little follies. The judge is woefully at fault about his early friend Lincoln being a "grocery-keeper." I don't know that it would be a great sin if I had been; but he is mistaken. Lincoln never kept a grocery anywhere in the world. It is true that Lincoln did work the latter part of one winter in a little still-house up at the head of a hollow. And so I think my friend, the judge, is equally at fault when he charges me at the time when I was in Congress of having opposed our soldiers who were fighting in the Mexican War. The judge did not make his charge very distinctly, but I tell you what he can prove, by referring to the record. You remember I was an Old Whig, and whenever the Democratic party tried to get me to vote that the war had been righteously begun by the President, I would not do it. But whenever they asked for any money, or land-warrants, or anything to pay the soldiers there, during all that time, I gave the same vote that Judge Douglas did. You can think as you please as to whether that was consistent. Such is the truth; and the judge has the right to make all he can out of it. But when he, by a general charge, conveys the idea that I withheld supplies from the soldiers who were fighting in the Mexican War, or did anything else to hinder the soldiers, he is, to say the least, grossly and altogether mistaken, as a consultation of the records will prove to him.

As I have not used up so much of my time as I had supposed, I will dwell a little longer upon one or two of these minor topics upon which the judge has spoken. He has read from my speech in Springfield in which I say that "a house divided against itself cannot stand." Does the judge say it can stand? I don't know whether he does or not. The judge does not seem to be attending to me just now, but I would like to know if it is his opinion that a house divided against itself can stand. If he does, then there is a question of veracity, not between him and me, but between the judge and an authority of a somewhat higher character.

Now, my friends, I ask your attention to this matter for the purpose of saying something seriously. I know that the judge may readily enough agree with me that the maxim which was put forth by the Saviour is true, but he may allege that I misapply it; and the judge has a right to urge that in my application I do misapply it, and then I have a right to show that I do not misapply it. When he undertakes to say that because I think this nation, so far as the question of slavery is concerned, will all become one thing or all the other, I am in favor of bringing about a dead uniformity in the various States in all their institutions, he argues erroneously. The great variety of the local institutions in the States, springing from differences in the soil, differences in the face of the country, and in the climate, are bonds of union. They do not make "a house divided against itself," but they make a house united. If they produce in one section of the country what is called for by the wants of another section, and this other section can supply the wants of the first, they are not matters of discord but bonds of union, true bonds of union. But can this question of slavery be considered as among these varieties in the institutions of the country? I leave it to you to say whether, in the history of our government, this institution of slavery has not always failed to be a bond of union, and, on the contrary, been an apple of discord and an element of division in the house. I ask you to consider whether, so long as the moral constitution of men's minds shall continue to be the same, after this generation and assemblage shall sink into the grave, and another race shall arise with the same moral and intellectual development we have—whether, if that institution is standing in the same irritating position in which it now is, it will not continue an element of division?

If so, then I have a right to say that, in regard to this question, the Union is a house divided against itself; and when the judge reminds me that I have often said to him that the institution of slavery has existed for eighty years in some States, and yet it does not exist in some others, I agree to the fact, and I account for it by looking at the position in which our fathers originally placed it—restricting it from the new Territories where it had not gone, and legislating to cut off its source by the abrogation of the slave-trade, thus putting the seal of legislation against its spread. The public mind did rest in the belief that it was in the course of ultimate extinction. But lately, I think—and in this I charge nothing on the judge's motives—lately, I think, that he, and those acting with him, have placed that institution on a new basis, which looks to the perpetuity and nationalization of slavery.   And while it is placed upon this new basis, I say, and I have said, that I believe we shall not have peace upon the question until the opponents of slavery arrest the further spread of it, and place it where the public mind shall rest in the belief that it is in the course of ultimate extinction; or, on the other hand, that its advocates will push it forward until it shall become alike lawful in all the States, old as well as new, North as well as South.   Now I believe if we could arrest the spread, and place it where Washington and Jefferson and Madison placed it, it would be in the course of ultimate extinction, and the public mind would, as for eighty years past, believe that it was in the course of ultimate extinction.   The crisis would be past, and the institution might be let alone for a hundred years—if it should live so long—in the States where it exists, yet it would be going out of existence in the way best for both the black and the white races. [A voice: "Then do you repudiate popular sovereignty?"]   Well, then, let us talk about popular sovereignty! What is popular sovereignty?   Is it the right of the people to have slavery or not have it, as they see fit, in the Territories?   I will state—and I have an able man to watch me—my understanding is that popular sovereignty, as now applied to the question of slavery, does allow the people of a Territory to have slavery if they want to, but does not allow them not to have it if they do not want it.   I do not mean that if this vast concourse of people were in a Territory of the United States, any one of them would be obliged to have a slave if he did not want one; but I do say that, as I understand the Dred Scott decision, if any one man wants slaves, all the rest have no way of keeping that one man from holding them.

When I made my speech at Springfield, of which the judge complains, and from which he quotes, I really was not thinking of the things which he ascribes to me at all.   I had no thought in the world that I was doing anything to bring about a war between the free and slave States.   I had no thought in the world that I was doing anything to bring about a political and social equality of the black and white races.   It never occurred to me that I was doing anything or favoring anything to reduce to a dead uniformity all the local institutions of the various States.   But I must say, in all fairness to him, if he thinks I am doing something which leads to these bad results, it is none the better that I did not mean it.   It is just as fatal to the country, if I have any influence in producing it, whether I intend it or not.   But can it be true, that placing this institution upon the original basis—the basis upon which our fathers placed it—can have any tendency to set the Northern and the Southern States at war with one another, or that it can have any tendency to make the people of Vermont raise sugar-cane because they raise it in Louisiana, or that it can compel the people of Illinois to cut pine logs on the Grand Prairie, where they will not grow, because they cut pine logs in Maine, where they do grow?   The judge says this is a new principle started in regard to this question.   Does the judge claim that he is working on the plan of the founders of the government? I think he says in some of his speeches—indeed, I have one here now—that he saw evidence of a policy to allow slavery to be south of a certain line, while north of it it should be excluded, and he saw an indisposition on the part of the country to stand upon that policy, and therefore he set about studying the subject upon original principles, and upon original principles he got up the Nebraska bill! I am fighting it upon these "original principles"—fighting it in the Jeffersonian, Washingtonian, and Madisonian fashion.

Now, my friends, I wish you to attend for a little while to one or two other things in that Springfield speech. My main object was to show, so far as my humble ability was capable of showing to the people of this country, what I believed was the truth—that there was a tendency, if not a conspiracy, among those who have engineered this slavery question for the last four or five years, to make slavery perpetual and universal in this nation. Having made that speech principally for that object, after arranging the evidences that I thought tended to prove my proposition, I concluded with this bit of comment:

We cannot absolutely know that these exact adaptations are the result of pre-concert, but when we see a lot of framed timbers, different portions of which we know have been gotten out at different times and places, and by different workmen—Stephen, Franklin, Roger, and James, for instance; and when we see these timbers joined together, and see they exactly make the frame of a house or a mill, all the tenons and mortices exactly fitting, and all the lengths and proportions of the different pieces exactly adapted to their respective places, and not a piece too many or too few,—not omitting even the scaffolding,—or if a single piece be lacking, we see the place in the frame exactly fitted and prepared to yet bring such piece in—in such a case we feel it impossible not to believe that Stephen and Franklin, and Roger and James, all understood one another from the beginning, and all worked upon a common plan or draft drawn before the first blow was struck.

When my friend, Judge Douglas, came to Chicago on the 9th of July, this speech having been delivered on the 16th of June, he made an harangue there in which he took hold of this speech of mine, showing that he had carefully read it; and while he paid no attention to this matter at all, but complimented me as being a "kind, amiable, and intelligent gentleman," notwithstanding I had said this, he goes on and deduces, or draws out, from my speech this tendency of mine to set the States at war with one another, to make all the institutions uniform, and set the niggers and white people to marry together. Then, as the judge had complimented me with these pleasant titles (I must confess to my weakness), I was a little "taken," for it came from a great man. I was not very much accustomed to flattery, and it came the sweeter to me. I was rather like the Hoosier with the gingerbread, when he said he reckoned he loved it better than any other man, and got less of it. As the judge had so flattered me, I could not make up my mind that he meant to deal unfairly with me; so I went to work to show him that he misunderstood the whole scope of my speech, and that I really never intended to set the people at war with one another. As an illustration, the next time I met him, which was at Springfield, I used this expression, that I claimed no right under the Constitution, nor had I any inclination, to enter into the slave States and interfere with the institutions of slavery. He says upon that: Lincoln will not enter into the slave States, but will go to the banks of the Ohio, on this side, and shoot over! He runs on, step by step, in the horse-chestnut style of argument, until in the Springfield speech he says, " Unless he shall be successful in firing his batteries, until he shall have extinguished slavery in all the States, the Union shall be dissolved." Now I don't think that was exactly the way to treat " a kind, amiable, intelligent gentleman." I know if I had asked the judge to show when or where it was I had said, that if I did n't succeed in firing into the slave States until slavery should be extinguished, the Union should be dissolved, he could not have shown it. I understand what he would do. He would say, "I don't mean to quote from you, but this was the result of what you say." But I have the right to ask, and I do ask now, did you not put it in such a form that an ordinary reader or listener would take it as an expression from me?

In a speech at Springfield on the night of the 17th, I thought I might as well attend to my business a little, and I recalled his attention as well as I could to this charge of conspiracy to nationalize slavery. I called his attention to the fact that he had acknowledged in my hearing twice that he had carefully read the speech; and, in the language of the lawyers, as he had twice read the speech, and still had put in no plea or answer, I took a default on him. I insisted that I had a right then to renew that charge of conspiracy. Ten days afterward I met the judge at Clinton — that is to say, I was on the ground, but not in the discussion — and heard him make a speech. Then he comes in with his plea to this charge, for the first time, and his plea when put in, as well as I can recollect it, amounted to this: that he never had any talk with Judge Taney or the President of the United States with regard to the Dred Scott decision before it was made. I (Lincoln) ought to know that the man who makes a charge without knowing it to be true, falsifies as much as he who knowingly tells a falsehood; and lastly, that he would pronounce the whole thing a falsehood; but he would make no personal application of the charge of falsehood, not because of any regard for the " kind, amiable, intelligent gentleman," but because of his own personal self-respect! I have understood since then (but [turning to Judge Douglas] will not hold the judge to it if he is not willing) that he has broken through the " self-respect," and has got to saying the thing out. The judge nods to me that it is so. It is fortunate for me that I can keep as good-humored as I do, when the judge acknowledges that he has been trying to make a question of veracity with me. I know the judge is a great man, while I am only a small man, but I feel that I have got him. I demur to that plea. I waive all objections that it was not filed till after default was taken, and demur to it upon the merits. What if Judge Douglas never did talk with Chief Justice Taney and the President before the Dred Scott decision was made;

does it follow that he could not have had as perfect an understanding without talking as with it? I am not disposed to stand upon my legal advantage. I am disposed to take his denial as being like an answer in chancery, that he neither had any knowledge, information, nor belief in the existence of such a conspiracy. I am disposed to take his answer as being as broad as though he had put it in these words. And now, I ask, even if he had done so, have not I a right to prove it on him, and to offer the evidence of more than two witnesses, by whom to prove it; and if the evidence proves the existence of the conspiracy, does his broad answer, denying all knowledge, information, or belief, disturb the fact? It can only show that he was used by conspirators, and was not a leader of them.

Now, in regard to his reminding me of the moral rule that persons who tell what they do not know to be true, falsify as much as those who knowingly tell falsehoods. I remember the rule, and it must be borne in mind that in what I have read to you, I do not say that I know such a conspiracy to exist. To that I reply, I believe it. If the judge says that I do not believe it, then he says what he does not know, and falls within his own rule that he who asserts a thing which he does not know to be true, falsifies as much as he who knowingly tells a falsehood. I want to call your attention to a little discussion on that branch of the case, and the evidence which brought my mind to the conclusion which I expressed as my belief. If, in arraying that evidence, I had stated anything which was false or erroneous, it needed but that Judge Douglas should point it out, and I would have taken it back with all the kindness in the world. I do not deal in that way. If I have brought forward anything not a fact, if he will point it out, it will not even ruffle me to take it back. But if he will not point out anything erroneous in the evidence, is it not rather for him to show by a comparison of the evidence that I have reasoned falsely, than to call the "kind, amiable, intelligent gentleman" a liar? If I have reasoned to a false conclusion, it is the vocation of an able debater to show by argument that I have wandered to an erroneous conclusion. I want to ask your attention to a portion of the Nebraska bill which Judge Douglas has quoted: "It being the true intent and meaning of this act, not to legislate slavery into any Territory or State, nor to exclude it therefrom, but to leave the people thereof perfectly free to form and regulate their domestic institutions in their own way, subject only to the Constitution of the United States." Thereupon Judge Douglas and others began to argue in favor of "popular sovereignty"—the right of the people to have slaves if they wanted them, and to exclude slavery if they did not want them. "But," said, in substance, a senator from Ohio (Mr. Chase, I believe), "we more than suspect that you do not mean to allow the people to exclude slavery if they wish to; and if you do mean it, accept an amendment which I propose expressly authorizing the people to exclude slavery." I believe I have the amendment here before me, which was offered, and under which the people of the Territory, through their proper representatives, might, if they saw fit, prohibit the existence of slavery therein. And now I state it as a fact, to be taken back if there is any mistake about it, that Judge Douglas and those acting with him voted that amendment down. I now think that those men who voted it down had a real reason for doing so. They know what that reason was. It looks to us, since we have seen the Dred Scott decision pronounced, holding that, " under the Constitution," the people cannot exclude slavery— I say it looks to outsiders, poor, simple, "amiable, intelligent gentlemen," as though the niche was left as a place to put that Dred Scott decision in, a niche which would have been spoiled by adopting the amendment. And now I say again, if this was not the reason, it will avail the judge much more to calmly and good-humoredly point out to these people what that other reason was for voting the amendment down, than swelling himself up to vociferate that he may be provoked to call somebody a liar.

Again: there is in that same quotation from the Nebraska bill this clause: "It being the true intent and meaning of this bill not to legislate slavery into any Territory or State." I have always been puzzled to know what business the word "State" had in that connection. Judge Douglas knows. He put it there. He knows what he put it there for. We outsiders cannot say what he put it there for. The law they were passing was not about States, and was not making provision for States. What was it placed there for? After seeing the Dred Scott decision which holds that the people cannot exclude slavery from a Territory, if another Dred Scott decision shall come, holding that they cannot exclude it from a State, we shall discover that when the word was originally put there, it was in view of something which was to come in due time, we shall see that it was the other half of something. I now say again, if there is any different reason for putting it there, Judge Douglas, in a good-humored way, without calling anybody a liar, can tell what the reason was.

When the judge spoke at Clinton, he came very near making a charge of falsehood against me. He used, as I found it printed in a newspaper, which, I remember was very nearly like the real speech, the following language:

I did not answer the charge [of conspiracy] before for the reason that I did not suppose there was a man in America with a heart so corrupt as to believe such a charge could be true. I have too much respect for Mr. Lincoln to suppose he is serious in making the charge.

I confess this is rather a curious view, that out of respect for me he should consider I was making what I deemed rather a grave charge in fun. I confess it strikes me rather strangely. But I let it pass. As the judge did not for a moment believe that there was a man in America whose heart was so "corrupt" as to make such a charge, and as he places me among the "men in America" who have hearts base enough to make such a charge, I hope he will excuse me if I hunt out another charge very like this; and if it should turn out that in hunting I should find that other, and it should turn out to be Judge Douglas himself who made it, I hope he will reconsider this question of the deep corruption of heart he has thought fit to ascribe to me. In Judge Douglas's speech of March 22, 1858, which I hold in my hand, he says:

In this connection there is another topic to which I desire to allude. I seldom refer to the course of newspapers, or notice the articles which they publish in regard to myself; but the course of the Washington "Union" has been so extraordinary, for the last two or three months, that I think it well enough to make some allusion to it. It has read me out of the Democratic party every other day, at least for two or three months, and keeps reading me out, and, as if it had not succeeded, still continues to read me out, using such terms as "traitor," "renegade," "deserter," and other kind and polite epithets of that nature. Sir, I have no vindication to make of my Democracy against the Washington "Union," or any other newspaper. I am willing to allow my history and actions for the last twenty years to speak for themselves as to my political principles, and my fidelity to political obligations. The Washington "Union" has a personal grievance. When the editor was nominated for public printer I declined to vote for him, and stated that at some time I might give my reasons for doing so. Since I declined to give that vote, this scurrilous abuse, these vindictive and constant attacks, have been repeated almost daily on me. Will my friend from Michigan read the article to which I allude?

This is a part of the speech. You must excuse me from reading the entire article of the Washington "Union," as Mr. Stuart read it for Mr. Douglas. The judge goes on and sums up, as I think, correctly:

Mr. President, you here find several distinct propositions advanced boldly by the Washington "Union" editorially, and apparently authoritatively, and any man who questions any of them is denounced as an Abolitionist, a Freesoiler, a fanatic. The propositions are, first, that the primary object of all government at its original institution is the protection of person and property; second, that the Constitution of the United States declares that the citizens of each State shall be entitled to all the privileges and immunities of citizens in the several States; and that, therefore, thirdly, all State laws, whether organic or otherwise, which prohibit the citizens of one State from settling in another with their slave property, and especially declaring it forfeited, are direct violations of the original intention of the government and Constitution of the United States; and, fourth, that the emancipation of the slaves of the Northern States was a gross outrage on the rights of property, inasmuch as it was involuntarily done on the part of the owner.

Remember that this article was published in the "Union" on the 17th of November, and on the 18th appeared the first article giving the adhesion of the "Union" to the Lecompton constitution. It was in these words:

"KANSAS AND HER CONSTITUTION. The vexed question is settled. The problem is solved. The dead point of danger is passed. All serious trouble to Kansas affairs is over and gone."

And a column nearly of the same sort. Then, when you come to look into the Lecompton constitution, you find the same doctrine incorporated in it which was put forth editorially in the "Union." What is it?

"ARTICLE 7, Section 1. The right of property is before and higher than any constitutional sanction; and the right of the owner of a slave to such slave and its increase is the same and as inviolable as the right of the owner of any property whatever."

Then in the schedule is a provision that the constitution may be amended after 1864 by a two-thirds vote.

"But no alteration shall be made to affect the right of property in the ownership of slaves."

It will be seen by these clauses in the Lecompton constitution that they are identical in spirit with the *authoritative* article in the Washington "Union" of the day previous to its indorsement of this constitution.

I pass over some portions of the speech, and I hope that any one who feels interested in this matter will read the entire section of the speech, and see whether I do the judge injustice. He proceeds:

When I saw that article in the "Union" of the 17th of November, followed by the glorification of the Lecompton constitution on the 18th of November, and this clause in the constitution asserting the doctrine that a State has no right to prohibit slavery within its limits, I saw that there was a fatal blow being struck at the sovereignty of the States of this Union.

I stop the quotation there, again requesting that it may all be read. I have read all of the portion I desire to comment upon. What is this charge that the judge thinks I must have a very corrupt heart to make? It was a purpose on the part of certain high functionaries to make it impossible for the people of one State to prohibit the people of any other State from entering it with their "property," so called, and making it a slave State. In other words, it was a charge implying a design to make the institution of slavery national. And now I ask your attention to what Judge Douglas has himself done here. I know he made that part of the speech as a reason why he had refused to vote for a certain man for public printer, but when we get at it, the charge itself is the very one I made against him, that he thinks I am so corrupt for uttering. Now, whom does he make that charge against? Does he make it against that newspaper editor merely? No; he says it is identical in spirit with the Lecompton constitution, and so the framers of that constitution are brought in with the editor of the newspaper in that "fatal blow being struck." He did not call it a "conspiracy." In his language it is a "fatal blow being struck." And if the words carry the meaning better when changed from a "conspiracy" into a "fatal blow being struck," I will change my expression and call it "fatal blow being struck." We see the charge made not merely against the editor of the "Union," but all the framers of the Lecompton constitution; and not only so, but the article was an authoritative article. By whose authority? Is there any question but that he means it was by the authority of the President and his cabinet—the administration? Is there any sort of question but that he means to make that charge? Then there are the editors of the "Union," the framers of the Lecompton constitution, the President of the United States and his cabinet, and all the supporters of the Lecompton constitution, in Congress and out of Congress, who are all involved in this "fatal blow being struck." I commend to Judge Douglas's consideration the question of how corrupt a man's heart must be to make such a charge!

Now, my friends, I have but one branch of the subject, in the little time I have left, to which to call your attention, and as I shall come to a close at the end of that branch, it is probable that I shall not occupy quite all the time allotted to me. Although on these questions I would like to talk twice as long as I have, I could not enter upon another head and discuss it properly without running over my time. I ask the attention of the people here assembled and elsewhere, to the course that Judge Douglas is pursuing every day as bearing upon this question of making slavery national. Not going back to the records, but taking the speeches he makes, the speeches he made yesterday and day before, and makes constantly all over the country — I ask your attention to them. In the first place, what is necessary to make the institution national? Not war. There is no danger that the people of Kentucky will shoulder their muskets, and, with a young nigger stuck on every bayonet, march into Illinois and force them upon us. There is no danger of our going over there and making war upon them. Then what is necessary for the nationalization of slavery? It is simply the next Dred Scott decision. It is merely for the Supreme Court to decide that no State under the Constitution can exclude it, just as they have already decided that under the Constitution neither Congress nor the territorial legislature can do it. When that is decided and acquiesced in, the whole thing is done. This being true, and this being the way, as I think, that slavery is to be made national, let us consider what Judge Douglas is doing every day to that end. In the first place, let us see what influence he is exerting on public sentiment. In this and like communities, public sentiment is everything. With public sentiment, nothing can fail; without it, nothing can succeed. Consequently he who molds public sentiment goes deeper than he who enacts statutes or pronounces decisions. He makes statutes and decisions possible or impossible to be executed. This must be borne in mind, as also the additional fact that Judge Douglas is a man of vast influence, so great that it is enough for many men to profess to believe anything when they once find out that Judge Douglas professes to believe it. Consider also the attitude he occupies at the head of a large party — a party which he claims has a majority of all the voters in the country.

This man sticks to a decision which forbids the people of a Territory to exclude slavery, and he does so not because he says it is right in itself,— he does not give any opinion on that,— but because it has been decided by the court, and, being decided by the court, he is, and you are, bound to take it in your political action as law — not that he judges at all of its merits, but because a decision of the court is to him a "Thus saith the Lord." He places it on that ground alone, and you will bear in mind that thus committing himself unreservedly to this decision, commits him to the next one just as firmly as to this. He did not commit himself on account of the merit or demerit of the decision, but it is a "Thus saith the Lord." The next decision, as much as this, will be a "Thus saith the Lord." There is nothing that can divert or turn him away from this decision. It is nothing that I point out to him that his great prototype, General Jackson, did not believe in the binding force of decisions. It is nothing to him that Jefferson did not so believe. I have said that I have often heard him approve of

Jackson's course in disregarding the decision of the Supreme Court pronouncing a national bank constitutional. He says I did not hear him say so. He denies the accuracy of my recollection. I say he ought to know better than I, but I will make no question about this thing, though it still seems to me that I heard him say it twenty times. I will tell him though, that he now claims to stand on the Cincinnati platform, which affirms that Congress cannot charter a national bank, in the teeth of that old standing decision that Congress can charter a bank. And I remind him of another piece of history on the question of respect for judicial decisions, and it is a piece of Illinois history, belonging to a time when a large party to which Judge Douglas belonged were displeased with a decision of the Supreme Court of Illinois, because they had decided that a governor could not remove a secretary of state. You will find the whole story in Ford's "History of Illinois," and I know that Judge Douglas will not deny that he was then in favor of overslaughing that decision by the mode of adding five new judges, so as to vote down the four old ones. Not only so, but it ended in the judge's sitting down on the very bench as one of the five new judges to break down the four old ones. It was in this way precisely that he got his title of judge. Now, when the judge tells me that men appointed conditionally to sit as members of a court will have to be catechised beforehand upon some subject, I say, "You know, judge; you have tried it." When he says a court of this kind will lose the confidence of all men, will be prostituted and disgraced by such a proceeding, I say, "You know best, judge; you have been through the mill."

But I cannot shake Judge Douglas's teeth loose from the Dred Scott decision. Like some obstinate animal (I mean no disrespect) that will hang on when he has once got his teeth fixed,—you may cut off a leg, or you may tear away an arm, still he will not relax his hold. And so I may point out to the judge, and say that he is bespattered all over, from the beginning of his political life to the present time, with attacks upon judicial decisions,— I may cut off limb after limb of his public record, and strive to wrench from him a single dictum of the court, yet I cannot divert him from it. He hangs to the last to the Dred Scott decision. These things show there is a purpose strong as death and eternity for which he adheres to this decision, and for which he will adhere to all other decisions of the same court. [A Hibernian: "Give us something besides Drid Scott."] Yes; no doubt you want to hear something that don't hurt. Now, having spoken of the Dred Scott decision, one more word and I am done. Henry Clay, my beau ideal of a statesman, the man for whom I fought all my humble life — Henry Clay once said of a class of men who would repress all tendencies to liberty and ultimate emancipation, that they must, if they would do this, go back to the era of our independence, and muzzle the cannon which thunders its annual joyous return; they must blow out the moral lights around us; they must penetrate the human soul, and eradicate there the love of liberty; and then, and not till then, could they perpetuate slavery in this country! To my thinking, Judge Douglas is, by his example and vast influence, doing that very thing in this community when he says that the negro has nothing in the Declaration of Independence. Henry Clay plainly understood the contrary. Judge Douglas is going back to the era of our Revolution, and to the extent of his ability muzzling the cannon which thunders its annual joyous return. When he invites any people, willing to have slavery, to establish it, he is blowing out the moral lights around us. When he says he "cares not whether slavery is voted down or voted up"—that it is a sacred right of self-government—he is, in my judgment, penetrating the human soul and eradicating the light of reason and the love of liberty in this American people. And now I will only say that when, by all these means and appliances, Judge Douglas shall succeed in bringing public sentiment to an exact accordance with his own views—when these vast assemblages shall echo back all these sentiments—when they shall come to repeat his views and to avow his principles, and to say all that he says on these mighty questions—then it needs only the formality of the second Dred Scott decision, which he indorses in advance, to make slavery alike lawful in all the States—old as well as new, North as well as South.

My friends, that ends the chapter. The judge can take his half hour.

Mr. Douglas's Rejoinder in the Ottawa Joint Debate.

Fellow-citizens: I will now occupy the half hour allotted to me in replying to Mr. Lincoln. The first point to which I will call your attention is, as to what I said about the organization of the Republican party in 1854, and the platform that was formed on the 5th of October of that year, and I will then put the question to Mr. Lincoln, whether or not he approves of each article in that platform, and ask for a specific answer. I did not charge him with being a member of the committee which reported that platform. I charged that that platform was the platform of the Republican party adopted by them. The fact that it was the platform of the Republican party is not denied, but Mr. Lincoln now says that although his name was on the committee which reported it, he does not think he was there, but thinks he was in Tazewell, holding court. Now, I want to remind Mr. Lincoln that he was at Springfield when that convention was held and those resolutions adopted.

The point I am going to remind Mr. Lincoln of is this: that after I had made my speech in 1854, during the fair, he gave me notice that he was going to reply to me the next day. I was sick at the time, but I stayed over in Springfield to hear his reply and to reply to him. On that day this very convention, the resolutions adopted by which I have read, was to meet in the Senate chamber. He spoke in the hall of the House; and when he got through his speech—my recollection is distinct, and I shall never forget it—Mr. Codding walked in as I took the stand to reply, and gave notice that the Republican State convention would meet instantly in the Senate chamber, and called upon the Republicans to retire there and go into this very convention, instead of remaining and listening to me.

In the first place, Mr. Lincoln was selected by the very men who made the Republican organization on that day, to reply to me. He spoke for them and for that party, and he was the leader of the party; and on the very day he made his speech in reply to me, preaching up this same doctrine of negro equality under the Declaration of Independence, this Republican party met in convention. Another evidence that he was acting in concert with them is to be found in the fact that that convention waited an hour after its time of meeting to hear Lincoln's speech, and Codding, one of their leading men, marched in the moment Lincoln got through, and gave notice that they did not want to hear me, and would proceed with the business of the convention. Still another fact. I have here a newspaper printed at Springfield — Mr. Lincoln's own town — in October, 1854, a few days afterward, publishing these resolutions charging Mr. Lincoln with entertaining these sentiments, and trying to prove that they were also the sentiments of Mr. Yates, then candidate for Congress. This has been published on Mr. Lincoln over and over again, and never before has he denied it.

But, my friends, this denial of his that he did not act on the committee, is a miserable quibble to avoid the main issue, which is, that this Republican platform declares in favor of the unconditional repeal of the fugitive-slave law. Has Lincoln answered whether he indorsed that or not? I called his attention to it when I first addressed you, and asked him for an answer, and I then predicted that he would not answer. How does he answer? Why, that he was not on the committee that wrote the resolutions. I then repeated the next proposition contained in the resolutions, which was to restrict slavery in those States in which it exists, and asked him whether he indorsed it. Does he answer yes or no? He says in reply, "I·was not on the committee at the time; I was up in Tazewell." The next question I put to him was, whether he was in favor of prohibiting the admission of any more slave States into the Union. I put the question to him distinctly, whether, if the people of the Territory, when they had sufficient population to make a State, should form their constitution recognizing slavery, he would vote for or against its admission. He is a candidate for the United States Senate, and it is possible, if he should be elected, that he would have to vote directly on that question. I asked him to answer me and you, whether he would vote to admit a State into the Union, with slavery or without it, as its own people might choose. He did not answer that question. He dodges that question also, under cover that he was not on the committee at the time, that he was not present when the platform was made. I want to know, if he should happen to be in the Senate when a State applied for admission with a constitution acceptable to her own people, whether he would vote to admit that State if slavery was one of its institutions. He avoids the answer.

It is true he gives the Abolitionists to understand by a hint that he would not vote to admit such a State. And why? He goes on to say that the man who would talk about giving each State the right to have slavery or not, as it pleased, was akin to the man who would muzzle the guns which thundered forth the annual joyous return of the day of our independence. He says that that kind of talk is casting a blight on the glory of this country. What is the meaning of that? That he is not in favor of each State to have the right of doing as it pleases on the slavery question? I will put the question to him again and again, and I intend to force it out of him.

Then again, this platform which was made at Springfield by his own party, when he was its acknowledged head, provides that Republicans will insist on the abolition of slavery in the District of Columbia, and I asked Lincoln specifically whether he agreed with them in that. ["Did you get an answer?"] He is afraid to answer it. He knows I will trot him down to Egypt. I intend to make him answer there, or I will show the people of Illinois that he does not intend to answer these questions. The convention to which I have been alluding goes a little further, and pledges itself to exclude slavery from all the Territories over which the General Government has exclusive jurisdiction north of 36° 30', as well as south. Now I want to know whether he approves that provision. I want him to answer, and when he does, I want to know his opinion on another point, which is, whether he will redeem the pledge of this platform and resist the acquirement of any more territory unless slavery therein shall be forever prohibited. I want him to answer this last question. All of the questions I have put to him are practical questions—questions based upon the fundamental principles of the Black Republican party; and I want to know whether he is the first, last, and only choice of a party with whom he does not agree in principle. He does not deny that that principle was unanimously adopted by the Republican party; he does not deny that the whole Republican party is pledged to it; he does not deny that a man who is not faithful to it is faithless to the Republican party; and now I want to know whether that party is unanimously in favor of a man who does not adopt that creed and agree with them in their principles: I want to know whether the man who does not agree with them, and who is afraid to avow his differences, and who dodges the issue, is the first, last, and only choice of the Republican party. [A voice: "How about the conspiracy?"] Never mind, I will come to that soon enough. But the platform which I have read to you not only lays down these principles, but it adds:

Resolved : That in furtherance of these principles we will use such constitutional and lawful means as shall seem best adapted to their accomplishment, and that we will support no man for office, under the General or State Government, who is not positively and fully committed to the support of these principles, and whose personal character and conduct are not a guaranty that he is reliable, and who shall not have abjured old party allegiance and ties.

The Black Republican party stands pledged that they will never support Lincoln until he has pledged himself to that platform, but he cannot devise his answer; he has not made up his mind whether he will or not. He talked about everything else he could think of to occupy his hour and a half, and when he could not think of anything more to say, without an excuse for refusing to answer these questions, he sat down long before his time was out.

In relation to Mr. Lincoln's charge of conspiracy against me, I have a word to say. In his speech to-day he quotes a playful part of his speech at Springfield, about Stephen, and James, and Franklin, and Roger, and says that I did not take exception to it. I did not answer it, and he repeats it again. I did not take exception to this figure of his. He has a right to be as playful as he pleases in throwing his arguments together, and I will not object; but I did take objection to his second Springfield speech, in which he stated that he intended his first speech as a charge of corruption or conspiracy against the Supreme Court of the United States, President Pierce, President Buchanan, and myself. That gave the offensive character to the charge. He then said that when he made it he did not know whether it was true or not, but inasmuch as Judge Douglas had not denied it, although he had replied to the other parts of his speech three times, he repeated it as a charge of conspiracy against me, thus charging me with moral turpitude. When he put it in that form, I did say, that inasmuch as he repeated the charge simply because I had not denied it, I would deprive him of the opportunity of ever repeating it again by declaring that it was in all its bearings an infamous lie. He says he will repeat it until I answer his folly and nonsense about Stephen, and Franklin, and Roger, and Bob, and James.

He studied that out—prepared that one sentence with the greatest care, committed it to memory, and put it in his first Springfield speech, and now he carries that speech around and reads that sentence to show how pretty it is. His vanity is wounded because I will not go into that beautiful figure of his about the building of a house. All I have to say is that I am not green enough to let him make a charge which he acknowledges he does not know to be true, and then take up my time in answering it, when I know it to be false and nobody else knows it to be true.

I have not brought a charge of moral turpitude against him. When he, or any other man, brings one against me, instead of disproving it, I will say that it is a lie, and let him prove it if he can.

I have lived twenty-five years in Illinois. I have served you with all the fidelity and ability which I possess, and Mr. Lincoln is at liberty to attack my public action, my votes, and my conduct; but when he dares to attack my moral integrity, by a charge of conspiracy between myself, Chief Justice Taney and the Supreme Court, and two Presidents of the United States, I will repel it.

Mr. Lincoln has not character enough for integrity and truth, merely on his own *ipse dixit*, to arraign President Buchanan, President Pierce, and nine judges of the Supreme Court, not one of whom would be complimented by being put on an equality with him. There is an unpardonable presumption in a man putting himself up before thousands of people, and pretending that his *ipse dixit*, without proof, without fact, and without truth, is enough to bring down and destroy the purest and best of living men.

Fellow-citizens, my time is fast expiring; I must pass on. Mr. Lincoln wants to know why I voted against Mr. Chase's amendment to the Nebraska bill. I will tell him. In the first place, the bill already conferred all the power which Congress had, by giving the people the whole power over the subject. Chase offered a proviso that they might abolish slavery, which by implication would convey the idea that they could prohibit by not introducing that institution. General Cass asked him to modify his amendment, so as to provide that the people might either prohibit or introduce slavery, and thus make it fair and equal. Chase refused to so modify his proviso, and then General Cass and all the rest of us voted it down. Those facts appear on the journals and debates of Congress, where Mr. Lincoln found the charge, and if he had told the whole truth, there would have been no necessity for me to occupy your time in explaining the matter.

Mr. Lincoln wants to know why the word "State," as well as "Territory," was put into the Nebraska bill? I will tell him. It was put there to meet just such false arguments as he has been adducing. That first, not only the people of the Territories should do as they pleased, but that when they come to be admitted as States, they should come into the Union with or without slavery, as the people determined. I meant to knock in the head this Abolition doctrine of Mr. Lincoln's, that there shall be no more slave States, even if the people want them. And it does not do for him to say, or for any other Black Republican to say, that there is nobody in favor of the doctrine of no more slave States, and that nobody wants to interfere with the right of the people to do as they please. What was the origin of the Missouri difficulty and the Missouri Compromise? The people of Missouri formed a constitution as a slave State, and asked admission into the Union, but the Free-soil party of the North, being in a majority, refused to admit her because she had slavery as one of her institutions. Hence this first slavery agitation arose upon a State and not upon a Territory, and yet Mr. Lincoln does not know why the word State was placed in the Kansas-Nebraska bill. The whole Abolition agitation arose on that doctrine of prohibiting a State from coming in with slavery or not, as it pleased, and that same doctrine is here in this Republican platform of 1854; it has never been repealed; and every Black Republican stands pledged by that platform never to vote for any man who is not in favor of it. Yet Mr. Lincoln does not know that there is a man in the world who is in favor of preventing a State from coming in as it pleases, notwithstanding the Springfield platform says that they, the Republican party, will not allow a State to come in under such circumstances. He is an ignorant man.

Now you see that upon these very points I am as far from bringing Mr. Lincoln up to the line as I ever was before. He does not want to avow his principles. I do want to avow mine, as clear as sunlight in midday. Democracy is founded upon the eternal principles of right. The plainer these principles are avowed before the people, the stronger will be the support which they will receive. I only wish I had the power to make them so clear that they would shine in the heavens for every man, woman, and child to read. The first of those principles that I would proclaim would be in opposition to Mr. Lincoln's doctrine of uniformity between the different States, and I would declare instead the sovereign right of each State to decide the slavery question as well as all other domestic questions for themselves, without interference from any other State or power whatsoever.

When that principle is recognized you will have peace and harmony and fraternal feeling between all the States of this Union; until you do recognize that doctrine there will be sectional warfare agitating and distracting the country. What does Mr. Lincoln propose? He says that the Union cannot exist divided into free and slave States. If it cannot endure thus divided, then he must strive to make them all free or all slave, which will inevitably bring about a dissolution of the Union.

Gentlemen, I am told that my time is out, and I am obliged to stop.

August 22, 1858.—LETTER TO J. O. CUNNINGHAM.

OTTAWA, August 22, 1858.

J. O. CUNNINGHAM, Esq.

My dear Sir: Yours of the 18th, signed as secretary of the Republican club, is received. In the matter of making speeches I am a good deal pressed by invitations from almost all quarters, and while I hope to be at Urbana some time during the canvass, I cannot yet say when. Can you not see me at Monticello on the 6th of September?

Douglas and I, for the first time this canvass, crossed swords here yesterday; the fire flew some, and I am glad to know I am yet alive. There was a vast concourse of people—more than could get near enough to hear.   Yours as ever,

A. LINCOLN.

August 27, 1858.—SECOND JOINT DEBATE AT FREEPORT, ILLINOIS.

Mr. Lincoln's Opening Speech.

Ladies and Gentlemen: On Saturday last, Judge Douglas and myself first met in public discussion. He spoke one hour, I an hour and a half, and he replied for half an hour. The order is now reversed. I am to speak an hour, he an hour and a half, and then I am to reply for half an hour. I propose to devote myself during the first hour to the scope of what was brought within the range of his half-hour speech at Ottawa. Of course there was brought within the scope of that half-hour's speech something of his own opening speech. In the course of that opening argument Judge Douglas proposed to me seven distinct interrogatories. In my speech of an hour and a half, I attended to some other parts of his speech, and incidentally, as I thought, answered one of the interrogatories then. I then distinctly intimated to him that I would answer the rest of his interrogatories on condition only that he should agree to answer as many for me. He made no intimation at the time of the proposition, nor did he in his reply allude at all to that suggestion of mine. I do him no injustice in saying that he occupied at least half of his reply in dealing with me as though I had refused to answer his in-

VOL. I.—20.

terrogatories. I now propose that I will answer any of the inter-rogatories, upon condition that he will answer questions from me not exceeding the same number. I give him an opportunity to respond. The judge remains silent. I now say that I will answer his inter-rogatories, whether he answers mine or not; and that after I have done so, I shall propound mine to him.

I have supposed myself, since the organization of the Republican party at Bloomington, in May, 1856, bound as a party man by the platforms of the party then and since. If in any interrogatories which I shall answer I go beyond the scope of what is within these platforms, it will be perceived that no one is responsible but myself. Having said this much, I will take up the judge's interrogatories as I find them printed in the Chicago "Times," and answer them *seria-tim*. In order that there may be no mistake about it, I have copied the interrogatories in writing, and also my answers to them. The first one of these interrogatories is in these words:

Question 1. "I desire to know whether Lincoln to-day stands as he did in 1854, in favor of the unconditional repeal of the fugitive-slave law?"

Answer. I do not now, nor ever did, stand in favor of the uncon-ditional repeal of the fugitive-slave law.

Q. 2. "I desire him to answer whether he stands pledged to-day as he did in 1854, against the admission of any more slave States into the Union, even if the people want them?"

A. I do not now, nor ever did, stand pledged against the admission of any more slave States into the Union.

Q. 3. "I want to know whether he stands pledged against the ad-mission of a new State into the Union with such a constitution as the people of that State may see fit to make?"

A. I do not stand pledged against the admission of a new State into the Union with such a constitution as the people of that State may see fit to make.

Q. 4. "I want to know whether he stands to-day pledged to the abolition of slavery in the District of Columbia?"

A. I do not stand to-day pledged to the abolition of slavery in the District of Columbia.

Q. 5. "I desire him to answer whether he stands pledged to the prohibition of the slave-trade between the different States?"

A. I do not stand pledged to the prohibition of the slave-trade between the different States.

Q. 6. "I desire to know whether he stands pledged to prohibit slavery in all the Territories of the United States, North as well as South of the Missouri Compromise line?"

A. I am impliedly, if not expressly, pledged to a belief in the right and duty of Congress to prohibit slavery in all the United States Territories.

Q. 7. "I desire him to answer whether he is opposed to the acquisition of any new territory unless slavery is first prohibited therein?"

A. I am not generally opposed to honest acquisition of territory; and, in any given case, I would or would not oppose such acquisition, accordingly as I might think such acquisition would or would not aggravate the slavery question among ourselves.

Now, my friends, it will be perceived upon an examination of these questions and answers, that so far I have only answered that I was not pledged to this, that, or the other. The judge has not framed his interrogatories to ask me anything more than this, and I have answered in strict accordance with the interrogatories, and have answered truly that I am not pledged at all upon any of the points to which I have answered. But I am not disposed to hang upon the exact form of his interrogatory. I am really disposed to take up at least some of these questions, and state what I really think upon them.

As to the first one, in regard to the fugitive-slave law, I have never hesitated to say, and I do not now hesitate to say, that I think, under the Constitution of the United States, the people of the Southern States are entitled to a congressional fugitive-slave law. Having said that, I have had nothing to say in regard to the existing fugitive-slave law, further than that I think it should have been framed so as to be free from some of the objections that pertain to it, without lessening its efficiency. And inasmuch as we are not now in an agitation in regard to an alteration or modification of that law, I would not be the man to introduce it as a new subject of agitation upon the general question of slavery.

In regard to the other question, of whether I am pledged to the admission of any more slave States into the Union, I state to you very frankly that I would be exceedingly sorry ever to be put in a position of having to pass upon that question. I should be exceedingly glad to know that there would never be another slave State admitted into the Union; but I must add, that if slavery shall be kept out of the Territories during the territorial existence of any one given Territory, and then the people shall, having a fair chance and a clear field, when they come to adopt the Constitution, do such an extraordinary thing as to adopt a slave constitution, uninfluenced by the actual presence of the institution among them, I see no alternative, if we own the country, but to admit them into the Union.

The third interrogatory is answered by the answer to the second, it being, as I conceive, the same as the second.

The fourth one is in regard to the abolition of slavery in the District of Columbia. In relation to that, I have my mind very distinctly made up. I should be exceedingly glad to see slavery abolished in the District of Columbia. I believe that Congress possesses the constitutional power to abolish it. Yet as a member of Congress, I should not with my present views be in favor of endeavoring to abolish slavery in the District of Columbia unless it would be upon these conditions: First, that the abolition should be gradual; second, that it should be on a vote of the majority of qualified voters in the District; and third, that compensation should be made to unwilling owners. With these three conditions, I confess I would be exceedingly glad to see Congress abolish slavery in the District of Columbia, and, in the language of Henry Clay, "sweep from our capital that foul blot upon our nation."

In regard to the fifth interrogatory, I must say here that as to the question of the abolition of the slave-trade between the different States, I can truly answer, as I have, that I am pledged to nothing about it. It is a subject to which I have not given that mature consideration that would make me feel authorized to state a position so as to hold myself entirely bound by it. In other words, that question has never been prominently enough before me to induce me to investigate whether we really have the constitutional power to do it. I could investigate it if I had sufficient time to bring myself to a conclusion upon that subject, but I have not done so, and I say so frankly to you here and to Judge Douglas. I must say, however, that if I should be of opinion that Congress does possess the constitutional power to abolish the slave-trade among the different States, I should still not be in favor of the exercise of that power unless upon some conservative principle as I conceive it, akin to what I have said in relation to the abolition of slavery in the District of Columbia.

My answer as to whether I desire that slavery should be prohibited in all the Territories of the United States is full and explicit within itself, and cannot be made clearer by any comments of mine. So I suppose in regard to the question whether I am opposed to the acquisition of any more territory unless slavery is first prohibited therein, my answer is such that I could add nothing by way of illustration, or making myself better understood, than the answer which I have placed in writing.

Now in all this the judge has me, and he has me on the record. I suppose he had flattered himself that I was really entertaining one set of opinions for one place and another set for another place—that I was afraid to say at one place what I uttered at another. What I am saying here I suppose I say to a vast audience as strongly tending to Abolitionism as any audience in the State of Illinois, and I believe I am saying that which, if it would be offensive to any persons and render them enemies to myself, would be offensive to persons in this audience.

I now proceed to propound to the judge the interrogatories so far as I have framed them. I will bring forward a new instalment when I get them ready. I will bring them forward now, only reaching to number four.

The first one is:

Question 1. If the people of Kansas shall, by means entirely unobjectionable in all other respects, adopt a State constitution, and ask admission into the Union under it, before they have the requisite number of inhabitants according to the English bill,—some ninety-three thousand,—will you vote to admit them?

Q. 2. Can the people of a United States Territory, in any lawful way, against the wish of any citizen of the United States, exclude slavery from its limits prior to the formation of a State constitution?

Q. 3. If the Supreme Court of the United States shall decide that States cannot exclude slavery from their limits, are you in favor of acquiescing in, adopting, and following such decision as a rule of political action?

Q. 4. Are you in favor of acquiring additional territory, in disregard of how such acquisition may affect the nation on the slavery question?

As introductory to these interrogatories which Judge Douglas propounded to me at Ottawa, he read a set of resolutions which he said Judge Trumbull and myself had participated in adopting, in the first Republican State convention, held at Springfield, in October, 1854. He insisted that I and Judge Trumbull, and perhaps the entire Republican party, were responsible for the doctrines contained in the set of resolutions which he read, and I understand that it was from that set of resolutions that he deduced the interrogatories which he propounded to me, using these resolutions as a sort of authority for propounding those questions to me. Now I say here to-day that I do not answer his interrogatories because of their springing at all from that set of resolutions which he read. I answered them because Judge Douglas thought fit to ask them. I do not now, nor ever did, recognize any responsibility upon myself in that set of resolutions. When I replied to him on that occasion, I assured him that I never had anything to do with them. I repeat here to-day, that I never in any possible form had anything to do with that set of resolutions. It turns out, I believe, that those resolutions were never passed at any convention held in Springfield. It turns out that they were never passed at any convention or any public meeting that I had any part in. I believe it turns out, in addition to all this, that there was not, in the fall of 1854, any convention holding a session in Springfield calling itself a Republican State convention; yet it is true there was a convention, or assemblage of men calling themselves a convention, at Springfield, that did pass some resolutions. But so little did I really know of the proceedings of that convention, or what set of resolutions they had passed, though having a general knowledge that there had been such an assemblage of men there, that when Judge Douglas read the resolutions, I really did not know but that they had been the resolutions passed then and there. I did not question that they were the resolutions adopted. For I could not bring myself to suppose that Judge Douglas could say what he did upon this subject without knowing that it was true. I contented myself, on that occasion, with denying, as I truly could, all connection with them, not denying or affirming whether they were passed at Springfield. Now it turns out that he had got hold of some resolutions passed at some convention or public meeting in Kane County. I wish to say here, that I don't conceive that in any fair and just mind this discovery relieves me at all. I had just as much to do with the convention in Kane County as that at Springfield. I am just as much responsible for the resolutions at Kane County as those at Springfield, the amount of the responsibility being exactly nothing in either case; no more than there would be in regard to a set of resolutions passed in the moon.

I allude to this extraordinary matter in this canvass for some further purpose than anything yet advanced. Judge Douglas did not make his statement upon that occasion as matters that he believed to be true, but he stated them roundly as being true, in such form as to pledge his veracity for their truth. When the whole matter turns out as it does, and when we consider who Judge Douglas is,— that he is a distinguished senator of the United States; that he has served nearly twelve years as such; that his character is not at all limited as an ordinary senator of the United States, but that his name has become of world-wide renown,—it is most extraordinary that he should so far forget all the suggestions of justice to an adversary, or of prudence to himself, as to venture upon the assertion of that which the slightest investigation would have shown him to be wholly false. I can only account for his having done so upon the supposition that that evil genius which has attended him through his life, giving to him an apparent astonishing prosperity, such as to lead very many good men to doubt there being any advantage in virtue over vice — I say I can only account for it on the supposition that that evil genius has at last made up its mind to forsake him.

And I may add that another extraordinary feature of the judge's conduct in this canvass — made more extraordinary by this incident — is, that he is in the habit, in almost all the speeches he makes, of charging falsehood upon his adversaries, myself and others. I now ask whether he is able to find in anything that Judge Trumbull, for instance, has said, or in anything that I have said, a justification at all compared with what we have, in this instance, for that sort of vulgarity.

I have been in the habit of charging as a matter of belief on my part, that, in the introduction of the Nebraska bill into Congress, there was a conspiracy to make slavery perpetual and national. I have arranged from time to time the evidence which establishes and proves the truth of this charge. I recurred to this charge at Ottawa. I shall not now have time to dwell upon it at very great length; but inasmuch as Judge Douglas in his reply of half an hour made some points upon me in relation to it, I propose noticing a few of them.

The judge insists that, in the first speech I made, in which I very distinctly made that charge, he thought for a good while I was in fun—that I was playful—that I was not sincere about it—and that he only grew angry and somewhat excited when he found that I insisted upon it as a matter of earnestness. He says he character- ized it as a falsehood as far as I implicated his moral character in that transaction. Well, I did not know, till he presented that view, that I had implicated his moral character. He is very much in the habit, when he argues me up into a position I never thought of occupying, of very cozily saying he has no doubt Lincoln is "con- scientious" in saying so. He should remember that I did not know but what he was altogether "conscientious" in that matter. I can conceive it possible for men to conspire to do a good thing, and I really find nothing in Judge Douglas's course of arguments that is contrary to or inconsistent with his belief of a conspiracy to nation- alize and spread slavery as being a good and blessed thing, and so I hope he will understand that I do not at all question but that in all this matter he is entirely "conscientious."

But to draw your attention to one of the points I made in this case, beginning at the beginning. When the Nebraska bill was introduced, or a short time afterward, by an amendment, I believe, it was provided that it must be considered "the true intent and meaning of this act not to legislate slavery into any State or Territory, or to exclude it therefrom, but to leave the people thereof perfectly free to form and regulate their own domestic institutions in their own way, subject only to the Constitution of the United States." I have called his attention to the fact that when he and some others began arguing that they were giving an increased degree of liberty to the people in the Territories over and above what they formerly had on the question of slavery, a question was raised whether the law was enacted to give such unconditional liberty to the people; and to test the sincerity of this mode of argument, Mr. Chase, of Ohio, introduced an amendment, in which he made the law—if the amendment were adopted—expressly declare that the people of the Territory should have the power to exclude slavery if they saw fit. I have asked attention also to the fact that Judge Douglas, and those who acted with him, voted that amendment down, notwithstanding it expressed exactly the thing they said was the true intent and meaning of the law. I have called attention to the fact that in subsequent times a decision of the Supreme Court has been made in which it has been declared that a Territorial Legislature has no constitutional right to exclude slavery. And I have argued and said that for men who did intend that the people of the Territory should have the right to exclude slavery absolutely and unconditionally, the voting down of Chase's amendment is wholly inexplicable. It is a puzzle—a riddle. But I have said that with men who did look forward to such a decision, or who had it in contemplation that such a decision of the Supreme Court would or might be made, the voting down of that amendment would be perfectly rational and intelligible. It would keep Congress from coming in collision with the decision when it was made. Anybody can conceive that if there was an intention or expectation that such a decision was to follow, it would not be a very desirable party attitude to get into for the Supreme Court—all or nearly all its members belonging to the same party—to decide one way, when the party in Congress had decided the other way. Hence it would be very rational for men expecting such a decision to keep the niche in that law clear for it. After pointing this out, I tell Judge Douglas that it looks to me as though here was the reason why Chase's amendment was voted down. I tell him that as he did it, and knows why he did it, if it was done for a reason different from this, he knows what that reason was, and can tell us what it was. I tell him, also, it will be vastly more satisfactory to the country for him to give some other plausible, intelligible reason why it was voted down than to stand upon his dignity and call people liars. Well, on Saturday he did make his answer, and what do you think it was? He says if I had only taken upon myself to tell the whole truth about that amendment of Chase's, no explanation would have been necessary on his part—or words to that effect. Now I say here that I am quite unconscious of having suppressed anything material to the case, and I am very frank to admit if there is any sound reason other than that which appeared to me material, it is quite fair for him to present it. What reason does he propose? That when Chase came forward with his amendment expressly authorizing the people to exclude slavery from the limits of every Territory, General Cass proposed to Chase, if he (Chase) would add to his amendment that the people should have the power to introduce or exclude, they would let it go.

This is substantially all of his reply. And because Chase would not do that they voted his amendment down. Well, it turns out, I believe, upon examination, that General Cass took some part in the little running debate upon that amendment, and then ran away and did not vote on it at all. Is not that the fact? So confident, as I think, was General Cass that there was a snake somewhere about, he chose to run away from the whole thing. This is an inference I draw from the fact that though he took part in the debate his name does not appear in the ayes and noes. But does Judge Douglas's reply amount to a satisfactory answer? [Cries of "Yes," "Yes," and "No," "No."] There is some little difference of opinion here. But I ask attention to a few more views bearing on the question of whether it amounts to a satisfactory answer. The men who were determined that that amendment should not get into the bill, and spoil the place where the Dred Scott decision was to come in, sought an excuse to get rid of it somewhere. One of these ways—one of these excuses—was to ask Chase to add to his proposed amendment a provision that the people might introduce slavery if they wanted to. They very well knew Chase would do no such thing—that Mr. Chase was one of the men differing from them on the broad principle of his insisting that freedom was better than slavery—a man who would not consent to enact a law penned with his own hand, by which he was made to recognize slavery on the one hand and liberty on the other as precisely equal; and when they insisted on his doing this, they very well knew they insisted on that which he would not for a moment think of doing, and that they were only bluffing him. I believe—I have not, since he made his answer, had a chance to examine the journals or "Congressional Globe," and therefore speak from memory—I believe the state of the bill at that time, according to parliamentary rules, was such that no member could propose an additional amendment to Chase's amendment. I rather think this is the truth—the judge shakes his head. Very well. I would like to know then, if they wanted Chase's amendment fixed over, why somebody else could not have offered to do it? If they wanted it amended, why did they not offer the amendment? Why did they stand there taunting and quibbling at Chase? Why did they not put it in themselves? But to put it on the other ground: suppose that there was such an amendment offered, and Chase's was an amendment to an amendment; until one is disposed of by parliamentary law, you cannot pile another on. Then all these gentlemen had to do was to vote Chase's on, and then, in the amended form in which the whole stood, add their own amendment to it if they wanted to put it in that shape. This was all they were obliged to do, and the ayes and noes show that there were thirty-six who voted it down, against ten who voted in favor of it. The thirty-six held entire sway and control. They could in some form or other have put that bill in the exact shape they wanted. If there was a rule preventing their amending it at the time, they could pass that, and then, Chase's amendment being merged, put it in the shape they wanted. They did not choose to do so, but they went into a quibble with Chase to get him to add what they knew he would not add, and because he would not, they stand upon that flimsy pretext for voting down what they argued was the meaning and intent of their own bill. They left room thereby for this Dred Scott decision, which goes very far to make slavery national throughout the United States.

I pass one or two points I have because my time will very soon expire, but I must be allowed to say that Judge Douglas recurs again, as he did upon one or two other occasions, to the enormity of Lincoln — an insignificant individual like Lincoln — upon his *ipse dixit* charging a conspiracy upon a large number of members of Congress, the Supreme Court, and two Presidents, to nationalize slavery. I want to say that, in the first place, I have made no charge of this sort upon my *ipse dixit*. I have only arrayed the evidence tending to prove it, and presented it to the understanding of others, saying what I think it proves, but giving you the means of judging whether it proves it or not. This is precisely what I have done. I have not placed it upon my *ipse dixit* at all. On this occasion, I wish to recall his attention to a piece of evidence which I brought forward at Ottawa on Saturday, showing that he had made substantially the same charge against substantially the same persons, excluding his dear self from the category. I ask him to give some attention to the evidence which I brought forward, that he himself had discovered a "fatal blow being struck" against the right of the people to exclude slavery from their limits, which fatal blow he assumed as in evidence in an article in the Washington "Union," published "by authority." I ask by whose authority? He discovers a similar or identical provision in the Lecompton constitution. Made by whom? The framers of that constitution. Advocated by whom? By all the members of the party in the nation, who advocated the introduction of Kansas into the Union under the Lecompton constitution.

I have asked his attention to the evidence that he arrayed to prove that such a fatal blow was being struck, and to the facts which he brought forward in support of that charge — being identical with the one which he thinks so villainous in me. He pointed it not at a newspaper editor merely, but at the President and his cabinet, and the members of Congress advocating the Lecompton constitution, and those framing that instrument. I must again be permitted to remind him, that although my *ipse dixit* may not be as great as his, yet it somewhat reduces the force of his calling my attention to the enormity of my making a like charge against him.

Go on, Judge Douglas.

Mr. Douglas's Reply in the Freeport Joint Debate.

Ladies and Gentlemen: The silence with which you have listened to Mr. Lincoln during his hour is creditable to this vast audience, composed of men of various political parties. Nothing is more honorable to any large mass of people assembled for the purpose of a fair discussion, than that kind and respectful attention that is yielded not only to your political friends, but to those who are opposed to you in politics.

I am glad that at last I have brought Mr. Lincoln to the conclusion that he had better define his position on certain political questions to which I called his attention at Ottawa. He there showed no disposition, no inclination, to answer them. I did not present idle questions for him to answer merely for my gratification. I laid the foundation for those interrogatories by showing that they constituted the platform of the party whose nominee he is for the Senate. I did not presume that I had the right to catechize him as I saw proper, unless I showed that his party, or a majority of it, stood upon the platform, and were in favor of the propositions upon which my questions were based. I desired simply to know, inasmuch as he had been nominated as the first, last, and only choice of his party, whether he concurred in the platform which that party had adopted for its government. In a few moments I will proceed to review the answers which he has given to these interrogatories, but in order to relieve his anxiety I will first respond to these which he has presented to me. Mark you, he has not presented interrogatories which have ever received the sanction of the party with which I am acting, and hence he has no other foundation for them than his own curiosity.

First, he desires to know if the people of Kansas shall form a constitution by means entirely proper and unobjectionable and ask admission into the Union as a State, before they have the requisite population for a member of Congress, whether I will vote for that admission. Well, now, I regret exceedingly that he did not answer that interrogatory himself before he put it to me, in order that we might understand, and not be left to infer, on which side he is. Mr. Trumbull, during the last session of Congress, voted from the beginning to the end against the admission of Oregon, although a free State, because she had not the requisite population for a member of Congress. Mr. Trumbull would not consent, under any circumstances, to let a State, free or slave, come into the Union until it had the requisite population. As Mr. Trumbull is in the field, fighting for Mr. Lincoln, I would like to have Mr. Lincoln answer his own question and tell me whether he is fighting Trumbull on that issue or not. But I will answer his question. In reference to Kansas, it is my opinion that as she has population enough to constitute a slave State, she has people enough for a free State. I will not make Kansas an exceptional case to the other States of the Union. I hold it to be a sound rule of universal application to require a Territory to contain the requisite population for a member of Congress, before it is admitted as a State into the Union. I made that proposition in the Senate in 1856, and I renewed it during the last session, in a bill providing that no Territory of the United States should form a constitution and apply for admission until it had the requisite population. On another occasion I proposed that neither Kansas, nor any other Territory, should be admitted until it had the requisite population.

Congress did not adopt any of my propositions containing this general rule, but did make an exception of Kansas. I will stand by that exception. Either Kansas must come in as a free State, with whatever population she may have, or the rule must be applied to all the other Territories alike. I therefore answer at once that, it having been decided that Kansas has people enough for a slave State, I hold that she has enough for a free State. I hope Mr. Lincoln is satisfied with my answer; and now I would like to get his answer to his own interrogatory—whether or not he will vote to admit Kansas before she has the requisite population. I want to know whether he will vote to admit Oregon before that Territory has the requisite population. Mr. Trumbull will not, and the same reason that commits Mr. Trumbull against the admission of Oregon commits him against Kansas, even if she should apply for admission as a free State. If there is any sincerity, any truth, in the argument of Mr. Trumbull in the Senate, against the admission of Oregon because she had not 93,420 people, although her population was larger than that of Kansas, he stands pledged against the admission of both Oregon and Kansas until they have 93,420 inhabitants. I would like Mr. Lincoln to answer this question. I would like him to take his own medicine. If he differs with Mr. Trumbull, let him answer his argument against the admission of Oregon, instead of poking questions at me.

The next question propounded to me by Mr. Lincoln is: Can the people of a Territory in any lawful way, against the wishes of any citizen of the United States, exclude slavery from their limits prior to the formation of a State constitution? I answer emphatically, as Mr. Lincoln has heard me answer a hundred times from every stump in Illinois, that in my opinion the people of a Territory can, by lawful means, exclude slavery from their limits prior to the formation of a State constitution. Mr. Lincoln knew that I had answered that question over and over again. He heard me argue the Nebraska bill on that principle all over the State in 1854, in 1855, and in 1856, and he has no excuse for pretending to be in doubt as to my position on that question. It matters not what way the Supreme Court may hereafter decide as to the abstract question whether slavery may or may not go into a Territory under the Constitution, the people have the lawful means to introduce it or exclude it as they please, for the reason that slavery cannot exist a day or an hour anywhere unless it is supported by local police regulations. Those police regulations can only be established by the local legislature, and if the people are opposed to slavery they will elect representatives to that body who will by unfriendly legislation effectually prevent the introduction of it into their midst. If, on the contrary, they are for it, their legislation will favor its extension. Hence, no matter what the decision of the Supreme Court may be on that abstract question, still the right of the people to make a slave Territory or a free Territory is perfect and complete under the Nebraska bill. I hope Mr. Lincoln deems my answer satisfactory on that point.

In this connection I will notice the charge which he has introduced in relation to Mr. Chase's amendment. I thought that I had chased that amendment out of Mr. Lincoln's brain at Ottawa; but it seems that still haunts his imagination, and he is not yet satisfied. I had supposed that he would be ashamed to press that question further. He is a lawyer, and has been a member of Congress, and has occupied his time and amused you by telling you about parliamentary proceedings. He ought to have known better than to try to palm off his miserable impositions upon this intelligent audience. The Nebraska bill provided that the legislative power and authority of the said Territory should extend to all rightful subjects of legislation consistent with the organic act and the Constitution of the United States. It did not make any exception as to slavery, but gave all the power that it was possible for Congress to give, without violating the Constitution, to the territorial legislature, with no exception or limitation on the subject of slavery at all. The language of that bill which I have quoted gave the full power and the full authority over the subject of slavery, affirmatively and negatively, to introduce it or exclude it, so far as the Constitution of the United States would permit. What more could Mr. Chase give by his amendment? Nothing. He offered his amendment for the identical purpose for which Mr. Lincoln is using it, to enable demagogues in the country to try and deceive the people.

His amendment was to this effect. It provided that the legislature should have the power to exclude slavery; and General Cass suggested, "Why not give the power to introduce as well as exclude?" The answer was, they have the power already in the bill to do both. Chase was afraid his amendment would be adopted if he put the alternative proposition and so make it fair both ways, but would not yield. He offered it for the purpose of having it rejected. He offered it, as he has himself avowed over and over again, simply to make capital out of it for the stump. He expected that it would be capital for small politicians in the country, and that they would make an effort to deceive the people with it; and he was not mistaken, for Lincoln is carrying out the plan admirably. Lincoln knows that the Nebraska bill, without Chase's amendment, gave all the power which the Constitution would permit. Could Congress confer any more? Could Congress go beyond the Constitution of the country? We gave all—a full grant, with no exception in regard to slavery one way or the other. We left that question as we left all others, to be decided by the people for themselves, just as they pleased. I will not occupy my time on this question. I have argued it before all over Illinois. I have argued it in this beautiful city of Freeport; I have argued it in the North, the South, the East, and the West, avowing the same sentiments and the same principles. I have not been afraid to avow my sentiments up here for fear I would be trotted down into Egypt.

The third question which Mr. Lincoln presented is, if the Supreme Court of the United States shall decide that a State of this Union cannot exclude slavery from its own limits, will I submit to it? I am amazed that Lincoln should ask such a question. ["A school-boy knows better."] Yes, a school-boy does know better. Mr. Lincoln's object is to cast an imputation upon the Supreme Court. He knows that there never was but one man in America claiming any degree of intelligence or decency, who ever for a moment pretended such a thing. It is true that the Washington "Union," in an article published on the 17th of last December, did put forth that doctrine, and I denounced the article on the floor of the Senate, in a speech which Mr. Lincoln now pretends was against the President. The "Union" had claimed that slavery had a right to go into the free States, and that any provision in the constitution or laws of the free States to the contrary was null and void. I denounced it in the Senate, as I said before, and I was the first man who did. Lincoln's friends, Trumbull, and Seward, and Hale, and Wilson, and the whole Black Republican side of the Senate were silent. They left it to me to denounce it. And what was the reply made to me on that occasion? Mr. Toombs, of Georgia, got up and undertook to lecture me on the ground that I ought not to have deemed the article worthy of notice, and ought not to have replied to it; that there was not one man, woman, or child south of the Potomac, in any slave State, who did not repudiate any such pretension. Mr. Lincoln knows that that reply was made on the spot, and yet now he asks this question. He might as well ask me, suppose Mr. Lincoln should steal a horse, would I sanction it? and it would be as genteel in me to ask him, in the event he stole a horse, what ought to be done with him. He casts an imputation upon the Supreme Court of the United States by supposing that they would violate the Constitution of the United States. I tell him that such a thing is not possible. It would be an act of moral treason that no man on the bench could ever descend to. Mr. Lincoln himself would never in his partizan feelings so far forget what was right as to be guilty of such an act.

The fourth question of Mr. Lincoln is: Are you in favor of acquiring additional territory, in disregard as to how such acquisition may affect the Union on the slavery question? This question is very ingeniously and cunningly put.

The Black Republican creed lays it down expressly, that under no circumstances shall we acquire any more territory unless slavery is first prohibited in the country. I ask Mr. Lincoln whether he is in favor of that proposition. Are you [addressing Mr. Lincoln] opposed to the acquisition of any more territory, under any circumstances, unless slavery is prohibited in it? That he does not like to answer. When I ask him whether he stands up to that article in the platform of his party, he turns, Yankee-fashion, and, without answering it, asks me whether I am in favor of acquiring territory without regard to how it may affect the Union on the slavery question. I answer that whenever it becomes necessary, in our growth and progress, to acquire more territory, that I am in favor of it, without reference to the question of slavery, and when we have acquired it, I will leave the people free to do as they please, either to make it slave or free territory, as they prefer. It is idle to tell me or you that we have territory enough. Our fathers supposed that we had enough when our territory extended to the Mississippi River, but a few years' growth and expansion satisfied them that we needed more, and the Louisiana territory, from the west branch of the Mississippi to the British possessions, was acquired. Then we acquired Oregon, then California and New Mexico. We have enough now for the present, but this is a young and a growing nation. It swarms as often as a hive of bees, and as new swarms are turned out each year, there must be hives in which they can gather and make their honey. In less than fifteen years, if the same progress that has distinguished this country for the last fifteen years continues, every foot of vacant land between this and the Pacific ocean, owned by the United States, will be occupied. Will you not continue to increase at the end of fifteen years as well as now? I tell you, increase, and multiply, and expand, is the law of this nation's existence. You cannot limit this great republic by mere boundary lines, saying, "Thus far shalt thou go, and no further." Any one of you gentlemen might as well say to a son twelve years old that he is big enough, and must not grow any larger, and in order to prevent his growth put a hoop around him to keep him to his present size. What would be the result? Either the hoop must burst and be rent asunder, or the child must die. So it would be with this great nation. With our natural increase, growing with a rapidity unknown in any other part of the globe, with the tide of emigration that is fleeing from despotism in the Old World to seek refuge in our own, there is a constant torrent pouring into this country that requires more land, more territory upon which to settle, and just as fast as our interests and our destiny require additional territory in the North, in the South, or on the islands of the ocean, I am for it, and when we acquire it, will leave the people, according to the Nebraska bill, free to do as they please on the subject of slavery and every other question.

I trust now that Mr. Lincoln will deem himself answered on his four points. He racked his brain so much in devising these four questions that he exhausted himself, and had not strength enough to invent the others. As soon as he is able to hold a council with his advisers, Lovejoy, Farnsworth, and Fred Douglass, he will frame and propound others. ["Good, good."] You Black Republicans who say good, I have no doubt think that they are all good men. I have reason to recollect that some people in this country think that Fred Douglass is a very good man. The last time I came here to make a speech, while talking from the stand to you, people of Freeport, as I am doing to-day, I saw a carriage, and a magnificent one it was, drive up and take a position on the outside of the crowd; a beautiful young lady was sitting on the box-seat, whilst Fred Douglass and her mother reclined inside, and the owner of the carriage acted as driver. I saw this in your own town. ["What of it?"] All I have to say of it is this, that if you Black Republicans think that the negro ought to be on a social equality with your wives and daughters, and ride in a carriage with your wife, whilst you drive the team, you have perfect right to do so. I am told that one of Fred Douglass's kinsmen, another rich black negro, is now traveling in this part of the State making speeches for his friend Lincoln as the champion of black men. ["What have you to say against it?"] All I have to say on that subject is, that those of you who believe that the negro is your equal and ought to be on an equality with you socially, politically, and legally, have a right to entertain those opinions, and of course will vote for Mr. Lincoln.

I have a word to say on Mr. Lincoln's answer to the interrogatories contained in my speech at Ottawa, and which he has pretended to reply to here to-day. Mr. Lincoln makes a great parade of the fact that I quoted a platform as having been adopted by the Black Republican party at Springfield in 1854, which, it turns out, was adopted at another place. Mr. Lincoln loses sight of the thing itself in his ecstasies over the mistake I made in stating the place where it was done. He thinks that that platform was not adopted on the right "spot."

When I put the direct questions to Mr. Lincoln to ascertain whether he now stands pledged to that creed — to the unconditional repeal of the fugitive-slave law, a refusal to admit any more slave States into the Union even if the people want them, a determination to apply the Wilmot proviso, not only to all the territory we now have, but all that we may hereafter acquire — he refused to answer, and his followers say, in excuse, that the resolutions upon which I based my interrogatories were not adopted at the right "spot." Lincoln and his political friends are great on "spots." In Congress, as a representative of this State, he declared the Mexican war to be unjust and infamous, and would not support it, or acknowledge his own country to be right in the contest, because he said that American blood was not shed on American soil in the right "spot." And now he cannot answer the questions I put to him at Ottawa because the resolutions I read were not adopted at the right "spot." It may be possible that I was led into an error as to the spot on which the resolutions I then read were proclaimed, but I was not, and am not in error as to the fact of their forming the basis of the creed of the Republican party when that party was first organized. I will state to you the evidence I had, and upon which I relied for my statement that the resolutions in question were adopted at Springfield on the 5th of October, 1854. Although I was aware that such resolutions had been passed in this district, and nearly all the northern congressional districts and county conventions, I had not noticed whether or not they had been adopted by any State convention. In 1856 a debate arose in Congress between Major Thomas L. Harris, of the Springfield district, and Mr. Norton, of the Joliet district, on political matters connected with our State, in the course of which Major Harris quoted those resolutions as having been passed by the first Republican State convention that ever assembled in Illinois. I knew that Major Harris was remarkable for his accuracy, that he was a very conscientious and sincere man, and I also noticed that Norton did not question the accuracy of this statement. I therefore took it for granted that it was so, and the other day when I concluded to use the resolutions at Ottawa, I wrote to Charles H. Lanphier, editor of the "State Register," at Springfield, calling his attention to them, telling him that I had been informed that Major Harris was lying sick at Springfield, and desiring him to call upon him and ascertain all the facts concerning the resolutions, the time and the place where they were adopted. In reply Mr. Lanphier sent me two copies of his paper, which I have here. The first is a copy of the "State Register," published at Springfield, Mr. Lincoln's own town, on the 16th of October, 1854, only eleven days after the adjournment of the convention, from which I desire to read the following:

During the late discussions in this city, Lincoln made a speech, to which Judge Douglas replied. In Lincoln's speech he took the broad ground that, according to the Declaration of Independence, the whites and blacks are equal. From this he drew the conclusion, which he several times repeated, that the white man had no right to pass laws for the government of the black man without the nigger's consent. This speech of Lincoln's was heard and applauded by all the Abolitionists assembled in Springfield. So soon as Mr. Lincoln was done speaking, Mr. Codding arose and requested all the delegates to the Black Republican convention to withdraw into the Senate chamber. They did so, and after long deliberation, they laid down the following Abolition platform as the platform on which they stood. We call the particular attention of our readers to it.

Then follows the identical platform, word for word, which I read at Ottawa. Now, that was published in Mr. Lincoln's own town, eleven days after the convention was held, and it has remained on record up to this day never contradicted.

When I quoted the resolutions at Ottawa and questioned Mr. Lincoln in relation to them, he said that his name was on the committee that reported them, but he did not serve, nor did he think he served, because he was, or thought he was, in Tazewell County at the time the convention was in session. He did not deny that the resolutions were passed by the Springfield convention. He did not know better, and evidently thought that they were, but afterward his friends declared that they had discovered that they varied in some respects from the resolutions passed by that convention. I have shown you that I had good evidence for believing that the resolutions had been passed at Springfield. Mr. Lincoln ought to have known better; but not a word is said about his ignorance on the subject, whilst I, notwithstanding the circumstances, am accused of forgery.

Now, I will show you that if I have made a mistake as to the place where these resolutions were adopted — and when I get down to Springfield I will investigate the matter and see whether or not I have — the principles they enunciate were adopted as the Black Republican platform [" White, white "], in the various counties and congressional districts throughout the north end of the State in 1854. This platform was adopted in nearly every county that gave a Black Republican majority for the legislature in that year, and here is a man [pointing to Mr. Denio, who sat on the stand near Deacon Bross] who knows as well as any living man that it was the creed of the Black Republican party at that time. I would be willing to call Denio as a witness, or any other honest man belonging to that party. I will now read the resolutions adopted at the Rockford convention on the 30th of August, 1854, which nominated Washburne for Congress. You elected him on the following platform:

Resolved, That the continued and increasing aggressions of slavery in our country are destructive of the best rights of a free people, and that such aggressions cannot be successfully resisted without the united political action of all good men.

Resolved, That the citizens of the United States hold in their hands peaceful, constitutional, and efficient remedy against the encroachments of the slave power, the ballot-box; and if that remedy is boldly and wisely applied, the principles of liberty and eternal justice will be established.

Resolved, That we accept this issue forced upon us by the slave power, and, in defense of freedom, will coöperate and be known as Republicans, pledged to the accomplishment of the following purposes:

To bring the administration of the government back to the control of first principles; to restore Kansas and Nebraska to the position of free Territories; to repeal and entirely abrogate the fugitive-slave law; to restrict slavery to those States in which it exists; to prohibit the admission of any more slave States into the Union; to exclude slavery from all the Territories over which the General Government has exclusive jurisdiction, and to resist the acquisition of any more Territories unless the introduction of slavery therein forever shall have been prohibited.

Resolved, That in furtherance of these principles we will use such constitutional and lawful means as shall seem best adapted to their accomplishment, and that we will support no man for office under the General or State Government who is not positively committed to the support of these principles, and whose personal character and conduct is not a guaranty that he is reliable and shall abjure all party allegiance and ties.

Resolved, That we cordially invite persons of all former political parties whatever in favor of the object expressed in the above resolutions to unite with us in carrying them into effect.

Well, you think that is a very good platform, do you not? If you do, if you approve it now, and think it is all right, you will not join with those men who say that I libel you by calling these your principles, will you? Now, Mr. Lincoln complains; Mr. Lincoln charges that I did you and him injustice by saying that this was the platform of your party. I am told that Washburne made a speech in Galena last night, in which he abused me awfully for bringing to light this platform, on which he was elected to Congress. He thought that you had forgotten it, as he and Mr. Lincoln desire to. He did not deny but that you had adopted it, and that he had subscribed to and was pledged by it, but he did not think it was fair to call it up and remind the people that it was their platform.

But I am glad to find that you are more honest in your Abolitionism than your leaders, by avowing that it is your platform, and right in your opinion.

In the adoption of that platform, you not only declared that you would resist the admission of any more slave States, and work for the repeal of the fugitive-slave law, but you pledged yourself not to vote for any man for State or Federal offices who was not committed to these principles. You were thus committed. Similar resolutions to those were adopted in your county convention here; and now with your admissions that they are your platform and embody your sentiments now as they did then, what do you think of Mr. Lincoln, your candidate for the United States Senate, who is attempting to dodge the responsibility of this platform, because it was not adopted in the right spot? I thought that it was adopted in Springfield, but it turns out it was not, that it was adopted at Rockford, and in the various counties which comprise this congressional district. When I get into the next district, I will show that the same platform was adopted there, and so on through the State, until I nail the responsibility of it upon the back of the Black Republican party throughout the State. [A voice: " Could n't you modify and call it brown?"] Not a bit. I thought that you were becoming a little brown when your members in Congress voted for the Crittenden-Montgomery bill, but since you have backed out from that position, and gone back to Abolitionism, you are black and not brown.

Gentlemen, I have shown you what your platform was in 1854. You still adhere to it. The same platform was adopted by nearly all the counties where the Black Republican party had a majority in 1854. I wish now to call your attention to the action of your representatives in the legislature when they assembled together at Springfield. In the first place you must remember that this was the organization of a new party. It is so declared in the resolutions themselves, which say that you are going to dissolve all old party ties and call the new party Republican. The Old Whig party was to have its throat cut from ear to ear, and the Democratic party was to be annihilated and blotted out of existence, whilst in lieu of these parties the Black Republican party was to be organized on this Abolition platform. You know who the chief leaders were in breaking up and destroying these two great parties. Lincoln on the one hand and Trumbull on the other, being disappointed politicians, and having retired or been driven to obscurity by an outraged constituency because of their political sins, formed a scheme to Abolitionize the two parties, and lead the old-line Whigs and old-line Democrats captive, bound hand and foot, into the Abolition camp. Giddings, Chase, Fred Douglass, and Lovejoy were here to christen them whenever they were brought in. Lincoln went to work to dissolve the old-line Whig party. Clay was dead, and although the sod was not yet green on his grave, this man undertook to bring into disrepute those great compromise measures of 1850, with which Clay and Webster were identified. Up to 1854 the Old Whig party and the Democratic party had stood on a common platform so far as this slavery question was concerned. You Whigs and we Democrats differed about the bank, the tariff, distribution, the specie circular, and the subtreasury, but we agreed on this slavery question and the true mode of preserving the peace and harmony of the Union. The compromise measures of 1850 were introduced by Clay, were defended by Webster, and supported by Cass, and were approved by Fillmore, and sanctioned by the national men of both parties. They constituted a common plank upon which both Whigs and Democrats stood. In 1852 the Whig party, in its last national convention at Baltimore, indorsed and approved these measures of Clay, and so did the national convention of the Democratic party held that same year. Thus the old-line Whigs and the old-line Democrats stood pledged to the great principle of self-government, which guarantees to the people of each Territory the right to decide the slavery question for themselves. In 1854, after the death of Clay and Webster, Mr. Lincoln, on the part of the Whigs, undertook to Abolitionize the Whig party by dissolving it, transferring the members into the Abolition camp and making them train under Giddings, Fred Douglass, Lovejoy, Chase, Farns-

worth, and other Abolition leaders. Trumbull undertook to dissolve
the Democratic party by taking old Democrats into the Abolition
camp.   Mr. Lincoln was aided in his efforts by many leading Whigs
throughout the State—your member of Congress, Mr. Washburne,
being one of the most active. Trumbull was aided by many rene-
gades from the Democratic party, among whom were John Wentworth, Tom Turner, and others with whom you are familiar.

Mr. Turner, who was one of the moderators, here interposed, and
said that he had drawn the resolutions which Senator Douglas had
read.

Mr. Douglas: Yes, and Turner says that he drew these resolutions.
["Hurrah for Turner!" "Hurrah for Douglas!"]   That is right;
give Turner cheers for drawing the resolutions, if you approve them.
If he drew those resolutions, he will not deny that they are the creed
of the Black Republican party.

Mr. Turner: They are our creed exactly.

Mr. Douglas: And yet Lincoln denies that he stands on them.
Mr. Turner says that the creed of the Black Republican party is the
admission of no more slave States, and yet Mr. Lincoln declares that
he would not like to be placed in a position where he would have to
vote for them.   All I have to say to friend Lincoln is, that I do not
think there is much danger of his being placed in such a position.
As Mr. Lincoln would be very sorry to be placed in such an embarrassing position as to be obliged to vote on the admission of any
more slave States, I propose, out of mere kindness, to relieve him
from any such necessity.   When the bargain between Lincoln and
Trumbull was completed for Abolitionizing the Whig and Democratic parties, they "spread" over the State, Lincoln still pretending
to be an old-line Whig, in order to "rope in" the Whigs, and Trumbull pretending to be as good a Democrat as he ever was, in order
to coax the Democrats over into the Abolition ranks.   They played
the part that "decoy ducks" play down on the Potomac River.   In
that part of the country they make artificial ducks, and put them on
the water in places where the wild ducks are to be found, for the
purpose of decoying them.   Well, Lincoln and Trumbull played the
part of these "decoy ducks," and deceived enough old-line Whigs
and old-line Democrats to elect a Black Republican legislature.
When that legislature met, the first thing it did was to elect as
Speaker of the House the very man who is now boasting that he wrote
the Abolition platform on which Lincoln will not stand.   I want to
know of Mr. Turner whether or not, when he was elected, he was a
good embodiment of Republican principles?

Mr. Turner: I hope I was then and am now.

Mr. Douglas: He swears that he hopes he was then and is now.
He wrote that Black Republican platform, and is satisfied with it
now.   I admire and acknowledge Turner's honesty.   Every man of
you knows what he says about these resolutions being the platform
of the Black Republican party is true, and you also know that each
one of these men who are shuffling and trying to deny it is only
trying to cheat the people out of their votes for the purpose of deceiving them still more after the election. I propose to trace this thing

a little further, in order that you can see what additional evidence there is to fasten this revolutionary platform upon the Black Republican party. When the legislature assembled, there was a United States senator to elect in the place of General Shields, and before they proceeded to ballot, Lovejoy insisted on laying down certain principles by which to govern the party. It has been published to the world and satisfactorily proven that there was, at the time the alliance was made between Trumbull and Lincoln to Abolitionize the two parties, an agreement that Lincoln should take Shields's place in the United States Senate, and Trumbull should have mine so soon as they could conveniently get rid of me. When Lincoln was beaten for Shields's place, in a manner I will refer to in a few minutes, he felt very sore and restive; his friends grumbled, and some of them came out and charged that the most infamous treachery had been practised against him; that the bargain was that Lincoln was to have had Shields's place, and Trumbull was to have waited for mine, but that Trumbull, having the control of a few Abolitionized Democrats, prevented them from voting for Lincoln, thus keeping him within a few votes of an election until he succeeded in forcing the party to drop him and elect Trumbull. Well, Trumbull having cheated Lincoln, his friends made a fuss, and in order to keep them and Lincoln quiet, the party were obliged to come forward, in advance, at the last State election, and make a pledge that they would go for Lincoln and nobody else. Lincoln could not be silenced in any other way.

Now, there are a great many Black Republicans of you who do not know this thing was done. [" White, white," and great clamor.] I wish to remind you that while Mr. Lincoln was speaking there was not a Democrat vulgar and blackguard enough to interrupt him. But I know that the shoe is pinching you. I am clinching Lincoln now, and you are scared to death for the result. I have seen this thing before. I have seen men make appointments for joint discussions, and, the moment their man has been heard, try to interrupt and prevent a fair hearing of the other side. I have seen your mobs before, and defy your wrath. [Tremendous applause.] My friends, do not cheer, for I need my whole time. The object of the opposition is to occupy my attention in order to prevent me from giving the whole evidence and nailing this double-dealing on the Black Republican party. As I have before said, Lovejoy demanded a declaration of principles on the part of the Black Republicans of the legislature before going into an election for United States senator. He offered the following preamble and resolutions which I hold in my hand:

WHEREAS, Human slavery is a violation of the principles of natural and revealed rights; and whereas, the fathers of the Revolution, fully imbued with the spirit of these principles, declared freedom to be the inalienable birthright of all men; and whereas, the preamble to the Constitution of the United States avers that that instrument was ordained to establish justice and secure the blessings of liberty to ourselves and our posterity; and whereas, in furtherance of the above principles, slavery was forever prohibited in the old Northwest Territory, and more recently in all that territory lying west and north of the State of Missouri by the act of the Federal Government; and whereas, the repeal of the prohibition last referred to was contrary to the wishes of the people of Illinois, a violation of an implied compact, long deemed sacred by the citizens of the United States, and a wide departure from the uniform action of the General Government in relation to the extension of slavery; therefore,

Resolved, by the House of Representatives, the Senate concurring therein, That our senators in Congress be instructed, and our representatives requested to introduce, if not otherwise introduced, and to vote for a bill to restore such prohibition to the aforesaid Territories, and also to extend a similar prohibition to all territory which now belongs to the United States, or which may hereafter come under their jurisdiction.

Resolved, That our senators in Congress be instructed, and our representatives requested, to vote against the admission of any State into the Union, the constitution of which does not prohibit slavery, whether the territory out of which such State may have been formed shall have been acquired by conquest, treaty, purchase, or from original territory of the United States.

Resolved, That our senators in Congress be instructed, and our representatives requested, to introduce and vote for a bill to repeal an act entitled "An act respecting fugitives from justice and persons escaping from the services of their masters"; and, failing in that, for such a modification of it as shall secure the right of *habeas corpus* and trial by jury before the regularly constituted authorities of the State, to all persons claimed as owing service or labor.

Those resolutions were introduced by Mr. Lovejoy immediately preceding the election of senator. They declared first, that the Wilmot proviso must be applied to all territory north of 36° 30′; secondly, that it must be applied to all territory south of 36° 30′; thirdly, that it must be applied to all the territory now owned by the United States; and finally, that it must be applied to all territory hereafter to be acquired by the United States. The next resolution declares that no more slave States shall be admitted into this Union under any circumstances whatever, no matter whether they are formed out of territory now owned by us or that we may hereafter acquire, by treaty, by Congress, or in any manner whatever. The next resolution demands the unconditional repeal of the fugitive-slave law, although its unconditional repeal would leave no provision for carrying out that clause of the Constitution of the United States which guarantees the surrender of fugitives. If they could not get an unconditional repeal, they demanded that that law should be so modified as to make it as nearly useless as possible. Now, I want to show you who voted for these resolutions. When the vote was taken on the first resolution, it was decided in the affirmative — yeas 41, nays 32. You will find that this is a strict party vote, between the Democrats on the one hand, and the Black Republicans on the other. [Cries of " White, white," and clamor.] I know your name, and always call things by their right name. The point I wish to call your attention to is this : that these resolutions were adopted on the 7th day of February, and that on the 8th they went into an election for a United States senator, and that day every man who voted for these resolutions, with but two exceptions, voted for Lincoln for the United States Senate. [" Give us their names."] I will read the names over to you if you want them, but I believe your object is to occupy my time.

On the next resolution the vote stood, yeas 33, nays 40; and on the third resolution, yeas 35, nays 47. I wish to impress upon you that every man who voted for those resolutions, with but two exceptions, voted on the next day for Lincoln for United States senator. Bear in mind that the members who thus voted for Lincoln were elected to the legislature pledged to vote for no man for office under the State or Federal Government who was not committed to this Black Republican platform. They were all so pledged. Mr. Turner, who stands by me, and who then represented you, and who says that he wrote those resolutions, voted for Lincoln, when he was pledged not to do so unless Lincoln was in favor of those resolutions. I now ask Mr. Turner [turning to Mr. Turner], did you violate your pledge in voting for Mr. Lincoln, or did he commit himself to your platform before you cast your vote for him?

I could go through the whole list of names here and show you that all the Black Republicans in the legislature, who voted for Mr. Lincoln, had voted on the day previous for these resolutions. For instance, here are the names of Sargent and Little, of Jo Daviess and Carroll; Thomas J. Turner, of Stephenson; Lawrence, of Boone and McHenry; Swan, of Lake; Pinckney, of Ogle County; and Lyman, of Winnebago. Thus you see every member from your congressional district voted for Mr. Lincoln, and they were pledged not to vote for him unless he was committed to the doctrine of no more slave States, the prohibition of slavery in the Territories, and the repeal of the fugitive-slave law. Mr. Lincoln tells you to-day that he is not pledged to any such doctrine. Either Mr. Lincoln was then committed to those propositions, or Mr. Turner violated his pledges to you when he voted for him. Either Lincoln was pledged to each one of those propositions, or else every Black Republican representative from this congressional district violated his pledge of honor to his constituents by voting for him. I ask you which horn of the dilemma will you take? Will you hold Lincoln up to the platform of his party, or will you accuse every representative you had in the legislature of violating his pledge of honor to his constituents? There is no escape for you. Either Mr. Lincoln was committed to those propositions, or your members violated their faith. Take either horn of the dilemma you choose. There is no dodging the question; I want Lincoln's answer. He says he was not pledged to repeal the fugitive-slave law, that he does not quite like to do it; he will not introduce a law to repeal it, but thinks there ought to be some law; he does not tell what it ought to be; upon the whole, he is altogether undecided, and don't know what to think or do. That is the substance of his answer upon the repeal of the fugitive-slave law. I put the question to him distinctly, whether he indorsed that part of the Black Republican platform which calls for the entire abrogation and repeal of the fugitive-slave law. He answers, no!—that he does not indorse that; but he does not tell what he is for, or what he will vote for. His answer is, in fact, no answer at all. Why cannot he speak out and say what he is for and what he will do?

In regard to there being no more slave States, he is not pledged to that. He would not like, he says, to be put in a position where he would have to vote one way or another upon that question. I pray you, do not put him in a position that would embarrass him so much. Gentlemen, if he goes to the Senate he may be put in that position, and then which way will he vote? [A voice: "How will you vote?"] I will vote for the admission of just such a State as by the form of their constitution the people show they want. If they want slavery, they shall have it; if they prohibit slavery, it shall be prohibited. They can form their institutions to please themselves, subject only to the Constitution; and I for one stand ready to receive them into the Union. Why cannot your Black Republican candidates talk out as plain as that when they are questioned?

I do not want to cheat any man out of his vote. No man is deceived in regard to my principles if I have the power to express myself in terms explicit enough to convey my ideas.

Mr. Lincoln made a speech when he was nominated for the United State Senate which covers all these Abolition platforms. He there lays down a proposition so broad in its Abolitionism as to cover the whole ground.

In my opinion it [the slavery agitation] will not cease until a crisis shall have been reached and passed. "A house divided against itself cannot stand." I believe this government cannot endure permanently half slave and half free. I do not expect the house to fall—but I do expect it will cease to be divided. It will become all one thing or all the other. Either the opponents of slavery will arrest the further spread of it, and place it where the public mind shall rest in the belief that it is in the course of ultimate extinction, or its advocates will push it forward till it shall become alike lawful in all the States — old as well as new, North as well as South.

There you find that Mr. Lincoln lays down the doctrine that this Union cannot endure divided as our fathers made it, with free and slave States. He says they must all become one thing or all the other; that they must all be free or all slave, or else the Union cannot continue to exist. It being his opinion that to admit any more slave States, to continue to divide the Union into free and slave States, will dissolve it, I want to know of Mr. Lincoln whether he will vote for the admission of another slave State.

He tells you the Union cannot exist unless the States are all free or all slave; he tells you that he is opposed to making them all slave, and hence he is for making them all free, in order that the Union may exist; and yet he will not say that he will not vote against another slave State, knowing that the Union must be dissolved if he votes for it. I ask you if that is fair dealing? The true intent and inevitable conclusion to be drawn from his first Springfield speech is, that he is opposed to the admission of any more slave States under any circumstances. If he is so opposed, why not say so? If he believes this Union cannot endure divided into free and slave States, that they must all become free in order to save the Union, he is bound as an honest man, to vote against any more slave States. If he believes it he is bound to do it. Show me that it is my duty in order to save the Union to do a particular act, and I will do it if the Constitution does not prohibit it. I am not for the dissolution of the Union under any circumstances. I will pursue no course of conduct that will give just cause for the dissolution of the Union. The hope of the friends of freedom throughout the world rests upon the perpetuity of this Union. The downtrodden and oppressed people who are suffering under European despotism all look with hope and anxiety to the American Union as the only resting-place and permanent home of freedom and self-government.

Mr. Lincoln says that he believes that this Union cannot continue to endure with slave States in it, and yet he will not tell you distinctly whether he will vote for or against the admission of any more slave States, but says he would not like to be put to the test. I do not think he will be put to the test. I do not think that the people of Illinois desire a man to represent them who would not like to be put to the test on the performance of a high constitutional duty. I will retire in shame from the Senate of the United States when I am not willing to be put to the test in the performance of my duty. I have been put to severe tests. I have stood by my principles in fair weather and in foul, in the sunshine and in the rain. I have defended the great principles of self-government here among you when Northern sentiment ran in a torrent against me, and I have defended that same great principle when Southern sentiment came down like an avalanche upon me. I was not afraid of any test they put to me. I knew I was right—I knew my principles were sound—I knew that the people would see in the end that I had done right, and I knew that the God of Heaven would smile upon me if I was faithful in the performance of my duty.

Mr. Lincoln makes a charge of corruption against the Supreme Court of the United States, and two Presidents of the United States, and attempts to bolster it up by saying that I did the same against the Washington "Union." Suppose I did make that charge of corruption against the Washington "Union," when it was true, does that justify him in making a false charge against me and others? That is the question I would put. He says that at the time the Nebraska bill was introduced, and before it was passed, there was a conspiracy between the judges of the Supreme Court, President Pierce, President Buchanan, and myself by that bill, and the decision of the court, to break down the barrier and establish slavery all over the Union. Does he not know that that charge is historically false as against President Buchanan? He knows that Mr. Buchanan was at that time in England, representing this country with distinguished ability at the Court of St. James, that he was there for a long time before, and did not return for a year or more after. He knows that to be true, and that fact proves his charge to be false as against Mr. Buchanan. Then again, I wish to call his attention to the fact that at the time the Nebraska bill was passed, the Dred Scott case was not before the Supreme Court at all; it was not upon the docket of the Supreme Court; it had not been brought there, and the judges in all probability knew nothing of it. Thus the history of the country proves the charge to be false as against them. As to President Pierce, his high character as a man of integrity and honor is enough to vindicate him from such a charge; and as to myself, I pronounce the charge an infamous lie, whenever and wherever made, and by whomsoever made.   I am willing that Mr. Lincoln should go and rake up every public act of mine, every measure I have introduced, report I have made, speech delivered, and criticize them; but when he charges upon me a corrupt conspiracy for the purpose of perverting the institutions of the country, I brand it as it deserves. I say the history of the country proves it to be false, and that it could not have been possible at the time.   But now he tries to protect himself in this charge, because I made a charge against the Washington "Union."   My speech in the Senate against the Washington "Union" was made because it advocated a revolutionary doctrine, by declaring that the free States had not the right to prohibit slavery within their own limits.   Because I made that charge against the Washington "Union," Mr. Lincoln says it was a charge against Mr. Buchanan. Suppose it was; is Lincoln the peculiar defender of Mr. Buchanan? Is he so interested in the Federal administration, and so bound to it, that he must jump to the rescue and defend it from every attack that I may make against it?   I understand the whole thing.   The Washington "Union," under that most corrupt of all men, Cornelius Wendell, is advocating Mr. Lincoln's claim to the Senate.   Wendell was the printer of the last Black Republican House of Representatives; he was a candidate before the present Democratic House, but was ignominiously kicked out, and then he took the money which he had made out of the public printing by means of the Black Republicans, bought the Washington "Union," and is now publishing it in the name of the Democratic party, and advocating Mr. Lincoln's election to the Senate.   Mr. Lincoln therefore considers an attack upon Wendell and his corrupt gang as a personal attack upon him.   This only proves what I have charged, that there is an alliance between Lincoln and his supporters, and the Federal office-holders of this State, and presidential aspirants out of it, to break me down at home.

Mr. Lincoln feels bound to come in to the rescue of the Washington "Union."   In that speech which I delivered in answer to the Washington "Union," I made it distinctly against the "Union" alone.   I did not choose to go beyond that.   If I have occasion to attack the President's conduct, I will do it in language that will not be misunderstood.   When I differed with the President I spoke out so that you all heard me.   That question passed away; it resulted in the triumph of my principle by allowing the people to do as they please, and there is an end of the controversy.   Whenever the great principle of self-government — the right of the people to make their own constitution, and come into the Union with slavery or without it, as they see proper — shall again arise, you will find me standing firm in defense of that principle, and fighting whoever fights it.   If Mr. Buchanan stands, as I doubt not he will, by the recommendation contained in his message, that hereafter all State constitutions ought to be submitted to the people before the admission of the State into the Union, he will find me standing by him firmly, shoulder to shoulder, in carrying it out.   I know Mr. Lincoln's object; he wants to divide the Democratic party, in order that he may defeat me and go to the Senate.

[Mr. Douglas's time here expired, and he stopped on the moment.]

Mr. Lincoln's Rejoinder in the Freeport Joint Debate.

My Friends : It will readily occur to you that I cannot in half an hour notice all the things that so able a man as Judge Douglas can say in an hour and a half; and I hope, therefore, if there be anything that he has said upon which you would like to hear something from me, but which I omit to comment upon, you will bear in mind that it would be expecting an impossibility for me to go over his whole ground. I can but take up some of the points that he has dwelt upon, and employ my half hour specially on them.

The first thing I have to say to you is a word in regard to Judge Douglas's declaration about the "vulgarity and blackguardism" in the audience — that no such thing, as he says, was shown by any Democrat while I was speaking. Now I only wish, by way of reply on this subject, to say that while I was speaking I used no "vulgarity or blackguardism" toward any Democrat.

Now, my friends, I come to all this long portion of the judge's speech — perhaps half of it — which he has devoted to the various resolutions and platforms that have been adopted in the different counties, in the different congressional districts, and in the Illinois legislature — which he supposes are at variance with the positions I have assumed before you to-day. It is true that many of these resolutions are at variance with the positions I have here assumed. All I have to ask is that we talk reasonably and rationally about it. I happen to know, the judge's opinion to the contrary notwithstanding, that I have never tried to conceal my opinions, nor tried to deceive any one in reference to them. He may go and examine all the members who voted for me for United States senator in 1855, after the election of 1854. They were pledged to certain things here at home, and were determined to have pledges from me, and if he will find any of these persons who will tell him anything inconsistent with what I say now, I will retire from the race, and give him no more trouble.

The plain truth is this. At the introduction of the Nebraska policy, we believed there was a new era being introduced in the history of the republic, which tended to the spread and perpetuation of slavery. But in our opposition to that measure we did not agree with one another in everything. The people in the north end of the State were for stronger measures of opposition than we of the central and southern portions of the State, but we were all opposed to the Nebraska doctrine. We had that one feeling and that one sentiment in common. You at the north end met in your conventions and passed your resolutions. We in the middle of the State and further south did not hold such conventions and pass the same resolutions, although we had in general a common view and a common sentiment. So that these meetings which the judge has alluded to, and the resolutions he has read from, were local, and did not spread over the whole State. We at last met together in 1856, from all parts of the State, and we agreed upon a common platform. You who held more extreme notions, either yielded those notions, or if not wholly yielding them, agreed to yield them practically, for the sake of embodying the opposition to the measures which the opposite party were pushing forward at that time. We met you then, and if there was anything yielded, it was for practical purposes. We agreed then upon a platform for the party throughout the entire State of Illinois, and now we are all bound, as a party, to that platform. And I say here to you, if any one expects of me, in the case of my election, that I will do anything not signified by our Republican platform and my answers here to-day, I tell you very frankly that person will be deceived. I do not ask for the vote of any one who supposes that I have secret purposes or pledges that I dare not speak out. Cannot the judge be satisfied? If he fears, in the unfortunate case of my election, that my going to Washington will enable me to advocate sentiments contrary to those which I expressed when you voted for and elected me, I assure him that his fears are wholly needless and groundless. Is the judge really afraid of any such thing? I 'll tell you what he is afraid of. He is afraid we 'll all pull together. This is what alarms him more than anything else. For my part, I do hope that all of us, entertaining a common sentiment in opposition to what appears to us a design to nationalize and perpetuate slavery, will waive minor differences on questions which either belong to the dead past or the distant future, and all pull together in this struggle. What are your sentiments? If it be true that on the ground which I occupy — ground which I occupy as frankly and boldly as Judge Douglas does his — my views, though partly coinciding with yours, are not as perfectly in accordance with your feelings as his are, I do say to you in all candor, go for him and not for me. I hope to deal in all things fairly with Judge Douglas, and with the people of the State, in this contest. And if I should never be elected to any office, I trust I may go down with no stain of falsehood upon my reputation, notwithstanding the hard opinions Judge Douglas chooses to entertain of me.

The judge has again addressed himself to the Abolition tendencies of a speech of mine, made at Springfield in June last. I have so often tried to answer what he is always saying on that melancholy theme, that I almost turn with disgust from the discussion — from the repetition of an answer to it. I trust that nearly all of this intelligent audience have read that speech. If you have, I may venture to leave it to you to inspect it closely, and see whether it contains any of those "bugaboos" which frighten Judge Douglas.

The judge complains that I did not fully answer his questions. If I have the sense to comprehend and answer those questions, I have done so fairly. If it can be pointed out to me how I can more fully and fairly answer him, I will do it — but I aver I have not the sense to see how it is to be done. He says I do not declare I would in any event vote for the admission of a slave State into the Union. If I have been fairly reported, he will see that I did give an explicit answer to his interrogatories. I did not merely say that I would dislike to be put to the test; but I said clearly, if I were put to the test, and a Territory from which slavery had been excluded should present herself with a State constitution sanctioning slavery,— a most extraordinary thing and wholly unlikely to happen,—I did not see how I could avoid voting for her admission. But he refuses to understand that I said so, and he wants this audience to understand that I did not say so. Yet it will be so reported in the printed speech that he cannot help seeing it.

He says if I should vote for the admission of a slave State I would be voting for a dissolution of the Union, because I hold that the Union cannot permanently exist half slave and half free. I repeat that I do not believe this government can endure permanently half slave and half free, yet I do not admit, nor does it at all follow, that the admission of a single slave State will permanently fix the character and establish this as a universal slave nation. The judge is very happy indeed at working up these quibbles. Before leaving the subject of answering questions, I aver as my confident belief, when you come to see our speeches in print, that you will find every question which he has asked me more fairly and boldly and fully answered than he has answered those which I put to him. Is not that so? The two speeches may be placed side by side; and I will venture to leave it to impartial judges whether his questions have not been more directly and circumstantially answered than mine.

Judge Douglas says he made a charge upon the editor of the Washington "Union," alone, of entertaining a purpose to rob the States of their power to exclude slavery from their limits. I undertake to say, and I make the direct issue, that he did not make his charge against the editor of the "Union" alone. I will undertake to prove by the record here that he made that charge against more and higher dignitaries than the editor of the Washington "Union." I am quite aware that he was shirking and dodging around the form in which he put it, but I can make it manifest that he leveled his "fatal blow" against more persons than this Washington editor. Will he dodge it now by alleging that I am trying to defend Mr. Buchanan against the charge? Not at all. Am I not making the same charge myself? I am trying to show that you, Judge Douglas, are a witness on my side. I am not defending Buchanan, and I will tell Judge Douglas that in my opinion when he made that charge he had an eye farther north than he was to-day. He was then fighting against people who called him a Black Republican and an Abolitionist. It is mixed all through his speech, and it is tolerably manifest that his eye was a great deal farther north than it is to-day. The judge says that though he made this charge, Toombs got up and declared there was not a man in the United States, except the editor of the "Union," who was in favor of the doctrines put forth in that article. And thereupon I understand that the judge withdrew the charge. Although he had taken extracts from the newspaper, and then from the Lecompton constitution, to show the existence of a conspiracy to bring about a "fatal blow," by which the States were to be deprived of the right of excluding slavery, it all went to pot as soon as Toombs got up and told him it was not true. It reminds me of the story that John Phœnix, the California railroad surveyor, tells. He says they started out from the Plaza to the Mission of Dolores. They had two ways of determining distances. One was by a chain and pins taken over the ground; the other was by a "go-it-ometer,"—an invention of his own,—a three-legged instrument, with which he computed a series of triangles between the points. At night he turned to the chain-man to ascertain what distance they had come, and found that by some mistake he had merely dragged the chain over the ground without keeping any record. By the "go-it-ometer" he found he had made ten miles. Being skeptical about this, he asked a drayman who was passing how far it was to the Plaza. The drayman replied it was just half a mile, and the surveyor put it down in his book—just as Judge Douglas says, after he had made his calculations and computations, he took Toombs's statement. I have no doubt that after Judge Douglas had made his charge, he was as easily satisfied about its truth as the surveyor was of the drayman's statement of the distance to the Plaza. Yet it is a fact that the man who put forth all that matter which Douglas deemed a "fatal blow" at State sovereignty, was elected by the Democrats as public printer.

Now, gentlemen, you may take Judge Douglas's speech of March 22, 1858, beginning about the middle of page 21, and reading to the bottom of page 24, and you will find the evidence on which I say that he did not make his charge against the editor of the "Union" alone. I cannot stop to read it, but I will give it to the reporters. Judge Douglas said:

Mr. President, you here find several distinct propositions advanced boldly by the Washington "Union" editorially, and apparently authoritatively, and every man who questions any of them is denounced as an Abolitionist, a Free-soiler, a fanatic. The propositions are: first, that the primary object of all government at its original institution is the protection of persons and property; second, that the Constitution of the United States declares that the citizens of each State shall be entitled to all the privileges and immunities of citizens in the several States; and that, therefore, thirdly, all State laws, whether organic or otherwise, which prohibit the citizens of one State from settling in another with their slave property, and especially declaring it forfeited, are direct violations of the original intention of the government and Constitution of the United States; and fourth, that the emancipation of the slaves of the Northern States was a gross outrage on the rights of property, inasmuch as it was involuntarily done on the part of the owner.

Remember that this article was published in the "Union" on the 17th of November, and on the 18th appeared the first article giving the adhesion of the "Union" to the Lecompton constitution. It was in these words:

"KANSAS AND HER CONSTITUTION.—The vexed question is settled. The problem is solved. The dead point of danger is passed. All serious trouble to Kansas affairs is over and gone."

And a column, nearly, of the same sort. Then, when you come to look into the Lecompton constitution, you find the same doctrine incorporated in it which was put forth editorially in the "Union." What is it?

"ARTICLE 7, *Section* 1. The right of property is before and higher than any constitutional sanction; and the right of the owner of a slave to such slave and its increase is the same and as invariable as the right of the owner of any property whatever."

Then in the schedule is a provision that the constitution may be amended after 1864 by a two-thirds vote.

"But no alteration shall be made to affect the right of property in the ownership of slaves."

It will be seen by these clauses in the Lecompton constitution that they are identical in spirit with this authoritative article in the Washington "Union" of the day previous to its indorsement of this constitution.

When I saw that article in the "Union" of the 17th of November, followed by the glorification of the Lecompton constitution on the 18th of November, and this clause in the constitution asserting the doctrine that a State has no right to prohibit slavery within its limits, I saw that there was a fatal blow being struck at the sovereignty of the States of this Union.

Here he says, "Mr. President, you here find several distinct propositions advanced boldly, and apparently authoritatively." By whose authority, Judge Douglas? Again, he says in another place, "It will be seen by these clauses in the Lecompton constitution that they are identical in spirit with this authoritative article." By whose authority? Who do you mean to say authorized the publication of these articles? He knows that the Washington "Union" is considered the organ of the administration. I demand of Judge Douglas by whose authority he meant to say those articles were published, if not by the authority of the President of the United States and his cabinet? I defy him to show whom he referred to, if not to these high functionaries in the Federal Government. More than this, he says the articles in that paper and the provisions of the Lecompton constitution are "identical," and being identical, he argues that the authors are coöperating and conspiring together. He does not use the word "conspiring," but what other construction can you put upon it? He winds up with this:

When I saw that article in the "Union" of the 17th of November, followed by the glorification of the Lecompton constitution on the 18th of November, and this clause in the constitution asserting the doctrine that a State has no right to prohibit slavery within its limits, I saw that there was a fatal blow being struck at the sovereignty of the States of this Union.

I ask him if all this fuss was made over the editor of this newspaper. It would be a terribly "fatal blow" indeed which a single man could strike, when no President, no cabinet officer, no member of Congress, was giving strength and efficiency to the movement. Out of respect to Judge Douglas's good sense I must believe he did n't manufacture his idea of the "fatal" character of that blow out of such a miserable scapegrace as he represents that editor to be. But the judge's eye is farther south now. Then, it was very peculiarly and decidedly north. His hope rested on the idea of enlisting the great "Black Republican" party, and making it the tail of his new kite. He knows he was then expecting from day to day to turn Republican and place himself at the head of our organization. He has found that these despised "Black Republicans" estimate him by a standard which he has taught them only too well. Hence he is crawling back into his old camp, and you will find him eventually installed in full fellowship among those whom he was then battling, and with whom he now pretends to be at such fearful variance. [Loud applause, and cries of " Go on, go on."] I cannot, gentlemen, my time has expired.

September 15, 1858.— THIRD JOINT DEBATE, AT JONESBORO, ILLINOIS.

Mr. Douglas's Opening Speech.

Ladies and Gentlemen : I appear before you to-day in pursuance of a previous notice, and have made arrangements with Mr. Lincoln to divide time, and discuss with him the leading political topics that now agitate the country.

Prior to 1854 this country was divided into two great political parties known as Whig and Democratic. These parties differed from each other on certain questions which were then deemed to be important to the best interests of the republic. Whigs and Democrats differed about a bank, the tariff, distribution, the specie circular, and the subtreasury. On those issues we went before the country, and discussed the principles, objects, and measures of the two great parties. Each of the parties could proclaim its principles in Louisiana as well as in Massachusetts, in Kentucky as well as in Illinois. Since that period, a great revolution has taken place in the formation of parties, by which they now seem to be divided by a geographical line, a large party in the North being arrayed under the Abolition or Republican banner, in hostility to the Southern States, Southern people, and Southern institutions. It becomes important for us to inquire how this transformation of parties has occurred, made from those of national principles to geographical factions. You remember that in 1850 — this country was agitated from its center to its circumference about this slavery question — it became necessary for the leaders of the great Whig party and the leaders of the great Democratic party to postpone for the time being their particular disputes, and unite first to save the Union before they should quarrel as to the mode in which it was to be governed. During the Congress of 1849–50, Henry Clay was the leader of the Union men, supported by Cass and Webster, and the leaders of the Democracy and the leaders of the Whigs, in opposition to Northern Abolitionists or Southern Disunionists. The great contest of 1850 resulted in the establishment of the compromise measures of that year, which measures rested on the great principle that the people of each State and each Territory of this Union ought to be permitted to regulate their own domestic institutions in their own way, subject to no other limitation than that which the Federal Constitution imposes.

I now wish to ask you whether that principle was right or wrong which guaranteed to every State and every community the right to form and regulate their domestic institutions to suit themselves. These measures were adopted, as I have previously said, by the joint action of the Union Whigs and Union Democrats in opposition to Northern Abolitionists and Southern Disunionists. In 1858, when the Whig party assembled at Baltimore in national convention for the last time, they adopted the principle of the compromise measures of 1850 as their rule of party action in the future. One month thereafter the Democrats assembled at the same place to nominate a candidate for the presidency, and declared the same great principle as the rule of action by which the Democracy would be governed. The presidential election of 1852 was fought on that basis. It is true that the Whigs claimed special merit for the adoption of those measures, because they asserted that their great Clay originated them, their godlike Webster defended them, and their Fillmore signed the bill making them the law of the land; but on the other hand, the Democrats claimed special credit for the Democracy upon the ground that we gave twice as many votes in both houses of Congress for the passage of these measures as the Whig party.

Thus you see that in the presidential election of 1852 the Whigs were pledged by their platform and their candidate to the principle of the compromise measures of 1850, and the Democracy were likewise pledged by our principles, our platform, and our candidate to the same line of policy, to preserve peace and quiet between the different sections of this Union. Since that period the Whig party has been transformed into a sectional party, under the name of the Republican party, whilst the Democratic party continues the same national party it was at that day. All sectional men, all men of Abolition sentiments and principles, no matter whether they were old Abolitionists or had been Whigs or Democrats, rally under the sectional Republican banner, and consequently all national men, all Union-loving men, whether Whigs, Democrats, or by whatever name they have been known, ought to rally under the Stars and Stripes in defense of the Constitution as our fathers made it, and of the Union as it has existed under the Constitution.

How has this departure from the faith of the Democracy and the faith of the Whig party been accomplished? In 1854, certain restless, ambitious, and disappointed politicians throughout the land took advantage of the temporary excitement created by the Nebraska bill to try and dissolve the Old Whig party and the old Democratic party, to Abolitionize their members, and lead them, bound hand and foot, captives into the Abolition camp. In the State of New York a convention was held by some of these men, and a platform adopted, every plank of which was as black as night, each one relating to the negro, and not one referring to the interests of the white man. That example was followed throughout the Northern States, the effort being made to combine all the free States in hostile array against the slave States. The men who thus thought that they could build up a great sectional party, and through its organization control the political destinies of this country, based all their hopes on the single fact that the North was the stronger division of the nation, and hence, if the North could be combined against the South, a sure victory awaited their efforts. I am doing no more than justice to the truth of history when I say that in this State Abraham Lincoln, on behalf of the Whigs, and Lyman Trumbull, on behalf of the Democrats, were the leaders who undertook to perform this grand scheme of Abolitionizing the two parties to which they belonged. They had a private arrangement as to what should be the political destiny of each of the contracting parties before they went into the operation.   The arrangement was that Mr. Lincoln was to take the old-line Whigs with him, claiming that he was still as good a Whig as ever, over to the Abolitionists, and Mr. Trumbull was to run for Congress in the Belleville district, and, claiming to be a good Democrat, coax the old Democrats into the Abolition camp, and when, by the joint efforts of the Abolitionized Whigs, the Abolitionized Democrats, and the old-line Abolition and Free-soil party of this State, they should secure a majority in the legislature, Lincoln was then to be made United States senator in Shields's place, Trumbull remaining in Congress until I should be accommodating enough to die or resign, and give him a chance to follow Lincoln. That was a very nice little bargain so far as Lincoln and Trumbull were concerned, if it had been carried out in good faith, and friend Lincoln had attained to senatorial dignity according to the contract. They went into the contest in every part of the State, calling upon all disappointed politicians to join in the crusade against the Democracy, and appealed to the prevailing sentiments and prejudices in all the northern counties of the State. In three congressional districts in the north end of the State they adopted, as the platform of this new party thus formed by Lincoln and Trumbull in connection with the Abolitionists, all of those principles which aimed at a warfare on the part of the North against the South. They declared in that platform that the Wilmot proviso was to be applied to all the Territories of the United States, North as well as South of 36° 30′, and not only to all the territory we then had, but all that we might hereafter acquire; that hereafter no more slave States should be admitted into this Union, even if the people of such States desired slavery; that the fugitive-slave law should be absolutely and unconditionally repealed; that slavery should be abolished in the District of Columbia; that the slave-trade should be abolished between the different States, and, in fact, every article in their creed related to this slavery question, and pointed to a Northern geographical party in hostility to the Southern States of this Union.

Such were their principles in northern Illinois. A little further south they became bleached and grew paler just in proportion as public sentiment moderated and changed in this direction. There were Republicans or Abolitionists in the North, anti-Nebraska men down about Springfield, and in this neighborhood they contented themselves with talking about the inexpediency of the repeal of the Missouri Compromise. In the extreme northern counties they brought out men to canvass the State whose complexion suited their political creed, and hence Fred Douglass, the negro, was to be found there, following General Cass, and attempting to speak on behalf of Lincoln, Trumbull, and Abolitionism, against that illustrious senator. Why, they brought Fred Douglass to Freeport, when I was addressing a meeting there, in a carriage driven by the white owner, the negro sitting inside with the white lady and her daughter. When I got through canvassing the northern counties that year,

VOL. I.—22.

and progressed as far south as Springfield, I was met and opposed in discussion by Lincoln, Lovejoy, Trumbull, and Sidney Breese, who were on one side. Father Giddings, the high priest of Abolitionism, had just been there, and Chase came about the time I left. ["Why did n't you shoot him?"] I did take a running shot at them, but as I was single-handed against the white, black, and mixed drove, I had to use a shot-gun and fire into the crowd instead of taking them off singly with a rifle. Trumbull had for his lieutenants in aiding him to Abolitionize the Democracy, such men as John Wentworth of Chicago, Governor Reynolds of Belleville, Sidney Breese of Carlisle, and John Dougherty of Union, each of whom modified his opinions to suit the locality he was in. Dougherty, for instance, would not go much further than to talk about the inexpediency of the Nebraska bill, whilst his allies at Chicago advocated negro citizenship and negro equality, putting the white man and the negro on the same basis under the law. Now these men, four years ago, were engaged in a conspiracy to break down the Democracy; to-day they are again acting together for the same purpose! They do not hoist the same flag; they do not own the same principles, or profess the same faith; but conceal their union for the sake of policy. In the northern counties you find that all the conventions are called in the name of the Black Republican party; at Springfield they dare not call a Republican convention, but invite all the enemies of the Democracy to unite, and when they get down into Egypt, Trumbull issues notices calling upon the "Free Democracy" to assemble and hear him speak. I have one of the handbills calling a Trumbull meeting at Waterloo the other day, which I received there, which is in the following language:

A meeting of the Free Democracy will take place in Waterloo, on Monday, Sept. 13th inst., whereat Hon. Lyman Trumbull, Hon. Jehu Baker, and others will address the people upon the different political topics of the day. Members of all parties are cordially invited to be present and hear and determine for themselves.

THE MONROE FREE DEMOCRACY.

What is that name of "Free Democrats" put forth for unless to deceive the people, and make them believe that Trumbull and his followers are not the same party as that which raises the black flag of Abolitionism in the northern part of this State, and makes war upon the Democratic party throughout the State. When I put that question to them at Waterloo on Saturday last, one of them rose and stated that they had changed their name for political effect in order to get votes. There was a candid admission. Their object in changing their party organization and principles in different localities was avowed to be an attempt to cheat and deceive some portion of the people until after the election. Why cannot a political party that is conscious of the rectitude of its purposes and the soundness of its principles declare them everywhere alike? I would disdain to hold any political principles that I could not avow in the same terms in Kentucky that I declared in Illinois, in Charleston as well as in Chicago, in New Orleans as well as in New-York. So long as we live under a constitution common to all the States, our political faith ought to be as broad, as liberal, and just as that constitution itself, and should be proclaimed alike in every portion of the Union. But it is apparent that our opponents find it necessary, for partizan effect, to change their colors in different counties in order to catch the popular breeze, and hope with these discordant materials combined together to secure a majority in the legislature for the purpose of putting down the Democratic party. This combination did succeed in 1854 so far as to elect a majority of their confederates to the legislature, and the first important act which they performed was to elect a senator in the place of the eminent and gallant Senator Shields. His term expired in the United States Senate at that time, and he had to be crushed by the Abolition coalition for the simple reason that he would not join in their conspiracy to wage war against one half of the Union. That was the only objection to General Shields. He had served the people of the State with ability in the legislature, he had served you with fidelity and ability as auditor, he had performed his duties to the satisfaction of the whole country at the head of the Land Department at Washington, he had covered the State and the Union with immortal glory on the bloody fields of Mexico in defense of the honor of our flag, and yet he had to be stricken down by this unholy combination. And for what cause? Merely because he would not join a combination of one half of the States to make war upon the other half, after having poured out his heart's blood for all the States in the Union. Trumbull was put in his place by Abolitionism. How did Trumbull get there?

Before the Abolitionists would consent to go into an election for United States senator, they required all the members of this new combination to show their hands upon this question of Abolitionism. Lovejoy, one of their high priests, brought in resolutions defining the Abolition creed, and required them to commit themselves on it by their votes—yea or nay. In that creed as laid down by Lovejoy, they declared first, that the Wilmot proviso must be put on all the Territories of the United States, north as well as south of 36° 30', and that no more territory should ever be acquired unless slavery was at first prohibited therein; second, that no more States should ever be received into the Union unless slavery was first prohibited, by constitutional provision, in such States; third, that the fugitive-slave law must be immediately repealed; or, failing in that, then such amendments were to be made to it as would render it useless and inefficient for the objects for which it was passed, etc. The next day after these resolutions were offered they were voted upon, part of them carried, and the others defeated, the same men who voted for them, with only two exceptions, voting soon after for Abraham Lincoln as their candidate for the United States Senate. He came within one or two votes of being elected, but he could not quite get the number required, for the simple reason that his friend Trumbull, who was a party to the bargain by which Lincoln was to take Shields's place, controlled a few Abolitionized Democrats in the legislature, and would not allow them all to vote for him, thus wronging

Lincoln by permitting him on each ballot to be almost elected, but not quite, until he forced them to drop Lincoln and elect him (Trumbull), in order to unite the party. Thus you find that although the legislature was carried that year by the bargain between Trumbull, Lincoln, and the Abolitionists, and the union of these discordant elements in one harmonious party, yet Trumbull violated his pledge, and played a Yankee trick on Lincoln when they came to divide the spoils. Perhaps you would like a little evidence on this point. If you would, I will call Colonel James H. Matheny of Springfield, to the stand, Mr. Lincoln's especial confidential friend for the last twenty years, and see what he will say upon the subject of this bargain. Matheny is now the Black Republican or Abolition candidate for Congress in the Springfield district against the gallant Colonel Harris, and is making speeches all over that part of the State against me and in favor of Lincoln, in concert with Trumbull. He ought to be a good witness, and I will read an extract from a speech which he made in 1856, when he was mad because his friend Lincoln had been cheated. It is one of numerous speeches of the same tenor that were made about that time, exposing this bargain between Lincoln, Trumbull, and the Abolitionists. Matheny then said:

The Whigs, Abolitionists, Know-nothings, and renegade Democrats made a solemn compact for the purpose of carrying this State against the Democracy, on this plan: First, that they would all combine and elect Mr. Trumbull to Congress, and thereby carry his district for the legislature, in order to throw all the strength that could be obtained into that body against the Democrats; second, that when the legislature should meet, the officers of that body, such as speaker, clerks, doorkeepers, etc., would be given to the Abolitionists; and third, that the Whigs were to have the United States senator. That, accordingly, in good faith, Trumbull was elected to Congress, and his district carried for the legislature, and, when it convened, the Abolitionists got all the officers of that body, and thus far the "bond" was fairly executed. The Whigs, on their part, demanded the election of Abraham Lincoln to the United States Senate, that the bond might be fulfilled, the other parties to the contract having already secured to themselves all that was called for. But, in the most perfidious manner, they refused to elect Mr. Lincoln; and the mean, low-lived, sneaking Trumbull succeeded, by pledging all that was required by any party, in thrusting Lincoln aside and foisting himself, an excrescence from the rotten bowels of the Democracy, into the United States Senate; and thus it has ever been, that an honest man makes a bad bargain when he conspires or contracts with rogues.

Matheny thought his friend Lincoln made a bad bargain when he conspired and contracted with such rogues as Trumbull and his Abolition associates in that campaign. Lincoln was shoved off the track, and he and his friends all at once began to mope; became sour and mad, and disposed to tell, but dare not; and thus they stood for a long time, until the Abolitionists coaxed and flattered him back by their assurances that he should certainly be a senator in Douglas's place. In that way the Abolitionists have been able to hold Lincoln to the alliance up to this time, and now they have brought him into a fight against me, and he is to see if he is again to be cheated by them. Lincoln this time, though, required more of them than a promise, and holds their bond, if not security, that Lovejoy shall not cheat him as Trumbull did.

When the Republican convention assembled at Springfield in June last, for the purpose of nominating State officers only, the Abolitionists could not get Lincoln and his friends into it until they would pledge themselves that Lincoln should be their candidate for the Senate; and you will find, in proof of this, that that convention passed a resolution unanimously declaring that Abraham Lincoln was the "first, last, and only choice" of the Republicans for United States senator. He was not willing to have it understood that he was merely their first choice, or their last choice, but their only choice. The Black Republican party had nobody else. Browning was nowhere; Governor Bissell was of no account; Archie Williams was not to be taken into consideration; John Wentworth was not worth mentioning; John M. Palmer was degraded; and their party presented the extraordinary spectacle of having but one—the first, the last, and only choice for the Senate. Suppose that Lincoln should die, what a horrible condition the Republican party would be in! They would have nobody left. They have no other choice, and it was necessary for them to put themselves before the world in this ludicrous, ridiculous attitude of having no other choice in order to quiet Lincoln's suspicions, and assure him that he was not to be cheated by Lovejoy, and the trickery by which Trumbull out-generaled him. Well, gentlemen, I think they will have a nice time of it before they get through. I do not intend to give them any chance to cheat Lincoln at all this time. I intend to relieve him of all anxiety upon that subject, and spare them the mortification of more exposures of contracts violated, and the pledged honor of rogues forfeited.

But I wish to invite your attention to the chief points at issue between Mr. Lincoln and myself in this discussion. Mr. Lincoln, knowing that he was to be the candidate of his party on account of the arrangement of which I have already spoken, knowing that he was to receive the nomination of the convention for the United States Senate, had his speech, accepting that nomination, all written and committed to memory, ready to be delivered the moment the nomination was announced. Accordingly when it was made he was in readiness and delivered his speech, a portion of which I will read in order that I may state his political principles fairly, by repeating them in his own language:

We are now far into the fifth year since a policy was instituted for the avowed object, and with the confident promise of putting an end to slavery agitation; under the operation of that policy, that agitation has not only not ceased, but has constantly augmented. I believe it will not cease until a crisis shall have been reached and passed. "A house divided against itself cannot stand." I believe this government cannot endure permanently half slave and half free. I do not expect the Union to be dissolved—I do not expect the house to fall—but I do expect it will cease to be divided. It will become all one thing or all the other. Either the opponents of slavery will arrest the spread of it, and place it where the public mind shall rest in the belief that it is in the course of ultimate extinction, or its advocates will push it forward until it shall become alike lawful in all the States, North as well as South.

There you have Mr. Lincoln's first and main proposition, upon which he bases his claims, stated in his own language. He tells you that this republic cannot endure permanently divided into slave and free States, as our fathers made it. He says that they must all become free or all become slave, that they must all be one thing or all be the other, or this government cannot last. Why can it not last, if we will execute the government in the same spirit and upon the same principles upon which it is founded? Lincoln, by his proposition, says to the South, "If you desire to maintain your institutions as they are now, you must not be satisfied with minding your own business, but you must invade Illinois and all the other Northern States, establish slavery in them, and make it universal"; and in the same language he says to the North, "You must not be content with regulating your own affairs, and minding your own business, but if you desire to maintain your freedom, you must invade the Southern States, abolish slavery there and everywhere, in order to have the States all one thing or all the other." I say that this is the inevitable and irresistible result of Mr. Lincoln's argument, inviting a warfare between the North and the South, to be carried on with ruthless vengeance, until the one section or the other shall be driven to the wall, and become the victim of the rapacity of the other. What good would follow such a system of warfare? Suppose the North should succeed in conquering the South, how much would she be the gainer? or suppose the South should conquer the North, could the Union be preserved in that way? Is this sectional warfare to be waged between Northern States and Southern States until they all shall become uniform in their local and domestic institutions merely because Mr. Lincoln says that a house divided against itself cannot stand, and pretends that this scriptural quotation, this language of our Lord and Master, is applicable to the American Union and the American Constitution? Washington and his compeers, in the convention that framed the Constitution, made this government divided into free and slave States. It was composed then of thirteen sovereign and independent States, each having sovereign authority over its local and domestic institutions, and all bound together by the Federal Constitution. Mr. Lincoln likens that bond of the Federal Constitution, joining free and slave States together, to a house divided against itself, and says that it is contrary to the law of God and cannot stand. When did he learn, and by what authority does he proclaim, that this government is contrary to the law of God and cannot stand? It has stood thus divided into free and slave States from its organization up to this day.

During that period we have increased from four millions to thirty millions of people; we have extended our territory from the Mississippi to the Pacific ocean; we have acquired the Floridas and Texas, and other territory sufficient to double our geographical extent; we have increased in population, in wealth, and in power beyond any example on earth; we have risen from a weak and feeble power to become the terror and admiration of the civilized world; and all this has been done under a Constitution which Mr. Lincoln, in substance, says is in violation of the law of God, and under a Union divided into free and slave States, which Mr. Lincoln thinks, because of such division, cannot stand. Surely, Mr. Lincoln is a wiser man than those who framed the government. Washington did not believe, nor did his compatriots, that the local laws and domestic institutions that were well adapted to the Green Mountains of Vermont were suited to the rice plantations of South Carolina; they did not believe at that day that in a republic so broad and expanded as this, containing such a variety of climate, soil, and interest, uniformity in the local laws and domestic institutions was either desirable or possible. They believed then, as our experience has proved to us now, that each locality, having different interests, a different climate, and different surroundings, required different local laws, local policy, and local institutions, adapted to the wants of that locality. Thus our government was formed on the principle of diversity in the local institutions and laws, and not on that of uniformity.

As my time flies, I can only glance at these points and not present them as fully as I would wish, because I desire to bring all the points in controversy between the two parties before you in order to have Mr. Lincoln's reply. He makes war on the decision of the Supreme Court, in the case known as the Dred Scott case. I wish to say to you, fellow-citizens, that I have no war to make on that decision, or any other ever rendered by the Supreme Court. I am content to take that decision as it stands delivered by the highest judicial tribunal on earth, a tribunal established by the Constitution of the United States for that purpose, and hence that decision becomes the law of the land, binding on you, on me, and on every other good citizen, whether we like it or not. Hence I do not choose to go into an argument to prove, before this audience, whether or not Chief Justice Taney understood the law better than Abraham Lincoln.

Mr. Lincoln objects to that decision, first and mainly because it deprives the negro of the rights of citizenship. I am as much opposed to his reason for that objection as I am to the objection itself. I hold that a negro is not and never ought to be a citizen of the United States. I hold that this government was made on the white basis, by white men for the benefit of white men and their posterity forever, and should be administered by white men, and none others. I do not believe that the Almighty made the negro capable of self-government. I am aware that all the Abolition lecturers that you find traveling about through the country, are in the habit of reading the Declaration of Independence to prove that all men were created equal and endowed by their Creator with certain inalienable rights, among which are life, liberty, and the pursuit of happiness. Mr. Lincoln is very much in the habit of following in the track of Lovejoy in this particular, by reading that part of the Declaration of Independence to prove that the negro was endowed by the Almighty with the inalienable right of equality with white men. Now, I say to you, my fellow-citizens, that in my opinion the signers of the Declaration had no reference to the negro whatever, when they declared all men to be created equal. They desired to express by that phrase white men, men of European birth and European descent, and had no reference either to the negro, the savage Indians, the Feejee, the Malay, or any other inferior and degraded race, when they spoke of the equality of men.   One great evidence that such was their understanding, is to be found in the fact that at that time every one of the thirteen colonies was a slaveholding colony, every signer of the Declaration represented a slaveholding constituency, and we know that no one of them emancipated his slaves, much less offered citizenship to them, when they signed the Declaration ; and yet, if they intended to declare that the negro was the equal of the white man, and entitled by divine right to an equality with him, they were bound, as honest men, that day and hour to have put their negroes on an equality with themselves.   Instead of doing so, with uplifted eyes to heaven they implored the divine blessing upon them, during the seven years' bloody war they had to fight to maintain that Declaration, never dreaming that they were violating divine law by still holding the negroes in bondage and depriving them of equality.

My friends, I am in favor of preserving this government as our fathers made it.   It does not follow by any means that because a negro is not your equal or mine, that hence he must necessarily be a slave.   On the contrary, it does follow that we ought to extend to the negro every right, every privilege, every immunity which he is capable of enjoying, consistent with the good of society.   When you ask me what these rights are, what their nature and extent is, I tell you that that is a question which each State of this Union must decide for itself.   Illinois has already decided the question.   We have decided that the negro must not be a slave within our limits ; but we have also decided that the negro shall not be a citizen within our limits ; that he shall not vote, hold office, or exercise any political rights.   I maintain that Illinois, as a sovereign State, has a right thus to fix her policy with reference to the relation between the white man and the negro ; but while we had that right to decide the question for ourselves, we must recognize the same right in Kentucky and in every other State to make the same decision, or a different one.   Having decided our own policy with reference to the black race, we must leave Kentucky and Missouri and every other State perfectly free to make just such a decision as they see proper on that question.

Kentucky has decided that question for herself.   She has said that within her limits a negro shall not exercise any political rights, and she has also said that a portion of the negroes under the laws of that State shall be slaves.   She had as much right to adopt that as her policy as we had to adopt the contrary for our policy.   New York has decided that in that State a negro may vote if he has two hundred and fifty dollars' worth of property, and if he owns that much he may vote upon an equality with the white man.   I, for one, am utterly opposed to negro suffrage anywhere and under any circumstances ; yet, inasmuch as the Supreme Court has decided in the celebrated Dred Scott case that a State has a right to confer the privilege of voting upon free negroes, I am not going to make war upon New York because she has adopted a policy repugnant to my feelings.

But New York must mind her own business, and keep her negro suffrage to herself, and not attempt to force it upon us.

In the State of Maine they have decided that a negro may vote and hold office on an equality with a white man. I had occasion to say to the senators from Maine, in a discussion last session, that if they thought that the white people within the limits of their State were no better than negroes, I would not quarrel with them for it, but they must not say that my white constituents of Illinois were no better than negroes, or we would be sure to quarrel.

The Dred Scott decision covers the whole question, and declares that each State has the right to settle this question of suffrage for itself, and all questions as to the relations between the white man and the negro. Judge Taney expressly lays down the doctrine. I receive it as law, and I say that while those States are adopting regulations on that subject disgusting and abhorrent, according to my views, I will not make war on them if they will mind their own business and let us alone.

I now come back to the question, why cannot this Union exist forever divided into free and slave States, as our fathers made it? It can thus exist if each State will carry out the principles upon which our institutions were founded—to wit, the right of each State to do as it pleases, without meddling with its neighbors. Just act upon that great principle, and this Union will not only live forever, but it will extend and expand until it covers the whole continent, and makes this confederacy one grand, ocean-bound republic. We must bear in mind that we are yet a young nation, growing with a rapidity unequaled in the history of the world, that our national increase is great, and that the emigration from the Old World is increasing, requiring us to expand and acquire new territory from time to time, in order to give our people land to live upon.

If we live up to the principle of State rights and State sovereignty, each State regulating its own affairs and minding its own business, we can go on and extend indefinitely, just as fast and as far as we need the territory. The time may come, indeed has now come, when our interests would be advanced by the acquisition of the island of Cuba. When we get Cuba we must take it as we find it, leaving the people to decide the question of slavery for themselves, without interference on the part of the Federal Government, or of any State of this Union. So when it becomes necessary to acquire any portion of Mexico or Canada, or of this continent or the adjoining islands, we must take them as we find them, leaving the people free to do as they please—to have slavery or not, as they choose. I never have inquired, and never will inquire, whether a new State applying for admission has slavery or not for one of her institutions. If the constitution that is presented be the act and deed of the people, and embodies their will, and they have the requisite population, I will admit them with slavery or without it, just as that people shall determine. My objection to the Lecompton constitution did not consist in the fact that it made Kansas a slave State. I would have been as much opposed to its admission under such a constitution as a free State as I was opposed to its admission under it as a slave

State. I hold that that was a question which that people had a right to decide for themselves, and that no power on earth ought to have interfered with that decision. In my opinion, the Lecompton constitution was not the act and deed of the people of Kansas, and did not embody their will, and the recent election in that Territory, at which it was voted down by nearly ten to one, shows conclusively that I was right in saying, when the constitution was presented, that it was not the act and deed of the people, and did not embody their will.

If we wish to preserve our institutions in their purity and transmit them unimpaired to our latest posterity, we must preserve with religious good faith that great principle of self-government which guarantees to each and every State, old and new, the right to make just such constitutions as they desire, and come into the Union with their own constitution, and not one palmed upon them. Whenever you sanction the doctrine that Congress may crowd a constitution down the throats of an unwilling people, against their consent, you will subvert the great fundamental principle upon which all our free institutions rest. In the future I have no fear that the attempt will ever be made. President Buchanan declared in his annual message, that hereafter the rule adopted in the Minnesota case, requiring a constitution to be submitted to the people, should be followed in all future cases, and if he stands by that recommendation there will be no division in the Democratic party on that principle in the future. Hence the great mission of the Democracy is to unite the fraternal feeling of the whole country, restore peace and quiet by teaching each State to mind its own business and regulate its own domestic affairs, and all to unite in carrying out the Constitution as our fathers made it, and thus to preserve the Union and render it perpetual in all time to come. Why should we not act as our fathers who made the government? There was no sectional strife in Washington's army. They were all brethren of a common confederacy; they fought under a common flag that they might bestow upon their posterity a common destiny, and to this end they poured out their blood in common streams, and shared, in some instances, a common grave.

Mr. Lincoln's Reply in the Jonesboro Joint Debate.

Ladies and Gentlemen: There is very much in the principles that Judge Douglas has here enunciated that I most cordially approve, and over which I shall have no controversy with him. In so far as he has insisted that all the States have the right to do exactly as they please about all their domestic relations, including that of slavery, I agree entirely with him. He places me wrong in spite of all I can tell him, though I repeat it again and again, insisting that I have made no difference with him upon this subject. I have made a great many speeches, some of which have been printed, and it will be utterly impossible for him to find anything that I have ever put in print contrary to what I now say upon this subject. I hold myself under constitutional obligations to allow the people in all the States, without interference, direct or indirect, to do exactly as they please, and I deny that I have any inclination to interfere with them, even if there were no such constitutional obligation. I can only say again that I am placed improperly — altogether improperly, in spite of all I can say — when it is insisted that I entertain any other view or purpose in regard to that matter.

While I am upon this subject, I will make some answers briefly to certain propositions that Judge Douglas has put. He says, "Why can't this Union endure permanently, half slave and half free?" I have said that I supposed it could not, and I will try, before this new audience, to give briefly some of the reasons for entertaining that opinion. Another form of his question is, "Why can't we let it stand as our fathers placed it?" That is the exact difficulty between us. I say that Judge Douglas and his friends have changed it from the position in which our fathers originally placed it. I say, in the way our fathers originally left the slavery question, the institution was in the course of ultimate extinction, and the public mind rested in the belief that it was in the course of ultimate extinction. I say when this government was first established, it was the policy of its founders to prohibit the spread of slavery into the new Territories of the United States, where it had not existed. But Judge Douglas and his friends have broken up that policy, and placed it upon a new basis by which it is to become national and perpetual. All I have asked or desired anywhere is that it should be placed back again upon the basis that the fathers of our government originally placed it upon. I have no doubt that it would become extinct, for all time to come, if we but readopted the policy of the fathers by restricting it to the limits it has already covered — restricting it from the new Territories.

I do not wish to dwell at great length on this branch of the subject at this time, but allow me to repeat one thing that I have stated before. Brooks, the man who assaulted Senator Sumner on the floor of the Senate, and who was complimented with dinners, and silver pitchers, and gold-headed canes, and a good many other things for that feat, in one of his speeches declared that when this government was originally established, nobody expected that the institution of slavery would last until this day. That was but the opinion of one man, but it was such an opinion as we can never get from Judge Douglas, or anybody in favor of slavery in the North at all. You can sometimes get it from a Southern man. He said at the same time that the framers of our government did not have the knowledge that experience has taught us — that experience and the invention of the cotton-gin have taught us that the perpetuation of slavery is a necessity. He insisted, therefore, upon its being changed from the basis upon which the fathers of the government left it to the basis of its perpetuation and nationalization.

I insist that this is the difference between Judge Douglas and myself — that Judge Douglas is helping that change along. I insist upon this government being placed where our fathers originally placed it.

I remember Judge Douglas once said that he saw the evidences on the statute-books of Congress of a policy in the origin of government to divide slavery and freedom by a geographical line — that he saw an indisposition to maintain that policy, and therefore he set about studying up a way to settle the institution on the right basis— the basis which he thought it ought to have been placed upon at first; and in that speech he confesses that he seeks to place it, not upon the basis that the fathers placed it upon, but upon one gotten up on "original principles." When he asks me why we cannot get along with it in the attitude where our fathers placed it, he had better clear up the evidences that he has himself changed it from that basis; that he has himself been chiefly instrumental in changing the policy of the fathers. Any one who will read his speech of the 22d of last March will see that he there makes an open confession, showing that he set about fixing the institution upon an altogether different set of principles. I think I have fully answered him when he asks me why we cannot let it alone upon the basis where our fathers left it, by showing that he has himself changed the whole policy of the government in that regard.

Now, fellow-citizens, in regard to this matter about a contract that was made between Judge Trumbull and myself, and all that long portion of Judge Douglas's speech on this subject, I wish simply to say what I have said to him before, that he cannot know whether it is true or not, and I do know that there is not a word of truth in it. And I have told him so before. I don't want any harsh language indulged in, but I do not know how to deal with this persistent insisting on a story that I know to be utterly without truth. It used to be a fashion amongst men that when a charge was made, some sort of proof was brought forward to establish it, and if no proof was found to exist, the charge was dropped. I don't know how to meet this kind of an argument. I don't want to have a fight with Judge Douglas, and I have no way of making an argument up into the consistency of a corn-cob and stopping his mouth with it. All I can do is, good-humoredly, to say that from the beginning to the end of all that story about a bargain between Judge Trumbull and myself, there is not a word of truth in it. I can only ask him to show some sort of evidence of the truth of his story. He brings forward here and reads from what he contends is a speech by James H. Matheny, charging such a bargain between Trumbull and myself. My own opinion is that Matheny did do some such immoral thing as to tell a story that he knew nothing about. I believe he did. I contradicted it instantly, and it has been contradicted by Judge Trumbull, while nobody has produced any proof, because there is none. Now, whether the speech which the judge brings forward here is really the one Matheny made, I do not know, and I hope the judge will pardon me for doubting the genuineness of this document, since his production of those Springfield resolutions at Ottawa. I do not wish to dwell at any great length upon this matter. I can say nothing when a long story like this is told, except that it is not true, and demand that he who insists upon it shall produce some proof. That is all any man can do, and I leave it in that way, for I know of no other way of dealing with it.

The judge has gone over a long account of the Old Whig and Democratic parties, and it connects itself with this charge against

Trumbull and myself. He says that they agreed upon a compromise in regard to the slavery question in 1850; that in a national Democratic convention resolutions were passed to abide by that compromise as a finality upon the slavery question. He also says that the Whig party in national convention agreed to abide by and regard as a finality the compromise of 1850. I understand the judge to be altogether right about that; I understand that part of the history of the country as stated by him to be correct. I recollect that I, as a member of that party, acquiesced in that compromise. I recollect in the presidential election which followed, when we had General Scott up for the presidency, Judge Douglas was around berating us Whigs as Abolitionists, precisely as he does to-day—not a bit of difference. I have often heard him. We could do nothing when the Old Whig party was alive that was not Abolitionism, but it has got an extremely good name since it has passed away.

When that compromise was made, it did not repeal the old Missouri Compromise. It left a region of United States territory half as large as the present territory of the United States, north of the line of 36° 30', in which slavery was prohibited by act of Congress. This compromise did not repeal that one. It did not affect or propose to repeal it. But at last it became Judge Douglas's duty, as he thought (and I find no fault with him), as chairman of the Committee on Territories, to bring in a bill for the organization of a territorial government—first of one, then of two Territories north of that line. When he did so it ended in his inserting a provision substantially repealing the Missouri Compromise. That was because the compromise of 1850 had not repealed it. And now I ask why he could not have left that compromise alone? We were quiet from the agitation of the slavery question. We were making no fuss about it. All had acquiesced in the compromise measures of 1850. We never had been seriously disturbed by any Abolition agitation before that period. When he came to form governments for the Territories north of the line of 36° 30', why could he not have let that matter stand as it was standing? Was it necessary to the organization of a Territory? Not at all. Iowa lay north of the line and had been organized as a Territory, and came into the Union as a State without disturbing that compromise. There was no sort of necessity for destroying it to organize these Territories. But, gentlemen, it would take up all my time to meet all the little quibbling arguments of Judge Douglas to show that the Missouri Compromise was repealed by the compromise of 1850. My own opinion is that a careful investigation of all the arguments to sustain the position that that compromise was virtually repealed by the compromise of 1850 would show that they are the merest fallacies. I have the report that Judge Douglas first brought into Congress at the time of the introduction of the Nebraska bill, which in its original form did not repeal the Missouri Compromise, and he there expressly stated that he had forborne to do so because it had not been done by the compromise of 1850. I close this part of the discussion on my part by asking him the question again, "Why, when we had peace under the Missouri Compromise, could you not have let it alone?"

In complaining of what I said in my speech at Springfield, in which he says I accepted my nomination for the senatorship (where, by the way, he is at fault, for if he will examine it, he will find no acceptance in it), he again quotes that portion in which I said that " a house divided against itself cannot stand." Let me say a word in regard to that matter.

He tries to persuade us that there must be a variety in the different institutions of the States of the Union; that that variety necessarily proceeds from the variety of soil, climate, of the face of the country, and the difference in the natural features of the States. I agree to all that. Have these very matters ever produced any difficulty amongst us? Not at all. Have we ever had any quarrel over the fact that they have laws in Louisiana designed to regulate the commerce that springs from the production of sugar? or because we have a different class relative to the production of flour in this State? Have they produced any differences? Not at all. They are the very cements of this Union. They don't make the house a house divided against itself. They are the props that hold up the house and sustain the Union.

But has it been so with this element of slavery? Have we not always had quarrels and difficulties over it? And when will we cease to have quarrels over it? Like causes produce like effects. It is worth while to observe that we have generally had comparative peace upon the slavery question, and that there has been no cause for alarm until it was excited by the effort to spread it into new territory. Whenever it has been limited to its present bounds, and there has been no effort to spread it, there has been peace. All the trouble and convulsion has proceeded from efforts to spread it over more territory. It was thus at the date of the Missouri Compromise. It was so again with the annexation of Texas; so with the territory acquired by the Mexican war; and it is so now. Whenever there has been an effort to spread it there has been agitation and resistance. Now, I appeal to this audience (very few of whom are my political friends), as national men, whether we have reason to expect that the agitation in regard to this subject will cease while the causes that tend to reproduce agitation are actively at work? Will not the same cause that produced agitation in 1820, when the Missouri Compromise was formed,—that which produced the agitation upon the annexation of Texas, and at other times,—work out the same results always? Do you think that the nature of man will be changed — that the same causes that produced agitation at one time will not have the same effect at another?

This has been the result so far as my observation of the slavery question and my reading in history extend. What right have we then to hope that the trouble will cease, that the agitation will come to an end; until it shall either be placed back where it originally stood, and where the fathers originally placed it, or, on the other hand, until it shall entirely master all opposition? This is the view I entertain, and this is the reason why I entertained it, as Judge Douglas has read from my Springfield speech.

Now, my friends, there is one other thing that I feel under some sort of obligation to mention.   Judge Douglas has here to-day — in a very rambling way, I was about saying — spoken of the platforms for which he seeks to hold me responsible.   He says, " Why can't you come out and make an open avowal of principles in all places alike ? " and he reads from an advertisement that he says was used to notify the people of a speech to be made by Judge Trumbull at Waterloo.   In commenting on it he desires to know whether we cannot speak frankly and manfully as he and his friends do !   How, I ask, do his friends speak out their own sentiments ?   A convention of his party in this State met on the 21st of April, at Springfield, and passed a set of resolutions which they proclaim to the country as their platform.   This does constitute their platform, and it is because Judge Douglas claims it is his platform — that these are his principles and purposes — that he has a right to declare that he speaks his sentiments "frankly and manfully."   On the 9th of June, Colonel John Dougherty, Governor Reynolds, and others, calling themselves National Democrats, met in Springfield, and adopted a set of resolutions which are as easily understood, as plain and as definite in stating to the country and to the world what they believed in and would stand upon, as Judge Douglas's platform.   Now, what is the reason that Judge Douglas is not willing that Colonel Dougherty and Governor Reynolds should stand upon their own written and printed platform as well as he upon his ?   Why must he look farther than their platform when he claims himself to stand by his platform ?

Again, in reference to our platform :   On the 16th of June the Republicans had their convention and published their platform, which is as clear and distinct as Judge Douglas's.   In it they spoke their principles as plainly and as definitely to the world.   What is the reason that Judge Douglas is not willing that I should stand upon that platform ?   Why must he go around hunting for some one who is supporting me, or has supported me at some time in his life, and who has said something at some time contrary to that platform ?   Does the judge regard that rule as a good one ?   If it turn out that the rule is a good one for me, — that I am responsible for any and every opinion that any man has expressed who is my friend, — then it is a good rule for him.   I ask, is it not as good a rule for him as it is for me ?   In my opinion, it is not a good rule for either of us.   Do you think differently, judge ?

Mr. Douglas: I do not.

Mr. Lincoln: Judge Douglas says he does not think differently. I am glad of it.   Then can he tell me why he is looking up resolutions of five or six years ago, and insisting that they were my platform, notwithstanding my protest that they are not, and never were, my platform, and my pointing out the platform of the State convention which he delights to say nominated me for the Senate ? I cannot see what he means by parading these resolutions, if it is not to hold me responsible for them in some way.   If he says to me here, that he does not hold the rule to be good, one way or the other, I do not comprehend how he could answer me more fully if he answered me at greater length.   I will therefore put in as my answer to the resolutions that he has hunted up against me what I, as a lawyer, would call a good plea to a bad declaration. I understand that it is a maxim of law, that a poor plea may be a good plea to a bad declaration. I think that the opinions the judge brings from those who support me, yet differ from me, are a bad declaration against me, but if I can bring the same things against him, I am putting in a good plea to that kind of declaration, and now I propose to try it.

At Freeport Judge Douglas occupied a large part of his time in producing resolutions and documents of various sorts, as I understood, to make me somehow responsible for them; and I propose now doing a little of the same sort of thing for him. In 1850 a very clever gentleman by the name of Thompson Campbell, a personal friend of Judge Douglas and myself, a political friend of Judge Douglas and opponent of mine, was a candidate for Congress in the Galena district. He was interrogated as to his views on this same slavery question. I have here before me the interrogatories, and Campbell's answers to them. I will read them:

Interrogatories.

1. Will you, if elected, vote for and cordially support a bill prohibiting slavery in the Territories of the United States?
2. Will you vote for and support a bill abolishing slavery in the District of Columbia?
3. Will you oppose the admission of any slave States which may be formed out of Texas or the Territories?
4. Will you vote for and advocate the repeal of the fugitive-slave law passed at the recent session of Congress?
5. Will you advocate and vote for the election of a Speaker of the House of Representatives who shall be willing to organize the committees of that House so as to give the free States their just influence in the business of legislation?
6. What are your views, not only as to the constitutional right of Congress to prohibit the slave-trade between the States, but also as to the expediency of exercising that right immediately?

Campbell's Reply.

To the first and second interrogatories, I answer unequivocally in the affirmative.
To the third interrogatory, I reply that I am opposed to the admission of any more slave States into the Union, that may be formed out of Texan or any other territory.
To the fourth and fifth interrogatories, I unhesitatingly answer in the affirmative.
To the sixth interrogatory, I reply that so long as the slave States continue to treat slaves as articles of commerce, the Constitution confers power on Congress to pass laws regulating that peculiar commerce, and that the protection of human rights imperatively demands the interposition of every constitutional means to prevent this most inhuman and iniquitous traffic.

T. CAMPBELL.

I want to say here that Thompson Campbell was elected to Congress on that platform, as the Democratic candidate in the Galena district, against Martin P. Sweet.

Judge Douglas: Give me the date of the letter.

Mr. Lincoln: The time Campbell ran was in 1850. I have not the exact date here. It was some time in 1850 that these interrogatories were put and the answer given. Campbell was elected to Congress, and served out his term. I think a second election came up before he served out his term, and he was not reëlected. Whether defeated or not nominated, I do not know. [Mr. Campbell was nominated for reëlection by the Democratic party, by acclamation.] At the end of his term his very good friend, Judge Douglas, got him a high office from President Pierce, and sent him off to California. Is not that the fact? Just at the end of his term in Congress it appears that our mutual friend Judge Douglas got our mutual friend Campbell a good office, and sent him to California upon it. And not only so, but on the 27th of last month, when Judge Douglas and myself spoke at Freeport in joint discussion, there was his same friend Campbell, come all the way from California, to help the judge beat me; and there was poor Martin P. Sweet standing on the platform, trying to help poor me to be elected. That is true of one of Judge Douglas's friends.

So again, in that same race of 1850, there was a congressional convention assembled at Joliet, and it nominated R. S. Molony for Congress, and unanimously adopted the following resolution:

Resolved, That we are uncompromisingly opposed to the extension of slavery; and while we would not make such opposition a ground of interference with the interests of the States where it exists, yet we moderately but firmly insist that it is the duty of Congress to oppose its extension into territory now free by all means compatible with the obligations of the Constitution, and with good faith to our sister States; that these principles were recognized by the ordinance of 1787, which received the sanction of Thomas Jefferson, who is acknowledged by all to be the great oracle and expounder of our faith.

Subsequently the same interrogatories were propounded to Dr. Molony which had been addressed to Campbell, as above, with the exception of the sixth, respecting the interstate slave-trade, to which Dr. Molony, the Democratic nominee for Congress, replied as follows:

I received the interrogatories this day, and as you will see by the La Salle "Democrat" and Ottawa "Free Trader," I took at Peru on the 5th and at Ottawa on the 7th, the affirmative side of interrogatories 1st and 2d; and in relation to the admission of any more slave States from free territory, my position taken at these meetings, as correctly reported in said papers, was emphatically and distinctly opposed to it. In relation to the admission of any more slave States from Texas, whether I shall go against it or not will depend upon the opinion that I may hereafter form of the true meaning and nature of the resolutions of annexation. If by said resolutions the honor and good faith of the nation is pledged to admit more slave States from Texas when she (Texas) may apply for admission of such State, then I should, if in Congress, vote for their admission. But if not so pledged and bound by sacred contract, then a bill for the admission of more slave States from Texas would never receive my vote.

To your fourth interrogatory I answer most decidedly in the affirmative, and for reasons set forth in my reported remarks at Ottawa last Monday.

To your fifth interrogatory I also reply in the affirmative most cordially, and that I will use my utmost exertions to secure the nomination and election of a man who will accomplish the objects of said interrogatories. I most cordially approve of the resolutions adopted at the union meeting held at Princeton on the 27th September ult. Yours, etc.,

R. S. MOLONY.

All I have to say in regard to Dr. Molony is that he was the regularly nominated Democratic candidate for Congress in his district; was elected at that time; at the end of his term was appointed to a land-office at Danville. (I never heard anything of Judge Douglas's instrumentality in this.) He held this office a considerable time, and when we were at Freeport the other day, there were handbills scattered about notifying the public that after our debate was over R. S. Molony would make a Democratic speech in favor of Judge Douglas. That is all I know of my own personal knowledge. It is added here to this resolution (and truly, I believe) that "among those who participated in the Joliet convention, and who supported its nominee, with his platform as laid down in the resolution of the convention, and in his reply as above given, we call at random the following names, all of which are recognized at this day as leading Democrats: Cook County — E. B. Williams, Charles McDonell, Arno Voss, Thomas Hoyne, Isaac Cook,"— I reckon we ought to except Cook,— "F. C. Sherman. Will — Joel A. Matteson, S. W. Bowen. Kane — B. F. Hall, G. W. Renwick, A. M. Herrington, Elijah Wilcox. McHenry — W. M. Jackson, Enos W. Smith, Neil Donnelly. La Salle — John Hise, William Reddick"—William Reddick— another one of Judge Douglas's friends that stood on the stand with him at Ottawa at the time the judge says my knees trembled so that I had to be carried away! The names are all here: "DuPage — Nathan Allen. DeKalb — Z. B. Mayo."

Here is another set of resolutions which I think are apposite to the matter in hand.

On the 28th of February of the same year, a Democratic district convention was held at Naperville, to nominate a candidate for circuit judge. Among the delegates were Bowen and Kelly, of Will; Captain Naper, H. H. Cody, Nathan Allen, of DuPage; W. M. Jackson, J. M. Strode, P. W. Platt, and Enos W. Smith, of McHenry; J. Horsman and others, of Winnebago. Colonel Strode presided over the convention. The following resolutions were unanimously adopted — the first on motion of P. W. Platt, the second on motion of William M. Jackson:

Resolved, That this convention is in favor of the Wilmot proviso, both in principle and practice, and that we know of no good reason why any person should oppose the largest latitude in free soil, free territory, and free speech.

Resolved, That in the opinion of this convention, the time has arrived when all men should be free, whites as well as others.

Judge Douglas: What is the date of those resolutions?

Mr. Lincoln: I understand it was in 1850, but I do not know it. I do not state a thing and say I know it when I do not. But I have the highest belief that this is so. I know of no way to arrive at the conclusion that there is an error in it. I mean to put a case no stronger than the truth will allow. But what I was going to comment upon is an extract from a newspaper in DeKalb County, and it strikes me as being rather singular, I confess, under the circumstances. There is a Judge Mayo in that county, who is a candidate for the legislature, for the purpose, if he secures his election, of helping to reëlect Judge Douglas. He is the editor of a newspaper [DeKalb County " Sentinel "], and in that paper I find the extract I am going to read. It is part of an editorial article in which he was electioneering as fiercely as he could for Judge Douglas and against me. It was a curious thing, I think, to be in such a paper. I will agree to that, and the judge may make the most of it:

Our education has been such that we have ever been rather in favor of the equality of the blacks; that is, that they should enjoy all the privileges of the whites where they reside. We are aware that this is not a very popular doctrine. We have had many a confab with some who are now strong " Republicans," we taking the broad ground of equality and they the opposite ground.

We were brought up in a State where blacks were voters, and we do not know of any inconvenience resulting from it, though perhaps it would not work so well where the blacks are more numerous. We have no doubt of the right of the whites to guard against such an evil, if it is one. Our opinion is that it would be best for all concerned to have the colored population in a State by themselves [in this I agree with him]; but if within the jurisdiction of the United States, we say by all means they should have the right to have their senators and their representatives in Congress, and to vote for President. With us "worth makes the man, and want of it the fellow." We have seen many a "nigger" that we thought more of than some white men.

That is one of Judge Douglas's friends. Now I do not want to leave myself in an attitude where I can be misrepresented, so I will say I do not think the judge is responsible for this article; but he is quite as responsible for it as I would be if one of my friends had said it. I think that is fair enough.

I have here also a set of resolutions passed by a Democratic State convention in Judge Douglas's own good old State of Vermont, and that, I think, ought to be good for him too.

Resolved, That liberty is a right inherent and inalienable in man, and that herein all men are equal.

Resolved, That we claim no authority in the Federal Government to abolish slavery in the several States. But we do claim for it constitutional power perpetually to prohibit the introduction of slavery into territory now free, and abolish it wherever, under the jurisdiction of Congress, it exists.

Resolved, That this power ought immediately to be exercised in prohibiting the introduction and existence of slavery in New Mexico and California, in abolishing slavery and the slave-trade in the District of Columbia, on the high seas, and wherever else, under the Constitution, it can be reached.

Resolved, That no more slave States should be admitted into the Federal Union.

Resolved, That the government ought to return to its ancient policy, not to extend, nationalize, or encourage, but to limit, localize, and discourage slavery.

At Freeport I answered several interrogatories that had been propounded to me by Judge Douglas at the Ottawa meeting. The judge has yet not seen fit to find any fault with the position that I took in regard to those seven interrogatories, which were certainly broad enough, in all conscience, to cover the entire ground. In my answers, which have been printed, and all have had the opportunity of seeing, I take the ground that those who elect me must expect that I will do nothing which will not be in accordance with those answers. I have some right to assert that Judge Douglas has no fault to find with them. But he chooses to still try to thrust me upon different ground without paying any attention to my answers, the obtaining of which from me cost him so much trouble and concern. At the same time, I propounded four interrogatories to him, claiming it as a right that he should answer as many interrogatories for me as I did for him, and I would reserve myself for a future instalment when I got them ready. The judge, in answering me upon that occasion, put in what I suppose he intends as answers to all four of my interrogatories. The first one of these interrogatories I have before me, and it is in these words:

Question 1. If the people of Kansas shall, by means entirely unobjectionable in all other respects, adopt a State constitution, and ask admission into the Union under it, before they have the requisite number of inhabitants according to the English bill,—some ninety-three thousand,—will you vote to admit them?

As I read the judge's answer in the newspaper, and as I remember it as pronounced at the time, he does not give any answer which is equivalent to yes or no—I will or I won't. He answers at very considerable length, rather quarreling with me for asking the question, and insisting that Judge Trumbull had done something that I ought to say something about; and finally getting out such statements as induce me to infer that he means to be understood he will, in that supposed case, vote for the admission of Kansas. I only bring this forward now for the purpose of saying that, if he chooses to put a different construction upon his answer, he may do it. But if he does not, I shall from this time forward assume that he will vote for the admission of Kansas in disregard of the English bill. He has the right to remove any misunderstanding I may have. I only mention it now that I may hereafter assume this to be the true construction of his answer, if he does not now choose to correct me.

The second interrogatory that I propounded to him was this:

Question 2. Can the people of a United States Territory, in any lawful way, against the wish of any citizen of the United States, exclude slavery from its limits prior to the formation of a State constitution?

To this Judge Douglas answered that they can lawfully exclude slavery from the Territory prior to the formation of a constitution. He goes on to tell us how it can be done. As I understand him, he holds that it can be done by the territorial legislature refusing to make any enactments for the protection of slavery in the Territory, and especially by adopting unfriendly legislation to it. For the sake of clearness, I state it again: that they can exclude slavery from the Territory—first, by withholding what he assumes to be an indispensable assistance to it in the way of legislation; and, second, by unfriendly legislation. If I rightly understand him, I wish to ask your attention for a while to his position.

In the first place, the Supreme Court of the United States has decided that any congressional prohibition of slavery in the Territories is unconstitutional—they have reached this proposition as a conclusion from their former proposition, that the Constitution of the United States expressly recognizes property in slaves; and from that other constitutional provision, that no person shall be deprived of property without due process of law. Hence they reach the conclusion that as the Constitution of the United States expressly recognizes property in slaves, and prohibits any person from being deprived of property without due process of law, to pass an act of Congress by which a man who owned a slave on one side of a line would be deprived of him if he took him on the other side is depriving him of that property without due process of law. That I understand to be the decision of the Supreme Court. I understand also that Judge Douglas adheres most firmly to that decision; and the difficulty is, how is it possible for any power to exclude slavery from the Territory unless in violation of that decision? That is the difficulty.

In the Senate of the United States, in 1856, Judge Trumbull, in a speech, substantially, if not directly, put the same interrogatory to Judge Douglas, as to whether the people of a Territory had the lawful power to exclude slavery prior to the formation of a constitution? Judge Douglas then answered at considerable length, and his answer will be found in the "Congressional Globe," under the date of June 9, 1856. The judge said that whether the people could exclude slavery prior to the formation of a constitution or not was a question to be decided by the Supreme Court. He put that proposition, as will be seen by the "Congressional Globe," in a variety of forms, all running to the same thing in substance—that it was a question for the Supreme Court. I maintain that when he says, after the Supreme Court has decided the question, that the people may yet exclude slavery by any means whatever, he does virtually say that it is not a question for the Supreme Court. He shifts his ground. I appeal to you whether he did not say it was a question for the Supreme Court? Has not the Supreme Court decided that question? When he now says that the people may exclude slavery, does he not make it a question for the people? Does he not virtually shift his ground and say that it is not a question for the court, but for the people? This is a very simple proposition—a very plain and naked one. It seems to me that there is no difficulty in deciding it. In a variety of ways he said that it was a question for the Supreme Court. He did not stop then to tell us that, whatever the Supreme Court decides, the people can by withholding necessary "police regulations" keep slavery out. He did not make any such answer. I submit to you now, whether the new state of the case has not induced the judge to sheer away from his original ground. Would not this be the impression of every fair-minded man?

I hold that the proposition that slavery cannot enter a new country without police regulations is historically false. It is not true at all. I hold that the history of this country shows that the institution of slavery was originally planted upon this continent without these "police regulations" which the judge now thinks necessary for the actual establishment of it. Not only so, but is there not another fact — how came this Dred Scott decision to be made ? It was made upon the case of a negro being taken and actually held in slavery in Minnesota Territory, claiming his freedom because the act of Congress prohibited his being so held there. Will the judge pretend that Dred Scott was not held there without police regulations ? There is at least one matter of record as to his having been held in slavery in the Territory, not only without police regulations, but in the teeth of congressional legislation supposed to be valid at the time. This shows that there is vigor enough in slavery to plant itself in a new country even against unfriendly legislation. It takes not only law but the enforcement of law to keep it out. That is the history of this country upon the subject.

I wish to ask one other question. It being understood that the Constitution of the United States guarantees property in slaves in the Territories, if there is any infringement of the right of that property, would not the United States courts, organized for the government of the Territory, apply such remedy as might be necessary in that case ? It is a maxim held by the courts, that there is no wrong without its remedy; and the courts have a remedy for whatever is acknowledged and treated as a wrong.

Again: I will ask you, my friends, if you were elected members of the legislature, what would be the first thing you would have to do before entering upon your duties ? Swear to support the Constitution of the United States. Suppose you believe, as Judge Douglas does, that the Constitution of the United States guarantees to your neighbor the right to hold slaves in that Territory,— that they are his property,— how can you clear your oaths unless you give him such legislation as is necessary to enable him to enjoy that property ? What do you understand by supporting the Constitution of a State, or of the United States ? Is it not to give such constitutional helps to the rights established by that Constitution as may be practically needed ? Can you, if you swear to support the Constitution, and believe that the Constitution establishes a right, clear your oath, without giving it support ? Do you support the Constitution if, knowing or believing there is a right established under it which needs specific legislation, you withhold that legislation ? Do you not violate and disregard your oath ? I can conceive of nothing plainer in the world. There can be nothing in the words "support the Constitution," if you may run counter to it by refusing support to any right established under the Constitution. And what I say here will hold with still more force against the judge's doctrine of "unfriendly legislation." How could you, having sworn to support the Constitution, and believing that it guaranteed the right to hold slaves in the Territories, assist in legislation intended to defeat that right ? That would be violating your own view of the Constitution. Not only so, but if you were to do so, how long would it take the courts to hold your votes unconstitutional and void? Not a moment.

Lastly I would ask—Is not Congress itself under obligation to give legislative support to any right that is established under the United States Constitution? I repeat the question—Is not Congress itself bound to give legislative support to any right that is established in the United States Constitution? A member of Congress swears to support the Constitution of the United States, and if he sees a right established by that Constitution which needs specific legislative protection, can he clear his oath without giving that protection? Let me ask you why many of us who are opposed to slavery upon principle give our acquiescence to a fugitive-slave law? Why do we hold ourselves under obligations to pass such a law, and abide by it when it is passed? Because the Constitution makes provision that the owners of slaves shall have the right to reclaim them. It gives the right to reclaim slaves, and that right is, as Judge Douglas says, a barren right, unless there is legislation that will enforce it.

The mere declaration, "No person held to service or labor in one State under the laws thereof, escaping into another, shall in consequence of any law or regulation therein be discharged from such service or labor, but shall be delivered up on claim of the party to whom such service or labor may be due," is powerless without specific legislation to enforce it. Now, on what ground would a member of Congress who is opposed to slavery in the abstract vote for a fugitive law, as I would deem it my duty to do? Because there is a constitutional right which needs legislation to enforce it. And although it is distasteful to me, I have sworn to support the Constitution, and having so sworn, I cannot conceive that I do support it if I withhold from that right any necessary legislation to make it practical. And if that is true in regard to a fugitive-slave law, is the right to have fugitive slaves reclaimed any better fixed in the Constitution than the right to hold slaves in the Territories? For this decision is a just exposition of the Constitution, as Judge Douglas thinks. Is the one right any better than the other? Is there any man who, while a member of Congress, would give support to the one any more than the other? If I wished to refuse to give legislative support to slave property in the Territories, if a member of Congress, I could not do it, holding the view that the Constitution establishes that right. If I did it at all, it would be because I deny that this decision properly construes the Constitution. But if I acknowledge, with Judge Douglas, that this decision properly construes the Constitution, I cannot conceive that I would be less than a perjured man if I should refuse in Congress to give such protection to that property as in its nature it needed.

At the end of what I have said here I propose to give the judge my fifth interrogatory, which he may take and answer at his leisure. My fifth interrogatory is this:

If the slaveholding citizens of a United States Territory should need and demand congressional legislation for the protection of their slave property in such Territory, would you, as a member of Congress, vote for or against such legislation?

Judge Douglas: Will you repeat that? I want to answer that question.

Mr. Lincoln: If the slaveholding citizens of a United States Territory should need and demand congressional legislation for the protection of their slave property in such Territory, would you, as a member of Congress, vote for or against such legislation?

I am aware that in some of the speeches Judge Douglas has made, he has spoken as if he did not know or think that the Supreme Court had decided that a territorial legislature cannot exclude slavery. Precisely what the judge would say upon the subject—whether he would say definitely that he does not understand they have so decided, or whether he would say he does understand that the court have so decided, I do not know; but I know that in his speech at Springfield he spoke of it as a thing they had not decided yet; and in his answer to me at Freeport, he spoke of it again, so far as I can comprehend it, as a thing that had not yet been decided. Now I hold that if the judge does entertain that view, I think that he is not mistaken in so far as it can be said that the court has not decided anything save the mere question of jurisdiction. I know the legal arguments that can be made—that after a court has decided that it cannot take jurisdiction in a case, it then has decided all that is before it, and that is the end of it. A plausible argument can be made in favor of that proposition, but I know that Judge Douglas has said in one of his speeches that the court went forward, like honest men as they were, and decided all the points in the case. If any points are really extra-judicially decided because not necessarily before them, then this one as to the power of the territorial legislature to exclude slavery is one of them, as also the one that the Missouri Compromise was null and void. They are both extra-judicial, or neither is, according as the court held that they had no jurisdiction in the case between the parties, because of want of capacity of one party to maintain a suit in that court. I want, if I have sufficient time, to show that the court did pass its opinion, but that is the only thing actually done in the case. If they did not decide, they showed what they were ready to decide whenever the matter was before them. What is that opinion? After having argued that Congress had no power to pass a law excluding slavery from a United States Territory, they then used language to this effect: That inasmuch as Congress itself could not exercise such a power, it followed as a matter of course that it could not authorize a territorial government to exercise it, for the territorial legislature can do no more than Congress could do. Thus it expressed its opinion emphatically against the power of a territorial legislature to exclude slavery, leaving us in just as little doubt on that point as upon any other point they really decided.

Now, fellow-citizens, my time is nearly out. I find a report of a speech made by Judge Douglas at Joliet, since we last met at Freeport,—published, I believe, in the Missouri "Republican,"— on the 9th of this month, in which Judge Douglas says:

You know at Ottawa I read this platform, and asked him if he concurred in each and all of the principles set forth in it. He would not answer these questions. At last I said frankly, "I wish you to answer them, because when I get them up here where the color of your principles is a little darker than in Egypt, I intend to trot you down to Jonesboro." The very notice that I was going to take him down to Egypt made him tremble in the knees so that he had to be carried from the platform. He laid up seven days, and in the mean time held a consultation with his political physicians; they had Lovejoy and Farnsworth and all the leaders of the Abolition party. They consulted it all over, and at last Lincoln came to the conclusion that he would answer; so he came to Freeport last Friday.

Now that statement altogether furnishes a subject for philosophical contemplation. I have been treating it in that way, and I have really come to the conclusion that I can explain it in no other way than by believing the judge is crazy. If he was in his right mind, I cannot conceive how he would have risked disgusting the four or five thousand of his own friends who stood there and knew, as to my having been carried from the platform, that there was not a word of truth in it.

Judge Douglas: Did n't they carry you off?

Mr. Lincoln: There; that question illustrates the character of this man Douglas, exactly. He smiles now and says, " Did n't they carry you off?" But he said then, " He had to be carried off"; and he said it to convince the country that he had so completely broken me down by his speech that I had to be carried away. Now he seeks to dodge it, and asks, " Did n't they carry you off?" Yes, they did. But, Judge Douglas, why did n't you tell the truth? I would like to know why you did n't tell the truth about it. And then again, " He laid up seven days." He puts this in print for the people of the country to read as a serious document. I think if he had been in his sober senses he would not have risked that barefacedness in the presence of thousands of his own friends, who knew that I made speeches within six of the seven days at Henry, Marshall County; Augusta, Hancock County; and Macomb, McDonough County, including all the necessary travel to meet him again at Freeport at the end of the six days. Now, I say, there is no charitable way to look at that statement, except to conclude that he is actually crazy. There is another thing in that statement that alarmed me very greatly as he states it—that he was going to "trot me down to Egypt." Thereby he would have you to infer that I would not come to Egypt unless he forced me—that I could not be got here, unless he, giant-like, had hauled me down here. That statement he makes, too, in the teeth of the knowledge that I made the stipulation to come down here, and that he himself had been very reluctant to enter into the stipulation. More than all this, Judge Douglas, when he made that statement, must have been crazy, and wholly out of his sober senses, or else he would have known that, when he got me down here, that promise—that windy promise— of his powers to annihilate me would n't amount to anything. Now, how little do I look like being carried away trembling? Let the judge go on, and after he is done with his half hour, I want you all, if I can't go home myself, to let me stay and rot here; and if anything happens to the judge, if I cannot carry him to the hotel and put him to bed, let me stay here and rot. I say, then, there is something extraordinary in this statement. I ask you if you know any other living man who would make such a statement? I will ask my friend Casey, over there, if he would do such a thing? Would he send that out and have his men take it as the truth? Did the judge talk of trotting me down to Egypt to scare me to death? Why, I know this people better than he does. I was raised just a little east of here. I am a part of this people. But the judge was raised further north, and perhaps he has some horrid idea of what this people might be induced to do. But really I have talked about this matter perhaps longer than I ought, for it is no great thing, and yet the smallest are often the most difficult things to deal with. The judge has set about seriously trying to make the impression that when we meet at different places I am literally in his clutches— that I am a poor, helpless, decrepit mouse, and that I can do nothing at all. This is one of the ways he has taken to create that impression. I don't know any other way to meet it, except this. I don't want to quarrel with him,—to call him a liar,—but when I come square up to him I don't know what else to call him, if I must tell the truth out. I want to be at peace, and reserve all my fighting powers for necessary occasions. My time, now, is very nearly out, and I give up the trifle that is left to the judge to let him set my knees trembling again—if he can.

Mr. Douglas's Rejoinder in the Jonesboro Joint Debate.

My friends, while I am very grateful to you for the enthusiasm which you show for me, I will say in all candor, that your quietness will be much more agreeable than your applause, inasmuch as you deprive me of some part of my time whenever you cheer.

I will commence where Mr. Lincoln left off, and make a remark upon this serious complaint of his about my speech at Joliet. I did say there in a playful manner that when I put these questions to Mr. Lincoln at Ottawa, he failed to answer, and that he trembled, and had to be carried off the stand, and required seven days to get up his reply. That he did not walk off from that stand he will not deny. That when the crowd went away from the stand with me, a few persons carried him home on their shoulders and laid him down, he will admit. I wish to say to you that whenever I degrade my friends and myself by allowing them to carry me on their backs along through the public streets, when I am able to walk, I am willing to be deemed crazy. I did not say whether I beat him or he beat me in the argument. It is true I put these questions to him, and I put them not as mere idle questions, but showed that I based them upon the creed of the Black Republican party, as declared by their conventions in that portion of the State which he depends upon to elect him, and desired to know whether he indorsed that creed. He would not answer. When I reminded him that I intended bringing him into Egypt and renewing my questions if he refused to answer, he then consulted, and did get up his answers one week after—answers which I may refer to in a few minutes, and show you how equivocal they

are. My object was to make him avow whether or not he stood by
the platform of his party; the resolutions I then read, and upon
which I based my questions, had been adopted by his party in the
Galena congressional district, and the Chicago and Bloomington
congressional districts, composing a large majority of the counties
in this State that give Republican or Abolition majorities.

Mr. Lincoln cannot and will not deny that the doctrines laid down
in these resolutions were in substance put forth in Lovejoy's resolutions, which were voted for by a majority of his party, some of them,
if not all, receiving the support of every man of his party. Hence
I laid a foundation for my questions to him before I asked him
whether that was or was not the platform of his party. He says that
he answered my questions. One of them was whether he would vote
to admit any more slave States into the Union. The creed of the
Republican party, as set forth in the resolutions of their various
conventions, was that they would under no circumstances vote
to admit another slave State. It was put forth in the Lovejoy
resolutions in the legislature; it was put forth and passed in a majority of all the counties of this State which give Abolition or Republican majorities, or elect members to the legislature of that school of
politics. I had a right to know whether he would vote for or against
the admission of another slave State in the event the people wanted
it. He first answered that he was not pledged on the subject, and
then said:

In regard to the other question, of whether I am pledged to the admission
of any more slave States into the Union, I state to you very frankly that I
would be exceedingly sorry ever to be put in the position of having to pass
on that question. I should be exceedingly glad to know that there would
never be another slave State admitted into the Union; but I must add that
if slavery shall be kept out of the Territories during the territorial existence
of any one given Territory, and then the people, having a fair chance and
clear field when they come to adopt a constitution, do such an extraordinary
thing as adopt a slave constitution, uninfluenced by the actual presence of
the institution among them, I see no alternative, if we own the country, but
to admit them into the Union.

Now analyze that answer. In the first place he says he would be
exceedingly sorry to be put in a position where he would have to vote
on the question of the admission of a slave State. Why is he a candidate for the Senate if he would be sorry to be put in that position?
I trust the people of Illinois will not put him in a position which he
would be so sorry to occupy. The next position he takes is that he
would be glad to know that there would never be another slave State,
yet, in certain contingencies, he might have to vote for one. What
is that contingency? "If Congress keeps slavery out by law while
it is a Territory, and then the people should have a fair chance and
should adopt slavery, uninfluenced by the presence of the institution,"
he supposed he would have to admit the State. Suppose Congress
should not keep slavery out during their territorial existence, then
how would he vote when the people applied for admission into the
Union with a slave constitution? That he does not answer, and that
is the condition of every Territory we have now got. Slavery is not

kept out of Kansas by act of Congress, and when I put the question to Mr. Lincoln, whether he will vote for the admission with or without slavery, as her people may desire, he will not answer, and you have not got an answer from him. In Nebraska slavery is not prohibited by act of Congress, but the people are allowed, under the Nebraska bill, to do as they please on the subject; and when I ask him whether he will vote to admit Nebraska with a slave constitution if her people desire it, he will not answer. So with New Mexico, Washington Territory, Arizona, and the four new States to be admitted from Texas. You cannot get an answer from him to these questions. His answer only applies to a given case, to a condition — things which he knows do not exist in any one Territory in the Union. He tries to give you to understand that he would allow the people to do as they please, and yet he dodges the question as to every Territory in the Union. I now ask why cannot Mr. Lincoln answer to each of these Territories? He has not done it, and he will not do it. The Abolitionists up North understand that this answer is made with a view of not committing himself on any one Territory now in existence. It is so understood there, and you cannot expect an answer from him on a case that applies to any one Territory, or applies to the new States which by compact we are pledged to admit out of Texas, when they have the requisite population and desire admission. I submit to you whether he has made a frank answer, so that you can tell how he would vote in any one of these cases. "He would be sorry to be put in the position." Why would he be sorry to be put in this position if his duty required him to give the vote? If the people of a Territory ought to be permitted to come into the Union as a State, with slavery or without it, as they pleased, why not give the vote admitting them cheerfully? If in his opinion they ought not to come in with slavery, even if they wanted to, why not say that he would cheerfully vote against their admission? His intimation is that conscience would not let him vote "No," and he would be sorry to do that which his conscience would compel him to do as an honest man.

In regard to the contract or bargain between Trumbull, the Abolitionists, and him, which he denies, I wish to say that the charge can be proved by notorious historical facts. Trumbull, Lovejoy, Giddings, Fred Douglass, Hale, and Banks were traveling the State at that time making speeches on the same side and in the same cause with him. He contents himself with the same denial that no such thing occurred. Does he deny that he, and Trumbull, and Breese, and Giddings, and Chase, and Fred Douglass, and Lovejoy, and all those Abolitionists and deserters from the Democratic party, did make speeches all over this State in the same common cause? Does he deny that Jim Matheny was then, and is now, his confidential friend, and does he deny that Matheny made the charge of the bargain and fraud in his own language, as I have read it from his printed speech. Matheny spoke of his own personal knowledge of that bargain existing between Lincoln, Trumbull, and the Abolitionists. He still remains Lincoln's confidential friend, and is now a candidate for Congress, and is canvassing the Springfield district for Lincoln.

I assert that I can prove the charge to be true in detail if I can ever get it where I can summon and compel the attendance of witnesses. I have the statement of another man to the same effect as that made by Matheny, which I am not permitted to use yet, but Jim Matheny is a good witness on that point, and the history of the country is conclusive upon it. That Lincoln up to that time had been a Whig, and then undertook to Abolitionize the Whigs and bring them into the Abolition camp, is beyond denial; that Trumbull up to that time had been a Democrat, and deserted, and undertook to Abolitionize the Democracy, and take them into the Abolition camp, is beyond denial; that they are both now active, leading, distinguished members of this Abolition Republican party, in full communion, is a fact that cannot be questioned or denied.

But Lincoln is not willing to be responsible for the creed of his party. He complains because I hold him responsible, and in order to avoid the issue he attempts to show that individuals in the Democratic party, many years ago, expressed Abolition sentiments. It is true that Tom Campbell, when a candidate for Congress in 1850, published the letter which Lincoln read. When I asked Lincoln for the date of that letter he could not give it. The date of the letter has been suppressed by other speakers who have used it, though I take it for granted that Lincoln did not know the date. If he will take the trouble to examine, he will find that the letter was published only two days before the election, and was never seen until after it, except in one county. Tom Campbell would have been beat to death by the Democratic party if that letter had been made public in his district. As to Molony, it is true that he uttered sentiments of the kind referred to by Mr. Lincoln, and the best Democrats would not vote for him for that reason. I returned from Washington after the passage of the compromise measures in 1850, and when I found Molony running under John Wentworth's tutelage, and on his platform, I denounced him, and declared that he was no Democrat. In my speech at Chicago, just before the election that year, I went before the infuriated people of that city and vindicated the compromise measures of 1850. Remember, the city council had passed resolutions nullifying acts of Congress and instructing the police to withhold their assistance from the execution of the laws, and as I was the only man in the city of Chicago who was responsible for the passage of the compromise measures, I went before the crowd, justified each and every one of those measures, and let it be said to the eternal honor of the people of Chicago, that when they were convinced by my exposition of those measures that they were right, and they had done wrong in opposing them, they repealed their nullifying resolutions, and declared that they would acquiesce in and support the laws of the land. These facts are well known, and Mr. Lincoln can only get up individual instances, dating back to 1849–50, which are contradicted by the whole tenor of the Democratic creed.

But Mr. Lincoln does not want to be held responsible for the Black Republican doctrine of no more slave States. Farnsworth is the candidate of his party to-day in the Chicago district, and he made a speech in the last Congress in which he called upon God to palsy his right arm if he ever voted for the admission of another slave State, whether the people wanted it or not. Lovejoy is making speeches all over the State for Lincoln now, and taking ground against any more slave States. Washburne, the Black Republican candidate for Congress in the Galena district, is making speeches in favor of this same Abolition platform declaring no more slave States. Why are men running for Congress in the northern districts, and taking that Abolition platform for their guide, when Mr. Lincoln does not want to be held to it down here in Egypt and in the center of the State, and objects to it so as to get votes here. Let me tell Mr. Lincoln that his party in the northern part of the State hold to that Abolition platform, and that if they do not in the south and in the center, they present the extraordinary spectacle of a "house divided against itself," and hence "cannot stand." I now bring down upon him the vengeance of his own scripture quotation, and give it a more appropriate application than he did, when I say to him that his party, Abolition in one end of the State and opposed to it in the other, is a house divided against itself, and cannot stand, and ought not to stand, for it attempts to cheat the American people out of their votes by disguising its sentiments.

Mr. Lincoln attempts to cover up and get over his Abolitionism by telling you that he was raised a little east of you, beyond the Wabash in Indiana, and he thinks that makes a mighty sound and good man of him on all these questions. I do not know that the place where a man is born or raised has much to do with his political principles. The worst Abolitionists I have ever known in Illinois have been men who have sold their slaves in Alabama and Kentucky, and have come here and turned Abolitionists while spending the money got for the negroes they sold, and I do not know that an Abolitionist from Indiana or Kentucky ought to have any more credit because he was born and raised among slave-holders. I do not know that a native of Kentucky is more excusable because raised among slaves; his father and mother having owned slaves, he comes to Illinois, turns Abolitionist, and slanders the graves of his father and mother, and breathes curses upon the institutions under which he was born, and his father and mother bred. True, I was not born out West here. I was born away down in Yankee land; I was born in a valley in Vermont, with the high mountains around me. I love the old green mountains and valleys of Vermont, where I was born, and where I played in my childhood. I went up to visit them some seven or eight years ago, for the first time for twenty odd years. When I got there they treated me very kindly. They invited me to the commencement of their college, placed me on the seats with their distinguished guests, and conferred upon me the degree of LL. D. in Latin (doctor of laws), the same as they did Old Hickory, at Cambridge, many years ago, and I give you my word and honor I understood just as much of the Latin as he did. When they got through conferring the honorary degree, they called upon me for a speech, and I got up with my heart full and swelling with gratitude for their kindness, and I said to them, "My friends, Vermont is the most glorious spot on the face of this globe for a man to be born in, provided he emigrates when he is very young."

I emigrated when I was very young. I came out here when I was a boy, and found my mind liberalized, and my opinions enlarged when I got on these broad prairies, with only the heavens to bound my vision, instead of having them circumscribed by the little narrow ridges that surrounded the valley where I was born. But I discard all flings at the land where a man was born. I wish to be judged by my principles, by those great public measures and constitutional principles upon which the peace, the happiness, and the perpetuity of this republic now rest.

Mr. Lincoln has framed another question, propounded it to me, and desired my answer. As I have said before, I did not put a question to him that I did not first lay a foundation for by showing that it was a part of the platform of the party whose votes he is now seeking, adopted in a majority of the counties where he now hopes to get a majority, and supported by the candidates of his party now running in those counties. But I will answer his question. It is as follows: "If the slaveholding citizens of a United States Territory should need and demand congressional legislation for the protection of their slave property in such Territory, would you, as a member of Congress, vote for or against such legislation?" I answer him that it is a fundamental article in the Democratic creed that there should be non-interference and non-intervention by Congress with slavery in the States or Territories. Mr. Lincoln could have found an answer to his question in the Cincinnati platform, if he had desired it. The Democratic party have always stood by that great principle of non-interference and non-intervention by Congress with slavery in the States or Territories alike, and I stand on that platform now.

Now I desire to call your attention to the fact that Lincoln did not define his own position in his own question. How does he stand on that question? He put the question to me at Freeport whether or not I would vote to admit Kansas into the Union before she had 93,420 inhabitants. I answered him at once that it having been decided that Kansas had now population enough for a slave State, she had population enough for a free State.

I answered the question unequivocally, and then I asked him whether he would vote for or against the admission of Kansas before she had 93,420 inhabitants, and he would not answer me. To-day he has called attention to the fact that, in his opinion, my answer on that question was not quite plain enough, and yet he has not answered it himself. He now puts a question in relation to congressional interference in the Territories to me. I answer him direct, and yet he has not answered the question himself. I ask you whether a man has any right, in common decency, to put questions, in these public discussions, to his opponent, which he will not answer himself when they are pressed home to him. I have asked him three times, whether he would vote to admit Kansas whenever the people applied with a constitution of their own making and their own adoption, under circumstances that were fair, just, and unexceptionable, but I cannot get an answer from him. Nor will he answer the question which he put to me, and which I have just answered, in relation to congressional interference in the Territories, by making a slave code there.

It is true that he goes on to answer the question by arguing that under the decision of the Supreme Court it is the duty of a man to vote for a slave code in the Territories. He says that it is his duty, under the decision that the court has made, and if he believes in that decision he would be a perjured man if he did not give the vote. I want to know whether he is not bound to a decision which is contrary to his opinions just as much as to one in accordance with his opinions. If the decision of the Supreme Court, the tribunal created by the Constitution to decide the question, is final and binding, is he not bound by it just as strongly as if he was for it instead of against it originally? Is every man in this land allowed to resist decisions he does not like, and only support those that meet his approval? What are important courts worth unless their decisions are binding on all good citizens? It is the fundamental principle of the judiciary that its decisions are final. It is created for that purpose, so that when you cannot agree among yourselves on a disputed point you appeal to the judicial tribunal, which steps in and decides for you, and that decision is then binding on every good citizen. It is the law of the land just as much with Mr. Lincoln against it as for it. And yet he says if that decision is binding he is a perjured man if he does not vote for a slave code in the different Territories of this Union. Well, if you [turning to Mr. Lincoln] are not going to resist the decision, if you obey it, and do not intend to array mob law against the constituted authorities, then according to your own statement, you will be a perjured man if you do not vote to establish slavery in these Territories. My doctrine is, that even taking Mr. Lincoln's view that the decision recognizes the right of a man to carry his slaves into the Territories of the United States, if he pleases, yet after he gets there he needs affirmative law to make that right of any value. The same doctrine not only applies to slave property, but all other kinds of property. Chief Justice Taney places it upon the ground that slave property is on an equal footing with other property. Suppose one of your merchants should move to Kansas and open a liquor-store; he has a right to take groceries and liquors there, but the mode of selling them, and the circumstances under which they shall be sold, and all the remedies, must be prescribed by local legislation, and if that is unfriendly it will drive him out just as effectually as if there was a constitutional provision against the sale of liquor. So the absence of local legislation to encourage and support slave property in a Territory excludes it practically just as effectually as if there was a positive constitutional provision against it. Hence I assert that under the Dred Scott decision you cannot maintain slavery a day in a Territory where there is an unwilling people and unfriendly legislation. If the people are opposed to it, our right is a barren, worthless, useless right; and if they are for it, they will support and encourage it. We come right back, therefore, to the practical question, if the people of a Territory want slavery they will have it, and if they do not want it you cannot force it on them. And this is the practical question, the great principle, upon which our institutions rest. I am willing to take the decision of the Supreme Court as it was pronounced by that august tribunal, without stopping to inquire whether I would have decided that way or not. I have had many a decision made against me on questions of law which I did not like, but I was bound by them just as much as if I had had a hand in making them, and approved them. Did you ever see a lawyer or a client lose his case that he approved the decision of the court? They always think the decision unjust when it is given against them. In a government of laws like ours we must sustain the Constitution as our fathers made it, and maintain the rights of the States as they are guaranteed under the Constitution, and then we will have peace and harmony between the different States and sections of this glorious Union.

[September 16?] 1858.—FRAGMENT. NOTES FOR SPEECHES.

I believe the declaration that "all men are created equal" is the great fundamental principle upon which our free institutions rest. That negro slavery is violative of that principle; but that by our form of government that principle has not been made one of legal obligation. That by our form of government the States which have slavery are to retain or disuse it, at their own pleasure; and that all others — individuals, free States, and National Government — are constitutionally bound to leave them alone about it. That our government was thus framed because of the necessity springing from the actual presence of slavery when it was formed.

September 18, 1858.—FOURTH JOINT DEBATE AT CHARLESTON, ILLINOIS.

Mr. Lincoln's Opening Speech.

Ladies and Gentlemen: It will be very difficult for an audience so large as this to hear distinctly what a speaker says, and consequently it is important that as profound silence be preserved as possible.

While I was at the hotel to-day, an elderly gentleman called upon me to know whether I was really in favor of producing a perfect equality between the negroes and white people. While I had not proposed to myself on this occasion to say much on that subject, yet as the question was asked me I thought I would occupy perhaps five minutes in saying something in regard to it. I will say then that I am not, nor ever have been, in favor of bringing about in any way the social and political equality of the white and black races — that I am not, nor ever have been, in favor of making voters or jurors of negroes, nor of qualifying them to hold office, nor to intermarry with white people; and I will say in addition to this that there is a physical difference between the white and black races which I believe will forever forbid the two races living together on terms of social and political equality. And inasmuch as they cannot so live, while they do remain together there must be the position of superior and

VOL. I.— 24.

inferior, and I as much as any other man am in favor of having the superior position assigned to the white race. I say upon this occasion I do not perceive that because the white man is to have the superior position the negro should be denied everything. I do not understand that because I do not want a negro woman for a slave I must necessarily want her for a wife. My understanding is that I can just let her alone. I am now in my fiftieth year, and I certainly never have had a black woman for either a slave or a wife. So it seems to me quite possible for us to get along without making either slaves or wives of negroes. I will add to this that I have never seen, to my knowledge, a man, woman, or child who was in favor of producing a perfect equality, social and political, between negroes and white men. I recollect of but one distinguished instance that I ever heard of so frequently as to be entirely satisfied of its correctness, and that is the case of Judge Douglas's old friend Colonel Richard M. Johnson. I will also add to the remarks I have made (for I am not going to enter at large upon this subject), that I have never had the least apprehension that I or my friends would marry negroes if there was no law to keep them from it; but as Judge Douglas and his friends seem to be in great apprehension that they might, if there were no law to keep them from it, I give him the most solemn pledge that I will to the very last stand by the law of this State, which forbids the marrying of white people with negroes. I will add one further word, which is this: that I do not understand that there is any place where an alteration of the social and political relations of the negro and the white man can be made except in the State legislature — not in the Congress of the United States; and as I do not really apprehend the approach of any such thing myself, and as Judge Douglas seems to be in constant horror that some such danger is rapidly approaching, I propose, as the best means to prevent it, that the judge be kept at home and placed in the State legislature to fight the measure. I do not propose dwelling longer at this time on the subject.

When Judge Trumbull, our other senator in Congress, returned to Illinois in the month of August, he made a speech at Chicago, in which he made what may be called a charge against Judge Douglas, which I understand proved to be very offensive to him. The judge was at that time out upon one of his speaking tours through the country, and when the news of it reached him, as I am informed, he denounced Judge Trumbull in rather harsh terms for having said what he did in regard to that matter. I was traveling at that time, and speaking at the same places with Judge Douglas on subsequent days, and when I heard of what Judge Trumbull had said of Douglas, and what Douglas had said back again, I felt that I was in a position where I could not remain entirely silent in regard to the matter. Consequently, upon two or three occasions I alluded to it, and alluded to it in no other wise than to say that in regard to the charge brought by Trumbull against Douglas, I personally knew nothing, and sought to say nothing about it — that I did personally know Judge Trumbull — that I believed him to be a man of veracity — that I believed him to be a man of capacity sufficient to know very well whether an assertion he was making, as a conclusion drawn from a set of facts, was true or false; and as a conclusion of my own from that, I stated it as my belief, if Trumbull should ever be called upon, he would prove everything he had said. I said this upon two or three occasions. Upon a subsequent occasion, Judge Trumbull spoke again before an audience at Alton, and upon that occasion not only repeated his charge against Douglas, but arrayed the evidence he relied upon to substantiate it. This speech was published at length, and subsequently at Jacksonville Judge Douglas alluded to the matter. In the course of his speech, and near the close of it, he stated in regard to myself what I will now read: "Judge Douglas proceeded to remark that he should not hereafter occupy his time in refuting such charges made by Trumbull, but that Lincoln having indorsed the character of Trumbull for veracity, he should hold him (Lincoln) responsible for the slanders." I have done simply what I have told you, to subject me to this invitation to notice the charge. I now wish to say that it had not originally been my purpose to discuss that matter at all. But inasmuch as it seems to be the wish of Judge Douglas to hold me responsible for it, then for once in my life I will play General Jackson, and to the just extent I take the responsibility.

I wish to say at the beginning that I will hand to the reporters that portion of Judge Trumbull's Alton speech which was devoted to this matter, and also that portion of Judge Douglas's speech made at Jacksonville in answer to it. I shall thereby furnish the readers of this debate with the complete discussion between Trumbull and Douglas. I cannot now read them, for the reason that it would take half of my first hour to do so. I can only make some comments upon them. Trumbull's charge is in the following words: "Now, the charge is, that there was a plot entered into to have a constitution formed for Kansas, and put in force, without giving the people an opportunity to vote upon it, and that Mr. Douglas was in the plot." I will state, without quoting further, for all will have an opportunity of reading it hereafter, that Judge Trumbull brings forward what he regards as sufficient evidence to substantiate this charge.

It will be perceived Judge Trumbull shows that Senator Bigler, upon the floor of the Senate, had declared there had been a conference among the senators, in which conference it was determined to have an Enabling Act passed for the people of Kansas to form a constitution under; and in this conference it was agreed among them that it was best not to have a provision for submitting the constitution to a vote of the people after it should be formed. He then brings forward evidence to show, and showing, as he deemed, that Judge Douglas reported the bill back to the Senate with that clause stricken out. He then shows that there was a new clause inserted into the bill, which would in its nature prevent a reference of the constitution back for a vote of the people—if, indeed, upon a mere silence in the law, it could be assumed that they had the right to vote upon it. These are the general statements that he has made.

I propose to examine the points in Judge Douglas's speech, in which he attempts to answer that speech of Judge Trumbull's. When you come to examine Judge Douglas's speech, you will find that the first point he makes is: "Suppose it were true that there was such a change in the bill, and that I struck it out — is that a proof of a plot to force a constitution upon them against their will?" His striking out such a provision, if there was such a one in the bill, he argues, does not establish the proof that it was stricken out for the purpose of robbing the people of that right. I would say, in the first place, that that would be a most manifest reason for it. It is true, as Judge Douglas states, that many territorial bills have passed without having such a provision in them. I believe it is true, though I am not certain, that in some instances constitutions framed under such bills have been submitted to a vote of the people, with the law silent upon the subject; but it does not appear that they once had their enabling acts framed with an express provision for submitting the constitution to be framed to a vote of the people, and then that it was stricken out when Congress did not mean to alter the effect of the law. That there have been bills which never had the provision in, I do not question; but when was that provision taken out of one that it was in? More especially does this evidence tend to prove the proposition that Trumbull advanced, when we remember that the provision was stricken out of the bill almost simultaneously with the time that Bigler says there was a conference among certain senators, and in which it was agreed that a bill should be passed leaving that out. Judge Douglas, in answering Trumbull, omits to attend to the testimony of Bigler, that there was a meeting in which it was agreed they should so frame the bill that there should be no submission of the constitution to a vote of the people. The judge does not notice this part of it. If you take this as one piece of evidence, and then ascertain that simultaneously Judge Douglas struck out a provision that did require it to be submitted, and put the two together, I think it will make a pretty fair show of proof that Judge Douglas did, as Trumbull says, enter into a plot to put in force a constitution for Kansas without giving the people any opportunity of voting upon it.

But I must hurry on. The next proposition that Judge Douglas puts is this: "But upon examination it turns out that the Toombs bill never did contain a clause requiring the constitution to be submitted." This is a mere question of fact, and can be determined by evidence. I only want to ask this question—why did not Judge Douglas say that these words were not stricken out of the Toombs bill, or this bill from which it is alleged the provision was stricken out—a bill which goes by the name of Toombs, because he originally brought it forward? I ask why, if the judge wanted to make a direct issue with Trumbull, did he not take the exact proposition Trumbull made in his speech, and say it was not stricken out? Trumbull has given the exact words that he says were in the Toombs bill, and he alleges that when the bill came back, they were stricken out. Judge Douglas does not say that the words which Trumbull says were stricken out, were not stricken out, but he says there was no provision in the Toombs bill to submit the constitution to a vote of the people.

We see at once that he is merely making an issue upon the meaning of the words. He has not undertaken to say that Trumbull tells a lie about these words being stricken out; but he is really, when pushed up to it, only taking an issue upon the meaning of the words. Now, then, if there be any issue upon the meaning of the words, or if there be upon the question of fact as to whether these words were stricken out, I have before me what I suppose to be a genuine copy of the Toombs bill, in which it can be shown that the words Trumbull says were in it, were, in fact, originally there. If there be any dispute upon the fact, I have got the documents here to show they were there. If there be any controversy upon the sense of the words — whether these words which were stricken out really constituted a provision for submitting the matter to a vote of the people, as that is a matter of argument, I think I may as well use Trumbull's own argument. He says that the proposition is in these words:

That the following propositions be, and the same are hereby, offered to the said convention of the people of Kansas, when formed, for their free acceptance or rejection; which, if accepted by the convention and ratified by the people at the election for the adoption of the constitution, shall be obligatory upon the United States and the said State of Kansas.

Now, Trumbull alleges that these last words were stricken out of the bill when it came back, and he said this was a provision for submitting the constitution to a vote of the people, and his argument is this: "Would it have been possible to ratify the land propositions at the election for the adoption of the constitution, unless such an election was to be held?" That is Trumbull's argument. Now, Judge Douglas does not meet the charge at all, but stands up and says there was no such proposition in that bill for submitting the constitution to be framed to a vote of the people. Trumbull admits that the language is not a direct provision for submitting it, but it is a provision necessarily implied from another provision. He asks you how it is possible to ratify the land proposition at the election for the adoption of the constitution, if there was no election to be held for the adoption of the constitution. And he goes on to show that it is not any less a law because the provision is put in that indirect shape than it would be if it was put directly. But I presume I have said enough to draw attention to this point, and I pass it by also.

Another one of the points that Judge Douglas makes upon Trumbull, and at very great length, is that Trumbull, while the bill was pending, said in a speech in the Senate that he supposed the constitution to be made would have to be submitted to the people. He asks, if Trumbull thought so then, what ground is there for anybody thinking otherwise now? Fellow-citizens, this much may be said in reply: That bill had been in the hands of a party to which Trumbull did not belong. It had been in the hands of the committee at the head of which Judge Douglas stood. Trumbull perhaps had a printed copy of the original Toombs bill. I have not the evidence on that point, except a sort of inference I draw from the general course of business there. What alterations, or what provisions in the way of altering, were going on in committee, Trumbull had no means of knowing, until the altered bill was reported back. Soon afterward, when it was reported back, there was a discussion over it, and perhaps Trumbull in reading it hastily in the altered form did not perceive all the bearings of the alterations. He was hastily borne into the debate, and it does not follow that because there was something in it Trumbull did not perceive, that something did not exist. More than this, is it true that what Trumbull did can have any effect on what Douglas did? Suppose Trumbull had been in the plot with these other men, would that let Douglas out of it? Would it exonerate Douglas that Trumbull did n't then perceive he was in the plot? He also asks the question: Why did n't Trumbull propose to amend the bill if he thought it needed any amendment? Why, I believe that everything Judge Trumbull had proposed, particularly in connection with this question of Kansas and Nebraska, since he had been on the floor of the Senate, had been promptly voted down by Judge Douglas and his friends. He had no promise that an amendment offered by him to anything on this subject would receive the slightest consideration. Judge Trumbull did bring the notice of the Senate at that time to the fact that there was no provision for submitting the constitution about to be made for the people of Kansas, to a vote of the people. I believe I may venture to say that Judge Douglas made some reply to this speech of Judge Trumbull's, but he never noticed that part of it at all. And so the thing passed by. I think, then, the fact that Judge Trumbull offered no amendment, does not throw much blame upon him; and if it did, it does not reach the question of fact as to what Judge Douglas was doing. I repeat that if Trumbull had himself been in the plot, it would not at all relieve the others who were in it from blame. If I should be indicted for murder, and upon the trial it should be discovered that I had been implicated in that murder, but that the prosecuting witness was guilty too, that would not at all touch the question of my crime. It would be no relief to my neck that they discovered this other man who charged the crime upon me to be guilty too.

Another one of the points Judge Douglas makes upon Judge Trumbull is that when he spoke in Chicago he made his charge to rest upon the fact that the bill had the provision in it for submitting the constitution to a vote of the people, when it went into his (Judge Douglas's) hands, that it was missing when he reported it to the Senate, and that in a public speech he had subsequently said the alteration in the bill was made while it was in committee, and that they were made in consultation between him (Judge Douglas) and Toombs. And Judge Douglas goes on to comment upon the fact of Trumbull's adducing in his Alton speech the proposition that the bill not only came back with that proposition stricken out, but with another clause and another provision in it saying that "until the complete execution of this act there shall be no election in said Territory," which Trumbull argued was not only taking the provision for submitting to a vote of the people out of the bill, but was adding an affirmative one, in that it prevented the people from exercising the right under a bill that was merely silent on the question.   Now in regard to what he says, that Trumbull shifts the issue—that he shifts his ground—and I believe he uses the term that "it being proven false, he has changed ground,"—I call upon all of you when you come to examine that portion of Trumbull's speech (for it will make a part of mine), to examine whether Trumbull has shifted his ground or not.   I say he did not shift his ground, but that he brought forward his original charge, and the evidence to sustain it yet more fully, but precisely as he originally made it.   Then, in addition thereto, he brought in a new piece of evidence.   He shifted no ground.   He brought no new piece of evidence inconsistent with his former testimony, but he brought a new piece tending, as he thought, and as I think, to prove his proposition.   To illustrate: A man brings an accusation against another, and on trial the man making the charge introduces A and B to prove the accusation.   At a second trial he introduces the same witnesses, who tell the same story as before, and a third witness who tells the same thing, and in addition gives further testimony corroborative of the charge.   So with Trumbull.   There was no shifting of ground, nor inconsistency of testimony between the new piece of evidence and what he originally introduced.

But Judge Douglas says that he himself moved to strike out that last provision of the bill, and that on his motion it was stricken out and a substitute inserted.   That I presume is the truth.   I presume it is true that that last proposition was stricken out by Judge Douglas.   Trumbull has not said it was not.   Trumbull has himself said that it was so stricken out.   He says: "I am speaking of the bill as Judge Douglas reported it back.   It was amended somewhat in the Senate before it passed, but I am speaking of it as he brought it back."   Now, when Judge Douglas parades the fact that the provision was stricken out of the bill when it came back, he asserts nothing contrary to what Trumbull alleges.   Trumbull has only said that he originally put it in—not that he did not strike it out.   Trumbull says it was not in the bill when it went to the committee.   When it came back it was in, and Judge Douglas said the alterations were made by him in consultation with Toombs.   Trumbull alleges therefore, as his conclusion, that Judge Douglas put it in.   Then if Douglas wants to contradict Trumbull and call him a liar, let him say he did not put it in, and not that he did n't take it out again.   It is said that a bear is sometimes hard enough pushed to drop a cub, and so I presume it was in this case.   I presume the truth is that Douglas put it in and afterward took it out.   That, I take it, is the truth about it.   Judge Trumbull says one thing; Douglas says another thing, and the two don't contradict one another at all.   The question is, what did he put it in for?   In the first place, what did he take the other provision out of the bill for?—the provision which Trumbull argued was necessary for submitting the constitution to a vote of the people?   What did he take that out for? and having taken it out, what did he put this in for?   I say that, in the run of things, it is not unlikely forces conspired to render it vastly expedient for Judge Douglas to take that latter clause out again.   The question that

Trumbull has made is that Judge Douglas put it in, and he don't meet Trumbull at all unless he denies that.

In the clause of Judge Douglas's speech upon this subject he uses this language toward Judge Trumbull. He says: "He forges his evidence from beginning to end, and by falsifying the record he endeavors to bolster up his false charge." Well, that is a pretty serious statement. Trumbull forges his evidence from beginning to end. Now upon my own authority I say that it is not true. What is a forgery? Consider the evidence that Trumbull has brought forward. When you come to read the speech, as you will be able to, examine whether the evidence is a forgery from beginning to end. He had the bill or document in his hand like that [holding up a paper]. He says that is a copy of the Toombs bill—the amendment offered by Toombs. He says that is a copy of the bill as it was introduced and went into Judge Douglas's hands. Now, does Judge Douglas say that is a forgery? That is one thing Trumbull brought forward. Judge Douglas says he forged it from beginning to end! That is the "beginning," we will say. Does Douglas say that is a forgery? Let him say it to-day, and we will have a subsequent examination upon this subject. Trumbull then holds up another document like this, and says that is an exact copy of the bill as it came back in the amended form out of Judge Douglas's hands. Does Judge Douglas say that is a forgery? Does he say it in his sweeping charge? Does he say so now? If he does not, then take this Toombs bill and the bill in the amended form, and it only needs to compare them to see that the provision is in the one and not in the other; it leaves the inference inevitable that it was taken out.

But while I am dealing with this question, let us see what Trumbull's other evidence is. One other piece of evidence I will read. Trumbull says there are in this original Toombs bill these words: "That the following propositions be, and the same are hereby, offered to the said convention of the people of Kansas, when formed, for their free acceptance or rejection; which, if accepted by the convention and ratified by the people at the election for the adoption of the constitution, shall be obligatory upon the United States and the said State of Kansas." Now, if it is said that this is a forgery, we will open the paper here and see whether it is or not. Again, Trumbull says, as he goes along, that Mr. Bigler made the following statement in his place in the Senate, December 9, 1857:

I was present when that subject was discussed by senators before the bill was introduced, and the question was raised and discussed, whether the constitution, when formed, should be submitted to a vote of the people. It was held by those most intelligent on the subject, that in view of all the difficulties surrounding that Territory, [and] the danger of any experiment at that time of a popular vote, it would be better there should be no such provision in the Toombs bill; and it was my understanding, in all the intercourse I had, that the convention would make a constitution, and send it here without submitting it to the popular vote.

Then Trumbull follows on:

In speaking of this meeting again on the 21st December, 1857 ["Congressional Globe," same volume, page 113], Senator Bigler said: "Nothing was further from my mind than to allude to any social or confidential interview. The meeting was not of that character. Indeed, it was semi-official and called to promote the public good. My recollection was clear that I left the conference under the impression that it had been deemed best to adopt measures to admit Kansas as a State through the agency of one popular election, and that for delegates to this convention. This impression was stronger because I thought the spirit of the bill infringed upon the doctrine of non-intervention, to which I had great aversion; but with the hope of accomplishing a great good, and as no movement had been made in that direction in the Territory, I waived this objection, and concluded to support the measure. I have a few items of testimony as to the correctness of these impressions, and with their submission I shall be content. I have before me the bill reported by the senator from Illinois on the 7th of March, 1856, providing for the admission of Kansas as a State, the third section of which reads as follows:

" ' That the following propositions be, and the same are hereby, offered to the said convention of the people of Kansas, when formed, for their free acceptance or rejection; which, if accepted by the convention and ratified by the people at the election for the adoption of the constitution, shall be obligatory upon the United States and the said State of Kansas.'

" The bill read in his place by the senator from Georgia, on the 25th of June, and referred to the committee on Territories, contained the same section word for word. Both these bills were under consideration at the conference referred to; but, sir, when the senator from Illinois reported the Toombs bill to the Senate with amendments the next morning, it did not contain that portion of the third section which indicated to the convention that the constitution should be approved by the people. The words, 'and ratified by the people at the election for the adoption of the constitution,' had been stricken out."

Now these things Trumbull says were stated by Bigler upon the floor of the Senate on certain days, and that they are recorded in the "Congressional Globe" on certain pages. Does Judge Douglas say this is a forgery? Does he say there is no such thing in the "Congressional Globe"? What does he mean when he says Judge Trumbull forges his evidence from beginning to end? So again he says, in another place, that Judge Douglas, in his speech December 9, 1857 ["Congressional Globe," Part I, page 15], stated:

That during the last session of Congress, I [Mr. Douglas] reported a bill from the committee on Territories, to authorize the people of Kansas to assemble and form a constitution for themselves. Subsequently the senator from Georgia [Mr. Toombs] brought forward a substitute for my bill, which, after being modified by him and myself in consultation, was passed by the Senate.

Now Trumbull says this is a quotation from a speech of Douglas, and is recorded in the "Congressional Globe." Is it a forgery? Is it there or not? It may not be there, but I want the judge to take these pieces of evidence, and distinctly say they are forgeries if he dare do it. [A voice: "He will."] Well, sir, you had better not commit him. He gives other quotations — another from Judge Douglas. He says:

I will ask the senator to show me an intimation, from any one member of the Senate, in the whole debate on the Toombs bill, and in the Union, from any quarter, that the constitution was not to be submitted to the public. I will venture to say that on all sides of the chamber it was so understood at the time. If the opponents of the bill had understood it was not, they would have made the point on it; and if they had made it, we should certainly have yielded to it, and put in the clause. That is a discovery made since the President found out that it was not safe to take it for granted that that would be done which ought in fairness to have been done.

Judge Trumbull says Douglas made that speech, and it is recorded. Does Judge Douglas say it is a forgery, and was not true? Trumbull says somewhere, and I propose to skip it, but it will be found by any one who will read this debate, that he did distinctly bring it to the notice of those who were engineering the bill, that it lacked that provision, and then he goes on to give another quotation from Judge Douglas, where Judge Trumbull uses this language:

Judge Douglas, however, on the same day and in the same debate, probably recollecting or being reminded of the fact that I had objected to the Toombs bill, when pending, that it did not provide for a submission of the constitution to the people, made another statement, which is to be found in the same volume of the "Globe," page 22, in which he says:

"That the bill was silent on this subject was true, and my attention was called to that about the time it was passed; and I took the fair construction to be, that powers not delegated were reserved, and that of course the constitution would be submitted to the people."

Whether this statement is consistent with the statement just before made, that had the point been made it would have been yielded to, or that it was a new discovery, you will determine.

So I say. I do not know whether Judge Douglas will dispute this, and yet maintain his position that Trumbull's evidence " was forged from beginning to end." I will remark that I have not got these "Congressional Globes" with me. They are large books and difficult to carry about, and if Judge Douglas shall say that on these points where Trumbull has quoted from them, there are no such passages there, I shall not be able to prove they are there upon this occasion, but I will have another chance. Whenever he points out the forgery and says, "I declare that this particular thing which Trumbull has uttered is not to be found where he says it is," then my attention will be drawn to that, and I will arm myself for the contest — stating now that I have not the slightest doubt on earth that I will find every quotation just where Trumbull says it is. Then the question is, how can Douglas call that a forgery? How can he make out that it is a forgery? What is a forgery? It is the bringing forward something in writing or in print purporting to be of certain effect when it is altogether untrue. If you come forward with my note for one hundred dollars when I have never given such a note, there is a forgery. If you come forward with a letter purporting to be written by me which I never wrote, there is another forgery. If you produce anything in writing or in print saying it is so and so, the document not being genuine, a forgery has been committed. How do you make this a forgery when every piece of the evidence is genuine? If Judge Douglas does say these documents and quotations are false and forged, he has a full right to do so, but until he does it specifically, we don't know how to get at him. If he does say they are false and forged, I will then look further into it, and I presume I can procure the certificates of the proper officers that they are genuine copies. I have no doubt each of these extracts will be found exactly where Trumbull says it is. Then I leave it to you if Judge Douglas, in making his sweeping charge that Judge Trumbull's evidence is forged from beginning to end, at all meets the case — if that is the way to get at the facts. I repeat again, if he will point out which one is a forgery, I will carefully examine it, and if it proves that any one of them is really a forgery, it will not be me who will hold to it any longer. I have always wanted to deal with every one I meet candidly and honestly. If I have made any assertion not warranted by facts, and it is pointed out to me, I will withdraw it cheerfully. But I do not choose to see Judge Trumbull calumniated, and the evidence he has brought forward branded in general terms "a forgery from beginning to end." This is not the legal way of meeting a charge, and I submit to all intelligent persons, both friends of Judge Douglas and of myself, whether it is.

The point upon Judge Douglas is this. The bill that went into his hands had the provision in it for a submission of the constitution to the people; and I say its language amounts to an express provision for a submission, and that he took the provision out. He says it was known that the bill was silent in this particular; but I say, Judge Douglas, it was not silent when you got it. It was vocal with the declaration when you got it, for a submission of the constitution to the people. And now, my direct question to Judge Douglas is to answer why, if he deemed the bill silent on this point, he found it necessary to strike out those particular harmless words. If he had found the bill silent and without this provision, he might say what he does now. If he supposes it was implied that the constitution would be submitted to a vote of the people, how could these two lines so encumber the statute as to make it necessary to strike them out? How could he infer that a submission was still implied, after its express provision had been stricken from the bill? I find the bill vocal with the provision, while he silenced it. He took it out, and although he took out the other provision preventing a submission to a vote of the people, I ask, why did you first put it in? I ask him whether he took the original provision out, which Trumbull alleges was in the bill? If he admits that he did take it, I ask him what he did it for? It looks to us as if he had altered the bill. If it looks differently to him — if he has a different reason for his action from the one we assign him — he can tell it. I insist upon knowing why he made the bill silent upon that point when it was vocal before he put his hands upon it.

I was told, before my last paragraph, that my time was within three minutes of being out. I presume it is expired now. I therefore close.

Extract from Mr. Trumbull's Speech made at Alton, referred to by Mr. Lincoln in his opening at Charleston.

I come now to another extract from a speech of Mr. Douglas, made at Beardstown, and reported in the "Missouri Republican." This extract has reference to a statement made by me at Chicago, wherein I charged that an agreement had been entered into by the very persons now claiming credit for opposing a constitution not submitted to the people, to have a constitution formed and put in force without giving the people of Kansas an opportunity to pass upon it. Without meeting this charge, which I substantiated by a reference to the record, my colleague is reported to have said:

"For when this charge was once made in a much milder form in the Senate of the United States, I did brand it as a lie in the presence of Mr. Trumbull, and Mr. Trumbull sat and heard it thus branded, without daring to say it was true. I tell you he knew it to be false when he uttered it at Chicago; and yet he says he is 'going to cram the lie down his throat until he should cry enough.' The miserable, craven-hearted wretch! he would rather have both ears cut off than to use that language in my presence, where I could call him to account. I see the object is to draw me into a personal controversy, with the hope thereby of concealing from the public the enormity of the principles to which they are committed. I shall not allow much of my time in this canvass to be occupied by these personal assaults. I have none to make on Mr. Lincoln; I have none to make on Mr. Trumbull; I have none to make on any other political opponent. If I cannot stand on my own public record, on my own private and public character as history will record it, I will not attempt to rise by traducing the characters of other men. I will not make a blackguard of myself by imitating the course they have pursued against me. I have no charges to make against them."

This is a singular statement, taken altogether. After indulging in language which would disgrace a loafer in the filthiest purlieus of a fish-market, he winds up by saying that he will not make a blackguard of himself, that he has no charges to make against me. So I suppose he considers that to say of another that he knew a thing to be false when he uttered it, that he was a "miserable craven-hearted wretch," does not amount to a personal assault, and does not make a man a blackguard. A discriminating public will judge of that for themselves; but as he says he has "no charges to make on Mr. Trumbull," I suppose politeness requires I should believe him. At the risk of again offending this mighty man of war, and losing something more than my ears, I shall have the audacity to again read the record upon him, and prove and pin upon him, so that he cannot escape it, the truth of every word I uttered at Chicago. You, fellow-citizens, are the judges to determine whether I do this. My colleague says he is willing to stand on his public record. By that he shall be tried, and if he had been able to discriminate between the exposure of a public act by the record, and a personal attack upon the individual, he would have discovered that there was nothing personal in my Chicago remarks, unless the condemnation of himself by his own public record is personal, and then you must judge who is most to blame for the torture his public record inflicts upon him, he for making, or I for reading it after it was made. As an individual I care very little about Judge Douglas one way or the other. It is his public acts with which I have to do, and if they condemn, disgrace, and consign him to oblivion, he has only himself, not me, to blame.

Now, the charge is that there was a plot entered into to have a constitution formed for Kansas, and put in force, without giving the people an opportunity to pass upon it, and that Mr. Douglas was in the plot. This is as susceptible of proof by the record as is the fact that the State of Minnesota was admitted into the Union at the last session of Congress.

On the 25th of June, 1856, a bill was pending in the United States Senate to authorize the people of Kansas to form a constitution and come into the Union. On that day Mr. Toombs offered an amendment which he intended to propose to the bill, which was ordered to be printed, and, with the original bill and other amendments, recommended to the Committee on Territories, of which Mr. Douglas was chairman. This amendment of Mr. Toombs, printed by order of the Senate, and a copy of which I have here present, provided for the appointment of commissioners, who were to take a census of Kansas, divide the Territory into election districts, and superintend the election of delegates to form a constitution, and contains a clause in the 18th section which I will read to you, requiring the constitution which should be formed to be submitted to the people for adoption. It reads as follows:

" That the following propositions be, and the same are hereby, offered to the said convention of the people of Kansas, when formed, for their free acceptance or rejection; which, if accepted by the convention and ratified by the people at the election for the adoption of the constitution, shall be obligatory upon the United States, and upon the said State of Kansas," etc.

It has been contended by some of the newspaper press that this section did not require the constitution which should be formed to be submitted to the people for approval, and that it was only the land propositions which were to be submitted. You will observe the language is that the propositions are to be "ratified by the people at the election for the adoption of the constitution." Would it have been possible to ratify the land propositions "at the election for the adoption of the constitution," unless such an election was to be held?

When one thing is required by a contract or law to be done, the doing of which is made dependent upon, and cannot be performed without, the doing of some other thing, is not that other thing just as much required by the contract or law as the first? It matters not in what part of the act, nor in what phraseology, the intention of the legislature is expressed, so you can clearly ascertain what it is; and whenever that intention is ascertained from an examination of the language used, such intention is part of and a requirement of the law. Can any candid, fair-minded man read the section I have quoted, and say that the intention to have the constitution which should be formed submitted to the people for their adoption is not clearly expressed? In my judgment there can be no controversy among honest men upon a proposition so plain as this. Mr. Douglas has never pretended to deny, so far as I am aware, that the Toombs amendment, as originally introduced, did require a submission of the constitution to the people. This amendment of Mr. Toombs was referred to the committee of which Mr. Douglas was chairman, and reported back by him on the 30th of June, with the words "and ratified by the people at the election for the adoption of the constitution" stricken out. I have here a copy of the bill as reported back by Mr. Douglas to substantiate the statement I make. Various other alterations were also made in the bill to which I shall presently have occasion to call attention. There was no other clause in the original Toombs bill requiring a submission of the constitution to the people than the one I have read, and there was no clause whatever, after that was struck out, in the bill, as reported back by Judge Douglas, requiring a submission. I will now introduce a witness whose testimony cannot be impeached, he acknowledging himself to have been one of the conspirators, and privy to the fact about which he testifies.

Senator Bigler, alluding to the Toombs bill, as it was called, and which, after sundry amendments, passed the Senate, and to the propriety of submitting the constitution which should be formed to a vote of the people, made the following statement in his place in the Senate, December 9, 1857. I read from Part I, "Congressional Globe" of last session, paragraph 21:

"I was present when that subject was discussed by senators, before the bill was introduced, and the question was raised and discussed whether the constitution, when formed, should be submitted to a vote of the people. It was held by the most intelligent on the subject that in view of all the difficulties surrounding that Territory, [and] the danger of any experiment at that time of a popular vote, it would be better that there should be no such provision in the Toombs bill; and it is my understanding, in all the intercourse I had, that the convention would make a constitution and send it here without submitting it to the popular vote."

In speaking of this meeting again on the 21st of December, 1857 ("Congressional Globe," same volume, page 113), Senator Bigler said:

" Nothing was farther from my mind than to allude to any social or confidential interview. The meeting was not of that character. Indeed, it was semi-official, and called to promote the public good. My recollection was clear that I left the conference under the impression that it had been deemed best to adopt measures to admit Kansas as a State through the agency of one popular election, and that for delegates to the convention. This impression was the stronger because I thought the spirit of the bill infringed upon the doctrine of non-intervention, to which I had great aversion; but with the hope of accomplishing great good, and as no movement had been made in that direction in the Territory, I waived this objection, and concluded to support the measure. I have a few items of testimony as to the correctness of these impressions, and with their submission I shall be content. I have before me the bill reported by the senator from Illinois on the 7th of March, 1856, providing for the admission of Kansas as a State, the third section of which reads as follows:

"'That the following propositions be, and the same are hereby, offered to the said convention of the people of Kansas, when formed, for their free acceptance or rejection; which, if accepted by the convention and ratified by the people at the election under the adoption of the constitution, shall be obligatory upon the United States, and upon the said State of Kansas.'

" The bill read in place by the senator from Georgia, on the 25th of June, and referred to the Committee on Territories, contained the same section, word for word. Both these bills were under consideration at the conference referred to; but, sir, when the senator from Illinois reported the Toombs bill to the Senate, with amendments, the next morning, it did not contain that portion of the third section which indicated to the convention that the constitution should be approved by the people. The words 'and ratified by the people at the election for the adoption of the constitution' had been stricken out."

I am not now seeking to prove that Douglas was in the plot to force a constitution upon Kansas without allowing the people to vote directly upon it. I shall attend to that branch of the subject by and by. My object now is to prove the existence of the plot, what the design was, and I ask if I have not already done so. Here are the facts:

The introduction of a bill on the 7th of March, 1856, providing for the calling of a convention in Kansas to form a State constitution, and providing that the constitution should be submitted to the people for adoption; an amendment to this bill, proposed by Mr. Toombs, containing the same requirement; a reference of these various bills to the Committee on Territories; a consultation of senators to determine whether it was advisable to have the constitution submitted for ratification; the determination that it was not advisable; and a report of the bill back to the Senate next morning, with the clause providing for the submission stricken out — could evidence be more complete to establish the first part of the charge I have made of a plot having been entered into by somebody to have a constitution adopted without submitting it to the people?

Now, for the other part of the charge. That Judge Douglas was in this plot, whether knowingly or ignorantly, is not material to my purpose. The charge is that he was an instrument coöperating in the project to have a constitution formed and put into operation without affording the people an opportunity to pass upon it. The first evidence to sustain the charge is the fact that he reported back the Toombs amendment with the clause providing for the submission stricken out: this, in connection with his speech in the Senate on the 9th of December, 1857 ("Congressional Globe," Part I, page 14), wherein he stated:

"That during the last Congress, I [Mr. Douglas] reported a bill from the Committee on Territories, to authorize the people of Kansas to assemble and form a constitution for themselves. Subsequently the senator from Georgia [Mr. Toombs] brought forward a substitute for my bill, which, after having been modified by him and myself in consultation, was passed by the Senate."

This of itself ought to be sufficient to show that my colleague was an instrument in the plot to have a constitution put in force without submitting it to the people, and to forever close his mouth from attempting to deny. No man can reconcile his acts and former declarations with his present denial, and the only charitable conclusion would be that he was being used by others without knowing it. Whether he is entitled to the benefit of even this excuse, you must judge on a candid hearing of the facts I shall present. When the charge was first made in the United States Senate, by Mr. Bigler, that my colleague had voted for an Enabling Act which put a government in operation without submitting the constitution to the people, my colleague ("Congressional Globe," last session, Part I, page 24) stated:

"I will ask the senator to show me an intimation from any one member of the Senate, in the whole debate on the Toombs bill, and in the Union from any quarter, that the constitution was not to be submitted to the people. I will venture to say that on all sides of the chamber it was so understood at the time. If the opponents of the bill had understood it was not, they would have made the point on it; and if they had made it we should certainly have yielded to it, and put in the clause. That is a discovery made since the President found out that it was not safe to take it for granted that that would be done which ought in fairness to have been done."

I knew, at the time this statement was made, that I had urged the very objection to the Toombs bill two years before, that it did not provide for the submission of the constitution. You will find my remarks, made on the 2d of July, 1856, in the appendix to the "Congressional Globe" of that year, page 179, urging this very objection. Do you ask why I did not expose him at the time? I will tell you. Mr. Douglas was then doing good service against the Lecompton iniquity. The Republicans were then engaged in a hand-to-hand fight with the National Democracy, to prevent the bringing of Kansas into the Union as a slave State against the wishes of its inhabitants, and of course I was unwilling to turn our guns from the common enemy to strike down an ally. Judge Douglas, however, on the same day, and in the same debate, probably recollecting, or being reminded of the fact, that I had objected to the Toombs bill, when pending, that it did not provide for the submission of the constitution to the people, made another statement, which is to be found in the same volume of the "Congressional Globe," page 22, in which he says:

"That the bill was silent on the subject is true, and my attention was called to that about the time it was passed; and I took the fair construction to be, that powers not delegated were reserved, and that of course the constitution would be submitted to the people."

Whether this statement is consistent with the statement just before made, that had the point been made it would have been yielded to, or that it was a new discovery, you will determine; for if the public records do not convict and condemn him, he may go uncondemned, so far as I am concerned. I make no use here of the testimony of Senator Bigler to show that Judge Douglas must have been privy to the consultation held at his house, when it was determined not to submit the constitution to the people, because Judge Douglas denies it, and I wish to use his own acts and declarations, which are abundantly sufficient for my purpose.

I come to a piece of testimony which disposes of all these various pretenses which have been set up for striking out of the original Toombs proposition the clause requiring a submission of the constitution to the people, and shows that it was not done either by accident, by inadvertence, or because it was believed that the bill, being silent on the subject, the constitution would necessarily be submitted to the people for approval. What will you think, after listening to the facts already presented to show that there was a design with those who concocted the Toombs bill, as amended, not to submit the constitution to the people, if I now bring before you the amended bill as Judge Douglas reported it back, and show the clause of the original bill requiring submission was not only struck out, but that other clauses were inserted in the bill putting it absolutely out of the power of the convention to submit the constitution to the people for approval, had they desired to do so? If I can produce such evidence as that, will you not all agree that it clinches and establishes forever all I charged at Chicago, and more too?

I propose now to furnish that evidence. It will be remembered that Mr. Toombs's bill provided for holding an election for delegates to form a constitution under the supervision of commissioners to be appointed by the President, and in the bill, as reported back by Judge Douglas, these words, not to be found in the original bill, are inserted at the close of the 11th section, viz.:

"And until the complete execution of this act no other election shall be held in said Territory."

This clause put it out of the power of the convention to refer to the people for adoption; it absolutely prohibited the holding of any other election than that for the election of delegates, till that act was completely executed, which would not have been until Kansas was admitted as a State, or, at all events, till her constitution was fully prepared and ready for submission to Congress for admission. Other amendments reported by Judge Douglas to the original Toombs bill clearly show that the intention was to enable Kansas to become a State without any further action than simply a resolution of admission. The amendment reported by Mr. Douglas, that "until the next congressional apportionment the said State shall have one representative," clearly shows this, no such provision being contained in the original Toombs bill. For what other earthly purpose could the clause to prevent any other election in Kansas, except that of delegates, till it was admitted as a State, have been inserted except to prevent a submission of the constitution, when formed, to the people?

The Toombs bill did not pass in the exact shape in which Judge Douglas reported it. Several amendments were made to it in the Senate. I am now dealing with the action of Judge Douglas as connected with that bill, and speak of the bill as he recommended it. The facts I have stated in regard to this matter appear upon the records, which I have here present to show to any man who wishes to look at them. They establish, beyond the power of controversy, all the charges I have made, and show that Judge Douglas was made use of as an instrument by others, or else knowingly was a party to the scheme to have a government put in force over the people of Kansas, without giving them an opportunity to pass upon it. That others high in position in the so-called Democratic party were parties to such a scheme is confessed by Governor Bigler; and the only reason why the scheme was not carried, and Kansas long ago forced into the Union as a slave State, is the fact that the Republicans were sufficiently strong in the House of Representatives to defeat the measure.

Extract from Mr. Douglas's Speech made at Jacksonville, and referred to by Mr. Lincoln in his opening at Charleston.

I have been reminded by a friend behind me that there is another topic upon which there has been a desire expressed that I should speak. I am told that Mr. Lyman Trumbull, who has the good fortune to hold a seat in the United States Senate, in violation of the bargain between him and Lincoln, was here the other day and occupied his time in making certain charges against me, involving, if they be true, moral turpitude. I am also informed that the charges he made here were substantially the same as those made by him in the city of Chicago, which were printed in the newspapers of that city. I now propose to answer those charges and to annihilate every pretext that an honest man has ever had for repeating them.

In order that I may meet these charges fairly, I will read them, as made by Mr. Trumbull in his Chicago speech, in his own language. He says:

"Now, fellow-citizens, I make the distinct charge that there was a preconcerted arrangement and plot entered into by the very men who now claim credit for opposing a constitution not submitted to the people, to have a constitution formed and put in force without giving the people an opportunity to pass upon it. This, my friends, is a serious charge, but I charge it to-night, that the very men who traverse the country under banners, proclaiming popular sovereignty, by design concocted a bill on purpose to force a constitution upon that people."

Again, speaking to some one in the crowd, he says:

"And you want to satisfy yourself that he was in the plot to force a constitution upon that people? I will satisfy you. I will cram the truth down any honest man's throat, until he cannot deny it, and to the man who does deny it, I will cram the lie down his throat till he shall cry enough! It is preposterous — it is the most damnable effrontery that man ever put on to conceal a scheme to defraud and cheat the people out of their rights, and then claim credit for it."

That is polite and decent language for a senator of the United States. Remember that that language was used without any provocation whatever from me. I had not alluded to him in any manner in any speech that I had made; hence it was without provocation. As soon as he sets his foot within the State, he makes the direct charge that I was a party to a plot to force a constitution upon the people of Kansas against their will, and knowing that it would be denied, he talks about cramming the lie down the throat of any man who shall deny it, until he cries enough.

Why did he take it for granted that it would be denied, unless he knew it to be false? Why did he deem it necessary to make a threat in advance that he would "cram the lie" down the throat of any man that should deny it? I have no doubt that the entire Abolition party consider it very polite for Mr. Trumbull to go round uttering calumnies of that kind, bullying and talking of cramming lies down men's throats; but if I deny any of his lies by calling him a liar, they are shocked at the indecency of the language; hence, to-day, instead of calling him a liar, I intend to prove that he is one.

I wish, in the first place, to refer to the evidence adduced by Trumbull, at Chicago, to sustain his charge. He there declared that Mr. Toombs, of Georgia, introduced a bill into Congress authorizing the people of Kansas to form a constitution and come into the Union, that, when introduced, it contained a clause requiring the constitution to be submitted to the people, and that I struck out the words of that clause.

Suppose it were true that there was such a clause in the bill, and that I struck it out, is that proof of a plot to force a constitution upon a people against their will? Bear in mind that, from the days of George Washington to the administration of Franklin Pierce, there has never been passed by Congress a bill requiring the submission of a constitution to the people. If Trumbull's charge, that I struck out that clause, were true, it would only prove that I had reported the bill in the exact shape of every bill of like character that passed under Washington, Jefferson, Madison, Monroe, Jackson, or any other president, to the time of the then present administration. I ask you would that be evidence of a design to force a constitution on a people against their will? If it were so, it would be evidence against Washington, Jefferson, Madison, Jackson, Van Buren, and every other president.

But upon examination, it turns out that the Toombs bill never did contain a clause requiring the constitution to be submitted. Hence no such clause was ever stricken out by me or anybody else. It is true, however, that the Toombs bill and its authors all took it for granted that the constitution would be submitted. There had never been in the history of this government any attempt made to force a constitution upon an unwilling people, and nobody dreamed that any such attempt would be made, or deemed it necessary to provide for such a contingency. If such a clause was necessary in Mr. Trumbull's opinion, why did he not offer an amendment to that effect?

In order to give more pertinency to that question, I will read an extract from Trumbull's speech in the Senate, on the Toombs bill, made on the 2d day of July, 1856. He said:

"We are asked to amend this bill, and make it perfect, and a liberal spirit seems to be manifested on the part of some senators to have a fair bill. It is difficult, I admit, to frame a bill that will give satisfaction to all; but to approach it, or come near it, I think two things must be done."

The first, then, he goes on to say, was the application of the Wilmot proviso to the Territories, and the second the repeal of all the laws passed by the territorial legislature. He did not then say that it was necessary to put in a clause requiring the submission of the constitution. Why, if he thought such a provision necessary, did he not introduce it? He says in his speech that he was invited to offer amendments. Why did he not do so? He cannot pretend that he had no chance to do this, for he did offer some amendments, but none requiring submission.

I now proceed to show that Mr. Trumbull knew at the time that the bill was silent as to the subject of submission, and also that he, and everybody else, took it for granted that the constitution would be submitted. Now for the evidence. In his second speech he says: "The bill in many of its features meets my approbation." So he did not think it so very bad.

Further on he says:

"In regard to the measure introduced by the senator from Georgia [Mr. Toombs], and recommended by the committee, I regard it, in many respects, as a most excellent bill; but we must look at it in the light of surrounding circumstances. In the condition of things now existing in the country, I do not consider it as a safe measure, nor one which will give peace, and I will give my reasons. First, it affords no immediate relief. It provides for taking a census of the voters in the Territory, for an election in November, and the assembling of a convention in December, to form, if it thinks proper, a constitution for Kansas, preparatory to its admission into the Union as a State. It is not until December that the convention is to meet. It would take some time to form a constitution. I suppose that constitution would have to be ratified by the people before it becomes valid."

He there expressly declared that he supposed, under the bill, the constitution would have to be submitted to the people before it became valid. He went on to say:

" No provision is made in this bill for such a ratification. This is objectionable to my mind. I do not think the people should be bound by a constitution, without passing upon it directly, themselves."

Why did he not offer an amendment providing for such a submission, if he thought it necessary ? Notwithstanding the absence of such a clause, he took it for granted that the constitution would have to be ratified by the people, under the bill.

In another part of the same speech, he says:

" There is nothing said in this bill, so far as I have discovered, about submitting the constitution which is to be framed to the people, for their sanction or rejection. Perhaps the convention would have the right to submit it, if it should think proper ; but it is certainly not compelled to do so, according to the provisions of the bill. If it is to be submitted to the people, it will take time, and it will not be until some time next year that this new constitution, affirmed and ratified by the people, would be submitted here to Congress for its acceptance, and what is to be the condition of that people in the mean time ? "

You see that his argument then was that the Toombs bill would not get Kansas into the Union quick enough, and was objectionable on that account. He had no fears about this submission, or why did he not introduce an amendment to meet the case ? [A voice: " Why did n't you ? You were chairman of the committee."] I will answer that question for you.

In the first place, no such provision had ever before been put in any similar act passed by Congress. I did not suppose that there was an honest man who would pretend that the omission of such a clause furnished evidence of a conspiracy or attempt to impose on the people. It could not be expected that such of us as did not think that omission was evidence of such a scheme would offer such an amendment; but if Trumbull then believed what he now says, why did he not offer the amendment, and try to prevent it, when he was, as he says, invited to do so ?

In this connection I will tell you what the main point of discussion was. There was a bill pending to admit Kansas whenever she should have a population of 93,420, that being the ratio required for a member of Congress. Under that bill Kansas could not have become a State for some years, because she could not have had the requisite population. Mr. Toombs took it into his head to bring in a bill to admit Kansas then, with only twenty-five or thirty thousand people, and the question was whether we would allow Kansas to come in under this bill, or keep her out under mine until she had 93,420 people. The committee considered that question, and overruled me by deciding in favor of the immediate admission of Kansas, and I reported accordingly. I hold in my hand a copy of the report which I made at that time. I will read from it:

" The point upon which your committee have entertained the most serious and grave doubts in regard to the propriety of indorsing the proposition relates to the fact that, in the absence of any census of the inhabitants, there is reason to apprehend that the Territory does not contain sufficient population to entitle them to demand admission under the treaty with France, if we take the ratio of representation for a member of Congress as the rule."

Thus you see that in the written report accompanying the bill, I said that the great difficulty with the committee was the question of population. In the same report I happened to refer to the question of submission. Now, listen to what I said about that:

"In the opinion of your committee, whenever a constitution shall be formed in any Territory, preparatory to its admission into the Union as a State, justice, the genius of our institutions, the whole theory of our republican system, imperatively demand that the voice of the people shall be fairly expressed, and their will embodied in that fundamental law without fraud or violence, or intimidation, or any other improper or unlawful influence, and subject to no other restrictions than those imposed by the Constitution of the United States."

I read this from the report I made at the time on the Toombs bill. I will read yet another passage from the same report. After setting out the features of the Toombs bill, I contrast it with the proposition of Senator Seward, saying:

"The revised proposition of the senator from Georgia refers all matters in dispute to the decision of the present population, with guarantees of fairness and safeguards against frauds and violence, to which no reasonable man can find just grounds of exception, while the senator from New York, if his proposition is designed to recognize and impart vitality to the Topeka constitution, proposes to disfranchise not only all the emigrants who have arrived in the Territory this year, but all the law-abiding men who refused to join in the act of open rebellion against the constituted authorities of the Territory last year by making the unauthorized and unlawful action of a political party the fundamental law of the whole people."

Then, again, I repeat that under that bill the question is to be referred to the present population to decide for or against coming into the Union under the constitution they may adopt.

Mr. Trumbull, when at Chicago, rested his charge upon the allegation that the clause requiring submission was originally in the bill, and was stricken out by me. When that falsehood was exposed by a publication of the record, he went to Alton and made another speech, repeating the charge, and referring to other and different evidence to sustain it. He saw that he was caught in his first falsehood, so he changed the issue, and instead of resting upon the allegation of striking out, he made it rest upon the declaration that I had introduced a clause into the bill prohibiting the people from voting upon the constitution. I am told that he made the same charge here that he made at Alton, that I had actually introduced and incorporated into the bill a clause which prohibited the people from voting upon their constitution. I hold his Alton speech in my hand, and will read the amendment which he alleges that I offered. It is in these words:

"And until the complete execution of this act no other election shall be held in said Territory."

Trumbull says the object of that amendment was to prevent the convention from submitting the constitution to a vote of the people. I will read what he said at Alton on that subject:

"This clause put it out of the power of the convention, had it been so disposed, to submit the constitution to the people for adoption; for it absolutely prohibited the holding of any other election, than that for the election of delegates, till that act was completely executed, which would not have been till Kansas was admitted as a State, or, at all events, till her constitution was fully prepared and ready for submission to Congress for admission."

Now, do you suppose that Mr. Trumbull supposed that that clause prohibited the convention from submitting the constitution to the people, when, in his speech in the Senate, he declared that the convention had a right to submit it? In his Alton speech, as will be seen by the extract which I have read, he declared that the clause put it out of the power of the convention to submit the constitution, and in his speech in the Senate he said:

"There is nothing said in this bill, so far as I have discovered, about submitting the constitution which is to be formed to the people, for their sanction or rejection. Perhaps the convention could have the right to submit it, if it should think proper, but it is certainly not compelled to do so according to the provisions of the bill."

Thus you see that, in Congress, he declared the bill to be silent on the subject, and a few days since, at Alton, he made a speech, and said that there was a provision in the bill prohibiting submission.

I have two answers to make to that. In the first place, the amendment which he quotes as depriving the people of an opportunity to vote upon the constitution was stricken out on my motion — absolutely stricken out and not voted on at all! In the second place, in lieu of it, a provision was voted in authorizing the convention to order an election whenever it pleased. I will read. After Trumbull had made his speech in the Senate, declaring that the constitution would probably be submitted to the people, although the bill was silent upon that subject, I made a few remarks, and offered two amendments, which you may find in the appendix to the "Congressional Globe," volume XXXIII, first session of the thirty-fourth Congress, page 795.

I quote:

"Mr. Douglas: I have an amendment to offer from the Committee on Territories. On page 8, section 11, strike out the words 'until the complete execution of this act no other election shall be held in said Territory,' and insert the amendment which I hold in my hand."

The amendment was as follows:

"That all persons who shall possess the other qualifications prescribed for voters under this act, and who shall have been *bona fide* inhabitants of said Territory since its organization, and who shall have absented themselves therefrom in consequence of the disturbances therein, and who shall return before the first day of October next, and become *bona fide* inhabitants of the Territory, with the intent of making it their permanent home, and shall present satisfactory evidence of these facts to the Board of Commissioners, shall be entitled to vote at said election, and shall have their names placed on said corrected list of voters for that purpose."

That amendment was adopted unanimously. After its adoption, the record shows the following:

"Mr. Douglas: I have another amendment to offer from the committee, to follow the amendment which has been adopted. The bill reads now: 'And until the complete execution of this act, no other election shall be held in said Territory.' It has been suggested that it should be modified in this way: 'And to avoid all conflict in the complete execution of this act, all other elections in said Territory are hereby postponed until such time as said convention shall appoint'; so that they can appoint the day in the event that there should be a failure to come into the Union."

This amendment was also agreed to without dissent.

Thus you see that the amendment quoted by Trumbull at Alton as evidence against me, instead of being put into the bill by me, was stricken out on my motion, and never became a part thereof at all. You also see that the substituted clause expressly authorized the convention to appoint such day of election as it should deem proper.

Mr. Trumbull, when he made that speech, knew these facts. He forged his evidence from beginning to end, and by falsifying the record he endeavors to bolster up his false charge. I ask you what you think of Trumbull thus going around the country, falsifying and garbling the public records? I ask you whether you will sustain a man who will descend to the infamy of such conduct?

Mr. Douglas proceeded to remark that he should not hereafter occupy his time in refuting such charges made by Trumbull, but that Lincoln having indorsed the character of Trumbull for veracity, he should hold him [Lincoln] responsible for the slanders.

Senator Douglas's Reply in the Charleston Joint Debate.

Ladies and Gentlemen : I had supposed that we assembled here to-day for the purpose of a joint discussion between Mr. Lincoln and myself, upon the political questions which now agitate the whole country. The rule of such discussions is, that the opening speaker shall touch upon all the points he intends to discuss, in order that his opponent, in reply, shall have the opportunity of answering them. Let me ask you what questions of public policy, relating to the welfare of this State or the Union, has Mr. Lincoln discussed before you? Mr. Lincoln simply contented himself at the outset by saying, that he was not in favor of social and political equality between the white man and the negro, and did not desire the law so changed as to make the latter voters or eligible to office. I am glad that I have at last succeeded in getting an answer out of him upon this subject of negro-citizenship and eligibility to office, for I have been trying to bring him to the point on it ever since this canvass commenced.

I will now call your attention to the question which Mr. Lincoln has occupied his entire time in discussing. He spent his whole hour in retailing a charge made by Senator Trumbull against me. The circumstances out of which that charge was manufactured, occurred prior to the last presidential election, over two years ago. If the charge was true, why did not Trumbull make it in 1856, when I was discussing the questions of that day all over this State with Lincoln and him, and when it was pertinent to the then issue? He was then as silent as the grave on the subject. If the charge was true, the time to have brought it forward was the canvass of 1856, the year when the Toombs bill passed the Senate. When the facts were fresh in the public mind, when the Kansas question was the paramount question of the day, and when such a charge would have had a material bearing on the election, why did he and Lincoln remain silent then, knowing that such a charge could be made and proved if true? Were they not false to you and false to the country in going through that entire campaign, concealing their knowledge of this enormous conspiracy which, Mr. Trumbull says, he then knew and would not tell? Mr. Lincoln intimates, in his speech, a good reason why Mr. Trumbull would not tell; for he says that it might be true, as I proved that it was at Jacksonville, that Trumbull was also in the plot, yet that the fact of Trumbull's being in the plot would not in any way relieve me. He illustrates this argument by supposing himself on trial for murder, and says that it would be no extenuating circumstance if, on his trial, another man was found to be a party to his crime. Well, if Trumbull was in the plot, and concealed it in order to escape the odium which would have fallen upon himself, I ask you whether you can believe him now when he turns State's evidence, and avows his own infamy in order to implicate me. I am amazed that Mr. Lincoln should now come forward and indorse that charge, occupying his whole hour in reading Mr. Trumbull's speech in support of it. Why, I ask, does not Mr. Lincoln make a speech of his own instead of taking up his time reading Trumbull's speech at Alton? I supposed that Mr. Lincoln was capable of making a public speech on his own account, or I should not have accepted the banter from him for a joint discussion. ["How about the charges?"] Do not trouble yourselves; I am going to make my speech in my own way, and I trust, as the Democrats listened patiently and respectfully to Mr. Lincoln, that his friends will not interrupt me when I am answering him. When Mr. Trumbull returned from the East, the first thing he did when he landed at Chicago was to make a speech wholly devoted to assaults upon my public character and public action. Up to that time I had never alluded to his course in Congress, or to him directly or indirectly; and hence his assaults upon me were entirely without provocation and without excuse. Since then he has been traveling from one end of the State to the other repeating his vile charge. I propose now to read it in his own language:

Now, fellow-citizens, I make the distinct charge that there was a preconcerted arrangement and plot entered into by the very men who now claim credit for opposing a constitution formed and put in force without giving the people any opportunity to pass upon it. This, my friends, is a serious charge, but I charge it to-night that the very men who traverse the country under banners proclaiming popular sovereignty, by design concocted a bill on purpose to force a constitution upon that people.

In answer to some one in the crowd, who asked him a question, Trumbull said:

And you want to satisfy yourself that he was in the plot to force a constitution upon that people? I will satisfy you. I will cram the truth down any honest man's throat until he cannot deny it. And to the man who does deny it, I will cram the lie down his throat till he shall cry enough.

It is preposterous—it is the most damnable effrontery that man ever put on—to conceal a scheme to defraud and cheat the people out of their rights, and then claim credit for it.

That is the polite language Senator Trumbull applied to me, his colleague, when I was two hundred miles off. Why did he not speak out as boldly in the Senate of the United States, and cram the lie down my throat when I denied the charge, first made by Bigler, and made him take it back? You all recollect how Bigler assaulted me when I was engaged in a hand-to-hand fight, resisting a scheme to force a constitution on the people of Kansas against their will. He then attacked me with this charge; but I proved its utter falsity, nailed the slander to the counter, and made him take the back track. There is not an honest man in America who read that debate who will pretend that the charge is true. Trumbull was then present in the Senate, face to face with me, and why did he not then rise and repeat the charge, and say he would cram the lie down my throat? I tell you that Trumbull then knew it was a lie. He knew that Toombs denied that there ever was a clause in the bill he brought forward, calling for and requiring a submission of the Kansas constitution to the people. I will tell you what the facts of the case were. I introduced a bill to authorize the people of Kansas to form a constitution and come into the Union as a State whenever they should have the requisite population for a member of Congress, and Mr. Toombs proposed a substitute, authorizing the people of Kansas, with their then population of only 25,000, to form a constitution, and come in at once. The question at issue was, whether we would admit Kansas with a population of 25,000, or make her wait until she had the ratio entitling her to a representative in Congress, which was 93,420. That was the point of dispute in the Committee on Territories, to which both my bill and Mr. Toombs's substitute had been referred. I was overruled by a majority of the committee, my proposition rejected, and Mr. Toombs's proposition to admit Kansas then, with her population of 25,000, adopted. Accordingly a bill to carry out his idea of immediate admission was reported as a substitute for mine—the only points at issue being, as I have already said, the question of population, and the adoption of safeguards against frauds at the election. Trumbull knew this,—the whole Senate knew it,—and hence he was silent at that time. He waited until I became engaged in this canvass, and finding that I was showing up Lincoln's Abolitionism and negro-equality doctrines, that I was driving Lincoln to the wall, and white men would not support his rank Abolitionism, he came back from the East and trumped up a system of charges against me, hoping that I would be compelled to occupy my entire time in defending myself, so that I would not be able to show up the enormity of the principles of the Abolitionists. Now the only reason, and the true reason, why Mr. Lincoln has occupied the whole of his first hour in this issue between Trumbull and myself, is to conceal from this vast audience the real questions which divide the two great parties.

I am not going to allow them to waste much of my time with these personal matters. I have lived in this State twenty-five years, most of that time have been in public life, and my record is open to you all. If that record is not enough to vindicate me from these petty, malicious assaults, I despise ever to be elected to office by slandering my opponents and traducing other men. Mr. Lincoln asks you to elect him to the United States Senate to-day solely because he and Trumbull can slander me. Has he given any other reason?

Has he avowed what he was desirous to do in Congress on any one question? He desires to ride into office, not upon his own merits, not upon the merits and soundness of his principles, but upon his success in fastening a stale old slander upon me.

I wish you to bear in mind that up to the time of the introduction of the Toombs bill, and after its introduction, there had never been an act of Congress for the admission of a new State which contained a clause requiring its constitution to be submitted to the people. The general rule made the law silent on the subject, taking it for granted that the people would demand and compel a popular vote on the ratification of their constitution. Such was the general rule under Washington, Jefferson, Madison, Jackson, and Polk, under the Whig presidents and the Democratic presidents from the beginning of the government down, and nobody dreamed that an effort would ever be made to abuse the power thus confided to the people of a Territory. For this reason our attention was not called to the fact of whether there was or was not a clause in the Toombs bill compelling submission, but it was taken for granted that the constitution would be submitted to the people whether the law compelled it or not.

Now I will read from the report by me as chairman of the Committee on Territories at the time I reported back the Toombs substitute to the Senate. It contained several things which I had voted against in committee, but had been overruled by a majority of the members, and it was my duty as chairman of the committee to report the bill back as it was agreed upon by them. The main point upon which I had been overruled was the question of population. In my report accompanying the Toombs bill, I said:

In the opinion of your committee, whenever a constitution shall be formed in any Territory, preparatory to its admission into the Union as a State, justice, the genius of our institutions, the whole theory of our republican system, imperatively demand that the voice of the people shall be fairly expressed, and their will embodied in that fundamental law, without fraud, or violence, or intimidation, or any other improper or unlawful influence, and subject to no other restrictions than those imposed by the Constitution of the United States.

There you find that we took it for granted that the constitution was to be submitted to the people, whether the bill was silent on the subject or not. Suppose I had reported it so, following the example of Washington, Adams, Jefferson, Madison, Monroe, Adams, Jackson, Van Buren, Harrison, Tyler, Polk, Taylor, Fillmore, and Pierce, would that fact have been evidence of conspiracy to force a constitution upon the people of Kansas against their will? If the charge which Mr. Lincoln makes be true against me, it is true against Zachary Taylor, Millard Fillmore, and every Whig president, as well as every Democratic president, and against Henry Clay, who, in the Senate or House, for forty years advocated bills similar to the one I reported, no one of them containing a clause compelling the submission of the constitution to the people. Are Mr. Lincoln and Mr. Trumbull prepared to charge upon all those eminent men from the beginning of the government down to the present day, that the absence of a provision compelling submission, in the various bills passed by them, authorizing the people of Territories to form State constitutions, is evidence of a corrupt design on their part to force a constitution upon an unwilling people?

I ask you to reflect on these things, for I tell you that there is a conspiracy to carry this election for the Black Republicans by slander, and not by fair means. Mr. Lincoln's speech this day is conclusive evidence of the fact. He has devoted his entire time to an issue between Mr. Trumbull and myself, and has not uttered a word about the politics of the day. Are you going to elect Mr. Trumbull's colleague upon an issue between Mr. Trumbull and me? I thought I was running against Abraham Lincoln, that he claimed to be my opponent, had challenged me to a discussion of the public questions of the day with him, and was discussing these questions with me; but it turns out that his only hope is to ride into office on Trumbull's back, who will carry him by falsehood.

Permit me to pursue this subject a little further. An examination of the record proves that Trumbull's charge — that the Toombs bill originally contained a clause requiring the constitution to be submitted to the people — is false. The printed copy of the bill which Mr. Lincoln held up before you, and which he pretends contains such a clause, merely contains a clause requiring a submission of the land grant, and there is no clause in it requiring a submission of the constitution. Mr. Lincoln cannot find such a clause in it. My report shows that we took it for granted that the people would require a submission of the constitution, and secure it for themselves. There never was a clause in the Toombs bill requiring the constitution to be submitted; Trumbull knew it at the time, and his speech made on the night of its passage discloses the fact that he knew it was silent on the subject; Lincoln pretends, and tells you that Trumbull has not changed his evidence in support of his charge since he made his speech in Chicago. Let us see. The Chicago "Times" took up Trumbull's Chicago speech, compared it with the official records of Congress, and proved that speech to be false in its charge that the original Toombs bill required a submission of the constitution to the people. Trumbull then saw that he was caught, and his falsehood exposed, and he went to Alton, and, under the very walls of the penitentiary, made a new speech, in which he predicated his assault upon me in the allegation that I had caused to be voted into the Toombs bill a clause which prohibited the convention from submitting the constitution to the people, and quoted what he pretended was the clause. Now, has not Mr. Trumbull entirely changed the evidence on which he bases his charge? The clause which he quoted in his Alton speech (which he has published and circulated broadcast over the State) as having been put into the Toombs bill by me, is in the following words: "And until the complete execution of this act, no other election shall be held in said Territory."

Trumbull says that the object of that amendment was to prevent the convention from submitting the constitution to a vote of the people.

Now I will show you that when Trumbull made that statement at Alton he knew it to be untrue. I read from Trumbull's speech in the Senate on the Toombs bill on the night of its passage. He then said:

There is nothing said in this bill, so far as I have discovered, about submitting the constitution, which is to be formed, to the people for their sanction or rejection. Perhaps the convention will have the right to submit it, if it should think proper; but it is certainly not compelled to do so according to the provisions of the bill.

Thus you see that Trumbull, when the bill was on its passage in the Senate, said that it was silent on the subject of submission, and that there was nothing in the bill one way or the other on it. In his Alton speech he says there was a clause in the bill preventing its submission to the people, and that I had it voted in as an amendment. Thus I convict him of falsehood and slander by quoting from him on the passage of the Toombs bill in the Senate of the United States, his own speech, made on the night of July 2, 1856, and reported in the "Congressional Globe" for the first session of the Thirty-fourth Congress, Vol. XXXIII. What will you think of a man who makes a false charge and falsifies the records to prove it? I will now show you that the clause which Trumbull says was put in the bill on my motion, was never put in at all by me, but was stricken out on my motion and another substituted in its place. I call your attention to the same volume of the "Congressional Globe" to which I have already referred, page 795, where you will find the following report of the proceedings of the Senate:

Mr. Douglas: I have an amendment to offer from the Committee on Territories. On page 8, section 11, strike out the words "until the complete execution of this act, no other election shall be held in said Territory," and insert the amendment which I hold in my hand.

You see from this that I moved to strike out the very words that Trumbull says I put in. The Committee on Territories overruled me in committee, and put the clause in; but as soon as I got the bill back into the Senate, I moved to strike it out, and put another clause in its place. On the same page you will find that my amendment was agreed to unanimously. I then offered another amendment, recognizing the right of the people of Kansas, under the Toombs bill, to order just such elections as they saw proper. You can find it on page 796 of the same volume. I will read it:

Mr. Douglas: I have another amendment to offer from the committee, to follow the amendment which has been adopted. The bill reads now: "And until the complete execution of this act, no other election shall be held in said Territory." It has been suggested that it should be modified in this way: "And to avoid conflict in the complete execution of this act, all other elections in said Territory are hereby postponed until such time as said convention shall appoint"; so that they can appoint the day in the event that there should be a failure to come into the Union.

The amendment was unanimously agreed to—clearly and distinctly recognizing the right of the convention to order just as many elections as they saw proper in the execution of the act. Trumbull concealed in his Alton speech the fact that the clause he quoted had been stricken out on my motion, and the other fact that this other clause was put in the bill on my motion, and made the false charge that I incorporated into the bill a clause preventing submission, in the face of the fact that, on my motion, the bill was so amended before it passed as to recognize in express words the right and duty of submission.

On this record that I have produced before you, I repeat my charge that Trumbull did falsify the public records of the country, in order to make his charge against me, and I tell Mr. Abraham Lincoln that if he will examine these records, he will then know what I state is true. Mr. Lincoln has this day indorsed Mr. Trumbull's veracity after he had my word for it that that veracity was proved to be violated and forfeited by the public records. It will not do for Mr. Lincoln, in parading his calumnies against me, to put Mr. Trumbull between him and the odium and responsibility which justly attach to such calumnies. I tell him that I am as ready to prosecute the indorser as the maker of a forged note. I regret the necessity of occupying my time with these petty personal matters. It is unbecoming the dignity of a canvass for an office of the character for which we are candidates. When I commenced the canvass at Chicago, I spoke of Mr. Lincoln in terms of kindness, as an old friend; I said that he was a good citizen, of unblemished character, against whom I had nothing to say. I repeated these complimentary remarks about him in my successive speeches, until he became the indorser for these and other slanders against me. If there is anything personally disagreeable, uncourteous, or disreputable in these personalities, the sole responsibility rests on Mr. Lincoln, Mr. Trumbull, and their backers.

I will show you another charge made by Mr. Lincoln against me, as an offset to his determination of willingness to take back anything that is incorrect, and to correct any false statement he may have made. He has several times charged that the Supreme Court, President Pierce, President Buchanan, and myself, at the time I introduced the Nebraska bill, in January, 1854, at Washington, entered into a conspiracy to establish slavery all over this country. I branded this charge as a falsehood, and then he repeated it, asked me to analyze its truth, and answer it. I told him, "Mr. Lincoln, I know what you are after; you want to occupy my time in personal matters, to prevent me from showing up the revolutionary principles which the Abolition party — whose candidate you are — have proclaimed to the world." But he asked me to analyze his proof, and I did so. I called his attention to the fact that at the time the Nebraska bill was introduced, there was no such case as the Dred Scott case pending in the Supreme Court, nor was it brought there for years afterward, and hence that it was impossible there could have been any such conspiracy between the judges of the Supreme Court and the other parties involved. I proved by the record that the charge was false, and what did he answer? Did he take it back like an honest man and say he had been mistaken? No; he repeated the charge, and said, that although there was no such case pending that year, there was an understanding between the Democratic owners of Dred Scott and the judges of the Supreme Court and other parties involved, that the case should be brought up. I then demanded to know who those Democratic owners of Dred Scott were. He could not or would not tell; he did not know. In truth, there were no Democratic owners of Dred Scott on the face of the land. Dred Scott was owned at that time by the Rev. Dr. Chaffee, an Abolition member of Congress from Springfield, Massachusetts, and his wife; and Mr. Lincoln ought to have known that Dred Scott was so owned, for the reason that as soon as the decision was announced by the court, Dr. Chaffee and his wife executed a deed emancipating him, and put that deed on record.

It was a matter of public record, therefore, that at the time the case was taken to the Supreme Court, Dred Scott was owned by an Abolition member of Congress, a friend of Lincoln's, and a leading man of his party, while the defense was conducted by Abolition lawyers; and thus the Abolitionists managed both sides of the case. I have exposed these facts to Mr. Lincoln, and yet he will not withdraw his charge of conspiracy. I now submit to you whether you can place any confidence in a man who continues to make a charge when its utter falsity is proven by the public records. I will state another fact to show how utterly reckless and unscrupulous this charge against the Supreme Court, President Pierce, President Buchanan, and myself is. Lincoln says that President Buchanan was in the conspiracy at Washington in the winter of 1854, when the Nebraska bill was introduced. The history of this country shows that James Buchanan was at that time representing this country at the Court of St. James, Great Britain, with distinguished ability and usefulness, that he had not been in the United States for nearly a year previous, and that he did not return until about three years after. Yet Mr. Lincoln keeps repeating this charge of conspiracy against Mr. Buchanan when the public records prove it to be untrue. Having proved it to be false as far as the Supreme Court and President Buchanan are concerned, I drop it, leaving the public to say whether I, by myself, without their concurrence, could have gone into a conspiracy with them. My friends, you see that the object clearly is to conduct the canvass on personal matters, and hunt me down with charges that are proven to be false by the public records of the country. I am willing to throw open my whole public and private life to the inspection of any man, or all men who desire to investigate it. Having resided among you twenty-five years, during nearly the whole of which time a public man, exposed to more assaults, perhaps more abuse, than any man living of my age, or who ever did live, and having survived it all and still commanded your confidence, I am willing to trust to your knowledge of me and my public conduct without making any more defense against these assaults.

Fellow-citizens, I came here for the purpose of discussing the leading political topics which now agitate the country. I have no charges to make against Mr. Lincoln, none against Mr. Trumbull, and none against any man who is a candidate, except in repelling their assaults upon me. If Mr. Lincoln is a man of bad character, I leave you to find it out; if his votes in the past are not satisfactory, I leave others to ascertain the fact; if his course on the Mexican war was not in accordance with your notions of patriotism and fidelity to our own country as against a public enemy, I leave you to ascertain the fact. I have no assaults to make upon him, except to trace his course on the questions that now divide the country and engross so much of the people's attention.

You know that prior to 1854 this country was divided into two great political parties, one the Whig, the other the Democratic. I, as a Democrat for twenty years prior to that time, had been in public discussions in this State as an advocate of Democratic principles, and I can appeal with confidence to every old-line Whig within the hearing of my voice to bear testimony that during all that period I fought you Whigs like a man on every question that separated the two parties. I had the highest respect for Henry Clay as a gallant party-leader, as an eminent statesman, and as one of the bright ornaments of this country; but I conscientiously believed that the Democratic party was right on the questions which separated the Democrats from the Whigs. The man does not live who can say that I ever personally assailed Henry Clay or Daniel Webster, or any one of the leaders of that great party, whilst I combated with all my energy the measures they advocated. What did we differ about in those days? Did Whigs and Democrats differ about this slavery question? On the contrary, did we not, in 1850, unite to a man in favor of that system of compromise measures which Mr. Clay introduced, Webster defended, Cass supported, and Fillmore approved and made the law of the land by his signature. While we agreed on these compromise measures, we differed about a bank, the tariff, distribution, the specie circular, the subtreasury, and other questions of that description. Now, let me ask you, which one of those questions on which Whigs and Democrats then differed now remains to divide the two great parties? Every one of those questions which divided Whigs and Democrats has passed away; the country has outgrown them; they have passed into history. Hence it is immaterial whether you were right or I was right on the bank, the subtreasury, and other questions, because they no longer continue living issues. What, then, has taken the place of those questions about which we once differed? The slavery question has now become the leading and controlling issue; that question on which you and I agreed, on which the Whigs and Democrats united, has now become the leading issue between the National Democracy on the one side, and the Republican or Abolition party on the other.

Just recollect for a moment the memorable contest of 1850, when this country was agitated from its center to its circumference by the slavery agitation. All eyes in this nation were then turned to the three great lights that survived the days of the Revolution. They looked to Clay, then in retirement at Ashland, and to Webster and Cass in the United States Senate. Clay had retired to Ashland, having, as he supposed, performed his mission on earth, and was preparing himself for a better sphere of existence in another world. In

that retirement he heard the discordant, harsh, and grating sounds
of sectional strife and disunion; and he aroused and came forth and
resumed his seat in the Senate, that great theater of his great deeds.
From the moment that Clay arrived among us he became the leader
of all the Union men, whether Whigs or Democrats. For nine months
we each assembled, each day, in the council-chamber, Clay in the
chair, with Cass upon his right hand and Webster upon his left, and
the Democrats and Whigs gathered around, forgetting differences,
and only animated by one common patriotic sentiment, to devise
means and measures by which we could defeat the mad and revolutionary scheme of the Northern Abolitionists and Southern disunionists. We did devise those means. Clay brought them forward, Cass
advocated them, the Union Democrats and Union Whigs voted for
them, Fillmore signed them, and they gave peace and quiet to the
country. Those compromise measures of 1850 were founded upon
the great fundamental principle that the people of each State and
each Territory ought to be left free to form and regulate their own
domestic institutions in their own way, subject only to the Federal
Constitution.

I will ask every old-line Democrat and every old-line Whig within
the hearing of my voice, if I have not truly stated the issues as they
then presented themselves to the country. You recollect that the
Abolitionists raised a howl of indignation, and cried for vengeance
and the destruction of Democrats and Whigs both who supported
those compromise measures of 1850. When I returned home to
Chicago, I found the citizens inflamed and infuriated against the
authors of those great measures. Being the only man in that city
who was held responsible for affirmative votes on all those measures,
I came forward and addressed the assembled inhabitants, defended
each and every one of Clay's compromise measures as they passed
the Senate and the House and were approved by President Fillmore.
Previous to that time, the city council had passed resolutions nullifying the act of Congress, and instructing the police to withhold all
assistance from its execution; but the people of Chicago listened to
my defense, and like candid, frank, conscientious men, when they
became convinced that they had done an injustice to Clay, Webster,
Cass, and all of us who had supported those measures, they repealed
their nullifying resolutions and declared that the laws should be
executed and the supremacy of the Constitution maintained. Let it
always be recorded in history, to the immortal honor of the people
of Chicago, that they returned to their duty when they found that
they were wrong, and did justice to those whom they had blamed
and abused unjustly. When the legislature of this State assembled
that year, they proceeded to pass resolutions approving the compromise measures of 1850. When the Whig party assembled in
1852 at Baltimore in national convention for the last time, to nominate Scott for the presidency, they adopted as a part of their platform the compromise measures of 1850 as the cardinal plank upon
which every Whig would stand and by which he would regulate his
future conduct. When the Democratic party assembled at the same
place, one month after, to nominate General Pierce, we adopted the

same platform so far as those compromise measures were concerned, agreeing that we would stand by those glorious measures as a cardinal article in the Democratic faith. Thus you see that in 1852 all the Old Whigs and all the old Democrats stood on a common plank so far as this slavery question was concerned, differing on other questions.

Now, let me ask, how is it that since that time so many of you Whigs have wandered from the true path marked out by Clay and carried out broad and wide by the great Webster? How is it that so many old-line Democrats have abandoned the old faith of their party, and joined with Abolitionism and Free-soilism to overturn the platform of the old Democrats, and the platform of the Old Whigs? You cannot deny that since 1854 there has been a great revolution on this one question. How has it been brought about? I answer that no sooner was the sod grown green over the grave of the immortal Clay, no sooner was the rose planted on the tomb of the godlike Webster, than many of the leaders of the Whig party, such as Seward, of New York, and his followers, led off and attempted to Abolitionize the Whig party, and transfer all your Old Whigs, bound hand and foot, into the Abolition camp. Seizing hold of the temporary excitement produced in this country by the introduction of the Nebraska bill, the disappointed politicians in the Democratic party united with the disappointed politicians in the Whig party, and endeavored to form a new party composed of all the Abolitionists, of Abolitionized Democrats and Abolitionized Whigs, banded together in an Abolition platform.

And who led that crusade against national principles in this State? I answer, Abraham Lincoln on behalf of the Whigs, and Lyman Trumbull on behalf of the Democrats, formed a scheme by which they would Abolitionize the two great parties in this State on condition that Lincoln should be sent to the United States Senate in place of General Shields, and that Trumbull should go to Congress from the Belleville district, until I would be accommodating enough either to die or resign for his benefit, and then he was to go to the Senate in my place. You all remember that during the year 1854 these two worthy gentlemen, Mr. Lincoln and Mr. Trumbull, one an old-line Whig and the other an old-line Democrat, were hunting in partnership to elect a legislature against the Democratic party. I canvassed the State that year from the time I returned home until the election came off, and spoke in every county that I could reach during that period. In the northern part of the State I found Lincoln's ally, in the person of Fred Douglass, the negro, preaching Abolition doctrines, while Lincoln was discussing the same principles down here, and Trumbull, a little further down, was advocating the election of members to the legislature who would act in concert with Lincoln's and Fred Douglass's friends. I witnessed an effort made at Chicago by Lincoln's then associates, and now supporters, to put Fred Douglass, the negro, on the stand at a Democratic meeting, to reply to the illustrious General Cass when he was addressing the people there. They had the same negro hunting me down, and they now have a negro traversing the northern counties of the State, and speaking in behalf of Lincoln. Lincoln knows that when we were at Freeport in joint discussion, there was a distinguished colored friend of his there then who was on the stump for him, and who made a speech there the night before we spoke, and another the night after, a short distance from Freeport, in favor of Lincoln; and in order to show how much interest the colored brethren felt in the success of their brother Abe, I have with me here, and would read it if it would not occupy too much of my time, a speech made by Fred Douglass in Poughkeepsie, N. Y., a short time since, to a large convention, in which he conjures all the friends of negro equality and negro citizenship to rally as one man around Abraham Lincoln, the perfect embodiment of their principles, and by all means to defeat Stephen A. Douglas. Thus you find that this Republican party in the northern part of the State had colored gentlemen for their advocates in 1854, in company with Lincoln and Trumbull, as they have now. When, in October, 1854, I went down to Springfield to attend the State fair, I found the leaders of this party all assembled together under the title of an anti-Nebraska meeting. It was Black Republican up north, and anti-Nebraska at Springfield. I found Lovejoy, a high priest of Abolitionism, and Lincoln, one of the leaders who was towing the old-line Whigs into the Abolition camp, and Trumbull, Sidney Breese, and Governor Reynolds, all making speeches against the Democratic party and myself, at the same place and in the same cause.

The same men who are now fighting the Democratic party and the regular Democratic nominees in this State were fighting us then. They did not then acknowledge that they had become Abolitionists, and many of them deny it now. Breese, Dougherty, and Reynolds were then fighting the Democracy under the title of anti-Nebraska men, and now they are fighting the Democracy under the pretense that they are simon-pure Democrats, saying that they are authorized to have every office-holder in Illinois beheaded who prefers the election of Douglas to that of Lincoln, or the success of the Democratic ticket in preference to the Abolition ticket for members of Congress, State officers, members of the legislature, or any office in the State. They canvassed the State against us in 1854, as they are doing now, owning different names and different principles in different localities, but having a common object in view, viz.: the defeat of all men holding national principles in opposition to this sectional Abolition party. They carried the legislature in 1854, and when it assembled in Springfield they proceeded to elect a United States senator, all voting for Lincoln with one or two exceptions, which exceptions prevented them from quite electing him. And why should they not elect him? Had not Trumbull agreed that Lincoln should have Shields's place? Had not the Abolitionists agreed to it? Was it not the solemn compact, the condition on which Lincoln agreed to Abolitionize the Old Whigs, that he should be senator? Still, Trumbull, having control of a few Abolitionized Democrats, would not allow them all to vote for Lincoln on any one ballot, and thus kept him for some time within one or two votes of an election, until he worried out Lincoln's friends, and compelled them to drop him and elect

VOL. I.—26.

Trumbull in violation of the bargain. I desire to read you a piece of testimony in confirmation of the notoriously public facts which I have stated to you. Colonel James H. Matheny, of Springfield, is, and for twenty years has been, the confidential personal and political friend and manager of Mr. Lincoln. Matheny is this very day the candidate of the Republican or Abolition party for Congress against the gallant Major Thomas L. Harris, in the Springfield district, and is making speeches for Lincoln and against me. I will read you the testimony of Matheny about this bargain between Lincoln and Trumbull when they undertook to Abolitionize Whigs and Democrats only four years ago. Matheny, being mad at Trumbull for having played a Yankee trick on Lincoln, exposed the bargain in a public speech two years ago, and I will read the published report of that speech, the correctness of which Mr. Lincoln will not deny:

The Whigs, Abolitionists, Know-nothings, and renegade Democrats made a solemn compact for the purpose of carrying this State against the Democracy on this plan: First, that they would all combine and elect Mr. Trumbull to Congress, and thereby carry his district for the legislature, in order to throw all the strength that could be obtained into that body against the Democrats. Second, that when the legislature should meet, the officers of that body, such as speaker, clerks, doorkeepers, etc., would be given to the Abolitionists; and, third, that the Whigs were to have the United States senator. That, accordingly, in good faith Trumbull was elected to Congress, and his district carried for the legislature, and when it convened the Abolitionists got all the officers of that body, and thus far the "bond" was fairly executed. The Whigs, on their part, demanded the election of Abraham Lincoln to the United States Senate, that the bond might be fulfilled, the other parties to the contract having already secured to themselves all that was called for. But, in the most perfidious manner, they refused to elect Mr. Lincoln; and the mean, low-lived, sneaking Trumbull succeeded, by pledging all that was required by any party, in thrusting Lincoln aside and foisting himself, an excrescence from the rotten bowels of the Democracy, into the United States Senate; and thus it has ever been, that an honest man makes a bad bargain when he conspires or contracts with rogues.

Lincoln's confidential friend, Matheny, thought that Lincoln made a bad bargain when he conspired with such rogues as Trumbull and the Abolitionists. I would like to know whether Lincoln had as high an opinion of Trumbull's veracity when the latter agreed to support him for the Senate, and then cheated him, as he has now, when Trumbull comes forward and makes charges against me. You could not then prove Trumbull an honest man either by Lincoln, by Matheny, or by any of Lincoln's friends. They charged everywhere that Trumbull had cheated them out of the bargain, and Lincoln found, sure enough, that it was a bad bargain to contract and conspire with rogues.

And now I will explain to you what has been a mystery all over the State and Union, the reason why Lincoln was nominated for the United States Senate by the Black Republican convention. You know it has never been usual for any party, or any convention, to nominate a candidate for United States senator. Probably this was the first time that such a thing was ever done. The Black Republican convention had not been called for that purpose, but to nominate a State ticket, and every man was surprised and many disgusted when Lincoln was nominated.   Archie Williams thought he was entitled to it, Browning knew that he deserved it, Wentworth was certain that he would get it, Peck had hopes, Judd felt sure that he was the man, and Palmer had claims and had made arrangements to secure it; but, to their utter amazement, Lincoln was nominated by the convention, and not only that, but he received the nomination unanimously, by a resolution declaring that Abraham Lincoln was "the first, last, and only choice" of the Republican party.   How did this occur?   Why, because they could not get Lincoln's friends to make another bargain with "rogues," unless the whole party would come up as one man and pledge their honor that they would stand by Lincoln first, last, and all the time, and that he should not be cheated by Lovejoy this time, as he was by Trumbull before.   Thus, by passing this resolution, the Abolitionists are all for him, Lovejoy and Farnsworth are canvassing for him, Giddings is ready to come here in his behalf, and the negro speakers are already on the stump for him, and he is sure not to be cheated this time.   He would not go into the arrangement until he got their bond for it, and Trumbull is compelled now to take the stump, get up false charges against me, and travel all over the State to try and elect Lincoln, in order to keep Lincoln's friends quiet about the bargain in which Trumbull cheated them four years ago.   You see now why it is that Lincoln and Trumbull are so mighty fond of each other.   They have entered into a conspiracy to break me down by these assaults on my public character, in order to draw my attention from a fair exposure of the mode in which they attempted to Abolitionize the Old Whig and the old Democratic parties and lead them captive into the Abolition camp. Do you not all remember that Lincoln went around here four years ago making speeches to you, and telling that you should all go for the Abolition ticket, and swearing that he was as good a Whig as he ever was; and that Trumbull went all over the State making pledges to the old Democrats, and trying to coax them into the Abolition camp, swearing by his Maker, with the uplifted hand, that he was still a Democrat, always intended to be, and that never would he desert the Democratic party.   He got your votes to elect an Abolition legislature, which passed Abolition resolutions, attempted to pass Abolition laws, and sustained Abolitionists for office, State and national.   Now, the same game is attempted to be played over again. Then Lincoln and Trumbull made captives of the Old Whigs and old Democrats and carried them into the Abolition camp, where Father Giddings, the high priest of Abolitionism, received and christened them in the dark cause just as fast as they were brought in.   Giddings found the converts so numerous that he had to have assistance, and he sent for John P. Hale, N. P. Banks, Chase, and other Abolitionists, and they came on, and with Lovejoy and Fred Douglass, the negro, helped to baptize these new converts as Lincoln, Trumbull, Breese, Reynolds, and Dougherty could capture them and bring them within the Abolition clutch.   Gentlemen, they are now around making the same kind of speeches.   Trumbull was down in Monroe County the other day assailing me, and making a speech in favor of

Lincoln, and I will show you under what notice his meeting was called. You see these people are Black Republicans or Abolitionists up north, while at Springfield to-day they dare not call their convention "Republican," but are obliged to say "a convention of all men opposed to the Democratic party," and in Monroe County and lower Egypt Trumbull advertises their meetings as follows:

A meeting of the Free Democracy will take place at Waterloo, on Monday, September 12th inst., whereat Hon. Lyman Trumbull, Hon. Jehu Baker, and others, will address the people upon the different political topics of the day. Members of all parties are cordially invited to be present, and hear and determine for themselves.

September 9, 1858.   THE FREE DEMOCRACY.

Did you ever before hear of this new party called the "Free Democracy"?

What object have these Black Republicans in changing their name in every county? They have one name in the north, another in the center, and another in the south. When I used to practise law before my distinguished judicial friend whom I recognize in the crowd before me, if a man was charged with horse-stealing, and the proof showed that he went by one name in Stephenson County, another in Sangamon, a third in Monroe, and a fourth in Randolph, we thought that the fact of his changing his name so often to avoid detection was pretty strong evidence of his guilt. I would like to know why it is that this great Free-soil Abolition party is not willing to avow the same name in all parts of the State? If this party believes that its course is just, why does it not avow the same principles in the north and in the south, in the east and in the west, wherever the American flag waves over American soil? [A voice: "The party does not call itself Black Republican in the north."] Sir, if you will get a copy of the paper published at Waukegan, fifty miles from Chicago, which advocates the election of Mr. Lincoln, and has his name flying at its masthead, you will find that it declares that "this paper is devoted to the cause" of Black Republicanism. I had a copy of it, and intended to bring it down here into Egypt to let you see what name the party rallied under up in the northern part of the State, and to convince you that their principles are as different in the two sections of the State as is their name. I am sorry I have mislaid it and have not got it here. Their principles in the north are jet-black, in the center they are in color a decent mulatto, and in lower Egypt they are almost white. Why, I admired many of the white sentiments contained in Lincoln's speech at Jonesboro, and could not help but contrast them with the speeches of the same distinguished orator made in the northern part of the State. Down here he denies that the Black Republican party is opposed to the admission of any more slave States, under any circumstances, and says that they are willing to allow the people of each State, when it wants to come into the Union, to do just as it pleases on the question of slavery. In the north you find Lovejoy, their candidate for Congress in the Bloomington district; Farnsworth, their candidate in the Chicago district; and Washburne, their candidate in the Galena district, all declaring that never will they consent under any circumstances to admit another slave State, even if the people want it.   Thus, while they avow one set of principles up there, they avow another and entirely different set down here.   And here let me recall to Mr. Lincoln the scriptural quotation which he has applied to the Federal Government, that a house divided against itself cannot stand, and ask him how does he expect this Abolition party to stand when in one half of the State it advocates a set of principles which it has repudiated in the other half?

I am told that I have but eight minutes more.   I would like to talk to you an hour and a half longer, but I will make the best use I can of the remaining eight minutes.   Mr. Lincoln said in his first remarks that he was not in favor of the social and political equality of the negro with the white man.   Everywhere up north he has declared that he was not in favor of the social and political equality of the negro, but he would not say whether or not he was opposed to negroes voting and negro citizenship.   I want to know whether he is for or against negro citizenship?   He declared his utter opposition to the Dred Scott decision, and advanced as a reason that the court had decided that it was not possible for a negro to be a citizen under the Constitution of the United States.   If he is opposed to the Dred Scott decision for that reason, he must be in favor of conferring the right and privilege of citizenship upon the negro.   I have been trying to get an answer from him on that point, but have never yet obtained one, and I will show you why.   In every speech he made in the north he quoted the Declaration of Independence to prove that all men were created equal, and insisted that the phrase "all men" included the negro as well as the white man, and that the equality rested upon divine law.   Here is what he said on that point:

I should like to know if, taking this old Declaration of Independence, which declares that all men are equal upon principle, and making exceptions to it, where will it stop?   If one man says it does not mean a negro, why may not another say it does not mean some other man?   If that Declaration is not the truth, let us get the statute-book in which we find it and tear it out.

Lincoln maintains there that the Declaration of Independence asserts that the negro is equal to the white man, and that under divine law; and if he believes so it was rational for him to advocate negro citizenship, which, when allowed, puts the negro on an equality under the law.   I say to you in all frankness, gentlemen, that in my opinion a negro is not a citizen, cannot be, and ought not to be, under the Constitution of the United States.   I will not even qualify my opinion to meet the declaration of one of the judges of the Supreme Court in the Dred Scott case, "that a negro descended from African parents, who was imported into this country as a slave, is not a citizen, and cannot be."   I say that this government was established on the white basis.   It was made by white men, for the benefit of white men and their posterity forever, and never should be administered by any except white men.   I declare that a negro ought not to be a citizen, whether his parents were imported into this country as slaves or not, or whether or not he was born here. It does not depend upon the place a negro's parents were born, or whether they were slaves or not, but upon the fact that he is a negro, belonging to a race incapable of self-government, and for that reason ought not to be on an equality with white men.

My friends, I am sorry that I have not time to pursue this argument further, as I might have done but for the fact that Mr. Lincoln compelled me to occupy a portion of my time in repelling those gross slanders and falsehoods that Trumbull has invented against me and put in circulation. In conclusion, let me ask you why should this government be divided by a geographical line — arraying all men North in one great hostile party against all men South? Mr. Lincoln tells you, in his speech at Springfield, that a house divided against itself cannot stand; that this government, divided into free and slave States, cannot endure permanently; that they must either be all free or all slave, all one thing or all the other. Why cannot this government endure divided into free States and slave States, as our fathers made it?

When this government was established by Washington, Jefferson, Madison, Jay, Hamilton, Franklin, and the other sages and patriots of that day, it was composed of free States and slave States, bound together by one common Constitution. We have existed and prospered from that day to this thus divided, and have increased with a rapidity never before equaled in wealth, the extension of territory, and all the elements of power and greatness, until we have become the first nation on the face of the globe. Why can we not thus continue to prosper? We can if we will live up to and execute the government upon those principles upon which our fathers established it. During the whole period of our existence Divine Providence has smiled upon us, and showered upon our nation richer and more abundant blessings than have ever been conferred upon any other.

Mr. Lincoln's Rejoinder in the Charleston Joint Debate.

Fellow-citizens: It follows as a matter of course that a half-hour answer to a speech of an hour and a half can be but a very hurried one. I shall only be able to touch upon a few of the points suggested by Judge Douglas, and give them a brief attention, while I shall have to totally omit others for the want of time.

Judge Douglas has said to you that he has not been able to get from me an answer to the question whether I am in favor of negro citizenship. So far as I know, the judge never asked me the question before. He shall have no occasion to ever ask it again, for I tell him very frankly that I am not in favor of negro citizenship. This furnishes me an occasion for saying a few words upon the subject. I mentioned in a certain speech of mine, which has been printed, that the Supreme Court had decided that a negro could not possibly be made a citizen, and without saying what was my ground of complaint in regard to that, or whether I had any ground of complaint, Judge Douglas has from that thing manufactured nearly everything that he ever says about my disposition to produce an equality between the negroes and the white people. If any one will read my speech, he will find I mentioned that as one of the points decided in the course of the Supreme Court opinions, but I did not state what objection I had to it. But Judge Douglas tells the people what my objection was when I did not tell them myself. Now my opinion is that the different States have the power to make a negro a citizen under the Constitution of the United States, if they choose. The Dred Scott decision decides that they have not that power. If the State of Illinois had that power, I should be opposed to the exercise of it. That is all I have to say about it.

Judge Douglas has told me that he heard my speeches north and my speeches south—that he had heard me at Ottawa and at Freeport in the north, and recently at Jonesboro in the south, and there was a very different cast of sentiment in the speeches made at the different points. I will not charge upon Judge Douglas that he wilfully misrepresents me, but I call upon every fair-minded man to take these speeches and read them, and I dare him to point out any difference between my speeches north and south. While I am here perhaps I ought to say a word, if I have the time, in regard to the latter portion of the judge's speech, which was a sort of declamation in reference to my having said I entertained the belief that this government would not endure half slave and half free. I have said so, and I did not say it without what seemed to me to be good reasons. It perhaps would require more time than I have now to set forth these reasons in detail; but let me ask you a few questions. Have we ever had any peace on this slavery question? When are we to have peace upon it if it is kept in the position it now occupies? How are we ever to have peace upon it? That is an important question. To be sure, if we will all stop and allow Judge Douglas and his friends to march on in their present career until they plant the institution all over the nation, here and wherever else our flag waves, and we acquiesce in it, there will be peace. But let me ask Judge Douglas how he is going to get the people to do that? They have been wrangling over this question for at least forty years. This was the cause of the agitation resulting in the Missouri compromise; this produced the troubles at the annexation of Texas, in the acquisition of the territory acquired in the Mexican war. Again, this was the trouble which was quieted by the compromise of 1850, when it was settled "forever," as both the great political parties declared in their national conventions. That "forever" turned out to be just four years, when Judge Douglas himself reopened it.

When is it likely to come to an end? He introduced the Nebraska bill in 1854 to put another end to the slavery agitation. He promised that it would finish it all up immediately, and he has never made a speech since until he got into a quarrel with the President about the Lecompton constitution, in which he has not declared that we are just at the end of the slavery agitation. But in one speech, I think last winter, he did say that he did n't quite see when the end of the slavery agitation would come. Now he tells us again that it is all over, and the people of Kansas have voted down the Lecompton constitution. How is it over? That was only one of the attempts at putting an end to the slavery agitation — one of these "final settlements." Is Kansas in the Union? Has she formed a constitution that she is likely to come in under? Is not the slavery agitation still an open question in that Territory? Has the voting down of that constitution put an end to all the trouble? Is that more likely to settle it than every one of these previous attempts to settle the slavery agitation? Now, at this day in the history of the world we can no more foretell where the end of this slavery agitation will be than we can see the end of the world itself. The Nebraska-Kansas bill was introduced four years and a half ago, and if the agitation is ever to come to an end, we may say we are four years and a half nearer the end. So, too, we can say we are four years and a half nearer the end of the world; and we can just as clearly see the end of the world as we can see the end of this agitation. The Kansas settlement did not conclude it. If Kansas should sink to-day, and leave a great vacant space in the earth's surface, this vexed question would still be among us. I say, then, there is no way of putting an end to the slavery agitation amongst us but to put it back upon the basis where our fathers placed it, no way but to keep it out of our new Territories — to restrict it forever to the old States where it now exists. Then the public mind will rest in the belief that it is in the course of ultimate extinction. That is one way of putting an end to the slavery agitation.

The other way is for us to surrender and let Judge Douglas and his friends have their way and plant slavery over all the States — cease speaking of it as in any way a wrong — regard slavery as one of the common matters of property, and speak of negroes as we do of our horses and cattle. But while it drives on in its state of progress as it is now driving, and as it has driven for the last five years, I have ventured the opinion, and I say to-day, that we will have no end to the slavery agitation until it takes one turn or the other. I do not mean that when it takes a turn toward ultimate extinction it will be in a day, nor in a year, nor in two years. I do not suppose that in the most peaceful way ultimate extinction would occur in less than a hundred years at least; but that it will occur in the best way for both races, in God's own good time, I have no doubt. But, my friends, I have used up more of my time than I intended on this point.

Now, in regard to this matter about Trumbull and myself having made a bargain to sell out the entire Whig and Democratic parties in 1854, Judge Douglas brings forward no evidence to sustain his charge, except the speech Matheny is said to have made in 1856, in which he told a cock-and-bull story of that sort, upon the same moral principles that Judge Douglas tells it here to-day. This is the simple truth. I do not care greatly for the story, but this is the truth of it, and I have twice told Judge Douglas to his face, that from beginning to end there is not one word of truth in it. I have called upon him for the proof, and he does not at all meet me as Trumbull met him upon that of which we were just talking, by producing the record. He did n't bring the record, because there was no record for him to bring. When he asks if I am ready to indorse Trumbull's veracity after he has broken a bargain with me, I reply that if Trumbull had broken a bargain with me, I would not be likely to indorse his veracity; but I am ready to indorse his veracity because neither in that thing, nor in any other, in all the years that I have known Lyman Trumbull, have I known him to fail of his word or tell a falsehood, large or small. It is for that reason that I indorse Lyman Trumbull.

Mr. James Brown [Douglas postmaster]: What does Ford's history say about him?

Mr. Lincoln: Some gentleman asks me what Ford's history says about him. My own recollection is, that Ford speaks of Trumbull in very disrespectful terms in several portions of his book, and that he talks a great deal worse of Judge Douglas. I refer you, sir, to the history for examination.

Judge Douglas complains at considerable length about a disposition on the part of Trumbull and myself to attack him personally. I want to attend to that suggestion a moment. I don't want to be unjustly accused of dealing illiberally or unfairly with an adversary, either in court, or in a political canvass, or anywhere else. I would despise myself if I supposed myself ready to deal less liberally with an adversary than I was willing to be treated myself. Judge Douglas, in a general way, without putting it in a direct shape, revives the old charge against me in reference to the Mexican war. He does not take the responsibility of putting it in a very definite form, but makes a general reference to it. That charge is more than ten years old. He complains of Trumbull and myself, because he says we bring charges against him one or two years old. He knows, too, that in regard to the Mexican war story, the more respectable papers of his own party throughout the State have been compelled to take it back and acknowledge that it was a lie.

[Here Mr. Lincoln turned to the crowd on the platform, and selecting Hon. Orlando B. Ficklin, led him forward and said:]

I do not mean to do anything with Mr. Ficklin, except to present his face and tell you that he personally knows it to be a lie! He was a member of Congress at the only time I was in Congress, and he knows that whenever there was an attempt to procure a vote of mine which would indorse the origin and justice of the war, I refused to give such indorsement, and voted against it; but I never voted against the supplies for the army, and he knows, as well as Judge Douglas, that whenever a dollar was asked by way of compensation or otherwise, for the benefit of the soldiers, I gave all the votes that Ficklin or Douglas did, and perhaps more.

Mr. Ficklin: My friends, I wish to say this in reference to the matter. Mr. Lincoln and myself are just as good personal friends as Judge Douglas and myself. In reference to this Mexican war, my recollection is that when Ashmun's resolution [amendment] was offered by Mr. Ashmun of Massachusetts, in which he declared that the Mexican war was unnecessarily and unconstitutionally commenced by the President,— my recollection is that Mr. Lincoln voted for that resolution.

Mr. Lincoln: That is the truth. Now you all remember that was a resolution censuring the President for the manner in which the war was begun. You know they have charged that I voted against the supplies, by which I starved the soldiers who were out fighting the battles of their country. I say that Ficklin knows it is false. When that charge was brought forward by the Chicago "Times," the Springfield "Register" [Douglas organ] reminded the "Times" that the charge really applied to John Henry; and I do know that John Henry is now making speeches and fiercely battling for Judge Douglas. If the judge now says that he offers this as a sort of a set-off to what I said to-day in reference to Trumbull's charge, then I remind him that he made this charge before I said a word about Trumbull's. He brought this forward at Ottawa, the first time we met face to face; and in the opening speech that Judge Douglas made, he attacked me in regard to a matter ten years old. Is n't he a pretty man to be whining about people making charges against him only two years old!

The judge thinks it is altogether wrong that I should have dwelt upon this charge of Trumbull's at all. I gave the apology for doing so in my opening speech. Perhaps it did n't fix your attention. I said that when Judge Douglas was speaking at places where I spoke on the succeeding day, he used very harsh language about this charge. Two or three times afterward I said I had confidence in Judge Trumbull's veracity and intelligence; and my own opinion was, from what I knew of the character of Judge Trumbull, that he would vindicate his position, and prove whatever he had stated to be true. This I repeated two or three times; and then I dropped it, without saying anything more on the subject for weeks—perhaps a month. I passed it by without noticing it at all till I found at Jacksonville that Judge Douglas, in the plenitude of his power, is not willing to answer Trumbull and let me alone; but he comes out there and uses this language: "He should not hereafter occupy his time in refuting such charges made by Trumbull, but that Lincoln having indorsed the character of Trumbull for veracity, he should hold him [Lincoln] responsible for the slanders." What was Lincoln to do! Did he not do right, when he had the fit opportunity of meeting Judge Douglas here, to tell him he was ready for the responsibility! I ask a candid audience whether in doing thus Judge Douglas was not the assailant rather than I! Here I meet him face to face, and say I am ready to take the responsibility so far as it rests on me.

Having done so, I ask the attention of this audience to the question-whether I have succeeded in sustaining the charge, and whether Judge Douglas has at all succeeded in rebutting it. You all heard me call upon him to say which of these pieces of evidence was a forgery. Does he say that what I present here as a copy of the original Toombs bill is a forgery! Does he say that what I present as a copy of the bill reported by himself is a forgery! Or what is presented as a transcript from the "Globe," of the quotations from Bigler's speech, is a forgery! Does he say the quotations from his own speech are forgeries! Does he say this transcript from Trumbull's speech is a forgery! ["He did n't deny one of them."] I would then like to know how it comes about that when each piece of a story is true, the whole story turns out false! I take it these people have some sense; they see plainly that Judge Douglas is playing cuttle-fish, a small species of fish that has no mode of defending itself when pursued except by throwing out a black fluid, which makes the water so dark the enemy cannot see it, and thus it escapes. Is not the judge playing the cuttlefish?

Now I would ask very special attention to the consideration of Judge Douglas's speech at Jacksonville; and when you shall read his speech of to-day, I ask you to watch closely and see which of these pieces of testimony, every one of which he says is a forgery, he has shown to be such. Not one of them has he shown to be a forgery. Then I ask the original question, if each of the pieces of testimony is true, how is it possible that the whole is a falsehood?

In regard to Trumbull's charge that he [Douglas] inserted a provision into the bill to prevent the constitution being submitted to the people, what was his answer? He comes here and reads from the "Congressional Globe" to show that on his motion that provision was struck out of the bill. Why, Trumbull has not said it was not stricken out, but Trumbull says he [Douglas] put it in, and it is no answer to the charge to say he afterward took it out. Both are perhaps true. It was in regard to that thing precisely that I told him he had dropped the cub. Trumbull shows you by his introducing the bill that it was his cub. It is no answer to that assertion to call Trumbull a liar merely because he did not specially say that Douglas struck it out. Suppose that were the case, does it answer Trumbull? I assert that you [pointing to an individual] are here to-day, and you undertake to prove me a liar by showing that you were in Mattoon yesterday. I say that you took your hat off your head, and you prove me a liar by putting it on your head. That is the whole force of Douglas's argument.

Now, I want to come back to my original question. Trumbull says that Judge Douglas had a bill with a provision in it for submitting a constitution to be made to a vote of the people of Kansas. Does Judge Douglas deny that fact? Does he deny that the provision which Trumbull reads was put in that bill? Then Trumbull says he struck it out. Does he dare to deny that? He does not, and I have the right to repeat the question—why Judge Douglas took it out? Bigler has said there was a combination of certain senators, among whom he did not include Judge Douglas, by which it was agreed that the Kansas bill should have a clause in it not to have the constitution formed under it submitted to a vote of the people. He did not say that Douglas was among them, but we prove by another source that about the same time Douglas comes into the Senate with that provision stricken out of the bill. Although Bigler cannot say they were all working in concert, yet it looks very much as if the thing was agreed upon and done with a mutual understanding after the conference; and while we do not know that it was absolutely so, yet it looks so probable that we have a right to call upon the man who knows the true reason why it was done, to tell what the true reason was. When he will not tell what the true reason was, he stands in the attitude of an accused thief who has stolen goods in his possession, and when called to account refuses to tell where he got them. Not only is this the evidence, but when he comes in with the bill having the provision stricken out, he tells us in a speech, not then, but since, that these alterations and modifications in the bill had been made by him, in consultation with Toombs, the originator of the bill. He tells us the same to-day. He says there were certain modifications made in the bill in committee that he did not vote for. I ask you to remember while certain amendments were made which he disapproved of, but which a majority of the committee voted in, he has himself told us that in this particular the alterations and modifications were made by him upon consultation with Toombs. We have his own word that these alterations were made by him and not by the committee.

Now, I ask what is the reason Judge Douglas is so chary about coming to the exact question? What is the reason he will not tell you anything about how it was made, by whom it was made, or that he remembers it being made at all? Why does he stand playing upon the meaning of words, and quibbling around the edges of the evidence? If he can explain all this, but leaves it unexplained, I have a right to infer that Judge Douglas understood it was the purpose of his party, in engineering that bill through, to make a constitution, and have Kansas come into the Union with that constitution, without its being submitted to a vote of the people. If he will explain his action on this question, by giving a better reason for the facts that happened than he has done, it will be satisfactory. But until he does that — until he gives a better or more plausible reason than he has offered against the evidence in the case — I suggest to him it will not avail him at all that he swells himself up, takes on dignity, and calls people liars. Why, sir, there is not a word in Trumbull's speech that depends on Trumbull's veracity at all. He has only arrayed the evidence and told you what follows as a matter of reasoning. There is not a statement in the whole speech that depends on Trumbull's word. If you have ever studied geometry, you remember that by a course of reasoning Euclid proves that all the angles in a triangle are equal to two right angles. Euclid has shown you how to work it out. Now, if you undertake to disprove that proposition, and to show that it is erroneous, would you prove it to be false by calling Euclid a liar? They tell me that my time is out, and therefore I close.

September 25, 1858.— ORDER FOR FURNITURE.

My old friend Henry Chew, the bearer of this, is in a strait for some furniture to commence housekeeping. If any person will furnish him twenty-five dollars' worth, and he does not pay for it by the 1st of January next, I will.

September 25, 1858.   A. LINCOLN.

URBANA, February 16, 1859.

HON. A. LINCOLN, SPRINGFIELD, ILLINOIS.

My dear Friend: I herewith inclose your order which you gave your friend Henry Chew. You will please send me a draft for the same and oblige yours,

S. LITTLE.

[October 1, 1858?]—Fragment. Notes for Speeches.

But there is a larger issue than the mere question of whether the spread of negro slavery shall or shall not be prohibited by Congress. That larger issue is stated by the Richmond "Enquirer," a Buchanan paper in the South, in the language I now read. It is also stated by the New York "Day-book," a Buchanan paper in the North, in this language.—And in relation to indigent white children, the same Northern paper says.—In support of the Nebraska bill, on its first discussion in the Senate, Senator Pettit of Indiana declared the equality of men, as asserted in our Declaration of Independence, to be a "self-evident lie." In his numerous speeches now being made in Illinois, Senator Douglas regularly argues against the doctrine of the equality of men; and while he does not draw the conclusion that the superiors ought to enslave the inferiors, he evidently wishes his hearers to draw that conclusion. He shirks the responsibility of pulling the house down, but he digs under it that it may fall of its own weight. Now, it is impossible to not see that these newspapers and senators are laboring at a common object, and in so doing are truly representing the controlling sentiment of their party.

It is equally impossible to not see that that common object is to subvert, in the public mind, and in practical administration, our old and only standard of free government, that "all men are created equal," and to substitute for it some different standard. What that substitute is to be is not difficult to perceive. It is to deny the equality of men, and to assert the natural, moral, and religious right of one class to enslave another.

[October 1, 1858?]—Fragment. Notes for Speeches.

Suppose it is true that the negro is inferior to the white in the gifts of nature; is it not the exact reverse of justice that the white should for that reason take from the negro any part of the little which he has had given him? "Give to him that is needy" is the Christian rule of charity; but "Take from him that is needy" is the rule of slavery.

Pro-slavery Theology.

The sum of pro-slavery theology seems to be this: "Slavery is not universally right, nor yet universally wrong; it is better for some people to be slaves; and, in such cases, it is the will of God that they be such."

Certainly there is no contending against the will of God; but still there is some difficulty in ascertaining and applying it to particular cases. For instance, we will suppose the Rev. Dr. Ross has a slave named Sambo, and the question is, "Is it the will of God that Sambo shall remain a slave, or be set free?" The Almighty gives no audible answer to the question, and his revelation, the Bible, gives none—or at most none but such as admits of a squabble as to its meaning; no one thinks of asking Sambo's opinion on it. So at last it comes to this, that Dr. Ross is to decide the question; and while he considers it, he sits in the shade, with gloves on his hands, and subsists on the bread that Sambo is earning in the burning sun. If he decides that God wills Sambo to continue a slave, he thereby retains his own comfortable position; but if he decides that God wills Sambo to be free, he thereby has to walk out of the shade, throw off his gloves, and delve for his own bread. Will Dr. Ross be actuated by the perfect impartiality which has ever been considered most favorable to correct decisions?

[October 1, 1858?]—FRAGMENT. NOTES FOR SPEECHES.

At Freeport I propounded four distinct interrogations to Judge Douglas, all which he assumed to answer. I say he assumed to answer them; for he did not very distinctly answer any of them.

To the first, which is in these words, " If the people of Kansas shall, by means entirely unobjectionable in all other respects, adopt a State constitution, and ask admission into the Union under it, before they have the requisite number of inhabitants according to the English bill,—some ninety-three thousand,—will you vote to admit them?" the judge did not answer " Yes" or "No," "I would" or "I would not," nor did he answer in any other such distinct way. But he did so answer that I infer he would vote for the admission of Kansas in the supposed case stated in the interrogatory—that, other objections out of the way, he would vote to admit Kansas before she had the requisite population according to the English bill. I mention this now to elicit an assurance that I correctly understood the judge on this point.

To my second interrogatory, which is in these words, "Can the people of a United States Territory, in any lawful way, against the wish of any citizen of the United States, exclude slavery from their limits, prior to the formation of a State constitution?" the judge answers that they can, and he proceeds to show how they can exclude it. The how, as he gives it, is by withholding friendly legislation and adopting unfriendly legislation. As he thinks, the people still can, by doing nothing to help slavery and by a little unfriendly leaning against it, exclude it from their limits. This is his position. This position and the Dred Scott decision are absolutely inconsistent. The judge furiously indorses the Dred Scott decision; and that decision holds that the United States Constitution guarantees to the citizens of the United States the right to hold slaves in the Territories, and that neither Congress nor a territorial legislature can destroy or abridge that right. In the teeth of this, where can the judge find room for his unfriendly legislation against their right? The members of a territorial legislature are sworn to support the Constitution of the United States. How dare they legislate unfriendlily to a right guaranteed by that Constitution? And if they should, how quickly would the courts hold their work to be unconstitutional and void! But doubtless the judge's chief reliance to sustain his proposition that the people can exclude slavery, is based upon non-action—upon withholding friendly legislation. But can members of a territorial legislature, having sworn to support the United States Constitution, conscientiously withhold necessary legislative protection to a right guaranteed by that Constitution?

Again, will not the courts, without territorial legislation, find a remedy for the evasion of a right guaranteed by the United States Constitution? It is a maxim of the courts that "there is no right without a remedy." But, as a matter of fact, non-action, both legislative and judicial, will not exclude slavery from any place. It is of record that Dred Scott and his family were held in actual slavery in Kansas without any friendly legislation or judicial assistance. It is well known that other negroes were held in actual slavery at the military post in Kansas under precisely the same circumstances. This was not only done without any friendly legislation, but in direct disregard of the congressional prohibition,—the Missouri Compromise,—then supposed to be valid, thus showing that it requires positive law to be both made and executed to keep actual slavery out of any Territory where any owner chooses to take it. Slavery having actually gone into a Territory to some extent, without local legislation in its favor, and against congressional prohibition, how much more will it go there now that by a judicial decision that congressional prohibition is swept away, and the constitutional guaranty of property declared to apply to slavery in the Territories.

But this is not all. Slavery was originally planted on this continent without the aid of friendly legislation. History proves this. After it was actually in existence to a sufficient extent to become, in some sort, a public interest, it began to receive legislative attention, but not before. How futile, then, is the proposition that the people of a Territory can exclude slavery by simply not legislating in its favor. Learned disputants use what they call the *argumentum ad hominem*—a course of argument which does not intrinsically reach the issue, but merely turns the adversary against himself. There are at least two arguments of this sort which may easily be turned against Judge Douglas's proposition that the people of a Territory can lawfully exclude slavery from their limits prior to forming a State constitution: In his report of the 12th of March, 1856, on page 28, Judge Douglas says: "The sovereignty of a Territory remains in abeyance, suspended in the United States, in trust for the people, until they shall be admitted into the Union as a State." If so,—if they have no active living sovereignty,—how can they readily enact the judge's unfriendly legislation to slavery?

But in 1856, on the floor of the Senate, Judge Trumbull asked Judge Douglas the direct question, "Can the people of a Territory exclude slavery prior to forming a State constitution?"—and Judge Douglas answered, "That is a question for the Supreme Court." I think he made the same answer to the same question more than once. But now, when the Supreme Court has decided that the people of a Territory cannot so exclude slavery, Judge Douglas shifts his ground, saying the people can exclude it, and thus virtually saying it is not a question for the Supreme Court.

I am aware Judge Douglas avoids admitting in direct terms that the Supreme Court have decided against the power of the people of a Territory to exclude slavery. He also avoids saying directly that they have not so decided; but he labors to leave the impression that he thinks they have not so decided. For instance, in his Springfield speech of July 17, 1858, Judge Douglas, speaking of me, says: "He infers that it [the court] would decide that the territorial legislatures could not prohibit slavery. I will not stop to inquire whether the courts will carry the decision that far or not." The court has already carried the decision exactly that far, and I must say I think Judge Douglas very well knows it has. After stating that Congress cannot prohibit slavery in the Territories, the court adds: "And if Congress itself cannot do this, if it be beyond the powers conferred on the Federal Government, it will be admitted, we presume, that it could not authorize a territorial government to exercise them, it could confer no power on any local government, established by its authority, to violate the provisions of the Constitution."

Can any mortal man misunderstand this language? Does not Judge Douglas equivocate when he pretends not to know that the Supreme Court has decided that the people of a Territory cannot exclude slavery prior to forming a State constitution?

My third interrogatory to the judge is in these words: "If the Supreme Court of the United States shall decide that States cannot exclude slavery from their limits, are you in favor of acquiescing in, adopting, and following such decision as a rule of political action?" To this question the judge gives no answer whatever. He disposes of it by an attempt to ridicule the idea that the Supreme Court will ever make such a decision. When Judge Douglas is drawn up to a distinct point, there is significance in all he says, and in all he omits to say. In this case he will not, on the one hand, face the people and declare he will support such decision when made, nor on the other will he trammel himself by saying he will not support it.

Now I propose to show, in the teeth of Judge Douglas's ridicule, that such a decision does logically and necessarily follow the Dred Scott decision. In that case the court holds that Congress can legislate for the Territories in some respects, and in others it cannot; that it cannot prohibit slavery in the Territories, because to do so would infringe the "right of property" guaranteed to the citizen by the fifth amendment to the Constitution, which provides that "no person shall be deprived of life, liberty, or property without due process of law." Unquestionably there is such a guaranty in the Constitution, whether or not the court rightfully apply it in this case. I propose to show, beyond the power of quibble, that that guaranty applies with all the force, if not more, to States that it does to Territories. The answers to two questions fix the whole thing: to whom is this guaranty given? and against whom does it protect those to whom it is given? The guaranty makes no distinction between persons in the States and those in the Territories; it is given to persons in the States certainly as much as, if not more than, to those in the Territories. "No person," under the shadow of the Constitution, "shall be deprived of life, liberty, or property without due process of law."

Against whom does this guaranty protect the rights of property? Not against Congress alone, but against the world—against State constitutions and laws, as well as against acts of Congress. The United States Constitution is the supreme law of the land; this guaranty of property is expressly given in that Constitution, in that supreme law; and no State constitution or law can override it. It is not a case where power over the subject is reserved to the States, because it is not expressly given to the General Government; it is a case where the guaranty is expressly given to the individual citizen, in and by the organic law of the General Government; and the duty of maintaining that guaranty is imposed upon that General Government, overriding all obstacles.

The following is the article of the Constitution containing the guaranty of property upon which the Dred Scott decision is based:

ARTICLE V. No person shall be held to answer for a capital or otherwise infamous crime, unless on a presentment or indictment by a grand jury, except in cases arising in the land or naval forces, or in the militia when in actual service, in time of war or public danger; nor shall any person be subject for the same offense to be twice put in jeopardy of life or limb; nor shall be compelled, in any criminal case, to be a witness against himself, nor be deprived of life, liberty, or property without due process of law; nor shall private property be taken for public use without just compensation.

Suppose, now, a provision in a State constitution should negative all the above propositions, declaring directly or substantially that "any person may be deprived of life, liberty, or property without due process of law," a direct contradiction—collision—would be pronounced between the United States Constitution and such State constitution. And can there be any doubt but that which is declared to be the supreme law would prevail over the other to the extent of the collision? Such State constitution would be unconstitutional.

There is no escape from this conclusion but in one way, and that is to deny that the Supreme Court, in the Dred Scott case, properly applies this constitutional guaranty of property. The Constitution itself impliedly admits that a person may be deprived of property by "due process of law," and the Republicans hold that if there be a law of Congress or territorial legislature telling the slaveholder in advance that he shall not bring his slave into the Territory upon pain of forfeiture, and he still will bring him, he will be deprived of his property in such slave by "due process of law." And the same would be true in the case of taking a slave into a State against a State constitution or law prohibiting slavery.

[October 1, 1858?]—FRAGMENT. NOTES FOR SPEECHES.

. . . When Douglas ascribes such to me, he does so, not by argument, but by mere burlesques on the art and name of argument—by such fantastic arrangements of words as prove "horse-chestnuts to be chestnut horses." In the main I shall trust an intelligent community to learn my objects and aims from what I say and do myself, rather than from what Judge Douglas may say of me. But I must not leave the judge just yet. When he has burlesqued me into a position

which I never thought of assuming myself, he will, in the most
benevolent and patronizing manner imaginable, compliment me by
saying "he has no doubt I am perfectly conscientious in it." I
thank him for that word "conscientious." It turns my attention
to the wonderful evidences of conscience he manifests. When he
assumes to be the first discoverer and sole advocate of the right
of a people to govern themselves, he is conscientious. When he
affects to understand that a man, putting a hundred slaves through
under the lash, is simply governing himself, he is more conscientious. When he affects not to know that the Dred Scott decision
forbids a territorial legislature to exclude slavery, he is most conscientious. When, as in his last Springfield speech, he declares that
I say, unless I shall play my batteries successfully, so as to abolish
slavery in every one of the States, the Union shall be dissolved, he
is absolutely bursting with conscience. It is nothing that I have
never said any such thing. With some men it might make a difference; but consciences differ in different individuals. Judge Douglas
has a greater conscience than most men. It corresponds with his
other points of greatness. Judge Douglas amuses himself by saying
I wish to go into the Senate on my qualifications as a prophet. He
says he has known some other prophets, and does not think very well
of them. Well, others of us have also known some prophets. We
know one who nearly five years ago prophesied that the 'Nebraska
bill' would put an end to slavery agitation in next to no time —
one who has renewed that prophecy at least as often as quarter-
yearly ever since; and still the prophecy has not been fulfilled. That
one might very well go out of the Senate on his qualifications as a
false prophet.

Allow me now, in my own way, to state with what aims and objects
I did enter upon this campaign. I claim no extraordinary exemption
from personal ambition. That I like preferment as well as the average of men may be admitted. But I protest I have not entered
upon this hard contest solely, or even chiefly, for a merely personal
object. I clearly see, as I think, a powerful plot to make slavery
universal and perpetual in this nation. The effort to carry that
plot through will be persistent and long continued, extending far
beyond the senatorial term for which Judge Douglas and I are just
now struggling. I enter upon the contest to contribute my humble
and temporary mite in opposition to that effort.

At the Republican State convention at Springfield I made a speech.
That speech has been considered the opening of the canvass on my
part. In it I arranged a string of incontestable facts which, I think,
prove the existence of a conspiracy to nationalize slavery. The
evidence was circumstantial only; but nevertheless it seemed inconsistent with every hypothesis, save that of the existence of such conspiracy. I believe the facts can be explained to-day on no other
hypothesis. Judge Douglas can so explain them if any one can.
From warp to woof his handiwork is everywhere woven in.

At New York he finds this speech of mine, and devises his plan of
assault upon it. At Chicago he develops that plan. Passing over,
unnoticed, the obvious purport of the whole speech, he cooks up two

or three issues upon points not discussed by me at all, and then authoritatively announces that these are to be the issues of the campaign. Next evening I answer, assuring him that he misunderstands me—that he takes issues which I have not tendered. In good faith I try to set him right. If he really has misunderstood my meaning, I give him language that can no longer be misunderstood. He will have none of it. At Bloomington, six days later, he speaks again, and perverts me even worse than before. He seems to have grown confident and jubilant, in the belief that he has entirely diverted me from my purpose of fixing a conspiracy upon him and his co-workers. Next day he speaks again at Springfield, pursuing the same course, with increased confidence and recklessness of assertion. At night of that day I speak again. I tell him that as he has carefully read my speech making the charge of conspiracy, and has twice spoken of the speech without noticing the charge, upon his own tacit admission I renew the charge against him. I call him, and take a default upon him. At Clinton, ten days after, he comes in with a plea. The substance of that plea is that he never passed a word with Chief Justice Taney as to what his decision was to be in the Dred Scott case; that I ought to know that he who affirms what he does not know to be true falsifies as much as he who affirms what he does know to be false; and that he would pronounce the whole charge of conspiracy a falsehood, were it not for his own self-respect! .

Now I demur to this plea. Waiving objection that it was not filed till after default, I demur to it on the merits. I say it does not meet the case. What if he did not pass a word with Chief Justice Taney? Could he not have as distinct an understanding, and play his part just as well, without directly passing a word with Taney, as with it? But suppose we construe this part of the plea more broadly than he puts it himself—suppose we construe it, as in an answer in chancery, to be a denial of all knowledge, information, or belief of such conspiracy. Still I have the right to prove the conspiracy, even against his answer; and there is much more than the evidence of two witnesses to prove it by. Grant that he has no knowledge, information, or belief of such conspiracy, and what of it? That does not disturb the facts in evidence. It only makes him the dupe, instead of a principal, of conspirators.

What if a man may not affirm a proposition without knowing it to be true? I have not affirmed that a conspiracy does exist. I have only stated the evidence, and affirmed my belief in its existence. If Judge Douglas shall assert that I do not believe what I say, then he affirms what he cannot know to be true, and falls within the condemnation of his own rule.

Would it not be much better for him to meet the evidence, and show, if he can, that I have no good reason to believe the charge? Would not this be far more satisfactory than merely vociferating an intimation that he may be provoked to call somebody a liar?

So far as I know, he denies no fact which I have alleged. Without now repeating all those facts, I recall attention to only a few of them. A provision of the Nebraska bill, penned by Judge Douglas, is in these words:

It being the true intent and meaning of this act not to legislate slavery into any Territory or State, nor exclude it therefrom, but to leave the people thereof perfectly free to form and regulate their domestic institutions in their own way, subject only to the Constitution of the United States.

In support of this the argument, evidently prepared in advance, went forth: "Why not let the people of a Territory have or exclude slavery, just as they choose? Have they any less sense or less patriotism when they settle in the Territories than when they lived in the States?"

Now the question occurs: Did Judge Douglas, even then, intend that the people of a Territory should have the power to exclude slavery? If he did, why did he vote against an amendment expressly declaring they might exclude it? With men who then knew and intended that a Supreme Court decision should soon follow, declaring that the people of a Territory could not exclude slavery, voting down such an amendment was perfectly rational. But with men not expecting or desiring such a decision, and really wishing the people to have such power, voting down such an amendment, to my mind, is wholly inexplicable.

That such an amendment was voted down by the friends of the bill, including Judge Douglas, is a recorded fact of the case. There was some real reason for so voting it down. What that reason was, Judge Douglas can tell. I believe that reason was to keep the way clear for a court decision, then expected to come, and which has since come, in the case of Dred Scott. If there was any other reason for voting down that amendment, Judge Douglas knows of it and can tell it? Again, in the before-quoted part of the Nebraska bill, what means the provision that the people of the "State" shall be left perfectly free, subject only to the Constitution? Congress was not therein legislating for, or about, States or the people of States. In that bill the provision about the people of "States" is the odd half of something, the other half of which was not yet quite ready for exhibition. What is that other half to be? Another Supreme Court decision, declaring that the people of a State cannot exclude slavery, is exactly fitted to be that other half. As the power of the people of the Territories and of the States is cozily set down in the Nebraska bill as being the same: so the constitutional limitations on that power will then be judicially held to be precisely the same in both Territories and States—that is, that the Constitution permits neither a Territory nor a State to exclude slavery.

With persons looking forward to such additional decision, the inserting a provision about States in the Nebraska bill was perfectly rational; but to persons not looking for such decision it was a puzzle. There was a real reason for inserting such provision. Judge Douglas inserted it, and therefore knows, and can tell, what that real reason was.

Judge Douglas's present course by no means lessens my belief in the existence of a purpose to make slavery alike lawful in all the States. This can be done by a Supreme Court decision holding that the United States Constitution forbids a State to exclude slavery; and probably it can be done in no other way. The idea of forcing slavery into a free State, or out of a slave State, at the point of the bayonet, is alike nonsensical. Slavery can only become extinct by being restricted to its present limits, and dwindling out. It can only become national by a Supreme Court decision. To such a decision, when it comes, Judge Douglas is fully committed. Such a decision acquiesced in by the people effects the whole object. Bearing this in mind, look at what Judge Douglas is doing every day. For the first sixty-five years under the United States Constitution, the practice of government had been to exclude slavery from the new free Territories. About the end of that period Congress, by the Nebraska bill, resolved to abandon this practice; and this was rapidly succeeded by a Supreme Court decision holding the practice to have always been unconstitutional. Some of us refuse to obey this decision as a political rule. Forthwith Judge Douglas espouses the decision, and denounces all opposition to it in no measured terms. He adheres to it with extraordinary tenacity; and under rather extraordinary circumstances. He espouses it not on any opinion of his that it is right within itself. On this he forbears to commit himself. He espouses it exclusively on the ground of its binding authority on all citizens—a ground which commits him as fully to the next decision as to this. I point out to him that Mr. Jefferson and General Jackson were both against him on the binding political authority of Supreme Court decisions. No response. I might as well preach Christianity to a grizzly bear as to preach Jefferson and Jackson to him.

I tell him I have often heard him denounce the Supreme Court decision in favor of a national bank. He denies the accuracy of my recollection—which seems strange to me, but I let it pass.

I remind him that he, even now, indorses the Cincinnati platform, which declares that Congress has no constitutional power to charter a bank; and that in the teeth of a Supreme Court decision that Congress has such power. This he cannot deny; and so he remembers to forget it.

I remind him of a piece of Illinois history about Supreme Court decisions—of a time when the Supreme Court of Illinois, consisting of four judges, because of one decision made, and one expected to be made, were overwhelmed by the adding of five new judges to their number; that he, Judge Douglas, took a leading part in that onslaught, ending in his sitting down on the bench as one of the five added judges. I suggest to him that as to his questions how far judges have to be catechized in advance, when appointed under such circumstances, and how far a court, so constituted, is prostituted beneath the contempt of all men, no man is better posted to answer than he, having once been entirely through the mill himself.

Still no response, except "Hurrah for the Dred Scott decision!" These things warrant me in saying that Judge Douglas adheres to the Dred Scott decision under rather extraordinary circumstances—circumstances suggesting the question, "Why does he adhere to it so pertinaciously? Why does he thus belie his whole past life? Why, with a long record more marked for hostility to judicial decisions than almost any living man, does he cling to this with a devotion that nothing can baffle!" In this age, and this country, public sentiment is everything. With it, nothing can fail; against it, nothing can succeed. Whoever molds public sentiment goes deeper than he who enacts statutes or pronounces judicial decisions. He makes possible the enforcement of them, else impossible.

Judge Douglas is a man of large influence. His bare opinion goes far to fix the opinions of others. Besides this, thousands hang their hopes upon forcing their opinions to agree with his. It is a party necessity with them to say they agree with him, and there is danger they will repeat the saying till they really come to believe it. Others dread, and shrink from, his denunciations, his sarcasms, and his ingenious misrepresentations. The susceptible young hear lessons from him, such as their fathers never heard when they were young.

If, by all these means, he shall succeed in molding public sentiment to a perfect accordance with his own; in bringing all men to indorse all court decisions, without caring to know whether they are right or wrong; in bringing all tongues to as perfect a silence as his own, as to there being any wrong in slavery; in bringing all to declare, with him, that they care not whether slavery be voted down or voted up; that if any people want slaves they have a right to have them; that negroes are not men; have no part in the Declaration of Independence; that there is no moral question about slavery; that liberty and slavery are perfectly consistent — indeed, necessary accompaniments; that for a strong man to declare himself the superior of a weak one, and thereupon enslave the weak one, is the very essence of liberty, the most sacred right of self-government; when, I say, public sentiment shall be brought to all this, in the name of Heaven what barrier will be left against slavery being made lawful everywhere! Can you find one word of his opposed to it! Can you not find many strongly favoring it! If for his life, for his eternal salvation, he was solely striving for that end, could he find any means so well adapted to reach the end!

If our presidential election, by a mere plurality, and of doubtful significance, brought one Supreme Court decision that no power can exclude slavery from a Territory, how much more shall a public sentiment, in exact accordance with the sentiments of Judge Douglas, bring another that no power can exclude it from a State!

And then, the negro being doomed, and damned, and forgotten, to everlasting bondage, is the white man quite certain that the tyrant demon will not turn upon him too!

[October 1, 1858?] — FRAGMENT. NOTES FOR SPEECHES.

From time to time, ever since the Chicago "Times" and "Illinois State Register" declared their opposition to the Lecompton constitution, and it began to be understood that Judge Douglas was also opposed to it, I have been accosted by friends of his with the question, "What do you think now!" Since the delivery of his speech in the Senate, the question has been varied a little. "Have you read Douglas's speech!" "Yes." "Well, what do you think of it!" In every instance the question is accompanied with an anxious inquiring stare, which asks, quite as plainly as words could, "Can't you go for Douglas now?" Like boys who have set a bird-trap, they are watching to see if the birds are picking at the bait and likely to go under.

I think, then, Judge Douglas knows that the Republicans wish Kansas to be a free State. He knows that they know, if the question be fairly submitted to a vote of the people of Kansas, it will be a free State; and he would not object at all if, by drawing their attention to this particular fact, and himself becoming vociferous for such fair vote, they should be induced to drop their own organization, fall into rank behind him, and form a great free-State Democratic party.

But before Republicans do this, I think they ought to require a few questions to be answered on the other side. If they so fall in with Judge Douglas, and Kansas shall be secured as a free State, there then remaining no cause of difference between him and the regular Democracy, will not the Republicans stand ready, haltered and harnessed, to be handed over by him to the regular Democracy, to filibuster indefinitely for additional slave territory,—to carry slavery into all the States, as well as Territories, under the Dred Scott decision, construed and enlarged from time to time, according to the demands of the regular slave Democracy,—and to assist in reviving the African slave-trade in order that all may buy negroes where they can be bought cheapest, as a clear incident of that "sacred right of property," now held in some quarters to be above all constitutions?

By so falling in, will we not be committed to or at least compromitted with, the Nebraska policy? If so, we should remember that Kansas is saved, not by that policy or its authors, but in spite of both —by an effort that cannot be kept up in future cases.

Did Judge Douglas help any to get a free-State majority into Kansas? Not a bit of it—the exact contrary. Does he now express any wish that Kansas, or any other place, shall be free? Nothing like it. He tells us, in this very speech, expected to be so palatable to Republicans, that he cares not whether slavery is voted down or voted up. His whole effort is devoted to clearing the ring, and giving slavery and freedom a fair fight. With one who considers slavery just as good as freedom, this is perfectly natural and consistent. But have Republicans any sympathy with such a view? They think slavery is wrong; and that, like every other wrong which some men will commit if left alone, it ought to be prohibited by law. They consider it not only morally wrong, but a "deadly poison" in a government like ours, professedly based on the equality of men. Upon this radical difference of opinion with Judge Douglas, the Republican party was organized. There is all the difference between him and them now that there ever was. He will not say that he has changed; have you?

Again, we ought to be informed as to Judge Douglas's present opinion as to the inclination of Republicans to marry with negroes. By his Springfield speech we know what it was last June; and by his resolution dropped at Jacksonville in September we know what it was then. Perhaps we have something even later in a Chicago speech, in which the danger of being "stunk out of church" was descanted upon. But what is his opinion on the point now? There is, or will be, a sure sign to judge by. If this charge shall be silently dropped by the judge and his friends, if no more resolutions on the subject shall be passed in Douglas Democratic meetings and conventions, it will be safe to swear that he is courting. Our "witching smile" has "caught his youthful fancy"; and henceforth Cuffy and he are rival beaux for our gushing affections.

We also ought to insist on knowing what the judge now thinks on "Sectionalism." Last year he thought it was a "clincher" against us on the question of Sectionalism, that we could get no support in the slave States, and could not be allowed to speak, or even breathe, south of the Ohio River. In vain did we appeal to the justice of our principles. He would have it that the treatment we received was conclusive evidence that we deserved it. He and his friends would bring speakers from the slave States to their meetings and conventions in the free States, and parade about, arm in arm with them, breathing in every gesture and tone, "How we national apples do swim!" Let him cast about for this particular evidence of his own nationality now. Why, just now, he and Frémont would make the closest race imaginable in the Southern States.

In the present aspect of affairs what ought the Republicans to do? I think they ought not to oppose any measure merely because Judge Douglas proposes it. Whether the Lecompton constitution should be accepted or rejected is a question upon which, in the minds of men not committed to any of its antecedents, and controlled only by the Federal Constitution, by republican principles, and by a sound morality, it seems to me there could not be two opinions. It should be throttled and killed as hastily and as heartily as a rabid dog. What those should do who are committed to all its antecedents is their business, not ours. If, therefore, Judge Douglas's bill secures a fair vote to the people of Kansas, without contrivance to commit any one farther, I think Republican members of Congress ought to support it. They can do so without any inconsistency. They believe Congress ought to prohibit slavery wherever it can be done without violation of the Constitution or of good faith. And having seen the noses counted, and actually knowing that a majority of the people of Kansas are against slavery, passing an act to secure them a fair vote is little else than prohibiting slavery in Kansas by act of Congress.

Congress cannot dictate a constitution to a new State. All it can do at that point is to secure the people a fair chance to form one for themselves, and then to accept or reject it when they ask admission into the Union. As I understand, Republicans claim no more than this. But they do claim that Congress can and ought to keep slavery out of a Territory, up to the time of its people forming a State constitution; and they should now be careful to not stultify themselves to any extent on that point.

I am glad Judge Douglas has, at last, distinctly told us that he cares not whether slavery be voted down or voted up. Not so much that this is any news to me; nor yet that it may be slightly new to some of that class of his friends who delight to say that they "are as much opposed to slavery as anybody." I am glad because it affords such a true and excellent definition of the Nebraska policy itself. That policy, honestly administered, is exactly that. It seeks to bring the people of the nation to not care anything about slavery. This is Nebraskaism in its abstract purity—in its very best dress.

Now, I take it, nearly everybody does care something about slavery—is either for it or against it; and that the statesmanship of a measure which conforms to the sentiments of nobody might well be doubted in advance.

But Nebraskaism did not originate as a piece of statesmanship. General Cass, in 1848, invented it, as a political manœuver, to secure himself the Democratic nomination for the presidency. It served its purpose then, and sunk out of sight. Six years later Judge Douglas fished it up, and glozed it over with what he called, and still persists in calling, " sacred rights of self-government."

Well, I, too, believe in self-government as I understand it; but I do not understand that the privilege one man takes of making a slave of another, or holding him as such, is any part of " self-government." To call it so is, to my mind, simply absurd and ridiculous. I am for the people of the whole nation doing just as they please in all matters which concern the whole nation; for those of each part doing just as they choose in all matters which concern no other part; and for each individual doing just as he chooses in all matters which concern nobody else. This is the principle. Of course I am content with any exception which the Constitution, or the actually existing state of things, makes a necessity. But neither the principle nor the exception will admit the indefinite spread and perpetuity of human slavery.

I think the true magnitude of the slavery element in this nation is scarcely appreciated by any one. Four years ago the Nebraska policy was adopted, professedly, to drive the agitation of the subject into the Territories, and out of every other place, and especially out of Congress.

When Mr. Buchanan accepted the presidential nomination, he felicitated himself with the belief that the whole thing would be quieted and forgotten in about six weeks. In his inaugural, and in his Silliman letter, at their respective dates, he was just not quite in reach of the same happy consummation. And now, in his first annual message, he urges the acceptance of the Lecompton constitution (not quite satisfactory to him) on the sole ground of getting this little unimportant matter out of the way.

Meanwhile, in those four years, there has really been more angry agitation of this subject, both in and out of Congress, than ever before. And just now it is perplexing the mighty ones as no subject ever did before. Nor is it confined to politics alone. Presbyterian assemblies, Methodist conferences, Unitarian gatherings, and single churches to an indefinite extent, are wrangling, and cracking, and going to pieces on the same question. Why, Kansas is neither the whole nor a tithe of the real question.

A house divided against itself cannot stand.

I believe the government cannot endure permanently half slave and half free. I expressed this belief a year ago; and subsequent developments have but confirmed me. I do not expect the Union to be dissolved. I do not expect the house to fall; but I do expect it will cease to be divided. It will become all one thing or all the other. Either the opponents of slavery will arrest the further spread of it, and put it in course of ultimate extinction; or its advocates will push it forward till it shall become alike lawful in all the States, old as well as new. Do you doubt it? Study the Dred Scott decision, and then see how little even now remains to be done. That decision may be reduced to three points. The first is that a negro cannot be a citizen. That point is made in order to deprive the negro, in every possible event, of the benefit of that provision of the United States Constitution which declares that "the citizens of each State shall be entitled to all privileges and immunities of citizens in the several States."

The second point is that the United States Constitution protects slavery, as property, in all the United States territories, and that neither Congress, nor the people of the Territories, nor any other power, can prohibit it at any time prior to the formation of State constitutions.

This point is made in order that the Territories may safely be filled up with slaves, before the formation of State constitutions, thereby to embarrass the free-State sentiment, and enhance the chances of slave constitutions being adopted.

The third point decided is that the voluntary bringing of Dred Scott into Illinois by his master, and holding him here a long time as a slave, did not operate his emancipation — did not make him free.

This point is made, not to be pressed immediately; but if acquiesced in for a while, then to sustain the logical conclusion that what Dred Scott's master might lawfully do with Dred in the free State of Illinois, every other master may lawfully do with any other one or one hundred slaves in Illinois, or in any other free State. Auxiliary to all this, and working hand in hand with it, the Nebraska doctrine is to educate and mold public opinion to "not care whether slavery is voted up or voted down." At least Northern public opinion must cease to care anything about it. Southern public opinion may, without offense, continue to care as much as it pleases.

Welcome or unwelcome, agreeable or disagreeable, whether this shall be an entire slave nation is the issue before us. Every incident — every little shifting of scenes or of actors — only clears away the intervening trash, compacts and consolidates the opposing hosts, and brings them more and more distinctly face to face. The conflict will be a severe one; and it will be fought through by those who do care for the result, and not by those who do not care — by those who are for, and those who are against, a legalized national slavery. The combined charge of Nebraskaism and Dred-Scottism must be repulsed and rolled back. The deceitful cloak of "self-government," wherewith "the sum of all villanies" seeks to protect and adorn itself, must be torn from its hateful carcass. That burlesque upon judicial decisions, and slander and profanation upon the honored names and sacred history of republican America, must be overruled and expunged from the books of authority.

To give the victory to the right, not bloody bullets, but peaceful ballots only are necessary. Thanks to our good old Constitution, and organization under it, these alone are necessary. It only needs that every right thinking man shall go to the polls, and without fear or prejudice vote as he thinks.

October 7, 1858.—FIFTH JOINT DEBATE, AT GALESBURG, ILLINOIS.

Mr. Douglas's Opening Speech.

Ladies and Gentlemen: Four years ago I appeared before the people of Knox County for the purpose of defending my political action upon the compromise measures of 1850 and the passage of the Kansas-Nebraska bill. Those of you before me who were present then will remember that I vindicated myself for supporting those two measures by the fact that they rested upon the great fundamental principle that the people of each State and each Territory of this Union have the right, and ought to be permitted to exercise the right, of regulating their own domestic concerns in their own way, subject to no other limitation or restriction than that which the Constitution of the United States imposes upon them. I then called upon the people of Illinois to decide whether that principle of self-government was right or wrong. If it was and is right, then the compromise measures of 1850 were right, and, consequently, the Kansas and Nebraska bill, based upon the same principle, must necessarily have been right.

The Kansas and Nebraska bill declared, in so many words, that it was the true intent and meaning of the act not to legislate slavery into any State or Territory, nor to exclude it therefrom, but to leave the people thereof perfectly free to form and regulate their domestic institutions in their own way, subject only to the Constitution of the United States. For the last four years I have devoted all my energies, in private and public, to commend that principle to the American people. Whatever else may be said in condemnation or support of my political course, I apprehend that no honest man will doubt the fidelity with which under all circumstances I have stood by it.

During the last year a question arose in the Congress of the United States whether or not that principle would be violated by the admission of Kansas into the Union under the Lecompton constitution. In my opinion, the attempt to force Kansas in under that constitution was a gross violation of the principle enunciated in the compromise measures of 1850, and the Kansas and Nebraska bill of 1854, and therefore I led off in the fight against the Lecompton constitution, and conducted it until the effort to carry that constitution through Congress was abandoned. And I can appeal to all men, friends and foes, Democrats and Republicans, Northern men and Southern men, that during the whole of that fight I carried the banner of popular sovereignty aloft, and never allowed it to trail in the dust, or lowered my flag until victory perched upon our arms. When the Lecompton constitution was defeated, the question arose in the minds of those who had advocated it what they should next resort to in order to carry out their views. They devised a measure known as the English bill, and granted a general amnesty and political pardon to all men who had fought against the Lecompton constitution, provided they would support that bill. I for one did not choose to accept the pardon, or to avail myself of the amnesty granted on that condition. The fact that the supporters of Lecompton were willing to forgive all differences of opinion at that time, in the event those who opposed it favored the English bill, was an admission that they did not think that opposition to Lecompton impaired a man's standing in the Democratic party. Now the question arises: What was that English bill which certain men are now attempting to make a test of political orthodoxy in this country. It provided, in substance, that the Lecompton constitution should be sent back to the people of Kansas for their adoption or rejection, at an election which was held in August last, and in case they refused admission under it, that Kansas should be kept out of the Union until she had 93,420 inhabitants.

I was in favor of sending the constitution back in order to enable the people to say whether or not it was their act and deed, and embodied their will; but the other proposition, that if they refused to come into the Union under it, they should be kept out until they had double or treble the population they then had, I never would sanction by my vote. The reason why I could not sanction it is to be found in the fact that by the English bill, if the people of Kansas had only agreed to become a slaveholding State under the Lecompton constitution, they could have done so with 35,000 people, but if they insisted on being a free State, as they had a right to do, then they were to be punished by being kept out of the Union until they had nearly three times that population. I then said in my place in the Senate, as I now say to you, that whenever Kansas has population enough for a slave State she has population enough for a free State. I have never yet given a vote, and I never intend to record one, making an odious and unjust distinction between the different States of this Union. I hold it to be a fundamental principle in our republican form of government that all the States of this Union, old and new, free and slave, stand on an exact equality. Equality among the different States is a cardinal principle on which all our institutions rest. Wherever, therefore, you make a discrimination, saying to a slave State that it shall be admitted with 35,000 inhabitants, and to a free State that it shall not be admitted until it has 93,000 or 100,000 inhabitants, you are throwing the whole weight of the Federal Government into the scale in favor of one class of States against the other. Nor would I on the other hand any sooner sanction the doctrine that a free State could be admitted into the Union with 35,000 people, while a slave State was kept out until it had 93,000. I have always declared in the Senate my willingness, and I am willing now, to adopt the rule that no Territory shall ever become a State until it has the requisite population for a member of Congress, according to the then existing ratio. But while I have always been, and am now, willing to adopt that general rule, I was not willing and would not consent to make an exception of Kansas, as a punishment for her obstinacy in demanding the right to do as she pleased in the formation of her constitution. It is proper that I should remark here that my opposition to the Lecompton constitution did not rest upon the peculiar position taken by Kansas on the subject of slavery. I held then, and hold now, that if the people of Kansas want a slave State, it is their right to make one and be received into the Union under it; if, on the contrary, they want a free State, it is their right to have it, and no man should ever oppose their admission because they ask it under the one or the other. I hold to that great principle of self-government which asserts the right of every people to decide for themselves the nature and character of the domestic institutions and fundamental law under which they are to live.

The effort has been, and is now being, made in this State by certain postmasters and other federal office-holders, to make a test of faith on the support of the English bill. These men are now making speeches all over the State against me and in favor of Lincoln, either directly or indirectly, because I would not sanction a discrimination between slave and free States by voting for the English bill. But while that bill is made a test in Illinois for the purpose of breaking up the Democratic organization in this State, how is it in the other States? Go to Indiana, and there you find that English himself, the author of the English bill, who is a candidate for reëlection to Congress, has been forced by public opinion to abandon his own darling project, and to give a promise that he will vote for the admission of Kansas at once, whenever she forms a constitution in pursuance of law, and ratifies it by a majority vote of her people. Not only is this the case with English himself, but I am informed that every Democratic candidate for Congress in Indiana takes the same ground. Pass to Ohio, and there you find that Groesbeck, and Pendleton, and Cox, and all the other anti-Lecompton men who stood shoulder to shoulder with me against the Lecompton constitution, but voted for the English bill, now repudiate it and take the same ground that I do on that question. So it is with the Joneses and others of Pennsylvania, and so it is with every other Lecompton Democrat in the free States.

They now abandon even the English bill, and come back to the true platform which I proclaimed at the time in the Senate, and upon which the Democracy of Illinois now stand. And yet, notwithstanding the fact that every Lecompton and anti-Lecompton Democrat in the free States has abandoned the English bill, you are told that it is to be made a test upon me, while the power and patronage of the government are all exerted to elect men to Congress in the other States who occupy the same position with reference to it that I do. It seems that my political offense consists in the fact that I did not first vote for the English bill, and thus pledge myself to keep Kansas out of the Union until she has a population of 93,420, and then return home, violate that pledge, repudiate the bill, and take the opposite ground. If I had done this, perhaps the administration would now be advocating my reëlection, as it is that of the others who have pursued this course. I did not choose to give that pledge, for the reason that I did not intend to carry out that principle. I never will consent, for the sake of conciliating the frowns of power, to pledge myself to do that which I do not intend to perform. I now submit the question to you, as my constituency, whether I was not right — first, in resisting the adoption of the Lecompton constitution; and secondly, in resisting the English bill. I repeat that I opposed the Lecompton constitution because it was not the act and deed of the people of Kansas, and did not embody their will. I denied the right of any power on earth, under our system of government, to force a constitution on an unwilling people. There was a time when some men could pretend to believe that the Lecompton constitution embodied the will of the people of Kansas, but that time has passed. The question was referred to the people of Kansas under the English bill last August, and then, at a fair election, they rejected the Lecompton constitution by a vote of from eight to ten against it to one in its favor. Since it has been voted down by so overwhelming a majority, no man can pretend that it was the act and deed of that people. I submit the question to you, whether or not, if it had not been for me, that constitution would have been crammed down the throats of the people of Kansas against their consent. While at least ninety-nine out of every hundred people here present agree that I was right in defeating that project, yet my enemies use the fact that I did defeat it by doing right, to break me down and put another man in the United States Senate in my place. The very men who acknowledge that I was right in defeating Lecompton now form an alliance with federal office-holders, professed Lecompton men, to defeat me because I did right.

My political opponent, Mr. Lincoln, has no hope on earth, and has never dreamed that he had a chance of success, were it not for the aid that he is receiving from federal office-holders, who are using their influence and the patronage of the government against me in revenge for my having defeated the Lecompton constitution. What do you Republicans think of a political organization that will try to make an unholy and unnatural combination with its professed foes to beat a man merely because he has done right? You know such is the fact with regard to your own party. You know that the ax of decapitation is suspended over every man in office in Illinois, and the terror of proscription is threatened every Democrat by the present administration, unless he supports the Republican ticket in preference to my Democratic associates and myself. I could find an instance in the postmaster of the city of Galesburg, and in every other postmaster in this vicinity, all of whom have been stricken down simply because they discharged the duties of their offices honestly, and supported the regular Democratic ticket in this State in the right. The Republican party is availing itself of every unworthy means in the present contest to carry the election, because its leaders know that if they let this chance slip they will never have another, and their hopes of making this a Republican State will be blasted forever.

Now, let me ask you whether the country has any interest in sustaining this organization known as the Republican party. That party is unlike all other political organizations in this country. All other parties have been national in their character—have avowed their principles alike in the slave and free States, in Kentucky as well as Illinois, in Louisiana as well as in Massachusetts. Such was the case with the Old Whig party, and such was and is the case with the Democratic party. Whigs and Democrats could proclaim their principles boldly and fearlessly in the North and in the South, in the East and in the West, wherever the Constitution ruled and the American flag waved over American soil.

But now you have a sectional organization, a party which appeals to the Northern section of the Union against the Southern, a party which appeals to Northern passion, Northern pride, Northern ambition, and Northern prejudices, against Southern people, the Southern States, and Southern institutions. The leaders of that party hope that they will be able to unite the Northern States in one great sectional party, and inasmuch as the North is the stronger section, that they will thus be enabled to outvote, conquer, govern, and control the South. Hence you find that they now make speeches advocating principles and measures which cannot be defended in any slave-holding State of this Union. Is there a Republican residing in Galesburg who can travel into Kentucky, and carry his principles with him across the Ohio? What Republican from Massachusetts can visit the Old Dominion without leaving his principles behind him when he crosses Mason's and Dixon's line? Permit me to say to you in perfect good humor, but in all sincerity, that no political creed is sound which cannot be proclaimed fearlessly in every State of this Union where the Federal Constitution is the supreme law of the land. Not only is this Republican party unable to proclaim its principles alike in the North and in the South, in the free States and in the slave States, but it cannot even proclaim them in the same forms and give them the same strength and meaning in all parts of the same State. My friend Lincoln finds it extremely difficult to manage a debate in the central part of the State, where there is a mixture of men from the North and the South. In the extreme northern part of Illinois he can proclaim as bold and radical Abolitionism as ever Giddings, Lovejoy, or Garrison enunciated; but when he gets down a little further south he claims that he is an old-line Whig, a disciple of Henry Clay, and declares that he still adheres to the old-line Whig creed, and has nothing whatever to do with Abolitionism, or negro equality, or negro citizenship. I once before hinted this of Mr. Lincoln in a public speech, and at Charleston he defied me to show that there was any difference between his speeches in the north and in the south, and that they were not in strict harmony. I will now

call your attention to two of them, and you can then say whether
you would be apt to believe that the same man ever uttered both.   In
a speech in reply to me at Chicago in July last, Mr. Lincoln, in speaking of the equality of the negro with the white man, used the following
language:

> I should like to know if, taking this old Declaration of Independence,
> which declares that all men are equal upon principle, and making excep-
> tions to it, where will it stop ?   If one man says it does not mean a negro,
> why may not another man say it does not mean another man ?   If the Decla-
> ration is not the truth, let us get the statute-book in which we find it and
> tear it out.   Who is so bold as to do it ?   If it is not true, let us tear it out.

You find that Mr. Lincoln there proposed that if the doctrine of
the Declaration of Independence, declaring all men to be born equal,
did not include the negro and put him on an equality with the white
man, that we should take the statute-book and tear it out.   He there
took the ground that the negro race is included in the Declaration
of Independence as the equal of the white race, and that there could
be no such thing as a distinction in the races, making one superior
and the other inferior.   I read now from the same speech:

> My friends [he says], I have detained you about as long as I desire to do,
> and I have only to say let us discard all this quibbling about this man and
> the other man — this race and that race and the other race being inferior,
> and therefore they must be placed in an inferior position, discarding our
> standard that we have left us.   Let us discard all these things, and unite
> as one people throughout this land, until we shall once more stand up de-
> claring that all men are created equal.

["That's right," etc.]
Yes, I have no doubt that you think it is right, but the Lincoln
men down in Coles, Tazewell, and Sangamon counties do not think
it is right.   In the conclusion of the same speech, talking to the
Chicago Abolitionists, he said: "I leave you, hoping that the lamp
of liberty will burn in your bosoms until there shall no longer be a
doubt that all men are created free and equal."   ["Good, good!"]
Well, you say good to that, and you are going to vote for Lincoln
because he holds that doctrine.   I will not blame you for supporting him on that ground, but I will show you, in immediate contrast
with that doctrine, what Mr. Lincoln said down in Egypt in order
to get votes in that locality where they do not hold to such a doctrine.   In a joint discussion between Mr. Lincoln and myself, at
Charleston, I think, on the 18th of last month, Mr. Lincoln, referring to this subject, used the following language:

> I will say, then, that I am not nor ever have been in favor of bringing
> about in any way the social and political equality of the white and black
> races; that I am not nor ever have been in favor of making voters of the
> free negroes, or jurors, or qualifying them to hold office, or having them
> to marry with white people.   I will say in addition, that there is a physi-
> cal difference between the white and black races, which, I suppose, will
> forever forbid the two races living together upon terms of social and
> political equality, and inasmuch as they cannot so live, that while they do

remain together, there must be the position of superior and inferior, that I as much as any other man am in favor of the superior position being assigned to the white man.

["Good for Lincoln!"]

Fellow-citizens, here you find men hurrahing for Lincoln, and saying that he did right when in one part of the State he stood up for negro equality, and in another part, for political effect, discarded the doctrine, and declared that there always must be a superior and inferior race. Abolitionists up north are expected and required to vote for Lincoln because he goes for the equality of the races, holding that by the Declaration of Independence the white man and the negro were created equal, and endowed by the divine law with that equality, and down south he tells the Old Whigs, the Kentuckians, Virginians, and Tennesseeans that there is a physical difference in the races, making one superior and the other inferior, and that he is in favor of maintaining the superiority of the white race over the negro.

Now, how can you reconcile those two positions of Mr. Lincoln? He is to be voted for in the south as a pro-slavery man, and he is to be voted for in the north as an Abolitionist. Up here he thinks it is all nonsense to talk about a difference between the races, and says that we must "discard all quibbling about this race and that race and the other race being inferior, and therefore they must be placed in an inferior position." Down south he makes this "quibble" about this race and that race and the other race being inferior as the creed of his party, and declares that the negro can never be elevated to the position of the white man. You find that his political meetings are called by different names in different counties in the State. Here they are called Republican meetings, but in old Tazewell, where Lincoln made a speech last Tuesday, he did not address a Republican meeting, but "a grand rally of the Lincoln men." There are very few Republicans there, because Tazewell County is filled with old Virginians and Kentuckians, all of whom are Whigs or Democrats, and if Mr. Lincoln had called an Abolition or Republican meeting there, he would not get many votes. Go down into Egypt, and you will find that he and his party are operating under an alias there, which his friend Trumbull has given them, in order that they may cheat the people. When I was down in Monroe County a few weeks ago addressing the people, I saw handbills posted announcing that Mr. Trumbull was going to speak in behalf of Lincoln, and what do you think the name of his party was there? Why, the "Free Democracy." Mr. Trumbull and Mr. Jehu Baker were announced to address the Free Democracy of Monroe County, and the bill was signed "Many Free Democrats." The reason that Mr. Lincoln and his party adopted the name of "Free Democracy" down there was because Monroe County has always been an old-fashioned Democratic county, and hence it was necessary to make the people believe that they were Democrats, sympathized with them, and were fighting for Lincoln as Democrats. Come up to Springfield, where Lincoln now lives and always has lived, and you find that the convention of his party which assembled to nominate candidates for the legislature, who are expected to vote for him

VOL. I.—28.

if elected, dare not adopt the name of Republican, but assembled under the title of "All opposed to the Democracy." Thus you find that Mr. Lincoln's creed cannot travel through even one half of the counties of this State, but that it changes its hues, and becomes lighter and lighter as it travels from the extreme north, until it is nearly white when it reaches the extreme south end of the State. I ask you, my friends, why cannot Republicans avow their principles alike everywhere? I would despise myself if I thought that I was procuring your votes by concealing my opinions, and by avowing one set of principles in one part of the State, and a different set in another part.

If I do not truly and honorably represent your feelings and principles, then I ought not to be your senator; and I will never conceal my opinions, or modify or change them a hair's-breadth, in order to get votes. I tell you that this Chicago doctrine of Lincoln's—declaring that the negro and the white man are made equal by the Declaration of Independence and by Divine Providence—is a monstrous heresy. The signers of the Declaration of Independence never dreamed of the negro when they were writing that document. They referred to white men, to men of European birth and European descent, when they declared the equality of all men. I see a gentleman there in the crowd shaking his head. Let me remind him that when Thomas Jefferson wrote that document he was the owner, and so continued until his death, of a large number of slaves. Did he intend to say in that Declaration that his negro slaves, which he held and treated as property, were created his equals by divine law, and that he was violating the law of God every day of his life by holding them as slaves? It must be borne in mind that when that Declaration was put forth, every one of the thirteen colonies were slaveholding colonies, and every man who signed that instrument represented a slaveholding constituency. Recollect, also, that no one of them emancipated his slaves, much less put them on an equality with himself, after he signed the Declaration. On the contrary, they all continued to hold their negroes as slaves during the Revolutionary War. Now, do you believe—are you willing to have it said—that every man who signed the Declaration of Independence declared the negro his equal, and then was hypocrite enough to continue to hold him as a slave, in violation of what he believed to be the divine law? And yet when you say that the Declaration of Independence includes the negro, you charge the signers of it with hypocrisy.

I say to you frankly, that in my opinion this government was made by our fathers on the white basis. It was made by white men for the benefit of white men and their posterity forever, and was intended to be administered by white men in all time to come. But while I hold that under our Constitution and political system the negro is not a citizen, cannot be a citizen, and ought not to be a citizen, it does not follow by any means that he should be a slave. On the contrary, it does follow that the negro as an inferior race ought to possess every right, every privilege, every immunity which he can safely exercise consistent with the safety of the society in which he lives. Humanity requires, and Christianity commands, that you shall extend to every inferior being, and every dependent being, all the privileges, immunities, and advantages which can be granted to them consistent with the safety of society. If you ask me the nature and extent of these privileges, I answer that that is a question which the people of each State must decide for themselves. Illinois has decided that question for herself. We have said that in this State the negro shall not be a slave, nor shall he be a citizen. Kentucky holds a different doctrine. New York holds one different from either, and Maine one different from all. Virginia, in her policy on this question, differs in many respects from the others, and so on, until there are hardly two States whose policy is exactly alike in regard to the relation of the white man and the negro. Nor can you reconcile them and make them alike. Each State must do as it pleases. Illinois had as much right to adopt the policy which we have on that subject as Kentucky had to adopt a different policy. The great principle of this government is that each State has the right to do as it pleases on all these questions, and no other State or power on earth has the right to interfere with us, or complain of us merely because our system differs from theirs. In the compromise measures of 1850, Mr. Clay declared that this great principle ought to exist in the Territories as well as in the States, and I reasserted his doctrine in the Kansas and Nebraska bill in 1854.

But Mr. Lincoln cannot be made to understand, and those who are determined to vote for him, no matter whether he is a pro-slavery man in the south and a negro-equality advocate in the north, cannot be made to understand, how it is that in a Territory the people can do as they please on the slavery question under the Dred Scott decision. Let us see whether I cannot explain it to the satisfaction of all impartial men. Chief Justice Taney has said, in his opinion in the Dred Scott case, that a negro slave, being property, stands on an equal footing with other property, and that the owner may carry them into United States territory the same as he does other property. Suppose any two of you neighbors shall conclude to go to Kansas, one carrying $100,000 worth of negro slaves and the other $100,000 worth of mixed merchandise, including quantities of liquors. You both agree that under that decision you may carry your property to Kansas, but when you get it there, the merchant who is possessed of the liquors is met by the Maine liquor law, which prohibits the sale or use of his property, and the owner of the slaves is met by equally unfriendly legislation, which makes his property worthless after he gets it there. What is the right to carry your property into the Territory worth to either, when unfriendly legislation in the Territory renders it worthless after you get it there? The slaveholder, when he gets his slaves there, finds that there is no local law to protect him in holding them, no slave code, no police regulation maintaining and supporting him in his right, and he discovers at once that the absence of such friendly legislation excludes his property from the Territory just as irresistibly as if there was a positive constitutional prohibition excluding it.

Thus you find it is with any kind of property in a Territory; it depends for its protection on the local and municipal law. If the people of a Territory want slavery, they make friendly legislation to introduce it, but if they do not want it, they withhold all protection from it, and then it cannot exist there. Such was the view taken on the subject by different Southern men when the Nebraska bill passed. See the speech of Mr. Orr, of South Carolina, the present Speaker of the House of Representatives of Congress, made at that time, and there you will find this whole doctrine argued out at full length. Read the speeches of other Southern congressmen, senators, and representatives, made in 1854, and you will find that they took the same view of the subject as Mr. Orr— that slavery could never be forced on a people who did not want it. I hold that in this country there is no power on the face of the globe that can force any institution on an unwilling people. The great fundamental principle of our government is that the people of each State and each Territory shall be left perfectly free to decide for themselves what shall be the nature and character of their institutions. When this government was made, it was based on that principle. At the time of its formation there were twelve slaveholding States, and one free State, in this Union. Suppose this doctrine of Mr. Lincoln and the Republicans, of uniformity of laws of all the States on the subject of slavery, had prevailed; suppose Mr. Lincoln himself had been a member of the convention which framed the Constitution, and that he had risen in that august body, and, addressing the Father of his Country, had said as he did at Springfield:

A house divided against itself cannot stand. I believe this government cannot endure permanently half slave and half free. I do not expect the Union to be dissolved — I do not expect the house to fall, but I do expect it will cease to be divided. It will become all one thing, or all the other.

What do you think would have been the result? Suppose he had made that convention believe that doctrine, and they had acted upon it, what do you think would have been the result? Do you believe that one free State would have outvoted the twelve slaveholding States, and thus abolished slavery? On the contrary, would not the twelve slaveholding States have outvoted the one free State, and under his doctrine have fastened slavery by an irrevocable constitutional provision upon every inch of the American republic? Thus you see that the doctrine he now advocates, if proclaimed at the beginning of the government, would have established slavery everywhere throughout the American continent; and are you willing, now that we have the majority section, to exercise a power which we never would have submitted to when we were in the minority? If the Southern States had attempted to control our institutions, and make the States all slave when they had the power, I ask would you have submitted to it? If you would not, are you willing, now that we have become the strongest under that great principle of self-government that allows each State to do as it pleases, to attempt to control the Southern institutions? Then, my friends, I say to you that there is but one path of peace in this republic, and that is to administer this government as our fathers made it, divided into free and slave States, allowing each State to decide for itself

whether it wants slavery or not. If Illinois will settle the slavery question for herself, and mind her own business and let her
neighbors alone, we will be at peace with Kentucky, and every other
Southern State. If every other State in the Union will do the same,
there will be peace between the North and South, and in the whole
Union.

Mr. Lincoln's Reply in the Galesburg Joint Debate.

My Fellow-citizens: A very large portion of the speech which
Judge Douglas has addressed to you has previously been delivered
and put in print. I do not mean that for a hit upon the judge at all.
If I had not been interrupted, I was going to say that such an answer
as I was able to make to a very large portion of it, had already been
more than once made and published. There has been an opportunity afforded to the public to see our respective views upon the topics
discussed in a large portion of the speech which he has just delivered.
I make these remarks for the purpose of excusing myself for not
passing over the entire ground that the judge has traversed. I,
however, desire to take up some of the points that he has attended
to, and ask your attention to them, and I shall follow him backward
upon some notes which I have taken, reversing the order by beginning where he concluded.

The judge has alluded to the Declaration of Independence, and
insisted that negroes are not included in that Declaration; and that
it is, a slander upon the framers of that instrument to suppose that
negroes were meant therein; and he asks you: Is it possible to
believe that Mr. Jefferson, who penned the immortal paper, could
have supposed himself applying the language of that instrument to
the negro race, and yet held a portion of that race in slavery?
Would he not at once have freed them? I only have to remark
upon this part of the judge's speech (and that, too, very briefly, for
I shall not detain myself, or you, upon that point for any great
length of time), that I believe the entire records of the world, from
the date of the Declaration of Independence up to within three years
ago, may be searched in vain for one single affirmation, from one
single man, that the negro was not included in the Declaration of
Independence; I think I may defy Judge Douglas to show that he
ever said so, that Washington ever said so, that any president ever
said so, that any member of Congress ever said so, or that any
living man upon the whole earth ever said so, until the necessities of
the present policy of the Democratic party, in regard to slavery, had
to invent that affirmation. And I will remind Judge Douglas and
this audience that while Mr. Jefferson was the owner of slaves, as
undoubtedly he was, in speaking upon this very subject, he used the
strong language that "he trembled for his country when he remembered that God was just"; and I will offer the highest premium in
my power to Judge Douglas if he will show that he, in all his life,
ever uttered a sentiment at all akin to that of Jefferson.

The next thing to which I will ask your attention is the judge's
comments upon the fact, as he assumes it to be, that we cannot call

our public meetings as Republican meetings; and he instances Taze-well County as one of the places where the friends of Lincoln have called a public meeting and have not dared to name it a Republican meeting. He instances Monroe County as another where Judge Trumbull and Jehu Baker addressed the persons whom the judge assumes to be the friends of Lincoln, calling them the "Free Democ-racy." I have the honor to inform Judge Douglas that he spoke in that very county of Tazewell last Saturday, and I was there on Tues-day last, and when he spoke there he spoke under a call not ventur-ing to use the word "Democrat." [Turning to Judge Douglas.] What think you of this?

So, again, there is another thing to which I would ask the judge's attention upon this subject. In the contest of 1856 his party de-lighted to call themselves together as the "National Democracy," but now, if there should be a notice put up anywhere for a meeting of the "National Democracy," Judge Douglas and his friends would not come. They would not suppose themselves invited. They would understand that it was a call for those hateful postmasters whom he talks about.

Now a few words in regard to these extracts from speeches of mine which Judge Douglas has read to you, and which he supposes are in very great contrast to each other. Those speeches have been before the public for a considerable time, and if they have any in-consistency in them, if there is any conflict in them, the public have been able to detect it. When the judge says, in speaking on this subject, that I make speeches of one sort for the people of the northern end of the State, and of a different sort for the southern people, he assumes that I do not understand that my speeches will be put in print and read north and south. I knew all the while that the speech that I made at Chicago and the one I made at Jonesboro and the one at Charleston would all be put in print, and all the read-ing and intelligent men in the community would see them and know all about my opinions; and I have not supposed, and do not now suppose, that there is any conflict whatever between them. But the judge will have it that if we do not confess that there is a sort of in-equality between the white and black races which justifies us in making them slaves, we must, then, insist that there is a degree of equality that requires us to make them our wives. Now, I have all the while taken a broad distinction in regard to that matter; and that is all there is in these different speeches which he arrays here, and the entire reading of either of the speeches will show that that distinction was made. Perhaps by taking two parts of the same speech he could have got up as much of a conflict as the one he has found. I have all the while maintained that in so far as it should be insisted that there was an equality between the white and black races that should produce a perfect social and political equality, it was an impossibility. This you have seen in my printed speeches, and with it I have said that in their right to "life, liberty, and the pursuit of happiness," as proclaimed in that old Declaration, the in-ferior races are our equals. And these declarations I have constantly made in reference to the abstract moral question, to contemplate and consider when we are legislating about any new country which is not already cursed with the actual presence of the evil—slavery. I have never manifested any impatience with the necessities that spring from the actual presence of black people amongst us, and the actual existence of slavery amongst us where it does already exist; but I have insisted that, in legislating for new countries where it does not exist, there is no just rule other than that of moral and abstract right. With reference to those new countries, those maxims as to the right of a people to "life, liberty, and the pursuit of happiness" were the just rules to be constantly referred to. There is no misunderstanding this, except by men interested to misunderstand it. I take it that I have to address an intelligent and reading community who will peruse what I say, weigh it, and then judge whether I advance improper or unsound views, or whether I advance hypocritical and deceptive and contrary views in different portions of the country. I believe myself to be guilty of no such thing as the latter, though, of course, I cannot claim that I am entirely free from all error in the opinions I advance.

The judge has also detained us awhile in regard to the distinction between his party and our party. His he assumes to be a national party—ours a sectional one. He does this in asking the question whether this country has any interest in the maintenance of the Republican party? He assumes that our party is altogether sectional—that the party to which he adheres is national; and the argument is that no party—can be based upon rightful principles—unless it can announce its principles everywhere. I presume that Judge Douglas could not go into Russia and announce the doctrine of our national Democracy; he could not denounce the doctrine of kings and emperors and monarchies in Russia; and it may be true of this country, that in some places we may not be able to proclaim a doctrine as clearly true as the truth of Democracy, because there is a section so directly opposed to it that they will not tolerate us in doing so. Is it the true test of the soundness of a doctrine, that in some places people won't let you proclaim it? Is that the way to test the truth of any doctrine? Why, I understand that at one time the people of Chicago would not let Judge Douglas preach a certain favorite doctrine of his. I commend to his consideration the question, whether he takes that as a test of the unsoundness of what he wanted to preach.

There is another thing to which I wish to ask attention for a little while on this occasion. What has always been the evidence brought forward to prove that the Republican party is a sectional party? The main one was that in the Southern portion of the Union the people did not let the Republicans proclaim their doctrines amongst them. That has been the main evidence brought forward—that they had no supporters, or substantially none, in the slave States. The South have not taken hold of our principles as we announce them; nor does Judge Douglas now grapple with those principles. We have a Republican State platform, laid down in Springfield in June last, stating our position all the way through the questions before the country. We are now far advanced in this canvass. Judge

Douglas and I have made perhaps forty speeches apiece, and we have now for the fifth time met face to face in debate, and up to this day I have not found either Judge Douglas or any friend of his taking hold of the Republican platform or laying his finger upon anything in it that is wrong. I ask you all to recollect that. Judge Douglas turns away from the platform of principles to the fact that he can find people somewhere who will not allow us to announce those principles. If he had great confidence that our principles were wrong, he would take hold of them and demonstrate them to be wrong. But he does not do so. The only evidence he has of their being wrong is in the fact that there are people who won't allow us to preach them. I ask again is that the way to test the soundness of a doctrine?

I ask his attention also to the fact that by the rule of nationality he is himself fast becoming sectional. I ask his attention to the fact that his speeches would not go as current now south of the Ohio River as they have formerly gone there. I ask his attention to the fact that he felicitates himself to-day that all the Democrats of the free States are agreeing with him, while he omits to tell us that the Democrats of any slave State agree with him. If he has not thought of this, I commend to his consideration the evidence in his own declaration, on this day, of his becoming sectional too. I see it rapidly approaching. Whatever may be the result of this ephemeral contest between Judge Douglas and myself, I see the day rapidly approaching when his pill of sectionalism, which he has been thrusting down the throats of Republicans for years past, will be crowded down his own throat.

Now in regard to what Judge Douglas said (in the beginning of his speech) about the compromise of 1850 containing the principle of the Nebraska bill; although I have often presented my views upon that subject, yet as I have not done so in this canvass, I will, if you please, detain you a little with them. I have always maintained so far as I was able that there was nothing of the principle of the Nebraska bill in the compromise of 1850 at all — nothing whatever. Where can you find the principle of the Nebraska bill in that compromise? If anywhere, in the two pieces of the compromise organizing the Territories of New Mexico and Utah. It was expressly provided in these two acts that, when they came to be admitted into the Union, they should be admitted with or without slavery, as they should choose, by their own constitutions. Nothing was said in either of those acts as to what was to be done in relation to slavery during the territorial existence of those Territories, while Henry Clay constantly made the declaration (Judge Douglas recognizing him as a leader) that, in his opinion, the old Mexican laws would control that question during the territorial existence, and that these old Mexican laws excluded slavery. How can that be used as a principle for declaring that during the territorial existence, as well as at the time of framing the constitution, the people, if you please, might have slaves if they wanted them? I am not discussing the question whether it is right or wrong; but how are the New Mexican and Utah laws patterns for the Nebraska bill? I maintain that the organization of Utah and New Mexico did not establish a general principle at all. It had no feature establishing a general principle. The acts to which I have referred were a part of a general system of compromises. They did not lay down what was proposed as a regular policy for the Territories ; only an agreement in this particular case to do in that way, because other things were done that were to be a compensation for it. They were allowed to come in in that shape, because in another way it was paid for — considering that as a part of that system of measures called the compromise of 1850, which finally included half a dozen acts. It included the admission of California as a free State, which was kept out of the Union for half a year because it had formed a free constitution. It included the settlement of the boundary of Texas, which had been undefined before, which was in itself a slavery question ; for if you pushed the line further west, you made Texas larger, and made more slave Territory ; while if you drew the line toward the east, you narrowed the boundary and diminished the domain of slavery, and by so much increased free Territory. It included the abolition of the slave-trade in the District of Columbia. It included the passage of a new fugitive-slave law. All these things were put together, and though passed in separate acts, were nevertheless in legislation (as the speeches at the time will show) made to depend upon each other. Each got votes, with the understanding that the other measures were to pass, and by this system of compromise, in that series of measures, those two bills — the New Mexico and Utah bills — were passed ; and I say for that reason they could not be taken as models, framed upon their own intrinsic principle, for all future Territories. And I have the evidence of this in the fact that Judge Douglas, a year afterward, or more than a year afterward perhaps, when he first introduced bills for the purpose of framing new Territories, did not attempt to follow these bills of New Mexico and Utah ; and even when he introduced this Nebraska bill, I think you will discover that he did not exactly follow them. But I do not wish to dwell at great length upon this branch of the discussion. My own opinion is that a thorough investigation will show most plainly that the New Mexico and Utah bills were part of a system of compromise, and not designed as patterns for future territorial legislation, and that this Nebraska bill did not follow them as a pattern at all.

The judge tells us, in proceeding, that he is opposed to making any odious distinctions between free and slave States. I am altogether unaware that the Republicans are in favor of making any odious distinctions between the free and slave States. But there still is a difference, I think, between Judge Douglas and the Republicans in this. I suppose that the real difference between Judge Douglas and his friends and the Republicans, on the contrary, is that the judge is not in favor of making any difference between slavery and liberty—that he is in favor of eradicating, of pressing out of view, the questions of preference in this country for free or slave institutions ; and consequently every sentiment he utters discards the idea that there is any wrong in slavery. Everything that emanates from him or his coadjutors in their course of policy carefully excludes the thought that there is anything wrong in slavery. All their arguments, if you will consider them, will be seen to exclude the thought that there is anything whatever wrong in slavery. If you will take the judge's speeches, and select the short and pointed sentences expressed by him,—as his declaration that he "don't care whether slavery is voted up or down,"—you will see at once that this is perfectly logical, if you do not admit that slavery is wrong. If you do admit that it is wrong, Judge Douglas cannot logically say he don't care whether a wrong is voted up or voted down. Judge Douglas declares that if any community wants slavery they have a right to have it. He can say that logically, if he says that there is no wrong in slavery; but if you admit that there is a wrong in it, he cannot logically say that anybody has a right to do wrong. He insists that, upon the score of equality, the owners of slaves and owners of property—of horses and every other sort of property— should be alike, and hold them alike in a new Territory. That is perfectly logical, if the two species of property are alike, and are equally founded in right. But if you admit that one of them is wrong, you cannot institute any equality between right and wrong. And from this difference of sentiment—the belief on the part of one that the institution is wrong, and a policy springing from that belief which looks to the arrest of the enlargement of that wrong; and this other sentiment, that it is no wrong, and a policy sprung from that sentiment which will tolerate no idea of preventing that wrong from growing larger, and looks to there never being an end of it through all the existence of things—arises the real difference between Judge Douglas and his friends on the one hand, and the Republicans on the other. Now, I confess myself as belonging to that class in the country who contemplate slavery as a moral, social, and political evil, having due regard for its actual existence amongst us, and the difficulties of getting rid of it in any satisfactory way, and to all the constitutional obligations which have been thrown about it; but who, nevertheless, desire a policy that looks to the prevention of it as a wrong, and looks hopefully to the time when as a wrong it may come to an end.

Judge Douglas has again, for, I believe, the fifth time, if not the seventh, in my presence, reiterated his charge of a conspiracy or combination between the National Democrats and Republicans. What evidence Judge Douglas has upon this subject I know not, inasmuch as he never favors us with any. I have said upon a former occasion, and I do not choose to suppress it now, that I have no objection to the division in the judge's party. He got it up himself. It was all his and their work. He had, I think, a great deal more to do with the steps that led to the Lecompton constitution than Mr. Buchanan had; though at last, when they reached it, they quarreled over it, and their friends divided upon it. I am very free to confess to Judge Douglas that I have no objection to the division; but I defy the judge to show any evidence that I have in any way promoted that division, unless he insists on being a witness himself in merely saying so. I can give all fair friends of Judge Douglas here to understand exactly the view that Republicans take in regard to that division. Don't you remember how two years ago the opponents of the Democratic party were divided between Frémont and Fillmore? I guess you do. Any Democrat who remembers that division will remember also that he was at the time very glad of it, and then he will be able to see all there is between the National Democrats and the Republicans. What we now think of the two divisions of Democrats, you then thought of the Frémont and Fillmore divisions. That is all there is of it.

But if the judge continues to put forward the declaration that there is an unholy, unnatural alliance between the Republicans and the National Democrats, I now want to enter my protest against receiving him as an entirely competent witness upon that subject. I want to call to the judge's attention an attack he made upon me in the first one of these debates, at Ottawa, on the 21st of August. In order to fix extreme Abolitionism upon me, Judge Douglas read a set of resolutions which he declared had been passed by a Republican State convention, in October, 1854, at Springfield, Illinois, and he declared I had taken part in that convention. It turned out that although a few men calling themselves an anti-Nebraska State convention had sat at Springfield about that time, yet neither did I take any part in it, nor did it pass the resolutions or any such resolutions as Judge Douglas read. So apparent had it become that the resolutions which he read had not been passed at Springfield at all, nor by any State convention in which I had taken part, that seven days afterward, at Freeport, Judge Douglas declared that he had been misled by Charles H. Lanphier, editor of the "State Register," and Thomas L. Harris, member of Congress in that district, and he promised in that speech that when he went to Springfield he would investigate the matter. Since then Judge Douglas has been to Springfield, and I presume has made the investigation; but a month has passed since he has been there, and so far as I know, he has made no report of the result of his investigation. I have waited as I think a sufficient time for the report of that investigation, and I have some curiosity to see and hear it. A fraud, an absolute forgery, was committed, and the perpetration of it was traced to the three—Lanphier, Harris, and Douglas. Whether it can be narrowed in any way, so as to exonerate any one of them, is what Judge Douglas's report would probably show.

It is true that the set of resolutions read by Judge Douglas were published in the Illinois "State Register" on the 16th of October, 1854, as being the resolutions of an anti-Nebraska convention which had sat in that same month of October, at Springfield. But it is also true that the publication in the "Register" was a forgery then, and the question is still behind, which of the three, if not all of them, committed that forgery? The idea that it was done by mistake is absurd. The article in the Illinois "State Register" contains part of the real proceedings of that Springfield convention, showing that the writer of the article had the real proceedings before him, and purposely threw out the genuine resolutions passed by the convention, and fraudulently substituted the others. Lanphier then, as now, was the editor of the "Register," so that there seems to be but little room for his escape. But then it is to be borne in mind that Lanphier had less interest in the object of that forgery than either of the other two. The main object of that forgery at that time was to beat Yates and elect Harris to Congress, and that object was known to be exceedingly dear to Judge Douglas at that time. Harris and Douglas were both in Springfield when the convention was in session, and although they both left before the fraud appeared in the "Register," subsequent events show that they have both had their eyes fixed upon that convention.

The fraud having been apparently successful upon that occasion, both Harris and Douglas have more than once since then been attempting to put it to new uses. As the fisherman's wife, whose drowned husband was brought home with his body full of eels, said when she was asked what was to be done with him, "Take the eels out and set him again," so Harris and Douglas have shown a disposition to take the eels out of that stale fraud by which they gained Harris's election, and set the fraud again more than once. On the 9th of July, 1856, Douglas attempted a repetition of it upon Trumbull on the floor of the Senate of the United States, as will appear from the appendix to the "Congressional Globe" of that date. On the 9th of August, Harris attempted it again upon Norton in the House of Representatives, as will appear by the same document—the appendix to the "Congressional Globe" of that date. On the 21st of August last, all three—Lanphier, Douglas, and Harris—reattempted it upon me at Ottawa. It has been clung to and played out again and again as an exceedingly high trump by this blessed trio. And now that it has been discovered publicly to be a fraud, we find that Judge Douglas manifests no surprise at it at all. He makes no complaint of Lanphier, who must have known it to be a fraud from the beginning. He, Lanphier, and Harris are just as cozy now, and just as active in the concoction of new schemes as they were before the general discovery of this fraud. Now all this is very natural if they are all alike guilty in that fraud, and it is very unnatural if any one of them is innocent. Lanphier perhaps insists that the rule of honor among thieves does not quite require him to take all upon himself, and consequently my friend Judge Douglas finds it difficult to make a satisfactory report upon his investigation. But meanwhile the three are agreed that each is "a most honorable man."

Judge Douglas requires an indorsement of his truth and honor by a reëlection to the United States Senate, and he makes and reports against me and against Judge Trumbull, day after day, charges which we know to be utterly untrue, without for a moment seeming to think that this one unexplained fraud, which he promised to investigate, will be the least drawback to his claim to belief. Harris ditto. He asks a reëlection to the lower House of Congress without seeming to remember at all that he is involved in this dishonorable fraud! The Illinois "State Register," edited by Lanphier, then, as now, the central organ of both Harris and Douglas, continues to din the public ear with these assertions without seeming to suspect that they are at all lacking in title to belief.

After all, the question still recurs upon us, how did that fraud originally get into the " State Register"? Lanphier then, as now, was the editor of that paper. Lanphier knows. Lanphier cannot be ignorant of how and by whom it was originally concocted. Can he be induced to tell, or if he has told, can Judge Douglas be induced to tell, how it originally was concocted? It may be true that Lanphier insists that the two men for whose benefit it was originally devised shall at least bear their share of it! How that is, I do not know, and while it remains unexplained, I hope to be pardoned if I insist that the mere fact of Judge Douglas making charges against Trumbull and myself is not quite sufficient evidence to establish them!

While we were at Freeport, in one of these joint discussions, I answered certain interrogatories which Judge Douglas had propounded to me, and there in turn propounded some to him, which he in a sort of way answered. The third one of these interrogatories I have with me, and wish now to make some comments upon it. It was in these words: "If the Supreme Court of the United States shall decide that States cannot exclude slavery from their limits, are you in favor of acquiescing in, adopting, and following such decision as a rule of political action?"

To this interrogatory Judge Douglas made no answer in any just sense of the word. He contented himself with sneering at the thought that it was possible for the Supreme Court ever to make such a decision. He sneered at me for propounding the interrogatory. I had not propounded it without some reflection, and I wish now to address to this audience some remarks upon it.

In the second clause of the sixth article, I believe it is, of the Constitution of the United States, we find the following language: " This Constitution and the laws of the United States which shall be made in pursuance thereof, and all treaties made, or which shall be made, under the authority of the United States, shall be the supreme law of the land; and the judges in every State shall be bound thereby, anything in the constitution or laws of any State to the contrary notwithstanding."

The essence of the Dred Scott case is compressed into the sentence which I will now read: "Now, as we have already said in an earlier part of this opinion, upon a different point, the right of property in a slave is distinctly and expressly affirmed in the Constitution." I repeat it, "the right of property in a slave is distinctly and expressly affirmed in the Constitution"! What is it to be "affirmed" in the Constitution? Made firm in the Constitution—so made that it cannot be separated from the Constitution without breaking the Constitution—durable as the Constitution, and part of the Constitution? Now, remembering the provision of the Constitution which I have read, affirming that that instrument is the supreme law of the land; that the judges of every State shall be bound by it, any law or constitution of any State to the contrary notwithstanding; that the right of property in a slave is affirmed in that Constitution, is made, formed into, and cannot be separated from it without breaking it; durable as the instrument, part of the instrument,—what follows as a short and even syllogistic argument from it? I think it follows, and I submit to the consideration of men capable of arguing, whether as I state it, in syllogistic form, the argument has any fault in it?

Nothing in the constitution or laws of any State can destroy a right distinctly and expressly affirmed in the Constitution of the United States.

The right of property in a slave is distinctly and expressly affirmed in the Constitution of the United States.

Therefore, nothing in the constitution or laws of any State can destroy the right of property in a slave.

I believe that no fault can be pointed out in that argument; assuming the truth of the premises, the conclusion, so far as I have capacity at all to understand it, follows inevitably. There is a fault in it, as I think, but the fault is not in the reasoning; the falsehood, in fact, is a fault in the premises. I believe that the right of property in a slave is not distinctly and expressly affirmed in the Constitution, and Judge Douglas thinks it is. I believe that the Supreme Court and the advocates of that decision may search in vain for the place in the Constitution where the right of property in a slave is distinctly and expressly affirmed. I say, therefore, that I think one of the premises is not true in fact. But it is true with Judge Douglas. It is true with the Supreme Court who pronounced it. They are estopped from denying it, and being estopped from denying it, the conclusion follows that the Constitution of the United States, being the supreme law, no constitution or law can interfere with it. It being affirmed in the decision that the right of property in a slave is distinctly and expressly affirmed in the Constitution, the conclusion inevitably follows that no State law or constitution can destroy that right. I then say to Judge Douglas, and to all others, that I think it will take a better answer than a sneer to show that those who have said that the right of property in a slave is distinctly and expressly affirmed in the Constitution are not prepared to show that no constitution or law can destroy that right. I say I believe it will take a far better argument than a mere sneer to show to the minds of intelligent men that whoever has so said is not prepared, whenever public sentiment is so far advanced as to justify it, to say the other.

This is but an opinion, and the opinion of one very humble man; but it is my opinion that the Dred Scott decision, as it is, never would have been made in its present form if the party that made it had not been sustained previously by the elections. My own opinion is that the new Dred Scott decision, deciding against the right of the people of the States to exclude slavery, will never be made if that party is not sustained by the elections. I believe, further, that it is just as sure to be made as to-morrow is to come, if that party shall be sustained. I have said upon a former occasion, and I repeat it now, that the course of argument that Judge Douglas makes use of upon this subject (I charge not his motives in this) is preparing the public mind for that new Dred Scott decision. I have asked him again to point out to me the reasons for his first adherence to the Dred Scott decision as it is. I have turned his attention to the fact that General Jackson differed with him in regard to the political obligation of a Supreme Court decision. I have asked his attention to the fact that

Jefferson differed with him in regard to the political obligation of a Supreme Court decision. Jefferson said that "judges are as honest as other men, and not more so." And he said, substantially, that whenever a free people should give up in absolute submission to any department of government, retaining for themselves no appeal from it, their liberties were gone. I have asked his attention to the fact that the Cincinnati platform, upon which he says he stands, disregards a time-honored decision of the Supreme Court, in defying the power of Congress to establish a national bank. I have asked his attention to the fact that he himself was one of the most active instruments at one time in breaking down the Supreme Court of the State of Illinois, because it had made a decision distasteful to him— a struggle ending in the remarkable circumstance of his sitting down as one of the new judges who were to overslaugh that decision, getting his title of judge in that very way.

So far in this controversy I can get no answer at all from Judge Douglas upon these subjects. Not one can I get from him, except that he swells himself up and says: "All of us who stand by the decision of the Supreme Court are the friends of the Constitution; all you fellows that dare question it in any way are the enemies of the Constitution." Now in this very devoted adherence to this decision, in opposition to all the great political leaders whom he has recognized as leaders—in opposition to his former self and history, there is something very marked. And the manner in which he adheres to it—not as being right upon the merits, as he conceives (because he did not discuss that at all), but as being absolutely obligatory upon every one simply because of the source from whence it comes—as that which no man can gainsay, whatever it may be—this is another marked feature of his adherence to that decision. It marks it in this respect, that it commits him to the next decision, whenever it comes, as being as obligatory as this one, since he does not investigate it, and won't inquire whether this opinion is right or wrong. So he takes the next one without inquiring whether it is right or wrong. He teaches men this doctrine, and in so doing prepares the public mind to take the next decision when it comes without any inquiry. In this I think I argue fairly (without questioning motives at all) that Judge Douglas is most ingeniously and powerfully preparing the public mind to take that decision when it comes; and not only so, but he is doing it in various other ways. In these general maxims about liberty—in his assertions that he "don't care whether slavery is voted up or voted down"; that "whoever wants slavery has a right to have it"; that "upon principles of equality it should be allowed to go everywhere"; that "there is no inconsistency between free and slave institutions"—in this he is also preparing (whether purposely or not) the way for making the institution of slavery national. I repeat again, for I wish no misunderstanding, that I do not charge that he means it so; but I call upon your minds to inquire, if you were going to get the best instrument you could, and then set it to work in the most ingenious way, to prepare the public mind for this movement, operating in the free States, where there is now an abhorrence of the institution of slavery, could you find an instrument so capable of doing it as Judge Douglas, or one employed in so apt a way to do it?

I have said once before, and I will repeat it now, that Mr. Clay, when he was once answering an objection to the Colonization Society, that it had a tendency to the ultimate emancipation of the slaves, said that "those who would repress all tendencies to liberty and ultimate emancipation must do more than put down the benevolent efforts of the Colonization Society—they must go back to the era of our liberty and independence, and muzzle the cannon that thunders its annual joyous return—they must blot out the moral lights around us—they must penetrate the human soul, and eradicate the light of reason and the love of liberty"! And I do think—I repeat, though I said it on a former occasion—that Judge Douglas, and whoever, like him, teaches that the negro has no share, humble though it may be, in the Declaration of Independence, is going back to the era of our liberty and independence, and, so far as in him lies, muzzling the cannon that thunders its annual joyous return; that he is blowing out the moral lights around us, when he contends that whoever wants slaves has a right to hold them; that he is penetrating, so far as lies in his power, the human soul, and eradicating the light of reason and the love of liberty, when he is in every possible way preparing the public mind, by his vast influence, for making the institution of slavery perpetual and national.

There is, my friends, only one other point to which I will call your attention for the remaining time that I have left me, and perhaps I shall not occupy the entire time that I have, as that one point may not take me clear through it.

Among the interrogatories that Judge Douglas propounded to me at Freeport, there was one in about this language: "Are you opposed to the acquisition of any further territory to the United States, unless slavery shall first be prohibited therein?" I answered as I thought, in this way, that I am not generally opposed to the acquisition of additional territory, and that I would support a proposition for the acquisition of additional territory, according as my supporting it was or was not calculated to aggravate this slavery question amongst us. I then proposed to Judge Douglas another interrogatory, which was correlative to that: "Are you in favor of acquiring additional territory in disregard of how it may affect us upon the slavery question?" Judge Douglas answered—that is, in his own way he answered it. I believe that, although he took a good many words to answer it, it was little more fully answered than any other. The substance of his answer was that this country would continue to expand—that it would need additional territory—that it was as absurd to suppose that we could continue upon our present territory, enlarging in population as we are, as it would be to hoop a boy twelve years of age, and expect him to grow to man's size without bursting the hoops. I believe it was something like that. Consequently he was in favor of the acquisition of further territory, as fast as we might need it, in disregard of how it might affect the slavery question. I do not say this as giving his exact language, but he said so substantially, and he would leave the question of slavery where the territory was acquired, to be settled by the people of the acquired territory. ["That's the doctrine."] Maybe it is; let us consider that for a while. This will probably, in the run of things, become one of the concrete manifestations of this slavery question. If Judge Douglas's policy upon this question succeeds and gets fairly settled down until all opposition is crushed out, the next thing will be a grab for the territory of poor Mexico, an invasion of the rich lands of South America, then the adjoining islands will follow, each one of which promises additional slave-fields. And this question is to be left to the people of those countries for settlement. When we shall get Mexico, I don't know whether the judge will be in favor of the Mexican people that we get with it settling that question for themselves and all others; because we know the judge has a great horror for mongrels, and I understand that the people of Mexico are most decidedly a race of mongrels. I understand that there is not more than one person there out of eight who is a pure white, and I suppose from the judge's previous declaration that when we get Mexico, or any considerable portion of it, he will be in favor of these mongrels settling the question, which would bring him somewhat into collision with his horror of an inferior race.

It is to be remembered, though, that this power of acquiring additional territory is a power confided to the President and Senate of the United States. It is a power not under the control of the representatives of the people any further than they, the President and the Senate, can be considered the representatives of the people. Let me illustrate that by a case we have in our history. When we acquired the territory from Mexico in the Mexican war, the House of Representatives, composed of the immediate representatives of the people, all the time insisted that the territory thus to be acquired should be brought in upon condition that slavery should be forever prohibited therein, upon the terms and in the language that slavery had been prohibited from coming into this country. That was insisted upon constantly, and never failed to call forth an assurance that any territory thus acquired should have that prohibition in it, so far as the House of Representatives was concerned. But at last the President and Senate acquired the territory without asking the House of Representatives anything about it, and took it without that prohibition. They have the power of acquiring territory without the immediate representatives of the people being called upon to say anything about it, thus furnishing a very apt and powerful means of bringing new territory into the Union, and, when it is once brought into the country, involving us anew in this slavery agitation. It is therefore, as I think, a very important question for the consideration of the American people, whether the policy of bringing in additional territory, without considering at all how it will operate upon the safety of the Union in reference to this one great disturbing element in our national politics, shall be adopted as the policy of the country. You will bear in mind that it is to be acquired, according to the judge's view, as fast as it is needed, and the indefinite part of this proposition is that we have only Judge Douglas and his class of men to decide how fast it is needed. We have no clear and certain way of determining or demonstrating how fast territory is needed by the necessities of the country. Whoever wants to go out filibustering, then, thinks that more territory is needed. Whoever wants wider slave-fields feels sure that some additional territory is needed as slave territory. Then it is as easy to show the necessity of additional slave territory as it is to assert anything that is incapable of absolute demonstration. Whatever motive a man or a set of men may have for making annexation of property or territory, it is very easy to assert, but much less easy to disprove, that it is necessary for the wants of the country.

And now it only remains for me to say that I think it is a very grave question for the people of this Union to consider whether, in view of the fact that this slavery question has been the only one that has ever endangered our republican institutions—the only one that has ever threatened or menaced a dissolution of the Union—that has ever disturbed us in such a way as to make us fear for the perpetuity of our liberty—in view of these facts, I think it is an exceedingly interesting and important question for this people to consider whether we shall engage in the policy of acquiring additional territory, discarding altogether from our consideration, while obtaining new territory, the question how it may affect us in regard to this the only endangering element to our liberties and national greatness. The judge's view has been expressed. I, in my answer to his question, have expressed mine. I think it will become an important and practical question. Our views are before the public. I am willing and anxious that they should consider them fully — that they should turn it about and consider the importance of the question, and arrive at a just conclusion as to whether it is or is not wise in the people of this Union, in the acquisition of new territory, to consider whether it will add to the disturbance that is existing among us—whether it will add to the one only danger that has ever threatened the perpetuity of the Union or our own liberties. I think it is extremely important that they shall decide, and rightly decide, that question before entering upon that policy.

And now, my friends, having said the little I wish to say upon this head, whether I have occupied the whole of the remnant of my time or not, I believe I could not enter upon any new topic so as to treat it fully without transcending my time, which I would not for a moment think of doing. I give way to Judge Douglas.

Mr. Douglas's Rejoinder in the Galesburg Joint Debate.

Gentlemen: The highest compliment you can pay me during the brief half-hour that I have to conclude is by observing a strict silence. I desire to be heard rather than to be applauded.

The first criticism that Mr. Lincoln makes on my speech was that it was in substance what I have said everywhere else in the State where I have addressed the people. I wish I could say the same of his speech. Why, the reason I complain of him is because he makes one speech north and another south. Because he has one set of sentiments for the Abolition counties, and another set for the counties opposed to Abolitionism. My point of complaint against him is that

I cannot induce him to hold up the same standard, to carry the same flag in all parts of the State. He does not pretend, and no other man will, that I have one set of principles for Galesburg and another for Charleston. He does not pretend that I hold to one doctrine in Chicago and an opposite one in Jonesboro. I have proved that he has a different set of principles for each of these localities. All I asked of him was that he should deliver the speech that he has made here to-day in Coles County instead of in old Knox. It would have settled the question between us in that doubtful county. Here I understand him to reaffirm the doctrine of negro equality, and to assert that by the Declaration of Independence the negro is declared equal to the white man. He tells you to-day that the negro was included in the Declaration of Independence when it asserted that all men were created equal. [" We believe it."] Very well.

Mr. Lincoln asserts to-day, as he did at Chicago, that the negro was included in that clause of the Declaration of Independence which says that all men were created equal, and endowed by the Creator with certain inalienable rights, among which are life, liberty, and the pursuit of happiness. If the negro was made his equal and mine, if that equality was established by divine law, and was the negro's inalienable right, how came he to say at Charleston to the Kentuckians residing in that section of our State, that the negro was physically inferior to the white man, belonged to an inferior race, and he was for keeping him always in that inferior condition. I wish you to bear these things in mind. At Charleston he said that the negro belonged to an inferior race, and that he was for keeping him in that inferior condition. There he gave the people to understand that there was no moral question involved, because the inferiority being established, it was only a question of degree and not a question of right; here, to-day, instead of making it a question of degree, he makes it a moral question, says that it is a great crime to hold the negro in that inferior condition. ["He's right."] Is he right now, or was he right in Charleston? ["Both."] He is right then, sir, in your estimation, not because he is consistent, but because he can trim his principles any way in any section, so as to secure votes. All I desire of him is that he will declare the same principles in the south that he does in the north.

But did you notice how he answered my position that a man should hold the same doctrines throughout the length and breadth of this republic? He said, "Would Judge Douglas go to Russia and proclaim the same principles he does here?" I would remind him that Russia is not under the American Constitution. If Russia was a part of the American republic, under our Federal Constitution, and I was sworn to support the Constitution, I would maintain the same doctrine in Russia that I do in Illinois. The slaveholding States are governed by the same Federal Constitution as ourselves, and hence a man's principles, in order to be in harmony with the Constitution, must be the same in the South as they are in the North, the same in the free States as they are in the slave States. Whenever a man advocates one set of principles in one section, and another set in another section, his opinions are in violation of the spirit of the Constitution which he has sworn to support. When Mr. Lincoln went to Congress in 1847, and, laying his hand upon the Holy Evangelists, made a solemn vow in the presence of high Heaven that he would be faithful to the Constitution — what did he mean? the Constitution as he expounds it in Galesburg, or the Constitution as he expounds it in Charleston.

Mr. Lincoln has devoted considerable time to the circumstance that at Ottawa I read a series of resolutions as having been adopted at Springfield, in this State, on the 4th or 5th of October, 1854, which happened not to have been adopted there. He has used hard names; has dared to talk about fraud, about forgery, and has insinuated that there was a conspiracy between Mr. Lanphier, Mr. Harris, and myself to perpetrate a forgery. Now, bear in mind that he does not deny that these resolutions were adopted in a majority of all the Republican counties of this State in that year; he does not deny that they were declared to be the platform of this Republican party in the first congressional district, in the second, in the third, and in many counties of the fourth, and that they thus became the platform of his party in a majority of the counties upon which he now relies for support; he does not deny the truthfulness of the resolutions, but takes exception to the spot on which they were adopted. He takes to himself great merit because he thinks they were not adopted on the right spot for me to use them against him, just as he was very severe in Congress upon the government of his country, when he thought that he had discovered that the Mexican war was not begun in the right spot, and was therefore unjust. He tries very hard to make out that there is something very extraordinary in the place where the thing was done, and not in the thing itself. I never believed before that Abraham Lincoln would be guilty of what he has done this day in regard to those resolutions. In the first place, the moment it was intimated to me that they had been adopted at Aurora and Rockford instead of Springfield, I did not wait for him to call my attention to the fact, but led off and explained in my first meeting after the Ottawa debate, what the mistake was and how it had been made. I supposed that for an honest man, conscious of his own rectitude, that explanation would be sufficient. I did not wait for him, after the mistake was made, to call my attention to it, but frankly explained it at once as an honest man would. I also gave the authority on which I had stated that these resolutions were adopted by the Springfield Republican convention; that I had seen them quoted by Major Harris in a debate in Congress, as having been adopted by the first Republican State convention in Illinois, and that I had written to him and asked him for the authority as to the time and place of their adoption; that Major Harris being extremely ill, Charles H. Lanphier had written to me for him that they were adopted at Springfield, on the 5th of October, 1854, and had sent me a copy of the Springfield paper containing them. I read them from the newspaper just as Mr. Lincoln reads the proceedings of meetings held years ago from the newspapers. After giving that explanation, I did not think there was an honest man in the State of Illinois who doubted that I had been led into the error, if it was such, innocently, in the way I detailed; and I will now say that I do not now believe that there is an honest man on the face of the globe who will not regard with abhorrence and disgust Mr. Lincoln's insinuations of my complicity in that forgery, if it was a forgery. Does Mr. Lincoln wish to push these things to the point of personal difficulties here? I commenced this contest by treating him courteously and kindly; I always spoke of him in words of respect, and in return he has sought, and is now seeking, to divert public attention from the enormity of his revolutionary principles by impeaching men's sincerity and integrity, and inviting personal quarrels.

I desired to conduct this contest with him like a gentleman, but I spurn the insinuation of complicity and fraud made upon the simple circumstance of an editor of a newspaper having made a mistake as to the place where a thing was done, but not as to the thing itself. These resolutions were the platform of this Republican party of Mr. Lincoln's of that year. They were adopted in a majority of the Republican counties in the State; and when I asked him at Ottawa whether they formed the platform upon which he stood, he did not answer, and I could not get an answer out of him. He then thought, as I thought, that those resolutions were adopted at the Springfield convention, but excused himself by saying that he was not there when they were adopted, but had gone to Tazewell court in order to avoid being present at the convention. He saw them published as having been adopted at Springfield, and so did I, and he knew that if there was a mistake in regard to them, that I had nothing under heaven to do with it. Besides, you find that in all these northern counties where the Republican candidates are running pledged to him, that the conventions which nominated them adopted that identical platform. One cardinal point in that platform which he shrinks from is this — that there shall be no more slave States admitted into the Union, even if the people want them. Lovejoy stands pledged against the admission of any more slave States. ["Right; so do we."] So do you, you say. Farnsworth stands pledged against the admission of any more slave States. Washburne stands pledged the same way. The candidate for the legislature who is running on Lincoln's ticket in Henderson and Warren stands committed by his vote in the legislature to the same thing, and I am informed, but do not know of the fact, that your candidate here is also so pledged. ["Hurrah for him! Good!"] Now, you Republicans all hurrah for him, and for the doctrine of " no more slave States," and yet Lincoln tells you that his conscience will not permit him to sanction that doctrine, and complains because the resolutions I read at Ottawa made him, as a member of the party, responsible for sanctioning the doctrine of no more slave States. You are one way, you confess, and he is or pretends to be the other, and yet you are both governed by principle in supporting one another. If it be true, as I have shown it is, that the whole Republican party in the northern part of the State stands committed to the doctrine of no more slave States, and that this same doctrine is repudiated by the Republicans in the other part of the State, I wonder whether Mr. Lincoln and his party do not present the case which he cited from the Scriptures, of a house divided against itself which cannot stand! I desire to know what are Mr. Lincoln's principles and the principles of his party. I hold, and the party with which I am identified holds, that the people of each State, old and new, have the right to decide the slavery question for themselves, and when I used the remark that I did not care whether slavery was voted up or down, I used it in the connection that I was for allowing Kansas to do just as she pleased on the slavery question. I said that I did not care whether they voted slavery up or down, because they had the right to do as they pleased on the question, and therefore my action would not be controlled by any such consideration. Why cannot Abraham Lincoln, and the party with which he acts, speak out their principles so that they may be understood? Why do they claim to be one thing in one part of the State and another in the other part? Whenever I allude to the Abolition doctrines, which he considers a slander to be charged with being in favor of, you all indorse them, and hurrah for them, not knowing that your candidate is ashamed to acknowledge them.

I have a few words to say upon the Dred Scott decision, which has troubled the brain of Mr. Lincoln so much. He insists that that decision would carry slavery into the free States, notwithstanding that the decision says directly the opposite; and goes into a long argument to make you believe that I am in favor of, and would sanction, the doctrine that would allow slaves to be brought here and held as slaves contrary to our constitution and laws. Mr. Lincoln knew better when he asserted this; he knew that one newspaper, and so far as is within my knowledge but one, ever asserted that doctrine, and that I was the first man in either House of Congress that read that article in debate, and denounced it on the floor of the Senate as revolutionary. When the Washington "Union," on the 17th of last November, published an article to that effect, I branded it at once, and denounced it, and hence the "Union" has been pursuing me ever since. Mr. Toombs, of Georgia, replied to me, and said that there was not a man in any of the slave States south of the Potomac River that held any such doctrine. Mr. Lincoln knows that there is not a member of the Supreme Court who holds that doctrine; he knows that every one of them, as shown by their opinions, holds the reverse. Why this attempt, then, to bring the Supreme Court into disrepute among the people? It looks as if there was an effort being made to destroy public confidence in the highest judicial tribunal on earth. Suppose he succeeds in destroying public confidence in the court, so that the people will not respect its decisions, but will feel at liberty to disregard them, and resist the laws of the land, what will he have gained? He will have changed the government from one of laws into that of a mob, in which the strong arm of violence will be substituted for the decisions of the courts of justice. He complains because I did not go into an argument reviewing Chief Justice Taney's opinion, and the other opinions of the different judges, to determine whether their reasoning is right or wrong on the questions of law. What use would that be? He wants to take an appeal from the Supreme Court to this meeting to determine whether the questions of law were decided properly. He is going to appeal from the Supreme Court of the United States to every town meeting, in the hope that he can excite a prejudice against that court, and on the wave of that prejudice ride into the Senate of the United States, when he could not get there on his own principles, or his own merits. Suppose he should succeed in getting into the Senate of the United States, what then will he have to do with the decision of the Supreme Court in the Dred Scott case? Can he reverse that decision when he gets there? Can he act upon it? Has the Senate any right to reverse it or revise it? He will not pretend that it has. Then why drag the matter into this contest, unless for the purpose of making a false issue, by which he can divert public attention from the real issue.

He has cited General Jackson in justification of the war he is making on the decision of the court. Mr. Lincoln misunderstands the history of the country if he believes there is any parallel in the two cases. It is true that the Supreme Court once decided that if a bank of the United States was a necessary fiscal agent of the government it was constitutional, and if not, that it was unconstitutional, and also, that whether or not it was necessary for that purpose was a political question for Congress, and not a judicial one for the courts to determine. Hence the court would not determine the bank unconstitutional. Jackson respected the decision, obeyed the law, executed it, and carried it into effect during its existence; but after the charter of the bank expired, and a proposition was made to create a new bank, General Jackson said: "It is unnecessary and improper, and therefore I am against it on constitutional grounds as well as those of expediency." Is Congress bound to pass every act that is constitutional? Why, there are a thousand things that are constitutional, but yet are inexpedient and unnecessary, and you surely would not vote for them merely because you had the right to? And because General Jackson would not do a thing which he had a right to do, but did not deem expedient or proper, Mr. Lincoln is going to justify himself in doing that which he has no right to do. I ask him whether he is not bound to respect and obey the decisions of the Supreme Court as well as I? The Constitution has created that court to decide all constitutional questions in the last resort, and when such decisions have been made they become the law of the land, and you, and he, and myself, and every other good citizen are bound by them. Yet he argues that I am bound by their decisions, and he is not. He says that their decisions are binding on Democrats, but not on Republicans. Are not Republicans bound by the laws of the land as well as Democrats? And when the court has fixed the construction of the Constitution on the validity of a given law, is not their decision binding upon Republicans as well as upon Democrats? Is it possible that you Republicans have the right to raise your mobs and oppose the laws of the land and the constituted authorities, and yet hold us Democrats bound to obey them? My time is within half a minute of expiring, and all I have to say is that I stand by the laws of the land. I stand by the Constitution as our fathers made it, by the laws as they are enacted, and by the decisions of the court upon all points within their jurisdiction as they are pronounced by the highest tribunal on earth; and any man who resists these must resort to mob-law and violence to overturn the government of laws.

October 13, 1858.— SIXTH JOINT DEBATE, AT QUINCY, ILLINOIS.

Mr. Lincoln's Opening Speech.

Ladies and Gentlemen : I have had no immediate conference with Judge Douglas, but I will venture to say that he and I will perfectly agree that your entire silence, both when I speak and when he speaks, will be most agreeable to us.

In the month of May, 1856, the elements in the State of Illinois which have since been consolidated into the Republican party assembled together in a State convention at Bloomington. They adopted at that time what, in political language, is called a platform. In June of the same year, the elements of the Republican party in the nation assembled together in a national convention at Philadelphia. They adopted what is called the national platform. In June, 1858,— the present year,—the Republicans of Illinois reassembled at Springfield in State convention, and adopted again their platform, as I suppose, not differing in any essential particular from either of the former ones, but perhaps adding something in relation to the new developments of political progress in the country.

The convention that assembled in June last did me the honor, if it be one, and I esteem it such, to nominate me as their candidate for the United States Senate. I have supposed that, in entering upon this canvass, I stood generally upon these platforms. We are now met together on the 13th of October of the same year, only four months from the adoption of the last platform, and I am unaware that in this canvass, from the beginning until to-day, any one of our adversaries has taken hold of our platforms, or laid his finger upon anything he calls wrong in them.

In the very first one of these joint discussions between Senator Douglas and myself, Senator Douglas, without alluding at all to these platforms, or to any one of them, of which I have spoken, attempted to hold me responsible for a set of resolutions passed long before the meeting of either one of these conventions of which I have spoken. And as a ground for holding me responsible for these resolutions, he assumed that they had been passed at a State convention of the Republican party, and that I took part in that convention. It was discovered afterward that this was erroneous, that the resolutions which he endeavored to hold me responsible for had not been passed by any State convention anywhere, had not been passed at Springfield, where he supposed they had, or assumed that they had, and that they had been passed in no convention in which I had taken part. The judge, nevertheless, was not willing to give up the point that he was endeavoring to make upon me, and he therefore thought to still hold me to the point that he was endeavoring to make, by showing that the resolutions that he read had been passed at a local convention in the northern part of the State, although it was not a local convention that embraced my residence at all, nor one that reached, as I suppose, nearer than one hundred and fifty or two hundred miles of where I was when it met, nor one in which I took any part at all. He also introduced other resolutions, passed at other meetings, and by combining the whole, although they were all antecedent to the two State conventions, and the one national convention I have mentioned, still he insisted and now insists, as I understand, that I am in some way responsible for them.

At Jonesboro, on our third meeting, I insisted to the judge that I was in no way rightfully held responsible for the proceedings of this local meeting or convention in which I had taken no part, and in which I was in no way embraced; but I insisted to him that if he thought I was responsible for every man or every set of men everywhere, who happen to be my friends, the rule ought to work both ways, and he ought to be responsible for the acts and resolutions of all men or sets of men who were or are now his supporters and friends, and gave him a pretty long string of resolutions, passed by men who are now his friends, and announcing doctrines for which he does not desire to be held responsible.

This still does not satisfy Judge Douglas. He still adheres to his proposition, that I am responsible for what some of my friends in different parts of the State have done; but that he is not responsible for what his have done. At least, so I understand him. But, in addition to that, the judge, at our meeting in Galesburg last week, undertakes to establish that I am guilty of a species of double-dealing with the public—that I make speeches of a certain sort in the North, among the Abolitionists, which I would not make in the South, and that I make speeches of a certain sort in the South which I would not make in the North. I apprehend, in the course I have marked out for myself, that I shall not have to dwell at very great length upon this subject.

As this was done in the judge's opening speech at Galesburg, I had an opportunity, as I had the middle speech then, of saying something in answer to it. He brought forward a quotation or two from a speech of mine, delivered at Chicago, and then, to contrast with it, he brought forward an extract from a speech of mine at Charleston, in which he insisted that I was greatly inconsistent, and insisted that his conclusion followed that I was playing a double part, and speaking in one region one way, and in another region another way. I have not time now to dwell on this as long as I would like, and wish only now to requote that portion of my speech at Charleston, which the judge quoted, and then make some comments upon it. This he quotes from me as being delivered at Charleston, and I believe correctly:

I will say, then, that I am not, nor ever have been, in favor of bringing about in any way the social and political equality of the white and black races — that I am not nor ever have been in favor of making voters or jurors of negroes, nor of qualifying them to hold office, nor to intermarry with white people; and I will say in addition to this that there is a physical difference between the white and black races which will ever forbid the two races living together on terms of social and political equality. And inasmuch as they cannot so live, while they do remain together, there must be the position of superior and inferior, and I, as much as any other man, am in favor of having the superior position assigned to the white race.

This, I believe, is the entire quotation from the Charleston speech, as Judge Douglas made it. His comments are as follows:

Yes, here you find men who hurrah for Lincoln, and say he is right when he discards all distinction between races, or when he declares that he discards the doctrine that there is such a thing as a superior and inferior race; and Abolitionists are required and expected to vote for Mr. Lincoln because he goes for the equality of races, holding that in the Declaration of Independence the white man and negro were declared equal, and endowed by divine law with equality. And down South with the old-line Whigs, with the Kentuckians, the Virginians, and the Tennesseeans, he tells you that there is a physical difference between the races, making the one superior, the other inferior, and he is in favor of maintaining the superiority of the white race over the negro.

Those are the judge's comments. Now I wish to show you, that a month, or only lacking three days of a month, before I made the speech at Charleston which the judge quotes from, he had himself heard me say substantially the same thing. It was in our first meeting, at Ottawa, and I will say a word about where it was, and the atmosphere it was in, after a while—but at our first meeting, at Ottawa, I read an extract from an old speech of mine, made nearly four years ago, not merely to show my sentiments, but to show that my sentiments were long entertained and openly expressed; in which extract I expressly declared that my own feelings would not admit of a social and political equality between the white and black races, and that even if my own feelings would admit of it, I still knew that the public sentiment of the country would not, and that such a thing was an utter impossibility, or substantially that. That extract from my old speech, the reporters, by some sort of accident, passed over, and it was not reported. I lay no blame upon anybody. I suppose they thought that I would hand it over to them, and dropped reporting while I was reading it, but afterward went away without getting it from me. At the end of that quotation from my old speech, which I read at Ottawa, I made the comments which were reported at that time, and which I will now read, and ask you to notice how very nearly they are the same as Judge Douglas says were delivered by me, down in Egypt. After reading I added these words:

Now, gentlemen, I don't want to read at any greater length, but this is the true complexion of all I have ever said in regard to the institution of slavery, or the black race, and this is the whole of it; and anything that argues me into his idea of perfect social and political equality with the negro is but a specious and fantastical arrangement of words by which a man can prove a horse-chestnut to be a chestnut horse. I will say here, while upon this subject, that I have no purpose, directly or indirectly, to interfere with the institution of slavery in the States where it exists. I believe I have no lawful right to do so, and I have no inclination to do so. I have no purpose to introduce political and social equality between the white and black races. There is a physical difference between the two, which, in my judgment, will probably forever forbid their living together on the footing of perfect equality, and, inasmuch as it becomes a necessity that there must be a difference, I, as well as Judge Douglas, am in favor of the race to which I belong having the superior position. I have never said anything to the contrary, but I hold that, notwithstanding all this, there is no reason in the world why the negro is not entitled to all the natural rights enumerated in the Declaration of Independence—the right to life, liberty, and the pursuit of happiness. I hold that he is as much entitled to these as the white man. I agree with

Judge Douglas that he is not my equal in many respects, certainly not in color—perhaps not in intellectual and moral endowments; but in the right to eat the bread, without the leave of anybody else, which his own hand earns, he is my equal, and the equal of Judge Douglas, and the equal of every living man.

I have chiefly introduced this for the purpose of meeting the judge's charge that the quotation he took from my Charleston speech was what I would say down south among the Kentuckians, the Virginians, etc., but would not say in the regions in which was supposed to be more of the Abolition element. I now make this comment: that speech from which I have now read the quotation, and which is there given correctly, perhaps too much so for good taste, was made away up north in the Abolition district of this State *par excellence*—in the Lovejoy district—in the personal presence of Lovejoy; for he was on the stand with us when I made it. It had been made and put in print in that region only three days less than a month before the speech made at Charleston, the like of which Judge Douglas thinks I would not make where there was any Abolition element. I only refer to this matter to say that I am altogether unconscious of having attempted any double-dealing anywhere; that upon one occasion I may say one thing and leave other things unsaid, and *vice versa;* but that I have said anything on one occasion that is inconsistent with what I have said elsewhere, I deny—at least, I deny it so far as the intention is concerned. I find that I have devoted to this topic a larger portion of my time than I had intended. I wished to show—but I will pass it upon this occasion—that in the sentiment I have occasionally advanced upon the Declaration of Independence, I am entirely borne out by the sentiments advanced by our old Whig leader, Henry Clay, and I have the book here to show it from; but because I have already occupied more time than I intended to do on that topic, I pass over it.

At Galesburg I tried to show that by the Dred Scott decision, pushed to its legitimate consequences, slavery would be established in all the States as well as in the Territories. I did this because, upon a former occasion, I had asked Judge Douglas whether, if the Supreme Court should make a decision declaring that the States had not the power to exclude slavery from their limits, he would adopt and follow that decision as a rule of political action; and because he had not directly answered that question, but had merely contented himself with sneering at it, I again introduced it, and tried to show that the conclusion that I stated followed inevitably and logically from the proposition already decided by the court. Judge Douglas had the privilege of replying to me at Galesburg, and again he gave me no direct answer as to whether he would or would not sustain such decision if made. I give him this third chance to say yes or no. He is not obliged to do either,—probably he will not do either,—but I give him the third chance. I tried to show then that this result, this conclusion, inevitably followed from the point already decided by the court. The judge, in his reply, again sneers at the thought of the court making any such decision, and in the course of his remarks upon this subject, uses the language which I will now read. Speaking of me, the judge says: "He goes on and insists that the Dred Scott decision would carry slavery into the free States, notwithstanding the decision itself says the contrary." And he adds: "Mr. Lincoln knows that there is no member of the Supreme Court that holds that doctrine. He knows that every one of them in their opinions held the reverse."

I especially introduce this subject again for the purpose of saying that I have the Dred Scott decision here, and I will thank Judge Douglas to lay his finger upon the place in the entire opinions of the court where any one of them "says the contrary." It is very hard to affirm a negative with entire confidence. I say, however, that I have examined that decision with a good deal of care, as a lawyer examines a decision, and so far as I have been able to do so, the court has nowhere in its opinions said that the States have the power to exclude slavery, nor have they used other language substantially that. I also say, so far as I can find, not one of the concurring judges has said that the States can exclude slavery, nor said anything that was substantially that. The nearest approach that any one of them has made to it, so far as I can find, was by Judge Nelson, and the approach he made to it was exactly, in substance, the Nebraska bill — that the States had the exclusive power over the question of slavery, so far as they are not limited by the Constitution of the United States. I ask the question, therefore, if the non-concurring judges, McLean or Curtis, had asked to get an express declaration that the States could absolutely exclude slavery from their limits, what reason have we to believe that it would not have been voted down by the majority of the judges, just as Chase's amendment was voted down by Judge Douglas and his compeers when it was offered to the Nebraska bill?

Also at Galesburg I said something in regard to those Springfield resolutions that Judge Douglas had attempted to use upon me at Ottawa, and commented at some length upon the fact that they were, as presented, not genuine. Judge Douglas in his reply to me seemed to be somewhat exasperated. He said he never would have believed that Abraham Lincoln, as he kindly called me, would have attempted such a thing as I had attempted upon that occasion; and among other expressions which he used toward me, was that I dared to say forgery — that I had dared to say forgery [turning to Judge Douglas]. Yes, judge, I did dare to say forgery. But in this political canvass the judge ought to remember that I was not the first who dared to say forgery. At Jacksonville Judge Douglas made a speech in answer to something said by Judge Trumbull, and at the close of what he said upon that subject, he dared to say that Trumbull had forged his evidence. He said, too, that he should not concern himself with Trumbull any more, but thereafter he should hold Lincoln responsible for the slanders upon him. When I met him at Charleston after that, although I think that I should not have noticed the subject if he had not said he would hold me responsible for it, I spread out before him the statements of the evidence that Judge Trumbull had used, and I asked Judge Douglas, piece by piece, to put his finger upon one piece of all that evidence that he would say was a forgery. When I went through with each and every piece, Judge Douglas did not dare then to say that any piece of it was a forgery. So it seems that there are some things that Judge Douglas dares to do, and some that he dares not to do. [A voice: "It's the same thing with you."]   Yes, sir, it's the same thing with me.

I do dare to say forgery when it's true, and don't dare to say forgery when it's false. Now, I will say here to this audience and to Judge Douglas, I have not dared to say he committed a forgery, and I never shall until I know it; but I did dare to say — just to suggest to the judge — that a forgery had been committed, which by his own showing had been traced to him and two of his friends. I dared to suggest to him that he had expressly promised in one of his public speeches to investigate that matter, and I dared to suggest to him that there was an implied promise that when he investigated it he would make known the result. I dared to suggest to the judge that he could not expect to be quite clear of suspicion of that fraud, for since the time that promise was made he had been with those friends, and had not kept his promise in regard to the investigation and the report upon it. I am not a very daring man, but I dared that much, judge, and I am not much scared about it yet. When the judge says he would n't have believed of Abraham Lincoln that he would have made such an attempt as that, he reminds me of the fact that he entered upon this canvass with the purpose to treat me courteously; that touched me somewhat. It set me to thinking. I was aware, when it was first agreed that Judge Douglas and I were to have these seven joint discussions, that they were the successive acts of a drama — perhaps I should say, to be enacted not merely in the face of audiences like this, but in the face of the nation, and to some extent, by my relation to him, and not from anything in myself, in the face of the world; and I am anxious that they should be conducted with dignity and in the good temper which would be befitting the vast audience before which it was conducted. But when Judge Douglas got home from Washington and made his first speech in Chicago, the evening afterward I made some sort of a reply to it. His second speech was made at Bloomington, in which he commented upon my speech at Chicago, and said that I had used language ingeniously contrived to conceal my intentions, or words to that effect. Now I understand that this is an imputation upon my veracity and my candor. I do not know what the judge understood by it, but in our first discussion at Ottawa, he led off by charging a bargain, somewhat corrupt in its character, upon Trumbull and myself — that we had entered into a bargain, one of the terms of which was that Trumbull was to Abolitionize the old Democratic party, and I, Lincoln, was to Abolitionize the Old Whig party — I pretending to be as good an old-line Whig as ever. Judge Douglas may not understand that he implicated my truthfulness and my honor when he said I was doing one thing and pretending another; and I misunderstood him if he thought he was treating me in a dignified way, as a man of honor and truth, as he now claims he was disposed to treat me. Even after that time, at Galesburg, when he brings forward an extract from a speech made at Chicago, and an extract from a speech made at Charleston, to prove that I was trying to play a double part,— that I was trying to cheat the public, and get votes upon one set of principles at one place and upon another set of principles at another place,— I do not understand but what he impeaches my honor, my veracity, and my candor; and because he does this, I do not understand that I am bound, if I see a truthful ground for it, to keep my hands off of him. As soon as I learned that Judge Douglas was disposed to treat me in this way, I signified in one of my speeches that I should be driven to draw upon whatever of humble resources I might have — to adopt a new course with him. I was not entirely sure that I should be able to hold my own with him, but I at least had the purpose made to do as well as I could upon him; and now I say that I will not be the first to cry "Hold!" I think it originated with the judge, and when he quits, I probably will. But I shall not ask any favors at all. He asks me, or he asks the audience, if I wish to push this matter to the point of personal difficulty. I tell him, No. He did not make a mistake, in one of his early speeches, when he called me an "amiable" man, though perhaps he did when he called me an "intelligent" man. It really hurts me very much to suppose that I have wronged anybody on earth. I again tell him, No! I very much prefer, when this canvass shall be over, however it may result, that we at least part without any bitter recollections of personal difficulties.

The judge, in his concluding speech at Galesburg, says that I was pushing this matter to a personal difficulty to avoid the responsibility for the enormity of my principles. I say to the judge and this audience now, that I will again state our principles as well as I hastily can in all their enormity, and if the judge hereafter chooses to confine himself to a war upon these principles, he will probably not find me departing from the same course.

We have in this nation the element of domestic slavery. It is a matter of absolute certainty that it is a disturbing element. It is the opinion of all the great men who have expressed an opinion upon it, that it is a dangerous element. We keep up a controversy in regard to it. That controversy necessarily springs from difference of opinion, and if we can learn exactly — can reduce to the lowest elements — what that difference of opinion is, we perhaps shall be better prepared for discussing the different systems of policy that we would propose in regard to that disturbing element. I suggest that the difference of opinion, reduced to its lowest terms, is no other than the difference between the men who think slavery a wrong and those who do not think it wrong. The Republican party think it wrong — we think it is a moral, a social, and a political wrong. We think it is a wrong not confining itself merely to the persons or the States where it exists, but that it is a wrong which in its tendency, to say the least, affects the existence of the whole nation. Because we think it wrong, we propose a course of policy that shall deal with it as a wrong. We deal with it as with any other wrong, in so far as we can prevent its growing any larger, and so deal with it that in the run of time there may be some promise of an end to it. We have a due regard to the actual presence of it amongst us, and the difficulties of getting rid of it in any satisfactory way, and all the constitutional obligations thrown about it. I suppose that in reference both to its actual existence in the nation, and to our constitutional obligations, we have no right at all to disturb it in the States where it exists, and we profess that we have no more inclination to disturb it than we have the right to do it. We go further than that: we don't propose to disturb it where, in one instance, we think the Constitution would permit us. We think the Constitution would permit us to disturb it in the District of Columbia. Still we do not propose to do that, unless it should be in terms which I don't suppose the nation is very likely soon to agree to—the terms of making the emancipation gradual and compensating the unwilling owners. Where we suppose we have the constitutional right, we restrain ourselves in reference to the actual existence of the institution and the difficulties thrown about it. We also oppose it as an evil so far as it seeks to spread itself. We insist on the policy that shall restrict it to its present limits. We don't suppose that in doing this we violate anything due to the actual presence of the institution, or anything due to the constitutional guaranties thrown around it.

We oppose the Dred Scott decision in a certain way, upon which I ought perhaps to address you a few words. We do not propose that when Dred Scott has been decided to be a slave by the court, we, as a mob, will decide him to be free. We do not propose that, when any other one, or one thousand, shall be decided by that court to be slaves, we will in any violent way disturb the rights of property thus settled; but we nevertheless do oppose that decision as a political rule, which shall be binding on the voter to vote for nobody who thinks it wrong, which shall be binding on the members of Congress or the President to favor no measure that does not actually concur with the principles of that decision. We do not propose to be bound by it as a political rule in that way, because we think it lays the foundation not merely of enlarging and spreading out what we consider an evil, but it lays the foundation for spreading that evil into the States themselves. We propose so resisting it as to have it reversed if we can, and a new judicial rule established upon this subject.

I will add this, that if there be any man who does not believe that slavery is wrong in the three aspects which I have mentioned, or in any one of them, that man is misplaced and ought to leave us. While, on the other hand, if there be any man in the Republican party who is impatient over the necessity springing from its actual presence, and is impatient of the constitutional guaranties thrown around it, and would act in disregard of these, he too is misplaced, standing with us. He will find his place somewhere else; for we have a due regard, so far as we are capable of understanding them, for all these things. This, gentlemen, as well as I can give it, is a plain statement of our principles in all their enormity.

I will say now that there is a sentiment in the country contrary to me—a sentiment which holds that slavery is not wrong, and therefore it goes for the policy that does not propose dealing with it as a wrong. That policy is the Democratic policy, and that sentiment is the Democratic sentiment. If there be a doubt in the mind of any one of this vast audience that this is really the central idea of the Democratic party, in relation to this subject, I ask him to bear with me while I state a few things tending, as I think, to prove that proposition. In the first place, the leading man—I think I may do my friend Judge Douglas the honor of calling him such—advocating the present Democratic policy never himself says it is wrong. He has the high distinction, so far as I know, of never having said slavery is either right or wrong. Almost everybody else says one or the other, but the judge never does. If there be a man in the Democratic party who thinks it is wrong, and yet clings to that party, I suggest to him in the first place that his leader don't talk as he does, for he never says that it is wrong. In the second place, I suggest to him that if he will examine the policy proposed to be carried forward, he will find that he carefully excludes the idea that there is anything wrong in it. If you will examine the arguments that are made on it, you will find that every one carefully excludes the idea that there is anything wrong in slavery. Perhaps that Democrat who says he is as much opposed to slavery as I am, will tell me that I am wrong about this. I wish him to examine his own course in regard to this matter a moment, and then see if his opinion will not be changed a little. You say it is wrong; but don't you constantly object to anybody else saying so? Do you not constantly argue that this is not the right place to oppose it? You say it must not be opposed in the free States, because slavery is not there; it must not be opposed in the slave States, because it is there; it must not be opposed in politics, because that will make a fuss; it must not be opposed in the pulpit, because it is not religion. Then where is the place to oppose it? There is no suitable place to oppose it. There is no plan in the country to oppose this evil overspreading the continent, which you say yourself is coming. Frank Blair and Gratz Brown tried to get up a system of gradual emancipation in Missouri, had an election in August, and got beat; and you, Mr. Democrat, threw up your hat and hallooed, "Hurrah for Democracy!"

So I say again, that in regard to the arguments that are made, when Judge Douglas says he "don't care whether slavery is voted up or voted down," whether he means that as an individual expression of sentiment, or only as a sort of statement of his views on national policy, it is alike true to say that he can thus argue logically if he don't see anything wrong in it; but he cannot say so logically if he admits that slavery is wrong. He cannot say that he would as soon see a wrong voted up as voted down. When Judge Douglas says that whoever or whatever community wants slaves, they have a right to have them, he is perfectly logical if there is nothing wrong in the institution; but if you admit that it is wrong, he cannot logically say that anybody has a right to do wrong. When he says that slave property and horse and hog property are alike to be allowed to go into the Territories, upon the principles of equality, he is reasoning truly if there is no difference between them as property; but if the one is property, held rightfully, and the other is wrong, then there is no equality between the right and wrong; so that, turn it in any way you can, in all the arguments sustaining the Democratic policy, and in that policy itself, there is a careful, studied exclusion of the idea that there is anything wrong in slavery. Let us understand this. I am not, just here, trying to prove that we are right and they are wrong. I have been stating where we and they stand, and trying to show what is the real difference between us; and I now say that whenever we can get the question distinctly stated,—can get all these men who believe that slavery is in some of these respects wrong, to stand and act with us in treating it as a wrong,—then, and not till then, I think, will we in some way come to an end of this slavery agitation.

Mr. Douglas's Reply in the Quincy Joint Debate.

Ladies and Gentlemen: Permit me to say that unless silence is observed it will be impossible for me to be heard by this immense crowd, and my friends can confer no higher favor upon me than by omitting all expressions of applause or approbation. I desire to be heard rather than to be applauded. I wish to address myself to your reason, your judgment, your sense of justice, and not to your passions.

I regret that Mr. Lincoln should have deemed it proper for him to again indulge in gross personalities and base insinuations in regard to the Springfield resolutions. It has imposed upon me the necessity of using some portion of my time for the purpose of calling your attention to the facts of the case, and it will then be for you to say what you think of a man who can predicate such a charge upon the circumstances he has in this. I had seen the platform adopted by a Republican congressional convention held in Aurora, the second congressional district, in September, 1854, published as purporting to be the platform of the Republican party. That platform declared that the Republican party was pledged never to admit another slave State into the Union, and also that it was pledged to prohibit slavery in all the Territories of the United States,—not only all that we then had, but all that we should thereafter acquire,—and to repeal unconditionally the fugitive-slave law, abolish slavery in the District of Columbia, and prohibit the slave-trade between the different States. These and other articles against slavery were contained in this platform, and unanimously adopted by the Republican congressional convention in that district. I had also seen that the Republican congressional conventions at Rockford, in the first district, and at Bloomington, in the third, had adopted the same platform that year, nearly word for word, and had declared it to be the platform of the Republican party. I had noticed that Major Thomas L. Harris, a member of Congress from the Springfield district, had referred to that platform in a speech in Congress, as having been adopted by the first Republican State convention which assembled in Illinois. When I had occasion to use the fact in this canvass, I wrote to Major Harris to know on what day that convention was held, and to ask him to send me its proceedings. He being sick, Charles H. Lanphier answered my letter by sending me the published proceedings of the convention held at

Springfield on the 5th of October, 1854, as they appeared in the report of the "State Register." I read those resolutions from that newspaper the same as any of you would refer back and quote any fact from the files of a newspaper which had published it. Mr. Lincoln pretends that after I had so quoted those resolutions he discovered that they had never been adopted at Springfield. He does not deny their adoption by the Republican party at Aurora, at Bloomington, and at Rockford, and by nearly all the Republican county conventions in northern Illinois where his party is in a majority; but merely because they were not adopted on the "spot" on which I said they were, he chooses to quibble about the place rather than meet and discuss the merits of the resolutions themselves. I stated when I quoted them that I did so from the "State Register." I gave my authority. Lincoln believed at the time, as he has since admitted, that they had been adopted at Springfield, as published. Does he believe now that I did not tell the truth when I quoted those resolutions? He knows in his heart that I quoted them in good faith, believing at the time that they had been adopted at Springfield. I would consider myself an infamous wretch if, under such circumstances, I could charge any man with being a party to a trick or a fraud. And I will tell him, too, that it will not do to charge a forgery on Charles H. Lanphier or Thomas L. Harris. No man on earth, who knows them, and knows Lincoln, would take his oath against their word. There are not two men in the State of Illinois who have higher characters for truth, for integrity, for moral character, and for elevation of tone, as gentlemen, than Mr. Lanphier and Mr. Harris. Any man who attempts to make such charges as Mr. Lincoln has indulged in against them, only proclaims himself a slanderer.

I will now show you that I stated with entire fairness, as soon as it was made known to me, that there was a mistake about the spot where the resolutions had been adopted, although their truthfulness, as a declaration of the principles of the Republican party, had not and could not be questioned. I did not wait for Lincoln to point out the mistake; but the moment I discovered it, I made a speech, and published it to the world, correcting the error. I corrected it myself, as a gentleman and an honest man, and as I always feel proud to do when I have made a mistake. I wish Mr. Lincoln could show that he has acted with equal fairness and truthfulness when I have convinced him that he has been mistaken. I will give you an illustration to show you how he acts in a similar case: In a speech at Springfield he charged Chief Justice Taney and his associates, President Pierce, President Buchanan, and myself, with having entered into a conspiracy at the time the Nebraska bill was introduced, by which the Dred Scott decision was to be made by the Supreme Court, in order to carry slavery everywhere under the Constitution. I called his attention to the fact that at the time alluded to—to wit, the introduction of the Nebraska bill—it was not possible that such a conspiracy could have been entered into, for the reason that the Dred Scott case had never been taken before the Supreme Court, and was not taken before it for a year after; and I asked him to take back that charge. Did he do it? I showed him that it was impossible that the charge could be true; I proved it by the record, and I then called upon him to retract his false charge. What was his answer? Instead of coming out like an honest man and doing so, he reiterated the charge, and said that if the case had not gone up to the Supreme Court from the courts of Missouri at the time he charged that the judges of the Supreme Court entered into the conspiracy, yet that there was an understanding with the Democratic owners of Dred Scott that they would take it up. I have since asked him who the Democratic owners of Dred Scott were, but he could not tell. And why? Because there were no such Democratic owners in existence. Dred Scott at the time was owned by the Rev. Dr. Chaffee, an Abolition member of Congress, of Springfield, Massachusetts, in right of his wife. He was owned by one of Lincoln's friends, and not by Democrats at all; his case was conducted in court by Abolition lawyers, so that both the prosecution and the defense were in the hands of the Abolition political friends of Mr. Lincoln.

Notwithstanding I thus proved by the record that his charge against the Supreme Court was false, instead of taking it back, he resorted to another false charge to sustain the infamy of it. He also charged President Buchanan with having been a party to the conspiracy. I directed his attention to the fact that the charge could not possibly be true, for the reason that at the time specified Mr. Buchanan was not in America, but was three thousand miles off, representing the United States at the Court of St. James, and had been there for a year previous, and did not return till three years afterward. Yet I never could get Mr. Lincoln to take back his false charge, although I have called upon him over and over again. He refuses to do it, and either remains silent or resorts to other tricks to try and palm his slander off on the country. Therein you will find the difference between Mr. Lincoln and myself. When I make a mistake, as an honest man I correct it without being asked to do so; but when he makes a false charge, he sticks to it and never corrects it. One word more in regard to these resolutions: I quoted them at Ottawa merely to ask Mr. Lincoln whether he stood on that platform. That was the purpose for which I quoted them. I did not think that I had a right to put idle questions to him, and I first laid a foundation for my questions by showing that the principles which I wished him either to affirm or deny had been adopted by some portion of his friends, at least, as their creed. Hence I read the resolutions, and put the questions to him, and he then refused to answer them. Subsequently—one week afterward—he did answer a part of them, but the others he has not answered up to this day.

Now let me call your attention for a moment to the answers which Mr. Lincoln made at Freeport to the questions which I propounded to him at Ottawa, based upon the platform adopted by a majority of the Abolition counties of the State, which now, as then, supported him. In answer to my question whether he indorsed the Black Republican principle of "no more slave States," he answered that he was not pledged against the admission of any more slave States, but that he would be very sorry if he should ever be placed in a position where he would have to vote on the question; that he would rejoice to know that no more slave States would be admitted into the Union; "but," he added, "if slavery shall be kept out of the Territories during the territorial existence of any one given Territory, and then the people shall, having a fair chance and a clear field when they come to adopt the constitution, do such an extraordinary thing as to adopt a slave constitution, uninfluenced by the actual presence of the institution among them, I see no alternative, if we own the country, but to admit them into the Union." The point I wish him to answer is this: Suppose Congress should not prohibit slavery in the Territory, and it applied for admission with a constitution recognizing slavery, then how would he vote? His answer at Freeport does not apply to any Territory in America. I ask you [turning to Lincoln], will you vote to admit Kansas into the Union, with just such a constitution as her people want, with slavery or without, as they shall determine? He will not answer. I have put that question to him time and time again, and have not been able to get an answer out of him. I ask you again, Lincoln, will you vote to admit New Mexico, when she has the requisite population, with such a constitution as her people adopt, either recognizing slavery or not, as they shall determine? He will not answer. I put the same question to him in reference to Oregon and the new States to be carved out of Texas in pursuance of the contract between Texas and the United States, and he will not answer. He will not answer these questions in reference to any Territory now in existence, but says that if Congress should prohibit slavery in a Territory, and when its people asked for admission as a State they should adopt slavery as one of their institutions, that he supposes he would have to let it come in. I submit to you whether that answer of his to my question does not justify me in saying that he has a fertile genius in devising language to conceal his thoughts. I ask you whether there is an intelligent man in America who does not believe that that answer was made for the purpose of concealing what he intended to do. He wished to make the old-line Whigs believe that he would stand by the compromise measures of 1850, which declared that the States might come into the Union with slavery, or without, as they pleased, while Lovejoy and his Abolition allies up north explained to the Abolitionists that in taking this ground he preached good Abolition doctrine, because his proviso would not apply to any Territory in America, and therefore there was no chance of his being governed by it. It would have been quite easy for him to have said that he would let the people of a State do just as they pleased, if he desired to convey such an idea. Why did he not do it? He would not answer my question directly because, up north, the Abolition creed declares that there shall be no more slave States, while down south, in Adams County, in Coles, and in Sangamon, he and his friends are afraid to advance that doctrine. Therefore he gives an evasive and equivocal answer, to be construed one way in the south and another way in the north, which, when analyzed, it is apparent is not an answer at all with reference to any Territory now in existence.

Mr. Lincoln complains that, in my speech the other day at Galesburg, I read an extract from a speech delivered by him at Chicago, and then another from his speech at Charleston, and compared them, thus showing the people that he had one set of principles in one part of the State and another in the other part. And how does he answer that charge? Why, he quotes from his Charleston speech as I quoted from it, and then quotes another extract from a speech which he made at another place, which he says is the same as the extract from his speech at Charleston; but he does not quote the extract from his Chicago speech, upon which I convicted him of double-dealing. I quoted from his Chicago speech to prove that he held one set of principles up north among the Abolitionists, and from his Charleston speech to prove that he held another set down at Charleston and in southern Illinois. In his answer to this charge, he ignores entirely his Chicago speech, and merely argues that he said the same thing which he said at Charleston at another place. If he did, it follows that he has twice, instead of once, held one creed in one part of the State, and a different creed in another part. Up at Chicago, in the opening of the campaign, he reviewed my reception speech, and undertook to answer my argument attacking his favorite doctrine of negro equality. I had shown that it was a falsification of the Declaration of Independence to pretend that that instrument applied to and included negroes in the clause declaring that all men are created equal. What was Lincoln's reply? I will read from his Chicago speech, and the one which he did not quote, and dare not quote, in this part of the State. He said:

I should like to know if, taking this old Declaration of Independence, which declares that all men are equal upon principle, and making exceptions to it, where will it stop? If one man says it does not mean a negro, why may not another man say it does not mean another man? If that declaration is not the truth, let us get this statute-book in which we find it and tear it out.

There you find that Mr. Lincoln told the Abolitionists of Chicago that if the Declaration of Independence did not declare that the negro was created by the Almighty the equal of the white man, that you ought to take that instrument and tear out the clause which says that all men are created equal. But let me call your attention to another part of the same speech. You know that in his Charleston speech, an extract from which he has read, he declared that the negro belongs to an inferior race, is physically inferior to the white man, and should always be kept in an inferior position. I will now read to you what he said at Chicago on that point. In concluding his speech at that place, he remarked:

My friends, I have detained you about as long as I desire to do, and I have only to say, let us discard all this quibbling about this man and the other man — this race and that race and the other race being inferior, and therefore they must be placed in an inferior position, discarding our standard that we have left us. Let us discard all these things, and unite as one people throughout this land until we shall once more stand up declaring that all men are created equal.

Thus you see that when addressing the Chicago Abolitionists he declared that all distinctions of race must be discarded and blotted out, because the negro stood on an equal footing with the white man; that if one man said the Declaration of Independence did not mean a negro when it declared all men created equal, that another man would say that it did not mean another man; and hence we ought to discard all difference between the negro race and all other races, and declare them all created equal. Did old Giddings, when he came down among you four years ago, preach more radical Abolitionism than this? Did Lovejoy, or Lloyd Garrison, or Wendell Phillips, or Fred Douglass, ever take higher Abolition grounds than that? Lincoln told you that I had charged him with getting up these personal attacks to conceal the enormity of his principles, and then commenced talking about something else, omitting to quote this part of his Chicago speech which contained the enormity of his principles to which I alluded. He knew that I alluded to his negro-equality doctrines when I spoke of the enormity of his principles, yet he did not find it convenient to answer on that point. Having shown you what he said in his Chicago speech in reference to negroes being created equal to white men, and about discarding all distinctions between the two races, I will again read to you what he said at Charleston:

I will say, then, that I am not, nor ever have been, in favor of bringing about in any way the social and political equality of the white and black races; that I am not, nor ever have been, in favor of making voters of the free negroes, or jurors, or qualifying them to hold office, or having them to marry with white people. I will say, in addition, that there is a physical difference between the white and black races which, I suppose, will forever forbid the two races living together upon terms of social and political equality; and inasmuch as they cannot so live, while they do remain together, there must be the position of superior and inferior, and I, as much as any other man, am in favor of the superior position being assigned to the white man.

A voice: "That's the doctrine."

Mr. Douglas: Yes, sir, that is good doctrine; but Mr. Lincoln is afraid to advocate it in the latitude of Chicago, where he hopes to get his votes. It is good doctrine in the anti-Abolition counties for him, and his Chicago speech is good doctrine in the Abolition counties. I assert, on the authority of these two speeches of Mr. Lincoln, that he holds one set of principles in the Abolition counties, and a different and contradictory set in the other counties. I do not question that he said at Ottawa what he quoted, but that only convicts him further, by proving that he has twice contradicted himself instead of once. Let me ask him why he cannot avow his principles the same in the north as in the south—the same in every county, if he has a conviction that they are just? But I forgot—he would not be a Republican if his principles would apply alike to every part of the country. The party to which he belongs is bounded and limited by geographical lines. With their principles they cannot even cross the Mississippi River on your ferry-boats. They cannot cross over the Ohio into Kentucky. Lincoln himself cannot visit the land of his fathers, the scenes of his childhood, the graves of his ancestors, and carry his Abolition principles, as he declared them at Chicago, with him.

This Republican organization appeals to the North against the South; it appeals to Northern passion, Northern prejudice, and Northern ambition, against Southern people, Southern States, and Southern institutions, and its only hope of success is by that appeal. Mr. Lincoln goes on to justify himself in making a war upon slavery upon the ground that Frank Blair and Gratz Brown did not succeed in their warfare upon the institutions in Missouri. Frank Blair was elected to Congress, in 1856, from the State of Missouri, as a Buchanan Democrat, and he turned Frémonter after the people elected him, thus belonging to one party before his election, and another afterward. What right, then, had he to expect, after having thus cheated his constituency, that they would support him at another election? Mr. Lincoln thinks that it is his duty to preach a crusade in the free States against slavery, because it is a crime, as he believes, and ought to be extinguished, and because the people of the slave States will never abolish it. How is he going to abolish it? Down in the southern part of the State he takes the ground openly that he will not interfere with slavery where it exists, and says that he is not now and never was in favor of interfering with slavery where it exists in the States. Well, if he is not in favor of that, how does he expect to bring slavery into a course of ultimate extinction? How can he extinguish it in Kentucky, in Virginia, in all the slave States, by his policy, if he will not pursue a policy which will interfere with it in the States where it exists? In his speech at Springfield before the Abolition or Republican convention, he declared his hostility to any more slave States in this language:

Under the operation of that policy the agitation has not only not ceased, but has constantly augmented. In my opinion it will not cease until a crisis shall have been reached and passed. "A house divided against itself cannot stand." I believe this government cannot endure permanently half slave and half free. I do not expect the Union to be dissolved,— I do not expect the house to fall,— but I do expect it will cease to be divided. It will become all one thing, or all the other. Either the opponents of slavery will arrest the further spread of it, and place it where the public mind shall rest in the belief that it is in the course of ultimate extinction, or its advocates will push it forward till it shall become alike lawful in all the States — old as well as new, North as well as South.

Mr. Lincoln there told his Abolition friends that this government could not endure permanently divided into free and slave States as our fathers made it, and that it must become all free or all slave; otherwise, that the government could not exist. How then does Lincoln propose to save the Union, unless by compelling all the States to become free, so that the house shall not be divided against itself? He intends making them all free; he will preserve the Union in that way; and yet he is not going to interfere with slavery anywhere it now exists. How is he going to bring it about? Why, he will agitate; he will induce the North to agitate until the South shall be worried out, and forced to abolish slavery. Let us examine the policy by which that is to be done. He first tells you that he would prohibit slavery everywhere in the Territories. He would thus confine slavery within its present limits. When he thus gets it confined, and surrounded, so that it cannot spread, the natural laws of increase will go on until the negroes will be so plenty that they cannot live on the soil. He will hem them in until starvation seizes them, and by starving them to death he will put slavery in the course of ultimate extinction. If he is not going to interfere with slavery in the States, but intends to interfere and prohibit it in the Territories, and thus smother slavery out, it naturally follows that he can extinguish it only by extinguishing the negro race; for his policy would drive them to starvation. This is the humane and Christian remedy that he proposes for the great crime of slavery.

He tells you that I will not argue the question whether slavery is right or wrong. I tell you why I will not do it. I hold that, under the Constitution of the United States, each State of this Union has a right to do as it pleases on the subject of slavery. In Illinois we have exercised that sovereign right by prohibiting slavery within our own limits. I approve of that line of policy. We have performed our whole duty in Illinois. We have gone as far as we have a right to go under the Constitution of our common country. It is none of our business whether slavery exists in Missouri or not. Missouri is a sovereign State of this Union, and has the same right to decide the slavery question for herself that Illinois has to decide it for herself. Hence I do not choose to occupy the time allotted to me in discussing a question that we have no right to act upon. I thought that you desired to hear us upon those questions coming within our constitutional power of action. Lincoln will not discuss these. What one question has he discussed that comes within the power or calls for the action or interference of a United States senator? He is going to discuss the rightfulness of slavery when Congress cannot act upon it either way. He wishes to discuss the merits of the Dred Scott decision when, under the Constitution, a senator has no right to interfere with the decision of judicial tribunals. He wants your exclusive attention to two questions that he has no power to act upon; to two questions that he could not vote upon if he was in Congress; to two questions that are not practical, in order to conceal from your attention other questions which he might be required to vote upon should he ever become a member of Congress. He tells you that he does not like the Dred Scott decision. Suppose he does not, how is he going to help himself? He says that he will reverse it. How will he reverse it? I know of but one mode of reversing judicial decisions, and that is by appealing from the inferior to the superior court. But I have never yet learned how or where an appeal could be taken from the Supreme Court of the United States. The Dred Scott decision was pronounced by the highest tribunal on earth. From that decision there is no appeal this side of heaven. Yet Mr. Lincoln says he is going to reverse that decision. By what tribunal will he reverse it? Will he appeal to a mob? Does he intend to appeal to violence, to lynch-law? Will he stir up strife and rebellion in the land, and overthrow the court by violence? He does not deign to tell you how he will reverse the Dred Scott decision, but keeps appealing each day from the Supreme Court of the United States to political meetings in the country. He wants me to argue with you the merits of each point of that decision before this political meeting. I say to you, with all due respect, that I choose to abide by the decisions of the Supreme Court as they are pronounced. It is not for me to inquire, after a decision is made, whether I like it in all the points or not. When I used to practise law with Lincoln, I never knew him to be beat in a case that he did not get mad at the judge and talk about appealing; and when I got beat I generally thought the court was wrong, but I never dreamed of going out of the court-house and making a stump speech to the people against the judge, merely because I had found out that I did not know the law as well as he did. If the decision did not suit me, I appealed until I got to the Supreme Court, and then if that court, the highest tribunal in the world, decided against me, I was satisfied, because it is the duty of every law-abiding man to obey the Constitution, the laws, and the constituted authorities. He who attempts to stir up odium and rebellion in the country against the constituted authorities, is stimulating the passions of men to resort to violence and to mobs instead of to the law. Hence I tell you that I take the decisions of the Supreme Court as the law of the land, and I intend to obey them as such.

But Mr. Lincoln says that I will not answer his question as to what I would do in the event of the court making so ridiculous a decision as he imagines they would by deciding that the free State of Illinois could not prohibit slavery within her own limits. I told him at Freeport why I would not answer such a question. I told him that there was not a man possessing any brains in America, lawyer or not, who ever dreamed that such a thing could be done. I told him then, as I do now, that by all the principles set forth in the Dred Scott decision, it is impossible. I told him then, as I do now, that it is an insult to men's understanding, and a gross calumny on the court, to presume in advance that it was going to degrade itself so low as to make a decision known to be in direct violation of the Constitution. [A voice: "The same thing was said about the Dred Scott decision before it passed."] Perhaps you think that the court did the same thing in reference to the Dred Scott decision. I have heard a man talk that way before. The principles contained in the Dred Scott decision had been affirmed previously in various other decisions. What court or judge ever held that a negro was a citizen? The State courts had decided that question over and over again, and the Dred Scott decision on that point only affirmed what every court in the land knew to be the law.

But I will not be drawn off into an argument upon the merits of the Dred Scott decision. It is enough for me to know that the Constitution of the United States created the Supreme Court for the purpose of deciding all disputed questions touching the true construction of that instrument, and when such decisions are pronounced, they are the law of the land, binding on every good citizen. Mr. Lincoln has a very convenient mode of arguing upon the subject. He holds that because he is a Republican he is not bound by the decisions of the court, but that I, being a Democrat, am so bound. It may be that Republicans do not hold themselves bound by the laws of the land

and the Constitution of the country as expounded by the courts; it may be an article in the Republican creed that men who do not like a decision have a right to rebel against it; but when Mr. Lincoln preaches that doctrine, I think he will find some honest Republican — some law-abiding man in that party — who will repudiate such a monstrous doctrine. The decision in the Dred Scott case is binding on every American citizen alike; and yet Mr. Lincoln argues that the Republicans are not bound by it because they are opposed to it, whilst Democrats are bound by it because we will not resist it. A Democrat cannot resist the constituted authorities of this country; a Democrat is a law-abiding man; a Democrat stands by the Constitution and the laws, and relies upon liberty as protected by law, and not upon mob or political violence.

I have never yet been able to make Mr. Lincoln understand, nor can I make any man who is determined to support him, right or wrong, understand, how it is that under the Dred Scott decision the people of a Territory, as well as a State, can have slavery or not, just as they please. I believe that I can explain that proposition to all constitution-loving, law-abiding men in a way that they cannot fail to understand. Chief Justice Taney, in his opinion in the Dred Scott case, said that slaves being property, the owner of them has a right to take them into a Territory the same as he would any other property; in other words, that slave property, so far as the right to enter into a Territory is concerned, stands on the same footing with other property. Suppose we grant that proposition. Then any man has a right to go to Kansas and take his property with him, but when he gets there he must rely upon the local law to protect his property, whatever it may be. In order to illustrate this, imagine that three of you conclude to go to Kansas. One takes $10,000 worth of slaves, another $10,000 worth of liquors, and the third $10,000 worth of dry-goods. When the man who owns the dry-goods arrives out there and commences selling them, he finds that he is stopped and prohibited from selling until he gets a license, which will destroy all the profits he can make on his goods to pay for. When the man with the liquors gets there and tries to sell, he finds a Maine liquor-law in force which prevents him. Now of what use is his right to go there with his property unless he is protected in the enjoyment of that right after he gets there? The man who goes there with his slaves finds that there is no law to protect him when he arrives there. He has no remedy if his slaves run away to another country: there is no slave code or police regulations, and the absence of them excludes his slaves from the Territory just as effectually and as positively as a constitutional prohibition could.

Such was the understanding when the Kansas and Nebraska bill was pending in Congress. Read the speech of Speaker Orr, of South Carolina, in the House of Representatives, in 1856, on the Kansas question, and you will find that he takes the ground that while the owner of a slave has a right to go into a Territory and carry his slaves with him, that he cannot hold them one day or hour unless there is a slave code to protect him. He tells you that slavery would not exist a day in South Carolina, or any other State, unless there was a friendly people and friendly legislation. Read the speeches of that giant in intellect, Alexander H. Stephens, of Georgia, and you will find them to the same effect. Read the speeches of Sam Smith, of Tennessee, and of all Southern men, and you will find that they all understood this doctrine then as we understand it now. Mr. Lincoln cannot be made to understand it, however. Down at Jonesboro, he went on to argue that if it be the law that a man has a right to take his slaves into territory of the United States under the Constitution, that then a member of Congress was perjured if he did not vote for a slave code. I ask him whether the decision of the Supreme Court is not binding upon him as well as on me? If so, and he holds that he would be perjured if he did not vote for a slave code under it, I ask him whether, if elected to Congress, he will so vote? I have a right to his answer, and I will tell you why. He put that question to me down in Egypt, and did it with an air of triumph. This was about the form of it: "In the event a slave-holding citizen of one of the Territories should need and demand a slave code to protect his slaves, would you vote for it?" I answered him that a fundamental article in the Democratic creed, as put forth in the Nebraska bill and the Cincinnati platform, was non-intervention by Congress with slavery in the States and Territories, and hence that I would not vote in Congress for any code of laws either for or against slavery in any Territory. I will leave the people perfectly free to decide that question for themselves.

Mr. Lincoln and the Washington "Union" both think this a monstrous bad doctrine. Neither Mr. Lincoln nor the Washington "Union" likes my Freeport speech on that subject. The "Union," in a late number, has been reading me out of the Democratic party because I hold that the people of a Territory, like those of a State, have the right to have slavery or not, as they please. It has devoted three and a half columns to prove certain propositions, one of which I will read. It says:

We propose to show that Judge Douglas's action in 1850 and 1854 was taken with especial reference to the announcement of doctrine and programme which was made at Freeport. The declaration at Freeport was that "in his opinion the people can, by lawful means, exclude slavery from a Territory before it comes in as a State"; and he declared that his competitor had "heard him argue the Nebraska bill on that principle all over Illinois in 1854, 1855, and 1856, and had no excuse to pretend to have any doubt upon that subject.

The Washington "Union" there charges me with the monstrous crime of now proclaiming on the stump the same doctrine that I carried out in 1850, by supporting Clay's compromise measures. The "Union" also charges that I am now proclaiming the same doctrine that I did in 1854 in support of the Kansas and Nebraska bill. It is shocked that I should now stand where I stood in 1850, when I was supported by Clay, Webster, Cass, and the great men of that day, and where I stood in 1854, and in 1856, when Mr. Buchanan was elected President. It goes on to prove, and succeeds in proving, from my speeches in Congress on Clay's compromise measures, that I held the same doctrines at that time that I do now, and then proves that by the Kansas and Nebraska bill I advanced the same doctrine that I now advance.   It remarks:

So much for the course taken by Judge Douglas on the compromises of 1850.   The record shows, beyond the possibility of cavil or dispute, that he expressly intended in those bills to give the territorial legislatures power to exclude slavery.   How stands his record in the memorable session of 1854, with reference to the Kansas-Nebraska bill itself?   We shall not overhaul the votes that were given on that notable measure.   Our space will not afford it.   We have his own words, however, delivered in his speech closing the great debate on that bill on the night of March 3, 1854, to show that he meant to do in 1854 precisely what he had meant to do in 1858.   The Kansas-Nebraska bill being upon its passage, he said:

It then quotes my remarks upon the passage of the bill as follows:

The principle which we propose to carry into effect by this bill is this: That Congress shall neither legislate slavery into any Territory or State, nor out of the same; but the people shall be left free to regulate their domestic concerns in their own way, subject only to the Constitution of the United States.   In order to carry this principle into practical operation, it becomes necessary to remove whatever legal obstacles might be found in the way of its free exercise.   It is only for the purpose of carrying out this great fundamental principle of self-government that the bill renders the eighth section of the Missouri act inoperative and void.

Now, let me ask, will those senators who have arraigned me, or any one of them, have the assurance to rise in his place and declare that this great principle was never thought of or advocated as applicable to territorial bills in 1850; that from that session until the present, nobody ever thought of incorporating this principle in all new territorial organizations, etc., etc.?   I will begin with the compromises of 1850.   Any senator who will take the trouble to examine our journals will find that on the 25th of March of that year I reported from the Committee on Territories two bills, including the following measures: the admission of California, a territorial government for Utah, a territorial government for New Mexico, and the adjustment of the Texas boundary.   These bills proposed to leave the people of Utah and New Mexico free to decide the slavery question for themselves, in the precise language of the Nebraska bill now under discussion.   A few weeks afterward the committee of thirteen took those bills and put a wafer between them and reported them back to the Senate as one bill, with some slight amendments.   One of these amendments was that the territorial legislatures should not legislate upon the subject of African slavery.   I objected to this provision, upon the ground that it subverted the great principle of self-government, upon which the bill had been originally framed by the territorial committee.   On the first trial the Senate refused to strike it out, but subsequently did so, upon full debate, in order to establish that principle as the rule of action in territorial organizations.

The "Union" comments thus on my speech on that occasion:

Thus it is seen that, in framing the Nebraska-Kansas bill, Judge Douglas framed it in the terms and upon the model of those of Utah and New Mexico, and that in the debate he took pains expressly to revive the recollection of the voting which had taken place upon amendments affecting the powers of the territorial legislatures over the subject of slavery in the bills of 1850, in order to give the same meaning, force, and effect to the Nebraska-Kansas bill on this subject as had been given to those of Utah and New Mexico.

The "Union" proves the following propositions: First, that I
sustained Clay's compromise measures on the ground that they
established the principle of self-government in the Territories. Secondly, that I brought in the Kansas and Nebraska bill, founded upon
the same principles as Clay's compromise measures of 1850; and
thirdly, that my Freeport speech is in exact accordance with those
principles. And what do you think is the imputation that the
"Union" casts upon me for all this? It says that my Freeport
speech is not Democratic, and that I was not a Democrat in 1854 or
in 1850! Now, is not that funny? Think that the author of the
Kansas and Nebraska bill was not a Democrat when he introduced it! The "Union" says I was not a sound Democrat in 1850,
nor in 1854, nor in 1856, nor am I in 1858, because I have always
taken and now occupy the ground that the people of a Territory, like
those of a State, have the right to decide for themselves whether slavery shall or shall not exist in a Territory. I wish to cite, for the
benefit of the Washington "Union" and the followers of that sheet,
one authority on that point, and I hope the authority will be deemed
satisfactory to that class of politicians. I will read from Mr. Buchanan's letter accepting the nomination of the Democratic convention for the presidency. You know that Mr. Buchanan, after he was
nominated, declared to the Keystone Club, in a public speech, that
he was no longer James Buchanan, but the embodiment of the Democratic platform. In his letter to the committee which informed him
of his nomination, accepting it, he defined the meaning of the Kansas and Nebraska bill and the Cincinnati platform in these words:

The recent legislation of Congress respecting domestic slavery, derived
as it has been from the original and pure fountain of legitimate political
power, the will of the majority, promises ere long to allay the dangerous
excitement. This legislation is founded upon principles as ancient as free
government itself, and in accordance with them has simply declared that
the people of a Territory, like those of a State, shall decide for themselves
whether slavery shall or shall not exist within their limits.

Thus you see that James Buchanan accepted the nomination at
Cincinnati on the condition that the people of a Territory, like
those of a State, should be left to decide for themselves whether
slavery should or should not exist within their limits. I sustained
James Buchanan for the presidency on that platform as adopted
at Cincinnati and expounded by himself. He was elected president on that platform, and now we are told by the Washington
"Union" that no man is a true Democrat who stands on the platform
on which Mr. Buchanan was nominated, and which he has explained
and expounded himself. We are told that a man is not a Democrat
who stands by Clay, Webster, and Cass, and the compromise measures of 1850, and the Kansas and Nebraska bill of 1854. Whether
a man be a Democrat or not on that platform, I intend to stand
there as long as I have life. I intend to cling firmly to that great
principle which declares the right of each State and each Territory to settle the question of slavery, and every other domestic question, for themselves. I hold that if they want a slave State, they

have a right, under the Constitution of the United States, to make it so, and if they want a free State, it is their right to have it. But the "Union," in advocating the claims of Lincoln over me to the Senate, lays down two unpardonable heresies which it says I advocate. The first is the right of the people of a Territory, the same as a State, to decide for themselves the question whether slavery shall exist within their limits, in the language of Mr. Buchanan; and the second is that a constitution shall be submitted to the people of a Territory for its adoption or rejection before their admission as a State under it. It so happens that Mr. Buchanan is pledged to both these heresies, for supporting which the Washington "Union" has read me out of the Democratic church. In his annual message he said he trusted that the example of the Minnesota case would be followed in all future cases requiring a submission of the constitution; and in his letter of acceptance he said that the people of a Territory, the same as a State, had the right to decide for themselves whether slavery should exist within their limits. Thus you find that this little corrupt gang who control the "Union," and wish to elect Lincoln in preference to me,—because, as they say, of these two heresies which I support,—denounce President Buchanan when they denounce me, if he stands now by the principles upon which he was elected. Will they pretend that he does not now stand by the principles on which he was elected? Do they hold that he has abandoned the Kansas-Nebraska bill, the Cincinnati platform, and his own letter accepting his nomination, all of which declare the right of the people of a Territory, the same as a State, to decide the slavery question for themselves? I will not believe that he has betrayed or intends to betray the platform which elected him; but if he does, I will not follow him. I will stand by that great principle, no matter who may desert it. I intend to stand by it for the purpose of preserving peace between the North and the South, the free and the slave States.

If each State will only agree to mind its own business, and let its neighbors alone, there will be peace forever between us. We in Illinois tried slavery when a Territory, and found it was not good for us in this climate, and with our surroundings, and hence we abolished it. We then adopted a free-State constitution, as we had a right to do. In this State we have declared that a negro shall not be a citizen, and we have also declared that he shall not be a slave. We had a right to adopt that policy. Missouri has just as good a right to adopt the other policy. I am now speaking of rights under the Constitution, and not of moral or religious rights. I do not discuss the morals of the people of Missouri, but let them settle that matter for themselves. I hold that the people of the slaveholding States are civilized men as well as ourselves; that they bear consciences as well as we, and that they are accountable to God and their posterity, and not to us. It is for them to decide, therefore, the moral and religious right of the slavery question for themselves within their own limits. I assert that they had as much right under the Constitution to adopt the system of policy which they have as we had to adopt ours. So it is with every other State in this Union. Let each State stand firmly by that great constitutional right, let each State mind its own business and let its neighbors alone, and there will be no trouble on this question. If we will stand by that principle, then Mr. Lincoln will find that this republic can exist forever divided into free and slave States, as our fathers made it, and the people of each State have decided. Stand by that great principle, and we can go on as we have done, increasing in wealth, in population, in power, and in all the elements of greatness, until we shall be the admiration and terror of the world. We can go on and enlarge as our population increases and requires more room, until we make this continent one ocean-bound republic. Under that principle the United States can perform that great mission, that destiny, which Providence has marked out for us. Under that principle we can receive with entire safety that stream of intelligence which is constantly flowing from the Old World to the New, filling up our prairies, clearing our wildernesses, and building cities, towns, railroads, and other internal improvements, and thus make this the asylum of the oppressed of the whole earth. We have this great mission to perform, and it can only be performed by adhering faithfully to that principle of self-government on which our institutions were all established. I repeat that the principle is the right of each State, each Territory, to decide this slavery question for itself, to have slavery or not, as it chooses, and it does not become Mr. Lincoln, or anybody else, to tell the people of Kentucky that they have no consciences, that they are living in a state of iniquity, and that they are cherishing an institution to their bosoms in violation of the law of God. Better for him to adopt the doctrine of "Judge not, lest ye shall be judged." Let him perform his own duty at home, and he will have a better fate in the future. I think there are objects of charity enough in the free States to excite the sympathies and open the pockets of all the benevolence we have amongst us, without going abroad in search of negroes, of whose condition we know nothing. We have enough objects of charity at home, and it is our duty to take care of our own poor, and our own suffering, before we go abroad to intermeddle with other people's business.

My friends, I am told that my time is within two minutes of expiring. I have omitted many topics that I would like to have discussed before you at length. There were many points touched by Mr. Lincoln that I have not been able to take up for the want of time. I have hurried over each subject that I have discussed as rapidly as possible, so as to omit but few; but one hour and a half is not time sufficient for a man to discuss at length one half of the great questions which are now dividing the public mind.

In conclusion, I desire to return to you my grateful acknowledgments for the kindness and the courtesy with which you have listened to me. It is something remarkable that in an audience as vast as this, composed of men of opposite politics and views, with their passions highly excited, there should be so much courtesy, kindness, and respect exhibited not only toward one another, but toward the speakers, and I feel that it is due to you that I should thus express my gratitude for the kindness with which you have treated me.

Mr. Lincoln's Rejoinder in the Quincy Joint Debate.

My Friends: Since Judge Douglas has said to you in his conclusion that he had not time in an hour and a half to answer all I had said in an hour, it follows of course that I will not be able to answer in half an hour all that he said in an hour and a half.

I wish to return to Judge Douglas my profound thanks for his public annunciation here to-day to be put on record, that his system of policy in regard to the institution of slavery contemplates that it shall last forever. We are getting a little nearer the true issue of this controversy, and I am profoundly grateful for this one sentence. Judge Douglas asks you, "Why cannot the institution of slavery, or rather, why cannot the nation, part slave and part free, continue as our fathers made it forever?" In the first place, I insist that our fathers did not make this nation half slave and half free, or part slave and part free. I insist that they found the institution of slavery existing here. They did not make it so, but they left it so because they knew of no way to get rid of it at that time. When Judge Douglas undertakes to say that, as a matter of choice, the fathers of the government made this nation part slave and part free, he assumes what is historically a falsehood. More than that: when the fathers of the government cut off the source of slavery by the abolition of the slave-trade, and adopted a system of restricting it from the new Territories where it had not existed, I maintain that they placed it where they understood, and all sensible men understood, it was in the course of ultimate extinction; and when Judge Douglas asks me why it cannot continue as our fathers made it, I ask him why he and his friends could not let it remain as our fathers made it?

It is precisely all I ask of him in relation to the institution of slavery, that it shall be placed upon the basis that our fathers placed it upon. Mr. Brooks, of South Carolina, once said, and truly said, that when this government was established, no one expected the institution of slavery to last until this day; and that the men who formed this government were wiser and better than the men of these days; but the men of these days had experience which the fathers had not, and that experience had taught them the invention of the cotton-gin, and this had made the perpetuation of the institution of slavery a necessity in this country. Judge Douglas could not let it stand upon the basis where our fathers placed it, but removed it, and put it upon the cotton-gin basis. It is a question, therefore, for him and his friends to answer — why they could not let it remain where the fathers of the government originally placed it.

I hope nobody has understood me as trying to sustain the doctrine that we have a right to quarrel with Kentucky or Virginia, or any of the slave States, about the institution of slavery — thus giving the judge an opportunity to make himself eloquent and valiant against us in fighting for their rights. I expressly declared in my opening speech that I had neither the inclination to exercise, nor the belief in the existence of, the right to interfere with the States of Kentucky or

Virginia in doing as they pleased with slavery or any other existing institution. Then what becomes of all his eloquence in behalf of the rights of States, which are assailed by no living man?

But I have to hurry on, for I have but a half-hour. The judge has informed me, or informed this audience, that the Washington "Union" is laboring for my election to the United States Senate. This is news to me—not very ungrateful news either. [Turning to Mr. W. H. Carlin, who was on the stand:] I hope that Carlin will be elected to the State Senate and will vote for me. [Mr. Carlin shook his head.] Carlin don't fall in, I perceive, and I suppose he will not do much for me; but I am glad of all the support I can get anywhere, if I can get it without practising any deception to obtain it. In respect to this large portion of Judge Douglas's speech, in which he tries to show that in the controversy between himself and the administration party he is in the right, I do not feel myself at all competent or inclined to answer him. I say to him, Give it to them—give it to them just all you can; and, on the other hand, I say to Carlin, and Jake Davis, and to this man Wagley up here in Hancock, Give it to Douglas—just pour it into him.

Now in regard to this matter of the Dred Scott decision, I wish to say a word or two. After all, the judge will not say whether, if a decision is made holding that the people of the States cannot exclude slavery, he will support it or not. He obstinately refuses to say what he will do in that case. The judges of the Supreme Court as obstinately refused to say what they would do on this subject. Before this I reminded him that at Galesburg he said the judges had expressly declared the contrary, and you remember that in my opening speech I told him I had the book containing that decision here, and I would thank him to lay his finger on the place where any such thing was said. He has occupied his hour and a half, and he has not ventured to try to sustain his assertion. He never will. But he is desirous of knowing how we are going to reverse the Dred Scott decision. Judge Douglas ought to know how. Did not he and his political friends find a way to reverse the decision of that same court in favor of the constitutionality of the national bank? Did n't they find a way to do it so effectually that they have reversed it as completely as any decision ever was reversed, so far as its practical operation is concerned? And, let me ask you, did n't Judge Douglas find a way to reverse the decision of our Supreme Court, when it decided that Carlin's father—old Governor Carlin—had not the constitutional power to remove a secretary of state? Did he not appeal to the "mobs," as he calls them? Did he not make speeches in the lobby to show how villainous that decision was, and how it ought to be overthrown? Did he not succeed, too, in getting an act passed by the legislature to have it overthrown? And did n't he himself sit down on that bench as one of the five added judges who were to overslaugh the four old ones—getting his name of "judge" in that way and in no other? If there is a villainy in using disrespect or making opposition to Supreme Court decisions, I commend it to Judge Douglas's earnest consideration. I know of no man in the State of Illinois who ought to know so well about how much villainy it takes to oppose a decision of the Supreme Court, as our honorable friend, Stephen A. Douglas.

Judge Douglas also makes the declaration that I say the Democrats are bound by the Dred Scott decision, while the Republicans are not. In the sense in which he argues, I never said it; but I will tell you what I have said and what I do not hesitate to repeat to-day. I have said that, as the Democrats believe that decision to be correct, and that the extension of slavery is affirmed in the National Constitution, they are bound to support it as such; and I will tell you here that General Jackson once said each man was bound to support the Constitution, "as he understood it." Now, Judge Douglas understands the Constitution according to the Dred Scott decision, and he is bound to support it as he understands it. I understand it another way, and therefore I am bound to support it in the way in which I understand it. And as Judge Douglas believes that decision to be correct, I will remake that argument if I have time to do so. Let me talk to some gentleman down there among you who looks me in the face. We will say you are a member of the territorial legislature, and, like Judge Douglas, you believe that the right to take and hold slaves there is a constitutional right. The first thing you do is to swear you will support the Constitution and all rights guaranteed therein; that you will, whenever your neighbor needs your legislation to support his constitutional rights, not withhold that legislation. If you withhold that necessary legislation for the support of the Constitution and constitutional rights, do you not commit perjury? I ask every sensible man if that is not so? That is undoubtedly just so, say what you please. Now, that is precisely what Judge Douglas says—that this is a constitutional right. Does the judge mean to say that the territorial legislature in legislating may, by withholding necessary laws or by passing unfriendly laws, nullify that constitutional right? Does he mean to say that? Does he mean to ignore the proposition, so long and well established in law, that what you cannot do directly, you cannot do indirectly? Does he mean that? The truth about the matter is this: Judge Douglas has sung pæans to his "popular sovereignty" doctrine until his Supreme Court, coöperating with him, has squatted his squatter sovereignty out. But he will keep up this species of humbuggery about squatter sovereignty. He has at last invented this sort of do-nothing sovereignty—that the people may exclude slavery by a sort of "sovereignty" that is exercised by doing nothing at all. Is not that running his popular sovereignty down awfully? Has it not got down as thin as the homeopathic soup that was made by boiling the shadow of a pigeon that had starved to death? But at last, when it is brought to the test of close reasoning, there is not even that thin decoction of it left. It is a presumption impossible in the domain of thought. It is precisely no other than the putting of that most unphilosophical proposition, that two bodies can occupy the same space at the same time. The Dred Scott decision covers the whole ground, and while it occupies it, there is no room even for the shadow of a starved pigeon to occupy the same ground.

Judge Douglas, in reply to what I have said about having upon a previous occasion made the same speech at Ottawa as the one he took an extract from at Charleston, says it only shows that I practised the deception twice. Now, my friends, are any of you obtuse enough to swallow that? Judge Douglas had said I had made a speech at Charleston that I would not make up north, and I turned around and answered him by showing I had made that same speech up north—had made it at Ottawa—made it in his hearing—made it in the Abolition district—in Lovejoy's district—in the personal presence of Lovejoy himself—in the same atmosphere exactly in which I had made my Chicago speech, of which he complains so much.

Now, in relation to my not having said anything about the quotation from the Chicago speech. He thinks that is a terrible subject for me to handle. Why, gentlemen, I can show you that the substance of the Chicago speech I delivered two years ago in "Egypt," as he calls it. It was down at Springfield. That speech is here in this book, and I could turn to it and read it to you but for the lack of time. I have not now the time to read it. ["Read it, read it."] No, gentlemen, I am obliged to use discretion in disposing most advantageously of my brief time. The judge has taken great exception to my adopting the heretical statement in the Declaration of Independence, that "all men are created equal," and he has a great deal to say about negro equality. I want to say that in sometimes alluding to the Declaration of Independence, I have only uttered the sentiments that Henry Clay used to hold. Allow me to occupy your time a moment with what he said. Mr. Clay was at one time called upon in Indiana, and in a way that I suppose was very insulting, to liberate his slaves, and he made a written reply to that application, and one portion of it is in these words:

What is the foundation of this appeal to me in Indiana to liberate the slaves under my care in Kentucky? It is a general declaration in the act announcing to the world the independence of the thirteen American colonies, that "men are created equal." Now, as an abstract principle, there is no doubt of the truth of that declaration, and it is desirable in the original construction of society, and in organized societies, to keep it in view as a great fundamental principle.

When I sometimes, in relation to the organization of new societies in new countries, where the soil is clean and clear, insist that we should keep that principle in view, Judge Douglas will have it that I want a negro wife. He never can be brought to understand that there is any middle ground on this subject. I have lived until my fiftieth year, and have never had a negro woman either for a slave or a wife, and I think I can live fifty centuries, for that matter, without having had one for either. I maintain that you may take Judge Douglas's quotations from my Chicago speech, and from my Charleston speech, and the Galesburg speech,—in his speech of to-day,—and compare them over, and I am willing to trust them with you upon his proposition that they show rascality or double-dealing. I deny that they do.

The judge does not seem disposed to have peace, but I find he is disposed to have a personal warfare with me. He says that my oath would not be taken against the bare word of Charles H. Lanphier or Thomas L. Harris. Well, that is altogether a matter of opinion. It is certainly not for me to vaunt my word against the oaths of these gentlemen, but I will tell Judge Douglas again the facts upon which I "dared" to say they proved a forgery. I pointed out at Galesburg that the publication of these resolutions in the Illinois "State Register" could not have been the result of accident, as the proceedings of that meeting bore unmistakable evidence of being done by a man who knew it was a forgery; that it was a publication partly taken from the real proceedings of the convention, and partly from the proceedings of a convention at another place; which showed that he had the real proceedings before him, and, taking one part of the resolutions, he threw out another part, and substituted false and fraudulent ones in their stead. I pointed that out to him, and also that his friend Lanphier, who was editor of the "Register" at that time and now is, must have known how it was done. Now whether he did it, or got some friend to do it for him, I could not tell, but he certainly knew all about it. I pointed out to Judge Douglas that in his Freeport speech he had promised to investigate that matter. Does he now say he did not make that promise? I have a right to ask why he did not keep it? I call upon him to tell here to-day why he did not keep that promise? That fraud has been traced up so that it lies between him, Harris, and Lanphier. There is little room for escape for Lanphier. Lanphier is doing the judge good service, and Douglas desires his word to be taken for the truth. He desires Lanphier to be taken as authority in what he states in his newspaper. He desires Harris to be taken as a man of vast credibility, and when this thing lies among them, they will not press it to show where the guilt really belongs. Now, as he has said that he would investigate it, and implied that he would tell us the result of his investigation, I demand of him to tell why he did not investigate it, if he did not; and if he did, why he won't tell the result. I call upon him for that.

This is the third time that Judge Douglas has assumed that he learned about these resolutions by Harris's attempting to use them against Norton on the floor of Congress. I tell Judge Douglas the public records of the country show that he himself attempted it upon Trumbull a month before Harris tried them on Norton—that Harris had the opportunity of learning it from him, rather than he from Harris. I now ask his attention to that part of the record on the case. My friends, I am not disposed to detain you longer in regard to that matter.

I am told that I still have five minutes left. There is another matter I wish to call attention to. He says, when he discovered there was a mistake in that case, he came forward magnanimously, without my calling his attention to it, and explained it. I will tell you how he became so magnanimous. When the newspapers of our side had discovered and published it, and put it beyond his power to deny it, then he came forward and made a virtue of necessity by acknowledging it. Now he argues that all the point there was in those resolutions, although never passed at Springfield, is retained by their being passed at other localities. Is that true? He said I had a hand in passing them, in his opening speech; that I was in the convention, and helped to pass them. Do the resolutions touch me at all? It strikes me there is some difference between holding a man responsible for an act which he has not done, and holding him responsible for an act that he has done. You will judge whether there is any difference in the "spots." And he has taken credit for great magnanimity in coming forward and acknowledging what is proved on him beyond even the capacity of Judge Douglas to deny, and he has more capacity in that way than any other living man.

Then he wants to know why I won't withdraw the charge in regard to a conspiracy to make slavery national, as he had withdrawn the one he made. May it please his worship, I will withdraw it when it is proven false on me as that was proven false on him. I will add a little more than that. I will withdraw it whenever a reasonable man shall be brought to believe that the charge is not true. I have asked Judge Douglas's attention to certain matters of fact tending to prove the charge of a conspiracy to nationalize slavery, and he says he convinces me that this is all untrue, because Buchanan was not in the country at that time, and because the Dred Scott case had not then got into the Supreme Court; and he says that I say the Democratic owners of Dred Scott got up the case. I never did say that. I defy Judge Douglas to show that I ever said so, for I never uttered it. [One of Mr. Douglas's reporters gesticulated affirmatively at Mr. Lincoln.] I don't care if your hireling does say I did. I tell you myself that I never said the "Democratic" owners of Dred Scott got up the case. I have never pretended to know whether Dred Scott's owners were Democrats or Abolitionists, Free-soilers or Border Ruffians. I have said that there is evidence about the case tending to show that it was a made-up case for the purpose of getting that decision. I have said that that evidence was very strong in the fact that when Dred Scott was declared to be a slave, the owner of him made him free, showing that he had had the case tried, and the question settled, for such use as could be made of that decision; he cared nothing about the property thus declared to be his by that decision. But my time is out, and I can say no more.

October 15, 1858.— THE SEVENTH AND LAST JOINT DEBATE,
AT ALTON, ILLINOIS.

Senator Douglas's Opening Speech.

Ladies and Gentlemen: It is now nearly four months since the canvass between Mr. Lincoln and myself commenced. On the 16th of June the Republican convention assembled at Springfield, and nominated Mr. Lincoln as their candidate for the United States Senate, and he, on that occasion, delivered a speech in which he laid down what he understood to be the Republican creed, and the platform on which he proposed to stand during the contest. The principal points in that speech of Mr. Lincoln's were: First, that this government could not endure permanently divided into free and slave States, as our fathers made it; that they must all become free or all become slave; all become one thing or all become the other, otherwise this Union could not continue to exist. I give you his opinions almost in the identical language he used. His second proposition was a crusade against the Supreme Court of the United States, because of the Dred Scott decision; urging as an especial reason for his opposition to that decision that it deprived the negroes of the rights and benefits of that clause in the Constitution of the United States which guarantees to the citizens of each State all the rights, privileges, and immunities of the citizens of the several States. On the 10th of July I returned home, and delivered a speech to the people of Chicago, in which I announced it to be my purpose to appeal to the people of Illinois to sustain the course I had pursued in Congress. In that speech I joined issue with Mr. Lincoln on the points which he had presented. Thus there was an issue clear and distinct made up between us on these two propositions laid down in the speech of Mr. Lincoln at Springfield, and controverted by me in my reply to him at Chicago. On the next day, the 11th of July, Mr. Lincoln replied to me at Chicago, explaining at some length, and re-affirming the positions which he had taken in his Springfield speech. In that Chicago speech he even went further than he had before, and uttered sentiments in regard to the negro being on an equality with the white man. He adopted in support of this position the argument which Lovejoy, and Codding, and other Abolition lecturers had made familiar in the northern and central portions of the State, to wit: that the Declaration of Independence having declared all men free and equal by Divine law, negro equality was also an inalienable right, of which they could not be deprived. He insisted, in that speech, that the Declaration of Independence included the negro in the clause asserting that all men were created equal, and went so far as to say that if one man was allowed to take the position that it did not include the negro, others might take the position that it did not include other men. He said that all these distinctions between this man and that man, this race and the other race, must be discarded, and we must all stand by the Declaration of Independence, declaring that all men were created equal.

The issue thus being made up between Mr. Lincoln and myself on three points, we went before the people of the State. During the following seven weeks, between the Chicago speeches and our first meeting at Ottawa, he and I addressed large assemblages of the people in many of the central counties. In my speeches I confined myself closely to those three positions which he had taken, controverting his proposition that this Union could not exist as our fathers made it, divided into free and slave States, controverting his proposition of a crusade against the Supreme Court because of the Dred Scott decision, and controverting his proposition that the Declaration of Independence included and meant the negroes as well as the white men, when it declared all men to be created equal. I supposed at that time that these propositions constituted a distinct issue between us, and that the opposite positions we had taken upon them we would be willing to be held to in every part of the State. I never intended to waver one hair's breadth from that issue either in the north or the south, or wherever I should address the people of Illinois. I hold that when the time arrives that I cannot proclaim my political creed in the same terms not only in the northern but the southern part of Illinois, not only in the Northern but the Southern States, and wherever the American flag waves over American soil, that then there must be something wrong in that creed — so long as we live under a common Constitution, so long as we live in a confederacy of sovereign and equal States, joined together as one for certain purposes, that any political creed is radically wrong which cannot be proclaimed in every State and every section of that Union, alike. I took up Mr. Lincoln's three propositions in my several speeches, analyzed them, and pointed out what I believed to be the radical errors contained in them. First, in regard to his doctrine that this government was in violation of the law of God, which says that a house divided against itself cannot stand; I repudiated it as a slander upon the immortal framers of our Constitution. I then said, I have often repeated, and now again assert, that in my opinion our government can endure forever, divided into free and slave States as our fathers made it — each State having the right to prohibit, abolish, or sustain slavery, just as it pleases. This government was made upon the great basis of the sovereignty of the States, the right of each State to regulate its own domestic institutions to suit itself, and that right was conferred with the understanding and expectation that inasmuch as each locality had separate interests, each locality must have different and distinct local and domestic institutions, corresponding to its wants and interests. Our fathers knew, when they made the government, that the laws and institutions which were well adapted to the green mountains of Vermont were unsuited to the rice plantations of South Carolina. They knew then, as well as we know now, that the laws and institutions which would be well adapted to the beautiful prairies of Illinois would not be suited to the mining regions of California. They knew that in a republic as broad as this, having such a variety of soil, climate, and interest, there must necessarily be a corresponding variety of local laws — the policy and institutions of each State adapted to its condition and wants. For this reason this Union was established on the right of each State to do as it pleased on the question of slavery, and every other question, and the various States were not allowed to complain of, much less interfere with, the policy of their neighbors.

Suppose the doctrine advocated by Mr. Lincoln and the Abolitionists of this day had prevailed when the Constitution was made, what would have been the result? Imagine for a moment that Mr. Lincoln had been a member of the convention that framed the Constitution of the United States, and that when its members were about to sign that wonderful document, he had arisen in that convention, as he did at Springfield this summer, and addressing himself to the President, had said: "A house divided against itself cannot stand; this government, divided into free and slave States cannot endure; they must all be free or all be slave, they must all be one thing or all the other; otherwise, it is a violation of the law of God, and cannot continue to exist" — suppose Mr. Lincoln had convinced that body of sages that that doctrine was sound, what would have been the result? Remember that the Union was then composed of thirteen States, twelve of which were slave-holding and one free. Do you think that the one free State would have out-voted the twelve slave-holding States, and thus have secured the abolition of slavery? On the other hand, would not the twelve slave-holding States have out-voted the one free State, and thus have fastened slavery, by a constitutional provision, on every foot of the American republic forever! You see that if this Abolition doctrine of Mr. Lincoln had prevailed when the government was made, it would have established slavery as a permanent institution, in all the States, whether they wanted it or not; and the question for us to determine in Illinois now, as one of the free States, is whether or not we are willing, having become the majority section, to enforce a doctrine on the minority which we would have resisted with our hearts' blood had it been attempted on us when we were in a minority. How has the South lost her power as the majority section in this Union, and how have the free States gained it, except under the operation of that principle which declares the right of the people of each State and each Territory to form and regulate their domestic institutions in their own way? It was under that principle that slavery was abolished in New Hampshire, Rhode Island, Connecticut, New York, New Jersey, and Pennsylvania; it was under that principle that one half of the slave-holding States became free; it was under that principle that the number of free States increased until, from being one out of twelve States, we have grown to be the majority of States of the whole Union, with the power to control the House of Representatives and Senate, and the power, consequently, to elect a President by Northern votes without the aid of a Southern State. Having obtained this power under the operation of that great principle, are you now prepared to abandon the principle, and declare that merely because we have the power you will wage a war against the Southern States and their institutions until you force them to abolish slavery everywhere?

After having pressed these arguments home on Mr. Lincoln for seven weeks, publishing a number of my speeches, we met at Ottawa in joint discussion, and he then began to crawfish a little, and let himself down. I there propounded certain questions to him. Amongst others, I asked him whether he would vote for the admission of any more slave States in the event the people wanted them. He would not answer. I then told him that if he did not answer the question there I would renew it at Freeport, and would then trot him down into Egypt and again put it to him. Well, at Freeport, knowing that the next joint discussion took place in Egypt, and being in dread of it, he did answer my question in regard to no more slave States in a mode which he hoped would be satisfactory to me, and accomplish the object he had in view. I will show you what his answer was. After saying that he was not pledged to the Republican doctrine of "no more slave States," he declared:

I state to you freely, frankly, that I should be exceedingly sorry to ever be put in the position of having to pass upon that question. I should be exceedingly glad to know that there never would be another slave State admitted into this Union.

Here permit me to remark that I do not think the people will ever force him into a position against his will.   He went on to say:

> But I must add, in regard to this, that if slavery shall be kept out of the Territory during the territorial existence of any one given Territory, and then the people should — having a fair chance and a clear field when they come to adopt a constitution — if they should do the extraordinary thing of adopting a slave constitution, uninfluenced by the actual presence of the institution among them, I see no alternative, if we own the country, but we must admit it into this Union.

That answer Mr. Lincoln supposed would satisfy the old-line Whigs, composed of Kentuckians and Virginians, down in the southern part of the State. Now, what does it amount to? I desired to know whether he would vote to allow Kansas to come into the Union with slavery or not, as her people desired. He would not answer, but in a roundabout way said that if slavery should be kept out of a Territory during the whole of its territorial existence, and then the people, when they adopted a State constitution, asked admission as a slave State, he supposed he would have to let the State come in. The case I put to him was an entirely different one. I desired to know whether he would vote to admit a State if Congress had not prohibited slavery in it during its territorial existence, as Congress never pretended to do under Clay's compromise measures of 1850. He would not answer, and I have not yet been able to get an answer from him. I have asked him whether he would vote to admit Nebraska if her people asked to come in as a State with a constitution recognizing slavery, and he refused to answer. I have put the question to him with reference to New Mexico, and he has not uttered a word in answer. I have enumerated the Territories, one after another, putting the same question to him with reference to each, and he has not said, and will not say, whether, if elected to Congress, he will vote to admit any Territory now in existence with such a constitution as her people may adopt. He invents a case which does not exist, and cannot exist, under this government, and answers it; but he will not answer the question I put to him in connection with any of the Territories now in existence. The contract we entered into with Texas when she entered the Union obliges us to allow four States to be formed out of the old State, and admitted with or without slavery, as the respective inhabitants of each may determine. I have asked Mr. Lincoln three times in our joint discussions whether he would vote to redeem that pledge, and he has never yet answered. He is as silent as the grave on the subject. He would rather answer as to a state of the case which will never arise than commit himself by telling what he would do in a case which would come up for his action soon after his election to Congress. Why can he not say whether he is willing to allow the people of each State to have slavery or not, as they please, and to come into the Union when they have the requisite population as a slave or a free State, as they decide? I have no trouble in answering the question. I have said everywhere, and now repeat it to you, that if the people of Kansas want a slave State they have a right, under the Constitution of the United States, to form such a State, and I will let them come into the Union with slavery or without it, as they determine. If the people of any other Territory desire slavery, let them have it. If they do not want it, let them prohibit it. It is their business, not mine. It is none of our business in Illinois whether Kansas is a free State or a slave State. It is none of your business in Missouri whether Kansas shall adopt slavery or reject it. It is the business of her people, and none of yours. The people of Kansas have as much right to decide that question for themselves as you have in Missouri to decide it for yourselves, or we in Illinois to decide it for ourselves.

And here I may repeat what I have said in every speech I have made in Illinois, that I fought the Lecompton constitution to its death, not because of the slavery clause in it, but because it was not the act and deed of the people of Kansas. I said then in Congress, and I say now, that if the people of Kansas want a slave State, they have a right to have it. If they wanted the Lecompton constitution, they had a right to have it. I was opposed to that constitution because I did not believe that it was the act and deed of the people, but, on the contrary, the act of a small, pitiful minority, acting in the name of the majority. When at last it was determined to send that constitution back to the people, and accordingly, in August last, the question of admission under it was submitted to a popular vote, the citizens rejected it by nearly ten to one, thus showing conclusively that I was right when I said that the Lecompton constitution was not the act and deed of the people of Kansas, and did not embody their will.

I hold that there is no power on earth, under our system of government, which has the right to force a constitution upon an unwilling people. Suppose that there had been a majority of ten to one in favor of slavery in Kansas, and suppose there had been an Abolition President, and an Abolition administration, and by some means the Abolitionists succeeded in forcing an Abolition constitution on those slaveholding people, would the people of the South have submitted to that act for one instant? Well, if you of the South would not have submitted to it a day, how can you, as fair, honorable, and honest men, insist on putting a slave constitution on a people who desire a free State? Your safety and ours depend upon both of us acting in good faith, and living up to that great principle which asserts the right of every people to form and regulate their domestic institutions to suit themselves, subject only to the Constitution of the United States.

Most of the men who denounced my course on the Lecompton question objected to it not because I was not right, but because they thought it expedient at that time, for the sake of keeping the party together, to do wrong. I never knew the Democratic party to violate any one of its principles out of policy or expediency, that it did not pay the debt with sorrow. There is no safety or success for our party unless we always do right, and trust the consequences to God and the people. I chose not to depart from principle for the sake of expediency in the Lecompton question, and I never intend to do it on that or any other question.

But I am told that I would have been all right if I had only voted for the English bill after Lecompton was killed. You know a general pardon was granted to all political offenders on the Lecompton question, provided they would only vote for the English bill. I did not accept the benefits of that pardon, for the reason that I had been right in the course I had pursued, and hence did not require any forgiveness. Let us see how the result has been worked out. English brought in his bill referring the Lecompton constitution back to the people, with the provision that if it was rejected Kansas should be kept out of the Union until she had the full ratio of population required for a member of Congress, thus in effect declaring that if the people of Kansas would only consent to come into the Union under the Lecompton constitution, and have a slave State when they did not want it, they should be admitted with a population of 35,000; but that if they were so obstinate as to insist upon having just such a constitution as they thought best, and to desire admission as a free State, then they should be kept out until they had 93,420 inhabitants. I then said, and I now repeat to you, that whenever Kansas has people enough for a slave State she has people enough for a free State. I was, and am, willing to adopt the rule that no State shall ever come into the Union until she has the full ratio of population for a member of Congress, provided that rule is made uniform. I made that proposition in the Senate last winter, but a majority of the senators would not agree to it; and I then said to them, "If you will not adopt the general rule, I will not consent to make an exception of Kansas."

I hold that it is a violation of the fundamental principles of this government to throw the weight of federal power into the scale, either in favor of the free or the slave States. Equality among all the States of this Union is a fundamental principle in our political system. We have no more right to throw the weight of the Federal Government into the scale in favor of the slaveholding than of the free States, and, least of all, should our friends in the South consent for a moment that Congress should withhold its powers either way when they know that there is a majority against them in both houses of Congress.

Fellow-citizens, how have the supporters of the English bill stood up to their pledges not to admit Kansas until she obtained a population of 93,420 in the event she rejected the Lecompton constitution? How? The newspapers inform us that English himself, whilst conducting his canvass for reëlection, and in order to secure it, pledged himself to his constituents that if returned he would disregard his own bill and vote to admit Kansas into the Union with such population as she might have when she made application. We are informed that every Democratic candidate for Congress in all the States where elections have recently been held was pledged against the English bill, with perhaps one or two exceptions. Now, if I had only done as these anti-Lecompton men who voted for the English bill in Congress, pledging themselves to refuse to admit Kansas if she refused to become a slave State until she had a population of 93,420, and then returned to their people, forfeited their pledge, and made a new pledge to admit Kansas any time she applied, without regard to population, I would have had no trouble. You saw the whole power and patronage of the Federal Government wielded in Indiana, Ohio, and Pennsylvania to elect anti-Lecompton men to Congress, who voted against Lecompton, then voted for the English bill, and then denounced the English bill, and pledged themselves to their people to disregard it. My sin consists in not having given a pledge, and then in not having afterward forfeited it. For that reason, in this State, every postmaster, every route agent, every collector of the ports, and every federal office-holder, forfeits his head the moment he expresses a preference for the Democratic candidates against Lincoln and his Abolition associates. A Democratic administration, which we helped to bring into power, deems it consistent with its fidelity to principle, and its regard to duty, to wield its power in this State in behalf of the Republican Abolition candidates in every county and every congressional district against the Democratic party. All I have to say in reference to the matter is that if that administration have not regard enough for principle, if they are not sufficiently attached to the creed of the Democratic party to bury forever their personal hostilities in order to succeed in carrying out our glorious principles, I have. I have no personal difficulty with Mr. Buchanan or his cabinet. He chose to make certain recommendations to Congress, as he had a right to do, on the Lecompton question. I could not vote in favor of them. I had as much right to judge for myself how I should vote as he had how he should recommend. He undertook to say to me, "If you do not vote as I tell you, I will take off the heads of your friends." I replied to him, "You did not elect me; I represent Illinois, and I am accountable to Illinois, as my constituency, and to God, but not to the President or to any other power on earth."

And now this warfare is made on me because I would not surrender my convictions of duty, because I would not abandon my constituency, and receive the orders of the executive authorities how I should vote in the Senate of the United States. I hold that an attempt to control the Senate on the part of the executive is subversive of the principles of our Constitution. The executive department is independent of the Senate, and the Senate is independent of the President. In matters of legislation the President has a veto on the action of the Senate, and in appointments and treaties the Senate has a veto on the President. He has no more right to tell me how I shall vote on his appointments than I have to tell him whether he shall veto or approve a bill that the Senate has passed. Whenever you recognize the right of the executive to say to a senator, "Do this, or I will take off the heads of your friends," you convert this government from a republic into a despotism. Whenever you recognize the right of a President to say to a member of Congress, "Vote as I tell you, or I will bring a power to bear against you at home which will crush you," you destroy the independence of the representative, and convert him into a tool of executive power. I resisted this invasion of the constitutional rights of a senator, and I intend to resist it as long as I have a voice to speak, or a vote to give.

Yet Mr. Buchanan cannot provoke me to abandon one iota of Democratic principles out of revenge or hostility to his course. I stand by the platform of the Democratic party, and by its organization, and support its nominees. If there are any who choose to bolt, the fact only shows that they are not as good Democrats as I am.

My friends, there never was a time when it was as important for the Democratic party, for all national men, to rally and stand together as it is to-day. We find all sectional men giving up past differences and uniting on the one question of slavery, and when we find sectional men thus uniting, we should unite to resist them and their treasonable designs. Such was the case in 1850, when Clay left the quiet and peace of his home, and again entered upon public life to quell agitation and restore peace to a distracted Union. Then we Democrats, with Cass at our head, welcomed Henry Clay, whom the whole nation regarded as having been preserved by God for the times. He became our leader in that great fight, and we rallied around him the same as the Whigs rallied around Old Hickory in 1832 to put down nullification. Thus you see that while Whigs and Democrats fought fearlessly in old times about banks, the tariff, distribution, the specie circular, and the subtreasury, all united as a band of brothers when the peace, harmony, or integrity of the Union was imperiled. It was so in 1850, when Abolitionism had even so far divided this country, North and South, as to endanger the peace of the Union. Whigs and Democrats united in establishing the compromise measures of that year, and restoring tranquillity and good feeling. These measures passed on the joint action of the two parties. They rested on the great principle that the people of each State and each Territory should be left perfectly free to form and regulate their domestic institutions to suit themselves. You Whigs and we Democrats justified them in that principle. In 1854, when it became necessary to organize the Territories of Kansas and Nebraska, I brought forward the bill on the same principle. In the Kansas-Nebraska bill you find it declared to be the true intent and meaning of the act not to legislate slavery into any State or Territory, nor to exclude it therefrom, but to leave the people thereof perfectly free to form and regulate their domestic institutions in their own way.

I stand on that same platform in 1858 that I did in 1850, 1854, and 1856. The Washington "Union," pretending to be the organ of the administration, in the number of the 5th of this month, devotes three columns and a half to establish these propositions: first, that Douglas in his Freeport speech held the same doctrine that he did in his Nebraska bill in 1854; second, that in 1854 Douglas justified the Nebraska bill upon the ground that it was based upon the same principle as Clay's compromise measures of 1850. The "Union" thus proved that Douglas was the same in 1858 that he was in 1856, 1854, and 1850, and consequently argued that he was never a Democrat. Is it not funny that I was never a Democrat? There is no pretense that I have changed a hair's-breadth. The "Union" proves by my speeches that I explained the compromise measures of 1850 just as I do now, and that I explained the Kansas and Nebraska bill in 1854 just as I did in my Freeport speech, and yet says that I am not a Democrat, and cannot be trusted, because I have not changed during the whole of that time. It has occurred to me that in 1854 the author of the Kansas and Nebraska bill was considered a pretty good Democrat. It has occurred to me that in 1856, when I was exerting every nerve and every energy for James Buchanan, standing on the same platform then that I do now, that I was a pretty good Democrat. They now tell me that I am not a Democrat, because I assert that the people of a Territory, as well as those of a State, have the right to decide for themselves whether slavery can or cannot exist in such Territory. Let me read what James Buchanan said on that point when he accepted the Democratic nomination for the presidency in 1856. In his letter of acceptance, he used the following language :

The recent legislation of Congress respecting domestic slavery, derived as it has been from the original and pure fountain of legitimate political power, the will of the majority, promises ere long to allay the dangerous excitement. This legislation is founded upon principles as ancient as free government itself, and in accordance with them has simply declared that the people of a Territory, like those of a State, shall decide for themselves whether slavery shall or shall not exist within their limits.

Dr. Hope will there find my answer to the question he propounded to me before I commenced speaking. Of course no man will consider it an answer, who is outside of the Democratic organization, bolts Democratic nominations, and indirectly aids to put Abolitionists into power over Democrats. But whether Dr. Hope considers it an answer or not, every fair-minded man will see that James Buchanan has answered the question, and has asserted that the people of a Territory, like those of a State, shall decide for themselves whether slavery shall or shall not exist within their limits. I answer specifically, if you want a further answer, and say that while under the decision of the Supreme Court, as recorded in the opinion of Chief Justice Taney, slaves are property like all other property, and can be carried into any Territory of the United States the same as any other description of property, yet when you get them there they are subject to the local law of the Territory just like all other property. You will find in a recent speech delivered by that able and eloquent statesman, Hon. Jefferson Davis, at Bangor, Maine, that he took the same view of this subject that I did in my Freeport speech. He there said:

If the inhabitants of any Territory should refuse to enact such laws and police regulations as would give security to their property or to his, it would be rendered more or less valueless in proportion to the difficulties of holding it without such protection. In the case of property in the labor of man, or what is usually called slave property, the insecurity would be so great that the owner could not ordinarily retain it. Therefore, though the right would remain, the remedy being withheld, it would follow that the owner would be practically debarred, by the circumstances of the case, from taking slave property into a Territory where the sense of the inhabitants was opposed to its introduction. So much for the oft-repeated fallacy of forcing slavery upon any community.

You will also find that the distinguished Speaker of the present House of Representatives, Hon. James L. Orr, construed the Kansas and Nebraska bill in this same way in 1856, and also that great intellect of the South, Alexander H. Stephens, put the same construction upon it in Congress that I did in my Freeport speech. The whole South is rallying to the support of the doctrine that if the people of a Territory want slavery they have a right to have it, and if they do not want it that no power on earth can force it upon them. I hold that there is no principle on earth more sacred to all the friends of freedom than that which says that no institution, no law, no constitution, should be forced on an unwilling people contrary to their wishes; and I assert that the Kansas and Nebraska bill contains that principle. It is the great principle contained in that bill. It is the principle on which James Buchanan was made President. Without that principle he never would have been made President of the United States. I will never violate or abandon that doctrine, if I have to stand alone. I have resisted the blandishments and threats of power on the one side, and seduction on the other, and have stood immovably for that principle, fighting for it when assailed by Northern mobs, or threatened by Southern hostility. I have defended it against the North and the South, and I will defend it against whoever assails it, and I will follow it wherever its logical conclusions lead me. I say to you that there is but one hope, one safety for this country, and that is to stand immovably by that principle which declares the right of each State and each Territory to decide these questions for themselves. This government was founded on that principle, and must be administered in the same sense in which it was founded.

But the Abolition party really think that under the Declaration of Independence the negro is equal to the white man, and that negro equality is an inalienable right conferred by the Almighty, and hence that all human laws in violation of it are null and void. With such men it is no use for me to argue. I hold that the signers of the Declaration of Independence had no reference to negroes at all when they declared all men to be created equal. They did not mean negroes, nor the savage Indians, nor the Feejee Islanders, nor any other barbarous race. They were speaking of white men. They alluded to men of European birth and European descent — to white men, and to none others, when they declared that doctrine. I hold that this government was established on the white basis. It was established by white men, for the benefit of white men and their posterity forever, and should be administered by white men, and none others. But it does not follow, by any means, that merely because the negro is not a citizen, and merely because he is not our equal, that therefore he should be a slave. On the contrary, it does follow that we ought to extend to the negro race, and to all other dependent races, all the rights, all the privileges, and all the immunities which they can exercise consistently with the safety of society. Humanity requires that we should give them all those privileges; Christianity commands that we should extend those privileges to them. The question then arises, What are those privileges, and what is the nature and extent of them? My answer is that that is a question which each State must answer for itself. We in Illinois have decided it for ourselves. We tried slavery, kept it up for twelve years, and finding that it was not profitable, we abolished it for that reason, and became a free State. We adopted in its stead the policy that a negro in this State shall not be a slave and shall not be a citizen. We have a right to adopt that policy. For my part, I think it is a wise and sound policy for us. You in Missouri must judge for yourselves whether it is a wise policy for you. If you choose to follow our example, very good; if you reject it, still well; it is your business, not ours. So with Kentucky. Let Kentucky adopt a policy to suit herself. If we do not like it, we will keep away from it; and if she does not like ours, let her stay at home, mind her own business, and let us alone. If the people of all the States will act on that great principle, and each State mind its own business, attend to its own affairs, take care of its own negroes, and not meddle with its neighbors, then there will be peace between the North and the South, the East and the West, throughout the whole Union. Why can we not thus have peace? Why should we thus allow a sectional party to agitate this country, to array the North against the South, and convert us into enemies instead of friends, merely that a few ambitious men may ride into power on a sectional hobby? How long is it since these ambitious Northern men wished for a sectional organization? Did any one of them dream of a sectional party as long as the North was the weaker section and the South the stronger? Then all were opposed to sectional parties. But the moment the North obtained the majority in the House and Senate by the admission of California, and could elect a President without the aid of Southern votes, that moment ambitious Northern men formed a scheme to excite the North against the South, and make the people be governed in their votes by geographical lines, thinking that the North, being the stronger section, would outvote the South, and consequently they, the leaders, would ride into office on a sectional hobby. I am told that my hour is out. It was very short.

Mr. Lincoln's Reply in the Alton Joint Debate.

Ladies and Gentlemen: I have been somewhat, in my own mind, complimented by a large portion of Judge Douglas's speech — I mean that portion which he devotes to the controversy between himself and the present administration. This is the seventh time Judge Douglas and myself have met in these joint discussions, and he has been gradually improving in regard to his war with the administration. At Quincy, day before yesterday, he was a little more severe upon the administration than I had heard him upon any occasion, and I took pains to compliment him for it. I then told him to "give it to them with all the power he had"; and as some of them were present, I told them I would be very much obliged if they would give it to him in about the same way. I take it that he has now vastly improved upon the attack he made then upon the administration. I flatter myself he has really taken my advice on this subject. All I can say now is to re-commend to him and to them what I then commended — to prosecute the war against one another in the most vigorous manner. I say to them again, "Go it, husband; go it, bear!"

There is one other thing I will mention before I leave this branch of the discussion—although I do not consider it much of my business, anyway. I refer to that part of the judge's remarks where he undertakes to involve Mr. Buchanan in an inconsistency. He reads something from Mr. Buchanan, from which he undertakes to involve him in an inconsistency; and he gets something of a cheer for having done so. I would only remind the judge that while he is very valiantly fighting for the Nebraska bill and the repeal of the Missouri Compromise, it has been but a little while since he was the valiant advocate of the Missouri Compromise. I want to know if Buchanan has not as much right to be inconsistent as Douglas has? Has Douglas the exclusive right in this country of being on all sides of all questions? Is nobody allowed that high privilege but himself? Is he to have an entire monopoly on that subject?

So far as Judge Douglas addressed his speech to me, or so far as it was about me, it is my business to pay some attention to it. I have heard the judge state two or three times what he has stated to-day—that in a speech which I made at Springfield, Illinois, I had in a very especial manner complained that the Supreme Court in the Dred Scott case had decided that a negro could never be a citizen of the United States. I have omitted, by some accident, heretofore to analyze this statement, and it is required of me to notice it now. In point of fact it is untrue. I never have complained especially of the Dred Scott decision because it held that a negro could not be a citizen, and the judge is always wrong when he says I ever did so complain of it. I have the speech here, and I will thank him or any of his friends to show where I said that a negro should be a citizen, and complained especially of the Dred Scott decision because it declared he could not be one. I have done no such thing, and Judge Douglas so persistently insisting that I have done so has strongly impressed me with the belief of a predetermination on his part to misrepresent me. He could not get his foundation for insisting that I was in favor of this negro equality anywhere else as well as he could by assuming that untrue proposition. Let me tell this audience what is true in regard to that matter; and the means by which they may correct me if I do not tell them truly is by a recurrence to the speech itself. I spoke of the Dred Scott decision in my Springfield speech, and I was then endeavoring to prove that the Dred Scott decision was a portion of a system or scheme to make slavery national in this country. I pointed out what things had been decided by the court. I mentioned as a fact that they had decided that a negro could not be a citizen—that they had done so, as I supposed, to deprive the negro, under all circumstances, of the remotest possibility of ever becoming a citizen and claiming the rights of a citizen of the United States under a certain clause of the Constitution. I stated that, without making any complaint of it at all. I then went on and stated the other points decided in the case,—namely, that the bringing of a negro into the State of Illinois, and holding him in slavery for two years here, was a matter in regard to which they would not decide whether it would make him free or not; that they decided the further point

VOL. I.— 32.

that taking him into a United States Territory where slavery was prohibited by act of Congress, did not make him free, because that act of Congress, as they held, was unconstitutional. I mentioned these three things as making up the points decided in that case. I mentioned them in a lump taken in connection with the introduction of the Nebraska bill, and the amendment of Chase, offered at the time, declaratory of the right of the people of the Territories to exclude slavery, which was voted down by the friends of the bill. I mentioned all these things together, as evidence tending to prove a combination and conspiracy to make the institution of slavery national. In that connection and in that way I mentioned the decision on the point that a negro could not be a citizen, and in no other connection.

Out of this, Judge Douglas builds up his beautiful fabrication — of my purpose to introduce a perfect social and political equality between the white and the black races. His assertion that I made an "especial objection" (that is his exact language) to the decision on this account, is untrue in point of fact.

Now, while I am upon this subject, and as Henry Clay has been alluded to, I desire to place myself, in connection with Mr. Clay, as nearly right before this people as may be. I am quite aware what the judge's object is here by all these allusions. He knows that we are before an audience having strong sympathies southward by relationship, place of birth, and so on. He desires to place me in an extremely Abolition attitude. He read upon a former occasion, and alludes without reading to-day, to a portion of a speech which I delivered in Chicago. In his quotations from that speech, as he has made them upon former occasions, the extracts were taken in such a way as, I suppose, brings them within the definition of what is called garbling — taking portions of a speech which, when taken by themselves, do not present the entire sense of the speaker as expressed at the time. I propose, therefore, out of that same speech, to show how one portion of it which he skipped over (taking an extract before and an extract after) will give a different idea, and the true idea I intended to convey. It will take me some little time to read it, but I believe I will occupy the time that way.

You have heard him frequently allude to my controversy with him in regard to the Declaration of Independence. I confess that I have had a struggle with Judge Douglas on that matter, and I will try briefly to place myself right in regard to it on this occasion. I said — and it is between the extracts Judge Douglas has taken from this speech, and put in his published speeches:

It may be argued that there are certain conditions that make necessities and impose them upon us, and to the extent that a necessity is imposed upon a man he must submit to it. I think that was the condition in which we found ourselves when we established this government. We had slaves among us; we could not get our Constitution unless we permitted them to remain in slavery; we could not secure the good we did secure if we grasped for more: and having by necessity submitted to that much, it does not destroy the principle that is the charter of our liberties. Let that charter remain as our standard.

Now I have upon all occasions declared as strongly as Judge Douglas against the disposition to interfere with the existing institution of slavery. You hear me read it from the same speech from which he takes garbled extracts for the purpose of proving upon me a disposition to interfere with the institution of slavery, and establish a perfect social and political equality between negroes and white people.

Allow me, while upon this subject, briefly to present one other extract from a speech of mine, made more than a year ago, at Springfield, in discussing this very same question, soon after Judge Douglas took his ground that negroes were not included in the Declaration of Independence:

I think the authors of that notable instrument intended to include all men, but they did not intend to declare all men equal in all respects. They did not mean to say that all men were equal in color, size, intellect, moral development, or social capacity. They defined with tolerable distinctness in what respects they did consider all men created equal—equal in certain inalienable rights, among which are life, liberty, and the pursuit of happiness. This they said, and this they meant. They did not mean to assert the obvious untruth, that all were then actually enjoying that equality, nor yet that they were about to confer it immediately upon them. In fact, they had no power to confer such a boon. They meant simply to declare the right, so that the enforcement of it might follow as fast as circumstances should permit.

They meant to set up a standard maxim for free society which should be familiar to all and revered by all—constantly looked to, constantly labored for, and even, though never perfectly attained, constantly approximated; and thereby constantly spreading and deepening its influence and augmenting the happiness and value of life to all people, of all colors, everywhere.

There, again, are the sentiments I have expressed in regard to the Declaration of Independence upon a former occasion—sentiments which have been put in print and read wherever anybody cared to know what so humble an individual as myself chose to say in regard to it.

At Galesburg the other day, I said, in answer to Judge Douglas, that three years ago there never had been a man, so far as I knew or believed, in the whole world, who had said that the Declaration of Independence did not include negroes in the term "all men." I reassert it to-day. I assert that Judge Douglas and all his friends may search the whole records of the country, and it will be a matter of great astonishment to me if they shall be able to find that one human being three years ago had ever uttered the astounding sentiment that the term "all men" in the Declaration did not include the negro. Do not let me be misunderstood. I know that more than three years ago there were men who, finding this assertion constantly in the way of their schemes to bring about the ascendancy and perpetuation of slavery, denied the truth of it. I know that Mr. Calhoun and all the politicians of his school denied the truth of the Declaration. I know that it ran along in the mouth of some Southern men for a period of years, ending at last in that shameful though rather forcible declaration of Pettit of Indiana, upon the floor of the

United States Senate, that the Declaration of Independence was in that respect "a self-evident lie," rather than a self-evident truth. But I say, with a perfect knowledge of all this hawking at the Declaration without directly attacking it, that three years ago there never had lived a man who had ventured to assail it in the sneaking way of pretending to believe it and then asserting it did not include the negro. I believe the first man who ever said it was Chief Justice Taney in the Dred Scott case, and the next to him was our friend, Stephen A. Douglas. And now it has become the catchword of the entire party. I would like to call upon his friends everywhere to consider how they have come in so short a time to view this matter in a way so entirely different from their former belief; to ask whether they are not being borne along by an irresistible current— whither, they know not.

In answer to my proposition at Galesburg last week, I see that some man in Chicago has got up a letter addressed to the Chicago "Times," to show, as he professes, that somebody had said so before; and he signs himself "An Old-Line Whig," if I remember correctly. In the first place I would say he was not an old-line Whig. I am somewhat acquainted with old-line Whigs. I was with the old-line Whigs from the origin to the end of that party; I became pretty well acquainted with them, and I know they always had some sense, whatever else you could ascribe to them. I know there never was one who had not more sense than to try to show by the evidence he produces that some man had, prior to the time I named, said that negroes were not included in the term "all men" in the Declaration of Independence. What is the evidence he produces? I will bring forward his evidence, and let you see what he offers by way of showing that somebody more than three years ago had said negroes were not included in the Declaration. He brings forward part of a speech from Henry Clay—the part of the speech of Henry Clay which I used to bring forward to prove precisely the contrary. I guess we are surrounded to some extent to-day by the old friends of Mr. Clay, and they will be glad to hear anything from that authority. While he was in Indiana a man presented a petition to liberate his negroes, and he (Mr. Clay) made a speech in answer to it, which I suppose he carefully wrote himself and caused to be published. I have before me an extract from that speech which constitutes the evidence this pretended "Old-Line Whig" at Chicago brought forward to show that Mr. Clay did n't suppose the negro was included in the Declaration of Independence. Hear what Mr. Clay said:

And what is the foundation of this appeal to me in Indiana, to liberate the slaves under my care in Kentucky? It is a general declaration in the act announcing to the world the independence of the thirteen American colonies, that all men are created equal. Now, as an abstract principle, there is no doubt of the truth of that declaration; and it is desirable, in the original construction of society, and in organized societies, to keep it in view as a great fundamental principle. But then I apprehend that in no society that ever did exist, or ever shall be formed, was or can the equality asserted among the members of the human race be practically enforced and carried out. There are portions, large portions,—women, minors, insane, culprits, transient sojourners,—that will always probably remain subject to the government of another portion of the community.

That declaration, whatever may be the extent of its import, was made by the delegations of the thirteen States. In most of them slavery existed, and had long existed, and was established by law. It was introduced and forced upon the colonies by the paramount law of England. Do you believe that in making that declaration the States that concurred in it intended that it should be tortured into a virtual emancipation of all the slaves within their respective limits? Would Virginia and other Southern States have ever united in a declaration which was to be interpreted into an abolition of slavery among them? Did any one of the thirteen colonies entertain such a design or expectation? To impute such a secret and unavowed purpose would be to charge a political fraud upon the noblest band of patriots that ever assembled in council—a fraud upon the confederacy of the Revolution—a fraud upon the union of those States whose constitution not only recognized the lawfulness of slavery, but permitted the importation of slaves from Africa until the year 1808.

This is the entire quotation brought forward to prove that somebody previous to three years ago had said the negro was not included in the term "all men" in the Declaration. How does it do so? In what way has it a tendency to prove that? Mr. Clay says it is true as an abstract principle that all men are created equal, but that we cannot practically apply it in all cases. He illustrates this by bringing forward the cases of females, minors, and insane persons, with whom it cannot be enforced; but he says that it is true as an abstract principle in the organization of society as well as in organized society, and it should be kept in view as a fundamental principle. Let me read a few words more before I add some comments of my own. Mr. Clay says a little further on:

I desire no concealment of my opinions in regard to the institution of slavery. I look upon it as a great evil, and deeply lament that we have derived it from the parent government, and from our ancestors. I wish every slave in the United States was in the country of his ancestors. But here they are, and the question is, how can they be best dealt with? If a state of nature existed, and we were about to lay the foundations of society, no man would be more strongly opposed than I should be, to incorporating the institution of slavery among its elements.

Now, here in this same book — in this same speech — in this same extract brought forward to prove that Mr. Clay held that the negro was not included in the Declaration of Independence — we find no such statement on his part, but instead the declaration that it is a great fundamental truth, which should be constantly kept in view in the organization of society and in societies already organized. But if I say a word about it; if I attempt, as Mr. Clay said all good men ought to do, to keep it in view; if, in this "organized society," I ask to have the public eye turned upon it; if I ask, in relation to the organization of new Territories, that the public eye should be turned upon it,—forthwith I am vilified as you hear me to-day. What have I done that I have not the license of Henry Clay's illustrious example here in doing? Have I done aught that I have not his authority for, while maintaining that in organizing new Territories and societies, this fundamental principle should be regarded, and in organized society holding it up to the public view and recognizing what he recognized as the great principle of free government?

And when this new principle—this new proposition that no human being ever thought of three years ago — is brought forward, I combat it as having an evil tendency, if not an evil design. I combat it as having a tendency to dehumanize the negro — to take away from him the right of ever striving to be a man. I combat it as being one of the thousand things constantly done in these days to prepare the public mind to make property, and nothing but property, of the negro in all the States in this Union.

But there is a point that I wish, before leaving this part of the discussion, to ask attention to. I have read, and I repeat, the words of Henry Clay:

I desire no concealment of my opinions in regard to the institution of slavery. I look upon it as a great evil, and deeply lament that we have derived it from the parent government, and from our ancestors. I wish every slave in the United States was in the country of his ancestors. But here they are, and the question is, how can they best be dealt with? If a state of nature existed, and we were about to lay the foundations of society, no man would be more strongly opposed than I should be, to incorporating the institution of slavery among its elements.

The principle upon which I have insisted in this canvass, is in relation to laying the foundations of new societies. I have never sought to apply these principles to the old States for the purpose of abolishing slavery in those States. It is nothing but a miserable perversion of what I have said, to assume that I have declared Missouri, or any other slave State, shall emancipate her slaves. I have proposed no such thing. But when Mr. Clay says that in laying the foundations of societies in our Territories where it does not exist, he would be opposed to the introduction of slavery as an element, I insist that we have his warrant— his license for insisting upon the exclusion of that element which he declared in such strong and emphatic language was most hateful to him.

Judge Douglas has again referred to a Springfield speech in which I said, "A house divided against itself cannot stand." The judge has so often made the entire quotation from that speech that I can make it from memory. I used this language:

We are now far into the fifth year since a policy was initiated with the avowed object and confident promise of putting an end to the slavery agitation. Under the operation of this policy, that agitation has not only not ceased, but has constantly augmented. In my opinion it will not cease until a crisis shall have been reached and passed. "A house divided against itself cannot stand." I believe this government cannot endure permanently half slave and half free. I do not expect the house to fall—but I do expect it will cease to be divided. It will become all one thing, or all the other. Either the opponents of slavery will arrest the further spread of it, and place it where the public mind shall rest in the belief that it is in the course of ultimate extinction, or its advocates will push it forward till it shall become alike lawful in all the States—old as well as new, North as well as South.

That extract, and the sentiments expressed in it, have been extremely offensive to Judge Douglas. He has warred upon them as Satan wars upon the Bible. His perversions upon it are endless. Here now are my views upon it in brief.

I said we were now far into the fifth year since a policy was initiated with the avowed object and confident promise of putting an end to the slavery agitation. Is it not so? When that Nebraska bill was brought forward four years ago last January, was it not for the "avowed object" of putting an end to the slavery agitation? We were to have no more agitation in Congress; it was all to be banished to the Territories. By the way, I will remark here that, as Judge Douglas is very fond of complimenting Mr. Crittenden in these days, Mr. Crittenden has said there was a falsehood in that whole business, for there was no slavery agitation at that time to allay. We were for a little while quiet on the troublesome thing, and that very allaying-plaster of Judge Douglas's stirred it up again. But was it not undertaken or initiated with the "confident promise" of putting an end to the slavery agitation? Surely it was. In every speech you heard Judge Douglas make, until he got into this "imbroglio," as they call it, with the administration about the Lecompton constitution, every speech on that Nebraska bill was full of his felicitations that we were just at the end of the slavery agitation. The last tip of the last joint of the old serpent's tail was just drawing out of view. But has it proved so? I have asserted that under that policy that agitation "has not only ceased, but has constantly augmented." When was there ever a greater agitation in Congress than last winter? When was it as great in the country as to-day?

There was a collateral object in the introduction of that Nebraska policy which was to clothe the people of the Territories with a superior degree of self-government, beyond what they had ever had before. The first object and the main one of conferring upon the people a higher degree of "self-government," is a question of fact to be determined by you in answer to a single question. Have you ever heard or known of a people anywhere on earth who had as little to do as, in the first instance of its use, the people of Kansas had with this same right of "self-government"? In its main policy and in its collateral object, it has been nothing but a living, creeping lie from the time of its introduction till to-day.

I have intimated that I thought the agitation would not cease until a crisis should have been reached and passed. I have stated in what way I thought it would be reached and passed. I have said that it might go one way or the other. We might, by arresting the further spread of it, and placing it where the fathers originally placed it, put it where the public mind should rest in the belief that it was in the course of ultimate extinction. Thus the agitation may cease. It may be pushed forward until it shall become alike lawful in all the States, old as well as new, North as well as South. I have said, and I repeat, my wish is that the further spread of it may be arrested, and that it may be placed where the public mind shall rest in the belief that it is in the course of ultimate extinction. I have expressed that as my wish. I entertain the opinion, upon evidence

sufficient to my mind, that the fathers of this government placed
that institution where the public mind did rest in the belief that it
was in the course of ultimate extinction.   Let me ask why they made
provision that the source of slavery—the African slave-trade—
should be cut off at the end of twenty years!   Why did they make
provision that in all the new territory we owned at that time, slavery
should be forever inhibited!   Why stop its spread in one direction
and cut off its source in another, if they did not look to its being
placed in the course of ultimate extinction!

Again, the institution of slavery is only mentioned in the Constitution of the United States two or three times, and in neither of
these cases does the word "slavery" or "negro race" occur; but
covert language is used each time, and for a purpose full of significance.   What is the language in regard to the prohibition of the
African slave-trade?   It runs in about this way: "The migration or
importation of such persons as any of the States now existing shall
think proper to admit, shall not be prohibited by the Congress prior
to the year 1808."

The next allusion in the Constitution to the question of slavery and
the black race, is on the subject of the basis of representation, and
there the language used is: "Representatives and direct taxes shall
be apportioned among the several States which may be included
within this Union, according to their respective numbers, which
shall be determined by adding to the whole number of free persons,
including those bound to service for a term of years, and excluding
Indians not taxed, three fifths of all other persons."

It says "persons," not slaves, not negroes; but this "three fifths"
can be applied to no other class among us than the negroes.

Lastly, in the provision for the reclamation of fugitive slaves, it
is said: "No person held to service or labor in one State, under the
laws thereof, escaping into another, shall in consequence of any law
or regulation therein be discharged from such service or labor, but
shall be delivered up, on claim of the party to whom such service or
labor may be due."   There, again, there is no mention of the word
"negro," or of slavery.   In all three of these places, being the only
allusion to slavery in the instrument, covert language is used.   Language is used not suggesting that slavery existed or that the black
race were among us.   And I understand the contemporaneous history
of those times to be that covert language was used with a purpose,
and that purpose was that in our Constitution, which it was hoped,
and is still hoped, will endure forever,—when it should be read by
intelligent and patriotic men, after the institution of slavery had
passed from among us,—there should be nothing on the face of the
great charter of liberty suggesting that such a thing as negro slavery
had ever existed among us.   This is part of the evidence that the
fathers of the government expected and intended the institution
of slavery to come to an end.   They expected and intended that it
should be in the course of ultimate extinction.   And when I say
that I desire to see the further spread of it arrested, I only say I
desire to see that done which the fathers have first done.   When I say
I desire to see it placed where the public mind will rest in the belief

that it is in the course of ultimate extinction, I only say I desire to see it placed where they placed it. It is not true that our fathers, as Judge Douglas assumes, made this government part slave and part free. Understand the sense in which he puts it. He assumes that slavery is a rightful thing within itself—was introduced by the framers of the Constitution. The exact truth is that they found the institution existing among us, and they left it as they found it. But in making the government they left this institution with many clear marks of disapprobation upon it. They found slavery among them, and they left it among them because of the difficulty—the absolute impossibility—of its immediate removal. And when Judge Douglas asks me why we cannot let it remain part slave and part free, as the fathers of the government made it, he asks a question based upon an assumption which is itself a falsehood; and I turn upon him and ask him the question, when the policy that the fathers of the government had adopted in relation to this element among us was the best policy in the world,—the only wise policy, the only policy that we can ever safely continue upon, that will ever give us peace, unless this dangerous element masters us all and becomes a national institution,—I turn upon him and ask him why he could not leave it alone. I turn and ask him why he was driven to the necessity of introducing a new policy in regard to it. He has himself said he introduced a new policy. He said so in his speech on the 22d of March of the present year, 1858. I ask him why he could not let it remain where our fathers placed it. I ask, too, of Judge Douglas and his friends, why we shall not again place this institution upon the basis on which the fathers left it? I ask you, when he infers that I am in favor of setting the free and the slave States at war, when the institution was placed in that attitude by those who made the Constitution, did they make any war? If we had no war out of it when thus placed, wherein is the ground of belief that we shall have war out of it if we return to that policy? Have we had any peace upon this matter springing from any other basis? I maintain that we have not. I have proposed nothing more than a return to the policy of the fathers.

I confess, when I propose a certain measure of policy, it is not enough for me that I do not intend anything evil in the result, but it is incumbent on me to show that it has not a tendency to that result. I have met Judge Douglas in that point of view. I have not only made the declaration that I do not mean to produce a conflict between the States, but I have tried to show by fair reasoning, and I think I have shown to the minds of fair men, that I propose nothing but what has a most peaceful tendency. The quotation that I happened to make in that Springfield speech, that "a house divided against itself cannot stand," and which has proved so offensive to the judge, was part and parcel of the same thing. He tries to show that variety in the domestic institutions of the different States is necessary and indispensable. I do not dispute it. I have no controversy with Judge Douglas about that. I shall very readily agree with him that it would be foolish for us to insist upon having a cranberry law here, in Illinois, where we have no cranberries, because they have a cranberry law in Indiana, where they have cranberries. I should insist that it would be exceedingly wrong in us to deny to Virginia the right to enact oyster laws, where they have oysters, because we want no such laws here. I understand, I hope, quite as well as Judge Douglas, or anybody else, that the variety in the soil and climate and face of the country, and consequent variety in the industrial pursuits and productions of a country, require systems of laws conforming to this variety in the natural features of the country. I understand quite as well as Judge Douglas, that if we here raise a barrel of flour more than we want, and the Louisianians raise a barrel of sugar more than they want, it is of mutual advantage to exchange. That produces commerce, brings us together, and makes us better friends. We like one another the more for it. And I understand as well as Judge Douglas, or anybody else, that these mutual accommodations are the cements which bind together the different parts of this Union; that instead of being a thing to "divide the house"—figuratively expressing the Union—they tend to sustain it; they are the props of the house tending always to hold it up.

But when I have admitted all this, I ask if there is any parallel between these things and this institution of slavery? I do not see that there is any parallel at all between them. Consider it. When have we had any difficulty or quarrel amongst ourselves about the cranberry laws of Indiana, or the oyster laws of Virginia, or the pine-lumber laws of Maine, or the fact that Louisiana produces sugar, and Illinois flour? When have we had any quarrels over these things? When have we had perfect peace in regard to this thing which I say is an element of discord in this Union? We have sometimes had peace, but when was it? It was when the institution of slavery remained quiet where it was. We have had difficulty and turmoil whenever it has made a struggle to spread itself where it was not. I ask, then, if experience does not speak in thunder-tones, telling us that the policy which has given peace to the country heretofore, being returned to, gives the greatest promise of peace again. You may say, and Judge Douglas has intimated the same thing, that all this difficulty in regard to the institution of slavery is the mere agitation of office-seekers and ambitious northern politicians. He thinks we want to get "his place," I suppose. I agree that there are office-seekers amongst us. The Bible says somewhere that we are desperately selfish. I think we would have discovered that fact without the Bible. I do not claim that I am any less so than the average of men, but I do claim that I am not more selfish than Judge Douglas.

But is it true that all the difficulty and agitation we have in regard to this institution of slavery springs from office-seeking — from the mere ambition of politicians? Is that the truth? How many times have we had danger from this question? Go back to the day of the Missouri Compromise. Go back to the nullification question, at the bottom of which lay this same slavery question. Go back to the time of the annexation of Texas. Go back to the troubles that led to the compromise of 1850. You will find that every time, with the single exception of the nullification question, they sprang from an endeavor to spread this institution. There never was a party in the history of this country, and there probably never will be, of sufficient strength to disturb the general peace of the country. Parties themselves may be divided and quarrel on minor questions, yet it extends not beyond the parties themselves. But does not this question make a disturbance outside of political circles? Does it not enter into the churches and rend them asunder? What divided the great Methodist Church into two parts, North and South? What has raised this constant disturbance in every Presbyterian general assembly that meets? What disturbed the Unitarian Church in this very city two years ago? What has jarred and shaken the great American Tract Society recently — not yet splitting it, but sure to divide it in the end? Is it not this same mighty, deep-seated power that somehow operates on the minds of men, exciting and stirring them up in every avenue of society — in politics, in religion, in literature, in morals, in all the manifold relations of life? Is this the work of politicians? Is that irresistible power, which for fifty years has shaken the government and agitated the people, to be stilled and subdued by pretending that it is an exceedingly simple thing, and we ought not to talk about it? If you will get everybody else to stop talking about it, I assure you I will quit before they have half done so. But where is the philosophy or statesmanship which assumes that you can quiet that disturbing element in our society which has disturbed us for more than half a century, which has been the only serious danger that has threatened our institutions — I say, where is the philosophy or the statesmanship based on the assumption that we are to quit talking about it, and that the public mind is all at once to cease being agitated by it? Yet this is the policy here in the North that Douglas is advocating — that we are to care nothing about it! I ask you if it is not a false philosophy? Is it not a false statesmanship that undertakes to build up a system of policy upon the basis of caring nothing about the very thing that everybody does care the most about — a thing which all experience has shown we care a very great deal about?

The judge alludes very often in the course of his remarks to the exclusive right which the States have to decide the whole thing for themselves. I agree with him very readily that the different States have that right. He is but fighting a man of straw when he assumes that I am contending against the right of the States to do as they please about it. Our controversy with him is in regard to the new Territories. We agree that when the States come in as States they have the right and the power to do as they please. We have no power as citizens of the free States, or in our federal capacity as members of the Federal Union through the General Government, to disturb slavery in the States where it exists. We profess constantly that we have no more inclination than belief in the power of the government to disturb it; yet we are driven constantly to defend ourselves from the assumption that we are warring upon the rights of the States. What I insist upon is, that the new Territories shall be kept free from

it while in the territorial condition. Judge Douglas assumes that
we have no interest in them—that we have no right whatever to interfere. I think we have some interest. I think that as white men
we have. Do we not wish for an outlet for our surplus population,
if I may so express myself? Do we not feel an interest in getting to,
that outlet with such institutions as we would like to have prevail
there? If you go to the Territory opposed to slavery, and another man
comes upon the same ground with his slave, upon the assumption
that the things are equal, it turns out that he has the equal right all
his way, and you have no part of it your way. If he goes in and
makes it a slave Territory, and by consequence a slave State, is it
not time that those who desire to have it a free State were on equal
ground? Let me suggest it in a different way. How many Democrats are there about here ["A thousand"] who have left slave States
and come into the free State of Illinois to get rid of the institution
of slavery? [Another voice: "A thousand and one."] I reckon there
are a thousand and one. I will ask you, if the policy you are now
advocating had prevailed when this country was in a territorial condition, where would you have gone to get rid of it? Where would
you have found your free State or Territory to go to? And when
hereafter, for any cause, the people in this place shall desire to find
new homes, if they wish to be rid of the institution, where will they
find the place to go to?

Now, irrespective of the moral aspect of this question as to whether
there is a right or wrong in enslaving a negro, I am still in favor of
our new Territories being in such a condition that white men may
find a home—may find some spot where they can better their condition—where they can settle upon new soil, and better their condition
in life. I am in favor of this not merely (I must say it here as I
have elsewhere) for our own people who are born amongst us, but
as an outlet for free white people everywhere, the world over—in
which Hans, and Baptiste, and Patrick, and all other men from all
the world, may find new homes and better their condition in life.

I have stated upon former occasions, and I may as well state again,
what I understand to be the real issue of this controversy between
Judge Douglas and myself. On the point of my wanting to make
war between the free and the slave States, there has been no issue
between us. So, too, when he assumes that I am in favor of introducing a perfect social and political equality between the white and
black races. These are false issues, upon which Judge Douglas has
tried to force the controversy. There is no foundation in truth for
the charge that I maintain either of these propositions. The real
issue in this controversy—the one pressing upon every mind—is the
sentiment on the part of one class that looks upon the institution of
slavery as a wrong, and of another class that does not look upon it
as a wrong. The sentiment that contemplates the institution of
slavery in this country as a wrong is the sentiment of the Republican party. It is the sentiment around which all their actions, all
their arguments, circle; from which all their propositions radiate.
They look upon it as being a moral, social, and political wrong; and
while they contemplate it as such, they nevertheless have due regard

for its actual existence among us, and the difficulties of getting rid of it in any satisfactory way, and to all the constitutional obligations thrown about it. Yet having a due regard for these, they desire a policy in regard to it that looks to its not creating any more danger. They insist that it, as far as may be, be treated as a wrong, and one of the methods of treating it as a wrong is to make provision that it shall grow no larger. They also desire a policy that looks to a peaceful end of slavery some time, as being a wrong. These are the views they entertain in regard to it, as I understand them; and all their sentiments, all their arguments and propositions, are brought within this range. I have said, and I repeat it here, that if there be a man amongst us who does not think that the institution of slavery is wrong in any one of the aspects of which I have spoken, he is misplaced, and ought not to be with us. And if there be a man amongst us who is so impatient of it as a wrong as to disregard its actual presence among us and the difficulty of getting rid of it suddenly in a satisfactory way, and to disregard the constitutional obligations thrown about it, that man is misplaced if he is on our platform. We disclaim sympathy with him in practical action. He is not placed properly with us.

On this subject of treating it as a wrong, and limiting its spread, let me say a word. Has anything ever threatened the existence of this Union save and except this very institution of slavery? What is it that we hold most dear amongst us? Our own liberty and prosperity. What has ever threatened our liberty and prosperity save and except this institution of slavery? If this is true, how do you propose to improve the condition of things by enlarging slavery — by spreading it out and making it bigger? You may have a wen or cancer upon your person, and not be able to cut it out lest you bleed to death; but surely it is no way to cure it, to engraft it and spread it over your whole body. That is no proper way of treating what you regard as a wrong. You see this peaceful way of dealing with it as a wrong — restricting the spread of it, and not allowing it to go into new countries where it has not already existed. That is the peaceful way, the old-fashioned way, the way in which the fathers themselves set us the example.

On the other hand, I have said there is a sentiment which treats it as not being wrong. That is the Democratic sentiment of this day. I do not mean to say that every man who stands within that range positively asserts that it is right. That class will include all who positively assert that it is right, and all who, like Judge Douglas, treat it as indifferent, and do not say it is either right or wrong. These two classes of men fall within the general class of those who do not look upon it as a wrong. And if there be among you anybody who supposes that he, as a Democrat, can consider himself "as much opposed to slavery as anybody," I would like to reason with him. You never treat it as a wrong. What other thing that you consider as a wrong, do you deal with as you deal with that? Perhaps you say it is wrong, but your leader never does, and you quarrel with anybody who says it is wrong. Although you pretend to say so yourself, you can find no fit place to deal with it as a wrong.

You must not say anything about it in the free States, because it is not here. You must not say anything about it in the slave States, because it is there. You must not say anything about it in the pulpit, because that is religion, and has nothing to do with it. You must not say anything about it in politics, because that will disturb the security of "my place." There is no place to talk about it as being a wrong, although you say yourself it is a wrong. But finally you will screw yourself up to the belief that if the people of the slave States should adopt a system of gradual emancipation on the slavery question, you would be in favor of it. You would be in favor of it! You say that is getting it in the right place, and you would be glad to see it succeed. But you are deceiving yourself. You all know that Frank Blair and Gratz Brown, down there in St. Louis, undertook to introduce that system in Missouri. They fought as valiantly as they could for the system of gradual emancipation which you pretend you would be glad to see succeed. Now I will bring you to the test. After a hard fight, they were beaten; and when the news came over here, you threw up your hats and hurrahed for Democracy. More than that, take all the argument made in favor of the system you have proposed, and it carefully excludes the idea that there is anything wrong in the institution of slavery. The arguments to sustain that policy carefully exclude it. Even here to-day you heard Judge Douglas quarrel with me because I uttered a wish that it might some time come to an end. Although Henry Clay could say he wished every slave in the United States was in the country of his ancestors, I am denounced by those pretending to respect Henry Clay, for uttering a wish that it might some time, in some peaceful way, come to an end.

The Democratic policy in regard to that institution will not tolerate the merest breath, the slightest hint, of the least degree of wrong about it. Try it by some of Judge Douglas's arguments. He says he "don't care whether it is voted up or voted down" in the Territories. I do not care myself, in dealing with that expression, whether it is intended to be expressive of his individual sentiments on the subject, or only of the national policy he desires to have established. It is alike valuable for my purpose. Any man can say that who does not see anything wrong in slavery, but no man can logically say it who does see a wrong in it; because no man can logically say he don't care whether a wrong is voted up or voted down. He may say he don't care whether an indifferent thing is voted up or down, but he must logically have a choice between a right thing and a wrong thing. He contends that whatever community wants slaves has a right to have them. So they have if it is not a wrong. But if it is a wrong, he cannot say people have a right to do wrong. He says that, upon the score of equality, slaves should be allowed to go into a new Territory like other property. This is strictly logical if there is no difference between it and other property. If it and other property are equal, his argument is entirely logical. But if you insist that one is wrong and the other right, there is no use to institute a comparison between right and wrong. You may turn over everything in the Democratic policy from beginning to end, whether in the shape it takes on the statute-book, in the shape it takes in the Dred Scott decision, in the shape it takes in conversation, or the shape it takes in short maxim-like arguments —it everywhere carefully excludes the idea that there is anything wrong in it.

That is the real issue. That is the issue that will continue in this country when these poor tongues of Judge Douglas and myself shall be silent. It is the eternal struggle between these two principles —right and wrong—throughout the world. They are the two principles that have stood face to face from the beginning of time; and will ever continue to struggle. The one is the common right of humanity, and the other the divine right of kings. It is the same principle in whatever shape it develops itself. It is the same spirit that says, "You toil and work and earn bread, and I 'll eat it." No matter in what shape it comes, whether from the mouth of a king who seeks to bestride the people of his own nation and live by the fruit of their labor, or from one race of men as an apology for enslaving another race, it is the same tyrannical principle. I was glad to express my gratitude at Quincy, and I reëxpress it here to Judge Douglas—that he looks to no end of the institution of slavery. That will help the people to see where the struggle really is. It will hereafter place with us all men who really do wish the wrong may have an end. And whenever we can get rid of the fog which obscures the real question,—when we can get Judge Douglas and his friends to avow a policy looking to its perpetuation,—we can get out from among them that class of men and bring them to the side of those who treat it as a wrong. Then there will soon be an end of it, and that end will be its "ultimate extinction." Whenever the issue can be distinctly made, and all extraneous matter thrown out, so that men can fairly see the real difference between the parties, this controversy will soon be settled, and it will be done peaceably too. There will be no war, no violence. It will be placed again where the wisest and best men of the world placed it. Brooks of South Carolina once declared that when this Constitution was framed, its framers did not look to the institution existing until this day. When he said this, I think he stated a fact that is fully borne out by the history of the times. But he also said they were better and wiser men than the men of these days; yet the men of these days had experience which they had not, and by the invention of the cotton-gin it became a necessity in this country that slavery should be perpetual. I now say that, willingly or unwillingly, purposely or without purpose, Judge Douglas has been the most prominent instrument in changing the position of the institution of slavery,—which the fathers of the government expected to come to an end ere this,—and putting it upon Brooks's cotton-gin basis—placing it where he openly confesses he has no desire there shall ever be an end of it.

I understand I have ten minutes yet. I will employ it in saying something about this argument Judge Douglas uses, while he sustains the Dred Scott decision, that the people of the Territories can still somehow exclude slavery. The first thing I ask attention to is the fact that Judge Douglas constantly said, before the decision,

that whether they could or not, was a question for the Supreme
Court. But after the court has made the decision, he virtually says
it is not a question for the Supreme Court, but for the people.
And how is it he tells us they can exclude it? He says it needs
"police regulations," and that admits of "unfriendly legislation."
Although it is a right established by the Constitution of the United
States to take a slave into a Territory of the United States and
hold him as property, yet unless the territorial legislature will give
friendly legislation, and, more especially, if they adopt unfriendly
legislation, they can practically exclude him. Now, without meeting
this proposition as a matter of fact, I pass to consider the real constitutional obligation. Let me take the gentleman who looks me in
the face before me, and let us suppose that he is a member of the
territorial legislature. The first thing he will do will be to swear
that he will support the Constitution of the United States. His
neighbor by his side in the Territory has slaves and needs territorial legislation to enable him to enjoy that constitutional right.
Can he withhold the legislation which his neighbor needs for the
enjoyment of a right which is fixed in his favor in the Constitution
of the United States which he has sworn to support? Can he withhold it without violating his oath? And more especially, can he pass
unfriendly legislation to violate his oath? Why, this is a monstrous
sort of talk about the Constitution of the United States! There has
never been as outlandish or lawless a doctrine from the mouth of
any respectable man on earth. I do not believe it is a constitutional
right to hold slaves in a Territory of the United States. I believe
the decision was improperly made, and I go for reversing it. Judge
Douglas is furious against those who go for reversing a decision.
But he is for legislating it out of all force while the law itself stands.
I repeat that there has never been so monstrous a doctrine uttered
from the mouth of a respectable man.

I suppose most of us (I know it of myself) believe that the people
of the Southern States are entitled to a congressional fugitive-slave
law; that is a right fixed in the Constitution. But it cannot be
made available to them without congressional legislation. In the
judge's language, it is a "barren right" which needs legislation
before it can become efficient and valuable to the persons to whom
it is guaranteed. And, as the right is constitutional, I agree that
the legislation shall be granted to it. Not that we like the institution of slavery; we profess to have no taste for running and
catching negroes — at least, I profess no taste for that job at all.
Why then do I yield support to a fugitive-slave law? Because I do
not understand that the Constitution, which guarantees that right,
can be supported without it. And if I believed that the right to
hold a slave in a Territory was equally fixed in the Constitution
with the right to reclaim fugitives, I should be bound to give it the
legislation necessary to support it. I say that no man can deny his
obligation to give the necessary legislation to support slavery in a
Territory, who believes it is a constitutional right to have it there.
No man can, who does not give the Abolitionists an argument to
deny the obligation enjoined by the Constitution to enact a fugitive-

slave law. Try it now. It is the strongest Abolition argument ever made. I say, if that Dred Scott decision is correct, then the right to hold slaves in a Territory is equally a constitutional right with the right of a slaveholder to have his runaway returned. No one can show the distinction between them. The one is express, so that we cannot deny it; the other is construed to be in the Constitution, so that he who believes the decision to be correct believes in the right. And the man who argues that by unfriendly legislation, in spite of that constitutional right, slavery may be driven from the Territories, cannot avoid furnishing an argument by which Abolitionists may deny the obligation to return fugitives, and claim the power to pass laws unfriendly to the right of the slaveholder to reclaim his fugitive. I do not know how such an argument may strike a popular assembly like this, but I defy anybody to go before a body of men whose minds are educated to estimating evidence and reasoning, and show that there is an iota of difference between the constitutional right to reclaim a fugitive, and the constitutional right to hold a slave, in a Territory, provided this Dred Scott decision is correct. I defy any man to make an argument that will justify unfriendly legislation to deprive a slaveholder of his right to hold his slave in a Territory, that will not equally, in all its length, breadth, and thickness, furnish an argument for nullifying the fugitive-slave law. Why, there is not such an Abolitionist in the nation as Douglas, after all.

Mr. Douglas's Rejoinder in the Alton Joint Debate.

Mr. Lincoln has concluded his remarks by saying that there is not such an Abolitionist as I am in all America. If he could make the Abolitionists of Illinois believe that, he would not have much show for the Senate. Let him make the Abolitionists believe the truth of that statement, and his political back is broken.

His first criticism upon me is the expression of his hope that the war of the administration will be prosecuted against me and the Democratic party of this State with vigor. He wants that war prosecuted with vigor; I have no doubt of it. His hopes of success, and the hopes of his party, depend solely upon it. They have no chance of destroying the Democracy of this State except by the aid of federal patronage. He has all the federal office-holders here as his allies, running separate tickets against the Democracy to divide the party, although the leaders all intend to vote directly the Abolition ticket, and only leave the greenhorns to vote this separate ticket who refuse to go into the Abolition camp. There is something really refreshing in the thought that Mr. Lincoln is in favor of prosecuting one war vigorously. It is the first war I ever knew him to be in favor of prosecuting. It is the first war that I ever knew him to believe to be just or constitutional. When the Mexican war was being waged, and the American army was surrounded by the enemy in Mexico, he thought the war was unconstitutional, unnecessary, and unjust. He thought it was not commenced on the right spot.

VOL. I.—33.

When I made an incidental allusion of that kind in the joint discussion over at Charleston, some weeks ago, Lincoln, in replying, said that I, Douglas, had charged him with voting against supplies for the Mexican war, and then he reared up, full length, and swore that he never voted against the supplies,—that it was a slander,—and caught hold of Ficklin, who sat on the stand, and said, "Here, Ficklin, tell the people that it is a lie." Well, Ficklin, who had served in Congress with him, stood up and told them all he recollected about it. It was that when George Ashmun, of Massachusetts, brought forward a resolution declaring the war unconstitutional, unnecessary, and unjust, Lincoln had voted for it. "Yes," said Lincoln, "I did." Thus he confessed that he voted that the war was wrong, that our country was in the wrong, and consequently that the Mexicans were in the right; but charged that I had slandered him by saying that he voted against the supplies. I never charged him with voting against the supplies in my life, because I knew that he was not in Congress when they were voted. The war was commenced on the 13th day of May, 1846, and on that day we appropriated in Congress ten millions of dollars and fifty thousand men to prosecute it. During the same session we voted more men and more money, and at the next session we voted more men and more money, so that by the time Mr. Lincoln entered Congress we had enough men and enough money to carry on the war, and had no occasion to vote for any more. When he got into the House, being opposed to the war, and not being able to stop the supplies, because they had all gone forward, all he could do was to follow the lead of Corwin, and prove that the war was not begun on the right spot, and that it was unconstitutional, unnecessary, and wrong. Remember, too, that this he did after the war had been begun. It is one thing to be opposed to the declaration of a war, another and very different thing to take sides with the enemy against your own country after the war has been commenced. Our army was in Mexico at the time, many battles had been fought; our citizens, who were defending the honor of their country's flag, were surrounded by the daggers, the guns, and the poison of the enemy. Then it was that Corwin made his speech in which he declared that the American soldiers ought to be welcomed by the Mexicans with bloody hands and hospitable graves; then it was that Ashmun and Lincoln voted in the House of Representatives that the war was unconstitutional and unjust; and Ashmun's resolution, Corwin's speech, and Lincoln's vote were sent to Mexico and read at the head of the Mexican army, to prove to them that there was a Mexican party in the Congress of the United States who were doing all in their power to aid them. That a man.who takes sides with the common enemy against his own country in time of war should rejoice in a war being made on me now, is very natural. And, in my opinion, no other kind of a man would rejoice in it.

Mr. Lincoln has told you a great deal to-day about his being an old-line Clay Whig. Bear in mind that there are a great many old Clay Whigs down in this region. It is more agreeable, therefore, for him to talk about the old Clay Whig party than it is for him to talk Abolitionism. We did not hear much about the old Clay Whig

party up in the Abolition districts. How much of an old-line Henry
Clay Whig was he? Have you read General Singleton's speech at
Jacksonville? You know that General Singleton was, for twenty-
five years, the confidential friend of Henry Clay in Illinois, and he
testified that in 1847, when the constitutional convention of this
State was in session, the Whig members were invited to a Whig
caucus at the house of Mr. Lincoln's brother-in-law, where Mr.
Lincoln proposed to throw Henry Clay overboard and take up General Taylor in his place, giving, as his reason, that if the Whigs did
not take up General Taylor, the Democrats would. Singleton testifies that Lincoln, in that speech, urged, as another reason for throwing Henry Clay overboard, that the Whigs had fought long enough
for principle, and ought to begin to fight for success. Singleton
also testifies that Lincoln's speech did have the effect of cutting
Clay's throat, and that he (Singleton) and others withdrew from the
caucus in indignation. He further states that when they got to
Philadelphia to attend the national convention of the Whig party,
that Lincoln was there, the bitter and deadly enemy of Clay, and
that he tried to keep him (Singleton) out of the convention because
he insisted on voting for Clay, and Lincoln was determined to have
Taylor. Singleton says that Lincoln rejoiced with very great joy
when he found the mangled remains of the murdered Whig statesman lying cold before him. Now Mr. Lincoln tells you that he is
an old-line Clay Whig! General Singleton testifies to the facts I
have narrated, in a public speech which has been printed and circulated broadcast over the State for weeks, yet not a lisp have we
heard from Mr. Lincoln on the subject, except that he is an old
Clay Whig.

What part of Henry Clay's policy did Lincoln ever advocate? He
was in Congress in 1848–49, when the Wilmot proviso warfare disturbed the peace and harmony of the country, until it shook the
foundation of the republic from its center to its circumference. It
was that agitation that brought Clay forth from his retirement at
Ashland again to occupy his seat in the Senate of the United States,
to see if he could not, by his great wisdom and experience, and the
renown of his name, do something to restore peace and quiet to a
disturbed country. Who got up that sectional strife that Clay had
to be called upon to quell? I have heard Lincoln boast that he voted
forty-two times for the Wilmot proviso, and that he would have
voted as many times more if he could. Lincoln is the man, in connection with Seward, Chase, Giddings, and other Abolitionists, who
got up that strife that I helped Clay to put down. Henry Clay came
back to the Senate in 1849, and saw that he must do something to
restore peace to the country. The Union Whigs and the Union
Democrats welcomed him the moment he arrived, as the man for the
occasion. We believed that he, of all men on earth, had been preserved by divine providence to guide us out of our difficulties, and
we Democrats rallied under Clay then, as you Whigs in nullification
times rallied under the banner of old Jackson, forgetting party when
the country was in danger, in order that we might have a country
first and parties afterward.

And this reminds me that Mr. Lincoln told you that the slavery question was the only thing that ever disturbed the peace and harmony of the Union. Did not nullification once raise its head and disturb the peace of this Union in 1832? Was that the slavery question, Mr. Lincoln? Did not disunion raise its monster head during the last war with Great Britain? Was that the slavery question, Mr. Lincoln? The peace of this country has been disturbed three times, once during the war with Great Britain, once on the tariff question, and once on the slavery question. His argument, therefore, that slavery is the only question that has ever created dissension in the Union falls to the ground. It is true that agitators are enabled now to use this slavery question for the purpose of sectional strife. He admits that, in regard to all things else, the principle that I advocate, making each State and Territory free to decide for itself, ought to prevail. He instances the cranberry laws, and the oyster laws, and he might have gone through the whole list with the same effect. I say that all these laws are local and domestic, and that local and domestic concerns should be left to each State and Territory to manage for itself. If agitators would acquiesce in that principle, there never would be any danger to the peace and harmony of the Union.

Mr. Lincoln tries to avoid the main issue by attacking the truth of my proposition, that our fathers made this government divided into free and slave States, recognizing the right of each to decide all its local questions for itself. Did they not thus make it? It is true that they did not establish slavery in any of the States, or abolish it in any of them; but finding thirteen States, twelve of which were slave and one free, they agreed to form a government uniting them together, as they stood, divided into free and slave States, and to guarantee forever to each State the right to do as it pleased on the slavery question. Having thus made the government, and conferred this right upon each State forever, I assert that this government can exist as they made it, divided into free and slave States, if any one State chooses to retain slavery. He says that he looks forward to a time when slavery shall be abolished everywhere. I look forward to the time when each State shall be allowed to do as it pleases. If it chooses to keep slavery forever, it is not my business, but its own; if it chooses to abolish slavery, it is its own business, not mine. I care more for the great principle of self-government, the right of the people to rule, than I do for all the negroes in Christendom. I would not endanger the perpetuity of this Union; I would not blot out the great inalienable rights of the white men for all the negroes that ever existed. Hence, I say, let us maintain this government on the principles on which our fathers made it, recognizing the right of each State to keep slavery as long as its people determine, or to abolish it when they please. But Mr. Lincoln says that when our fathers made this government they did not look forward to the state of things now existing, and therefore he thinks the doctrine was wrong; and he quotes Brooks, of South Carolina, to prove that our fathers then thought that probably slavery would be abolished by each State acting for itself before this time. Suppose they did; suppose they did not foresee what

has occurred—does that change the principles of our government?
They did not probably foresee the telegraph that transmits intelligence by lightning; nor did they foresee the railroads that now form the bonds of union between the different States; or the thousand mechanical inventions that have elevated mankind. But do these things change the principles of the government? Our fathers, I say, made this government on the principle of the right of each State to do as it pleases in its own domestic affairs, subject to the Constitution, and allowed the people of each to apply to every new change of circumstances such remedy as they may see fit to improve their condition. This right they have for all time to come.

Mr. Lincoln went on to tell you that he does not at all desire to interfere with slavery in the States where it exists, nor does his party. I expected him to say that down here. Let me ask him then how he expects to put slavery in the course of ultimate extinction everywhere, if he does not intend to interfere with it in the States where it exists? He says that he will prohibit it in all Territories, and the inference is, then, that unless they make free States out of them he will keep them out of the Union; for, mark you, he did not say whether or not he would vote to admit Kansas with slavery or not, as her people might apply (he forgot that, as usual); he did not say whether or not he was in favor of bringing the Territories now in existence into the Union on the principle of Clay's compromise measures on the slavery question. I told you that he would not. His idea is that he will prohibit slavery in all the Territories, and thus force them all to become free States, surrounding the slave States with a cordon of free States and hemming them in, keeping the slaves confined to their present limits whilst they go on multiplying until the soil on which they live will no longer feed them, and he will thus be able to put slavery in a course of ultimate extinction by starvation. He will extinguish slavery in the Southern States as the French general extinguished the Algerines when he smoked them out. He is going to extinguish slavery by surrounding the slave States, hemming in the slaves, and starving them out of existence, as you smoke a fox out of his hole. He intends to do that in the name of humanity and Christianity, in order that we may get rid of the terrible crime and sin entailed upon our fathers of holding slaves. Mr. Lincoln makes out that line of policy, and appeals to the moral sense of justice and to the Christian feeling of the community to sustain him. He says that any man who holds to the contrary doctrine is in the position of the king who claimed to govern by divine right. Let us examine for a moment and see what principle it was that overthrew the divine right of George III. to govern us. Did not these colonies rebel because the British parliament had no right to pass laws concerning our property and domestic and private institutions without our consent? We demanded that the British government should not pass such laws unless they gave us representation in the body passing them—and this the British government insisting on doing, we went to war, on the principle that the home government should not control and govern distant colonies without giving them a representation. Now Mr. Lincoln proposes to govern the Territories without giving them a representation, and calls on Congress to pass laws controlling their property and domestic concerns without their consent and against their will. Thus he asserts for his party the identical principle asserted by George III. and the Tories of the Revolution.

I ask you to look into these things, and then tell me whether the Democracy or the Abolitionists are right. I hold that the people of a Territory, like those of a State (I use the language of Mr. Buchanan in his letter of acceptance), have the right to decide for themselves whether slavery shall or shall not exist within their limits. The point upon which Chief Justice Taney expresses his opinion is simply this, that slaves, being property, stand on an equal footing with other property, and consequently that the owner has the same right to carry that property into a Territory that he has any other, subject to the same conditions. Suppose that one of your merchants was to take fifty or one hundred thousand dollars' worth of liquors to Kansas. He has a right to go there under that decision, but when he gets there he finds the Maine liquor-law in force, and what can he do with his property after he gets it there? He cannot sell it, he cannot use it, it is subject to the local law, and that law is against him, and the best thing he can do with it is to bring it back into Missouri or Illinois and sell it. If you take negroes to Kansas, as Colonel Jefferson Davis said in his Bangor speech, from which I have quoted to-day, you must take them there subject to the local law. If the people want the institution of slavery, they will protect and encourage it; but if they do not want it, they will withhold that protection, and the absence of local legislation protecting slavery excludes it as completely as a positive prohibition. You slaveholders of Missouri might as well understand what you know practically, that you cannot carry slavery where the people do not want it. All you have a right to ask is that the people shall do as they please; if they want slavery, let them have it; if they do not want it, allow them to refuse to encourage it.

My friends, if, as I have said before, we will only live up to this great fundamental principle, there will be peace between the North and the South. Mr. Lincoln admits that under the Constitution, on all domestic questions except slavery, we ought not to interfere with the people of each State. What right have we to interfere with slavery any more than we have to interfere with any other question? He says that this slavery question is now the bone of contention. Why? Simply because agitators have combined in all the free States to make war upon it. Suppose the agitators in the States should combine in one half of the Union to make war upon the railroad system of the other half. They would thus be driven to the same sectional strife. Suppose one section makes war upon any other peculiar institution of the opposite section, and the same strife is produced. The only remedy and safety is that we shall stand by the Constitution as our fathers made it, obey the laws as they are passed, while they stand the proper test, and sustain the decisions of the Supreme Court and the constituted authorities.

[October 15?] 1858.—FRAGMENT. OPINION ON ELECTION LAWS OF
ILLINOIS.

It is made a question whether, under our laws, a person offering
to vote, and being challenged, and having taken the oath prescribed
by the act of 1849, is then absolutely entitled to vote, or whether
his oath may be disproved, and his vote thereon lawfully rejected.
In Purple's Statutes, Volume I, all our existing election laws are
brought together, commencing on page 514 and extending to page
532. They consist of acts and parts of acts passed at different times.
The true way of reading so much of the law as applies to the above
question, is to first read (64) section x, including the form of the
oath on page 528. Then turn back and read (19) section xix, on
page 518. If it be said that the section last mentioned is not now
in force, turn forward to (75) section xxi, on page 530, where it is
expressly declared to be in force.
The result is that when a person has taken the oath, his oath may
still be proved to be false, and his vote thereupon rejected. It may
be proved to be false by cross-examining the proposed voter himself,
or by any other person, or competent testimony known to the general law of evidence. On page 532 is an extract of a Supreme Court
decision on the very section xix, on page 518, in which, among other
things, the court says: "If such person takes the oath prescribed
by law, the judges must receive his vote, unless the oath be proved
false." Something of a definition of residence is therein given.

October 30, 1858.— LETTER TO E. LUSK.

SPRINGFIELD, October 30, 1858.
EDWARD LUSK, Esq.
Dear Sir: I understand the story is still being told and insisted
upon that I have been a Know-nothing. I repeat what I stated in
a public speech at Meredosia, that I am not, nor ever have been, connected with the party called the Know-nothing party, or party calling themselves the American party. Certainly no man of truth, and
I believe no man of good character for truth, can be found to say on
his own knowledge that I ever was connected with that party.
Yours very truly,   A. LINCOLN.

November 4, 1858.—LETTER TO J. J. CRITTENDEN.

SPRINGFIELD, November 4, 1858.
HON. J. J. CRITTENDEN.
My dear Sir : Yours of the 27th was taken from the office by
my law partner, and in the confusion consequent upon the recent
election, was handed to me only this moment. I am sorry the allusion made in the "Missouri Republican" to the private correspondence between yourself and me has given you any pain. It gave me
scarcely a thought, perhaps for the reason that, being away from
home, I did not see it until only two days before the election. It

never occurred to me to cast any blame upon you. I have been told that the correspondence has been alluded to in the "Missouri Republican" several times; but I only saw one of the allusions made, in which it was stated, as I remember, that a gentleman of St. Louis had seen a copy of your letter to me. As I have given no copy, nor ever shown the original, of course I inferred he had seen it in your hands; but it did not occur to me to blame you for showing what you had written yourself. It was not said that the gentleman had seen a copy, or the original, of my letter to you.

The emotions of defeat at the close of a struggle in which I felt more than a merely selfish interest, and to which defeat the use of your name contributed largely, are fresh upon me; but even in this mood I cannot for a moment suspect you of anything dishonorable.

Your obedient servant, A. LINCOLN.

November 15, 1858.—LETTER TO N. B. JUDD.

SPRINGFIELD, November 15, 1858.

HON. N. B. JUDD.

My dear Sir: I have the pleasure to inform you that I am convalescent, and hoping these lines may find you in the same improving state of health. Doubtless you have suspected for some time that I entertain a personal wish for a term in the United States Senate; and had the suspicion taken the shape of a direct charge, I think I could not have truthfully denied it. But let the past as nothing be. For the future, my view is that the fight must go on. The returns here are not yet completed; but it is believed that Dougherty's vote will be slightly greater than Miller's majority over Tracy. We have some hundred and twenty thousand clear Republican votes. That pile is worth keeping together. It will elect a State treasurer two years hence.

In that day I shall fight in the ranks, but I shall be in no one's way for any of the places. I am especially for Trumbull's reëlection; and, by the way, this brings me to the principal object of this letter. Can you not take your draft of an apportionment law, and carefully revise it till it shall be strictly and obviously just in all particulars, and then by an early and persistent effort get enough of the enemy's men to enable you to pass it? I believe if you and Peck make a job of it, begin early, and work earnestly and quietly, you can succeed in it. Unless something be done, Trumbull is eventually beaten two years hence. Take this into serious consideration.

Yours as ever, A. LINCOLN.

November 16, 1858.—LETTER TO N. B. JUDD.

SPRINGFIELD, November 16, 1858.

HON. N. B. JUDD.

Dear Sir: Yours of the 15th is just received. I wrote you the same day. As to the pecuniary matter, I am willing to pay according to my ability; but I am the poorest hand living to get others to pay. I have been on expenses so long without earning anything that I am absolutely without money now for even household purposes. Still, if you can put in two hundred and fifty dollars for me toward discharging the debt of the committee, I will allow it when you and I settle the private matter between us. This, with what I have already paid, and with an outstanding note of mine, will exceed my subscription of five hundred dollars. This, too, is exclusive of my ordinary expenses during the campaign, all of which being added to my loss of time and business, bears pretty heavily upon one no better off in [this] world's goods than I; but as I had the post of honor, it is not for me to be over nice. You are feeling badly,—"And this too shall pass away," never fear. Yours as ever,

A. LINCOLN.

November 19, 1858.—LETTER TO H. ASBURY.

SPRINGFIELD, November 19, 1858.

HENRY ASBURY, Esq.

Dear Sir : Yours of the 13th was received some days ago. The fight must go on. The cause of civil liberty must not be surrendered at the end of one or even one hundred defeats. Douglas had the ingenuity to be supported in the late contest both as the best means to break down and to uphold the slave interest. No ingenuity can keep these antagonistic elements in harmony long. Another explosion will soon come.   Yours truly,

A. LINCOLN.

November 19, 1858.— LETTER TO A. G. HENRY.

SPRINGFIELD, ILLINOIS, November 19, 1858.

DR. A. G. HENRY.

My dear Sir : Yours of the 27th of September was received two days ago. I was at Oquawka, Henderson County, on the 9th of October; and I may then have seen Major A. N. Armstrong; but having nothing then to fix my attention, I do not remember such a man. I have concluded, as the best way of serving you, to inclose your letter to E. A. Paine, Esq., of Monmouth, Ill., a reliable lawyer, asking him to do what you ask of me. If a suit is to be brought, he will correspond directly with you.

You doubtless have seen ere this the result of the election here. Of course I wished, but I did not much expect, a better result. The popular vote of the State is with us; so that the seat in the

(Lower portion of page cut off.)

whole canvass. On the contrary, John and George Weber, and several such old Democrats, were furiously for me. As a general rule, out of Sangamon as well as in it, much of the plain old Democracy is with us, while nearly all the old exclusive silk-stocking Whiggery is against us. I don't mean nearly all the Old Whig party, but nearly all of the nice exclusive sort. And why not? There has been nothing in politics since the Revolution so congenial to their nature as the present position of the great Democratic party.

I am glad I made the late race. It gave me a hearing on the great and durable question of the age, which I could have had in no other way; and though I now sink out of view, and shall be forgotten, I believe I have made some marks which will tell for the cause of civil liberty long after I am gone. Mary joins me in sending our best wishes to Mrs. Henry and others of your family.

.   .   .   .

November 25, 1858.— LETTER TO J. A. MATTESON.

SPRINGFIELD, November 25, 1858.

HON. JOEL A. MATTESON.

Dear Sir: Last summer, when a movement was made in court against your road, you engaged us to be on your side. It has so happened that, so far, we have performed no service in the case; but we lost a cash fee offered us on the other side. Now, being hard run, we propose a little compromise. We will claim nothing for the matter just mentioned, if you will relieve us at once from the old matter at the Marine and Fire Insurance Company, and be greatly obliged to boot. Can you not do it?

Yours truly,   A. LINCOLN.

[February 22] 1859.— LECTURE ON " DISCOVERIES, INVENTIONS, AND IMPROVEMENTS," DELIVERED IN NEIGHBORING TOWNS IN 1859, AND BEFORE THE SPRINGFIELD LIBRARY ASSOCIATION, SPRINGFIELD, ILLINOIS, FEBRUARY 22, 1860.

From autograph manuscript in the Lincoln Collection of Charles F. Gunther, Esq., Chicago, Illinois.

We have all heard of Young America. He is the most current youth of the age. Some think him conceited and arrogant; but has he not reason to entertain a rather extensive opinion of himself? Is he not the inventor and owner of the present, and sole hope of the future? Men and things, everywhere, are ministering unto him. Look at his apparel, and you shall see cotton fabrics from Manchester and Lowell; flax linen from Ireland; wool cloth from Spain; silk from France; furs from the arctic region; with a buffalo-robe from the Rocky Mountains, as a general outsider. At his table, besides plain bread and meat made at home, are sugar from Louisiana, coffee and fruits from the tropics, salt from Turk's Island, fish from Newfoundland, tea from China, and spices from the Indies. The whale of the Pacific furnishes his candle-light, he has a diamond ring from Brazil, a gold watch from California, and a Spanish cigar from Havana. He not only has a present supply of all these, and much more; but thousands of hands are engaged in producing fresh supplies, and other thousands in bringing them to him. The iron horse is panting and impatient to carry him everywhere in no time; and the lightning stands ready harnessed to take and bring his tidings in a

trifle less than no time.   He owns a large part of the world, by right
of possessing it, and all the rest by right of wanting it, and intending to have it.   As Plato had for the immortality of the soul, so
Young America has "a pleasing hope, a fond desire—a longing
after" territory.   He has a great passion—a perfect rage—for the
"new"; particularly new men for office, and the new earth mentioned
in the Revelations, in which, being no more sea, there must be about
three times as much land as in the present.   He is a great friend of
humanity; and his desire for land is not selfish, but merely an impulse to extend the area of freedom.   He is very anxious to fight
for the liberation of enslaved nations and colonies, provided, always,
they have land, and have not any liking for his interference.   As to
those who have no land, and would be glad of help from any quarter,
he considers they can afford to wait a few hundred years longer.   In
knowledge he is particularly rich.   He knows all that can possibly
be known; inclines to believe in spiritual rappings, and is the unquestioned inventor of "Manifest Destiny."   His horror is for all
that is old, particularly "Old Fogy"; and if there be anything old
which he can endure, it is only old whisky and old tobacco.

If the said Young America really is, as he claims to be, the owner
of all present, it must be admitted that he has considerable advantage of Old Fogy.   Take, for instance, the first of all fogies, Father
Adam.   There he stood, a very perfect physical man, as poets and
painters inform us; but he must have been very ignorant, and simple in his habits.   He had had no sufficient time to learn much by
observation, and he had no near neighbors to teach him anything.
No part of his breakfast had been brought from the other side of
the world; and it is quite probable he had no conception of the
world having any other side.   In all these things, it is very plain, he
was no equal of Young America; the most that can be said is, that
according to his chance he may have been quite as much of a man
as his very self-complacent descendant.   Little as was what he
knew, let the youngster discard all he has learned from others, and
then show, if he can, any advantage on his side.   In the way of land
and live-stock, Adam was quite in the ascendant.   He had dominion
over all the earth, and all the living things upon and round about it.
The land has been sadly divided out since; but never fret, Young
America will re-annex it.

The great difference between Young America and Old Fogy is the
result of discoveries, inventions, and improvements.   These, in turn,
are the result of observation, reflection, and experiment.   For instance, it is quite certain that ever since water has been boiled in
covered vessels, men have seen the lids of the vessels rise and fall a
little, with a sort of fluttering motion, by force of the steam; but so
long as this was not specially observed, and reflected, and experi-
mented upon, it came to nothing.   At length, however, after many
thousand years, some man observes this long-known effect of hot
water lifting a pot-lid, and begins a train of reflection upon it.   He
says, "Why, to be sure, the force that lifts the pot-lid will lift anything else which is no heavier than the pot-lid.   And as man has
much hard fighting to do, cannot this hot-water power be made to

help him ?" He has become a little excited on the subject, and he fancies he hears a voice answering, "Try me." He does try it; and the observation, reflection, and trial give to the world the control of that tremendous and now well-known agent called steam-power. This is not the actual history in detail, but the general principle.

But was this first inventor of the application of steam wiser or more ingenious than those who had gone before him? Not at all. Had he not learned much of those, he never would have succeeded, probably never would have thought of making the attempt. To be fruitful in invention, it is indispensable to have a habit of observation and reflection; and this habit our steam friend acquired, no doubt, from those who, to him, were old fogies. But for the difference in habit of observation, why did Yankees almost instantly discover gold in California, which had been trodden upon and overlooked by Indians and Mexican greasers for centuries? Gold-mines are not the only mines overlooked in the same way. There are more mines above the earth's surface than below it. All nature — the whole world, material, moral, and intellectual — is a mine; and in Adam's day it was a wholly unexplored mine. Now, it was the destined work of Adam's race to develop, by discoveries, inventions, and improvements, the hidden treasures of this mine. But Adam had nothing to turn his attention to the work. If he should do anything in the way of inventions, he had first to invent the art of invention, the instance, at least, if not the habit, of observation and reflection. As might be expected, he seems not to have been a very observing man at first; for it appears he went about naked a considerable length of time before he ever noticed that obvious fact. But when he did observe it, the observation was not lost upon him; for it immediately led to the first of all inventions of which we have any direct account—the fig-leaf apron.

The inclination to exchange thoughts with one another is probably an original impulse of our nature. If I be in pain, I wish to let you know it, and to ask your sympathy and assistance; and my pleasurable emotions also I wish to communicate to and share with you. But to carry on such communications, some instrumentality is indispensable. Accordingly, speech — articulate sounds rattled off from the tongue — was used by our first parents, and even by Adam before the creation of Eve. He gave names to the animals while she was still a bone in his side; and he broke out quite volubly when she first stood before him, the best present of his Maker. From this it would appear that speech was not an invention of man, but rather the direct gift of his Creator. But whether divine gift or invention, it is still plain that if a mode of communication had been left to invention, speech must have been the first, from the superior adaptation to the end of the organs of speech over every other means within the whole range of nature. Of the organs of speech the tongue is the principal; and if we shall test it, we shall find the capacities of the tongue, in the utterance of articulate sounds, absolutely wonderful. You can count from one to one hundred quite distinctly in about forty seconds. In doing this two hundred and eighty-three distinct sounds or syllables are uttered, being seven to each second, and yet there should be enough difference between every two to be easily recognized by the ear of the hearer. What other signs to represent things could possibly be produced so rapidly? or, even if ready made, could be arranged so rapidly to express the sense? Motions with the hands are no adequate substitute. Marks for the recognition of the eye,—writing,—although a wonderful auxiliary of speech, is no worthy substitute for it. In addition to the more slow and laborious process of getting up a communication in writing, the materials—pen, ink, and paper—are not always at hand. But one always has his tongue with him, and the breath of his life is the ever-ready material with which it works. Speech, then, by enabling different individuals to interchange thoughts, and thereby to combine their powers of observation and reflection, greatly facilitates useful discoveries and inventions. What one observes, and would himself infer nothing from, he tells to another, and that other at once sees a valuable hint in it. A result is thus reached which neither alone would have arrived at. And this reminds me of what I passed unnoticed before, that the very first invention was a joint operation, Eve having shared with Adam the getting up of the apron. And, indeed, judging from the fact that sewing has come down to our times as "woman's work," it is very probable she took the leading part,—he, perhaps, doing no more than to stand by and thread the needle. That proceeding may be reckoned as the mother of all "sewing-societies," and the first and most perfect "World's Fair," all inventions and all inventors then in the world being on the spot.

But speech alone, valuable as it ever has been and is, has not advanced the condition of the world much. This is abundantly evident when we look at the degraded condition of all those tribes of human creatures who have no considerable additional means of communicating thoughts. Writing, the art of communicating thoughts to the mind through the eye, is the great invention of the world. Great is the astonishing range of analysis and combination which necessarily underlies the most crude and general conception of it—great, very great, in enabling us to converse with the dead, the absent, and the unborn, at all distances of time and space; and great, not only in its direct benefits, but greatest help to all other inventions. Suppose the art, with all conceptions of it, were this day lost to the world, how long, think you, would it be before Young America could get up the letter A with any adequate notion of using it to advantage? The precise period at which writing was invented is not known, but it certainly was as early as the time of Moses; from which we may safely infer that its inventors were very old fogies.

Webster, at the time of writing his dictionary, speaks of the English language as then consisting of seventy or eighty thousand words. If so, the language in which the five books of Moses were written must at that time, now thirty-three or -four hundred years ago, have consisted of at least one quarter as many, or twenty thousand. When we remember that words are sounds merely, we shall conclude that the idea of representing those sounds by marks, so that whoever should at any time after see the marks would understand what sounds they meant, was a bold and ingenious conception, not likely to occur to one man in a million in the run of a thousand years. And when it did occur, a distinct mark for each word, giving twenty thousand different marks first to be learned, and afterward to be remembered, would follow as the second thought, and would present such a difficulty as would lead to the conclusion that the whole thing was impracticable. But the necessity still would exist; and we may readily suppose that the idea was conceived, and lost, and reproduced, and dropped, and taken up again and again, until at last the thought of dividing sounds into parts, and making a mark, not to represent a whole sound, but only a part of one, and then of combining those marks, not very many in number, upon principles of permutation, so as to represent any and all of the whole twenty thousand words, and even any additional number, was somehow conceived and pushed into practice. This was the invention of phonetic writing, as distinguished from the clumsy picture-writing of some of the nations. That it was difficult of conception and execution is apparent, as well by the foregoing reflection, as the fact that so many tribes of men have come down from Adam's time to our own without ever having possessed it. Its utility may be conceived by the reflection that to it we owe everything which distinguishes us from savages. Take it from us, and the Bible, all history, all science, all government, all commerce, and nearly all social intercourse go with it.

The great activity of the tongue in articulating sounds has already been mentioned, and it may be of some passing interest to notice the wonderful power of the eye in conveying ideas to the mind from writing. Take the same example of the numbers from one to one hundred written down, and you can run your eye over the list, and be assured that every number is in it, in about one half the time it would require to pronounce the words with the voice; and not only so, but you can in the same short time determine whether every word is spelled correctly, by which it is evident that every separate letter, amounting to eight hundred and sixty-four, has been recognized and reported to the mind within the incredibly short space of twenty seconds, or one third of a minute.

I have already intimated my opinion that in the world's history certain inventions and discoveries occurred of peculiar value, on account of their great efficiency in facilitating all other inventions and discoveries. Of these were the art of writing and of printing, the discovery of America, and the introduction of patent laws. The date of the first, as already stated, is unknown; but it certainly was as much as fifteen hundred years before the Christian era; the second—printing—came in 1436, or nearly three thousand years after the first. The others followed more rapidly—the discovery of America in 1492, and the first patent laws in 1624. Though not apposite to my present purpose, it is but justice to the fruitfulness of that period to mention two other important events—the Lutheran Reformation in 1517, and, still earlier, the invention of negroes, or of the present mode of using them, in 1434. But to return to the consideration of printing, it is plain that it is but the other half, and in reality the better half, of writing; and that both together are but the assistants of speech in the communication of thoughts between man and man. When man was possessed of speech alone, the chances of invention, discovery, and improvement were very limited; but by the introduction of each of these they were greatly multiplied. When writing was invented, any important observation likely to lead to a discovery had at least a chance of being written down, and consequently a little chance of never being forgotten, and of being seen and reflected upon by a much greater number of persons; and thereby the chances of a valuable hint being caught proportionately augmented. By this means the observation of a single individual might lead to an important invention years, and even centuries, after he was dead. In one word, by means of writing, the seeds of invention were more permanently preserved and more widely sown. And yet for three thousand years during which printing remained undiscovered after writing was in use, it was only a small portion of the people who could write, or read writing; and consequently the field of invention, though much extended, still continued very limited. At length printing came. It gave ten thousand copies of any written matter quite as cheaply as ten were given before; and consequently a thousand minds were brought into the field where there was but one before. This was a great gain—and history shows a great change corresponding to it—in point of time.

I will venture to consider it the true termination of that period called "the dark ages." Discoveries, inventions, and improvements followed rapidly, and have been increasing their rapidity ever since. The effects could not come all at once. It required time to bring them out; and they are still coming. The capacity to read could not be multiplied as fast as the means of reading. Spelling-books just began to go into the hands of the children, but the teachers were not very numerous or very competent, so that it is safe to infer they did not advance so speedily as they do nowadays. It is very probable—almost certain—that the great mass of men at that time were utterly unconscious that their condition or their minds were capable of improvement. They not only looked upon the educated few as superior beings, but they supposed themselves to be naturally incapable of rising to equality. To emancipate the mind from this false underestimate of itself is the great task which printing came into the world to perform. It is difficult for us now and here to conceive how strong this slavery of the mind was, and how long it did of necessity take to break its shackles, and to get a habit of freedom of thought established. It is, in this connection, a curious fact that a new country is most favorable—almost necessary—to the emancipation of thought, and the consequent advancement of civilization and the arts. The human family originated, as is thought, somewhere in Asia, and have worked their way principally westward. Just now in civilization and the arts the people of Asia are entirely behind those of Europe; those of the east of Europe behind those of the west of it; while we, here, in America, think we discover, and invent, and improve faster than any of them. They may think this is arrogance; but they cannot deny that Russia has called on us to show her how to build steamboats and railroads, while in the older parts of Asia they scarcely know that such things as steamboats and railroads exist. In anciently inhabited countries, the dust of ages — a real, downright old-fogyism — seems to settle upon and smother the intellects and energies of man. It is in this view that I have mentioned the discovery of America as an event greatly favoring and facilitating useful discoveries and inventions. Next came the patent laws. These began in England in 1624, and in this country with the adoption of our Constitution. Before then any man [might] instantly use what another man had invented, so that the inventor had no special advantage from his invention. The patent system changed this, secured to the inventor for a limited time exclusive use of his inventions, and thereby added the fuel of interest to the fire of genius in the discovery and production of new and useful things.

March 1, 1859.—SPEECH AT CHICAGO ON THE NIGHT OF THE MUNICIPAL ELECTION.

I understand that you have to-day rallied around your principles, and they have again triumphed in the city of Chicago. I am exceedingly happy to meet you under such cheering auspices on this occasion — the first on which I have appeared before an audience since the campaign of last year. It is unsuitable to enter into a lengthy discourse, as is quite apparent, at a moment like this. I shall therefore detain you only a very short while.

It gives me peculiar pleasure to find an opportunity under such favorable circumstances to return my thanks for the gallant support that the Republicans of the city of Chicago and of the State gave to the cause in which we were all engaged in the late momentous struggle in Illinois.

I remember in that canvass but one instance of dissatisfaction with my course, and I allude to that now not for the purpose of reviving any matter of dispute or producing any unpleasant feeling, but in order to help to get rid of the point upon which that matter of disagreement or dissatisfaction arose. I understand that in some speeches I made I said something, or was supposed to have said something, that some very good people, as I really believe them to be, commented upon unfavorably, and said that rather than support one holding such sentiments as I had expressed, the real friends of liberty could afford to wait a while. I don't want to say anything that shall excite unkind feeling, and I mention this simply to suggest that I am afraid of the effect of that sort of argument. I do not doubt that it comes from good men, but I am afraid of the result upon organized action where great results are in view, if any of us allow ourselves to seek out minor or separate points, on which there may be difference of views as to policy and right, and let them keep us from uniting in action upon a great principle in a cause on which we all agree; or are deluded into the belief that all can be brought to consider alike and agree upon every minor point before we unite and press forward in organization, asking the coöperation of all good men in that resistance to the extension of slavery upon which we all agree. I am afraid that such methods would result in keeping the friends of liberty waiting longer than we ought to. I say this for the purpose of suggesting that we consider whether it would not be better and wiser, so long as we all agree that this matter of slavery is a moral, political, and social wrong, and ought to be treated as a wrong, not to let anything minor or subsidiary to that main principle and purpose make us fail to coöperate.

One other thing,—and that again I say in no spirit of unkindness. There was a question amongst Republicans all the time of the canvass of last year, and it has not quite ceased yet, whether it was not the true and better policy for the Republicans to make it their chief object to reëlect Judge Douglas to the Senate of the United States. Now, I differ with those who thought that the true policy, but I have never said an unkind word of any one entertaining that opinion. I believe most of them were as sincerely the friends of our cause as I claim to be myself; yet I thought they were mistaken, and I speak of this now for the purpose of justifying the course that I took and the course of those who supported me. In what I say now there is no unkindness, even toward Judge Douglas. I have believed that in the Republican situation in Illinois, if we, the Republicans of this State, had made Judge Douglas our candidate for the Senate of the United States last year, and had elected him, there would to-day be no Republican party in this Union. I believe that the principles around which we have rallied and organized that party would live; they will live under all circumstances, while we will die. They would reproduce another party in the future. But in the mean time all the labor that has been done to build up the present Republican party would be entirely lost, and perhaps twenty years of time, before we would again have formed around that principle as solid, extensive, and formidable an organization as we have, standing shoulder to shoulder, to-night, in harmony and strength around the Republican banner.

It militates not at all against this view to tell us that the Republicans could make something in the State of New York by electing to Congress John B. Haskin, who occupied a position similar to Judge Douglas; or that they could make something by electing Hickman of Pennsylvania, or Davis of Indiana. I think it likely that they could and do make something by it; but it is false logic to assume that for that reason anything could be gained by us in electing Judge Douglas in Illinois. And for this reason: It is no disparagement to these men, Hickman and Davis, to say that individually they were comparatively small men, and the Republican party could take hold of them, use them, elect them, absorb them, expel them, or do whatever it pleased with them, and the Republican organization be in no wise shaken. But it is not so with Judge Douglas. Let the Republican party of Illinois dally with Judge Douglas; let them fall in behind him and make him their candidate, and they do not absorb him—he absorbs them. They would come out at the end all Douglas men, all claimed by him as having indorsed every one of his doctrines upon the great subject with which the whole nation is engaged at this hour—that the question of negro slavery is simply a question of dollars and cents; that the Almighty has

VOL. I.—34.

drawn a line across the continent, on one side of which labor—the cultivation of the soil—must always be performed by slaves. It would be claimed that we, like him, do not care whether slavery is voted up or voted down. Had we made him our candidate and given him a great majority, we should never have heard an end of declarations by him that we had indorsed all these dogmas.

You all remember that at the last session of Congress there was a measure introduced in the Senate by Mr. Crittenden which proposed that the pro-slavery Lecompton constitution should be left to a vote to be taken in Kansas, and if it and slavery were adopted, Kansas should be at once admitted as a slave State. That same measure was introduced into the House by Mr. Montgomery, and therefore got the name of the Crittenden-Montgomery bill; and in the House of Representatives the Republicans all voted for it under the peculiar circumstances in which they found themselves placed. You may remember also that the New York "Tribune," which was so much in favor of our electing Judge Douglas to the Senate of the United States, has not yet got through the task of defending the Republican party, after that one vote in the House of Representatives, from the charge of having gone over to the doctrine of popular sovereignty. Now, how long would the New York "Tribune" have been in getting rid of the charge that the Republicans had abandoned their principles, if we had taken up Judge Douglas, adopted all his doctrines, and elected him to the Senate, when the single vote upon that one point so confused and embarrassed the position of the Republicans that it has kept them for one entire year arguing against the effect of it?

This much being said on that point, I wish now to add a word that has a bearing on the future. The Republican principle, the profound central truth that slavery is wrong and ought to be dealt with as a wrong,—though we are always to remember the fact of its actual existence amongst us and faithfully observe all the constitutional guarantees,—the unalterable principle never for a moment to be lost sight of, that it is a wrong and ought to be dealt with as such, cannot advance at all upon Judge Douglas's ground; that there is a portion of the country in which slavery must always exist; that he does not care whether it is voted up or voted down, as it is simply a question of dollars and cents. Whenever in any compromise, or arrangement, or combination that may promise some temporary advantage we are led upon that ground, then and there the great living principle upon which we have organized as a party is surrendered. The proposition now in our minds that this thing is wrong being once driven out and surrendered, then the institution of slavery necessarily becomes national.

One or two words more of what I did not think of when I rose. Suppose it is true that the Almighty has drawn a line across this continent, on the south side of which part of the people will hold the rest as slaves; that the Almighty ordered this; that it is right, unchangeably right, that men ought there to be held as slaves; that their fellow-men will always have the right to hold them as slaves. I ask you, this once admitted, how can you believe that it is not right for us, or for them coming here, to hold slaves on this other side of the line? Once we come to acknowledge that it is right, that it is the law of the Eternal Being for slavery to exist on one side of that line, have we any sure ground to object to slaves being held on the other side? Once admit the position that a man rightfully holds another man as property on one side of the line, and you must, when it suits his convenience to come to the other side, admit that he has the same right to hold his property there. Once admit Judge Douglas's proposition, and we must all finally give way. Although we may not bring ourselves to the idea that it is to our interest to have slaves in this Northern country, we shall soon bring ourselves to admit that while we may not want them, if any one else does, he has the moral right to have them. Step by step, south of the judge's moral climate line in the States, in the Territories everywhere, and then in all the States — it is thus that Judge Douglas would lead us inevitably to the nationalization of slavery. Whether by his doctrine of squatter sovereignty, or by the ground taken by him in his recent speeches in Memphis and through the South,— that wherever the climate makes it the interest of the inhabitants to encourage slave property they will pass a slave code,— whether it is covertly nationalized by congressional legislation, or by Dred Scott decision, or by the sophistical and misleading doctrine he has last advanced, the same goal is inevitably reached by the one or the other device. It is only traveling to the same place by different roads.

It is in this direction lies all the danger that now exists to the great Republican cause. I take it that so far as concerns forcibly establishing slavery in the Territories by congressional legislation, or by virtue of the Dred Scott decision, that day has passed. Our only serious danger is that we shall be led upon this ground of Judge Douglas, on the delusive assumption that it is a good way of whipping our opponents, when in fact it is a way that leads straight to final surrender. The Republican party should not dally with Judge Douglas when it knows where his proposition and his leadership would take us, nor be disposed to listen to it because it was best somewhere else to support somebody occupying his ground. That is no just reason why we ought to go over to Judge Douglas, as we were called upon to do last year. Never forget that we have before us this whole matter of the right or wrong of slavery in this Union, though the immediate question is as to its spreading out into new Territories and States.

I do not wish to be misunderstood upon this subject of slavery in this country. I suppose it may long exist; and perhaps the best way for it to come to an end peaceably is for it to exist for a length of time. But I say that the spread and strengthening and perpetuation of it is an entirely different proposition. There we should in every way resist it as a wrong, treating it as a wrong, with the fixed idea that it must and will come to an end. If we do not allow ourselves to be allured from the strict path of our duty by such a device as shifting our ground and throwing us into the rear of a leader who denies our first principle, denies that there is an absolute wrong in the institution of slavery, then the future of the Republican cause is safe, and victory is assured. You Republicans of Illinois have deliberately taken your ground; you have heard the whole subject discussed again and again; you have stated your faith in platforms laid down in a State convention and in a national convention; you have heard and talked over and considered it until you are now all of opinion that you are on a ground of unquestionable right. All you have to do is to keep the faith, to remain steadfast to the right, to stand by your banner. Nothing should lead you to leave your guns. Stand together, ready, with match in hand. Allow nothing to turn you to the right or to the left. Remember how long you have been in setting out on the true course; how long you have been in getting your neighbors to understand and believe as you now do. Stand by your principles, stand by your guns, and victory, complete and permanent, is sure at the last.

March 28, 1859.—LETTER TO W. M. MORRIS.

SPRINGFIELD, March 28, 1859.

W. M. MORRIS, Esq.

Dear Sir: Your kind note inviting me to deliver a lecture at Galesburg is received. I regret to say I cannot do so now; I must stick to the courts awhile. I read a sort of lecture to three different audiences during the last month and this; but I did so under circumstances which made it a waste of no time whatever.

Yours very truly,   ·   A. LINCOLN.

April 6, 1859.—LETTER TO H. L. PIERCE AND OTHERS.

SPRINGFIELD, ILL., April 6, 1859.

Gentlemen: Your kind note inviting me to attend a festival in Boston, on the 28th instant, in honor of the birthday of Thomas Jefferson, was duly received. My engagements are such that I cannot attend.

Bearing in mind that about seventy years ago two great political parties were first formed in this country, that Thomas Jefferson was the head of one of them and Boston the headquarters of the other, it is both curious and interesting that those supposed to descend politically from the party opposed to Jefferson should now be celebrating his birthday in their own original seat of empire, while those claiming political descent from him have nearly ceased to breathe his name everywhere.

Remembering, too, that the Jefferson party was formed upon its supposed superior devotion to the personal rights of men, holding the rights of property to be secondary only, and greatly inferior, and assuming that the so-called Democracy of to-day are the Jefferson, and their opponents the anti-Jefferson, party, it will be equally interesting to note how completely the two have changed hands as to the principle upon which they were originally supposed to be divided. The Democracy of to-day hold the liberty of one man to be absolutely nothing, when in conflict with another man's right of property; Republicans, on the contrary, are for both the man and the dollar, but in case of conflict the man before the dollar.

I remember being once much amused at seeing two partially intoxicated men engaged in a fight with their great-coats on, which fight, after a long and rather harmless contest, ended in each having fought himself out of his own coat and into that of the other. If the two leading parties of this day are really identical with the two in the days of Jefferson and Adams, they have performed the same feat as the two drunken men.

But, soberly, it is now no child's play to save the principles of Jefferson from total overthrow in this nation. One would state with great confidence that he could convince any sane child that the simpler propositions of Euclid are true; but nevertheless he would fail, utterly, with one who should deny the definitions and axioms. The principles of Jefferson are the definitions and axioms of free society. And yet they are denied and evaded, with no small show of success. One dashingly calls them "glittering generalities." Another bluntly calls them "self-evident lies." And others insidiously argue that they apply to "superior races." These expressions, differing in form, are identical in object and effect—the supplanting the principles of free government, and restoring those of classification, caste, and legitimacy. They would delight a convocation of crowned heads plotting against the people. They are the vanguard, the miners and sappers of returning despotism. We must repulse them, or they will subjugate us. This is a world of compensation; and he who would be no slave must consent to have no slave. Those who deny freedom to others deserve it not for themselves, and, under a just God, cannot long retain it. All honor to Jefferson—to the man who, in the concrete pressure of a struggle for national independence by a single people, had the coolness, forecast, and capacity to introduce into a merely revolutionary document an abstract truth, applicable to all men and all times, and so to embalm it there that to-day and in all coming days it shall be a rebuke and a stumbling-block to the very harbingers of reappearing tyranny and oppression. Your obedient servant,

MESSRS. H. L. PIERCE AND OTHERS.   A. LINCOLN.

April 16, 1859.—LETTER TO T. J. PICKETT.

SPRINGFIELD, April 16, 1859.

T. J. PICKETT, Esq.

My dear Sir : Yours of the 13th is just received. My engagements are such that I cannot at any very early day visit Rock Island to deliver a lecture, or for any other object. As to the other matter you kindly mention, I must in candor say I do not think myself fit for the presidency. I certainly am flattered and gratified that some partial friends think of me in that connection; but I really think it best for our cause that no concerted effort, such as you suggest, should be made. Let this be considered confidential.

Yours very truly,   A. LINCOLN.

May 14, 1859.—LETTER TO M. W. DELAHAY.

May 14, 1859.

M. W. DELAHAY.

. . . You will probably adopt resolutions in the nature of a platform. I think the only temptation will be to lower the Republican standard in order to gather recruits. In my judgment such a step would be a serious mistake, and open a gap through which more would pass out than pass in. And this would be the same whether the letting down should be in deference to Douglasism or to the Southern opposition element; either would surrender the object of the Republican organization—the preventing of the spread and nationalization of slavery. This object surrendered, the organization would go to pieces. I do not mean by this that no Southern man must be placed upon our national ticket in 1860. There are many men in the slave States for any one of whom I could cheerfully vote to be either President or Vice-President, provided he would enable me to do so with safety to the Republican cause, without lowering the Republican standard. This is the indispensable condition of a union with us; it is idle to talk of any other. Any other would be as fruitless to the South as distasteful to the North, the whole ending in common defeat. Let a union be attempted on the basis of ignoring the slavery question, and magnifying other questions which the people are just now not caring about, and it will result in gaining no single electoral vote in the South, and losing every one in the North. . . .

May 17, 1859.—LETTER TO T. CANISIUS.

SPRINGFIELD, May 17, 1859.

DR. THEODORE CANISIUS.

Dear Sir: Your note asking, in behalf of yourself and other German citizens, whether I am for or against the constitutional provision in regard to naturalized citizens, lately adopted by Massachusetts, and whether I am for or against a fusion of the Republicans, and other opposition elements, for the canvass of 1860, is received.

Massachusetts is a sovereign and independent State; and it is no privilege of mine to scold her for what she does. Still, if from what she has done an inference is sought to be drawn as to what I would do, I may without impropriety speak out. I say, then, that, as I understand the Massachusetts provision, I am against its adoption in Illinois, or in any other place where I have a right to oppose it. Understanding the spirit of our institutions to aim at the elevation of men, I am opposed to whatever tends to degrade them. I have some little notoriety for commiserating the oppressed negro; and I should be strangely inconsistent if I could favor any project for curtailing the existing rights of white men, even though born in different lands, and speaking different languages from myself. As to the matter of fusion, I am for it, if it can be had on Republican grounds; and I am not for it on any other terms. A fusion on any other terms would be as foolish as unprincipled. It would lose the whole North, while the common enemy would still carry the whole South. The question of men is a different one. There are good patriotic men and able statesmen in the South whom I would cheerfully support, if they would now place themselves on Republican ground, but I am against letting down the Republican standard a hair's-breadth.

I have written this hastily, but I believe it answers your questions substantially.   Yours truly,

A. LINCOLN.

July 6, 1859.—LETTER TO SCHUYLER COLFAX.

SPRINGFIELD, ILL., July 6, 1859.

HON. SCHUYLER COLFAX.

My dear Sir : I much regret not seeing you while you were here among us. Before learning that you were to be at Jacksonville on the 4th, I had given my word to be at another place. Besides a strong desire to make your personal acquaintance, I was anxious to speak with you on politics a little more fully than I can well do in a letter. My main object in such conversation would be to hedge against divisions in the Republican ranks generally, and particularly for the contest of 1860. The point of danger is the temptation in different localities to "platform" for something which will be popular just there, but which, nevertheless, will be a firebrand elsewhere, and especially in a national convention. As instances, the movement against foreigners in Massachusetts; in New Hampshire, to make obedience to the fugitive-slave law punishable as a crime; in Ohio, to repeal the fugitive-slave law; and squatter sovereignty, in Kansas. In these things there is explosive matter enough to blow up half a dozen national conventions, if it gets into them; and what gets very rife outside of conventions is very likely to find its way into them. What is desirable, if possible, is that in every local convocation of Republicans a point should be made to avoid everything which will disturb Republicans elsewhere. Massachusetts Republicans should have looked beyond their noses, and then they could not have failed to see that tilting against foreigners would ruin us in the whole Northwest. New Hampshire and Ohio should forbear tilting against the fugitive-slave law in such a way as to utterly overwhelm us in Illinois with the charge of enmity to the Constitution itself. Kansas, in her confidence that she can be saved to freedom on "squatter sovereignty," ought not to forget that to prevent the spread and nationalization of slavery is a national concern, and must be attended to by the nation. In a word, in every locality we should look beyond our noses; and at least say nothing on points where it is probable we shall disagree. I write this for your eye only; hoping, however, if you see danger as I think I do, you will do what you can to avert it. Could not suggestions be made to leading men in the State and congressional conventions, and so avoid, to some extent at least, these apples of discord?

Yours very truly,   A. LINCOLN.

July 11, 1859.— LETTER TO JAMES MILLER, TREASURER OF THE
STATE OF ILLINOIS.

SPRINGFIELD, ILL., July 11, 1859.

HON. JAMES MILLER.

Dear Sir: We suppose you are persistently urged to pay something upon the new McCallister and Stebbins bonds. As friends of yours and of the people, we advise you to pay nothing upon them under any possible circumstances. The holders of them did a great wrong, and are now persisting in it in a way which deserves severe punishment. They know the legislature has again and again refused to fully recognize the old bonds. Seizing upon an act never intended to apply to them, they besieged Governor Bissell more than a year ago to fund the old bonds; he refused. They sought a mandamus upon him from the Supreme Court; the court refused. Again they besieged the governor last winter; he sought to have them go before the legislature; they refused. Still they persisted, and dogged him in his afflicted condition till they got from him what the agent in New York acted upon and issued the new bonds. Now they refuse to surrender them, hoping to force an acquiescence, for Governor Bissell's sake. "That cock won't fight," and they may as well so understand at once. If the news of the surrender of the new bonds does not reach here in ten days from this date, we shall do what we can to have them repudiated in toto, finally and forever. If they were less than demons they would at once relieve Governor Bissell from the painful position they have dogged him into; and if they still persist, they shall never see even the twenty-six cents to the dollar, if we can prevent it.   Yours very truly,

A. LINCOLN,
S. T. LOGAN,
O. M. HATCH.

July 27, 1859.— LETTER TO S. GALLOWAY.

SPRINGFIELD, ILL., July 27, 1859.

HON. SAMUEL GALLOWAY.

My dear Sir: Your letter in relation to the claim of Mr. Ambos for the Columbus Machine Manufacturing Company against Barret and others is received. This has been a somewhat disagreeable matter to me. As I remember, you first wrote me on the general subject, Barret having then had a credit of four or five hundred dollars, and there was some question about his taking the machinery. I think you inquired as to Barret's responsibility; and that I answered I considered him an honest and honorable man, having a great deal of property, owing a good many debts, and hard pressed for ready cash. I was a little surprised soon after to learn that they had enlarged the credit to near ten thousand dollars, more or less. They wrote me to take notes and a mortgage, and to hold on to the notes awhile to fix amounts. I inferred the notes and mortgage were both to be held up for a time, and did so; Barret gave a second mortgage on part of the premises, which was first recorded, and then I was blamed some for not having recorded the other mortgage when first executed. My chief annoyance with the case now is that the parties at Columbus seem to think it is by my neglect that they do not get their money. There is an older mortgage on the real estate mortgaged, though not on the machinery. I got a decree of foreclosure in this present month; but I consented to delay advertising for sale till September, on a reasonable prospect that something will then be paid on a collateral Barret has put in my hands. When we come to sell on the decree, what will we do about the older mortgage? Barret has offered one or two other good notes—that is, notes on good men—if we would take them, *pro tanto*, as payment, but I notified Mr. Ambos, and he declined. My impression is that the whole of the money cannot be got very soon, anyway, but that it all will be ultimately collected, and that it could be got faster by turning in every little parcel we can, than by trying to force it through by the law in a lump. There are no special personal relations between Barret and myself. We are personal friends in a general way—no business transactions between us—not akin, and opposed on politics.

Yours truly,   A. LINCOLN.

July 28, 1859.—LETTER TO S. GALLOWAY.

SPRINGFIELD, ILL., July 28, 1859.

HON. SAMUEL GALLOWAY.

My dear Sir: Your very complimentary, not to say flattering, letter of the 23d inst. is received. Dr. Reynolds had induced me to expect you here; and I was disappointed not a little by your failure to come. And yet I fear you have formed an estimate of me which can scarcely be sustained on a personal acquaintance.

Two things done by the Ohio Republican convention—the repudiation of Judge Swan, and the "plank" for a repeal of the fugitive-slave law—I very much regretted. These two things are of a piece; and they are viewed by many good men, sincerely opposed to slavery, as a struggle against, and in disregard of, the Constitution itself. And it is the very thing that will greatly endanger our cause, if it be not kept out of our national convention. There is another thing our friends are doing which gives me some uneasiness. It is their leaning toward "popular sovereignty." There are three substantial objections to this. First, no party can command respect which sustains this year what it opposed last. Secondly, Douglas (who is the most dangerous enemy of liberty, because the most insidious one) would have little support in the North, and by consequence, no capital to trade on in the South, if it were not for his friends thus magnifying him and his humbug. But lastly, and chiefly, Douglas's popular sovereignty, accepted by the public mind as a just principle, nationalizes slavery, and revives the African slave-trade inevitably. Taking slaves into new Territories, and buying slaves in Africa, are identical things, identical rights or identical wrongs, and the argument which establishes one will establish the other. Try a thousand years for a sound reason why Congress shall not hinder the people of Kansas from having slaves, and when you have found it, it will be an equally good one why Congress should not hinder the people of Georgia from importing slaves from Africa.

As to Governor Chase, I have a kind side for him. He was one of the few distinguished men of the nation who gave us, in Illinois, their sympathy last year. I never saw him, but suppose him to be able and right-minded; but still he may not be the most suitable as a candidate for the presidency.

I must say I do not think myself fit for the presidency. As you propose a correspondence with me, I shall look for your letters anxiously.

I have not met Dr. Reynolds since receiving your letter; but when I shall, I will present your respects as requested.

Yours very truly,   A. LINCOLN.

September 16, 1859.— SPEECH AT COLUMBUS, OHIO.

Fellow-citizens of the State of Ohio: I cannot fail to remember that I appear for the first time before an audience in this now great State — an audience that is accustomed to hear such speakers as Corwin, and Chase, and Wade, and many other renowned men; and remembering this, I feel that it will be well for you, as for me, that you should not raise your expectations to that standard to which you would have been justified in raising them had one of these distinguished men appeared before you. You would perhaps be only preparing a disappointment for yourselves, and, as a consequence of your disappointment, mortification to me. I hope, therefore, that you will commence with very moderate expectations; and perhaps, if you will give me your attention, I shall be able to interest you to a moderate degree.

Appearing here for the first time in my life, I have been somewhat embarrassed for a topic by way of introduction to my speech; but I have been relieved from that embarrassment by an introduction which the "Ohio Statesman" newspaper gave me this morning. In this paper I have read an article in which, among other statements, I find the following:

> In debating with Senator Douglas during the memorable contest last fall, Mr. Lincoln declared in favor of negro suffrage, and attempted to defend that vile conception against the Little Giant.

I mention this now, at the opening of my remarks, for the purpose of making three comments upon it. The first I have already announced — it furnished me an introductory topic; the second is to show that the gentleman is mistaken; thirdly, to give him an opportunity to correct it.

In the first place, in regard to this matter being a mistake. I have found that it is not entirely safe, when one is misrepresented under his very nose, to allow the misrepresentation to go uncontradicted. I therefore propose, here at the outset, not only to say that this is a misrepresentation, but to show conclusively that it is so; and you will bear with me while I read a couple of extracts from that very "memorable" debate with Judge Douglas last year, to which this newspaper refers.   In the first pitched battle which Senator Douglas and myself had, at the town of Ottawa, I used the language which I will now read. Having been previously reading an extract, I continued as follows:

Now, gentlemen, I don't want to read at any greater length, but this is the true complexion of all I have ever said in regard to the institution of slavery and the black race.   This is the whole of it, and anything that argues me into his idea of perfect social and political equality with the negro is but a specious and fantastic arrangement of words, by which a man can prove a horse-chestnut to be a chestnut horse.   I will say here, while upon this subject, that I have no purpose either directly or indirectly to interfere with the institution of slavery in the States where it exists.   I believe I have no lawful right to do so, and I have no inclination to do so. I have no purpose to introduce political and social equality between the white and the black races.   There is a physical difference between the two which, in my judgment, will probably forever forbid their living together upon the footing of perfect equality, and inasmuch as it becomes a necessity that there must be a difference, I, as well as Judge Douglas, am in favor of the race to which I belong having the superior position.   I have never said anything to the contrary, but I hold that, notwithstanding all this, there is no reason in the world why the negro is not entitled to all the natural rights enumerated in the Declaration of Independence, the right to life, liberty, and the pursuit of happiness.   I hold that he is as much entitled to these as the white man.   I agree with Judge Douglas, he is not my equal in many respects—certainly not in color, perhaps not in moral or intellectual endowments.   But in the right to eat the bread, without leave of anybody else, which his own hand earns, he is my equal, and the equal of Judge Douglas, and the equal of every living man.

Upon a subsequent occasion, when the reason for making a statement like this recurred, I said:

While I was at the hotel to-day an elderly gentleman called upon me to know whether I was really in favor of producing a perfect equality between the negroes and white people.   While I had not proposed to myself on this occasion to say much on that subject, yet as the question was asked me I thought I would occupy perhaps five minutes in saying something in regard to it.   I will say, then, that I am not, nor ever have been, in favor of bringing about in any way the social and political equality of the white and the black races—that I am not, nor ever have been, in favor of making voters or jurors of negroes, nor of qualifying them to hold office, nor to intermarry with white people; and I will say in addition to this, that there is a physical difference between the white and the black races, which, I believe, will forever forbid the two races living together on terms of social and political equality. And inasmuch as they cannot so live, while they do remain together there must be the position of superior and inferior, and I, as much as any other man, am in favor of having the superior position assigned to the white race. I say upon this occasion I do not perceive that because the white man is to have the superior position, the negro should be denied everything.   I do not understand that because I do not want a negro woman for a slave, I must necessarily want her for a wife.   My understanding is that I can just let her alone.   I am now in my fiftieth year; and I certainly never have had a black woman for either a slave or a wife. So it seems to me quite possible for us to get along without making either slaves or wives of negroes. I will add to this, that I have never seen to my knowledge a man, woman, or child who was in favor of producing a perfect equality, social and political, between negroes and white men. I recollect of but one distinguished instance that I ever heard of so frequently as to be entirely satisfied of its correctness — and that is the case of Judge Douglas's old friend, Colonel Richard M. Johnson. I will also add to the remarks I have made (for I am not going to enter at large upon this subject), that I have never had the least apprehension that I or my friends would marry negroes, if there was no law to keep them from it; but as Judge Douglas and his friends seem to be in great apprehension that they might, if there were no law to keep them from it, I give him the most solemn pledge that I will to the very last stand by the law of the State, which forbids the marrying of white people with negroes.

There, my friends, you have briefly what I have, upon former occasions, said upon the subject to which this newspaper, to the extent of its ability, has drawn the public attention. In it you not only perceive, as a probability, that in that contest I did not at any time say I was in favor of negro suffrage; but the absolute proof that twice — once substantially and once expressly — I declared against it. Having shown you this, there remains but a word of comment upon that newspaper article. It is this: that I presume the editor of that paper is an honest and truth-loving man, and that he will be greatly obliged to me for furnishing him thus early an opportunity to correct the misrepresentation he has made, before it has run so long that malicious people can call him a liar.

The giant himself has been here recently. I have seen a brief report of his speech. If it were otherwise unpleasant to me to introduce the subject of the negro as a topic for discussion, I might be somewhat relieved by the fact that he dealt exclusively in that subject while he was here. I shall, therefore, without much hesitation or diffidence, enter upon this subject.

The American people, on the first day of January, 1854, found the African slave-trade prohibited by a law of Congress. In a majority of the States of this Union, they found African slavery, or any other sort of slavery, prohibited by State constitutions. They also found a law existing, supposed to be valid, by which slavery was excluded from almost all the territory the United States then owned. This was the condition of the country, with reference to the institution of slavery, on the first of January, 1854. A few days after that, a bill was introduced into Congress, which ran through its regular course in the two branches of the national legislature, and finally passed into a law in the month of May, by which the act of Congress prohibiting slavery from going into the Territories of the United States was repealed. In connection with the law itself, and, in fact, in the terms of the law, the then existing prohibition was not only repealed, but there was a declaration of a purpose on the part of Congress never thereafter to exercise any power that they might have, real or supposed, to prohibit the extension or spread of slavery. This was a very great change; for the law thus repealed was of more than thirty years' standing. Following rapidly upon the heels of this action of Congress, a decision of the Supreme Court is made, by which it is declared that Congress, if it desires to prohibit the spread of slavery into the Territories, has no constitutional power to do so. Not only so, but that decision lays down principles, which, if pushed to their logical conclusion,— I say pushed to their logical conclusion,— would decide that the constitutions of free States, forbidding slavery, are themselves unconstitutional. Mark me, I do not say the judges said this, and let no man say I affirm the judges used these words; but I only say it is my opinion that what they did say, if pressed to its logical conclusion, will inevitably result thus.

Looking at these things, the Republican party, as I understand its principles and policy, believes that there is great danger of the institution of slavery being spread out and extended, until it is ultimately made alike lawful in all the States of this Union; so believing, to prevent that incidental and ultimate consummation is the original and chief purpose of the Republican organization. I say "chief purpose" of the Republican organization; for it is certainly true that if the national house shall fall into the hands of the Republicans, they will have to attend to all the other matters of national house-keeping as well as this. The chief and real purpose of the Republican party is eminently conservative. It proposes nothing save and except to restore this government to its original tone in regard to this element of slavery, and there to maintain it, looking for no further change in reference to it than that which the original framers of the government themselves expected and looked forward to.

The chief danger to this purpose of the Republican party is not just now the revival of the African slave-trade, or the passage of a congressional slave-code, or the declaring of a second Dred Scott decision, making slavery lawful in all the States. These are not pressing us just now. They are not quite ready yet. The authors of these measures know that we are too strong for them; but they will be upon us in due time, and we will be grappling with them hand to hand, if they are not now headed off. They are not now the chief danger to the purpose of the Republican organization; but the most imminent danger that now threatens that purpose is that insidious Douglas popular sovereignty. This is the miner and sapper. While it does not propose to revive the African slave-trade, nor to pass a slave-code, nor to make a second Dred Scott decision, it is preparing us for the onslaught and charge of these ultimate enemies when they shall be ready to come on, and the word of command for them to advance shall be given. I say this Douglas popular sovereignty— for there is a broad distinction, as I now understand it, between that article and a genuine popular sovereignty.

I believe there is a genuine popular sovereignty. I think a definition of genuine popular sovereignty, in the abstract, would be about this: That each man shall do precisely as he pleases with himself, and with all those things which exclusively concern him. Applied to government, this principle would be, that a general government shall do all those things which pertain to it, and all the local governments shall do precisely as they please in respect to those matters which exclusively concern them. I understand that this government of the United States, under which we live, is based upon this principle; and I am misunderstood if it is supposed that I have any war to make upon that principle.

Now, what is Judge Douglas's popular sovereignty? It is, as a principle, no other than that if one man chooses to make a slave of another man, neither that other man nor anybody else has a right to object. Applied in government, as he seeks to apply it, it is this: If, in a new Territory into which a few people are beginning to enter for the purpose of making their homes, they choose to either exclude slavery from their limits or to establish it there, however one or the other may affect the persons to be enslaved, or the infinitely greater number of persons who are afterward to inhabit that Territory, or the other members of the families of communities, of which they are but an incipient member, or the general head of the family of States as parent of all—however their action may affect one or the other of these, there is no power or right to interfere. That is Douglas's popular sovereignty applied.

He has a good deal of trouble with popular sovereignty. His explanations explanatory of explanations explained are interminable. The most lengthy and, as I suppose, the most maturely considered of his long series of explanations is his great essay in "Harper's Magazine." I will not attempt to enter on any very thorough investigation of his argument as there made and presented. I will nevertheless occupy a good portion of your time here in drawing your attention to certain points in it. Such of you as may have read this document will have perceived that the judge, early in the document, quotes from two persons as belonging to the Republican party, without naming them, but who can readily be recognized as being Governor Seward, of New York, and myself. It is true that exactly fifteen months ago this day, I believe, I for the first time expressed a sentiment upon this subject, and in such a manner that it should get into print, that the public might see it beyond the circle of my hearers, and my expression of it at that time is the quotation that Judge Douglas makes. He has not made the quotation with accuracy, but justice to him requires me to say that it is sufficiently accurate not to change its sense.

The sense of that quotation condensed is this—that this slavery element is a durable element of discord among us, and that we shall probably not have perfect peace in this country with it until it either masters the free principle in our government, or is so far mastered by the free principle as for the public mind to rest in the belief that it is going to its end. This sentiment which I now express in this way was, at no great distance of time, perhaps in different language, and in connection with some collateral ideas, expressed by Governor Seward. Judge Douglas has been so much annoyed by the expression of that sentiment that he has constantly, I believe, in almost all his speeches since it was uttered, been referring to it. I find he alluded to it in his speech here, as well as in the copyright essay. I do not now enter upon this for the purpose of making an elaborate argument to show that we were right in the expression of that sentiment. I only ask your attention to this matter for the purpose of making one or two points upon it.

If you will read the copyright essay, you will discover that Judge Douglas himself says a controversy between the American colonies and the government of Great Britain began on the slavery question in 1699, and continued from that time until the Revolution; and, while he did not say so, we all know that it has continued with more or less violence ever since the Revolution.

Then we need not appeal to history, to the declaration of the framers of the government, but we know from Judge Douglas himself that slavery began to be an element of discord among the white people of this country as far back as 1699, or one hundred and sixty years ago, or five generations of men — counting thirty years to a generation. Now it would seem to me that it might have occurred to Judge Douglas, or to anybody who had turned his attention to these facts, that there was something in the nature of that thing, slavery, somewhat durable for mischief and discord.

There is another point I desire to make in regard to this matter before I leave it. From the adoption of the Constitution down to 1820 is the precise period of our history when we had comparative peace upon this question — the precise period of time when we came nearer to having peace about it than any other time of that entire one hundred and sixty years, in which he says it began, or of the eighty years of our own Constitution. Then it would be worth our while to stop and examine into the probable reason of our coming nearer to having peace then than at any other time. This was the precise period of time in which our fathers adopted, and during which they followed, a policy restricting the spread of slavery, and the whole Union was acquiescing in it. The whole country looked forward to the ultimate extinction of the institution. It was when a policy had been adopted and was prevailing, which led all just and right-minded men to suppose that slavery was gradually coming to an end, and that they might be quiet about it, watching it as it expired. I think Judge Douglas might have perceived that too, and, whether he did or not, it is worth the attention of fair-minded men, here and elsewhere, to consider whether that is not the truth of the case. If he had looked at these two facts, that this matter has been an element of discord for one hundred and sixty years among this people, and that the only comparative peace we have had about it was when that policy prevailed in this government, which he now wars upon, he might then, perhaps, have been brought to a more just appreciation of what I said fifteen months ago — that "a house divided against itself cannot stand. I believe this government cannot endure permanently half slave and half free. I do not expect the Union to be dissolved — I do not expect the house to fall; but I do expect it will cease to be divided. It will become all one thing or all the other. Either the opponents of slavery will arrest the further spread of it, and place it where the public mind will rest in the belief that it is in the course of ultimate extinction, or its advocates will push it forward, until it shall become alike lawful in all the States, old as well as new, North as well as South." That was my sentiment at that time. In connection with it I said, "We are now far into the fifth year since a policy was initiated with the avowed object and confident promise of putting an end to slavery agitation. Under the operation of that policy, that agitation has not only not ceased, but has constantly augmented." I now say to you here that we are advanced still farther into the sixth year since that policy of Judge Douglas—that popular sovereignty of his for quieting the slavery question—was made the national policy. Fifteen months more have been added since I uttered that sentiment, and I call upon you, and all other right-minded men, to say whether those fifteen months have belied or corroborated my words.

While I am here upon this subject, I cannot but express gratitude that the true view of this element of discord among us — as I believe it is—is attracting more and more attention. I do not believe that Governor Seward uttered that sentiment because I had done so before, but because he reflected upon this subject, and saw the truth of it. Nor do I believe, because Governor Seward or I uttered it, that Mr. Hickman, of Pennsylvania, in different language, since that time, has declared his belief in the utter antagonism which exists between the principles of liberty and slavery. You see we are multiplying. Now, while I am speaking of Hickman, let me say, I know but little about him. I have never seen him, and know scarcely anything about the man; but I will say this much about him: Of all the anti-Lecompton Democracy that have been brought to my notice, he alone has the true, genuine ring of the metal. And now, without indorsing anything else he has said, I will ask this audience to give three cheers for Hickman. [The audience responded with three rousing cheers for Hickman.]

Another point in the copyright essay to which I would ask your attention is rather a feature to be extracted from the whole thing, than from any express declaration of it at any point. It is a general feature of that document, and indeed, of all of Judge Douglas's discussions of this question, that the Territories of the United States and the States of this Union are exactly alike— that there is no difference between them at all —that the Constitution applies to the Territories precisely as it does to the States — and that the United States Government, under the Constitution, may not do in a State what it may not do in a Territory, and what it must do in a State, it must do in a Territory. Gentlemen, is that a true view of the case? It is necessary for this squatter sovereignty; but is it true?

Let us consider. What does it depend upon? It depends altogether upon the proposition that the States must, without the interference of the General Government, do all those things that pertain exclusively to themselves—that are local in their nature, that have no connection with the General Government. After Judge Douglas has established this proposition, which nobody disputes or ever has disputed, he proceeds to assume, without proving it, that slavery is one of those little, unimportant, trivial matters, which are of just about as much consequence as the question would be to me whether my neighbor should raise horned cattle or plant tobacco; that there is no moral question about it, but that it is altogether a matter of dollars and cents; that when a new Territory is opened for settlement, the first man who goes into it may plant there a thing which, like the

Canada thistle, or some other of those pests of the soil, cannot be dug out by the millions of men who will come thereafter; that it is one of those little things that is so trivial in its nature that it has no effect upon anybody save the few men who first plant upon the soil; that it is not a thing which in any way affects the family of communities composing these States, nor any way endangers the General Government. Judge Douglas ignores altogether the very well-known fact that we have never had a serious menace to our political existence, except it sprang from this thing, which he chooses to regard as only upon a par with onions and potatoes.

Turn it, and contemplate it in another view. He says that, according to his popular sovereignty, the General Government may give to the Territories governors, judges, marshals, secretaries, and all the other chief men to govern them, but they must not touch upon this other question. Why? The question of who shall be governor of a Territory for a year or two, and pass away, without his track being left upon the soil, or an act which he did for good or for evil being left behind, is a question of vast national magnitude. It is so much opposed in its nature to locality that the nation itself must decide it; while this other matter of planting slavery upon a soil — a thing which, once planted, cannot be eradicated by the succeeding millions who have as much right there as the first comers, or if eradicated, not without infinite difficulty and a long struggle — he considers the power to prohibit it as one of these little, local, trivial things that the nation ought not to say a word about; that it affects nobody save the few men who are there.

Take these two things and consider them together, present the question of planting a State with the institution of slavery by the side of a question of who shall be governor of Kansas for a year or two, and is there a man here — is there a man on earth — who would not say the governor question is the little one, and the slavery question is the great one? I ask any honest Democrat if the small, the local, and the trivial and temporary question is not, Who shall be governor? — while the durable, the important, and the mischievous one is, Shall this soil be planted with slavery?

This is an idea, I suppose, which has arisen in Judge Douglas's mind from his peculiar structure. I suppose the institution of slavery really looks small to him. He is so put up by nature that a lash upon his back would hurt him, but a lash upon anybody else's back does not hurt him. That is the build of the man, and consequently he looks upon the matter of slavery in this unimportant light.

Judge Douglas ought to remember, when he is endeavoring to force this policy upon the American people, that while he is put up in that way, a good many are not. He ought to remember that there was once in this country a man by the name of Thomas Jefferson, supposed to be a Democrat — a man whose principles and policy are not very prevalent amongst Democrats to-day, it is true; but that man did not take exactly this view of the insignificance of the element of slavery which our friend Judge Douglas does. In contemplation of this thing, we all know he was led to exclaim, "I tremble for my country when I remember that God is just!" We know how he looked upon it when he thus expressed himself. There was danger to this country, danger of the avenging justice of God, in that little unimportant popular-sovereignty question of Judge Douglas. He supposed there was a question of God's eternal justice wrapped up in the enslaving of any race of men, or any man, and that those who did so braved the arm of Jehovah — that when a nation thus dared the Almighty, every friend of that nation had cause to dread his wrath. Choose ye between Jefferson and Douglas as to what is the true view of this element among us.

There is another little difficulty about this matter of treating the Territories and States alike in all things, to which I ask your attention, and I shall leave this branch of the case. If there is no difference between them, why not make the Territories States at once? What is the reason that Kansas was not fit to come into the Union when it was organized into a Territory, in Judge Douglas's view? Can any of you tell any reason why it should not have come into the Union at once? They are fit, as he thinks, to decide upon the slavery question — the largest and most important with which they could possibly deal; what could they do by coming into the Union that they are not fit to do, according to his view, by staying out of it? Oh, they are not fit to sit in Congress and decide upon the rates of postage, or questions of *ad valorem* or specific duties on foreign goods, or live-oak timber contracts; they are not fit to decide these vastly important matters, which are national in their import, but they are fit, "from the jump," to decide this little negro question. But, gentlemen, the case is too plain; I occupy too much time on this head, and I pass on.

Near the close of the copyright essay, the judge, I think, comes very near kicking his own fat into the fire. I did not think when I commenced these remarks that I would read from that article, but I now believe I will:

This exposition of the history of these measures shows conclusively that the authors of the compromise measures of 1850, and of the Kansas-Nebraska act of 1854, as well as the members of the Continental Congress in 1774, and the founders of our system of government subsequent to the Revolution, regarded the people of the Territories and Colonies as political communities which were entitled to a free and exclusive power of legislation in their provincial legislatures, where their representation could alone be preserved, in all cases of taxation and internal polity.

When the judge saw that putting in the word "slavery" would contradict his own history, he put in what he knew would pass as synonymous with it—"internal polity." Whenever we find *that* in one of his speeches, the substitute is used in this manner; and I can tell you the reason. It would be too bald a contradiction to say slavery, but "internal polity" is a general phrase which would pass in some quarters, and which he hopes will pass with the reading community, for the same thing.

This right pertains to the people collectively, as a law-abiding and peaceful community, and not to the isolated individuals who may wander upon the public domain in violation of law. It can only be exercised where there are inhabitants sufficient to constitute a government, and capable of performing its various functions and duties, a fact to be ascertained and determined by —

Who do you think? Judge Douglas says, " By Congress."

Whether the number shall be fixed at ten, fifteen, or twenty thousand inhabitants does not affect the principle.

Now I have only a few comments to make. Popular sovereignty, by his own words, does not pertain to the few persons who wander upon the public domain in violation of law. We have his words for that. When it does pertain to them is when they are sufficient to be formed into an organized political community, and he fixes the minimum for that at 10,000, and the maximum at 20,000. Now I would like to know what is to be done with the 9,000? Are they all to be treated, until they are large enough to be organized into a political community, as wanderers upon the public land in violation of law? And if so treated and driven out, at what point of time would there ever be ten thousand? If they were not driven out, but remained there as trespassers upon the public land in violation of the law, can they establish slavery there? No; the judge says popular sovereignty don't pertain to them then. Can they exclude it then? No; popular sovereignty don't pertain to them then. I would like to know, in the case covered by the essay, what condition the people of the Territory are in before they reach the number of ten thousand?

But the main point I wish to ask attention to is that the question as to when they shall have reached a sufficient number to be formed into a regular organized community is to be decided "by Congress." Judge Douglas says so. Well, gentlemen, that is about all we want. No; that is all the Southerners want. That is what all those who are for slavery want. They do not want Congress to prohibit slavery from coming into the new Territories, and they do not want popular sovereignty to hinder it; and as Congress is to say when they are ready to be organized, all that the South has to do is to get Congress to hold off. Let Congress hold off until they are ready to be admitted as a State, and the South has all it wants in taking slavery into and planting it in all the Territories that we now have, or hereafter may have. In a word, the whole thing, at a dash of the pen, is at last put in the power of Congress; for if they do not have this popular sovereignty until Congress organizes them, I ask if it at last does not come from Congress? If, at last, it amounts to anything at all, Congress gives it to them. I submit this rather for your reflection than for comment. After all that is said, at last, by a dash of the pen, everything that has gone before is undone, and he puts the whole question under the control of Congress. After fighting through more than three hours, if you will undertake to read it, he at last places the whole matter under the control of that power which he had been contending against, and arrives at a result directly contrary to what he had been laboring to do. He at last leaves the whole matter to the control of Congress.

There are two main objects, as I understand it, of this "Harper's Magazine" essay. One was to show, if possible, that the men of our Revolutionary times were in favor of his popular sovereignty; and the other was to show that the Dred Scott decision had not entirely squelched out this popular sovereignty. I do not propose, in regard to this argument drawn from the history of former times, to enter into a detailed examination of the historical statements he has made. I have the impression that they are inaccurate in a great many instances; sometimes in positive statement, but very much more inaccurate by the suppression of statements that really belong to the history. But I do not propose to affirm that this is so to any very great extent, or to enter into a very minute examination of his historical statements. I avoid doing so upon this principle — that if it were important for me to pass out of this lot in the least period of time possible, and I came to that fence and saw by a calculation of my own strength and agility that I could clear it at a bound, it would be folly for me to stop and consider whether I could or could not crawl through a crack. So I say of the whole history contained in his essay, where he endeavored to link the men of the Revolution to popular sovereignty. It only requires an effort to leap out of it — a single bound to be entirely successful. If you read it over you will find that he quotes here and there from documents of the Revolutionary times, tending to show that the people of the colonies were desirous of regulating their own concerns in their own way, that the British Government should not interfere; that at one time they struggled with the British Government to be permitted to exclude the African slave-trade; if not directly, to be permitted to exclude it indirectly by taxation sufficient to discourage and destroy it. From these and many things of this sort, Judge Douglas argues that they were in favor of the people of our own Territories excluding slavery if they wanted to, or planting it there if they wanted to, doing just as they pleased from the time they settled upon the Territory. Now, however his history may apply, and whatever of his argument there may be that is sound and accurate or unsound and inaccurate, if we can find out what these men did themselves do upon this very question of slavery in the Territories, does it not end the whole thing? If, after all this labor and effort to show that the men of the Revolution were in favor of his popular sovereignty and his mode of dealing with slavery in the Territories, we can show that these very men took hold of that subject, and dealt with it, we can see for ourselves how they dealt with it. It is not a matter of argument or inference, but we know what they thought about it.

It is precisely upon that part of the history of the country that one important omission is made by Judge Douglas. He selects parts of the history of the United States upon the subject of slavery, and treats it as the whole, omitting from his historical sketch the legislation of Congress in regard to the admission of Missouri, by which the Missouri Compromise was established, and slavery excluded from a country half as large as the present United States. All this is left out of his history, and in no wise alluded to by him, so far as I can remember, save once, when he makes a remark, that upon his principle the Supreme Court was authorized to pronounce a decision that the act called the Missouri Compromise was unconstitutional. All that history has been left out. But this part of the history of the country was not made by the men of the Revolution.

There was another part of our political history made by the very men who were the actors in the Revolution, which has taken the name of the ordinance of '87. Let me bring that history to your attention. In 1784, I believe, this same Mr. Jefferson drew up an ordinance for the government of the country upon which we now stand; or rather a frame or draft of an ordinance for the government of this country, here in Ohio, our neighbors in Indiana, us who live in Illinois, and our neighbors in Wisconsin and Michigan. In that ordinance, drawn up not only for the government of that Territory, but for the Territories south of the Ohio River, Mr. Jefferson expressly provided for the prohibition of slavery. Judge Douglas says, and perhaps he is right, that that provision was lost from that ordinance. I believe that is true. When the vote was taken upon it, a majority of all present in the Congress of the Confederation voted for it; but there were so many absentees that those voting for it did not make the clear majority necessary, and it was lost. But three years after that the Congress of the Confederation were together again, and they adopted a new ordinance for the government of this Northwest Territory, not contemplating territory south of the river, for the States owning that territory had hitherto refrained from giving it to the General Government; hence they made the ordinance to apply only to what the government owned. In that, the provision excluding slavery was inserted and passed unanimously, or at any rate it passed and became a part of the law of the land. Under that ordinance we live. First, here, in Ohio, you were a Territory, then an enabling act was passed, authorizing you to form a constitution and State government, provided it was Republican, and not in conflict with the ordinance of '87. When you framed your constitution and presented it for admission, I think you will find the legislation upon the subject will show that, "whereas you had formed a constitution that was Republican, and not in conflict with the ordinance of '87," therefore you were admitted upon equal footing with the original States. The same process in a few years was gone through with Indiana, and so with Illinois, and the same substantially with Michigan and Wisconsin.

Not only did that ordinance prevail, but it was constantly looked to whenever a step was taken by a new Territory to become a State. Congress always turned their attention to it, and in all their movements upon this subject they traced their course by that ordinance of '87. When they admitted new States they advertised them of this ordinance as a part of the legislation of the country. They did so because they had traced the ordinance of '87 throughout the history of this country. Begin with the men of the Revolution, and go down for sixty entire years, and until the last scrap of that Territory comes into the Union in the form of the State of Wisconsin, everything was made to conform to the ordinance of '87, excluding slavery from that vast extent of country.

I omitted to mention in the right place that the Constitution of the United States was in process of being framed when that ordinance was made by the Congress of the Confederation; and one of the first acts of Congress itself, under the new Constitution itself, was to give force to that ordinance by putting power to carry it out into the hands of new officers under the Constitution, in the place of the old ones, who had been legislated out of existence by the change in the government from the Confederation to the Constitution. Not only so, but I believe Indiana once or twice, if not Ohio, petitioned the General Government for the privilege of suspending that provision and allowing them to have slaves. A report made by Mr. Randolph, of Virginia, himself a slaveholder, was directly against it, and the action was to refuse them the privilege of violating the ordinance of '87.

This period of history, which I have run over briefly, is, I presume, as familiar to most of this assembly as any other part of the history of our country. I suppose that few of my hearers are not as familiar with that part of history as I am, and I only mention it to recall your attention to it at this time. And hence I ask how extraordinary a thing it is that a man who has occupied a position upon the floor of the Senate of the United States, who is now in his third term, and who looks to see the government of this whole country fall into his own hands, pretending to give a truthful and accurate history of the slavery question in this country, should so entirely ignore the whole of that portion of our history—the most important of all. Is it not a most extraordinary spectacle, that a man should stand up and ask for any confidence in his statements, who sets out as he does with portions of history, calling upon the people to believe that it is a true and fair representation, when the leading part and controlling feature of the whole history is carefully suppressed?

But the mere leaving out is not the most remarkable feature of this most remarkable essay. His proposition is to establish that the leading men of the Revolution were for his great principle of non-intervention by the government in the question of slavery in the Territories; while history shows that they decided in the cases actually brought before them in exactly the contrary way, and he knows it. Not only did they so decide at that time, but they stuck to it during sixty years, through thick and thin, as long as there was one of the Revolutionary heroes upon the stage of political action. Through their whole course, from first to last, they clung to freedom. And now he asks the community to believe that the men of the Revolution were in favor of his great principle, when we have the naked history that they themselves dealt with this very subject-matter of his principle, and utterly repudiated his principle, acting upon a precisely contrary ground. It is as impudent and absurd as if a prosecuting attorney should stand up before a jury, and ask them to convict A as the murderer of B, while B was walking alive before them.

I say again, if Judge Douglas asserts that the men of the Revolution acted upon principles by which, to be consistent with themselves, they ought to have adopted his popular sovereignty, then, upon a consideration of his own argument, he had a right to make you believe that they understood the principles of government, but misapplied them—that he has arisen to enlighten the world as to the just application of this principle. He has a right to try to persuade you that he understands their principles better than they did, and therefore he will apply them now, not as they did, but as they ought to have done. He has a right to go before the community, and try to convince them of this; but he has no right to attempt to impose upon any one the belief that these men themselves approved of his great principle. There are two ways of establishing a proposition. One is by trying to demonstrate it upon reason, and the other is, to show that great men in former times have thought so and so, and thus to pass it by the weight of pure authority. Now, if Judge Douglas will demonstrate somehow that this is popular sovereignty —the right of one man to make a slave of another, without any right in that other, or any one else, to object,—demonstrate it as Euclid demonstrated propositions,—there is no objection. But when he comes forward, seeking to carry a principle by bringing to it the authority of men who themselves utterly repudiate that principle, I ask that he shall not be permitted to do it.

I see, in the judge's speech here, a short sentence in these words: "Our fathers, when they formed this government under which we live, understood this question just as well and even better than we do now." That is true; I stick to that. I will stand by Judge Douglas in that to the bitter end. And now, Judge Douglas, come and stand by me, and truthfully show how they acted, understanding it better than we do. All I ask of you, Judge Douglas, is to stick to the proposition that the men of the Revolution understood this subject better than we do now, and with that better understanding they acted better than you are trying to act now.

I wish to say something now in regard to the Dred Scott decision, as dealt with by Judge Douglas. In that "memorable debate" between Judge Douglas and myself, last year, the judge thought fit to commence a process of catechizing me, and at Freeport I answered his questions, and propounded some to him. Among others I propounded to him was one that I have here now. The substance, as I remember it, is: "Can the people of a United States Territory, under the Dred Scott decision, in any lawful way, against the wish of any citizen of the United States, exclude slavery from its limits, prior to the formation of a State constitution?" He answered that they could lawfully exclude slavery from the United States Territories, notwithstanding the Dred Scott decision. There was something about that answer that has probably been a trouble to the judge ever since.

The Dred Scott decision expressly gives every citizen of the United States a right to carry his slaves into the United States Territories. And now there was some inconsistency in saying that the decision was right, and saying, too, that the people of the Territory could lawfully drive slavery out again. When all the trash, the words, the collateral matter, was cleared away from it,—all the chaff was fanned out of it,—it was a bare absurdity: no less than that a thing may be lawfully driven away from where it has a lawful right to be. Clear it of all the verbiage, and that is the naked truth of his proposition—that a thing may be lawfully driven from the place where it has a lawful right to stay. Well, it was because the judge could n't help seeing this that he has had so much trouble with it; and what I want to ask your especial attention to, just now, is to remind you, if you have not noticed the fact, that the judge does not any longer say that the people can exclude slavery. He does not say so in the copyright essay; he did not say so in the speech that he made here; and, so far as I know, since his reëlection to the Senate, he has never said, as he did at Freeport, that the people of the Territories can exclude slavery. He desires that you, who wish the Territories to remain free, should believe that he stands by that position, but he does not say it himself. He escapes, to some extent, the absurd position I have stated by changing his language entirely. What he says now is something different in language, and we will consider whether it is not different in sense too. It is now that the Dred Scott decision, or rather the Constitution under that decision, does not carry slavery into the Territories beyond the power of the people of the Territories to control it as other property. He does not say the people can drive it out, but they can control it as other property. The language is different; we should consider whether the sense is different. Driving a horse out of this lot is too plain a proposition to be mistaken about; it is putting him on the other side of the fence. Or it might be a sort of exclusion of him from the lot if you were to kill him and let the worms devour him; but neither of these things is the same as "controlling him as other property." That would be to feed him, to pamper him, to ride him, to use and abuse him, to make the most money out of him, "as other property"; but, please you, what do the men who are in favor of slavery want more than this? What do they really want, other than that slavery, being in the Territories, shall be controlled as other property?

If they want anything else, I do not comprehend it. I ask your attention to this, first, for the purpose of pointing out the change of ground the judge has made; and, in the second place, the importance of the change—that that change is not such as to give you gentlemen who want his popular sovereignty the power to exclude the institution or drive it out at all. I know the judge sometimes squints at the argument that in controlling it as other property by unfriendly legislation they may control it to death, as you might in the case of a horse, perhaps, feed him so lightly and ride him so much that he would die. But when you come to legislative control, there is something more to be attended to. I have no doubt, myself, that if the Territories should undertake to control slave property as other property—that is, control it in such a way that it would be the most valuable as property, and make it bear its just proportion in the way of burdens as property,—really deal with it as property,—the Supreme Court of the United States will say, "God speed you, and amen." But I undertake to give the opinion, at least, that if the Territories attempt by any direct legislation to drive the man with his slave out of the Territory, or to decide that his slave is free because of his being taken in there, or to tax him to such an extent that he cannot keep him there, the Supreme Court will unhesitatingly decide all such legislation unconstitutional, as long as that Supreme Court is constructed as the Dred Scott Supreme Court is. The first two things they have already decided, except that there is a little quibble among lawyers between the words *dicta* and decision. They have already decided that a negro cannot be made free by territorial legislation.

What is that Dred Scott decision? Judge Douglas labors to show that it is one thing, while I think it is altogether different. It is a long opinion, but it is all embodied in this short statement: "The Constitution of the United States forbids Congress to deprive a man of his property without due process of law; the right of property in slaves is distinctly and expressly affirmed in that Constitution; therefore if Congress shall undertake to say that a man's slave is no longer his slave when he crosses a certain line into a Territory, that is depriving him of his property without due process of law, and is unconstitutional." There is the whole Dred Scott decision. They add that if Congress cannot do so itself, Congress cannot confer any power to do so, and hence any effort by the territorial legislature to do either of these things is absolutely decided against. It is a foregone conclusion by that court.

Now, as to this indirect mode by "unfriendly legislation," all lawyers here will readily understand that such a proposition cannot be tolerated for a moment, because a legislature cannot indirectly do that which it cannot accomplish directly. Then I say any legislation to control this property, as property, for its benefit as property, would be hailed by this Dred Scott Supreme Court, and fully sustained; but any legislation driving slave property out, or destroying it as property, directly or indirectly, will most assuredly by that court be held unconstitutional.

Judge Douglas says that if the Constitution carries slavery into the Territories, beyond the power of the people of the Territories to control it as other property, then it follows logically that every one who swears to support the Constitution of the United States must give that support to that property which it needs. And if the Constitution carries slavery into the Territories beyond the power of the people to control it as other property, then it also carries it into the States, because the Constitution is the supreme law of the land. Now, gentlemen, if it were not for my excessive modesty I would say that I told that very thing to Judge Douglas quite a year ago. This argument is here in print, and if it were not for my modesty, as I said, I might call your attention to it. If you read it, you will find that I not only made that argument, but made it better than he has made it since.

There is, however, this difference. I say now, and said then, there is no sort of question that the Supreme Court has decided that it is the right of the slaveholder to take his slave and hold him in the Territory; and, saying this, Judge Douglas himself admits the conclusion. He says if that is so, this consequence will follow; and because this consequence would follow, his argument is, the decision cannot therefore be that way — "that would spoil my popular sovereignty, and it cannot be possible that this great principle has been squelched out in this extraordinary way. It might be, if it were not for the extraordinary consequences of spoiling my humbug."

Another feature of the judge's argument about the Dred Scott case is an effort to show that that decision deals altogether in declarations of negatives; that the Constitution does not affirm anything as expounded by the Dred Scott decision, but it only declares a want of power, a total absence of power, in reference to the Territories. It seems to be his purpose to make the whole of that decision to result in a mere negative declaration of a want of power in Congress to do anything in relation to this matter in the Territories. I know the opinion of the judges states that there is a total absence of power; but that is, unfortunately, not all it states; for the judges add that the right of property in a slave is distinctly and expressly affirmed in the Constitution. It does not stop at saying that the right of property in a slave is recognized in the Constitution, is declared to exist somewhere in the Constitution, but says it is affirmed in the Constitution. Its language is equivalent to saying that it is embodied and so woven into that instrument that it cannot be detached without breaking the Constitution itself,—in a word, it is a part of the Constitution.

Douglas is singularly unfortunate in his effort to make out that decision to be altogether negative, when the express language at the vital part is that this is distinctly affirmed in the Constitution. I think myself, and I repeat it here, that this decision does not merely carry slavery into the Territories, but by its logical conclusion it carries it into the States in which we live. One provision of that Constitution is, that it shall be the supreme law of the land,—I do not quote the language,—any constitution or law of any State to the contrary notwithstanding. This Dred Scott decision says that the right of property in a slave is affirmed in that Constitution which is the supreme law of the land, any State constitution or law notwithstanding. Then I say that to destroy a thing which is distinctly affirmed and supported by the supreme law of the land, even by a State constitution or law, is a violation of that supreme law, and there is no escape from it. In my judgment there is no avoiding that result, save that the American people shall see that State constitutions are better construed than our Constitution is construed in that decision. They must take care that it is more faithfully and truly carried out than it is there expounded.

I must hasten to a conclusion. Near the beginning of my remarks I said that this insidious Douglas popular sovereignty is the measure that now threatens the purpose of the Republican party to prevent slavery from being nationalized in the United States. I propose to ask your attention for a little while to some propositions in affirmance of that statement. Take it just as it stands, and apply it as a principle; extend and apply that principle elsewhere, and consider where it will lead you. I now put this proposition, that Judge Douglas's popular sovereignty applied will reopen the African slave-trade; and I will demonstrate it by any variety of ways in which you can turn the subject or look at it.

The judge says that the people of the Territories have the right, by his principle, to have slaves if they want them. Then I say that the people in Georgia have the right to buy slaves in Africa if they want them, and I defy any man on earth to show any distinction between the two things — to show that the one is either more wicked or more unlawful; to show, on original principles, that one is better or worse than the other; or to show by the Constitution that one differs a whit from the other. He will tell me, doubtless, that there is no constitutional provision against people taking slaves into the new Territories, and I tell him that there is equally no constitutional provision against buying slaves in Africa. He will tell you that a people in the exercise of popular sovereignty ought to do as they please about that thing, and have slaves if they want them; and I tell you that the people of Georgia are as much entitled to popular sovereignty, and to buy slaves in Africa, if they want them, as the people of the Territory are to have slaves if they want them. I ask any man, dealing honestly with himself, to point out a distinction.

I have recently seen a letter of Judge Douglas's, in which, without stating that to be the object, he doubtless endeavors to make a distinction between the two. He says he is unalterably opposed to the repeal of the laws against the African slave-trade. And why? He then seeks to give a reason that would not apply to his popular sovereignty in the Territories. What is that reason? "The abolition of the African slave-trade is a compromise of the Constitution." I deny it. There is no truth in the proposition that the abolition of the African slave-trade is a compromise of the Constitution. No man can put his finger on anything in the Constitution, or on the line of history, which shows it. It is a mere barren assertion, made simply for the purpose of getting up a distinction between the revival of the African slave-trade and his "great principle."

At the time the Constitution of the United States was adopted it was expected that the slave-trade would be abolished. I should assert, and insist upon that, if Judge Douglas denied it. But I know that it was equally expected that slavery would be excluded from the Territories, and I can show by history that in regard to these two things public opinion was exactly alike, while in regard to positive action, there was more done in the ordinance of '87 to resist the spread of slavery than was ever done to abolish the foreign slave-trade. Lest I be misunderstood, I say again that at the time of the formation of the Constitution, public expectation was that the slave-trade would be abolished, but no more so than that the spread of slavery in the Territories should be restrained. They stand alike, except that in the ordinance of '87 there was a mark left by public opinion, showing that it was more committed against the spread of slavery in the Territories than against the foreign slave-trade.

Compromise! What word of compromise was there about it? Why, the public sense was then in favor of the abolition of the slave-trade; but there was at the time a very great commercial interest involved in it, and extensive capital in that branch of trade. There were doubtless the incipient stages of improvement in the South in the way of farming, dependent on the slave-trade, and they made a proposition to Congress to abolish the trade after allowing it twenty years, a sufficient time for the capital and commerce engaged in it to be transferred to other channels. They made no provision that it should be abolished in twenty years; I do not doubt that they expected it would be; but they made no bargain about it. The public sentiment left no doubt in the minds of any that it would be done away. I repeat, there is nothing in the history of those times in favor of that matter being a compromise of the Constitution. It was the public expectation at the time, manifested in a thousand ways, that the spread of slavery should also be restricted.

Then I say if this principle is established, that there is no wrong in slavery, and whoever wants it has a right to have it; that it is a matter of dollars and cents; a sort of question as to how they shall deal with brutes; that between us and the negro here there is no sort of question, but that at the South the question is between the negro and the crocodile; that it is a mere matter of policy; that there is a perfect right, according to interest, to do just as you please — when this is done, where this doctrine prevails, the miners and sappers will have formed public opinion for the slave-trade. They will be ready for Jeff Davis and Stephens, and other leaders of that company, to sound the bugle for the revival of the slave-trade, for the second Dred Scott decision, for the flood of slavery to be poured over the free States, while we shall be here tied down and helpless, and run over like sheep.

It is to be a part and parcel of this same idea to say to men who want to adhere to the Democratic party, who have always belonged to that party, and are only looking about for some excuse to stick to it, but nevertheless hate slavery, that Douglas's popular sovereignty is as good a way as any to oppose slavery. They allow themselves to be persuaded easily, in accordance with their previous dispositions, into this belief, that it is about as good a way of opposing slavery as any, and we can do that without straining our old party ties or breaking up old political associations. We can do so without being called negro-worshipers. We can do that without being subjected to the gibes and sneers that are so readily thrown out in place of argument where no argument can be found. So let us stick to this popular sovereignty — this insidious popular sovereignty. Now let me call your attention to one thing that has really happened, which shows this gradual and steady debauching of public opinion, this course of preparation for the revival of the slave-trade, for the territorial slave-code, and the new Dred Scott decision that is to carry slavery into the free States. Did you ever, five years ago, hear of anybody in the world saying that the negro had no share in the Declaration of National Independence; that it did not mean negroes at all, and when "all men" were spoken of negroes were not included?

I am satisfied that five years ago that proposition was not put upon paper by any living being anywhere. I have been unable at any time to find a man in an audience who would declare that he had ever known of anybody saying so five years ago. But last year there was not a "Douglas popular sovereignty" man in Illinois who did not say it. Is there one in Ohio but declares his firm belief that the Declaration of Independence did not mean negroes at all? I do not know how this is; I have not been here much; but I presume you are very much alike everywhere. Then I suppose that all now express the belief that the Declaration of Independence never did mean negroes. I call upon one of them to say that he said it five years ago.

If you think that now, and did not think it then, the next thing that strikes me is to remark that there has been a change wrought in you, and a very significant change it is, being no less than changing the negro, in your estimation, from the rank of a man to that of a brute. They are taking him down, and placing him, when spoken of, among reptiles and crocodiles, as Judge Douglas himself expresses it.

Is not this change wrought in your minds a very important change? Public opinion in this country is everything. In a nation like ours this popular sovereignty and squatter sovereignty have already wrought a change in the public mind to the extent I have stated. There is no man in this crowd who can contradict it.

Now, if you are opposed to slavery honestly, as much as anybody, I ask you to note that fact, and the like of which is to follow, to be plastered on, layer after layer, until very soon you are prepared to deal with the negro everywhere as with the brute. If public sentiment has not been debauched already to this point, a new turn of the screw in that direction is all that is wanting; and this is constantly being done by the teachers of this insidious popular sovereignty. You need but one or two turns further until your minds, now ripening under these teachings, will be ready for all these things, and you will receive and support, or submit to, the slave-trade revived with all its horrors, a slave code enforced in our Territories, and a new Dred Scott decision to bring slavery up into the very heart of the free North. This, I must say, is but carrying out those words prophetically spoken by Mr. Clay many, many years ago,—I believe more than thirty years,—when he told an audience that if they would repress all tendencies to liberty and ultimate emancipation, they must go back to the era of our independence and muzzle the cannon which thundered its annual joyous return on the Fourth of July; they must blow out the moral lights around us; they must penetrate the human soul, and eradicate the love of liberty; but until they did these things, and others eloquently enumerated by him, they could not repress all tendencies to ultimate emancipation.

I ask attention to the fact that in a preëminent degree these popular sovereigns are at this work: blowing out the moral lights around us; teaching that the negro is no longer a man, but a brute; that the Declaration has nothing to do with him; that he ranks with the crocodile and the reptile; that man, with body and soul, is a matter of dollars and cents. I suggest to this portion of the Ohio Republicans, or Democrats, if there be any present, the serious consideration of this fact, that there is now going on among you a steady process of debauching public opinion on this subject. With this, my friends, I bid you adieu.

September 17, 1859.—SPEECH AT CINCINNATI, OHIO.

My Fellow-citizens of the State of Ohio: This is the first time in
my life that I have appeared before an audience in so great a city
as this.   I therefore—though I am no longer a young man—make
this appearance under some degree of embarrassment.   But I have
found that when one is embarrassed, usually the shortest way to get
through with it is to quit talking or thinking about it, and go at
something else.

I understand that you have had recently with you my very distinguished friend, Judge Douglas, of Illinois, and I understand,
without having had an opportunity (not greatly sought, to be sure)
of seeing a report of the speech that he made here, that he did me the
honor to mention my humble name.   I suppose that he did so for the
purpose of making some objection to some sentiment at some time
expressed by me.   I should expect, it is true, that Judge Douglas had reminded you, or informed you, if you had never before
heard it, that I had once in my life declared it as my opinion that
this government cannot " endure permanently half slave and half
free; that a house divided against itself cannot stand," and, as I had
expressed it, I did not expect the house to fall; that I did not expect
the Union to be dissolved, but that I did expect it would cease to
be divided; that it would become all one thing or all the other; that
either the opposition of slavery will arrest the further spread of it,
and place it where the public mind would rest in the belief that it
was in the course of ultimate extinction, or the friends of slavery
will push it forward until it becomes alike lawful in all the States,
old or new, free as well as slave.   I did, fifteen months ago, express
that opinion, and upon many occasions Judge Douglas has denounced
it, and has greatly, intentionally or unintentionally, misrepresented
my purpose in the expression of that opinion.

I presume, without having seen a report of his speech, that he did
so here.   I presume that he alluded also to that opinion in different
language, having been expressed at a subsequent time by Governor
Seward, of New York, and that he took the two in a lump and denounced them; that he tried to point out that there was something
couched in this opinion which led to the making of an entire uniformity of the local institutions of the various States of the Union, in
utter disregard of the different States, which in their nature would
seem to require a variety of institutions, and a variety of laws conforming to the differences in the nature of the different States.

Not only so; I presume he insisted that this was a declaration of
war between the free and slave States—that it was the sounding to
the onset of continual war between the different States, the slave
and free States.

This charge, in this form, was made by Judge Douglas on, I believe, the 9th of July, 1858, in Chicago, in my hearing.   On the next
evening, I made some reply to it.   I informed him that many of the
inferences he drew from that expression of mine were altogether
foreign to any purpose entertained by me, and in so far as he should

ascribe these inferences to me, as my purpose, he was entirely mistaken; and in so far as he might argue that whatever might be my purpose, actions, conforming to my views, would lead to these results, he might argue and establish if he could; but, so far as purposes were concerned, he was totally mistaken as to me.

When I made that reply to him, I told him, on the question of declaring war between the different States of the Union, that I had not said I did not expect any peace upon this question until slavery was exterminated; that I had only said I expected peace when that institution was put where the public mind should rest in the belief that it was in course of ultimate extinction; that I believed, from the organization of our government until a very recent period of time, the institution had been placed and continued upon such a basis; that we had had comparative peace upon that question through a portion of that period of time, only because the public mind rested in that belief in regard to it, and that when we returned to that position in relation to that matter, I supposed we should again have peace as we previously had. I assured him, as I now assure you, that I neither then had, nor have, nor ever had, any purpose in any way of interfering with the institution of slavery where it exists. I believe we have no power, under the Constitution of the United States, or rather under the form of government under which we live, to interfere with the institution of slavery, or any other of the institutions of our sister States, be they free or slave States. I declared then, and I now re-declare, that I have as little inclination to interfere with the institution of slavery where it now exists, through the instrumentality of the General Government, or any other instrumentality, as I believe we have no power to do so. I accidentally used this expression: I had no purpose of entering into the slave States to disturb the institution of slavery. So, upon the first occasion that Judge Douglas got an opportunity to reply to me, he passed by the whole body of what I had said upon that subject, and seized upon the particular expression of mine, that I had no purpose of entering into the slave States to disturb the institution of slavery. "Oh, no," said he; "he [Lincoln] won't enter into the slave States to disturb the institution of slavery; he is too prudent a man to do such a thing as that; he only means that he will go on to the line between the free and slave States, and shoot over at them. This is all he means to do. He means to do them all the harm he can, to disturb them all he can, in such a way as to keep his own hide in perfect safety."

Well, now, I did not think, at that time, that that was either a very dignified or very logical argument; but so it was, and I had to get along with it as well as I could.

It has occurred to me here to-night that if I ever do shoot over the line at the people on the other side of the line, into a slave State, and propose to do so keeping my skin safe, that I have now about the best chance I shall ever have. I should not wonder if there are some Kentuckians about this audience; we are close to Kentucky; and whether that be so or not, we are on elevated ground, and by speaking distinctly I should not wonder if some of the Kentuckians would hear me on the other side of the river. For that reason I propose to address a portion of what I have to say to the Kentuckians.

I say, then, in the first place, to the Kentuckians, that I am what they call, as I understand it, a "Black Republican." I think slavery is wrong, morally and politically. I desire that it should be no further spread in these United States, and I should not object if it should gradually terminate in the whole Union. While I say this for myself, I say to you Kentuckians that I understand you differ radically with me upon this proposition; that you believe slavery is a good thing; that slavery is right; that it ought to be extended and perpetuated in this Union. Now, there being this broad difference between us, I do not pretend, in addressing myself to you Kentuckians, to attempt proselyting you; that would be a vain effort. I do not enter upon it. I only propose to try to show you that you ought to nominate for the next presidency, at Charleston, my distinguished friend, Judge Douglas. In all that there is no real difference between you and him; I understand he is as sincerely for you, and more wisely for you, than you are for yourselves. I will try to demonstrate that proposition. Understand now, I say that I believe he is as sincerely for you, and more wisely for you, than you are for yourselves.

What do you want more than anything else to make successful your views of slavery — to advance the outspread of it, and to secure and perpetuate the nationality of it? What do you want more than anything else? What is needed absolutely? What is indispensable to you? Why, if I may be allowed to answer the question, it is to retain a hold upon the North — it is to retain support and strength from the free States. If you can get this support and strength from the free States, you can succeed. If you do not get this support and this strength from the free States, you are in the minority, and you are beaten at once.

If that proposition be admitted,— and it is undeniable,— then the next thing I say to you is, that Douglas of all the men in this nation is the only man that affords you any hold upon the free States; that no other man can give you any strength in the free States. This being so, if you doubt the other branch of the proposition, whether he is for you,— whether he is really for you, as I have expressed it,— I propose asking your attention for a while to a few facts.

The issue between you and me, understand, is that I think slavery is wrong, and ought not to be outspread, and you think it is right, and ought to be extended and perpetuated. I now proceed to try to show to you that Douglas is as sincerely for you, and more wisely for you, than you are for yourselves.

In the first place, we know that in a government like this, a government of the people, where the voice of all the men of the country, substantially, enters into the administration of the government, what lies at the bottom of all of it is public opinion. I lay down the proposition that Judge Douglas is not only the man that promises you in advance a hold upon the North, and support in the North, but that he constantly molds public opinion to your ends; that in every possible way he can, he molds the public opinion of the North to your ends; and if there are a few things in which he seems to be against you,— a few things which he says that appear to be against you, and a few that he forbears to say which you would like to have him say,— you ought to remember that the saying of the one, or the forbearing to say the other, would lose his hold upon the North, and, by consequence, would lose his capacity to serve you.

Upon this subject of molding public opinion, I call your attention to the fact — for a well-established fact it is — that the judge never says your institution of slavery is wrong: he never says it is right, to be sure, but he never says it is wrong. There is not a public man in the United States, I believe, with the exception of Senator Douglas, who has not, at some time in his life, declared his opinion whether the thing is right or wrong; but Senator Douglas never declares it is wrong. He leaves himself at perfect liberty to do all in your favor which he would be hindered from doing if he were to declare the thing to be wrong. On the contrary, he takes all the chances that he has for inveigling the sentiment of the North, opposed to slavery, into your support, by never saying it is right. This you ought to set down to his credit. You ought to give him full credit for this much, little though it be in comparison to the whole which he does for you.

Some other things I will ask your attention to. He said upon the floor of the United States Senate, and he has repeated it, as I understand, a great many times, that he does not care whether slavery is "voted up or voted down." This again shows you, or ought to show you, if you would reason upon it, that he does not believe it to be wrong; for a man may say, when he sees nothing wrong in a thing, that he does not care whether it be voted up or voted down; but no man can logically say that he cares not whether a thing goes up or goes down which appears to him to be wrong. You therefore have a demonstration in this, that to Judge Douglas's mind your favorite institution, which you desire to have spread out and made perpetual, is no wrong.

Another thing he tells you, in a speech made at Memphis, in Tennessee, shortly after the canvass in Illinois, last year. He there distinctly told the people that there was a "line drawn by the Almighty across this continent, on the one side of which the soil must always be cultivated by slaves"; that he did not pretend to know exactly where that line was, but that there was such a line. I want to ask your attention to that proposition again — that there is one portion of this continent where the Almighty has designed the soil shall always be cultivated by slaves; that its being cultivated by slaves at that place is right; that it has the direct sympathy and authority of the Almighty. Whenever you can get these Northern audiences to adopt the opinion that slavery is right on the other side of the Ohio; whenever you can get them, in pursuance of Douglas's views, to adopt that sentiment, they will very readily make the other argument, which is perfectly logical, that that which is right on that side of the Ohio cannot be wrong on this, and that if you have that property on that side of the Ohio, under the seal and stamp of the

Almighty, when by any means it escapes over here, it is wrong to have constitutions and laws "to devil" you about it. So Douglas is molding the public opinion of the North, first to say that the thing is right in your State over the Ohio River, and hence to say that that which is right there is not wrong here, and that all laws and constitutions here, recognizing it as being wrong, are themselves wrong, and ought to be repealed and abrogated. He will tell you, men of Ohio, that if you choose here to have laws against slavery, it is in conformity to the idea that your climate is not suited to it; that your climate is not suited to slave labor, and therefore you have constitutions and laws against it.

Let us attend to that argument for a little while, and see if it be sound. You do not raise sugar-cane (except the new-fashioned sugar-cane, and you won't raise that long), but they do raise it in Louisiana. You don't raise it in Ohio because you can't raise it profitably, because the climate don't suit it. They do raise it in Louisiana because there it is profitable. Now Douglas will tell you that is precisely the slavery question: that they do have slaves there because they are profitable, and you don't have them here because they are not profitable. If that is so, then it leads to dealing with the one precisely as with the other. Is there, then, anything in the constitution or laws of Ohio against raising sugar-cane? Have you found it necessary to put any such provision in your law? Surely not! No man desires to raise sugar-cane in Ohio; but if any man did desire to do so, you would say it was a tyrannical law that forbids his doing so; and whenever you shall agree with Douglas, whenever your minds are brought to adopt his argument, as surely you will have reached the conclusion that although slavery is not profitable in Ohio, if any man want it, it is wrong to him not to let him have it.

In this matter Judge Douglas is preparing the public mind for you of Kentucky, to make perpetual that good thing in your estimation, about which you and I differ.

In this connection let me ask your attention to another thing. I believe it is safe to assert that, five years ago, no living man had expressed the opinion that the negro had no share in the Declaration of Independence. Let me state that again: Five years ago no living man had expressed the opinion that the negro had no share in the Declaration of Independence. If there is in this large audience any man who ever knew of that opinion being put upon paper as much as five years ago, I will be obliged to him now, or at a subsequent time, to show it.

If that be true, I wish you then to note the next fact— that within the space of five years Senator Douglas, in the argument of this question, has got his entire party, so far as I know, without exception, to join in saying that the negro has no share in the Declaration of Independence. If there be now in all these United States one Douglas man that does not say this, I have been unable upon any occasion to scare him up. Now, if none of you said this five years ago, and all of you say it now, that is a matter that you Kentuckians ought to note. That is a vast change in the Northern public sentiment upon that question.

Of what tendency is that change? The tendency of that change is to bring the public mind to the conclusion that when men are spoken of, the negro is not meant; that when negroes are spoken of, brutes alone are contemplated. That change in public sentiment has already degraded the black man, in the estimation of Douglas and his followers, from the condition of a man of some sort, and assigned him to the condition of a brute. Now you Kentuckians ought to give Douglas credit for this. That is the largest possible stride that can be made in regard to the perpetuation of your good thing of slavery.

In Kentucky, perhaps,—in many of the slave States certainly,—you are trying to establish the rightfulness of slavery by reference to the Bible. You are trying to show that slavery existed in the Bible times by divine ordinance. Now Douglas is wiser than you for your own benefit, upon that subject. Douglas knows that whenever you establish that slavery was right by the Bible, it will occur that that slavery was the slavery of the white man,—of men without reference to color,—and he knows very well that you may entertain that idea in Kentucky as much as you please, but you will never win any Northern support upon it. He makes a wiser argument for you; he makes the argument that the slavery of the black man, the slavery of the man who has a skin of a different color from your own, is right. He thereby brings to your support Northern voters who could not for a moment be brought by your own argument of the Bible-right of slavery. Will you not give him credit for that? Will you not say that in this matter he is more wisely for you than you are for yourselves?

Now, having established with his entire party this doctrine,— having been entirely successful in that branch of his efforts in your behalf,—he is ready for another.

At this same meeting at Memphis, he declared that in all contests between the negro and the white man, he was for the white man, but that in all questions between the negro and the crocodile he was for the negro. He did not make that declaration accidentally at Memphis. He made it a great many times in the canvass in Illinois last year (though I don't know that it was reported in any of his speeches there; but he frequently made it). I believe he repeated it at Columbus, and I should not wonder if he repeated it here. It is, then, a deliberate way of expressing himself upon that subject. It is a matter of mature deliberation with him thus to express himself upon that point of his case. It therefore requires some deliberate attention.

The first inference seems to be that if you do not enslave the negro you are wronging the white man in some way or other; and that whoever is opposed to the negro being enslaved is, in some way or other, against the white man. Is not that a falsehood? If there was a necessary conflict between the white man and the negro, I should be for the white man as much as Judge Douglas; but I say there is no such necessary conflict. I say that there is room enough for us all to be free, and that it not only does not wrong the white man that the negro should be free, but it positively wrongs the mass of the white men that the negro should be enslaved; that the mass of white men are really injured by the effects of slave-labor in the vicinity of the fields of their own labor.

But I do not desire to dwell upon this branch of the question more than to say that this assumption of his is false, and I do hope that that fallacy will not long prevail in the minds of intelligent white men. At all events, you ought to thank Judge Douglas for it. It is for your benefit it is made.

The other branch of it is, that in a struggle between the negro and the crocodile, he is for the negro. Well, I don't know that there is any struggle between the negro and the crocodile, either. I suppose that if a crocodile (or, as we old Ohio River boatmen used to call them, alligators) should come across a white man, he would kill him if he could, and so he would a negro. But what, at last, is this proposition? I believe that it is a sort of proposition in proportion, which may be stated thus: "As the negro is to the white man, so is the crocodile to the negro; and as the negro may rightfully treat the crocodile as a beast or reptile, so the white man may rightfully treat the negro as a beast or reptile." That is really the point of all that argument of his.

Now, my brother Kentuckians, who believe in this, you ought to thank Judge Douglas for having put that in a much more taking way than any of yourselves have done.

Again, Douglas's great principle, "popular sovereignty," as he calls it, gives you by natural consequence the revival of the slave-trade whenever you want it. If you are disposed to question this, listen awhile, consider awhile, what I shall advance in support of that proposition.

He says that it is the sacred right of the man who goes into the Territories to have slavery if he wants it. Grant that for argument's sake. Is it not the sacred right of the man who don't go there, equally to buy slaves in Africa, if he wants them? Can you point out the difference? The man who goes into the Territories of Kansas and Nebraska, or any other new Territory, with the sacred right of taking a slave there which belongs to him, would certainly have no more right to take one there than I would who own no slave, but who would desire to buy one and take him there. You will not say—you, the friends of Judge Douglas—but that the man who does not own a slave, has an equal right to buy one and take him to the Territory as the other does?

I say that Douglas's popular sovereignty, establishing his sacred right in the people, if you please, if carried to its logical conclusion, gives equally the sacred right to the people of the States or the Territories themselves to buy slaves, wherever they can buy them cheapest; and if any man can show a distinction, I should like to hear him try it. If any man can show how the people of Kansas have a better right to slaves because they want them, than the people of Georgia have to buy them in Africa, I want him to do it. I think it cannot be done. If it is "popular sovereignty" for the people to have slaves because they want them, it is popular sovereignty for them to buy them in Africa, because they desire to do so.

I know that Douglas has recently made a little effort — not seeming to notice that he had a different theory — has made an effort to get rid of that. He has written a letter, addressed to somebody, I believe, who resides in Iowa, declaring his opposition to the repeal of the laws that prohibit the African slave-trade. He bases his opposition to such repeal upon the ground that these laws are themselves one of the compromises of the Constitution of the United States. Now it would be very interesting to see Judge Douglas, or any of his friends, turn to the Constitution of the United States and point out that compromise, to show where there is any compromise in the Constitution, or provision in the Constitution, expressed or implied, by which the administrators of that Constitution are under any obligation to repeal the African slave-trade. I know, or at least I think I know, that the framers of that Constitution did expect that the African slave-trade would be abolished at the end of twenty years, to which time their prohibition against its being abolished extended. I think there is abundant contemporaneous history to show that the framers of the Constitution expected it to be abolished. But while they so expected, they gave nothing for that expectation, and they put no provision in the Constitution requiring it should be so abolished. The migration or importation of such persons as the States shall see fit to admit shall not be prohibited, but a certain tax might be levied upon such importation. But what was to be done after that time? The Constitution is as silent about that as it is silent, personally, about myself. There is absolutely nothing in it about that subject — there is only the expectation of the framers of the Constitution that the slave-trade would be abolished at the end of that time, and they expected it would be abolished, owing to public sentiment, before that time, and they put that provision in, in order that it should not be abolished before that time, for reasons which I suppose they thought to be sound ones, but which I will not now try to enumerate before you.

But while they expected the slave-trade would be abolished at that time, they expected that the spread of slavery into the new Territories should also be restricted. It is as easy to prove that the framers of the Constitution of the United States expected that slavery should be prohibited from extending into the new Territories, as it is to prove that it was expected that the slave-trade should be abolished. Both these things were expected. One was no more expected than the other, and one was no more a compromise of the Constitution than the other. There was nothing said in the Constitution in regard to the spread of slavery into the Territories. I grant that, but there was something very important said about it by the same generation of men in the adoption of the old ordinance of '87, through the influence of which you here in Ohio, our neighbors in Indiana, we in Illinois, our neighbors in Michigan and Wisconsin, are happy, prosperous, teeming millions of free men. That generation of men, though not to the full extent members of the convention that framed the Constitution, were to some extent members of that convention, holding seats at the same time in one body and the other, so that if there was any compromise on either of these subjects, the strong evidence is that that compromise was in favor of the restriction of slavery from the new Territories.

But Douglas says that he is unalterably opposed to the repeal of those laws; because, in his view, it is a compromise of the Constitution. You Kentuckians, no doubt, are somewhat offended with that! You ought not to be! You ought to be patient! You ought to know that if he said less than that, he would lose the power of "lugging" the Northern States to your support. Really, what you would push him to do would take from him his entire power to serve you. And you ought to remember how long, by precedent, Judge Douglas holds himself obliged to stick by compromises. You ought to remember that by the time you yourselves think you are ready to inaugurate measures for the revival of the African slave-trade, that sufficient time will have arrived, by precedent, for Judge Douglas to break through that compromise. He says now nothing more strong than he said in 1849 when he declared in favor of the Missouri Compromise—that precisely four years and a quarter after he declared that compromise to be a sacred thing, which "no ruthless hand would ever dared to touch," he, himself, brought forward the measure ruthlessly to destroy it. By a mere calculation of time it will only be four years more until he is ready to take back his profession about the sacredness of the compromise abolishing the slave-trade. Precisely as soon as you are ready to have his services in that direction, by fair calculation, you may be sure of having them.

But you remember and set down to Judge Douglas's debt, or discredit, that he, last year, said the people of Territories can, in spite of the Dred Scott decision, exclude your slaves from those Territories; that he declared by "unfriendly legislation" the extension of your property into the new Territories may be cut off in the teeth of that decision of the Supreme Court of the United States.

He assumed that position at Freeport, on the 27th of August, 1858. He said that the people of the Territories can exclude slavery, in so many words. You ought, however, to bear in mind that he has never said it since. You may hunt in every speech that he has since made, and he has never used that expression once. He has never seemed to notice that he is stating his views differently from what he did then; but by some sort of accident, he has always really stated it differently. He has always since then declared that "the Constitution does not carry slavery into the Territories of the United States beyond the power of the people legally to control it, as other property." Now there is a difference in the language used upon that former occasion and in this latter day. There may or may not be a difference in the meaning, but it is worth while considering whether there is not also a difference in meaning.

What is it to exclude? Why, it is to drive it out. It is in some way to put it out of the Territory. It is to force it across the line, or change its character, so that as property it is out of existence. But what is the controlling of it "as other property"? Is controlling it as other property the same thing as destroying it, or driving it away? I should think not. I should think the controlling of it as other property would be just about what you in Kentucky should want.

I understand the controlling of property means the controlling of it for the benefit of the owner of it. While I have no doubt the Supreme Court of the United States would say "God speed" to any of the territorial legislatures that should thus control slave property, they would sing quite a different tune if by the pretense of controlling it they were to undertake to pass laws which virtually excluded it, and that upon a very well known principle to all lawyers, that what a legislature cannot directly do, it cannot do by indirection; that as the legislature has not the power to drive slaves out, they have no power by indirection, by tax, or by imposing burdens in any way on that property, to effect the same end, and that any attempt to do so would be held by the Dred Scott court unconstitutional.

Douglas is not willing to stand by his first proposition that they can exclude it, because we have seen that that proposition amounts to nothing more nor less than the naked absurdity that you may lawfully drive out that which has a lawful right to remain. He admitted at first that the slave might be lawfully taken into the Territories under the Constitution of the United States, and yet asserted that he might be lawfully driven out. That being the proposition, it is the absurdity I have stated. He is not willing to stand in the face of that direct, naked, and impudent absurdity; he has, therefore, modified his language into that of being "controlled as other property."

The Kentuckians don't like this in Douglas! I will tell you where it will go. He now swears by the court. He was once a leading man in Illinois to break down a court because it had made a decision he did not like. But he now not only swears by the court, the courts having got to working for you, but he denounces all men that do not swear by the courts as unpatriotic, as bad citizens. When one of these acts of unfriendly legislation shall impose such heavy burdens as to, in effect, destroy property in slaves in a Territory, and show plainly enough that there can be no mistake in the purpose of the legislature to make them so burdensome, this same Supreme Court will decide that law to be unconstitutional, and he will be ready to say for your benefit, "I swear by the court; I give it up"; and while that is going on he has been getting all his men to swear by the courts, and to give it up with him. In this again he serves you faithfully, and, as I say, more wisely than you serve yourselves.

Again, I have alluded in the beginning of these remarks to the fact that Judge Douglas has made great complaint of my having expressed the opinion that this government "cannot endure permanently half slave and half free." He has complained of Seward for using different language, and declaring that there is an "irrepressible conflict" between the principles of free and slave labor. [A voice: "He says it is not original with Seward. That is original with Lincoln."] I will attend to that immediately, sir. Since that time, Hickman, of Pennsylvania, expressed the same sentiment. He has never denounced Mr. Hickman. Why? There is a little chance, notwithstanding that opinion in the mouth of Hickman, that he may yet be a Douglas man. That is the difference. It is not unpatriotic to hold that opinion, if a man is a Douglas man.

But neither I, nor Seward, nor Hickman is entitled to the enviable or unenviable distinction of having first expressed that idea.   That same idea was expressed by the Richmond "Enquirer" in Virginia, in 1856, quite two years before it was expressed by the first of us. And while Douglas was pluming himself that in his conflict with my humble self, last year, he had "squelched out" that fatal heresy, as he delighted to call it, and had suggested that if he only had had a chance to be in New York and meet Seward he would have "squelched" it there also, it never occurred to him to breathe a word against Pryor. I don't think that you can discover that Douglas ever talked of going to Virginia to "squelch" out that idea there.   No.   More than that. That same Roger A. Pryor was brought to Washington City and made the editor of the *par excellence* Douglas paper after making use of that expression which, in us, is so unpatriotic and heretical.   From all this my Kentucky friends may see that this opinion is heretical in his view only when it is expressed by men suspected of a desire that the country shall all become free, and not when expressed by those fairly known to entertain the desire that the whole country shall become slave.   When expressed by that class of men, it is in no wise offensive to him.   In this again, my friends of Kentucky, you have Judge Douglas with you.

There is another reason why you Southern people ought to nominate Douglas at your convention at Charleston.   That reason is the wonderful capacity of the man; the power he has of doing what would seem to be impossible.   Let me call your attention to one of these apparently impossible things.

Douglas had three or four very distinguished men, of the most extreme antislavery views of any men in the Republican party, expressing their desire for his reëlection to the Senate last year.   That would, of itself, have seemed to be a little wonderful, but that wonder is heightened when we see that Wise, of Virginia, a man exactly opposed to them, a man who believes in the divine right of slavery, was also expressing his desire that Douglas should be reëlected; that another man that may be said to be kindred to Wise, Mr. Breckinridge, the Vice-President, and of your own State, was also agreeing with the antislavery men in the North that Douglas ought to be reëlected.   Still, to heighten the wonder, a senator from Kentucky, whom I have always loved with an affection as tender and endearing as I have ever loved any man, who was opposed to the antislavery men for reasons which seemed sufficient to him, and equally opposed to Wise and Breckinridge, was writing letters into Illinois to secure the reëlection of Douglas.   Now that all these conflicting elements should be brought, while at daggers' points with one another, to support him, is a feat that is worthy for you to note and consider.   It is quite probable that each of these classes of men thought, by the reëlection of Douglas, their peculiar views would gain something: it is probable that the antislavery men thought their views would gain something; that Wise and Breckinridge thought so too, as regards their opinions; that Mr. Crittenden thought that his views would gain something, although he was opposed to both these other men.   It is probable that each and all of them thought that they were using Douglas, and it is yet an unsolved problem whether he was not using them all. If he was, then it is for you to consider whether that power to perform wonders is one for you lightly to throw away.

There is one other thing that I will say to you in this relation. It is but my opinion; I give it to you without a fee. It is my opinion that it is for you to take him or be defeated; and that if you do take him you may be beaten. You will surely be beaten if you do not take him. We, the Republicans and others forming the opposition of the country, intend to "stand by our guns," to be patient and firm, and in the long run to beat you whether you take him or not. We know that before we fairly beat you, we have to beat you both together. We know that "you are all of a feather," and that we have to beat you all together, and we expect to do it. We don't intend to be very impatient about it. We mean to be as deliberate and calm about it as it is possible to be, but as firm and resolved as it is possible for men to be. When we do as we say, beat you, you perhaps want to know what we will do with you.

I will tell you, so far as I am authorized to speak for the opposition, what we mean to do with you. We mean to treat you, as near as we possibly can, as Washington, Jefferson, and Madison treated you. We mean to leave you alone, and in no way to interfere with your institution; to abide by all and every compromise of the Constitution, and, in a word, coming back to the original proposition, to treat you, so far as degenerated men (if we have degenerated) may, according to the example of those noble fathers—Washington, Jefferson, and Madison. We mean to remember that you are as good as we; that there is no difference between us other than the difference of circumstances. We mean to recognize and bear in mind always that you have as good hearts in your bosoms as other people, or as we claim to have, and treat you accordingly. We mean to marry your girls when we have a chance—the white ones, I mean, and I have the honor to inform you that I once did have a chance in that way.

I have told you what we mean to do. I want to know, now, when that thing takes place, what do you mean to do? I often hear it intimated that you mean to divide the Union whenever a Republican or anything like it is elected President of the United States. [A voice: "That is so."] "That is so," one of them says; I wonder if he is a Kentuckian? [A voice: "He is a Douglas man."] Well, then, I want to know what you are going to do with your half of it? Are you going to split the Ohio down through, and push your half off a piece? Or are you going to keep it right alongside of us outrageous fellows? Or are you going to build up a wall some way between your country and ours, by which that movable property of yours can't come over here any more, to the danger of your losing it? Do you think you can better yourselves on that subject by leaving us here under no obligation whatever to return those specimens of your movable property that come hither? You have divided the Union because we would not do right with you, as you think, upon that subject; when we cease to be under obligations to do anything for you, how much better off do you think you will be? Will you make war upon us and kill us all? Why, gentlemen, I think you are as gallant and as brave men as live; that you can fight as bravely in a good cause, man for man, as any other people living; that you have shown yourselves capable of this upon various occasions; but man for man, you are not better than we are, and there are not so many of you as there are of us. You will never make much of a hand at whipping us. If we were fewer in numbers than you, I think that you could whip us; if we were equal it would likely be a drawn battle; but being inferior in numbers, you will make nothing by attempting to master us.

But perhaps I have addressed myself as long, or longer, to the Kentuckians than I ought to have done, inasmuch as I have said that whatever course you take, we intend in the end to beat you. I propose to address a few remarks to our friends, by way of discussing with them the best means of keeping that promise that I have in good faith made.

It may appear a little episodical for me to mention the topic of which I shall speak now. It is a favorite proposition of Douglas's that the interference of the General Government, through the ordinance of '87, or through any other act of the General Government, never has made, nor ever can make, a free State; that the ordinance of '87 did not make free States of Ohio, Indiana, or Illinois; that these States are free upon his "great principle" of popular sovereignty, because the people of those several States have chosen to make them so. At Columbus, and probably here, he undertook to compliment the people that they themselves had made the State of Ohio free, and that the ordinance of '87 was not entitled in any degree to divide the honor with him. I have no doubt that the people of the State of Ohio did make her free according to their own will and judgment; but let the facts be remembered.

In 1802, I believe, it was you who made your first constitution, with the clause prohibiting slavery, and you did it, I suppose, very nearly unanimously; but you should bear in mind that you — speaking of you as one people — that you did so unembarrassed by the actual presence of the institution amongst you; that you made it a free State, not with the embarrassment upon you of already having among you many slaves, which, if they had been here, and you had sought to make a free State, you would not know what to do with. If they had been among you, embarrassing difficulties, most probably, would have induced you to tolerate a slave Constitution instead of a free one; as, indeed, these very difficulties have constrained every people on this continent who have adopted slavery.

Pray, what was it that made you free? What kept you free? Did you not find your country free when you came to decide that Ohio should be a free State? It is important to inquire by what reason you found it so. Let us take an illustration between the States of Ohio and Kentucky. Kentucky is separated by this river Ohio, not a mile wide. A portion of Kentucky, by reason of the course of the Ohio, is further north than this portion of Ohio in which we now stand. Kentucky is entirely covered with slavery — Ohio is entirely free from it. What made that difference? Was it climate? No! A portion of Kentucky was further north than this portion of Ohio.

Was it soil? No! There is nothing in the soil of the one more favorable to slave-labor than the other. It was not climate or soil that caused one side of the line to be entirely covered with slavery and the other side free of it. What was it? Study over it. Tell us, if you can, in all the range of conjecture, if there be anything you can conceive of that made that difference, other than that there was no law of any sort keeping it out of Kentucky, while the ordinance of '87 kept it out of Ohio. If there is any other reason than this, I confess that it is wholly beyond my power to conceive of it. This, then, I offer to combat the idea that that ordinance has never made any State free.

I don't stop at this illustration. I come to the State of Indiana; and what I have said as between Kentucky and Ohio, I repeat as between Indiana and Kentucky; it is equally applicable. One additional argument is applicable also to Indiana. In her territorial condition she more than once petitioned Congress to abrogate the ordinance entirely, or at least so far as to suspend its operation for a time, in order that they should exercise the "popular sovereignty" of having slaves if they wanted them. The men then controlling the General Government, imitating the men of the Revolution, refused Indiana that privilege. And so we have the evidence that Indiana supposed she could have slaves, if it were not for that ordinance; that she besought Congress to put that barrier out of the way; that Congress refused to do so, and it all ended at last in Indiana being a free State. Tell me not then that the ordinance of '87 had nothing to do with making Indiana a free State, when we find some men chafing against and only restrained by that barrier.

Come down again to our State of Illinois. The great Northwest Territory, including Ohio, Indiana, Illinois, Michigan, and Wisconsin, was acquired first, I believe, by the British government, in part, at least, from the French. Before the establishment of our independence, it became a part of Virginia, enabling Virginia afterward to transfer it to the General Government. There were French settlements in what is now Illinois, and at the same time there were French settlements in what is now Missouri — in the tract of country that was not purchased till about 1803. In these French settlements negro slavery had existed for many years — perhaps more than a hundred, if not as much as two hundred, years — at Kaskaskia, in Illinois, and at St. Genevieve, or Cape Girardeau, perhaps, in Missouri. The number of slaves was not very great, but there was about the same number in each place. They were there when we acquired the Territory. There was no effort made to break up the relation of master and slave, and even the ordinance of '87 was not so enforced as to destroy that slavery in Illinois; nor did the ordinance apply to Missouri at all.

What I want to ask your attention to, at this point, is that Illinois and Missouri came into the Union about the same time, Illinois in the latter part of 1818, and Missouri, after a struggle, I believe, some time in 1820. They had been filling up with American people about the same period of time, their progress enabling them to come into the Union about the same. At the end of that ten years, in which they had been so preparing (for it was about that period of time), the number of slaves in Illinois had actually decreased; while in Missouri, beginning with very few, at the end of that ten years there were about ten thousand. This being so, and it being remembered that Missouri and Illinois are, to a certain extent, in the same parallel of latitude,—that the northern half of Missouri and the southern half of Illinois are in the same parallel of latitude,—so that climate would have the same effect upon one as upon the other; and that in the soil there is no material difference so far as bears upon the question of slavery being settled upon one or the other; there being none of those natural causes to produce a difference in filling them, and yet there being a broad difference in their filling up, we are led again to inquire what was the cause of that difference.

It is most natural to say that in Missouri there was no law to keep that country from filling up with slaves, while in Illinois there was the ordinance of '87. The ordinance being there, slavery decreased during that ten years—the ordinance not being in the other, it increased from a few to ten thousand. Can anybody doubt the reason of the difference?

I think all these facts most abundantly prove that my friend Judge Douglas's proposition, that the ordinance of '87, or the national restriction of slavery, never had a tendency to make a free State, is a fallacy—a proposition without the shadow or substance of truth about it.

Douglas sometimes says that all the States (and it is part of that same proposition I have been discussing) that have become free, have become so upon his "great principle"; that the State of Illinois itself came into the Union as a slave State, and that the people, upon the "great principle" of popular sovereignty, have since made it a free State. Allow me but a little while to state to you what facts there are to justify him in saying that Illinois came into the Union as a slave State.

I have mentioned to you that there were a few old French slaves there. They numbered, I think, one or two hundred. Besides that, there had been a territorial law for indenturing black persons. Under that law, in violation of the ordinance of '87, but without any enforcement of the ordinance to overthrow the system, there had been a small number of slaves introduced as indentured persons. Owing to this, the clause for the prohibition of slavery was slightly modified. Instead of running like yours, that neither slavery nor involuntary servitude, except for crime, of which the party shall have been duly convicted, should exist in the State, they said that neither slavery nor involuntary servitude should thereafter be introduced, and that the children of indentured servants should be born free; and nothing was said about the few old French slaves. Out of this fact, that the clause for prohibiting slavery was modified because of the actual presence of it, Douglas asserts again and again that Illinois came into the Union as a slave State. How far the facts sustain the conclusion that he draws, it is for intelligent and impartial men to decide. I leave it with you, with these remarks, worthy of being remembered, that that little thing, those few indentured servants being there, was of itself sufficient to modify a constitution made by a people ardently desiring to have a free constitution; showing the power of the actual presence of the institution of slavery to prevent any people, however anxious to make a free State, from making it perfectly so. I have been detaining you longer perhaps than I ought to do.

I am in some doubt whether to introduce another topic upon which I could talk awhile. [Cries of "Go on," and "Give us it."] It is this then — Douglas's popular sovereignty, as a principle, is simply this: If one man chooses to make a slave of another man, neither that man nor anybody else has a right to object. Apply it to government, as he seeks to apply it, and it is this: If, in a new Territory, into which a few people are beginning to enter for the purpose of making their homes, they choose to either exclude slavery from their limits, or to establish it there, however one or the other may affect the persons to be enslaved, or the infinitely greater number of persons who are afterward to inhabit that Territory, or the other members of the family of communities, of which they are but an incipient member, or the general head of the family of States as parent of all — however their action may affect one or the other of these, there is no power or right to interfere. That is Douglas's popular sovereignty applied. Now I think that there is a real popular sovereignty in the world. I think a definition of popular sovereignty, in the abstract, would be about this — that each man shall do precisely as he pleases with himself, and with all those things which exclusively concern him. Applied in government, this principle would be, that a general government shall do all those things which pertain to it, and all the local governments shall do precisely as they please in respect to those matters which exclusively concern them.

Douglas looks upon slavery as so insignificant that the people must decide that question for themselves, and yet they are not fit to decide who shall be their governor, judge, or secretary, or who shall be any of their officers. These are vast national matters, in his estimation; but the little matter in his estimation is that of planting slavery there. That is purely of local interest, which nobody should be allowed to say a word about.

Labor is the great source from which nearly all, if not all, human comforts and necessities are drawn. There is a difference in opinion about the elements of labor in society. Some men assume that there is a necessary connection between capital and labor, and that connection draws within it the whole of the labor of the community. They assume that nobody works unless capital excites them to work. They begin next to consider what is the best way. They say there are but two ways — one is to hire men and to allure them to labor by their consent; the other is to buy the men and drive them to it, and that is slavery. Having assumed that, they proceed to discuss the question of whether the laborers themselves are better off in the condition of slaves or of hired laborers, and they usually decide that they are better off in the condition of slaves.

In the first place, I say that the whole thing is a mistake. That there is a certain relation between capital and labor, I admit. That it does exist, and rightfully exists, I think is true. That men who are industrious and sober and honest in the pursuit of their own interests should after a while accumulate capital, and after that should be allowed to enjoy it in peace, and also if they should choose, when they have accumulated it, to use it to save themselves from actual labor, and hire other people to labor for them, is right. In doing so, they do not wrong the man they employ, for they find men who have not their own land to work upon, or shops to work in, and who are benefited by working for others—hired laborers, receiving their capital for it. Thus a few men that own capital hire a few others, and these establish the relation of capital and labor rightfully—a relation of which I make no complaint. But I insist that that relation, after all, does not embrace more than one eighth of the labor of the country.

[The speaker proceeded to argue that the hired laborer, with his ability to become an employer, must have every precedence over him who labors under the inducement of force. He continued:]

I have taken upon myself, in the name of some of you, to say that we expect upon these principles to ultimately beat them. In order to do so, I think we want and must have a national policy in regard to the institution of slavery that acknowledges and deals with that institution as being wrong. Whoever desires the prevention of the spread of slavery and the nationalization of that institution, yields all when he yields to any policy that either recognizes slavery as being right, or as being an indifferent thing. Nothing will make you successful but setting up a policy which shall treat the thing as being wrong. When I say this, I do not mean to say that this General Government is charged with the duty of redressing or preventing all the wrongs in the world; but I do think that it is charged with preventing and redressing all wrongs which are wrongs to itself. This government is expressly charged with the duty of providing for the general welfare. We believe that the spreading out and perpetuity of the institution of slavery impairs the general welfare. We believe—nay, we know—that that is the only thing that has ever threatened the perpetuity of the Union itself. The only thing which has ever menaced the destruction of the government under which we live, is this very thing. To repress this thing, we think, is providing for the general welfare. Our friends in Kentucky differ from us. We need not make our argument for them; but we who think it is wrong in all its relations, or in some of them at least, must decide as to our own actions, and our own course, upon our own judgment.

I say that we must not interfere with the institution of slavery in the States where it exists, because the Constitution forbids it, and the general welfare does not require us to do so. We must not withhold an efficient fugitive-slave law, because the Constitution requires us, as I understand it, not to withhold such a law. But we must prevent the outspreading of the institution, because neither the Constitution nor general welfare requires us to extend it. We must prevent the revival of the African slave-trade, and the enacting by Congress of a territorial slave-code. We must prevent each of these things being done by either congresses or courts. The people of these United States are the rightful masters of both congresses and courts, not to overthrow the Constitution, but to overthrow the men who pervert the Constitution.

To do these things we must employ instrumentalities. We must hold conventions; we must adopt platforms, if we conform to ordinary custom; we must nominate candidates; and we must carry elections. In all these things, I think that we ought to keep in view our real purpose, and in none do anything that stands adverse to our purpose. If we shall adopt a platform that fails to recognize or express our purpose, or elect a man that declares himself inimical to our purpose, we not only take nothing by our success, but we tacitly admit that we act upon no other principle than a desire to have "the loaves and fishes," by which, in the end, our apparent success is really an injury to us.

I know that it is very desirable with me, as with everybody else, that all the elements of the Opposition shall unite in the next presidential election, and in all future time. I am anxious that that should be, but there are things seriously to be considered in relation to that matter. If the terms can be arranged, I am in favor of the union. But suppose we shall take up some man, and put him upon one end or the other of the ticket, who declares himself against us in regard to the prevention of the spread of slavery, who turns up his nose and says he is tired of hearing anything more about it, who is more against us than against the enemy — what will be the issue? Why, he will get no slave States after all — he has tried that already until being beat is the rule for him. If we nominate him upon that ground, he will not carry a slave State, and not only so, but that portion of our men who are high strung upon the principle we really fight for will not go for him, and he won't get a single electoral vote anywhere, except, perhaps, in the State of Maryland. There is no use in saying to us that we are stubborn and obstinate because we won't do some such thing as this. We cannot do it. We cannot get our men to vote it. I speak by the card, that we cannot give the State of Illinois in such case by fifty thousand. We would be flatter down than the "Negro Democracy" themselves have the heart to wish to see us.

After saying this much, let me say a little on the other side. There are plenty of men in the slave States that are altogether good enough for me to be either President or Vice-President, provided they will profess their sympathy with our purpose, and will place themselves on such ground that our men, upon principle, can vote for them. There are scores of them — good men in their character for intelligence, and talent, and integrity. If such an one will place himself upon the right ground, I am for his occupying one place upon the next Republican or Opposition ticket. I will heartily go for him. But unless he does so place himself, I think it is a matter of perfect nonsense to attempt to bring about a union upon any other basis; that if a union be made, the elements will scatter so that there can be no success for such a ticket, nor anything like success. The good old maxims of the Bible are applicable, and truly applicable, to human affairs, and in this, as in other things, we may say here that he who is not for us is against us; he who gathereth not with us scattereth. I should be glad to have some of the many good, and able, and noble men of the South to place themselves where we can confer upon them the high honor of an election upon one or the other end of our ticket. It would do my soul good to do that thing. It would enable us to teach them that, inasmuch as we select one of their own number to carry out our principles, we are free from the charge that we mean more than we say.

But, my friends, I have detained you much longer than I expected to do. I believe I may allow myself the compliment to say that you have stayed and heard me with great patience, for which I return you my most sincere thanks.

September 30, 1859.—ANNUAL ADDRESS BEFORE THE WISCONSIN STATE AGRICULTURAL SOCIETY, AT MILWAUKEE, WIS.

Members of the Agricultural Society and Citizens of Wisconsin: Agricultural fairs are becoming an institution of the country. They are useful in more ways than one. They bring us together, and thereby make us better acquainted and better friends than we otherwise would be. From the first appearance of man upon the earth down to very recent times, the words "stranger" and "enemy" were quite or almost synonymous. Long after civilized nations had defined robbery and murder as high crimes, and had affixed severe punishments to them, when practised among and upon their own people respectively, it was deemed no offense, but even meritorious, to rob and murder and enslave strangers, whether as nations or as individuals. Even yet, this has not totally disappeared. The man of the highest moral cultivation, in spite of all which abstract principle can do, likes him whom he does know much better than him whom he does not know. To correct the evils, great and small, which spring from want of sympathy and from positive enmity among strangers, as nations or as individuals, is one of the highest functions of civilization. To this end our agricultural fairs contribute in no small degree. They render more pleasant, and more strong, and more durable the bond of social and political union among us. Again, if, as Pope declares, "happiness is our being's end and aim," our fairs contribute much to that end and aim, as occasions of recreation, as holidays. Constituted as man is, he has positive need of occasional recreation, and whatever can give him this associated with virtue and advantage, and free from vice and disadvantage, is a positive good. Such recreation our fairs afford. They are a present pleasure, to be followed by no pain as a consequence; they are a present pleasure, making the future more pleasant.

But the chief use of agricultural fairs is to aid in improving the great calling of agriculture in all its departments and minute divisions; to make mutual exchange of agricultural discovery, information, and knowledge; so that, at the end, all may know everything which may have been known to but one or to but few, at the beginning; to bring together especially all which is supposed to be not generally known because of recent discovery or invention.

And not only to bring together and to impart all which has been accidentally discovered and invented upon ordinary motive, but by exciting emulation for premiums, and for the pride and honor of success,—of triumph, in some sort,—to stimulate that discovery and invention into extraordinary activity. In this these fairs are kindred to the patent clause in the Constitution of the United States, and to the department and practical system based upon that clause.

One feature, I believe, of every fair is a regular address. The Agricultural Society of the young, prosperous, and soon to be great State of Wisconsin has done me the high honor of selecting me to make that address upon this occasion—an honor for which I make my profound and grateful acknowledgment.

I presume I am not expected to employ the time assigned me in the mere flattery of the farmers as a class. My opinion of them is that, in proportion to numbers, they are neither better nor worse than other people. In the nature of things they are more numerous than any other class; and I believe there really are more attempts at flattering them than any other, the reason of which I cannot perceive, unless it be that they can cast more votes than any other. On reflection, I am not quite sure that there is not cause of suspicion against you in selecting me, in some sort a politician and in no sort a farmer, to address you.

But farmers being the most numerous class, it follows that their interest is the largest interest. It also follows that that interest is most worthy of all to be cherished and cultivated—that if there be inevitable conflict between that interest and any other, that other should yield.

Again, I suppose it is not expected of me to impart to you much specific information on agriculture. You have no reason to believe, and do not believe, that I possess it; if that were what you seek in this address, any one of your own number or class would be more able to furnish it. You, perhaps, do expect me to give some general interest to the occasion, and to make some general suggestions on practical matters. I shall attempt nothing more. And in such suggestions by me, quite likely very little will be new to you, and a large part of the rest will be possibly already known to be erroneous.

My first suggestion is an inquiry as to the effect of greater thoroughness in all the departments of agriculture than now prevails in the Northwest—perhaps I might say in America. To speak entirely within bounds, it is known that fifty bushels of wheat, or one hundred bushels of Indian corn, can be produced from an acre. Less than a year ago I saw it stated that a man, by extraordinary care and labor, had produced of wheat what was equal to two hundred bushels from an acre. But take fifty of wheat, and one hundred of corn, to be the possibility, and compare it with the actual crops of the country. Many years ago I saw it stated, in a patent-office report, that eighteen bushels was the average crop throughout the United States; and this year an intelligent farmer of Illinois assured me that he did not believe the land harvested in that State this season had yielded more than an average of eight bushels to the acre; much was cut, and then abandoned as not worth threshing, and much was abandoned as not worth cutting. As to Indian corn, and indeed, most other crops, the case has not been much better. For the last four years I do not believe the ground planted with corn in Illinois has produced an average of twenty bushels to the acre. It is true that heretofore we have had better crops with no better cultivation, but I believe it is also true that the soil has never been pushed up to one half of its capacity.

What would be the effect upon the farming interest to push the soil up to something near its full capacity? Unquestionably it will take more labor to produce fifty bushels from an acre than it will to produce ten bushels from the same acre; but will it take more labor to produce fifty bushels from one acre than from five? Unquestionably thorough cultivation will require more labor to the acre; but will it require more to the bushel? If it should require just as much to the bushel, there are some probable, and several certain, advantages in favor of the thorough practice. It is probable it would develop those unknown causes which of late years have cut down our crops below their former average. It is almost certain, I think, that by deeper plowing, analysis of the soils, experiments with manures and varieties of seeds, observance of seasons, and the like, these causes would be discovered and remedied. It is certain that thorough cultivation would spare half, or more than half, the cost of land, simply because the same product would be got from half, or from less than half, the quantity of land. This proposition is self-evident, and can be made no plainer by repetitions or illustrations. The cost of land is a great item, even in new countries, and it constantly grows greater and greater, in comparison with other items, as the country grows older.

It also would spare the making and maintaining of inclosures for the same, whether these inclosures should be hedges, ditches, or fences. This again is a heavy item—heavy at first, and heavy in its continual demand for repairs. I remember once being greatly astonished by an apparently authentic exhibition of the proportion the cost of an inclosure bears to all the other expenses of the farmer, though I cannot remember exactly what that proportion was. Any farmer, if he will, can ascertain it in his own case for himself.

Again, a great amount of locomotion is spared by thorough cultivation. Take fifty bushels of wheat ready for harvest, standing upon a single acre, and it can be harvested in any of the known ways with less than half the labor which would be required if it were spread over five acres. This would be true if cut by the old hand-sickle; true, to a greater extent, if by the scythe and cradle; and to a still greater extent, if by the machines now in use. These machines are chiefly valuable as a means of substituting animal-power for the power of men in this branch of farm-work. In the highest degree of perfection yet reached in applying the horse-power to harvesting, fully nine tenths of the power is expended by the animal in carrying himself and dragging the machine over the field, leaving certainly not more than one tenth to be applied directly to the only end of the whole operation—the gathering in of the grain, and clipping of the straw. When grain is very thin on the ground, it is always more or less intermingled with weeds, chess, and the like, and a large part of the power is expended in cutting these. It is plain that when the crop is very thick upon the ground, a larger proportion of the power is directly applied to gathering in and cutting it; and the smaller to that which is totally useless as an end. And what I have said of harvesting is true in a greater or less degree of mowing, plowing, gathering in of crops generally, and indeed of almost all farm-work.

The effect of thorough cultivation upon the farmer's own mind, and in reaction through his mind back upon his business, is perhaps quite equal to any other of its effects. Every man is proud of what he does well, and no man is proud of that he does not well. With the former his heart is in his work, and he will do twice as much of it with less fatigue; the latter he performs a little imperfectly, looks at it in disgust, turns from it, and imagines himself exceedingly tired—the little he has done comes to nothing for want of finishing.

The man who produces a good full crop will scarcely ever let any part of it go to waste; he will keep up the inclosure about it, and allow neither man nor beast to trespass upon it; he will gather it in due season, and store it in perfect security. Thus he labors with satisfaction, and saves himself the whole fruit of his labor. The other, starting with no purpose for a full crop, labors less, and with less satisfaction, allows his fences to fall, and cattle to trespass, gathers not in due season, or not at all. Thus the labor he has performed is wasted away, little by little, till in the end he derives scarcely anything from it.

The ambition for broad acres leads to poor farming, even with men of energy. I scarcely ever knew a mammoth farm to sustain itself, much less to return a profit upon the outlay. I have more than once known a man to spend a respectable fortune upon one, fail, and leave it, and then some man of modest aims get a small fraction of the ground, and make a good living upon it. Mammoth farms are like tools or weapons which are too heavy to be handled; ere long they are thrown aside at a great loss.

The successful application of steam-power to farm-work is a desideratum—especially a steam-plow. It is not enough that a machine operated by steam will really plow. To be successful, it must, all things considered, plow better than can be done with animal-power. It must do all the work as well, and cheaper; or more rapidly, so as to get through more perfectly in season; or in some way afford an advantage over plowing with animals, else it is no success. I have never seen a machine intended for a steam-plow. Much praise and admiration are bestowed upon some of them, and they may be, for aught I know, already successful; but I have not perceived the demonstration of it. I have thought a good deal, in an abstract way, about a steam-plow. That one which shall be so contrived as to apply the larger proportion of its power to the cutting and turning the soil, and the smallest, to the moving itself over the field, will be the best one. A very small stationary-engine would draw a large gang of plows through the ground from a short distance to itself; but when it is not stationary, but has to move along like a horse, dragging the plows after it, it must have additional power to carry itself; and the difficulty grows by what is intended to overcome it; for what adds power also adds size and weight to the machine, thus increasing again the demand for power. Suppose you construct the machine so as to cut a succession of short furrows, say a rod in length, transversely to the course the machine is locomoting, something like the shuttle in weaving. In such case the whole machine would move north only the width of a furrow, while in length the furrow would be a rod from east to west. In such case a very large proportion of the power would be applied to the actual plowing. But in this, too, there would be difficulty, which would be the getting of the plow into and out of the ground, at the end of all these short furrows.

I believe, however, ingenious men will, if they have not already, overcome the difficulty I have suggested. But there is still another, about which I am less sanguine. It is the supply of fuel, and especially water, to make steam. Such supply is clearly practicable; but can the expense of it be borne? Steamboats live upon the water, and find their fuel at stated places. Steam-mills and other stationary steam-machinery have their stationary supplies of fuel and water. Railroad-locomotives have their regular wood and water stations. But the steam-plow is less fortunate. It does not live upon the water, and if it be once at a water-station, it will work away from it, and when it gets away cannot return without leaving its work, at a great expense of its time and strength. It will occur that a wagon-and-horse team might be employed to supply it with fuel and water; but this, too, is expensive; and the question recurs, "Can the expense be borne?" When this is added to all other expenses, will not plowing cost more than in the old way?

It is to be hoped that the steam-plow will be finally successful, and if it shall be, "thorough cultivation"—putting the soil to the top of its capacity, producing the largest crop possible from a given quantity of ground—will be most favorable for it. Doing a large amount of work upon a small quantity of ground, it will be as nearly as possible stationary while working, and as free as possible from locomotion, thus expending its strength as much as possible upon its work, and as little as possible in traveling. Our thanks, and something more substantial than thanks, are due to every man engaged in the effort to produce a successful steam-plow. Even the unsuccessful will bring something to light which, in the hands of others, will contribute to the final success. I have not pointed out difficulties in order to discourage, but in order that, being seen, they may be the more readily overcome.

The world is agreed that labor is the source from which human wants are mainly supplied. There is no dispute upon this point. From this point, however, men immediately diverge. Much disputation is maintained as to the best way of applying and controlling the labor element. By some it is assumed that labor is available only in connection with capital — that nobody labors, unless somebody else owning capital, somehow, by the use of it, induces him to do it. Having assumed this, they proceed to consider whether it is best that capital shall hire laborers, and thus induce them to work by their own consent, or buy them, and drive them to it, without their consent. Having proceeded so far, they naturally conclude that all laborers are naturally either hired laborers or slaves. They further assume that whoever is once a hired laborer, is fatally fixed in that condition for life; and thence again, that his condition is as bad as, or worse than, that of a slave. This is the "mud-sill" theory. But another class of reasoners hold the opinion that there is no such relation between capital and labor as assumed; that there is no such thing as a free man being fatally fixed for life in the condition of a hired laborer; that both these assumptions are false, and all inferences from them groundless. They hold that labor is prior to, and independent of, capital; that, in fact, capital is the fruit of labor, and could never have existed if labor had not first existed; that labor can exist without capital, but that capital could never have existed without labor. Hence they hold that labor is the superior — greatly the superior — of capital.

They do not deny that there is, and probably always will be, a relation between labor and capital. The error, as they hold, is in assuming that the whole labor of the world exists within that relation. A few men own capital; and that few avoid labor themselves, and with their capital hire or buy another few to labor for them. A large majority belong to neither class — neither work for others, nor have others working for them. Even in all our slave States except South Carolina, a majority of the whole people of all colors are neither slaves nor masters. In these free States, a large majority are neither hirers nor hired. Men, with their families — wives, sons, and daughters — work for themselves, on their farms, in their houses, and in their shops, taking the whole product to themselves, and asking no favors of capital on the one hand, nor of hirelings or slaves on the other. It is not forgotten that a considerable number of persons mingle their own labor with capital — that is, labor with their own hands, and also buy slaves or hire free men to labor for them; but this is only a mixed, and not a distinct, class. No principle stated is disturbed by the existence of this mixed class. Again, as has already been said, the opponents of the "mud-sill" theory insist that there is not, of necessity, any such thing as the free hired laborer being fixed to that condition for life. There is demonstration for saying this. Many independent men in this assembly doubtless a few years ago were hired laborers. And their case is almost, if not quite, the general rule.

The prudent, penniless beginner in the world labors for wages awhile, saves a surplus with which to buy tools or land for himself, then labors on his own account another while, and at length hires another new beginner to help him. This, say its advocates, is free labor — the just, and generous, and prosperous system, which opens the way for all, gives hope to all, and energy, and progress, and improvement of condition to all. If any continue through life in the condition of the hired laborer, it is not the fault of the system, but because of either a dependent nature which prefers it, or improvidence, folly, or singular misfortune. I have said this much about the elements of labor generally, as introductory to the consideration of a new phase which that element is in process of assuming. The old general rule was that educated people did not perform manual labor. They managed to eat their bread, leaving the toil of producing it to the uneducated. This was not an insupportable evil to the working bees, so long as the class of drones remained very small. But now, especially in these free States, nearly all are educated — quite too nearly all to leave the labor of the uneducated in any wise adequate to the support of the whole. It follows from this that henceforth educated people must labor. Otherwise, education itself would become a positive and intolerable evil. No country can sustain in idleness more than a small percentage of its numbers. The great majority must labor at something productive. From these premises the problem springs, "How can labor and education be the most satisfactorily combined?"

By the "mud-sill" theory it is assumed that labor and education are incompatible, and any practical combination of them impossible. According to that theory, a blind horse upon a tread-mill is a perfect illustration of what a laborer should be — all the better for being blind, that he could not kick understandingly. According to that theory, the education of laborers is not only useless but pernicious and dangerous. In fact, it is, in some sort, deemed a misfortune that laborers should have heads at all. Those same heads are regarded as explosive materials, only to be safely kept in damp places, as far as possible from that peculiar sort of fire which ignites them. A Yankee who could invent a strong-handed man without a head would receive the everlasting gratitude of the "mud-sill" advocates.

But free labor says, "No." Free labor argues that as the Author of man makes every individual with one head and one pair of hands, it was probably intended that heads and hands should coöperate as friends, and that that particular head should direct and control that pair of hands. As each man has one mouth to be fed, and one pair of hands to furnish food, it was probably intended that that particular pair of hands should feed that particular mouth — that each head is the natural guardian, director, and protector of the hands and mouth inseparably connected with it; and that being so, every head should be cultivated and improved by whatever will add to its capacity for performing its charge. In one word, free labor insists on universal education.

I have so far stated the opposite theories of "mud-sill" and "free labor," without declaring any preference of my own between them. On an occasion like this, I ought not to declare any. I suppose, however, I shall not be mistaken in assuming as a fact that the people of Wisconsin prefer free labor, with its natural companion, education.

This leads to the further reflection that no other human occupation opens so wide a field for the profitable and agreeable combination of labor with cultivated thought, as agriculture. I know nothing so pleasant to the mind as the discovery of anything that is at once new and valuable — nothing that so lightens and sweetens toil as the hopeful pursuit of such discovery. And how vast and how varied a field is agriculture for such discovery! The mind, already trained to thought in the country school, or higher school, cannot fail to find there an exhaustless source of enjoyment. Every blade of grass is a study; and to produce two where there was but one is both a profit and a pleasure. And not grass alone, but soils, seeds, and seasons — hedges, ditches, and fences — draining, droughts, and irrigation — plowing, hoeing, and harrowing — reaping, mowing, and threshing — saving crops, pests of crops, diseases of crops, and what will prevent or cure them — implements, utensils, and machines, their relative merits, and how to improve them — hogs, horses, and cattle — sheep, goats, and poultry — trees, shrubs, fruits, plants, and flowers — the thousand things of which these are specimens — each a world of study within itself.

In all this, book-learning is available. A capacity and taste for reading gives access to whatever has already been discovered by others. It is the key, or one of the keys, to the already solved problems. And not only so: it gives a relish and facility for successfully pursuing the unsolved ones. The rudiments of science are available, and highly available. Some knowledge of botany assists in dealing with the vegetable world — with all growing crops. Chemistry assists in the analysis of soils, selection and application of manures, and in numerous other ways. The mechanical branches of natural philosophy are ready help in almost everything, but especially in reference to implements and machinery.

The thought recurs that education — cultivated thought — can best be combined with agricultural labor, or any labor, on the principle of thorough work; that careless, half performed, slovenly work makes no place for such combination; and thorough work, again, renders sufficient the smallest quantity of ground to each man; and this, again, conforms to what must occur in a world less inclined to wars and more devoted to the arts of peace than heretofore. Population must increase rapidly, more rapidly than in former times, and ere long the most valuable of all arts will be the art of deriving a comfortable subsistence from the smallest area of soil. No community whose every member possesses this art, can ever be the victim of oppression in any of its forms. Such community will be alike independent of crowned kings, money kings, and land kings.

But, according to your program, the awarding of premiums awaits the closing of this address. Considering the deep interest necessarily pertaining to that performance, it would be no wonder if I am already heard with some impatience. I will detain you but a moment longer. Some of you will be successful, and such will need but little philosophy to take them home in cheerful spirits; others will be disappointed, and will be in a less happy mood. To such let it be said, "Lay it not too much to heart." Let them adopt the maxim, "Better luck next time," and then by renewed exertion make that better luck for themselves.

And by the successful and unsuccessful let it be remembered that while occasions like the present bring their sober and durable benefits, the exultations and mortifications of them are but temporary; that the victor will soon be vanquished if he relax in his exertion; and that the vanquished this year may be victor the next, in spite of all competition.

It is said an Eastern monarch once charged his wise men to invent him a sentence to be ever in view, and which should be true and appropriate in all times and situations. They presented him the words, "And this, too, shall pass away." How much it expresses! How chastening in the hour of pride! How consoling in the depths of affliction! "And this, too, shall pass away." And yet, let us hope, it is not quite true. Let us hope, rather, that by the best cultivation of the physical world beneath and around us, and the intellectual and moral world within us, we shall secure an individual, social, and political prosperity and happiness, whose course shall be onward and upward, and which, while the earth endures, shall not pass away.

October 11, 1859.—LETTER TO EDWARD WALLACE.

CLINTON, October 11, 1859.

DR. EDWARD WALLACE.

My dear Sir: I am here just now attending court. Yesterday, before I left Springfield, your brother, Dr. William S. Wallace, showed me a letter of yours, in which you kindly mention my name, inquire for my tariff views, and suggest the propriety of my writing a letter upon the subject. I was an old Henry Clay-Tariff-Whig. In old times I made more speeches on that subject than any other.

I have not since changed my views. I believe yet, if we could have a moderate, carefully adjusted protective tariff, so far acquiesced in as not to be a perpetual subject of political strife, squabbles, changes, and uncertainties, it would be better for us. Still it is my opinion that just now the revival of that question will not advance the cause itself, or the man who revives it.

I have not thought much on the subject recently, but my general impression is that the necessity for a protective tariff will ere long force its old opponents to take it up; and then its old friends can join in and establish it on a more firm and durable basis. We, the Old Whigs, have been entirely beaten out on the tariff question, and we shall not be able to reëstablish the policy until the absence of it shall have demonstrated the necessity for it in the minds of men heretofore opposed to it. With this view, I should prefer to not now write a public letter on the subject. I therefore wish this to be considered confidential. I shall be very glad to receive a letter from you.

Yours truly,   A. LINCOLN.

November 1, 1859.— LETTER TO W. E. FRAZER.

SPRINGFIELD, ILLINOIS, November 1, 1859.

W. E. FRAZER, Esq.

Dear Sir: Yours of the 24th ult. was forwarded to me from Chicago. It certainly is important to secure Pennsylvania for the

Republicans in the next presidential contest, and not unimportant to also secure Illinois. As to the ticket you name, I shall be heartily for it after it shall have been fairly nominated by a Republican national convention; and I cannot be committed to it before. For my single self, I have enlisted for the permanent success of the Republican cause; and for this object I shall labor faithfully in the ranks, unless, as I think not probable, the judgment of the party shall assign me a different position. If the Republicans of the great State of Pennsylvania shall present Mr. Cameron as their candidate for the presidency, such an indorsement for his fitness for the place could scarcely be deemed insufficient. Still, as I would not like the public to know, so I would not like myself to know, I had entered a combination with any man to the prejudice of all others whose friends respectively may consider them preferable.

Yours truly,   A. LINCOLN.

November 13, 1859.— LETTER TO JAMES A. BRIGGS.

DANVILLE, ILLINOIS, November 13, 1859.

JAMES A. BRIGGS, Esq.

Dear Sir : Yours of the 1st, closing with my proposition for compromise, was duly received. I will be on hand, and in due time will notify you of the exact day. I believe, after all, I shall make a political speech of it. You have no objection ? I would like to know in advance whether I am also to speak or lecture in New York. Very, very glad your election went right. Yours truly,

A. LINCOLN.

December 1–5, 1859.— SPEECHES IN KANSAS.

[In response to invitations from Republicans of the then Territory, Mr. Lincoln made a visit to Kansas in December, 1859, and made speeches at Elwood (opposite St. Joseph, Mo.), at Troy, Doniphan, Atchison, and Leavenworth, Kansas. Among his papers were a number of disconnected sheets of autograph manuscript, which contained internal evidence that they were portions of the addresses made by him on these occasions. Though the fragments seem to belong to different addresses, the topics treated in them justify their presentation in the order here arranged, as the general line of argument followed by him.]

Introduction.

Purpose of the Republican organization.— The Republican party believe there is danger that slavery will be further extended, and ultimately made national in the United States; and to prevent this incidental and final consummation, is the purpose of this organization.

Chief danger to that purpose.— A congressional slave code for the Territories, and the revival of the African trade, and a second Dred Scott decision, are not just now the chief danger to our purpose.

These will press us in due time, but they are not quite ready yet—they know that, as yet, we are too strong for them. The insidious Douglas popular sovereignty, which prepares the way for this ultimate danger, it is which just now constitutes our chief danger.

Popular Sovereignty.—I say Douglas popular sovereignty; for there is a broad distinction between real popular sovereignty and Douglas popular sovereignty. That the nation shall control what concerns it; that a State, or any minor political community, shall control what exclusively concerns it; and that an individual shall control what exclusively concerns him,—is a real popular sovereignty, which no Republican opposes.

But this is not Douglas popular sovereignty? Douglas popular sovereignty, as a matter of principle, simply is: "If one man would enslave another, neither that other nor any third man has a right to object."

Douglas popular sovereignty, as he practically applies it, is: "If any organized political community, however new and small, would enslave men or forbid their being enslaved within its own territorial limits; however the doing the one or the other may affect the men sought to be enslaved, or the vastly superior number of men who are afterward to come within those limits, or the family of communities of which it is but a member, or the head of that family, as the present and common guardian of the whole—however any or all these are to be affected, neither any nor all may interfere."

This is Douglas popular sovereignty. He has great difficulty with it. His speeches and letters and essays and explanations explanatory of explanations explained upon it, are legion. The most lengthy, and as I suppose the most maturely considered, is that recently published in "Harper's Magazine." It has two leading objects: the first, to appropriate the authority and reverence due the great and good men of the Revolution to his popular sovereignty; and, secondly, to show that the Dred Scott decision has not entirely squelched his popular sovereignty.

Before considering these main objects, I wish to consider a few minor points of the copyright essay.

Last year Governor Seward and myself, at different times and occasions, expressed the opinion that slavery is a durable element of discord, and that we shall not have peace with it until it either masters or is mastered by the free principle. This gave great offense to Judge Douglas, and his denunciations of it, and absurd inferences from it, have never ceased. Almost at the very beginning of the copyright essay he quotes the language respectively of Seward and myself—not quite accurately, but substantially, in my case—upon this point, and repeats his absurd and extravagant inference. For lack of time I omit much which I might say here with propriety, and content myself with two remarks only upon this point. The first is, that inasmuch as Douglas in this very essay tells us slavery agitation began in this country in 1699, and has not yet ceased; has lasted through a hundred and sixty years, through ten entire generations of men,—it might have occurred to even him that slavery in its tendency to agitation and discord has something slightly durable about it.   The second remark is that Judge Douglas might have noted, if he would, while he was diving so deeply into history, the historical fact that the only comparative peace we have had with slavery during that hundred and sixty years was in the period from the Revolution to 1820, precisely the period through which we were closing out the African slave-trade, abolishing slavery in several of the States, and restraining the spread of it into new ones by the ordinance of '87, precisely the period in which the public mind had reason to rest, and did rest, in the belief that slavery was in course of ultimate extinction.

Another point, which for the present I shall touch only hastily, is Judge Douglas's assumption that the States and Territories differ only in the fact that the States are in the Union, and the Territories are not in it.   But if this be the only difference, why not instantly bring the Territories in?   Why keep them out?   Do you say they are unfitted for it?   What unfits them?   Especially what unfits them for any duty in the Union, after they are fit, if they choose, to plant the soil they sparsely inhabit with slavery, beyond the power of their millions of successors to eradicate it, and to the durable discord of the Union?   What function of sovereignty, out of the Union or in it, is so portentous as this?   What function of government requires such perfect maturity, in numbers and everything else, among those who exercise it?   It is a concealed assumption of Douglas's popular sovereignty that slavery is a little, harmless, indifferent thing, having no wrong in it, and no power for mischief about it.   If all men looked upon it as he does, his policy in regard to it might do.   But neither all, nor half the world, so look upon it.

Near the close of the essay in "Harper's Magazine" Douglas tells us that his popular sovereignty pertains to a people only after they are regularly organized into a political community; and that Congress in its discretion must decide when they are fit in point of numbers to be so organized.   Now I should like for him to point out in the Constitution any clause conferring that discretion upon Congress, which, when pointed out, will not be equally a power in Congress to govern them, in its discretion, till they are admitted as a State.   Will he try?   He intimates that before the exercise of that discretion, their number must be ten, fifteen, or twenty thousand.   Well, what is to be done for them, or with them, or by them, before they number ten thousand?   If any one of them desires to have slaves, is any other one bound to help him, or at liberty to hinder him?   Is it his plan that any time before they reach the required numbers, those who are on hand shall be driven out as trespassers?   If so, it will probably be a good while before a sufficient number to organize will get in.

But plainly enough this conceding to Congress the discretion as to when a community shall be organized, is a total surrender of his popular sovereignty.   He says himself it does not pertain to a people until they are organized; and that when they shall be organized is in the discretion of Congress.   Suppose Congress shall choose to not organize them until they are numerous enough to come into the Union as a State.   By his own rule, his popular sovereignty is derived from Congress, and cannot be exercised by the people till

Congress chooses to confer it. After toiling through nineteen mortal pages of "Harper," to show that Congress cannot keep the people of a new country from excluding slavery, in a single closing paragraph he makes the whole thing depend on Congress at last. And should Congress refuse to organize, how will that affect the question of planting slavery in a new country? If individuals choose to plant it, the people cannot prevent them, for they are not yet clothed with popular sovereignty. If it be said that it cannot be planted, in fact, without protective law, that assertion is already falsified by history; for it was originally planted on this continent without protective law.

And, by the way, it is probable that no act of territorial organization could be passed by the present Senate; and almost certainly not by both the Senate and House of Representatives. If an act declared the right of Congress to exclude slavery, the Republicans would vote for it, and both wings of the Democracy against it. If it denied the power to either exclude or protect it, the Douglasites would vote for it, and both the Republicans and slave-coders against it. If it denied the power to exclude, and asserted the power to protect, the slave-coders would vote for it, and the Republicans and Douglasites against it.

You are now a part of a people of a Territory, but that Territory is soon to be a State of the Union. Both in your individual and collective capacities, you have the same interest in the past, the present, and the future of the United States as any other portion of the people. Most of you came from the States, and all of you soon will be citizens of the common Union. What I shall now address to you will have neither greater nor less application to you than to any other people of the Union.

You are gathered to-day as a Republican convention—Republican in the party sense, and, as we hope, in the true, original sense of the word republican.

I assume that Republicans throughout the nation believe they are right, and are earnest and determined in their cause.

Let them then keep constantly in view that the chief object of their organization is to prevent the spread and nationalization of slavery. With this ever distinctly before us, we can always better see at what point our cause is most in danger.

We are, as I think, in the present temper or state of public sentiment, in no danger from the open advocates of a congressional slave code for the Territories, and of the revival of the African slave-trade. As yet we are strong enough to meet and master any combination openly formed on those grounds. It is only the insidious position of Douglas that endangers our cause. That position is simply an ambuscade. By entering into contest with our open enemies, we are to be lured into his train; and then, having lost our own organization and arms, we are to be turned over to those same open enemies.

Douglas's position leads to the nationalization of slavery as surely as does that of Jeff Davis and Mason of Virginia. The two positions are but slightly different roads to the same place — with this difference, that the nationalization of slavery can be reached by Douglas's route, and never can be by the other.

I have said that in our present moral tone and temper we are strong enough for our open enemies, and so we are. But the chief effect of Douglasism is to change that tone and temper. Men who support the measures of a political leader do, almost of necessity, adopt the reasoning and sentiments the leader advances in support of them. The reasoning and sentiments advanced by Douglas in support of his policy as to slavery all spring from the view that slavery is not wrong. In the first place, he never says it is wrong. He says he does not care whether it shall be voted down or voted up. He says whoever wants slavery has a right to have it. He says the question whether people will have it or not is simply a question of dollars and cents. He says the Almighty has drawn a line across the continent, on one side of which the soil must be cultivated by slave labor.

Now let the people of the free States adopt these sentiments, and they will be unable to see a single reason for maintaining their prohibitions of slavery in their own States. "What! do you mean to say that anything in these sentiments requires us to believe it will be the interest of Northern States to have slavery?" No. But I do mean to say that although it is not the interest of Northern States to grow cotton, none of them have, or need, any law against it; and it would be tyranny to deprive any one man of the privilege to grow cotton in Illinois. There are many individual men in all the free States who desire to have slaves; and if you admit that slavery is not wrong, it is also but tyranny to deny them the privilege. It is no just function of government to prohibit what is not wrong.

Again, if slavery is right—ordained by the Almighty—on one side of a line dividing sister States of a common Union, then it is positively wrong to harass and bedevil the owners of it with constitutions and laws and prohibitions of it on the other side of the line. In short, there is no justification for prohibiting slavery anywhere, save only in the assumption that slavery is wrong; and whenever the sentiment that slavery is wrong shall give way in the North, all legal prohibitions of it will also give way.

If it be insisted that men may support Douglas's measures without adopting his sentiments, let it be tested by what is actually passing before us. You can even now find no Douglas man who will disavow any one of these sentiments; and none but will actually indorse them if pressed to the point.

Five years ago no living man had placed on record, nor, as I believe, verbally expressed, a denial that negroes have a share in the Declaration of Independence. Two or three years since, Douglas began to deny it; and now every Douglas man in the nation denies it.

To the same effect is the absurdity compounded of support to the Dred Scott decision, and legislation unfriendly to slavery by the Territories—the absurdity which asserts that a thing may be lawfully driven from a place, at which place it has a lawful right to remain. That absurd position will not be long maintained by any one. The Dred Scott half of it will soon master the other half. The process will probably be about this: some territorial legislature will adopt unfriendly legislation; the Supreme Court will decide that legislation to be unconstitutional, and then the advocates of the present compound absurdity will acquiesce in the decision. The only effect of that position now is to prepare its advocates for such acquiescence when the time comes. Like wood for ox-bows, they are merely being soaked in it preparatory to the bending. The advocates of a slave code are not now strong enough to master us; and they never will be, unless recruits enough to make them so be tolled in through the gap of Douglasism. Douglas, on the sly, is effecting more for them than all their open advocates. He has reason to be provoked that they will not understand him, and recognize him as their best friend. He cannot be more plain, without being so plain as to lure no one into their trap—so plain as to lose his power to serve them profitably. Take other instances. Last year both Governor Seward and myself expressed the belief that this government cannot endure permanently half slave and half free. This gave great offense to Douglas, and after the fall election in Illinois he became quite rampant upon it. At Chicago, St. Louis, Memphis, and New Orleans, he denounced it as a "fatal heresy." With great pride he claimed that he had crushed it in Illinois, and modestly regretted that he could not have been in New York to crush it there too. How the heresy is fatal to anything, or what the thing is to which it is fatal, he has never paused to tell us. At all events, it is a fatal heresy in his view when expressed by a Northern man. Not so when expressed by men of the South. In 1856, Roger A. Pryor, editor of the Richmond "Enquirer," expressed the same belief in that paper, quite two years before it was expressed by either Seward or me. But Douglas perceived no "heresy" in him—talked not of going to Virginia to crush it out; nay, more, he now has that same Mr. Pryor at Washington, editing the "States" newspaper as his especial organ.

This brings us to see that in Douglas's view this opinion is a "fatal heresy" when expressed by men wishing to have the nation all free, and it is no heresy at all when expressed by men wishing to have it all slave. Douglas has cause to complain that the South will not note this and give him credit for it.

At Memphis Douglas told his audience that he was for the negro against the crocodile, but for the white man against the negro. This was not a sudden thought hastily thrown off at Memphis. He said the same thing many times in Illinois last summer and autumn, though I am not sure it was reported then.

It is a carefully formed illustration of the estimate he places upon the negro and the manner he would have him dealt with. It is a sort of proposition in proportion. "As the negro is to the crocodile, so the white man is to the negro." As the negro ought to treat the crocodile as a beast, so the white man ought to treat the negro as a beast. Gentlemen of the South, is not that satisfactory? Will you give Douglas no credit for impressing that sentiment on the Northern mind for your benefit? Why, you should magnify him to the utmost, in order that he may impress it the more deeply, broadly, and surely.

A hope is often expressed that all the elements of opposition to the so-called Democracy may unite in the next presidential election; and to favor this it is suggested that at least one candidate on the opposition national ticket must be resident in the slave States. I strongly sympathize with this hope; and the particular suggestion presents no difficulty to me.   There are very many men in the slave States who as men and statesmen and patriots are quite acceptable to me for either President or Vice-President.   But there is a difficulty of another sort; and I think it most prudent for us to face that difficulty at once.   Will those good men of the South occupy any ground upon which we of the free States can vote for them?   There is the rub.   They seem to labor under a huge mistake in regard to us.   They say they are tired of slavery agitation.   We think the slaves, and free white laboring-men too, have more reason to be tired of slavery than masters have to be tired of agitation about it. In Kentucky a Democratic candidate for Congress takes ground against a congressional slave-code for the Territories, whereupon his opponent, in full hope to unite with Republicans in 1860, takes ground in favor of such slave-code.   Such hope, under such circumstances, is delusion gross as insanity itself.   Rational men can only entertain it in the strange belief that Republicans are not in earnest for their principles; that they are really devoted to no principle of their own, but are ready for, and anxious to jump to, any position not occupied by the Democracy.   This mistake must be dispelled. For the sake of their principles, in forming their party, they broke and sacrificed the strongest mere party ties and advantages which can exist.   Republicans believe that slavery is wrong; and they insist, and will continue to insist, upon a national policy which recognizes it and deals with it as a wrong.   There can be no letting down about this.   Simultaneously with such letting down the Republican organization would go to pieces, and half its elements would go in a different direction, leaving an easy victory to the common enemy. No ingenuity of political trading could possibly hold it together. About this there is no joke, and can be no trifling.   Understanding this, that Republicanism can never mix with territorial slave-codes becomes self-evident.

In this contest mere men are nothing.   We could come down to Douglas quite as well as to any other man standing with him, and better than to any other standing below or beyond him.   The simple problem is: will any good and capable man of the South allow the Republicans to elect him on their own platform?   If such man can be found, I believe the thing can be done.   It can be done in no other way.

What do we gain, say some, by such a union?   Certainly not everything; but still something, and quite all that we for our lives can possibly give.   In yielding a share of the high honors and offices to you, you gain the assurance that ours is not a mere struggle to secure those honors and offices for one section.   You gain the assurance that we mean no more than we say in our platforms, else we would not intrust you to execute them.   You gain the assurance that we intend no invasion of your rights or your honor, else we would not make one of you the executor of the laws and commander of the army and navy.

As a matter of mere partizan policy, there is no reason for and much against any letting down of the Republican party in order to form a union with the Southern opposition. By no possibility can a union ticket secure a simple electoral vote in the South, unless the Republican platform be so far let down as to lose every electoral vote in the North; and even at that, not a single vote would be secured in the South, unless by bare possibility those of Maryland. There is no successful basis of union but for some good Southern man to allow us of the North to elect him square on our platform. Plainly it is that or nothing.

The St. Louis "Intelligencer" is out in favor of a good man for President, to be run without a platform. Well, I am not wedded to the formal written platform system; but a thousand to one the editor is not himself in favor of his plan, except with the qualification that he and his sort are to select and name the "good man." To bring him to the test, is he willing to take Seward without a platform? Oh, no; Seward's antecedents exclude him, say you. Well, is your good man without antecedents? If he is, how shall the nation know that he is a good man? The sum of the matter is that, in the absence of formal written platforms, the antecedents of candidates become their platforms. On just such platforms all our earlier and better Presidents were elected, but this by no means facilitates a union of men who differ in principles.

Nor do I believe we can ever advance our principles by supporting men who oppose our principles. Last year, as you know, we Republicans in Illinois were advised by numerous and respectable outsiders to reëlect Douglas to the Senate by our votes. I never questioned the motives of such advisers, nor the devotion to the Republican cause of such as professed to be Republicans. But I never for a moment thought of following the advice, and have never yet regretted that we did not follow it. True, Douglas is back in the Senate in spite of us; but we are clear of him and his principles, and we are uncrippled and ready to fight both him and them straight along till they shall be finally "closed out." Had we followed the advice, there would now be no Republican party in Illinois, and none to speak of anywhere else. The whole thing would now be floundering along after Douglas upon the Dred Scott and crocodile theory. It would have been the grandest "haul" for slavery ever yet made. Our principles would still live, and ere long would produce a party; but we should have lost all our past labor and twenty years of time by the folly.

Take an illustration. About a year ago all the Republicans in Congress voted for what was called the Crittenden-Montgomery bill; and forthwith Douglas claimed, and still claims, that they were all committed to his "gur-reat pur-rinciple." And Republicans have been so far embarrassed by the claim that they have ever since been protesting that they were not so committed, and trying to explain why. Some of the very newspapers which advised Douglas's return to the Senate by Republican votes have been largely and continuously engaged in these protests and explanations. For such let us state a question in the rule of three. If voting for the Crittenden-Montgomery bill entangle the Republicans with Douglas's dogmas for one year, how long would voting for Douglas himself so entangle them?

It is nothing to the contrary that Republicans gained something by electing Haskins, Hickman, and Davis. They were comparatively small men. I mean no disrespect; they may have large merit; but Republicans can dally with them, and absorb or expel them at pleasure. If they dally with Douglas, he absorbs them.

We want, and must have, a national policy as to slavery which deals with it as being a wrong. Whoever would prevent slavery becoming national and perpetual yields all when he yields to a policy which treats it either as being right, or as being a matter of indifference.

We admit that the United States General Government is not charged with the duty of redressing or preventing all the wrongs in the world. But the government rightfully may, and subject to the Constitution ought to, redress and prevent all wrongs which are wrongs to the nation itself. It is expressly charged with the duty of providing for the general welfare. We think slavery impairs and endangers the general welfare. Those who do not think this are not of us, and we cannot agree with them. We must shape our own course by our own judgment.

We must not disturb slavery in the States where it exists, because the Constitution and the peace of the country both forbid us. We must not withhold an efficient fugitive-slave law, because the Constitution demands it.

But we must, by a national policy, prevent the spread of slavery into new Territories, or free States, because the Constitution does not forbid us, and the general welfare does demand such prevention. We must prevent the revival of the African slave-trade, because the Constitution does not forbid us, and the general welfare does require the prevention. We must prevent these things being done by either congresses or courts. The people—the people—are the rightful masters of both congresses and courts,—not to overthrow the Constitution, but to overthrow the men who pervert it.

To effect our main object we have to employ auxiliary means. We must hold conventions, adopt platforms, select candidates, and carry elections. At every step we must be true to the main purpose. If we adopt a platform falling short of our principle, or elect a man rejecting our principle, we not only take nothing affirmative by our success, but we draw upon us the positive embarrassment of seeming ourselves to have abandoned our principle.

That our principle, however baffled or delayed, will finally triumph, I do not permit myself to doubt. Men will pass away—die, die politically and naturally; but the principle will live, and live forever. Organizations rallied around that principle may, by their own dereliction, go to pieces, thereby losing all their time and labor; but the principle will remain, and will reproduce another, and another, till the final triumph will come.

VOL. I.—38.

But to bring it soon, we must save our labor already performed—our organization, which has cost us so much time and toil to create. We must keep our principle constantly in view, and never be false to it.

And as to men for leaders, we must remember that "He that is not for us is against us; and he that gathereth not with us scattereth."

December 9, 1859.—LETTER TO N. B. JUDD.

SPRINGFIELD, December 9, 1859.

HON. N. B. JUDD.

My dear Sir : I have just reached home from Kansas and found your long letter of the 1st inst. It has a tone of blame toward myself which I think is not quite just; but I will not stand upon that, but will consider a day or two, and put something in the best shape I can, and send it to you. A great difficulty is that they make no distinct charge against you which I can contradict. You did vote for Trumbull against me; and, although I think, and have said a thousand times, that was no injustice to me, I cannot change the fact, nor compel people to cease speaking of it. Ever since that matter occurred, I have constantly labored, as I believe you know, to have all recollection of it dropped.

The vague charge that you played me false last year I believe to be false and outrageous; but it seems I can make no impression by expressing that belief. I made a special job of trying to impress that upon Baker, Bridges, and Wilson here last winter. They all well know that I believe no such charge against you. But they chose to insist that they know better about it than I do.

As to the charge of your intriguing for Trumbull against me, I believe as little of that as any other charge. If Trumbull and I were candidates for the same office, you would have a right to prefer him, and I should not blame you for it; but all my acquaintance with you induces me to believe you would not pretend to be for me while really for him. But I do not understand Trumbull and myself to be rivals. You know I am pledged to not enter a struggle with him for the seat in the Senate now occupied by him; and yet I would rather have a full term in the Senate than in the presidency.   Your friend as ever,

A. LINCOLN.

P. S.—I omitted to say that I have, in no single instance, permitted a charge such as alluded to above to go uncontradicted when made in my presence.   A. L.

December 14, 1859.—LETTER TO N. B. JUDD.

SPRINGFIELD, December 14, 1859.

Dear Judd : Herewith is the letter of our old Whig friends, and my answer, sent as you requested. I showed both to Dubois, and he feared the clause about leave to publish, in the answer, would not be quite satisfactory to you. I hope it will be satisfactory, as I would rather not seem to come before the public as a volunteer; still if, after considering this, you still deem it important, you may substitute the inclosed slip by pasting it down over the original clause.

I find some of our friends here attach more consequence to getting the national convention into our State than I did, or do. Some of them made me promise to say so to you. As to the time, it must certainly be after the Charleston fandango; and I think, within bounds of reason, the later the better.

As to that matter about the committee, in relation to appointing delegates by general convention, or by districts, I shall attend to it as well as I know how, which, God knows, will not be very well. Write me if you can find anything to write. Yours as ever,

A. LINCOLN.

[Inclosure.]
SPRINGFIELD, ILLINOIS, December 14, 1859.

MESSRS. GEORGE W. DOLE, G. S. HUBBARD, AND W. H. BROWN.

Gentlemen: Your letter of the 12th instant is received. To your question: "In the election of senator in 1854 [1855 you mean], when Mr. Trumbull was the successful candidate, was there any unfairness in the conduct of Mr. Judd toward you, or anything blamable on his part?" I answer, I have never believed, and do not now believe, that on that occasion there was any unfairness in the conduct of Mr. Judd toward me, or anything blamable on his part. Without deception, he preferred Judge Trumbull to myself, which was his clear right, morally as well as legally.

To your question: "During the canvass of last year, did he do his whole duty toward you and the Republican party?" I answer, I have always believed, and now believe, that during that canvass he did his whole duty toward me and the Republican party.

To your question: "Do you know of anything unfair in his conduct toward yourself in any way?" I answer, I neither know nor suspect anything unfair in his conduct toward myself in any way.

I take pleasure in adding that of all the avowed friends I had in the canvass of last year, I do not suspect a single one of having acted treacherously to me, or to our cause; and that there is not one of them in whose honor and integrity I have more confidence to-day than in that of Mr. Judd.

You can use your discretion as to whether you make this public.

Yours very truly,   A. LINCOLN.

December 19, 1859.— LETTER TO G. M. PARSONS AND OTHERS.

SPRINGFIELD, ILLINOIS, December 19, 1859.

MESSRS. G. M. PARSONS, AND OTHERS, *Central Executive Committee, etc.*

Gentlemen: Your letter of the 7th instant, accompanied by a similar one from the governor-elect, the Republican State officers, and the

Republican members of the State Board of Equalization of Ohio, both requesting of me, for publication in permanent form, copies of the political debates between Senator Douglas and myself last year, has been received.   With my grateful acknowledgments to both you and them for the very flattering terms in which the request is communicated, I transmit you the copies.   The copies I send you are as reported and printed by the respective friends of Senator Douglas and myself, at the time—that is, his by his friends, and mine by mine. It would be an unwarrantable liberty for us to change a word or a letter in his, and the changes I have made in mine, you perceive, are verbal only, and very few in number.   I wish the reprint to be precisely as the copies I send, without any comment whatever.

Yours very truly,   A. LINCOLN.

December 20, 1859.—LETTER TO J. W. FELL.

SPRINGFIELD, December 20, 1859.

J. W. FELL, Esq.

My dear Sir : Herewith is a little sketch, as you requested.   There is not much of it, for the reason, I suppose, that there is not much of me.   If anything be made out of it, I wish it to be modest, and not to go beyond the material.   If it were thought necessary to incorporate anything from any of my speeches, I suppose there would be no objection.   Of course it must not appear to have been written by myself.   Yours very truly,

A. LINCOLN.

I was born February 12, 1809, in Hardin County, Kentucky.   My parents were both born in Virginia, of undistinguished families— second families, perhaps I should say.   My mother, who died in my tenth year, was of a family of the name of Hanks, some of whom now reside in Adams, and others in Macon County, Illinois.   My paternal grandfather, Abraham Lincoln, emigrated from Rockingham County, Virginia, to Kentucky about 1781 or 1782, where a year or two later he was killed by the Indians, not in battle, but by stealth, when he was laboring to open a farm in the forest.   His ancestors, who were Quakers, went to Virginia from Berks County, Pennsylvania.   An effort to identify them with the New England family of the same name ended in nothing more definite than a similarity of Christian names in both families, such as Enoch, Levi, Mordecai, Solomon, Abraham, and the like.

My father, at the death of his father, was but six years of age, and he grew up literally without education.   He removed from Kentucky to what is now Spencer County, Indiana, in my eighth year.   We reached our new home about the time the State came into the Union. It was a wild region, with many bears and other wild animals still in the woods.   There I grew up.   There were some schools, so called, but no qualification was ever required of a teacher beyond " readin', writin', and cipherin' " to the rule of three.   If a straggler supposed to understand Latin happened to sojourn in the neighborhood, he was looked upon as a wizard.   There was absolutely nothing to excite

ambition for education. Of course, when I came of age I did not
know much. Still, somehow, I could read, write, and cipher to the
rule of three, but that was all. I have not been to school since.
The little advance I now have upon this store of education, I have
picked up from time to time under the pressure of necessity.

I was raised to farm work, which I continued till I was twenty-
two. At twenty-one I came to Illinois, Macon County. Then I got
to New Salem, at that time in Sangamon, now in Menard County,
where I remained a year as a sort of clerk in a store. Then came
the Black Hawk war; and I was elected a captain of volunteers, a
success which gave me more pleasure than any I have had since.
I went the campaign, was elated, ran for the legislature the same
year (1832), and was beaten—the only time I ever have been beaten
by the people. The next and three succeeding biennial elections I
was elected to the legislature. I was not a candidate afterward.
During this legislative period I had studied law, and removed to
Springfield to practise it. In 1846 I was once elected to the lower
House of Congress. Was not a candidate for reëlection. From 1849
to 1854, both inclusive, practised law more assiduously than ever
before. Always a Whig in politics; and generally on the Whig
electoral tickets, making active canvasses. I was losing interest in
politics when the repeal of the Missouri compromise aroused me
again. What I have done since then is pretty well known.

If any personal description of me is thought desirable, it may be
said I am, in height, six feet four inches, nearly; lean in flesh, weigh-
ing on an average one hundred and eighty pounds; dark complexion, with coarse black hair and gray eyes. No other marks or
brands recollected.   Yours truly,

HON. J. W. FELL.   A. LINCOLN.

January 24, 1860.—LETTER TO J. W. SHEAHAN.

SPRINGFIELD, January 24, 1860.

JAMES W. SHEAHAN, Esq.

Dear Sir: Yours of the 21st, requesting copies of my speeches
now in progress of publication in Ohio, is received. I have no such
copies now at my control, having sent the only set I ever had to
Ohio. Mr. George M. Parsons has taken an active part among
those who have the matter in charge in Ohio; and I understand
Messrs. Follett, Foster & Co. are to be the publishers. I make no
objection to any satisfactory arrangement you may make with Mr.
Parsons and the publishers; and if it will facilitate you, you are at
liberty to show them this note.

You labor under a mistake somewhat injurious to me, if you suppose I have revised the speeches in any just sense of the word. I
only made some small verbal corrections, mostly such as an intelligent reader would make for himself, not feeling justified to do more
when republishing the speeches along with those of Senator Douglas, his and mine being mutually answers and replies to one another.

Yours truly,   A. LINCOLN.

February 5, 1860.— LETTER TO N. B. JUDD.

SPRINGFIELD, February 5, 1860.

HON. N. B. JUDD.

My dear Sir: Your two letters were duly received. Whether Mr. Storrs shall come to Illinois and assist in our approaching campaign, is a question of dollars and cents. Can we pay him ? If we can, that is the sole question. I consider his services very valuable.

A day or so before you wrote about Mr. Herndon, Dubois told me that he (Herndon) had been talking to William Jayne in the way you indicate. At first sight afterward, I mentioned it to him; he rather denied the charge, and I did not press him about the past, but got his solemn pledge to say nothing of the sort in the future. I had done this before I received your letter. I impressed upon him as well as I could, first, that such [*sic*] was untrue and unjust to you; and, second, that I would be held responsible for what he said. Let this be private.

Some folks are pretty bitter toward me about the Dole, Hubbard, and Brown letter.   Yours as ever,   A. LINCOLN.

February 9, 1860.—LETTER TO N. B. JUDD.

SPRINGFIELD, February 9, 1860.

HON. N. B. JUDD.

Dear Sir: I am not in a position where it would hurt much for me to not be nominated on the national ticket; but I am where it would hurt some for me to not get the Illinois delegates. What I expected when I wrote the letter to Messrs. Dole and others is now happening. Your discomfited assailants are most bitter against me; and they will, for revenge upon me, lay to the Bates egg in the South, and to the Seward egg in the North, and go far toward squeezing me out in the middle with nothing. Can you not help me a little in this matter in your end of the vineyard ? I mean this to be private.   Yours as ever,   A. LINCOLN.

February 9, 1860.—LETTER TO J. M. LUCAS.

SPRINGFIELD, February 9, 1860.

J. M. LUCAS, Esq.

My dear Sir: Your late letter, suggesting, among other things, that I might aid your election as postmaster, by writing to Mr. Burlingame, was duly received the day the Speaker was elected; so that I had no hope a letter of mine could reach Mr. B. before your case would be decided, as it turned out in fact it could not. We are all much gratified here to see you are elected. We consider you our peculiar friend at court.

I shall be glad to receive a letter from you at any time you can find leisure to write one.   Yours very truly,   A. LINCOLN.

February 27, 1860.—ADDRESS AT COOPER INSTITUTE, NEW YORK.

Mr. President and Fellow-citizens of New York: The facts with which I shall deal this evening are mainly old and familiar; nor is there anything new in the general use I shall make of them. If there shall be any novelty, it will be in the mode of presenting the facts, and the inferences and observations following that presentation. In his speech last autumn at Columbus, Ohio, as reported in the "New-York Times," Senator Douglas said:

Our fathers, when they framed the government under which we live, understood this question just as well, and even better, than we do now.

I fully indorse this, and I adopt it as a text for this discourse. I so adopt it because it furnishes a precise and an agreed starting-point for a discussion between Republicans and that wing of the Democracy headed by Senator Douglas. It simply leaves the inquiry: What was the understanding those fathers had of the question mentioned?

What is the frame of government under which we live? The answer must be, "The Constitution of the United States." That Constitution consists of the original, framed in 1787, and under which the present government first went into operation, and twelve subsequently framed amendments, the first ten of which were framed in 1789.

Who were our fathers that framed the Constitution? I suppose the "thirty-nine" who signed the original instrument may be fairly called our fathers who framed that part of the present government. It is almost exactly true to say they framed it, and it is altogether true to say they fairly represented the opinion and sentiment of the whole nation at that time. Their names, being familiar to nearly all, and accessible to quite all, need not now be repeated.

I take these "thirty-nine," for the present, as being "our fathers who framed the government under which we live." What is the question which, according to the text, those fathers understood "just as well, and even better, than we do now"?

It is this: Does the proper division of local from Federal authority, or anything in the Constitution, forbid our Federal Government to control as to slavery in our Federal Territories?

Upon this, Senator Douglas holds the affirmative, and Republicans the negative. This affirmation and denial form an issue; and this issue — this question — is precisely what the text declares our fathers understood "better than we." Let us now inquire whether the "thirty-nine," or any of them, ever acted upon this question; and if they did, how they acted upon it — how they expressed that better understanding. In 1784, three years before the Constitution, the United States then owning the Northwestern Territory, and no other, the Congress of the Confederation had before them the question of prohibiting slavery in that Territory; and four of the "thirty-nine" who afterward framed the Constitution were in that Congress, and voted on that question. Of these, Roger Sherman, Thomas Mifflin, and Hugh Williamson voted for the prohibition, thus showing that, in their understanding, no line dividing local from Federal authority, nor anything else, properly forbade the Federal Government to control as to slavery in Federal territory. The other of the four, James McHenry, voted against the prohibition, showing that for some cause he thought it improper to vote for it.

In 1787, still before the Constitution, but while the convention was in session framing it, and while the Northwestern Territory still was the only Territory owned by the United States, the same question of prohibiting slavery in the Territory again came before the Congress of the Confederation; and two more of the "thirty-nine" who afterward signed the Constitution were in that Congress, and voted on the question. They were William Blount and William Few; and they both voted for the prohibition—thus showing that in their understanding no line dividing local from Federal authority, nor anything else, properly forbade the Federal Government to control as to slavery in Federal territory. This time the prohibition became a law, being part of what is now well known as the ordinance of '87.

The question of Federal control of slavery in the Territories seems not to have been directly before the convention which framed the original Constitution; and hence it is not recorded that the "thirty-nine," or any of them, while engaged on that instrument, expressed any opinion on that precise question.

In 1789, by the first Congress which sat under the Constitution, an act was passed to enforce the ordinance of '87, including the prohibition of slavery in the Northwestern Territory. The bill for this act was reported by one of the "thirty-nine"—Thomas Fitzsimmons, then a member of the House of Representatives from Pennsylvania. It went through all its stages without a word of opposition, and finally passed both branches without ayes and nays, which is equivalent to a unanimous passage. In this Congress there were sixteen of the thirty-nine fathers who framed the original Constitution. They were John Langdon, Nicholas Gilman, Wm. S. Johnson, Roger Sherman, Robert Morris, Thos. Fitzsimmons, William Few, Abraham Baldwin, Rufus King, William Paterson, George Clymer, Richard Bassett, George Read, Pierce Butler, Daniel Carroll, and James Madison.

This shows that, in their understanding, no line dividing local from Federal authority, nor anything in the Constitution, properly forbade Congress to prohibit slavery in the Federal territory; else both their fidelity to correct principle, and their oath to support the Constitution, would have constrained them to oppose the prohibition.

Again, George Washington, another of the "thirty-nine," was then President of the United States, and as such approved and signed the bill, thus completing its validity as a law, and thus showing that, in his understanding, no line dividing local from Federal authority, nor anything in the Constitution, forbade the Federal Government to control as to slavery in Federal territory.

No great while after the adoption of the original Constitution, North Carolina ceded to the Federal Government the country now constituting the State of Tennessee; and a few years later Georgia ceded that which now constitutes the States of Mississippi and Alabama. In both deeds of cession it was made a condition by the ceding States that the Federal Government should not prohibit slavery in the ceded country. Besides this, slavery was then actually in the ceded country. Under these circumstances, Congress, on taking charge of these countries, did not absolutely prohibit slavery within them. But they did interfere with it—take control of it—even there, to a certain extent. In 1798 Congress organized the Territory of Mississippi. In the act of organization they prohibited the bringing of slaves into the Territory from any place without the United States, by fine, and giving freedom to slaves so brought. This act passed both branches of Congress without yeas and nays. In that Congress were three of the "thirty-nine" who framed the original Constitution. They were John Langdon, George Read, and Abraham Baldwin. They all probably voted for it. Certainly they would have placed their opposition to it upon record if, in their understanding, any line dividing local from Federal authority, or anything in the Constitution, properly forbade the Federal Government to control as to slavery in Federal territory.

In 1803 the Federal Government purchased the Louisiana country. Our former territorial acquisitions came from certain of our own States; but this Louisiana country was acquired from a foreign nation. In 1804 Congress gave a territorial organization to that part of it which now constitutes the State of Louisiana. New Orleans, lying within that part, was an old and comparatively large city. There were other considerable towns and settlements, and slavery was extensively and thoroughly intermingled with the people. Congress did not, in the Territorial Act, prohibit slavery; but they did interfere with it—take control of it—in a more marked and extensive way than they did in the case of Mississippi. The substance of the provision therein made in relation to slaves was:

1st. That no slave should be imported into the Territory from foreign parts.

2d. That no slave should be carried into it who had been imported into the United States since the first day of May, 1798.

3d. That no slave should be carried into it, except by the owner, and for his own use as a settler; the penalty in all the cases being a fine upon the violator of the law, and freedom to the slave.

This act also was passed without ayes or nays. In the Congress which passed it there were two of the "thirty-nine." They were Abraham Baldwin and Jonathan Dayton. As stated in the case of Mississippi, it is probable they both voted for it. They would not have allowed it to pass without recording their opposition to it if, in their understanding, it violated either the line properly dividing local from Federal authority, or any provision of the Constitution.

In 1819-20 came and passed the Missouri question. Many votes were taken, by yeas and nays, in both branches of Congress, upon the various phases of the general question. Two of the "thirty-nine"—Rufus King and Charles Pinckney—were members of that

Congress. Mr. King steadily voted for slavery prohibition and against all compromises, while Mr. Pinckney as steadily voted against slavery prohibition and against all compromises. By this, Mr. King showed that, in his understanding, no line dividing local from Federal authority, nor anything in the Constitution, was violated by Congress prohibiting slavery in Federal territory; while Mr. Pinckney, by his votes, showed that, in his understanding, there was some sufficient reason for opposing such prohibition in that case.

The cases I have mentioned are the only acts of the "thirty-nine," or of any of them, upon the direct issue, which I have been able to discover.

To enumerate the persons who thus acted as being four in 1784, two in 1787, seventeen in 1789, three in 1798, two in 1804, and two in 1819–20, there would be thirty of them. But this would be counting John Langdon, Roger Sherman, William Few, Rufus King, and George Read each twice, and Abraham Baldwin three times. The true number of those of the "thirty-nine" whom I have shown to have acted upon the question which, by the text, they understood better than we, is twenty-three, leaving sixteen not shown to have acted upon it in any way.

Here, then, we have twenty-three out of our thirty-nine fathers "who framed the government under which we live," who have, upon their official responsibility and their corporal oaths, acted upon the very question which the text affirms they "understood just as well, and even better, than we do now"; and twenty-one of them — a clear majority of the whole "thirty-nine"— so acting upon it as to make them guilty of gross political impropriety and wilful perjury if, in their understanding, any proper division between local and Federal authority, or anything in the Constitution they had made themselves, and sworn to support, forbade the Federal Government to control as to slavery in the Federal Territories. Thus the twenty-one acted; and, as actions speak louder than words, so actions under such responsibility speak still louder.

Two of the twenty-three voted against congressional prohibition of slavery in the Federal Territories, in the instances in which they acted upon the question. But for what reasons they so voted is not known. They may have done so because they thought a proper division of local from Federal authority, or some provision or principle of the Constitution, stood in the way; or they may, without any such question, have voted against the prohibition on what appeared to them to be sufficient grounds of expediency. No one who has sworn to support the Constitution can conscientiously vote for what he understands to be an unconstitutional measure, however expedient he may think it; but one may and ought to vote against a measure which he deems constitutional if, at the same time, he deems it inexpedient. It, therefore, would be unsafe to set down even the two who voted against the prohibition as having done so because, in their understanding, any proper division of local from Federal authority, or anything in the Constitution, forbade the Federal Government to control as to slavery in Federal territory.

The remaining sixteen of the "thirty-nine," so far as I have discovered, have left no record of their understanding upon the direct question of Federal control of slavery in the Federal Territories. But there is much reason to believe that their understanding upon that question would not have appeared different from that of their twenty-three compeers, had it been manifested at all.

For the purpose of adhering rigidly to the text, I have purposely omitted whatever understanding may have been manifested by any person, however distinguished, other than the thirty-nine fathers who framed the original Constitution; and, for the same reason, I have also omitted whatever understanding may have been manifested by any of the " thirty-nine" even on any other phase of the general question of slavery. If we should look into their acts and declarations on those other phases, as the foreign slave-trade, and the morality and policy of slavery generally, it would appear to us that on the direct question of Federal control of slavery in Federal Territories, the sixteen, if they had acted at all, would probably have acted just as the twenty-three did. Among that sixteen were several of the most noted antislavery men of those times,— as Dr. Franklin, Alexander Hamilton, and Gouverneur Morris,— while there was not one now known to have been otherwise, unless it may be John Rutledge, of South Carolina.

The sum of the whole is that of our thirty-nine fathers who framed the original Constitution, twenty-one — a clear majority of the whole —certainly understood that no proper division of local from Federal authority, nor any part of the Constitution, forbade the Federal Government to control slavery in the Federal Territories; while all the rest had probably the same understanding. Such, unquestionably, was the understanding of our fathers who framed the original Constitution; and the text affirms that they understood the question " better than we."

But, so far, I have been considering the understanding of the question manifested by the framers of the original Constitution. In and by the original instrument, a mode was provided for amending it; and, as I have already stated, the present frame of " the government under which we live" consists of that original, and twelve amendatory articles framed and adopted since. Those who now insist that Federal control of slavery in Federal Territories violates the Constitution, point us to the provisions which they suppose it thus violates; and, as I understand, they all fix upon provisions in these amendatory articles, and not in the original instrument. The Supreme Court, in the Dred Scott case, plant themselves upon the fifth amendment, which provides that no person shall be deprived of "life, liberty, or property without due process of law"; while Senator Douglas and his peculiar adherents plant themselves upon the tenth amendment, providing that "the powers not delegated to the United States by the Constitution" "are reserved to the States respectively, or to the people."

Now, it so happens that these amendments were framed by the first Congress which sat under the Constitution— the identical Congress which passed the act, already mentioned, enforcing the prohibition of slavery in the Northwestern Territory. Not only was it the same

Congress, but they were the identical, same individual men who, at the same session, and at the same time within the session, had under consideration, and in progress toward maturity, these constitutional amendments, and this act prohibiting slavery in all the territory the nation then owned. The constitutional amendments were introduced before, and passed after, the act enforcing the ordinance of '87; so that, during the whole pendency of the act to enforce the ordinance, the constitutional amendments were also pending.

The seventy-six members of that Congress, including sixteen of the framers of the original Constitution, as before stated, were preeminently our fathers who framed that part of "the government under which we live" which is now claimed as forbidding the Federal Government to control slavery in the Federal Territories.

Is it not a little presumptuous in any one at this day to affirm that the two things which that Congress deliberately framed, and carried to maturity at the same time, are absolutely inconsistent with each other? And does not such affirmation become impudently absurd when coupled with the other affirmation, from the same mouth, that those who did the two things alleged to be inconsistent, understood whether they really were inconsistent better than we—better than he who affirms that they are inconsistent?

It is surely safe to assume that the thirty-nine framers of the original Constitution, and the seventy-six members of the Congress which framed the amendments thereto, taken together, do certainly include those who may be fairly called "our fathers who framed the government under which we live." And so assuming, I defy any man to show that any one of them ever, in his whole life, declared that, in his understanding, any proper division of local from Federal authority, or any part of the Constitution, forbade the Federal Government to control as to slavery in the Federal Territories. I go a step further. I defy any one to show that any living man in the whole world ever did, prior to the beginning of the present century (and I might almost say prior to the beginning of the last half of the present century), declare that, in his understanding, any proper division of local from Federal authority, or any part of the Constitution, forbade the Federal Government to control as to slavery in the Federal Territories. To those who now so declare I give not only "our fathers who framed the government under which we live," but with them all other living men within the century in which it was framed, among whom to search, and they shall not be able to find the evidence of a single man agreeing with them.

Now, and here, let me guard a little against being misunderstood. I do not mean to say we are bound to follow implicitly in whatever our fathers did. To do so would be to discard all the lights of current experience— to reject all progress, all improvement. What I do say is that if we would supplant the opinions and policy of our fathers in any case, we should do so upon evidence so conclusive, and argument so clear, that even their great authority, fairly considered and weighed, cannot stand; and most surely not in a case whereof we ourselves declare they understood the question better than we.

If any man at this day sincerely believes that a proper division of local from Federal authority, or any part of the Constitution, forbids the Federal Government to control as to slavery in the Federal Territories, he is right to say so, and to enforce his position by all truthful evidence and fair argument which he can.   But he has no right to mislead others, who have less access to history, and less leisure to study it, into the false belief that "our fathers who framed the government under which we live" were of the same opinion—thus substituting falsehood and deception for truthful evidence and fair argument.   If any man at this day sincerely believes "our fathers who framed the government under which we live" used and applied principles, in other cases, which ought to have led them to understand that a proper division of local from Federal authority, or some part of the Constitution, forbids the Federal Government to control as to slavery in the Federal Territories, he is right to say so.   But he should, at the same time, brave the responsibility of declaring that, in his opinion, he understands their principles better than they did themselves; and especially should he not shirk that responsibility by asserting that they "understood the question just as well, and even better, than we do now."

But enough!   Let all who believe that "our fathers who framed the government under which we live understood this question just as well, and even better, than we do now," speak as they spoke, and act as they acted upon it.   This is all Republicans ask—all Republicans desire—in relation to slavery.   As those fathers marked it, so let it be again marked, as an evil not to be extended, but to be tolerated and protected only because of and so far as its actual presence among us makes that toleration and protection a necessity. Let all the guaranties those fathers gave it be not grudgingly, but fully and fairly, maintained.   For this Republicans contend, and with this, so far as I know or believe, they will be content.

And now, if they would listen,—as I suppose they will not,—I would address a few words to the Southern people.

I would say to them: You consider yourselves a reasonable and a just people; and I consider that in the general qualities of reason and justice you are not inferior to any other people.   Still, when you speak of us Republicans, you do so only to denounce us as reptiles, or, at the best, as no better than outlaws.   You will grant a hearing to pirates or murderers, but nothing like it to "Black Republicans." In all your contentions with one another, each of you deems an unconditional condemnation of "Black Republicanism" as the first thing to be attended to.   Indeed, such condemnation of us seems to be an indispensable prerequisite—license, so to speak—among you to be admitted or permitted to speak at all.   Now can you or not be prevailed upon to pause and to consider whether this is quite just to us, or even to yourselves?   Bring forward your charges and specifications, and then be patient long enough to hear us deny or justify.,

You say we are sectional.   We deny it.   That makes an issue; and the burden of proof is upon you.   You produce your proof; and what is it?   Why, that our party has no existence in your section

—gets no votes in your section. The fact is substantially true; but does it prove the issue? If it does, then in case we should, without change of principle, begin to get votes in your section, we should thereby cease to be sectional. You cannot escape this conclusion; and yet, are you willing to abide by it? If you are, you will probably soon find that we have ceased to be sectional, for we shall get votes in your section this very year. You will then begin to discover, as the truth plainly is, that your proof does not touch the issue. The fact that we get no votes in your section is a fact of your making, and not of ours. And if there be fault in that fact, that fault is primarily yours, and remains so until you show that we repel you by some wrong principle or practice. If we do repel you by any wrong principle or practice, the fault is ours; but this brings you to where you ought to have started—to a discussion of the right or wrong of our principle. If our principle, put in practice, would wrong your section for the benefit of ours, or for any other object, then our principle, and we with it, are sectional, and are justly opposed and denounced as such. Meet us, then, on the question of whether our principle, put in practice, would wrong your section; and so meet us as if it were possible that something may be said on our side. Do you accept the challenge? No! Then you really believe that the principle which "our fathers who framed the government under which we live" thought so clearly right as to adopt it, and indorse it again and again, upon their official oaths, is in fact so clearly wrong as to demand your condemnation without a moment's consideration.

Some of you delight to flaunt in our faces the warning against sectional parties given by Washington in his Farewell Address. Less than eight years before Washington gave that warning, he had, as President of the United States, approved and signed an act of Congress enforcing the prohibition of slavery in the Northwestern Territory, which act embodied the policy of the government upon that subject up to and at the very moment he penned that warning; and about one year after he penned it, he wrote Lafayette that he considered that prohibition a wise measure, expressing in the same connection his hope that we should at some time have a confederacy of free States.

Bearing this in mind, and seeing that sectionalism has since arisen upon this same subject, is that warning a weapon in your hands against us, or in our hands against you? Could Washington himself speak, would he cast the blame of that sectionalism upon us, who sustain his policy, or upon you, who repudiate it? We respect that warning of Washington, and we commend it to you, together with his example pointing to the right application of it.

But you say you are conservative—eminently conservative—while we are revolutionary, destructive, or something of the sort. What is conservatism? Is it not adherence to the old and tried, against the new and untried? We stick to, contend for, the identical old policy on the point in controversy which was adopted by "our fathers who framed the government under which we live"; while you with one accord reject, and scout, and spit upon that old policy, and insist upon substituting something new. True, you disagree among yourselves as to what that substitute shall be. You are divided on new propositions 'and plans, but you are unanimous in rejecting and denouncing the old policy of the fathers. Some of you are for reviving the foreign slave-trade; some for a congressional slave code for the Territories; some for Congress forbidding the Territories to prohibit slavery within their limits; some for maintaining slavery in the Territories through the judiciary; some for the " gur-reat pur-rinciple " that " if one man would enslave another, no third man should object," fantastically called "popular sovereignty"; but never a man among you is in favor of Federal prohibition of slavery in Federal Territories, according to the practice of "our fathers who framed the government under which we live." Not one of all your various plans can show a precedent or an advocate in the century within which our government originated. Consider, then, whether your claim of conservatism for yourselves, and your charge of destructiveness against us, are based on the most clear and stable foundations.

Again, you say we have made the slavery question more prominent than it formerly was. We deny it. We admit that it is more prominent, but we deny that we made it so. It was not we, but you, who discarded the old policy of the fathers. We resisted, and still resist, your innovation; and thence comes the greater prominence of the question. Would you have that question reduced to its former proportions? Go back to that old policy. What has been will be again, under the same conditions. If you would have the peace of the old times, readopt the precepts and policy of the old times.

You charge that we stir up insurrections among your slaves. We deny it; and what is your proof? Harper's Ferry! John Brown!! John Brown was no Republican; and you have failed to implicate a single Republican in his Harper's Ferry enterprise. If any member of our party is guilty in that matter, you know it, or you do not know it. If you do know it, you are inexcusable for not designating the man and proving the fact. If you do not know it, you are inexcusable for asserting it, and especially for persisting in the assertion after you have tried and failed to make the proof. You need not be told that persisting in a charge which one does not know to be true, is simply malicious slander.

Some of you admit that no Republican designedly aided or encouraged the Harper's Ferry affair, but still insist that our doctrines and declarations necessarily lead to such results. We do not believe it. We know we hold no doctrine, and make no declaration, which were not held to and made by "our fathers who framed the government under which we live." You never dealt fairly by us in relation to this affair. When it occurred, some important State elections were near at hand, and you were in evident glee with the belief that, by charging the blame upon us, you could get an advantage of us in those elections. The elections came, and your expectations were not quite fulfilled. Every Republican man knew that, as to himself at least, your charge was a slander, and he was not much inclined by it to cast his vote in your favor. Republican doctrines and declarations are accompanied with a continual protest against any interference whatever with your slaves, or with you about your slaves. Surely, this does not encourage them to revolt. True, we do, in common with "our fathers who framed the government under which we live," declare our belief that slavery is wrong; but the slaves do not hear us declare even this. For anything we say or do, the slaves would scarcely know there is a Republican party. I believe they would not, in fact, generally know it but for your misrepresentations of us in their hearing. In your political contests among yourselves, each faction charges the other with sympathy with Black Republicanism; and then, to give point to the charge, defines Black Republicanism to simply be insurrection, blood, and thunder among the slaves.

Slave insurrections are no more common now than they were before the Republican party was organized. What induced the Southampton insurrection, twenty-eight years ago, in which at least three times as many lives were lost as at Harper's Ferry? You can scarcely stretch your very elastic fancy to the conclusion that Southampton was "got up by Black Republicanism." In the present state of things in the United States, I do not think a general, or even a very extensive, slave insurrection is possible. The indispensable concert of action cannot be attained. The slaves have no means of rapid communication; nor can incendiary freemen, black or white, supply it. The explosive materials are everywhere in parcels; but there neither are, nor can be supplied, the indispensable connecting trains.

Much is said by Southern people about the affection of slaves for their masters and mistresses; and a part of it, at least, is true. A plot for an uprising could scarcely be devised and communicated to twenty individuals before some one of them, to save the life of a favorite master or mistress, would divulge it. This is the rule; and the slave revolution in Hayti was not an exception to it, but a case occurring under peculiar circumstances. The gunpowder plot of British history, though not connected with slaves, was more in point. In that case, only about twenty were admitted to the secret; and yet one of them, in his anxiety to save a friend, betrayed the plot to that friend, and, by consequence, averted the calamity. Occasional poisonings from the kitchen, and open or stealthy assassinations in the field, and local revolts extending to a score or so, will continue to occur as the natural results of slavery; but no general insurrection of slaves, as I think, can happen in this country for a long time. Whoever much fears, or much hopes, for such an event, will be alike disappointed.

In the language of Mr. Jefferson, uttered many years ago, "It is still in our power to direct the process of emancipation and deportation peaceably, and in such slow degrees, as that the evil will wear off insensibly; and their places be, *pari passu*, filled up by free white laborers. If, on the contrary, it is left to force itself on, human nature must shudder at the prospect held up."

Mr. Jefferson did not mean to say, nor do I, that the power of emancipation is in the Federal Government. He spoke of Virginia;

and, as to the power of emancipation, I speak of the slaveholding States only. The Federal Government, however, as we insist, has the power of restraining the extension of the institution—the power to insure that a slave insurrection shall never occur on any American soil which is now free from slavery.

John Brown's effort was peculiar. It was not a slave insurrection. It was an attempt by white men to get up a revolt among slaves, in which the slaves refused to participate. In fact, it was so absurd that the slaves, with all their ignorance, saw plainly enough it could not succeed. That affair, in its philosophy, corresponds with the many attempts, related in history, at the assassination of kings and emperors. An enthusiast broods over the oppression of a people till he fancies himself commissioned by Heaven to liberate them. He ventures the attempt, which ends in little else than his own execution. Orsini's attempt on Louis Napoleon, and John Brown's attempt at Harper's Ferry, were, in their philosophy, precisely the same. The eagerness to cast blame on old England in the one case, and on New England in the other, does not disprove the sameness of the two things.

And how much would it avail you, if you could, by the use of John Brown, Helper's Book, and the like, break up the Republican organization? Human action can be modified to some extent, but human nature cannot be changed. There is a judgment and a feeling against slavery in this nation, which cast at least a million and a half of votes. You cannot destroy that judgment and feeling—that sentiment—by breaking up the political organization which rallies around it. You can scarcely scatter and disperse an army which has been formed into order in the face of your heaviest fire; but if you could, how much would you gain by forcing the sentiment which created it out of the peaceful channel of the ballot-box into some other channel? What would that other channel probably be? Would the number of John Browns be lessened or enlarged by the operation?

But you will break up the Union rather than submit to a denial of your constitutional rights.

That has a somewhat reckless sound; but it would be palliated, if not fully justified, were we proposing, by the mere force of numbers, to deprive you of some right plainly written down in the Constitution. But we are proposing no such thing.

When you make these declarations you have a specific and well-understood allusion to an assumed constitutional right of yours to take slaves into the Federal Territories, and to hold them there as property. But no such right is specifically written in the Constitution. That instrument is literally silent about any such right. We, on the contrary, deny that such a right has any existence in the Constitution, even by implication.

Your purpose, then, plainly stated, is that you will destroy the government, unless you be allowed to construe and force the Constitution as you please, on all points in dispute between you and us. You will rule or ruin in all events.

This, plainly stated, is your language. Perhaps you will say the

Supreme Court has decided the disputed constitutional question in your favor. Not quite so. But waiving the lawyer's distinction between dictum and decision, the court has decided the question for you in a sort of way. The court has substantially said, it is your constitutional right to take slaves into the Federal Territories, and to hold them there as property. When I say the decision was made in a sort of way, I mean it was made in a divided court, by a bare majority of the judges, and they not quite agreeing with one another in the reasons for making it; that it is so made as that its avowed supporters disagree with one another about its meaning, and that it was mainly based upon a mistaken statement of fact—the statement in the opinion that "the right of property in a slave is distinctly and expressly affirmed in the Constitution."

An inspection of the Constitution will show that the right of property in a slave is not "distinctly and expressly affirmed" in it. Bear in mind, the judges do not pledge their judicial opinion that such right is impliedly affirmed in the Constitution; but they pledge their veracity that it is "distinctly and expressly" affirmed there—"distinctly," that is, not mingled with anything else—"expressly," that is, in words meaning just that, without the aid of any inference, and susceptible of no other meaning.

If they had only pledged their judicial opinion that such right is affirmed in the instrument by implication, it would be open to others to show that neither the word "slave" nor "slavery" is to be found in the Constitution, nor the word "property" even, in any connection with language alluding to the things slave, or slavery; and that wherever in that instrument the slave is alluded to, he is called a "person"; and wherever his master's legal right in relation to him is alluded to, it is spoken of as "service or labor which may be due" —as a debt payable in service or labor. Also it would be open to show, by contemporaneous history, that this mode of alluding to slaves and slavery, instead of speaking of them, was employed on purpose to exclude from the Constitution the idea that there could be property in man.

To show all this is easy and certain.

When this obvious mistake of the judges shall be brought to their notice, is it not reasonable to expect that they will withdraw the mistaken statement, and reconsider the conclusion based upon it?

And then it is to be remembered that "our fathers who framed the government under which we live"—the men who made the Constitution—decided this same constitutional question in our favor long ago: decided it without division among themselves when making the decision; without division among themselves about the meaning of it after it was made, and, so far as any evidence is left, without basing it upon any mistaken statement of facts.

Under all these circumstances, do you really feel yourselves justified to break up this government unless such a court decision as yours is shall be at once submitted to as a conclusive and final rule of political action? But you will not abide the election of a Republican president! In that supposed event, you say, you will destroy the Union; and then, you say, the great crime of having destroyed it will be upon us! That is cool. A highwayman holds a pistol to my ear, and mutters through his teeth, "Stand and deliver, or I shall kill you, and then you will be a murderer!"

To be sure, what the robber demanded of me—my money—was my own; and I had a clear right to keep it; but it was no more my own than my vote is my own; and the threat of death to me, to extort my money, and the threat of destruction to the Union, to extort my vote, can scarcely be distinguished in principle.

A few words now to Republicans. It is exceedingly desirable that all parts of this great Confederacy shall be at peace, and in harmony one with another. Let us Republicans do our part to have it so. Even though much provoked, let us do nothing through passion and ill temper. Even though the Southern people will not so much as listen to us, let us calmly consider their demands, and yield to them if, in our deliberate view of our duty, we possibly can. Judging by all they say and do, and by the subject and nature of their controversy with us, let us determine, if we can, what will satisfy them.

Will they be satisfied if the Territories be unconditionally surrendered to them? We know they will not. In all their present complaints against us, the Territories are scarcely mentioned. Invasions and insurrections are the rage now. Will it satisfy them if, in the future, we have nothing to do with invasions and insurrections? We know it will not. We so know, because we know we never had anything to do with invasions and insurrections; and yet this total abstaining does not exempt us from the charge and the denunciation.

The question recurs, What will satisfy them? Simply this: we must not only let them alone, but we must somehow convince them that we do let them alone. This, we know by experience, is no easy task. We have been so trying to convince them from the very beginning of our organization, but with no success. In all our platforms and speeches we have constantly protested our purpose to let them alone; but this has had no tendency to convince them. Alike unavailing to convince them is the fact that they have never detected a man of us in any attempt to disturb them.

These natural and apparently adequate means all failing, what will convince them? This, and this only: cease to call slavery wrong, and join them in calling it right. And this must be done thoroughly —done in acts as well as in words. Silence will not be tolerated— we must place ourselves avowedly with them. Senator Douglas's new sedition law must be enacted and enforced, suppressing all declarations that slavery is wrong, whether made in politics, in presses, in pulpits, or in private. We must arrest and return their fugitive slaves with greedy pleasure. We must pull down our free-State constitutions. The whole atmosphere must be disinfected from all taint of opposition to slavery, before they will cease to believe that all their troubles proceed from us.

I am quite aware they do not state their case precisely in this way. Most of them would probably say to us, "Let us alone; do nothing to us, and say what you please about slavery." But we do let them alone,—have never disturbed them,—so that, after all, it is what we say which dissatisfies them. They will continue to accuse us of doing, until we cease saying.

I am also aware they have not as yet in terms demanded the overthrow of our free-State constitutions. Yet those constitutions declare the wrong of slavery with more solemn emphasis than do all other sayings against it; and when all these other sayings shall have been silenced, the overthrow of these constitutions will be demanded, and nothing be left to resist the demand. It is nothing to the contrary that they do not demand the whole of this just now. Demanding what they do, and for the reason they do, they can voluntarily stop nowhere short of this consummation. Holding, as they do, that slavery is morally right and socially elevating, they cannot cease to demand a full national recognition of it as a legal right and a social blessing.

Nor can we justifiably withhold this on any ground save our conviction that slavery is wrong. If slavery is right, all words, acts, laws, and constitutions against it are themselves wrong, and should be silenced and swept away. If it is right, we cannot justly object to its nationality—its universality; if it is wrong, they cannot justly insist upon its extension—its enlargement. All they ask we could readily grant, if we thought slavery right; all we ask they could as readily grant, if they thought it wrong. Their thinking it right and our thinking it wrong is the precise fact upon which depends the whole controversy. Thinking it right, as they do, they are not to blame for desiring its full recognition as being right; but thinking it wrong, as we do, can we yield to them? Can we cast our votes with their view, and against our own? In view of our moral, social, and political responsibilities, can we do this?

Wrong as we think slavery is, we can yet afford to let it alone where it is, because that much is due to the necessity arising from its actual presence in the nation; but can we, while our votes will prevent it, allow it to spread into the national Territories, and to overrun us here in these free States? If our sense of duty forbids this, then let us stand by our duty fearlessly and effectively. Let us be diverted by none of those sophistical contrivances wherewith we are so industriously plied and belabored—contrivances such as groping for some middle ground between the right and the wrong: vain as the search for a man who should be neither a living man nor a dead man; such as a policy of "don't care" on a question about which all true men do care; such as Union appeals beseeching true Union men to yield to Disunionists, reversing the divine rule, and calling, not the sinners, but the righteous to repentance; such as invocations to Washington, imploring men to unsay what Washington said and undo what Washington did.

Neither let us be slandered from our duty by false accusations against us, nor frightened from it by menaces of destruction to the government, nor of dungeons to ourselves. Let us have faith that right makes might, and in that faith let us to the end dare to do our duty as we understand it.

March 5, 1860.—ABSTRACT OF SPEECH AT HARTFORD, CONN.

Slavery is the great political question of the nation. Though all desire its settlement, it still remains the all-pervading question of the day. It has been so especially for the past six years. It is indeed older than the Revolution—rising, subsiding, then rising again, till '54, since which time it has been constantly augmenting. Those who occasioned the Lecompton imbroglio now admit that they see no end to it. It had been their cry that the vexed question was just about to be settled—"the tail of this hideous creature is just going out of sight." That cry is played out, and has ceased.

Why, when all desire to have this controversy settled, can we not settle it satisfactorily? One reason is, we want it settled in different ways. Each faction has a different plan—they pull different ways, and neither has a decided majority. In my humble opinion, the importance and magnitude of the question is underrated, even by our wisest men. If I be right, the first thing is to get a just estimate of the evil; then we can provide a cure.

One sixth, and a little more, of the population of the United States are slaves, looked upon as property, as nothing but property. The cash value of these slaves, at a moderate estimate, is $2,000,000,000. This amount of property value has a vast influence on the minds of its owners, very naturally. The same amount of property would have an equal influence upon us if owned in the North. Human nature is the same—people at the South are the same as those at the North, barring the difference in circumstances. Public opinion is founded, to a great extent, on a property basis. What lessens the value of property is opposed; what enhances its value is favored. Public opinion at the South regards slaves as property, and insists upon treating them like other property.

On the other hand, the free States carry on their government on the principle of the equality of men. We think slavery is morally wrong, and a direct violation of that principle. We all think it wrong. It is clearly proved, I think, by natural theology, apart from revelation. Every man, black, white, or yellow, has a mouth to be fed, and two hands with which to feed it—and bread should be allowed to go to that mouth without controversy.

Slavery is wrong in its effect upon white people and free labor. It is the only thing that threatens the Union. It makes what Senator Seward has been much abused for calling an "irrepressible conflict." When they get ready to settle it, we hope they will let us know. Public opinion settles every question here; any policy to be permanent must have public opinion at the bottom—something in accordance with the philosophy of the human mind as it is. The property basis will have its weight. The love of property and a consciousness of right or wrong have conflicting places in our organization, which often make a man's course seem crooked, his conduct a riddle.

Some men would make it a question of indifference, neither right nor wrong, merely a question of dollars and cents;—the Almighty has drawn a line across the land, below which it must be cultivated by slave labor, above which by free labor. They would say: "If the question is between the white man and the negro, I am for the white man; if between the negro and the crocodile, I am for the negro." There is a strong effort to make this policy of indifference prevail, but it cannot be a durable one. A "don't care" policy won't prevail, for everybody does care.

Is there a Democrat, especially one of the Douglas wing, but will declare that the Declaration of Independence has no application to the negro? It would be safe to offer a moderate premium for such a man. I have asked this question in large audiences where they were in the habit of answering right out, but no one would say otherwise. Not one of them said it five years ago. I never heard it till I heard it from the lips of Judge Douglas. True, some men boldly took the bull by the horns and said the Declaration of Independence was not true! They did n't sneak around the question. I say I heard first from Douglas that the Declaration did not apply to the black man. Not a man of them said it till then—they all say it now. This is a long stride toward establishing the policy of indifference—one more such stride, I think, would do it.

The proposition that there is a struggle between the white man and the negro contains a falsehood. There is no struggle. If there was, I should be for the white man. If two men are adrift at sea on a plank which will bear up but one, the law justifies either in pushing the other off. I never had to struggle to keep a negro from enslaving me, nor did a negro ever have to fight to keep me from enslaving him. They say, between the crocodile and the negro, they go for the negro. The logical proportion is, therefore, as a white man is to a negro, so is a negro to a crocodile, or as a negro may treat the crocodile, so the white man may treat the negro. The "don't care" policy leads just as surely to nationalizing slavery as Jeff Davis himself, but the doctrine is more dangerous because more insidious.

If the Republicans, who think slavery is wrong, get possession of the General Government, we may not root out the evil at once, but may at least prevent its extension. If I find a venomous snake lying on the open prairie, I seize the first stick and kill him at once; but if that snake is in bed with my children, I must be more cautious;— I shall, in striking the snake, also strike the children, or arouse the reptile to bite the children. Slavery is the venomous snake in bed with the children. But if the question is whether to kill it on the prairie or put it in bed with other children, I am inclined to think we 'd kill it.

Another illustration. When for the first time I met Mr. Clay, the other day in the cars, in front of us sat an old gentleman with an enormous wen upon his neck. Everybody would say the wen was a great evil, and would cause the man's death after a while; but you could n't cut it out, for he 'd bleed to death in a minute. But would you ingraft the seeds of that wen on the necks of sound and healthy men? He must endure and be patient, hoping for possible relief. The wen represents slavery on the neck of this country. This only applies to those who think slavery is wrong.   Those who think it right would consider the snake a jewel and the wen an ornament.

We want those Democrats who think slavery wrong, to quit voting with those who think it right.   They don't treat it as they do other wrongs—they won't oppose it in the free States, for it is n't there; nor in the slave States, for it is there;—don't want it in politics, for it makes agitation; not in the pulpit, for it is n't religion; not in a tract society, for it makes a fuss—there is no place for its discussion.   Are they quite consistent in this?

If those Democrats really think slavery wrong, they will be much pleased when earnest men in the slave States take up a plan of gradual emancipation, and go to work energetically and very kindly to get rid of the evil.   Now let us test them.   Frank Blair tried it; and he ran for Congress in '58, and got beaten.   Did the Democracy feel bad about it?   I reckon not.   I guess you all flung up your hats and shouted, "Hurrah for the Democracy!"

He went on to speak of the manner in which slavery was treated by the Constitution.   The word "slave" is nowhere used; the supply of slaves was to be prohibited after 1808; they stopped the spread of it in the Territories; seven of the States abolished it.   He argued very conclusively that it was then regarded as an evil which would eventually be got rid of, and that they desired, once rid of it, to have nothing in the Constitution to remind them of it.   The Republicans go back to first principles, and deal with it as a wrong.   Mason, of Virginia, said openly that the framers of our government were anti-slavery.   Hammond, of South Carolina, said, "Washington set this evil example."   Bully Brooks said, "At the time the Constitution was formed, no one supposed slavery would last till now."   We stick to the policy of our fathers.

The Democracy are given to bushwhacking.   After having their errors and misstatements continually thrust in their faces, they pay no heed, but go on howling about Seward and the "irrepressible conflict."   That is bushwhacking.   So with John Brown and Harper's Ferry.   They charge it upon the Republican party, and ignominiously fail in all attempts to substantiate the charge.   Yet they go on with their bushwhacking, the pack in full cry after John Brown. The Democrats had just been whipped in Ohio and Pennsylvania, and seized upon the unfortunate Harper's Ferry affair to influence other elections then pending.   They said to each other, "Jump in; now 's your chance"; and were sorry there were not more killed. But they did n't succeed well.   Let them go on with their howling. They will succeed when by slandering women you get them to love you, and by slandering men you get them to vote for you.

Mr. Lincoln then took up the Massachusetts shoemakers' strike, treating it in a humorous and philosophical manner, and exposing to ridicule the foolish pretense of Senator Douglas—that the strike arose from "this unfortunate sectional warfare."   Mr. Lincoln thanked God that we have a system of labor where there can be a strike. Whatever the pressure, there is a point where the workman may stop.   He did n't pretend to be familiar with the subject of the shoe strike—probably knew as little about it as Senator Douglas himself. Shall we stop making war upon the South? We never have made war upon them. If any one has, he had better go and hang himself and save Virginia the trouble. If you give up your convictions and call slavery right, as they do, you let slavery in upon you—instead of white laborers who can strike, you 'll soon have black laborers who can't strike.

I have heard that in consequence of this " sectional warfare," as Douglas calls it, Senator Mason, of Virginia, had appeared in a suit of homespun. Now, up in New Hampshire, the woolen and cotton mills are all busy, and there is no strike—they are busy making the very goods Senator Mason has quit buying! To carry out his idea, he ought to go barefoot! If that 's the plan, they should begin at the foundation, and adopt the well-known " Georgia costume" of a shirt-collar and pair of spurs.

It reminded him of the man who had a poor, old, lean, bony, spavined horse, with swelled legs. He was asked what he was going to do with such a miserable beast—the poor creature would die. "Do?" said he. "I 'm going to fat him up; don't you see that I have got him seal fat as high as the knees?" Well, they have got the Union dissolved up to the ankle, but no further!

All portions of this Confederacy should act in harmony and with careful deliberation. The Democrats cry " John Brown invasion." We are guiltless of it, but our denial does not satisfy them. Nothing will satisfy them but disinfecting the atmosphere entirely of all opposition to slavery. They have not demanded of us to yield the guards of liberty in our State constitutions, but it will naturally come to that after a while. If we give up to them, we cannot refuse even their utmost request. If slavery is right, it ought to be extended; if not, it ought to be restricted—there is no middle ground. Wrong as we think it, we can afford to let it alone where it of necessity now exists; but we cannot afford to extend it into free territory and around our own homes. Let us stand against it!

The " Union " arrangements are all a humbug—they reverse the scriptural order, calling the righteous, and not sinners, to repentance. Let us not be slandered or intimidated to turn from our duty. Eternal right makes might; as we understand our duty, let us do it!

March 6, 1860.—SPEECH AT NEW HAVEN, CONN.

Mr. President and Fellow-citizens of New Haven: If the Republican party of this nation shall ever have the national house intrusted to its keeping, it will be the duty of that party to attend to all the affairs of national housekeeping. Whatever matters of importance may come up, whatever difficulties may arise, in the way of its administration of the government, that party will then have to attend to: it will then be compelled to attend to other questions besides this question which now assumes an overwhelming importance—the question of slavery. [It is true that in the organization of the Republican party this question of slavery was more important than any other; indeed, so much more important has it become that no other national question can even get a hearing just at present. The old question of tariff—a matter that will remain one of the chief affairs of national housekeeping to all time; the question of the management of financial affairs; the question of the disposition of the public domain: how shall it be managed for the purpose of getting it well settled, and of making there the homes of a free and happy people—these will remain open and require attention for a great while yet, and these questions will have to be attended to by whatever party has the control of the government. Yet just now they cannot even obtain a hearing, and I do not purpose to detain you upon these topics, or what sort of hearing they should have when opportunity shall come. For whether we will or not, the question of slavery is the question, the all-absorbing topic, of the day. It is true that all of us—and by that I mean not the Republican party alone, but the whole American people here and elsewhere—all of us wish this question settled; wish it out of the way. It stands in the way and prevents the adjustment and the giving of necessary attention to other questions of national housekeeping. The people of the whole nation agree that this question ought to be settled, and yet it is not settled; and the reason is that they are not yet agreed how it shall be settled. All wish it done, but some wish one way and some another, and some a third, or fourth, or fifth; different bodies are pulling in different directions, and none of them having a decided majority are able to accomplish the common object.

In the beginning of the year 1854, a new policy was inaugurated with the avowed object and confident promise that it would entirely and forever put an end to the slavery agitation. It was again and again declared that under this policy, when once successfully established, the country would be forever rid of this whole question. Yet under the operation of that policy this agitation has not only not ceased, but it has been constantly augmented. And this, too, although from the day of its introduction its friends, who promised that it would wholly end all agitation, constantly insisted, down to the time that the Lecompton bill was introduced, that it was working admirably, and that its inevitable tendency was to remove the question forever from the politics of the country. Can you call to mind any Democratic speech, made after the repeal of the Missouri Compromise down to the time of the Lecompton bill, in which it was not predicted that the slavery agitation was just at an end; that "the Abolition excitement was played out," "the Kansas question was dead," "they have made the most they can out of this question and it is now forever settled"? But since the Lecompton bill, no Democrat within my experience has ever pretended that he could see the end. That cry has been dropped. They themselves do not pretend now that the agitation of this subject has come to an end yet. The truth is that this question is one of national importance, and we cannot help dealing with it; we must do something about it, whether we will or not. We cannot avoid it; the subject is one we cannot avoid considering; we can no more avoid it than a man can live without eating. It is upon us; it attaches to the body politic as much and as closely as the natural wants attach to our natural bodies. Now I think it important that this matter should be taken up in earnest and really settled. And one way to bring about a true settlement of the question is to understand its true magnitude.

There have been many efforts to settle it. Again and again it has been fondly hoped that it was settled, but every time it breaks out afresh, and more violently than ever. It was settled, our fathers hoped, by the Missouri Compromise, but it did not stay settled. Then the compromises of 1850 were declared to be a full and final settlement of the question. The two great parties, each in national convention, adopted resolutions declaring that the settlement made by the compromise of 1850 was a finality — that it would last forever. Yet how long before it was unsettled again? It broke out again in 1854, and blazed higher and raged more furiously than ever before, and the agitation has not rested since.

These repeated settlements must have some fault about them. There must be some inadequacy in their very nature to the purpose for which they were designed. We can only speculate as to where that fault — that inadequacy is, but we may perhaps profit by past experience.

I think that one of the causes of these repeated failures is that our best and greatest men have greatly underestimated the size of this question. They have constantly brought forward small cures for great sores — plasters too small to cover the wound. That is one reason that all settlements have proved so temporary, so evanescent.

Look at the magnitude of this subject. One sixth of our population, in round numbers — not quite one sixth, and yet more than a seventh — about one sixth of the whole population of the United States, are slaves. The owners of these slaves consider them property. The effect upon the minds of the owners is that of property, and nothing else; it induces them to insist upon all that will favorably affect its value as property, to demand laws and institutions and a public policy that shall increase and secure its value, and make it durable, lasting, and universal. The effect on the minds of the owners is to persuade them that there is no wrong in it. The slave-holder does not like to be considered a mean fellow for holding that species of property, and hence he has to struggle within himself, and sets about arguing himself into the belief that slavery is right. The property influences his mind. The dissenting minister who argued some theological point with one of the established church was always met by the reply, "I can't see it so." He opened the Bible and pointed him to a passage, but the orthodox minister replied, "I can't see it so." Then he showed him a single word — "Can you see that?" "Yes, I see it," was the reply. The dissenter laid a guinea over the word, and asked, "Do you see it now?" So here. Whether the owners of this species of property do really see it as it is, it is not for me to say; but if they do, they see it as it is through two billions of dollars, and that is a pretty thick coating. Certain it is that they do not see it as we see it. Certain it is that this two thousand million of dollars invested in this species of property is all so concentrated that the mind can grasp it at once. This immense pecuniary interest has its influence upon their minds.

But here in Connecticut and at the North slavery does not exist, and we see it through no such medium. To us it appears natural to think that slaves are human beings; men, not property; that some of the things, at least, stated about men in the Declaration of Independence apply to them as well as to us. I say we think, most of us, that this charter of freedom applies to the slave as well as to ourselves; that the class of arguments put forward to batter down that idea are also calculated to break down the very idea of free government, even for white men, and to undermine the very foundations of free society. We think slavery a great moral wrong, and while we do not claim the right to touch it where it exists, we wish to treat it as a wrong in the Territories, where our votes will reach it. We think that a respect for ourselves, a regard for future generations and for the God that made us, require that we put down this wrong where our votes will properly reach it. We think that species of labor an injury to free white men—in short, we think slavery a great moral, social, and political evil, tolerable only because, and so far as, its actual existence makes it necessary to tolerate it, and that beyond that it ought to be treated as a wrong.

Now these two ideas—the property idea that slavery is right and the idea that it is wrong—come into collision, and do actually produce that irrepressible conflict which Mr. Seward has been so roundly abused for mentioning. The two ideas conflict, and must forever conflict.

Again, in its political aspect does anything in any way endanger the perpetuity of this Union but that single thing—slavery? Many of our adversaries are anxious to claim that they are specially devoted to the Union, and take pains to charge upon us hostility to the Union. Now we claim that we are the only true Union men, and we put to them this one proposition: What ever endangered this Union save and except slavery? Did any other thing ever cause a moment's fear? All men must agree that this thing alone has ever endangered the perpetuity of the Union. But if it was threatened by any other influence, would not all men say that the best thing that could be done, if we could not or ought not to destroy it, would be at least to keep it from growing any larger? Can any man believe that the way to save the Union is to extend and increase the only thing that threatens the Union, and to suffer it to grow bigger and bigger?

Whenever this question shall be settled, it must be settled on some philosophical basis. No policy that does not rest upon philosophical public opinion can be permanently maintained. And hence there are but two policies in regard to slavery that can be at all maintained. The first, based on the property view that slavery is right, conforms to that idea throughout, and demands that we shall do everything for it that we ought to do if it were right. We must sweep away all opposition, for opposition to the right is wrong; we must agree that slavery is right, and we must adopt the idea that property has persuaded the owner to believe, that slavery is morally right and socially elevating. This gives a philosophical basis for a permanent policy of encouragement.

The other policy is one that squares with the idea that slavery is wrong, and it consists in doing everything that we ought to do if it is wrong. Now I don't wish to be misunderstood, nor to leave a gap down to be misrepresented, even. I don't mean that we ought to attack it where it exists. To me it seems that if we were to form a government anew, in view of the actual presence of slavery we should find it necessary to frame just such a government as our fathers did: giving to the slaveholder the entire control where the system was established, while we possess the power to restrain it from going outside those limits. From the necessities of the case we should be compelled to form just such a government as our blessed fathers gave us; and surely if they have so made it, that adds another reason why we should let slavery alone where it exists.

If I saw a venomous snake crawling in the road, any man would say I might seize the nearest stick and kill it; but if I found that snake in bed with my children, that would be another question. I might hurt the children more than the snake, and it might bite them. Much more, if I found it in bed with my neighbor's children, and I had bound myself by a solemn compact not to meddle with his children under any circumstances, it would become me to let that particular mode of getting rid of the gentleman alone. But if there was a bed newly made up, to which the children were to be taken, and it was proposed to take a batch of young snakes and put them there with them, I take it no man would say there was any question how I ought to decide!

That is just the case. The new Territories are the newly made bed to which our children are to go, and it lies with the nation to say whether they shall have snakes mixed up with them or not. It does not seem as if there could be much hesitation what our policy should be.

Now I have spoken of a policy based on the idea that slavery is wrong, and a policy based upon the idea that it is right. But an effort has been made for a policy that shall treat it as neither right nor wrong. It is based upon utter indifference. Its leading advocate has said: "I don't care whether it be voted up or down." "It is merely a matter of dollars and cents." "The Almighty has drawn a line across this continent, on one side of which all soil must forever be cultivated by slave labor, and on the other by free." "When the struggle is between the white man and the negro, I am for the white man; when it is between the negro and the crocodile, I am for the negro." Its central idea is indifference. It holds that it makes no more difference to us whether the Territories become free or slave States, than whether my neighbor stocks his farm with horned cattle or puts it into tobacco. All recognize this policy, the plausible sugar-coated name of which is "popular sovereignty."

This policy chiefly stands in the way of a permanent settlement of the question. I believe there is no danger of its becoming the permanent policy of the country, for it is based on a public indifference. There is nobody that "don't care." All the people do care, one way or the other. I do not charge that its author, when he says he "don't care," states his individual opinion; he only expresses his policy for the government. I understand that he has never said, as an individual, whether he thought slavery right or wrong—and he is the only man in the nation that has not. Now such a policy may have a temporary run; it may spring up as necessary to the political prospects of some gentleman—but it is utterly baseless; the people are not indifferent, and it can therefore have no durability or permanence.

But suppose it could! Then it can be maintained only by a public opinion that shall say, "We don't care." There must be a change in public opinion; the public mind must be so far debauched as to square with this policy of caring not at all. The people must come to consider this as "merely a question of dollars and cents," and to believe that in some places the Almighty has made slavery necessarily eternal. This policy can be brought to prevail if the people can be brought round to say honestly, "We don't care"; if not, it can never be maintained. It is for you to say whether that can be done.

You are ready to say it cannot; but be not too fast. Remember what a long stride has been taken since the repeal of the Missouri Compromise! Do you know of any Democrat, of either branch of the party—do you know one who declares that he believes that the Declaration of Independence has any application to the negro? Judge Taney declares that it has not, and Judge Douglas even vilifies me personally and scolds me roundly for saying that the Declaration applies to all men, and that negroes are men. Is there a Democrat here who does not deny that the Declaration applies to a negro? Do any of you know of one? Well, I have tried before perhaps fifty audiences, some larger and some smaller than this, to find one such Democrat, and never yet have I found one who said I did not place him right in that. I must assume that Democrats hold that; and now not one of these Democrats can show that he said that five years ago! I venture to defy the whole party to produce one man that ever uttered the belief that the Declaration did not apply to negroes before the repeal of the Missouri Compromise! Four or five years ago we all thought negroes were men, and that when "all men" were named, negroes were included. But the whole Democratic party has deliberately taken negroes from the class of men and put them in the class of brutes. Turn it as you will, it is simply the truth! Don't be too hasty then in saying that the people cannot be brought to this new doctrine, but note that long stride. One more as long completes the journey from where negroes are estimated as men to where they are estimated as mere brutes—as rightful property!

That saying, "In the struggle between the white man and the negro," etc., which, I know, came from the same source as this policy—that saying marks another step. There is a falsehood wrapped up in that statement. "In the struggle between the white man and the negro," assumes that there is a struggle, in which either the white man must enslave the negro or the negro must enslave the white. There is no such struggle. It is merely an ingenious falsehood to degrade and brutalize the negro. Let each let the other alone, and there is no struggle about it. If it was like two wrecked seamen on a narrow plank, where each must push the other off or drown himself, I would push the negro off—or a white man either; but it is not: the plank is large enough for both. This good earth is plenty broad enough for white man and negro both, and there is no need of either pushing the other off.

So that saying, "In the struggle between the negro and the crocodile," etc., is made up from the idea that down where the crocodile inhabits, a white man can't labor; it must be nothing else but crocodile or negro; if the negro does not, the crocodile must possess the earth; in that case he declares for the negro. The meaning of the whole is just this: As a white man is to a negro, so is a negro to a crocodile; and as the negro may rightfully treat the crocodile, so may the white man rightfully treat the negro. This very dear phrase coined by its author, and so dear that he deliberately repeats it in many speeches, has a tendency to still further brutalize the negro, and to bring public opinion to the point of utter indifference whether men so brutalized are enslaved or not. When that time shall come, if ever, I think that policy to which I refer may prevail. But I hope the good free men of this country will never allow it to come, and until then the policy can never be maintained.

Now, consider the effect of this policy. We in the States are not to care whether freedom or slavery gets the better, but the people in the Territories may care. They are to decide, and they may think what they please; it is a matter of dollars and cents! But are not the people of the Territories detailed from the States? If this feeling of indifference—this absence of moral sense about the question—prevails in the States, will it not be carried into the Territories? Will not every man say, "I don't care; it is nothing to me"? If any one comes that wants slavery, must they not say, "I don't care whether freedom or slavery be voted up or voted down"? It results at last in nationalizing the institution of slavery. Even if fairly carried out, that policy is just as certain to nationalize slavery as the doctrine of Jeff Davis himself. These are only two roads to the same goal, and "popular sovereignty" is just as sure, and almost as short, as the other.

What we want, and all we want, is to have with us the men who think slavery wrong. But those who say they hate slavery, and are opposed to it, but yet act with the Democratic party—where are they? Let us apply a few tests. You say that you think slavery a wrong, but you renounce all attempts to restrain it. Is there anything else that you think wrong, that you are not willing to deal with as a wrong? Why are you so careful, so tender of this one wrong and no other? You will not let us do a single thing as if it was wrong; there is no place where you will allow it to be even called wrong. We must not call it wrong in the free States, because it is not there, and we must not call it wrong in the slave States, because it is there; we must not call it wrong in politics, because that is bringing morality into politics, and we must not call it wrong in the pulpit, because that is bringing politics into religion; we must not bring it into the tract society, or other societies, because those are such unsuitable places, and there is no single place, according to you, where this wrong thing can properly be called wrong.

Perhaps you will plead that if the people of slave States should of themselves set on foot an effort for emancipation, you would wish them success and bid them God-speed. Let us test that! In 1858 the emancipation party of Missouri, with Frank Blair at their head, tried to get up a movement for that purpose; and, having started a party, contested the State. Blair was beaten, apparently if not truly, and when the news came to Connecticut, you, who knew that Frank Blair was taking hold of this thing by the right end, and doing the only thing that you say can properly be done to remove this wrong — did you bow your heads in sorrow because of that defeat? Do you, any of you, know one single Democrat that showed sorrow over that result? Not one! On the contrary, every man threw up his hat, and hallooed at the top of his lungs, "Hooray for Democracy!"

Now, gentleman, the Republicans desire to place this great question of slavery on the very basis on which our fathers placed it, and no other. It is easy to demonstrate that "our fathers who framed this government under which we live" looked on slavery as wrong, and so framed it and everything about it as to square with the idea that it was wrong, so far as the necessities arising from its existence permitted. In forming the Constitution they found the slave-trade existing, capital invested in it, fields depending upon it for labor, and the whole system resting upon the importation of slave labor. They therefore did not prohibit the slave-trade at once, but they gave the power to prohibit it after twenty years. Why was this? What other foreign trade did they treat in that way? Would they have done this if they had not thought slavery wrong?

Another thing was done by some of the same men who framed the Constitution, and afterward adopted as their own act by the first Congress held under that Constitution, of which many of the framers were members — they prohibited the spread of slavery in the Territories. Thus the same men, the framers of the Constitution, cut off the supply and prohibited the spread of slavery; and both acts show conclusively that they considered that the thing was wrong.

If additional proof is wanting, it can be found in the phraseology of the Constitution. When men are framing a supreme law and chart of government to secure blessings and prosperity to untold generations yet to come, they use language as short and direct and plain as can be found to express their meaning. In all matters but this of slavery the framers of the Constitution used the very clearest, shortest, and most direct language. But the Constitution alludes to slavery three times without mentioning it once! The language used becomes ambiguous, roundabout, and mystical. They speak of the "immigration of persons," and mean the importation of slaves, but do not say so. In establishing a basis of representation they say "all other persons," when they mean to say slaves. Why did they not use the shortest phrase? In providing for the return of fugitives they say "persons held to service or labor." If they had said "slaves," it would have been plainer and less liable to misconstruction. Why did n't they do it? We cannot doubt that it was done on purpose. Only one reason is possible, and that is supplied us by one of the framers of the Constitution—and it is not possible for man to conceive of any other. They expected and desired that the system would come to an end, and meant that when it did the Constitution should not show that there ever had been a slave in this good free country of ours.

I will dwell on that no longer. I see the signs of the approaching triumph of the Republicans in the bearing of their political adversaries. A great deal of this war with us nowadays is mere bushwhacking. At the battle of Waterloo, when Napoleon's cavalry had charged again and again upon the unbroken squares of British infantry, at last they were giving up the attempt, and going off in disorder, when some of the officers, in mere vexation and complete despair, fired their pistols at those solid squares. The Democrats are in that sort of extreme desperation; it is nothing else. I will take up a few of these arguments.

There is "the irrepressible conflict." How they rail at Seward for that saying! They repeat it constantly; and although the proof has been thrust under their noses again and again that almost every good man since the formation of our government has uttered that same sentiment, from General Washington, who "trusted that we should yet have a confederacy of free States," with Jefferson, Jay, Monroe, down to the latest days, yet they refuse to notice that at all, and persist in railing at Seward for saying it. Even Roger A. Pryor, editor of the Richmond "Enquirer," uttered the same sentiment in almost the same language, and yet so little offense did it give the Democrats that he was sent for to Washington to edit the "States"—the Douglas organ there, while Douglas goes into hydrophobia and spasms of rage because Seward dared to repeat it. That is what I call bushwhacking—a sort of argument that they must know any child can see through.

Another is John Brown! You stir up insurrections; you invade the South! John Brown! Harper's Ferry! Why, John Brown was not a Republican! You have never implicated a single Republican in that Harper's Ferry enterprise. We tell you if any member of the Republican party is guilty in that matter, you know it or you do not know it. If you do know it, you are inexcusable not to designate the man and prove the fact. If you do not know it, you are inexcusable to assert it, and especially to persist in the assertion after you have tried and failed to make the proof. You need not be told that persisting in a charge which one does not know to be true is simply malicious slander. Some of you admit that no Republican designedly aided or encouraged the Harper's Ferry affair; but still insist that our doctrines and declarations necessarily lead to such results. We do not believe it. We know we hold to no doctrines and make no declarations which were not held to and made by our fathers who framed the government under which we live, and we cannot see how declarations that were patriotic when they made them are villainous when we make them. You never dealt fairly by us in relation to that affair—and I will say frankly that I know of nothing in your character that should lead us to suppose that you would. You had just been soundly thrashed in elections in several States, and others were soon to come. You rejoiced at the occasion, and only were troubled that there were not three times as many killed in the affair. You were in evident glee; there was no sorrow for the killed nor for the peace of Virginia disturbed; you were rejoicing that by charging Republicans with this thing you might get an advantage of us in New York and the other States. You pulled that string as tightly as you could, but your very generous and worthy expectations were not quite fulfilled. Each Republican knew that the charge was a slander as to himself at least, and was not inclined by it to cast his vote in your favor. It was mere bushwhacking, because you had nothing else to do. You are still on that track, and I say, Go on! If you think you can slander a woman into loving you, or a man into voting for you, try it till you are satisfied.

Another specimen of this bushwhacking—that "shoe strike." Now be it understood that I do not pretend to know all about the matter. I am merely going to speculate a little about some of its phases, and at the outset I am glad to see that a system of labor prevails in New England under which laborers can strike when they want to, where they are not obliged to work under all circumstances, and are not tied down and obliged to labor whether you pay them or not! I like the system which lets a man quit when he wants to, and wish it might prevail everywhere. One of the reasons why I am opposed to slavery is just here. What is the true condition of the laborer? I take it that it is best for all to leave each man free to acquire property as fast as he can. Some will get wealthy. I don't believe in a law to prevent a man from getting rich; it would do more harm than good. So while we do not propose any war upon capital, we do wish to allow the humblest man an equal chance to get rich with everybody else. When one starts poor, as most do in the race of life, free society is such that he knows he can better his condition; he knows that there is no fixed condition of labor for his whole life. I am not ashamed to confess that twenty-five years ago I was a hired laborer, mauling rails, at work on a flatboat—just what might happen to any poor man's son. I want every man to have the chance—and I believe a black man is entitled to it—in which he can better his condition—when he may look forward and hope to be a hired laborer this year and the next, work for himself afterward, and finally to hire men to work for him. That is the true system. Up here in New England you have a soil that scarcely sprouts black-eyed beans, and yet where will you find wealthy men so wealthy, and poverty so rarely in extremity? There is not another such place on earth! I desire that if you get too thick here, and find it hard to better your condition on this soil, you may have a chance to strike and go somewhere else, where you may not be degraded, nor have your family corrupted by forced rivalry with negro slaves. I want you to have a clean bed and no snakes in it! Then you can better your condition, and so it may go on and on in one ceaseless round so long as man exists on the face of the earth.

Now to come back to this shoe strike. If, as the senator from Illinois asserts, this is caused by withdrawal of Southern votes, consider briefly how you will meet the difficulty. You have done nothing, and have protested that you have done nothing, to injure the South; and yet to get back the shoe trade, you must leave off doing something that you are now doing. What is it? You must stop thinking slavery wrong. Let your institutions be wholly changed; let your State constitutions be subverted; glorify slavery; and so you will get back the shoe trade — for what? You have brought owned labor with it to compete with your own labor, to underwork you, and degrade you. Are you ready to get back the trade on these terms?

But the statement is not correct. You have not lost that trade; orders were never better than now. Senator Mason, a Democrat, comes into the Senate in homespun, a proof that the dissolution of the Union has actually begun. But orders are the same. Your factories have not struck work, neither those where they make anything for coats, nor for pants, nor for shirts, nor for ladies' dresses. Mr. Mason has not reached the manufacturers who ought to have made him a coat and pants. To make his proof good for anything, he should have come into the Senate barefoot.

Another bushwhacking contrivance — simply that, nothing else! I find a good many people who are very much concerned about the loss of Southern trade. Now, either these people are sincere, or they are not. I will speculate a little about that. If they are sincere, and are moved by any real danger of the loss of the Southern trade, they will simply get their names on the white list, and then instead of persuading Republicans to do likewise, they will be glad to keep you away. Don't you see they thus shut off competition? They would not be whispering around to Republicans to come in and share the profits with them. But if they are not sincere, and are merely trying to fool Republicans out of their votes, they will grow very anxious about your pecuniary prospects; they are afraid you are going to get broken up and ruined; they did not care about Democratic votes — oh, no, no, no! You must judge which class those belong to whom you meet. I leave it to you to determine from the facts.

Let us notice some more of the stale charges against Republicans. You say we are sectional. We deny it. That makes an issue; and the burden of proof is upon you. You produce your proof; and what is it? Why, that our party has no existence in your section — gets no votes in your section. The fact is substantially true; but does it prove the issue? If it does, then in case we should, without change of principle, begin to get votes in your section, we should thereby cease to be sectional. You cannot escape this conclusion; and yet, are you willing to abide by it? If you are, you will probably soon find that we have ceased to be sectional, for we shall get votes in your section this very year. The fact that we get no votes in your section is a fact of your making, and not of ours. And if there be fault in that fact, that fault is primarily yours, and remains so until you show that we repel you by some wrong principle or practice. If we do repel you by any wrong principle or practice, the fault is ours; but this brings you to where you ought to have started — to a discussion of the right or wrong of our principle. If our principle, put in practice, would wrong your section for the benefit of ours, or for any other object, then our principle and we with it, are sectional, and are justly opposed and denounced as such. Meet us, then, on the question of whether our principle, put in practice, would wrong your section; and so meet it as if it were possible that something may be said on our side. Do you accept the challenge? No? Then you really believe that the principle which our fathers who framed the government under which we live thought so clearly right as to adopt it, and indorse it again and again, upon their official oaths, is, in fact, so clearly wrong as to demand your condemnation without a moment's consideration.

Some of you delight to flaunt in our faces the warning against sectional parties given by Washington in his Farewell Address. Less than eight years before Washington gave that warning, he had, as President of the United States, approved and signed an act of Congress enforcing the prohibition of slavery in the Northwestern Territory, which act embodied the policy of government upon that subject up to and at the very moment he penned that warning; and about one year after he penned it, he wrote Lafayette that he considered that prohibition a wise measure, expressing in the same connection his hope that we should some time have a confederacy of free States.

Bearing this in mind, and seeing that sectionalism has since arisen upon this same subject, is that warning a weapon in your hands against us, or in our hands against you? Could Washington himself speak, would he cast the blame of that sectionalism upon us who sustain his policy, or upon you who repudiate it? We respect that warning of Washington, and we commend it to you, together with his example pointing to the right application of it.

But you say you are conservative — eminently conservative — while we are revolutionary, destructive, or something of that sort. What is conservatism? Is it not adherence to the old and tried against the new and untried? We stick to, contend for, the identical old policy on the point in controversy which was adopted by our fathers who framed the government under which we live; while you with one accord reject, and scout, and spit upon that old policy, and insist upon substituting something new. True, you disagree among yourselves as to what that substitute shall be; you have considerable variety of new propositions and plans, but you are unanimous in rejecting and denouncing the old policy of the fathers. Some of you are for reviving the foreign slave-trade; some for a congressional slave code for the Territories; some for Congress forbidding the Territories to prohibit slavery within their limits; some for maintaining slavery in the Territories through the judiciary; some for the "great principle" that if one man would enslave another, no third man should object, fantastically called "popular sovereignty"; but never a man among you in favor of Federal prohibition of slavery in Federal Territories according to the practice of our fathers who framed the government under which we live. Not one of all your various plans can show a precedent or an advocate in the century within which our government originated. And yet you draw yourselves up and say, " We are eminently conservative."

It is exceedingly desirable that all parts of this great Confederacy shall be at peace and in harmony one with another. Let us Republicans do our part to have it so. Even though much provoked, let us do nothing through passion and ill temper. Even though the Southern people will not so much as listen to us, let us calmly consider their demands, and yield to them if, in our deliberate view of our duty, we possibly can. Judging by all they say and do, and by the subject and nature of their controversy with us, let us determine, if we can, what will satisfy them.

Will they be satisfied if the Territories be unconditionally surrendered to them ? We know they will not. In all their present complaints against us the Territories are scarcely mentioned. Invasions and insurrections are the rage now. Will it satisfy them if in the future we have nothing to do with invasions and insurrections ? We know it will not. We so know because we know we never have had anything to do with invasions and insurrections; and yet this total abstaining does not exempt us from the charge and the denunciation.

The question recurs, What will satisfy them ? Simply this: we must not only let them alone, but we must somehow convince them that we do let them alone. This we know by experience is no easy task. We have been so trying to convince them from the very beginning of our organization, but with no success. In all our platforms and speeches we have constantly protested our purpose to let them alone; but this has had no tendency to convince them. Alike unavailing to convince them is the fact that they have never detected a man of us in any attempt to disturb them.

These natural and apparently adequate means all failing, what will convince them ? This, and this only : cease to call slavery wrong, and join them in calling it right. And this must be done thoroughly —done in acts as well as in words. Silence will not be tolerated— we must place ourselves avowedly with them. Douglas's new sedition law must be enacted and enforced, suppressing all declarations that slavery is wrong, whether made in politics, in presses, in pulpits, or in private. We must arrest and return their fugitive slaves with greedy pleasure. We must pull down our free-State constitutions. The whole atmosphere must be disinfected of all taint of opposition to slavery before they will cease to believe that all their troubles proceed from us. So long as we call slavery wrong, whenever a slave runs away they will overlook the obvious fact that he ran because he was oppressed, and declare that he was stolen off. Whenever a master cuts his slaves with the lash, and they cry out under it, he will overlook the obvious fact that the negroes cry out because they are hurt, and insist that they were put up to it by some rascally Abolitionist.

I am quite aware that they do not state their case precisely in this way. Most of them would probably say to us: "Let us alone; do nothing to us, and say what you please about slavery." But we do let them alone,—have never disturbed them,—so that, after all, it is what we say which dissatisfies them. They will continue to accuse us of doing, until we cease saying.

I am also aware that they have not as yet in terms demanded the overthrow of our free-State constitutions. Yet those constitutions declare the wrong of slavery with more solemn emphasis than do all other sayings against it; and when all these other sayings shall have been silenced, the overthrow of these constitutions will be demanded, and nothing be left to resist the demand. It is nothing to the contrary that they do not demand the whole of this just now. Demanding what they do, and for the reason they do, they can voluntarily stop nowhere short of this consummation. Holding as they do that slavery is morally right and socially elevating, they cannot cease to demand a full national recognition of it, as a legal right and a social blessing.

Nor can we justifiably withhold this on any ground save our conviction that slavery is wrong. If slavery is right, all words, acts, laws, and constitutions against it are themselves wrong, and should be silenced and swept away. If it is right, we cannot justly object to its nationality—its universality; if it is wrong, they cannot justly insist upon its extension—its enlargement. All they ask we could readily grant, if we thought slavery right; all we ask they could as readily grant, if they thought it wrong. Their thinking it right, and our thinking it wrong, is the precise fact upon which depends the whole controversy. Thinking it right, as they do, they are not to blame for desiring its full recognition as being right; but thinking it wrong, as we do, can we yield to them? Can we cast our votes with their view, and against our own? In view of our moral, social, and political responsibilities, can we do this?

Wrong as we think slavery is, we can yet afford to let it alone where it is, because that much is due to the necessity arising from its actual presence in the nation; but can we, while our votes will prevent it, allow it to spread into the national Territories and to overrun us here in these free States?

If our sense of duty forbids this, then let us stand by our duty fearlessly and effectively. Let us be diverted by none of those sophistical contrivances wherewith we are so industriously plied and belabored—contrivances such as groping for some middle ground between the right and the wrong; vain as the search for a man who should be neither a living man nor a dead man; such as a policy of "don't care" on a question about which all true men do care; such as Union appeals beseeching true Union men to yield to Disunionists, reversing the divine rule, and calling, not the sinners, but the righteous to repentance; such as invocations to Washington, imploring men to unsay what Washington did.

Neither let us be slandered from our duty by false accusations against us, nor frightened from it by menaces of destruction to the government, nor of dungeons to ourselves. Let us have faith that right makes might; and in that faith let us to the end dare to do our duty as we understand it.

March 9, 1860.—ABSTRACT OF SPEECH AT NORWICH, CONNECTICUT.

Whether we will or not, the question of slavery is the question, the all-absorbing topic, of the day. It is true that all of us—and by that I mean, not the Republican party alone, but the whole American people, here and elsewhere—all of us wish the question settled—wish it out of the way.

It stands in the way and prevents the adjustment and the giving of necessary attention to other questions of national housekeeping. The people of the whole nation agree that this question ought to be settled, and yet it is not settled. And the reason is that they are not yet agreed how it shall·be settled.

Again and again it has been fondly hoped that it was settled, but every time it breaks out afresh and more violently than ever. It was settled, our fathers hoped, by the Missouri Compromise, but it did not stay settled. Then the compromise of 1850 was declared to be a full and final settlement of the question. The two great parties, each in national convention, adopted resolutions declaring that the settlement made by the compromises of 1850 was a finality—that it would last forever. Yet how long before it was unsettled again! It broke out again in 1854, and blazed higher and raged more furiously than ever before, and the agitation has not rested since.

These repeated settlements must have some fault about them. There must be some inadequacy in their very nature to the purpose for which they were designed. We can only speculate as to where that fault—that inadequacy is, but we may perhaps profit by past experience.

I think that one of the causes of these repeated failures is that our best and greatest men have greatly underestimated the size of this question. They have constantly brought forward small cures for great sores—plasters too small to cover the wound. This is one reason that all settlements have proved so temporary, so evanescent.

Look at the magnitude of this subject. About one sixth of the whole population of the United States are slaves. The owners of the slaves consider them property. The effect upon the minds of the owners is that of property, and nothing else—it induces them to insist upon all that will favorably affect its value as property, to demand laws and institutions and a public policy that shall increase and secure its value, and make it durable, lasting, and universal. The effect on the minds of the owners is to persuade them that there is no wrong in it.

But here in Connecticut and at the North slavery does not exist, and we see it through no such medium. To us it appears natural to think that slaves are human beings; men, not property; that some of the things, at least, stated about men in the Declaration of Independence apply to them as well as to us. We think slavery a great moral wrong; and while we do not claim the right to touch it where it exists, we wish to treat it as a wrong in the Territories where our votes will reach it. Now these two ideas, the property idea that slavery is right, and the idea that it is wrong, come into collision, and do actually produce that irrepressible conflict which Mr. Seward has been so roundly abused for mentioning. The two ideas conflict, and must conflict.

There are but two policies in regard to slavery that can be at all maintained. The first, based upon the property view that slavery is right, conforms to the idea throughout, and demands that we shall do everything for it that we ought to do if it were right. The other policy is one that squares with the idea that slavery is wrong, and it consists in doing everything that we ought to do if it is wrong. I don't mean that we ought to attack it where it exists. To me it seems that if we were to form a government anew, in view of the actual presence of slavery we should find it necessary to frame just such a government as our fathers did — giving to the slaveholder the entire control where the system was established, while we possessed the power to restrain it from going outside those limits.

Now I have spoken of a policy based upon the idea that slavery is wrong, and a policy based upon the idea that it is right. But an effort has been made for a policy that shall treat it as neither right nor wrong. Its central idea is indifference. It holds that it makes no more difference to me whether the Territories become free or slave States than whether my neighbor stocks his farm with horned cattle or puts it into tobacco. All recognize this policy, the plausible, sugar-coated name of which is " popular sovereignty."

Mr. Lincoln showed up the fallacy of this policy at length, and then made a manly vindication of the principles of the Republican party, urging the necessity of the union of all elements to free our country from its present rule, and closed with an eloquent exhortation for each and every one to do his duty without regard to the sneers and slanders of our political opponents.

March 16, 1860.— LETTER TO ———.

As to your kind wishes for myself, allow me to say I cannot enter the ring on the money basis — first, because in the main it is wrong; and secondly, I have not and cannot get the money.

I say, in the main, the use of money is wrong; but for certain objects in a political contest, the use of some is both right and indispensable. With me, as with yourself, the long struggle has been one of great pecuniary loss.

I now distinctly say this — if you shall be appointed a delegate to Chicago, I will furnish one hundred dollars to bear the expenses of the trip.   Your friend, as ever,

A. LINCOLN.

March 17, 1860.— LETTER TO J. W. SOMERS.

SPRINGFIELD, March 17, 1860.

JAMES W. SOMERS, Esq.

My dear Sir: Reaching home three days ago, I found your letter of February 26th.

Considering your difficulty of hearing, I think you had better settle in Chicago, if, as you say, a good man already in fair practice there will take you into partnership. If you had not that difficulty, I still should think it an even balance whether you would not better remain in Chicago, with such a chance for a copartnership.

If I went West, I think I would go to Kansas,—to Leavenworth or Atchison. Both of them are, and will continue to be, fine growing places.

I believe I have said all I can, and I have said it with the deepest interest for your welfare.   Yours truly,

A. LINCOLN.

March 17, 1860.—LETTER TO E. STAFFORD.

SPRINGFIELD, ILLINOIS, March 17, 1860.

E. STAFFORD, Esq.

Dear Sir: Reaching home on the 14th instant, I found yours of the 1st. Thanking you very sincerely for your kind purposes toward me, I am compelled to say the money part of the arrangement you propose is, with me, an impossibility. I could not raise ten thousand dollars if it would save me from the fate of John Brown. Nor have my friends, so far as I know, yet reached the point of staking any money on my chances of success. I wish I could tell you better things, but it is even so.   Yours very truly,

A. LINCOLN.

March 24, 1860.—LETTER TO SAMUEL GALLOWAY.

CHICAGO, March 24, 1860.

HON. SAMUEL GALLOWAY.

My dear Sir: I am here attending a trial in court. Before leaving home I received your kind letter of the 15th. Of course I am gratified to know I have friends in Ohio who are disposed to give me the highest evidence of their friendship and confidence. Mr. Parrott, of the legislature, had written me to the same effect. If I have any chance, it consists mainly in the fact that the whole opposition would vote for me, if nominated. (I don't mean to include the pro-slavery opposition of the South, of course.) My name is new in the field, and I suppose I am not the first choice of a very great many. Our policy, then, is to give no offense to others—leave them in a mood to come to us if they shall be compelled to give up their first love. This, too, is dealing justly with all, and leaving us in a mood to support heartily whoever shall be nominated. I believe I have once before told you that I especially wish to do no ungenerous thing toward Governor Chase, because he gave us his sympathy in 1858 when scarcely any other distinguished man did. Whatever you may do for me, consistently with these suggestions, will be appreciated and gratefully remembered. Please write me again.

Yours very truly,   A. LINCOLN.

April 6, 1860.—LETTER TO C. F. McNEIL.

SPRINGFIELD, April 6, 1860.

C. F. McNEIL, Esq.

Dear Sir: Reaching home yesterday, I found yours of the 23d March, inclosing a slip from "The Middleport Press." It is not true that I ever charged anything for a political speech in my life; but this much is true: Last October I was requested by letter to deliver some sort of speech in Mr. Beecher's church, in Brooklyn—two hundred dollars being offered in the first letter. I wrote that I could do it in February, provided they would take a political speech if I could find time to get up no other. They agreed; and subsequently I informed them the speech would have to be a political one. When I reached New York, I for the first time learned that the place was changed to "Cooper Institute." I made the speech, and left for New Hampshire, where I have a son at school, neither asking for pay, nor having any offered me. Three days after a check for two hundred dollars was sent to me at New Hampshire; and I took it, and did not know it was wrong. My understanding now is—though I knew nothing of it at the time—that they did charge for admittance to the Cooper Institute, and that they took in more than twice two hundred dollars.

I have made this explanation to you as a friend; but I wish no explanation made to our enemies. What they want is a squabble and a fuss, and that they can have if we explain; and they cannot have it if we don't.

When I returned through New York from New England, I was told by the gentlemen who sent me the check that a drunken vagabond in the club, having learned something about the two hundred dollars, made the exhibition out of which "The Herald" manufactured the article quoted by "The Press" of your town.

My judgment is, and therefore my request is, that you give no denial and no explanation.

Thanking you for your kind interest in the matter, I remain,

Yours truly,   A. LINCOLN.

April 14, 1860.—LETTER TO ———.

SPRINGFIELD, ILLINOIS, April 14, 1860.

My dear Sir: Reaching home last night, I found your letter of the 7th. You know I was in New England. Some of the acquaintances I made while there write to me since the election that the close vote in Connecticut and the *quasi* defeat in Rhode Island are a drawback upon the prospects of Governor Seward; and Trumbull writes Dubois to the same effect. Do not mention this as coming from me. Both those States are safe enough for us in the fall. I see by the despatches that since you wrote Kansas has appointed delegates and instructed them for Seward. Do not stir them up to anger, but come along to the convention, and I will do as I said about expenses.

Yours as ever,   A. LINCOLN.

May 12, 1860.— LETTER TO EDWARD WALLACE.

SPRINGFIELD, ILLINOIS, May 12, 1860.

DR. EDWARD WALLACE.

My dear Sir: Your brother, Dr. W. S. Wallace, shows me a letter of yours in which you request him to inquire if you may use a letter of mine to you in which something is said upon the tariff question. I do not precisely remember what I did say in that letter, but I presume I said nothing substantially different from what I shall say now.

In the days of Henry Clay, I was a Henry-Clay-tariff man, and my views have undergone no material change upon that subject. I now think the tariff question ought not to be agitated in the Chicago convention, but that all should be satisfied on that point with a presidential candidate whose antecedents give assurance that he would neither seek to force a tariff law by executive influence, nor yet to arrest a reasonable one by a veto or otherwise. Just such a candidate I desire shall be put in nomination. I really have no objection to these views being publicly known, but I do wish to thrust no letter before the public now upon any subject. Save me from the appearance of obtrusion, and I do not care who sees this or my former letter.   Yours very truly,

A. LINCOLN.

May 19, 1860.—REPLY TO THE COMMITTEE SENT BY THE CHICAGO CONVENTION TO INFORM MR. LINCOLN OF HIS NOMINATION FOR PRESIDENT.

Mr. Chairman and Gentlemen of the Committee: I tender to you, and through you to the Republican National Convention, and all the people represented in it, my profoundest thanks for the high honor done me, which you now formally announce. Deeply and even painfully sensible of the great responsibility which is inseparable from this high honor—a responsibility which I could almost wish had fallen upon some one of the far more eminent men and experienced statesmen whose distinguished names were before the convention—I shall, by your leave, consider more fully the resolutions of the convention, denominated the platform, and without any unnecessary or unreasonable delay respond to you, Mr. Chairman, in writing, not doubting that the platform will be found satisfactory, and the nomination gratefully accepted.

And now I will not longer defer the pleasure of taking you, and each of you, by the hand.

May 21, 1860.—LETTER TO J. R. GIDDINGS.

SPRINGFIELD, ILLINOIS, May 21, 1860.

HON. J. R. GIDDINGS.

My good Friend: Your very kind and acceptable letter of the 19th was duly handed me by Mr. Tuck. It is indeed most grateful to my feelings that the responsible position assigned me comes without conditions, save only such honorable ones as are fairly implied. I am not wanting in the purpose, though I may fail in the strength, to maintain my freedom from bad influences. Your letter comes to my aid in this point most opportunely. May the Almighty grant that the cause of truth, justice, and humanity shall in no wise suffer at my hands.

Mrs. Lincoln joins me in sincere wishes for your health, happiness, and long life.

A. LINCOLN.

May 23, 1860.—LETTER TO GEORGE ASHMUN AND OTHERS.

SPRINGFIELD, ILLINOIS, May 23, 1860.

HON. GEORGE ASHMUN,
President of the Republican National Convention.

Sir: I accept the nomination tendered me by the convention over which you presided, and of which I am formally apprised in the letter of yourself and others, acting as a committee of the convention for that purpose.

The declaration of principles and sentiments which accompanies your letter meets my approval; and it shall be my care not to violate or disregard it in any part.

Imploring the assistance of Divine Providence, and with due regard to the views and feelings of all who were represented in the convention—to the rights of all the States and Territories and people of the nation; to the inviolability of the Constitution; and the perpetual union, harmony, and prosperity of all—I am most happy to coöperate for the practical success of the principles declared by the convention.

Your obliged friend and fellow-citizen, A. LINCOLN.

PLATFORM OF THE REPUBLICAN NATIONAL CONVENTION HELD IN CHICAGO, ILLINOIS, MAY 16–18, 1860.

Resolved, That we, the delegated representatives of the Republican electors of the United States, in convention assembled, in the discharge of the duty we owe to our constituents and our country, unite in the following declarations:

1. That the history of the nation during the last four years has fully established the propriety and necessity of the organization and perpetuation of the Republican party; and that the causes which called it into existence are permanent in their nature, and now, more than ever before, demand its peaceful and constitutional triumph.

2. That the maintenance of the principles promulgated in the Declaration of Independence and embodied in the Federal Constitution is essential to the preservation of our Republican institutions, and that the Federal Constitution, the rights of the States, and the union of the States, must and shall be preserved.

3. That to the union of the States this nation owes its unprecedented increase in population, its surprising development of material resources, its rapid augmentation of wealth, its happiness at home, and its honor abroad; and we hold in abhorrence all schemes for disunion, come from

whatever source they may. And we congratulate the country that no Republican member of Congress has uttered or countenanced the threats of disunion so often made by Democratic members without rebuke and with applause from their political associates; and we denounce those threats of disunion, in case of a popular overthrow of their ascendancy, as denying the vital principles of a free government, and as an avowal of contemplated treason, which it is the imperative duty of an indignant people sternly to rebuke and forever silence.

4. That the maintenance inviolate of the rights of the States, and especially the right of each State to order and control its own domestic institutions according to its own judgment exclusively, is essential to that balance of power on which the perfection and endurance of our political fabric depends; and we denounce the lawless invasion by armed force of the soil of any State or Territory, no matter under what pretext, as among the gravest of crimes.

5. That the present Democratic administration has far exceeded our worst apprehensions in its measureless subserviency to the exactions of a sectional interest, as especially evinced in its desperate exertions to force the infamous Lecompton constitution upon the protesting people of Kansas; in construing the personal relation between master and servant to involve an unqualified property in persons; in its attempted enforcement everywhere, on land and sea, through the intervention of Congress and of the Federal courts, of the extreme pretensions of a purely local interest; and in its general and unvarying abuse of the power intrusted to it by a confiding people.

6. That the people justly view with alarm the reckless extravagance which pervades every department of the Federal Government; that a return to rigid economy and accountability is indispensable to arrest the systematic plunder of the public treasury by favored partizans; while the recent startling developments of frauds and corruptions at the Federal metropolis show that an entire change of administration is imperatively demanded.

7. That the new dogma that the Constitution, of its own force, carries slavery into any or all of the Territories of the United States, is a dangerous political heresy, at variance with the explicit provisions of that instrument itself, with contemporaneous exposition, and with legislative and judicial precedent; is revolutionary in its tendency, and subversive of the peace and harmony of the country.

8. That the normal condition of all the territory of the United States is that of freedom; that as our Republican fathers, when they had abolished slavery in all our national territory, ordained that "no person should be deprived of life, liberty, or property without due process of law," it becomes our duty, by legislation, whenever such legislation is necessary, to maintain this provision of the Constitution against all attempts to violate it; and we deny the authority of Congress, of a territorial legislature, or of any individuals, to give legal existence to slavery in any Territory of the United States.

9. That we brand the recent reopening of the African slave-trade, under the cover of our national flag, aided by perversions of judicial power, as a crime against humanity and a burning shame to our country and age; and we call upon Congress to take prompt and efficient measures for the total and final suppression of that execrable traffic.

10. That in the recent vetoes, by their Federal governors, of the acts of the legislatures of Kansas and Nebraska prohibiting slavery in those Territories, we find a practical illustration of the boasted Democratic principle of non-intervention and popular sovereignty embodied in the Kansas-Nebraska bill, and a demonstration of the deception and fraud involved therein.

11. That Kansas should, of right, be immediately admitted as a State under the constitution recently formed and adopted by her people, and accepted by the House of Representatives.

12. That while providing revenue for the support of the General Government by duties upon imports, sound policy requires such an adjustment of these imposts as to encourage the development of the industrial interests of the whole country; and we commend that policy of national exchanges which secures to the working-men liberal wages, to agriculture remunerating prices, to mechanics and manufacturers an adequate reward for their skill, labor, and enterprise, and to the nation commercial prosperity and independence.

13. That we protest against any sale or alienation to others of the public lands held by actual settlers, and against any view of the free-homestead policy which regards the settlers as paupers or suppliants for public bounty; and we demand the passage by Congress of the complete and satisfactory homestead measure which has already passed the House.

14. That the national Republican party is opposed to any change in our naturalization laws, or any State legislation by which the rights of citizenship hitherto accorded to immigrants from foreign lands shall be abridged or impaired; and in favor of giving a full and efficient protection to the rights of all classes of citizens, whether native or naturalized, both at home and abroad.

15. That appropriations by Congress for river and harbor improvements of a national character, required for the accommodation and security of an existing commerce, are authorized by the Constitution and justified by the obligation of government to protect the lives and property of its citizens.

16. That a railroad to the Pacific Ocean is imperatively demanded by the interests of the whole country; that the Federal Government ought to render immediate and efficient aid in its construction; and that, as preliminary thereto, a daily overland mail should be promptly established.

17. Finally, having thus set forth our distinctive principles and views, we invite the coöperation of all citizens, however differing on other questions, who substantially agree with us in their affirmance and support.

May 26, 1860.— LETTER TO E. B. WASHBURNE.

SPRINGFIELD, ILLINOIS, May 26, 1860.

HON. E. B. WASHBURNE.

My dear Sir: I have several letters from you written since the nomination, but till now have found no moment to say a word by way of answer. Of course I am glad that the nomination is well received by our friends, and I sincerely thank you for so informing me. So far as I can learn, the nominations start well everywhere; and, if they get no back-set, it would seem as if they are going through. I hope you will write often; and as you write more rapidly than I do, don't make your letters so short as mine.

Yours very truly,   A. LINCOLN.

May 26, 1860.—LETTER TO S. P. CHASE.

SPRINGFIELD, ILLINOIS, May 26, 1860.

HON. S. P. CHASE.

My dear Sir: It gave me great pleasure to receive yours mistakenly dated May 17. Holding myself the humblest of all whose names were before the convention, I feel in especial need of the assistance of all; and I am glad — very glad — of the indication that you stand ready. It is a great consolation that so nearly all — all except Mr. Bates and Mr. Clay, I believe — of those distinguished and able men are already in high position to do service in the common cause.   Your obedient servant,

                                        A. LINCOLN.

[June ?] 1860.—FORM OF REPLY PREPARED BY MR. LINCOLN, WITH WHICH HIS PRIVATE SECRETARY WAS INSTRUCTED TO ANSWER A NUMEROUS CLASS OF LETTERS IN THE CAMPAIGN OF 1860.

(*Doctrine.*)

                    SPRINGFIELD, ILLINOIS, ———, 1860.

Dear Sir: Your letter to Mr. Lincoln of ———, and by which you seek to obtain his opinions on certain political points, has been received by him. He has received others of a similar character, but he also has a greater number of the exactly opposite character. The latter class beseech him to write nothing whatever upon any point of political doctrine. They say his positions were well known when he was nominated, and that he must not now embarrass the canvass by undertaking to shift or modify them. He regrets that he cannot oblige all, but you perceive it is impossible for him to do so.

        Yours, etc.,   JNO. G. NICOLAY.

June [1 ?], 1860.—SHORT AUTOBIOGRAPHY WRITTEN AT THE REQUEST OF A FRIEND TO USE IN PREPARING A POPULAR CAMPAIGN BIOGRAPHY IN THE ELECTION OF 1860.

Abraham Lincoln was born February 12, 1809, then in Hardin, now in the more recently formed county of La Rue, Kentucky. His father, Thomas, and grandfather, Abraham, were born in Rockingham County, Virginia, whither their ancestors had come from Berks County, Pennsylvania. His lineage has been traced no farther back than this. The family were originally Quakers, though in later times they have fallen away from the peculiar habits of that people. The grandfather, Abraham, had four brothers — Isaac, Jacob, John, and Thomas. So far as known, the descendants of Jacob and John are still in Virginia. Isaac went to a place near where Virginia, North Carolina, and Tennessee join; and his descendants are in that region. Thomas came to Kentucky, and after many years died there, whence his descendants went to Missouri. Abraham, grandfather of the subject of this sketch, came to Kentucky, and was killed by Indians about the year 1784. He left a widow, three sons, and two daughters. The eldest son, Mordecai, remained in Kentucky till late in life, when he removed to Hancock County, Illinois, where soon after he died, and where several of his descendants still remain. The second son, Josiah, removed at an early day to a place on Blue River, now within Hancock County, Indiana, but no recent information of him or his family has been obtained. The eldest sister, Mary, married Ralph Crume, and some of her descendants are now known to be in Breckenridge County, Kentucky. The second sister, Nancy, married William Brumfield, and her family are not known to have left Kentucky, but there is no recent information from them. Thomas, the youngest son, and father of the present subject, by the early death of his father, and very narrow circumstances of his mother, even in childhood was a wandering laboring-boy, and grew up literally without education. He never did more in the way of writing than to bunglingly write his own name. Before he was grown he passed one year as a hired hand with his uncle Isaac on Watauga, a branch of the Holston River. Getting back into Kentucky, and having reached his twenty-eighth year, he married Nancy Hanks— mother of the present subject — in the year 1806. She also was born in Virginia; and relatives of hers of the name of Hanks, and of other names, now reside in Coles, in Macon, and in Adams counties, Illinois, and also in Iowa. The present subject has no brother or sister of the whole or half blood. He had a sister, older than himself, who was grown and married, but died many years ago, leaving no child; also a brother, younger than himself, who died in infancy. Before leaving Kentucky, he and his sister were sent, for short periods, to A B C schools, the first kept by Zachariah Riney, and the second by Caleb Hazel.

At this time his father resided on Knob Creek, on the road from Bardstown, Kentucky, to Nashville, Tennessee, at a point three or three and a half miles south or southwest of Atherton's Ferry, on the Rolling Fork. From this place he removed to what is now Spencer County, Indiana, in the autumn of 1816, Abraham then being in his eighth year. This removal was partly on account of slavery, but chiefly on account of the difficulty in land titles in Kentucky. He settled in an unbroken forest, and the clearing away of surplus wood was the great task ahead. Abraham, though very young, was large of his age, and had an ax put into his hands at once; and from that till within his twenty-third year he was almost constantly handling that most useful instrument — less, of course, in plowing and harvesting seasons. At this place Abraham took an early start as a hunter, which was never much improved afterward. A few days before the completion of his eighth year, in the absence of his father, a flock of wild turkeys approached the new log cabin, and Abraham with a rifle-gun, standing inside, shot through a crack and killed one of them. He has never since pulled a trigger on any larger game. In the autumn of 1818 his mother died; and a year afterward his father married Mrs. Sally Johnston, at Elizabethtown, Kentucky, a widow with three children of her first marriage. She proved a good and kind mother to Abraham, and is still living in Coles County, Illinois. There were no children of this second marriage. His father's residence continued at the same place in Indiana till 1830. While here Abraham went to A B C schools by littles, kept successively by Andrew Crawford, —— Sweeney, and Azel W. Dorsey. He does not remember any other. The family of Mr. Dorsey now resides in Schuyler County, Illinois. Abraham now thinks that the aggregate of all his schooling did not amount to one year. He was never in a college or academy as a student, and never inside of a college or academy building till since he had a law license. What he has in the way of education he has picked up. After he was twenty-three and had separated from his father, he studied English grammar—imperfectly, of course, but so as to speak and write as well as he now does. He studied and nearly mastered the six books of Euclid since he was a member of Congress. He regrets his want of education, and does what he can to supply the want. In his tenth year he was kicked by a horse, and apparently killed for a time. When he was nineteen, still residing in Indiana, he made his first trip upon a flatboat to New Orleans. He was a hired hand merely, and he and a son of the owner, without other assistance, made the trip. The nature of part of the "cargo-load," as it was called, made it necessary for them to linger and trade along the sugar-coast; and one night they were attacked by seven negroes with intent to kill and rob them. They were hurt some in the mêlée, but succeeded in driving the negroes from the boat, and then "cut cable," "weighed anchor," and left.

March 1, 1830, Abraham having just completed his twenty-first year, his father and family, with the families of the two daughters and sons-in-law of his stepmother, left the old homestead in Indiana and came to Illinois. Their mode of conveyance was wagons drawn by ox-teams, and Abraham drove one of the teams. They reached the county of Macon, and stopped there some time within the same month of March. His father and family settled a new place on the north side of the Sangamon River, at the junction of the timber-land and prairie, about ten miles westerly from Decatur. Here they built a log cabin, into which they removed, and made sufficient of rails to fence ten acres of ground, fenced and broke the ground, and raised a crop of sown corn upon it the same year. These are, or are supposed to be, the rails about which so much is being said just now, though these are far from being the first or only rails ever made by Abraham.

The sons-in-law were temporarily settled in other places in the county. In the autumn all hands were greatly afflicted with ague and fever, to which they had not been used, and by which they were greatly discouraged, so much so that they determined on leaving the county. They remained, however, through the succeeding winter, which was the winter of the very celebrated "deep snow" of Illinois. During that winter Abraham, together with his stepmother's son, John D. Johnston, and John Hanks, yet residing in Macon County, hired themselves to Denton Offutt to take a flatboat from Beardstown, Illinois, to New Orleans; and for that purpose were to join him— Offutt—at Springfield, Illinois, so soon as the snow should go off. When it did go off, which was about the first of March, 1831, the county was so flooded as to make traveling by land impracticable; to obviate which difficulty they purchased a large canoe, and came down the Sangamon River in it. This is the time and the manner of Abraham's first entrance into Sangamon County. They found Offutt at Springfield, but learned from him that he had failed in getting a boat at Beardstown. This led to their hiring themselves to him for twelve dollars per month each, and getting the timber out of the trees and building a boat at Old Sangamon town on the Sangamon River, seven miles northwest of Springfield, which boat they took to New Orleans, substantially upon the old contract.

During this boat-enterprise acquaintance with Offutt, who was previously an entire stranger, he conceived a liking for Abraham, and believing he could turn him to account, he contracted with him to act as clerk for him, on his return from New Orleans, in charge of a store and mill at New Salem, then in Sangamon, now in Menard County. Hanks had not gone to New Orleans, but having a family, and being likely to be detained from home longer than at first expected, had turned back from St. Louis. He is the same John Hanks who now engineers the "rail enterprise" at Decatur, and is a first cousin to Abraham's mother. Abraham's father, with his own family and others mentioned, had, in pursuance of their intention, removed from Macon to Coles County. John D. Johnston, the stepmother's son, went to them, and Abraham stopped indefinitely and for the first time, as it were, by himself at New Salem, before mentioned. This was in July, 1831. Here he rapidly made acquaintances and friends. In less than a year Offutt's business was failing — had almost failed — when the Black Hawk war of 1832 broke out. Abraham joined a volunteer company, and, to his own surprise, was elected captain of it. He says he has not since had any success in life which gave him so much satisfaction. He went to the campaign, served near three months, met the ordinary hardships of such an expedition, but was in no battle. He now owns, in Iowa, the land upon which his own warrants for the service were located. Returning from the campaign, and encouraged by his great popularity among his immediate neighbors, he the same year ran for the legislature, and was beaten,— his own precinct, however, casting its votes 277 for and 7 against him—and that, too, while he was an avowed Clay man, and the precinct the autumn afterward giving a majority of 115 to General Jackson over Mr. Clay. This was the only time Abraham was ever beaten on a direct vote of the people. He was now without means and out of business, but was anxious to remain with his friends who had treated him with so much generosity, especially as he had nothing elsewhere to go to. He studied what he should do—thought of learning the blacksmith trade—thought of trying to study law — rather thought he could not succeed at that without a better education. Before long, strangely enough, a man offered to sell, and did sell, to Abraham and another as poor as himself, an old stock of goods, upon credit. They opened as merchants; and he says that was the store. Of course they did nothing but get deeper and deeper in debt. He was appointed postmaster at New Salem—the office being too insignificant to make his politics an objection. The store winked out. The surveyor of Sangamon offered to depute to Abraham that portion of his work which was within his part of the county. He accepted, procured a compass and chain, studied Flint and Gibson a little, and went at it. This procured bread, and kept soul and body together. The election of 1834 came, and he was then elected to the legislature by the highest vote cast for any candidate. Major John T. Stuart, then in full practice of the law, was also elected. During the canvass, in a private conversation he encouraged Abraham [to] study law. After the election he borrowed books of Stuart, took them home with him, and went at it in good earnest. He studied with nobody. He still mixed in the surveying to pay board and clothing bills. When the legislature met, the law-books were dropped, but were taken up again at the end of the session. He was reëlected in 1836, 1838, and 1840. In the autumn of 1836 he obtained a law license, and on April 15, 1837, removed to Springfield, and commenced the practice—his old friend Stuart taking him into partnership. March 3, 1837, by a protest entered upon the "Illinois House Journal" of that date, at pages 817 and 818, Abraham, with Dan Stone, another representative of Sangamon, briefly defined his position on the slavery question; and so far as it goes, it was then the same that it is now. The protest is as follows:

Resolutions upon the subject of domestic slavery having passed both branches of the General Assembly at its present session, the undersigned hereby protest against the passage of the same.

They believe that the institution of slavery is founded on both injustice and bad policy, but that the promulgation of Abolition doctrines tends rather to increase than abate its evils.

They believe that the Congress of the United States has no power under the Constitution to interfere with the institution of slavery in the different States.

They believe that the Congress of the United States has the power, under the Constitution, to abolish slavery in the District of Columbia, but that the power ought not to be exercised unless at the request of the people of the District.

The difference between these opinions and those contained in the above resolutions is their reason for entering this protest.

DAN STONE,
A. LINCOLN,
Representatives from the County of Sangamon.

In 1838 and 1840, Mr. Lincoln's party voted for him as Speaker, but being in the minority he was not elected. After 1840 he declined a reëlection to the legislature. He was on the Harrison electoral ticket in 1840, and on that of Clay in 1844, and spent much time and labor in both those canvasses. In November, 1842, he was married to Mary, daughter of Robert S. Todd, of Lexington, Kentucky. They have three living children, all sons, one born in 1843, one in 1850, and one in 1853. They lost one, who was born in 1846.

In 1846 he was elected to the lower House of Congress, and served one term only, commencing in December, 1847, and ending with the inauguration of General Taylor, in March, 1849. All the battles of the Mexican war had been fought before Mr. Lincoln took his seat in Congress, but the American army was still in Mexico, and the treaty of peace was not fully and formally ratified till the June afterward. Much has been said of his course in Congress in regard to this war. A careful examination of the "Journal" and "Congressional Globe" shows that he voted for all the supply measures that came up, and for all the measures in any way favorable to the officers, soldiers, and their families, who conducted the war through: with the exception that some of these measures passed without yeas and nays, leaving no record as to how particular men voted.   The "Journal" and "Globe" also show him voting that the war was unnecessarily and unconstitutionally begun by the President of the United · States.   This is the language of Mr. Ashmun's amendment, for which Mr. Lincoln and nearly or quite all other Whigs of the House of Representatives voted.

Mr. Lincoln's reasons for the opinion expressed by this vote were briefly that the President had sent General Taylor into an inhabited part of the country belonging to Mexico, and not to the United States, and thereby had provoked the first act of hostility, in fact the commencement of the war; that the place, being the country bordering on the east bank of the Rio Grande, was inhabited by native Mexicans, born there under the Mexican government, and had never submitted to, nor been conquered by, Texas or the United States, nor transferred to either by treaty; that although Texas claimed the Rio Grande as her boundary, Mexico had never recognized it, and neither Texas nor the United States had ever enforced it; that there was a broad desert between that and the country over which Texas had actual control; that the country where hostilities commenced, having once belonged to Mexico, must remain so until it was somehow legally transferred, which had never been done.

Mr. Lincoln thought the act of sending an armed force among the Mexicans was unnecessary, inasmuch as Mexico was in no way molesting or menacing the United States or the people thereof; and that it was unconstitutional, because the power of levying war is vested in Congress, and not in the President.   He thought the principal motive for the act was to divert public attention from the surrender of "Fifty-four, forty, or fight" to Great Britain, on the Oregon boundary question.

Mr. Lincoln was not a candidate for reëlection.   This was determined upon and declared before he went to Washington, in accordance with an understanding among Whig friends, by which Colonel Hardin and Colonel Baker had each previously served a single term in this same district.

In 1848, during his term in Congress, he advocated General Taylor's nomination for the presidency, in opposition to all others, and also took an active part for his election after his nomination, speaking a few times in Maryland, near Washington, several times in Massachusetts, and canvassing quite fully his own district in Illinois, which was followed by a majority in the district of over 1500 for General Taylor.

Upon his return from Congress he went to the practice of the law with greater earnestness than ever before.   In 1852 he was upon the Scott electoral ticket, and did something in the way of canvassing, but owing to the hopelessness of the cause in Illinois he did less than in previous presidential canvasses.

In 1854 his profession had almost superseded the thought of

politics in his mind, when the repeal of the Missouri Compromise aroused him as he had never been before.

In the autumn of that year he took the stump with no broader practical aim or object than to secure, if possible, the reëlection of Hon. Richard Yates to Congress. His speeches at once attracted a more marked attention than they had ever before done. As the canvass proceeded he was drawn to different parts of the State outside of Mr. Yates's district. He did not abandon the law, but gave his attention by turns to that and politics. The State agricultural fair was at Springfield that year, and Douglas was announced to speak there.

In the canvass of 1856 Mr. Lincoln made over fifty speeches, no one of which, so far as he remembers, was put in print. One of them was made at Galena, but Mr. Lincoln has no recollection of any part of it being printed; nor does he remember whether in that speech he said anything about a Supreme Court decision. He may have spoken upon that subject, and some of the newspapers may have reported him as saying what is now ascribed to him; but he thinks he could not have expressed himself as represented.

June 14, 1860.—AUTOBIOGRAPHICAL MEMORANDUM GIVEN TO THE ARTIST HICKS.

I was born February 12, 1809, in then Hardin County, Kentucky, at a point within the now county of La Rue, a mile, or a mile and a half, from where Hodgen's mill now is. My parents being dead, and my own memory not serving, I know no means of identifying the precise locality. It was on Nolin Creek.

June 14, 1860.   A. LINCOLN.

June 28, 1860.—LETTER TO W. C. BRYANT.

SPRINGFIELD, ILLINOIS, June 28, 1860.

MR. WM. C. BRYANT.

My dear Sir: Please accept my thanks for the honor done me by your letter of the 16th. I appreciate the danger against which you would guard me, nor am I wanting in the purpose to avoid it. I thank you for the additional strength your words give me to maintain that purpose. Your friend and servant,

A. LINCOLN.

July 4, 1860.— LETTER TO A. G. HENRY.

SPRINGFIELD, ILLINOIS, July 4, 1860.

My dear Doctor: Your very agreeable letter of May 15th was received three days ago. We are just now receiving the first sprinkling of your Oregon election returns — not enough, I think, to indicate the result. We should be too happy if both Logan and Baker should triumph.

Long before this you have learned who was nominated at Chicago.

We know not what a day may bring forth, but to-day it looks as if the Chicago ticket will be elected. I think the chances were more than equal that we could have beaten the Democracy united. Divided as it is, its chance appears indeed very slim. But great is Democracy in resources; and it may yet give its fortunes a turn. It is under great temptation to do something; but what can it do which was not thought of, and found impracticable, at Charleston and Baltimore? The signs now are that Douglas and Breckinridge will each have a ticket in every State. They are driven to this to keep up their bombastic claims of nationality, and to avoid the charge of sectionalism which they have so much lavished upon us.

It is an amusing fact, after all Douglas has said about nationality and sectionalism, that I had more votes from the southern section at Chicago than he had at Baltimore! In fact, there was more of the southern section represented at Chicago than in the Douglas rump concern at Baltimore!

Our boy, in his tenth year (the baby when you left), has just had a hard and tedious spell of scarlet fever, and he is not yet beyond all danger. I have a headache and a sore throat upon me now, inducing me to suspect that I have an inferior type of the same thing.

Our eldest boy, Bob, has been away from us nearly a year at school, and will enter Harvard University this month. He promises very well, considering we never controlled him much. Write again when you receive this. Mary joins in sending our kindest regards to Mrs. H., yourself, and all the family.

Your friend, as ever,   A. LINCOLN.

July 18, 1860.—LETTER TO HANNIBAL HAMLIN.

SPRINGFIELD, ILLINOIS, July 18, 1860.

HON. HANNIBAL HAMLIN.

My dear Sir: It appears to me that you and I ought to be acquainted, and accordingly I write this as a sort of introduction of myself to you. You first entered the Senate during the single term I was a member of the House of Representatives, but I have no recollection that we were introduced. I shall be pleased to receive a line from you.

The prospect of Republican success now appears very flattering, so far as I can perceive. Do you see anything to the contrary?

Yours truly,   A. LINCOLN.

July 20, 1860.—LETTER TO C. M. CLAY.

SPRINGFIELD, ILLINOIS, July 20, 1860.

HON. CASSIUS M. CLAY.

My dear Sir: I see by the papers, and also learn from Mr. Nicolay, who saw you at Terre Haute, that you are filling a list of speaking-appointments in Indiana. I sincerely thank you for this, and I

shall be still further obliged if you will, at the close of the tour, drop
me a line giving your impressions of our prospects in that State.

Still more will you oblige me if you will allow me to make a list
of appointments in our State, commencing, say, at Marshall, in Clark
County, and thence south and west along over the Wabash and
Ohio River border.

In passing let me say that at Rockport you will be in the county
within which I was brought up from my eighth year, having left
Kentucky at that point of my life.

Yours very truly,   A. LINCOLN.

July 21, 1860.—LETTER TO A. JONAS.

(Confidential.)

SPRINGFIELD, ILLINOIS, July 21, 1860.

HON. A. JONAS.

My dear Sir: Yours of the 20th is received. I suppose as good
or even better men than I may have been in American or Know-
nothing lodges; but, in point of fact, I never was in one at Quincy
or elsewhere. I was never in Quincy but one day and two nights
while Know-nothing lodges were in existence, and you were with me
that day and both those nights. I had never been there before in
my life, and never afterward, till the joint debate with Douglas in
1858. It was in 1854 when I spoke in some hall there, and after the
speaking, you, with others, took me to an oyster-saloon, passed an
hour there, and you walked with me to, and parted with me at, the
Quincy House, quite late at night. I left by stage for Naples before
daylight in the morning, having come in by the same route after
dark the evening previous to the speaking, when I found you waiting at the Quincy House to meet me. A few days after I was there,
Richardson, as I understood, started this same story about my having
been in a Know-nothing lodge.   When I heard of the charge, as I
did soon after, I taxed my recollection for some incident which could
have suggested it; and I remembered that on parting with you the
last night, I went to the office of the hotel to take my stage-passage
for the morning, was told that no stage-office for that line was kept
there, and that I must see the driver before retiring, to insure his
calling for me in the morning; and a servant was sent with me to
find the driver, who, after taking me a square or two, stopped me,
and stepped perhaps a dozen steps farther, and in my hearing called
to some one, who answered him, apparently from the upper part of a
building, and promised to call with the stage for me at the Quincy
House. I returned, and went to bed, and before day the stage called
and took me.   This is all.

That I never was in a Know-nothing lodge in Quincy, I should
expect could be easily proved by respectable men who were always
in the lodges and never saw me there. An affidavit of one or two
such would put the matter at rest.

And now a word of caution. Our adversaries think they can
gain a point if they could force me to openly deny the charge, by

which some degree of offense would be given to the Americans. For this reason it must not publicly appear that I am paying any attention to the charge.   Yours truly,

A. LINCOLN.

August 10, 1860.—LETTER TO C. M. CLAY.

SPRINGFIELD, ILLINOIS, August 10, 1860.

HON. C. M. CLAY.

My dear Sir: Your very kind letter of the 6th was received yesterday. It so happened that our State Central Committee was in session here at the time; and, thinking it proper to do so, I submitted the letter to them. They were delighted with the assurance of having your assistance. For what appear good reasons, they, however, propose a change in the program, starting you at the same place (Marshall in Clark County), and thence northward. This change, I suppose, will be agreeable to you, as it will give you larger audiences, and much easier travel—nearly all being by railroad. They will be governed by your time, and when they shall have fully designated the places, you will be duly notified.

As to the inaugural, I have not yet commenced getting it up; while it affords me great pleasure to be able to say the cliques have not yet commenced upon me. Yours very truly,

A. LINCOLN.

August 14, 1860.—LETTER TO T. A. CHENEY.

SPRINGFIELD, ILLINOIS, August 14, 1860.

T. A. CHENEY, Esq.

Dear Sir: Yours of the 10th is received, and for which I thank you. I would cheerfully answer your questions in regard to the fugitive-slave law were it not that I consider it would be both imprudent and contrary to the reasonable expectation of my friends for me to write or speak anything upon doctrinal points now. Besides this, my published speeches contain nearly all I could willingly say. Justice and fairness to all, is the utmost I have said, or will say.

Yours truly,   A. LINCOLN.

August 14, 1860.—REMARKS AT SPRINGFIELD, ILLINOIS.

My Fellow-citizens: I appear among you upon this occasion with no intention of making a speech.

It has been my purpose since I have been placed in my present position to make no speeches. This assemblage having been drawn together at the place of my residence, it appeared to be the wish of those constituting this vast assembly to see me; and it is certainly my wish to see all of you. I appear upon the ground here at this time only for the purpose of affording myself the best opportunity of seeing you, and enabling you to see me.

I confess with gratitude, be it understood, that I did not suppose my appearance among you would create the tumult which I now witness. I am profoundly grateful for this manifestation of your feelings. I am grateful, because it is a tribute such as can be paid to no man as a man; it is the evidence that four years from this time you will give a like manifestation to the next man who is the representative of the truth on the questions that now agitate the public; and it is because you will then fight for this cause as you do now, or with even greater ardor than now, though I be dead and gone, that I most profoundly and sincerely thank you.

Having said this much, allow me now to say that it is my wish that you will hear this public discussion by others of our friends who are present for the purpose of addressing you, and that you will kindly let me be silent.

August 15, 1860.—LETTER TO JOHN B. FRY.

SPRINGFIELD, ILLINOIS, August 15, 1860.

My dear Sir: Yours of the 9th, inclosing the letter of Hon. John Minor Botts, was duly received. The latter is herewith returned according to your request. It contains one of the many assurances I receive from the South, that in no probable event will there be any very formidable effort to break up the Union. The people of the South have too much of good sense and good temper to attempt the ruin of the government rather than see it administered as it was administered by the men who made it. At least so I hope and believe. I thank you both for your own letter and a sight of that of Mr. Botts.   Yours very truly,

A. LINCOLN.

JOHN B. FRY, Esq.

August 17, 1860.—LETTER TO THURLOW WEED.

SPRINGFIELD, ILLINOIS, August 17, 1860.

My dear Sir: Yours of the 13th was received this morning. Douglas is managing the Bell element with great adroitness. He has his men in Kentucky to vote for the Bell candidate, producing a result which has badly alarmed and damaged Breckinridge, and at the same time has induced the Bell men to suppose that Bell will certainly be President if they can keep a few of the Northern States away from us by throwing them to Douglas. But you, better than I, understand all this.

I think there will be the most extraordinary effort ever made to carry New York for Douglas. You and all others who write me from your State think the effort cannot succeed, and I hope you are right. Still it will require close watching and great efforts on the other side.

Herewith I send you a copy of a letter written at New York, which sufficiently explains itself, and which may or may not give you a valuable hint. You have seen that Bell tickets have been put on the track both here and in Indiana. In both cases the object has been, I think, the same as the Hunt movement in New York—to throw States to Douglas. In our State we know the thing is engineered by Douglas men, and we do not believe they can make a great deal out of it.   Yours very truly,

A. LINCOLN.

August 27, 1860.—LETTER TO C. H. FISHER.
(APPARENTLY UNFINISHED.)

SPRINGFIELD, ILLINOIS, August 27, 1860.

C. H. FISHER.

Dear Sir: Your second note, inclosing the supposed speech of Mr. Dallas to Lord Brougham, is received. I have read the speech quite through, together with the real author's introductory and closing remarks. I have also looked through the long preface of the book to-day. Both seem to be well written, and contain many things with which I could agree, and some with which I could not. A specimen of the latter is the declaration, in the closing remarks upon the "speech," that the institution is a "necessity" imposed on us by the negro race. That the going many thousand miles, seizing a set of savages, bringing them here, and making slaves of them is a necessity imposed on us by them involves a species of logic to which my mind will scarcely assent.

September 4, 1860.—LETTER TO HANNIBAL HAMLIN.

SPRINGFIELD, ILLINOIS, September 4, 1860.

HON. HANNIBAL HAMLIN.

My dear Sir: I am annoyed some by a letter from a friend in Chicago, in which the following passage occurs: "Hamlin has written Colfax that two members of Congress will, he fears, be lost in Maine—the first and sixth districts; and that Washburne's majority for governor will not exceed six thousand."

I had heard something like this six weeks ago, but had been assured since that it was not so. Your secretary of state,—Mr. Smith, I think,—whom you introduced to me by letter, gave this assurance; more recently, Mr. Fessenden, our candidate for Congress in one of those districts, wrote a relative here that his election was sure by at least five thousand, and that Washburne's majority would be from 14,000 to 17,000; and still later, Mr. Fogg, of New Hampshire, now at New York serving on a national committee, wrote me that we were having a desperate fight in Maine, which would end in a splendid victory for us.

Such a result as you seem to have predicted in Maine, in your letter to Colfax, would, I fear, put us on the down-hill track, lose us the State elections in Pennsylvania and Indiana, and probably ruin us on the main turn in November.

You must not allow it.   Yours very truly,   A. LINCOLN.

September 9, 1860.—LETTER TO E. B. WASHBURNE.

SPRINGFIELD, ILLINOIS, September 9, 1860.

HON. E. B. WASHBURNE.

My dear Sir: Yours of the 5th was received last evening. I was right glad to see it. It contains the freshest "posting" which I now have. It relieved me some from a little anxiety I had about Maine. Jo Medill, on August 30th, wrote me that Colfax had a letter from Mr. Hamlin saying we were in great danger of losing two members of Congress in Maine, and that your brother would not have exceeding six thousand majority for governor. I addressed you at once, at Galena, asking for your latest information. As you are at Washington, that letter you will receive some time after the Maine election.

Yours very truly,   A. LINCOLN.

September 21, 1860.—LETTER TO JOHN CHRISMAN.

SPRINGFIELD, ILLINOIS, September 21, 1860.

JOHN CHRISMAN, Esq.

My dear Sir: Yours of the 13th was duly received. I have no doubt that you and I are related. My grandfather's Christian name was "Abraham." He had four brothers—Isaac, Jacob, John, and Thomas. They were born in Pennsylvania, and my grandfather, and some, if not all, the others, in early life removed to Rockingham County, Virginia. There my father—named Thomas—was born. From there my grandfather removed to Kentucky, and was killed by the Indians about the year 1784. His brother Thomas, who was my father's uncle, also removed to Kentucky—to Fayette County, I think —where, as I understand, he lived and died. I close by repeating I have no doubt you and I are related.

Yours very truly,   A. LINCOLN.

September 22, 1860.—LETTER TO A. G. HENRY.

SPRINGFIELD, ILLINOIS, September 22, 1860.

Dear Doctor: Yours of July 18th was received some time ago. When you wrote you had not learned the result of the Democratic conventions at Charleston and Baltimore. With the two tickets in the field I should think it possible for our friends to carry Oregon. But the general result, I think, does not depend upon Oregon. No one this side of the mountains pretends that any ticket can be elected by the people, unless it be ours. Hence great efforts to combine against us are being made, which, however, as yet have not had much success. Besides what we see in the newspapers, I have a good deal of private correspondence; and without giving details, I will only say it all looks very favorable to our success.

Make my best respects to Mrs. Henry and the rest of your family.

Your friend, as ever,   A. LINCOLN.

September 22, 1860.—LETTER TO G. Y. TAMS.

(Private and confidential.)

SPRINGFIELD, ILLINOIS, September 22, 1860.

G. YOKE TAMS, Esq.

My dear Sir: Your letter asking me "Are you in favor of a tariff and protection to American industry?" is received. The convention which nominated me, by the twelfth plank of their platform, selected their position on this question; and I have declared my approval of the platform, and accepted the nomination. Now, if I were to publicly shift the position by adding or subtracting anything, the convention would have the right, and probably would be inclined, to displace me as their candidate. And I feel confident that you, on reflection, would not wish me to give private assurances to be seen by some and kept secret from others. I enjoin that this shall by no means be made public. Yours respectfully,

A. LINCOLN.

September 25, 1860.—LETTER TO J. M. BROCKMAN.

SPRINGFIELD, ILLINOIS, September 25, 1860.

J. M. BROCKMAN, Esq.

Dear Sir: Yours of the 24th, asking "the best mode of obtaining a thorough knowledge of the law," is received. The mode is very simple, though laborious and tedious. It is only to get the books and read and study them carefully. Begin with Blackstone's "Commentaries," and after reading it carefully through, say twice, take up Chitty's "Pleadings," Greenleaf's "Evidence," and Story's "Equity," etc., in succession. Work, work, work, is the main thing.

Yours very truly,   A. LINCOLN.

October 1, 1860.—LETTER TO J. H. REED.

SPRINGFIELD, ILLINOIS, October 1, 1860.

J. H. REED, Esq.

My dear Sir: Yours of September 21st was received some time ago, but I could not till now find time to answer it. I never was in McDonough County till 1858. I never said anything derogatory of Mr. Jefferson in McDonough County or elsewhere. About three weeks ago, for the first time in my life did I ever see or hear the language attributed to me as having been used toward Mr. Jefferson; and then it was sent to me, as you now send, in order that I might say whether it came from me. I never used any such language at any time. You may rely on the truth of this, although it is my wish that you do not publish it.   Yours truly,

A. LINCOLN.

October 19, 1860.— LETTER TO MISS GRACE BEDELL.

(*Private.*)

SPRINGFIELD, ILLINOIS, October 19, 1860.

MISS GRACE BEDELL.

My dear little Miss: Your very agreeable letter of the 15th is received. I regret the necessity of saying I have no daughter. I have three sons — one seventeen, one nine, and one seven years of age. They, with their mother, constitute my whole family. As to the whiskers, having never worn any, do you not think people would call it a piece of silly affectation if I were to begin it now?

Your very sincere well-wisher,   A. LINCOLN.

October 23, 1860.— LETTER TO W. S. SPEER.

(*Confidential.*)

SPRINGFIELD, ILLINOIS, October 23, 1860.

WILLIAM S. SPEER, Esq.

My dear Sir: Yours of the 13th was duly received. I appreciate your motive when you suggest the propriety of my writing for the public something disclaiming all intention to interfere with slaves or slavery in the States; but in my judgment it would do no good. I have already done this many, many times; and it is in print, and open to all who will read. Those who will not read or heed what I have already publicly said would not read or heed a repetition of it. "If they hear not Moses and the prophets, neither will they be persuaded though one rose from the dead."

Yours truly,   A. LINCOLN.

October 29, 1860.— LETTER TO G. D. PRENTICE.

(*Private and confidential.*)

SPRINGFIELD, ILLINOIS, October 29, 1860.

GEORGE D. PRENTICE, Esq.

My dear Sir: Yours of the 26th is just received. Your suggestion that I in a certain event shall write a letter setting forth my conservative views and intentions is certainly a very worthy one. But would it do any good? If I were to labor a month I could not express my conservative views and intentions more clearly and strongly than they are expressed in our platform and in my many speeches already in print and before the public. And yet even you, who do occasionally speak of me in terms of personal kindness, give no prominence to these oft-repeated expressions of conservative views and intentions, but busy yourself with appeals to all conservative men to vote for Douglas,— to vote any way which can possibly defeat me,— thus impressing your readers that you think I am the very worst man living. If what I have already said has failed to convince you, no repetition of it would convince you. The writing of your letter, now before me, gives assurance that you would publish such a letter from me as you suggest; but, till now, what reason had I to suppose the " Louisville Journal," even, would publish a repetition of that which is already at its command, and which it does not press upon the public attention ?

And now, my friend,—for such I esteem you personally,—do not misunderstand me. I have not decided that I will not do substantially what you suggest. I will not forbear from doing so merely on punctilio and pluck. If I do finally abstain, it will be because of apprehension that it would do harm. For the good men of the South— and I regard the majority of them as such—I have no objection to repeat seventy and seven times. But I have bad men to deal with, both North and South; men who are eager for something new upon which to base new misrepresentations; men who would like to frighten me, or at least to fix upon me the character of timidity and cowardice. They would seize upon almost any letter I could write as being an " awful coming down." I intend keeping my eye upon these gentlemen, and to not unnecessarily put any weapons in their hands.   Yours very truly,

A. LINCOLN.

[The following indorsement appears on the back:]

(Confidential.)

The within letter was written on the day of its date, and on reflection withheld till now. It expresses the views I still entertain.

A. LINCOLN.

November 8, 1860.— LETTER TO HANNIBAL HAMLIN.

(Confidential.)

SPRINGFIELD, ILLINOIS, November 8, 1860.

HON. HANNIBAL HAMLIN.

My dear Sir: I am anxious for a personal interview with you at as early a day as possible. Can you, without much inconvenience, meet me at Chicago? If you can, please name as early a day as you conveniently can, and telegraph me, unless there be sufficient time before the day named to communicate by mail.

Yours very truly,   A. LINCOLN.

November 9, 1860.—LETTER TO GENERAL WINFIELD SCOTT.

SPRINGFIELD, ILLINOIS, November 9, 1860.

LIEUTENANT-GENERAL SCOTT.

Mr. Lincoln tenders his sincere thanks to General Scott for the copy of his " views," etc., which is received; and especially for this renewed manifestation of his patriotic purpose as a citizen, connected, as it is, with his high official position and most distinguished character as a military captain.   A. L.

November 10, 1860.— LETTER TO TRUMAN SMITH.

(Private and confidential.)

SPRINGFIELD, ILLINOIS, November 10, 1860.

HON. TRUMAN SMITH.

My dear Sir: This is intended as a strictly private letter to you, and not as an answer to yours brought me by Mr. ——. It is with the most profound appreciation of your motive, and highest respect for your judgment, too, that I feel constrained, for the present at least, to make no declaration for the public.

First. I could say nothing which I have not already said, and which is in print, and open for the inspection of all. To press a repetition of this upon those who have listened, is useless; to press it upon those who have refused to listen, and still refuse, would be wanting in self-respect, and would have an appearance of sycophancy and timidity which would excite the contempt of good men and encourage bad ones to clamor the more loudly.

I am not insensible to any commercial or financial depression that may exist, but nothing is to be gained by fawning around the " respectable scoundrels " who got it up. Let them go to work and repair the mischief of their own making, and then perhaps they will be less greedy to do the like again.

Yours very truly,   A. LINCOLN.

November 13, 1860.— LETTER TO SAMUEL HAYCRAFT.

(Private and confidential.)

SPRINGFIELD, ILLINOIS, November 13, 1860.

HON. SAMUEL HAYCRAFT.

My dear Sir : Yours of the 9th is just received. I can only answer briefly. Rest fully assured that the good people of the South who will put themselves in the same temper and mood toward me which you do, will find no cause to complain of me.

Yours very truly,   A. LINCOLN.

November 16, 1860.— LETTER TO N. P. PASCHALL.

(Private and confidential.)

SPRINGFIELD, ILLINOIS, November 16, 1860.

N. P. PASCHALL, Esq.

My dear Sir : Mr. Ridgely showed me a letter of yours in which you manifest some anxiety that I should make some public declaration with a view to favorably affect the business of the country. I said to Mr. Ridgely I would write you to-day, which I now do.

I could say nothing which I have not already said, and which is in print, and accessible to the public. Please pardon me for suggesting that if the papers like yours, which heretofore have persistently garbled and misrepresented what I have said, will now fully and fairly place it before their readers, there can be no further misunderstanding. I beg you to believe me sincere when I declare I do not say this in a spirit of complaint or resentment; but that I urge it as the true cure for any real uneasiness in the country that my course may be other than conservative. The Republican newspapers now and for some time past are and have been republishing copious extracts from my many published speeches, which would at once reach the whole public if your class of papers would also publish them. I am not at liberty to shift my ground—that is out of the question. If I thought a repetition would do any good, I would make it. But in my judgment it would do positive harm. The secessionists *per se*, believing they had alarmed me, would clamor all the louder.

Yours, etc.,   A. LINCOLN.

November 20, 1860.—REMARKS AT THE MEETING AT SPRINGFIELD, ILLINOIS, TO CELEBRATE LINCOLN'S ELECTION.

Friends and Fellow-citizens: Please excuse me on this occasion from making a speech. I thank you in common with all those who have thought fit by their votes to indorse the Republican cause. I rejoice with you in the success which has thus far attended that cause. Yet in all our rejoicings, let us neither express nor cherish any hard feelings toward any citizen who by his vote has differed with us. Let us at all times remember that all American citizens are brothers of a common country, and should dwell together in the bonds of fraternal feeling. Let me again beg you to accept my thanks, and to excuse me from further speaking at this time.

November 27, 1860.—LETTER TO HANNIBAL HAMLIN.

SPRINGFIELD, ILLINOIS, November 27, 1860.

HON. HANNIBAL HAMLIN.

My dear Sir: On reaching home I find I have in charge for you the inclosed letter.

I deem it proper to advise you that I also find letters here from very strong and unexpected quarters in Pennsylvania, urging the appointment of General Cameron to a place in the cabinet.

Let this be a profound secret, even though I do think best to let you know it.   Yours very sincerely,

A. LINCOLN.

November 28, 1860.—LETTER TO HENRY J. RAYMOND.

(*Private and confidential.*)

SPRINGFIELD, ILLINOIS, November 28, 1860.

HON. HENRY J. RAYMOND.

My dear Sir: Yours of the 14th was received in due course. I have delayed so long to answer it, because my reasons for not coming before the public in any form just now had substantially appeared in your paper (the "Times"), and hence I feared they were not deemed sufficient by you, else you would not have written me as you did. I now think we have a demonstration in favor of my view. On the 20th instant Senator Trumbull made a short speech, which I suppose you have both seen and approved. Has a single newspaper, heretofore against us, urged that speech upon its readers with a purpose to quiet public anxiety? Not one, so far as I know. On the contrary, the "Boston Courier" and its class hold me responsible for that speech, and endeavor to inflame the North with the belief that it foreshadows an abandonment of Republican ground by the incoming administration; while the Washington "Constitution" and its class hold the same speech up to the South as an open declaration of war against them. This is just as I expected, and just what would happen with any declaration I could make. These political fiends are not half sick enough yet. Party malice, and not public good, possesses them entirely. "They seek a sign, and no sign shall be given them." At least such is my present feeling and purpose.   Yours very truly,

A. LINCOLN.

November 30, 1860.—LETTER TO A. H. STEPHENS.

SPRINGFIELD, ILLINOIS, November 30, 1860.

HON. ALEXANDER H. STEPHENS.

My dear Sir: I have read in the newspapers your speech recently delivered (I think) before the Georgia legislature, or its assembled members. If you have revised it, as is probable, I shall be much obliged if you will send me a copy. Yours very truly,

A. LINCOLN.

December 8, 1860.—LETTER TO HANNIBAL HAMLIN.

(*Private.*)

SPRINGFIELD, ILLINOIS, December 8, 1860.

HON. HANNIBAL HAMLIN.

My dear Sir: Yours of the 4th was duly received. The inclosed to Governor Seward covers two notes to him, copies of which you find open for your inspection. Consult with Judge Trumbull; and if you and he see no reason to the contrary, deliver the letter to Governor Seward at once. If you see reason to the contrary, write me at once.

I have had an intimation that Governor Banks would yet accept a place in the cabinet. Please ascertain and write me how this is.

Yours very truly,   A. LINCOLN.

December 8, 1860.—LETTERS TO W. H. SEWARD.

SPRINGFIELD, ILLINOIS, December 8, 1860.

My dear Sir: With your permission I shall at the proper time nominate you to the Senate for confirmation as Secretary of State for the United States. Please let me hear from you at your own earliest convenience. Your friend and obedient servant,

A. LINCOLN.

HON. WILLIAM H. SEWARD, Washington, D. C.

(Private and confidential.)

SPRINGFIELD, ILLINOIS, December 8, 1860.

My dear Sir: In addition to the accompanying and more formal note inviting you to take charge of the State Department, I deem it proper to address you this. Rumors have got into the newspapers to the effect that the department named above would be tendered you as a compliment, and with the expectation that you would decline it. I beg you to be assured that I have said nothing to justify these rumors. On the contrary, it has been my purpose, from the day of the nomination at Chicago, to assign you, by your leave, this place in the administration. I have delayed so long to communicate that purpose in deference to what appeared to me a proper caution in the case. Nothing has been developed to change my view in the premises; and I now offer you the place in the hope that you will accept it, and with the belief that your position in the public eye, your integrity, ability, learning, and great experience, all combine to render it an appointment preëminently fit to be made.

One word more. In regard to the patronage sought with so much eagerness and jealousy, I have prescribed for myself the maxim, "Justice to all"; and I earnestly beseech your coöperation in keeping the maxim good. Your friend and obedient servant,

A. LINCOLN.

HON. WILLIAM H. SEWARD, Washington, D. C.

December 11, 1860.— REPLY TO A LETTER FROM WILLIAM KELLOGG, M. C., ASKING ADVICE.

Entertain no proposition for a compromise in regard to the extension of slavery. The instant you do they have us under again: all our labor is lost, and sooner or later must be done over. Douglas is sure to be again trying to bring in his "popular sovereignty."

VOL. I.—42.

Have none of it. The tug has to come, and better now than later. You know I think the fugitive-slave clause of the Constitution ought to be enforced—to put it in its mildest form, ought not to be resisted.

December 12, 1860.—SHORT EDITORIAL PRINTED IN THE "ILLINOIS JOURNAL."

We hear such frequent allusions to a supposed purpose on the part of Mr. Lincoln to call into his cabinet two or three Southern gentlemen from the parties opposed to him politically, that we are prompted to ask a few questions.

First. Is it known that any such gentleman of character would accept a place in the cabinet?

Second. If yea, on what terms does he surrender to Mr. Lincoln, or Mr. Lincoln to him, on the political differences between them; or do they enter upon the administration in open opposition to each other?

December 13, 1860.—LETTER TO E. B. WASHBURNE.

(Private and Confidential.)

SPRINGFIELD, ILLINOIS, December 13, 1860.

HON. E. B. WASHBURNE.

My dear Sir: Your long letter received. Prevent, as far as possible, any of our friends from demoralizing themselves and our cause by entertaining propositions for compromise of any sort on "slavery extension." There is no possible compromise upon it but which puts us under again, and leaves all our work to do over again. Whether it be a Missouri line or Eli Thayer's popular sovereignty, it is all the same. Let either be done, and immediately filibustering and extending slavery recommences. On that point hold firm, as with a chain of steel.   Yours as ever,   A. LINCOLN.

December 15, 1860.—LETTER TO JOHN A. GILMER.

(Strictly confidential.)

SPRINGFIELD, ILLINOIS, December 15, 1860.

HON. JOHN A. GILMER.

My dear Sir: Yours of the 10th is received. I am greatly disinclined to write a letter on the subject embraced in yours; and I would not do so, even privately as I do, were it not that I fear you might misconstrue my silence. Is it desired that I shall shift the ground upon which I have been elected? I cannot do it. You need only to acquaint yourself with that ground, and press it on the attention of the South. It is all in print and easy of access. May I be pardoned if I ask whether even you have ever attempted to procure the reading of the Republican platform, or my speeches, by the Southern people? If not, what reason have I to expect that any additional production of mine would meet a better fate? It would make me appear as if I repented for the crime of having been elected, and was anxious to apologize and beg forgiveness. To so represent me would be the principal use made of any letter I might now thrust upon the public. My old record cannot be so used; and that is precisely the reason that some new declaration is so much sought.

Now, my dear sir, be assured that I am not questioning your candor; I am only pointing out that while a new letter would hurt the cause which I think a just one, you can quite as well effect every patriotic object with the old record. Carefully read pages 18, 19, 74, 75, 88, 89, and 267 of the volume of joint debates between Senator Douglas and myself, with the Republican platform adopted at Chicago, and all your questions will be substantially answered. I have no thought of recommending the abolition of slavery in the District of Columbia, nor the slave-trade among the slave States, even on the conditions indicated; and if I were to make such recommendation, it is quite clear Congress would not follow it.

As to employing slaves in arsenals and dock-yards, it is a thing I never thought of in my life, to my recollection, till I saw your letter; and I may say of it precisely as I have said of the two points above.

As to the use of patronage in the slave States, where there are few or no Republicans, I do not expect to inquire for the politics of the appointee, or whether he does or not own slaves. I intend in that matter to accommodate the people in the several localities, if they themselves will allow me to accommodate them. In one word, I never have been, am not now, and probably never shall be in a mood of harassing the people either North or South.

On the territorial question I am inflexible, as you see my position in the book. On that there is a difference between you and us; and it is the only substantial difference. You think slavery is right and ought to be extended; we think it is wrong and ought to be restricted. For this neither has any just occasion to be angry with the other.

As to the State laws, mentioned in your sixth question, I really know very little of them. I never have read one. If any of them are in conflict with the fugitive-slave clause, or any other part of the Constitution, I certainly shall be glad of their repeal; but I could hardly be justified, as a citizen of Illinois, or as President of the United States, to recommend the repeal of a statute of Vermont or South Carolina.

With the assurance of my highest regards, I subscribe myself,

Your obedient servant,   A. LINCOLN.

P. S. The documents referred to I suppose you will readily find in Washington.   A. L.

December 17, 1860.—LETTER TO THURLOW WEED.

SPRINGFIELD, ILLINOIS, December 17, 1860.
THURLOW WEED, Esq.

My dear Sir: Yours of the 11th was received two days ago. Should the convocation of governors of which you speak seem desirous to know my views on the present aspect of things, tell them you judge from my speeches that I will be inflexible on the territorial question; that I probably think either the Missouri line extended, or Douglas's and Eli Thayer's popular sovereignty, would lose us everything we gain by the election; that filibustering for all south of us and making slave States of it would follow, in spite of us, in either case; also that I probably think all opposition, real and apparent, to the fugitive-slave clause of the Constitution ought to be withdrawn.

I believe you can pretend to find but little, if anything, in my speeches about secession. But my opinion is, that no State can in any way lawfully get out of the Union without the consent of the others; and that it is the duty of the President and other government functionaries to run the machine as it is.

Truly yours,   A. LINCOLN.

December 18, 1860.—LETTER TO EDWARD BATES.

(Confidential.)

SPRINGFIELD, ILLINOIS, December 18, 1860.

My dear Sir: Yours of to-day is just received. Let a little editorial appear in the "Missouri Democrat" in about these words;

"We have the permission of both Mr. Lincoln and Mr. Bates to say that the latter will be offered, and will accept, a place in the new cabinet, subject, of course, to the action of the Senate. It is not yet definitely settled which department will be assigned to Mr. Bates."

Let it go just as above, or with any modification which may seem proper to you.   Yours very truly,

HON. EDWARD BATES.   A. LINCOLN.

December 21, 1860.—LETTER TO E. B. WASHBURNE.

(Confidential.)

SPRINGFIELD, ILLINOIS, December 21, 1860.

HON. E. B. WASHBURNE.

My dear Sir: Last night I received your letter giving an account of your interview with General Scott, and for which I thank you. Please present my respects to the general, and tell him, confidentially, I shall be obliged to him to be as well prepared as he can to either hold or retake the forts, as the case may require, at and after the inauguration.   Yours as ever,

A. LINCOLN.

December 22, 1860.—LETTER TO A. H. STEPHENS.

(For your own eye only.)

SPRINGFIELD, ILLINOIS, December 22, 1860.

HON. ALEXANDER H. STEPHENS.

My dear Sir: Your obliging answer to my short note is just received, and for which please accept my thanks. I fully appreciate the present peril the country is in, and the weight of responsibility on me. Do the people of the South really entertain fears that a Republican administration would, directly or indirectly, interfere with the slaves, or with them about the slaves? If they do, I wish to assure you, as once a friend, and still, I hope, not an enemy, that there is no cause for such fears. The South would be in no more danger in this respect than it was in the days of Washington. I suppose, however, this does not meet the case. You think slavery is right and ought to be extended, while we think it is wrong and ought to be restricted. That, I suppose, is the rub. It certainly is the only substantial difference between us. Yours very truly,

A. LINCOLN.

December 24, 1860.—LETTER TO HANNIBAL HAMLIN.

SPRINGFIELD, ILLINOIS, December 24, 1860.

HON. HANNIBAL HAMLIN.

My dear Sir: I need a man of Democratic antecedents from New England. I cannot get a fair share of that element in without. This stands in the way of Mr. Adams. I think of Governor Banks, Mr. Welles, and Mr. Tuck. Which of them do the New England delegation prefer? Or shall I decide for myself? Yours as ever,

A. LINCOLN.

December 28, 1860.—LETTER TO LYMAN TRUMBULL.

SPRINGFIELD, ILLINOIS, December 28, 1860.

HON. LYMAN TRUMBULL.

My dear Sir: General Duff Green is out here endeavoring to draw a letter out of me. I have written one which herewith I inclose to you, and which I believe could not be used to our disadvantage. Still, if on consultation with our discreet friends you conclude that it may do us harm, do not deliver it. You need not mention that the second clause of the letter is copied from the Chicago platform. If, on consultation, our friends, including yourself, think it can do no harm, keep a copy and deliver the letter to General Green.

Yours as ever,   A. LINCOLN.

[*Inclosure.*]

SPRINGFIELD, ILLINOIS, December 28, 1860.

GENERAL DUFF GREEN.

My dear Sir: I do not desire any amendment of the Constitution. Recognizing, however, that questions of such amendment rightfully belong to the American people, I should not feel justified nor inclined to withhold from them, if I could, a fair opportunity of expressing their will thereon through either of the modes prescribed in the instrument.

In addition I declare that the maintenance inviolate of the rights of the States, and especially the right of each State to order and control its own domestic institutions according to its own judgment exclusively, is essential to that balance of powers on which the perfection and endurance of our political fabric depend; and I denounce the lawless invasion by armed force of the soil of any State or Territory, no matter under what pretext, as the gravest of crimes.

I am greatly averse to writing anything for the public at this time; and I consent to the publication of this only upon the condition that six of the twelve United States senators for the States of Georgia, Alabama, Mississippi, Louisiana, Florida, and Texas shall sign their names to what is written on this sheet below my name, and allow the whole to be published together.

Yours truly,   A. LINCOLN.

We recommend to the people of the States we represent respectively, to suspend all action for dismemberment of the Union, at least until some act deemed to be violative of our rights shall be done by the incoming administration.

December 29, 1860.— LETTER TO W. C. BRYANT.

SPRINGFIELD, ILLINOIS, December 29, 1860.

HON. WILLIAM CULLEN BRYANT.

My dear Sir: Yours of the 25th is duly received. The "well-known politician" to whom I understand you to allude did write me, but did not press upon me any such compromise as you seem to suppose, or, in fact, any compromise at all.

As to the matter of the cabinet, mentioned by you, I can only say I shall have a great deal of trouble, do the best I can. I promise you that I shall unselfishly try to deal fairly with all men and all shades of opinion among our friends.

Yours very truly,   A. LINCOLN.

December 31, 1860.— LETTER TO SALMON P. CHASE.

SPRINGFIELD, ILLINOIS, December 31, 1860.

HON. SALMON P. CHASE.

My dear Sir: In these troublous times I would much like a conference with you. Please visit me here at once.

Yours very truly,   A. LINCOLN.

December 31, 1860.— LETTER TO SIMON CAMERON.

SPRINGFIELD, ILLINOIS, December 31, 1860.

HON. SIMON CAMERON.

My dear Sir: I think fit to notify you now that by your permission I shall at the proper time nominate you to the United States Senate for confirmation as Secretary of the Treasury, or as Secretary of War—which of the two I have not yet definitely decided. Please answer at your earliest convenience. ⁻

Your obedient servant,   A. LINCOLN.

January 3, 1861.—LETTER TO W. H. SEWARD.

(*Private.*)

SPRINGFIELD, ILLINOIS, January 3, 1861.

HON. W. H. SEWARD.

My dear Sir: Yours without signature was received last night. I have been considering your suggestions as to my reaching Washington somewhat earlier than is usual. It seems to me the inauguration is not the most dangerous point for us. Our adversaries have us now clearly at disadvantage. On the second Wednesday of February, when the votes should be officially counted, if the two Houses refuse to meet at all, or meet without a quorum of each, where shall we be? I do not think that this counting is constitutionally essential to the election; but how are we to proceed in absence of it?

In view of this, I think it best for me not to attempt appearing in Washington till the result of that ceremony is known. It certainly would be of some advantage if you could know who are to be at the heads of the War and Navy departments; but until I can ascertain definitely whether I can get any suitable men from the South, and who, and how many, I cannot well decide. As yet I have no word from Mr. Gilmer in answer to my request for an interview with him. I look for something on the subject, through you, before long.

Yours very truly,   A. LINCOLN.

January 3, 1861.—LETTER TO SIMON CAMERON.

(*Private.*)

SPRINGFIELD, ILLINOIS, January 3, 1861.

HON. SIMON CAMERON.

My dear Sir: Since seeing you things have developed which make it impossible for me to take you into the cabinet. You will say this comes of an interview with McClure; and this is partly, but not wholly, true. The more potent matter is wholly outside of Pennsylvania; and yet I am not at liberty to specify it. Enough that it appears to me to be sufficient. And now I suggest that you write me declining the appointment, in which case I do not object to its being known that it was tendered you. Better do this at once, before things so change that you cannot honorably decline, and I be compelled to openly recall the tender. No person living knows or has an intimation that I write this letter. Yours truly,

A. LINCOLN.

P. S. Telegraph me instantly on receipt of this, saying, "All right."   A. L.

January 11, 1861.—LETTER TO GENERAL WINFIELD SCOTT.

SPRINGFIELD, ILLINOIS, January 11, 1861.
LIEUTENANT-GENERAL WINFIELD SCOTT.

My dear Sir: I herewith beg leave to acknowledge the receipt of your communication of the 4th instant, inclosing (documents Nos. 1, 2, 3, 4, 5, and 6) copies of correspondence and notes of conversation with the President of the United States and the Secretary of War concerning various military movements suggested by yourself for the better protection of the government and the maintenance of public order.

Permit me to renew to you the assurance of my high appreciation of the many past services you have rendered the Union, and of my deep gratification at this evidence of your present active exertions to maintain the integrity and honor of the nation.

I shall be highly pleased to receive from time to time such communications from yourself as you may deem it proper to make to me.

Very truly your obedient servant,   A. LINCOLN.

January 11, 1861.—LETTER TO J. T. HALE.

(*Confidential.*)

SPRINGFIELD, ILLINOIS, January 11, 1861.
HON. J. T. HALE.

My dear Sir: Yours of the 6th is received. I answer it only because I fear you would misconstrue my silence. What is our present condition? We have just carried an election on principles fairly stated to the people. Now we are told in advance the government shall be broken up unless we surrender to those we have beaten, before we take the offices. In this they are either attempting to play upon us or they are in dead earnest. Either way, if we surrender, it is the end of us and of the government. They will repeat the experiment upon us *ad libitum.* A year will not pass till we shall have to take Cuba as a condition upon which they will stay in the Union. They now have the Constitution under which we have lived over seventy years, and acts of Congress of their own framing, with no prospect of their being changed; and they can never have a more shallow pretext for breaking up the government, or extorting a compromise, than now. There is in my judgment but one compromise which would really settle the slavery question, and that would be a prohibition against acquiring any more territory.

Yours very truly,   A. LINCOLN.

January 12, 1861.—LETTER TO W. H. SEWARD.

(*Private.*)

SPRINGFIELD, ILLINOIS, January 12, 1861.
HON. W. H. SEWARD.

My dear Sir: Yours of the 8th received. I still hope Mr. Gilmer will, on a fair understanding with us, consent to take a place in the cabinet. The preference for him over Mr. Hunt or Mr. Gentry is that, up to date, he has a living position in the South, while they have not. He is only better than Winter Davis in that he is farther South. I fear if we could get we could not safely take more than one such man — that is, not more than one who opposed us in the election, the danger being to lose the confidence of our own friends.

Your selection for the State Department having become public, I am happy to find scarcely any objection to it. I shall have trouble with every other Northern cabinet appointment, so much so that I shall have to defer them as long as possible, to avoid being teased to insanity to make changes. Your obedient servant,

A. LINCOLN.

January 13, 1861.—LETTERS TO SIMON CAMERON.

(Private and confidential.)

SPRINGFIELD, ILLINOIS, January 13, 1861.

HON. SIMON CAMERON.

My dear Sir: At the suggestion of Mr. Sanderson, and with hearty good-will besides, I herewith send you a letter dated January 3 — the same in date as the last you received from me. I thought best to give it that date, as it is in some sort to take the place of that letter. I learn, both by a letter from Mr. Swett and from Mr. Sanderson, that your feelings were wounded by the terms of my letter really of the 3d. I wrote that letter under great anxiety, and perhaps I was not so guarded in its terms as I should have been; but I beg you to be assured I intended no offense. My great object was to have you act quickly, if possible before the matter should be complicated with the Pennsylvania senatorial election. Destroy the offensive letter, or return it to me.

I say to you now I have not doubted that you would perform the duties of a department ably and faithfully. Nor have I for a moment intended to ostracize your friends. If I should make a cabinet appointment for Pennsylvania before I reach Washington, I will not do so without consulting you, and giving all the weight to your views and wishes which I consistently can. This I have always intended.   Yours truly,

A. LINCOLN.

[Inclosure.]

SPRINGFIELD, ILLINOIS, January 3, 1861.

HON. SIMON CAMERON.

My dear Sir: When you were here, about the last of December, I handed you a letter saying I should at the proper time nominate you to the Senate for a place in the cabinet. It is due to you and to truth for me to say you were here by my invitation, and not upon any suggestion of your own. You have not as yet signified to me whether you would accept the appointment, and with much pain I now say to you that you will relieve me from great embarrassment by allowing me to recall the offer. This springs from an unexpected complication, and not from any change of my view as to the ability or faithfulness with which you would discharge the duties of the place.   I now think I will not definitely fix upon any appointment for Pennsylvania until I reach Washington.

Your obedient servant,   A. LINCOLN.

January 14, 1861.— LETTER TO GENERAL JOHN E. WOOL.

SPRINGFIELD, ILLINOIS, January 14, 1861.

GENERAL JOHN E. WOOL.

My dear Sir: Many thanks for your patriotic and generous letter of the 11th instant.   As to how far the military force of the government may become necessary to the preservation of the Union, and more particularly how that force can best be directed to the object, I must chiefly rely upon General Scott and yourself.   It affords me the profoundest satisfaction to know that with both of you judgment and feeling go heartily with your sense of professional and official duty to the work.

It is true that I have given but little attention to the military department of government; but, be assured, I cannot be ignorant as to who General Wool is, or what he has done.   With my highest esteem and gratitude, I subscribe myself

Your obedient servant,   A. LINCOLN.

January 23, 1861.— LETTER TO GENERAL EDWIN C. WILSON.

(*Private.*)

SPRINGFIELD, ILLINOIS, January 23, 1861.

GENERAL EDWIN C. WILSON.   ⁌

Dear Sir: Your official communication of the 31st ultimo, addressed to Hon. A. Lincoln, was duly received.

Mr. Lincoln desires me to answer that while he does not now deem it necessary to avail himself of the services you so kindly offer him, he is nevertheless gratified to have this assurance from yourself that the militia of the State of Pennsylvania is loyal to the Constitution and the Union, and stands ready to rally to their support and maintenance in the event of trouble or danger.   Yours truly,

JNO. G. NICOLAY.

January 26, 1861.— LETTER TO R. A. CAMERON AND OTHERS, COMMITTEE.

SPRINGFIELD, January 26, 1861.

MESSRS. CAMERON, MARSH, AND BRANHAM, Committee.

Gentlemen : I have the honor to acknowledge the receipt, by your hands, of a copy of a joint resolution adopted by the legislature of the State of Indiana, on the 15th instant, inviting me to visit that honorable body on my way to the Federal capital.

Expressing my profound gratitude for this flattering testimonial of their regard and esteem, be pleased to bear to them my acceptance of their kind invitation, and inform them that I will endeavor to visit them, in accordance with their expressed desire, on the 12th of February next.

With feelings of high consideration, I remain

Your humble servant,   A. LINCOLN.

January 28, 1861.—LETTER TO JAMES SULGROVE AND OTHERS, COMMITTEE.

SPRINGFIELD, ILLINOIS, January 28, 1861.

MESSRS. JAMES SULGROVE, ERIE LOCKE, WILLIAM WALLACE, AND JOHN T. WOOD, Committee.

Gentlemen: I received to-day from the hands of Mr. Locke a transcript of the resolutions passed at a meeting of the citizens of Indianapolis, inviting me to visit that city on my route to Washington.

Permit me to express to the citizens of Indianapolis, through you, their committee, my cordial thanks for the honor shown me. I accept with great pleasure the invitation so kindly tendered, and will be in your city on the 12th day of February next.

Your obedient servant,   A. LINCOLN.

January 28, 1861.—LETTER TO J. W. TILLMAN.

SPRINGFIELD, ILLINOIS, January 28, 1861.

J. W. TILLMAN, Esq.

Dear Sir: Your letter of the 24th instant addressed to Hon. A. Lincoln, inviting him, on behalf of the State Central Committee of Michigan, to pass through that State on his journey to Washington, has been received.

He desires me to reply, with profound thanks for the honor thus cordially tendered him, that having accepted similar invitations to pass through the capitals of the States of Indiana and Ohio, he regrets that it will be out of his power to accept the courtesies and hospitalities of the people of Michigan so kindly proffered him through yourself and the committee.

Yours truly,   JNO. G. NICOLAY.

January 28, 1861.—LETTER TO EDWARD BATES.

SPRINGFIELD, ILLINOIS, January 28, 1861.

HON. EDWARD BATES.

Dear Sir: Hon. A. Lincoln desires me to write to you that he has determined on starting from here for Washington city on the 11th of February. He will go through Indianapolis, Columbus, Pittsburg, Albany, New York, Philadelphia, Harrisburg, and Baltimore.

Albany, New York, and Philadelphia are not *finally* decided upon, though it is probable that he will also take them in his route. The journey will occupy twelve or fifteen days.

Yours truly,   JNO. G. NICOLAY.

February 1, 1861.—LETTER TO E. D. MORGAN.

SPRINGFIELD, ILLINOIS, February 1, 1861.

HON. E. D. MORGAN.

Dear Sir: Your letter of the 19th ultimo addressed to Hon. A. Lincoln, was duly received, in which you invite him to visit Albany on his route to Washington, and tender him the hospitalities of the State and your home.

In accordance with the answer just sent to the telegraphic message received from yourself a few minutes since, Mr. Lincoln desires me to write that it has for some little time been his purpose to pass through Albany, and that he would have answered you to that same effect before this, but for the fact that as the legislatures of Indiana, Ohio, New Jersey, and Pennsylvania had by resolution invited him to visit them, he thought it probable that a similar resolution would be adopted by the legislature of New York, and he had therefore waited to reply to both invitations together.

He will cheerfully accede to any arrangements yourself and the citizens of Albany may make for his stay, providing only no formal ceremonies wasting any great amount of time be adopted.

Yours truly,   JNO. G. NICOLAY.

February 1, 1861.—LETTER TO W. H. SEWARD.

(Private and confidential.)

SPRINGFIELD, ILLINOIS, February 1, 1861.

HON. W. H. SEWARD.

My dear Sir: On the 21st ult. Hon. W. Kellogg, a Republican member of Congress of this State, whom you probably know, was here in a good deal of anxiety seeking to ascertain to what extent I would be consenting for our friends to go in the way of compromise on the now vexed question. While he was with me I received a despatch from Senator Trumbull, at Washington, alluding to the same question and telling me to await letters. I therefore told Mr. Kellogg that when I should receive these letters posting me as to the state of affairs at Washington, I would write to you, requesting you to let him see my letter. To my surprise, when the letters mentioned by Judge Trumbull came they made no allusion to the " vexed question." This baffled me so much that I was near not writing you at all, in compliance to what I have said to Judge Kellogg. I say now, however, as I have all the while said, that on the territorial question—that is, the question of extending slavery under the national auspices — I am inflexible. I am for no compromise which assists or permits the extension of the institution on soil owned by the nation.   And any trick by which the nation is to acquire territory, and then allow some local authority to spread slavery over it, is as obnoxious as any other.   I take it that to effect some such result as this, and to put us again on the highroad to a slave empire, is the object of all these proposed compromises.   I am against it. As to fugitive slaves, District of Columbia, slave-trade among the slave States, and whatever springs of necessity from the fact that the institution is amongst us, I care but little, so that what is done be comely and not altogether outrageous.   Nor do I care much about New Mexico, if further extension were hedged against.

Yours very truly,   A. LINCOLN.

February 4, 1861.— LETTER TO THURLOW WEED.

SPRINGFIELD, ILLINOIS, February 4, 1861.

Dear Sir: I have both your letter to myself and that to Judge Davis, in relation to a certain gentleman in your State claiming to dispense patronage in my name, and also to be authorized to use my name to advance the chances of Mr. Greeley for an election to the United States Senate.

It is very strange that such things should be said by any one.   The gentleman you mention did speak to me of Mr. Greeley in connection with the senatorial election, and I replied in terms of kindness toward Mr. Greeley, which I really feel, but always with an expressed protest that my name must not be used in the senatorial election in favor of, or against, any one.   Any other representation of me is a misrepresentation.

As to the matter of dispensing patronage, it perhaps will surprise you to learn that I have information that you claim to have my authority to arrange that matter in New York.   I do not believe that you have so claimed; but still so some men say.   On that subject you know all I have said to you is "Justice to all," and I have said nothing more particular to any one.   I say this to reassure you that I have not changed my position.   In the hope, however, that you will not use my name in the matter, I am

Yours truly,   A. LINCOLN.

February 4, 1861.—LETTER TO E. D. MORGAN.

SPRINGFIELD, ILLINOIS, February 4, 1861.

Sir: Your letter of the 30th ultimo, inviting me on behalf of the legislature of New York to pass through that State on my way to Washington, and tendering me the hospitalities of her authorities and people, has been duly received.

With feelings of deep gratitude to you and them for this testimonial of regard and esteem, I beg you to notify them that I accept the invitation so kindly extended. Your obedient servant,

A. LINCOLN.

His Excellency EDWIN D. MORGAN,
Governor of New York.

P. S. Please let ceremonies be only such as to take the least time possible. A. L.

February 5, 1861.—LETTER TO EDWARD BATES.

SPRINGFIELD, ILLINOIS, February 5, 1861.

HON. EDWARD BATES.

Dear Sir: Hon. A. Lincoln directs me to say to you that in case you intend going to Washington about the time he proposes to start (the 11th instant), he would be pleased to have you accompany him on the trip he contemplates.

He does not desire to have you do this, however, at the cost of any inconvenience to yourself, or the derangement of any plans you may have already formed.   Yours truly,

JNO. G. NICOLAY.

P. S. Mr. Lincoln intended to have said this to you himself when you were here, but in his hurry it escaped his attention.

J. G. N.

February 6, 1861.—LETTER TO CHARLES S. OLDEN.

SPRINGFIELD, ILLINOIS, February 6, 1861.

Sir: Your letter of the 1st instant inviting me, in compliance with the request of the legislature of New Jersey, to visit your State capital while on my journey to Washington, has been duly received.

I accept the invitation, with much gratitude to you and them for the kindness and honor thus offered. Your obedient servant,

A. LINCOLN.

His Excellency CHARLES S. OLDEN,
Governor of New Jersey.

P. S. Please arrange no ceremonies that will waste time.

February 7, 1861.—LETTER TO THE GOVERNOR AND THE LEGISLA-
TURE OF MASSACHUSETTS.

SPRINGFIELD, ILLINOIS, February 7, 1861.

HIS EXCELLENCY THE GOVERNOR, THE PRESIDENT OF THE SENATE,
AND THE SPEAKER OF THE HOUSE OF REPRESENTATIVES FOR
THE COMMONWEALTH OF MASSACHUSETTS.

Gentlemen: Your kind letter of February 1, with a copy of the resolutions of the General Court, inviting me, in the name of the government and people of Massachusetts, to visit the State and accept its hospitality previous to the time of the presidential inauguration, is gratefully received by the hand of Colonel Horace Binney Sargent; and, in answer, I am constrained to say want of time denies me the pleasure of accepting the invitation so generously tendered.   Your obedient servant,

A. LINCOLN.

February 7, 1861.—LETTER TO WILLIAM DENNISON.

SPRINGFIELD, ILLINOIS, February 7, 1861.

Sir : Your letter of the 31st ultimo, inviting me, on behalf of the legislature of Ohio, to visit Columbus on my way to Washington, has been duly received.

With profound gratitude for the mark of respect and honor thus cordially tendered me by you and them, I accept the invitation.

Your obedient servant,   A. LINCOLN.

His Excellency WILLIAM DENNISON,
Governor of Ohio.

Please arrange no ceremonies which will waste time.

February 7, 1861.—LETTER TO J. G. LOWE AND OTHERS, COMMITTEE.

SPRINGFIELD, ILLINOIS, February 7, 1861.

Gentlemen : Your note of to-day, inviting me while on my way to Washington to pass through the town and accept the hospitalities of the citizens of Dayton, Ohio, is before me.

A want of the necessary time makes it impossible for me to stop in your town.   If it will not retard my arrival at or departure from the city of Columbus, I will endeavor to pass through and at least bow to the friends there; if, however, it would in any wise delay me, they must not even expect this, but be content instead to receive through you my warmest thanks for the kindness and cordiality with which they have tendered this invitation.

Your obedient servant,   A. LINCOLN.

MESSRS. J. G. LOWE, T. A. PHILLIPS,
AND W. H. GILLESPIE, Committee.

February 8, 1861.—LETTER TO GEORGE B. SENTER AND OTHERS, COMMITTEE.

SPRINGFIELD, ILLINOIS, February 8, 1861.

GEORGE B. SENTER AND OTHERS, Committee.

Gentlemen : Yours of the 6th, inviting me, in compliance with a resolution of the city council of the city of Cleveland, Ohio, to visit that city on my contemplated journey to Washington, is duly at hand, and in answer I have the honor to accept the invitation.   The time of arrival and other details are subject to future arrangement.

Your obedient servant,   A. LINCOLN.

February 8, 1861.—LETTER TO A. D. FINNEY AND OTHERS,
COMMITTEE.

SPRINGFIELD, ILLINOIS, February 8, 1861.
HON. A. D. FINNEY AND OTHERS, Committee.

Gentlemen: Yours of the 4th, inviting me on behalf of the legislature of Pennsylvania to visit Harrisburg on my way to the Federal
capital, is received; and, in answer, allow me to say I gratefully accept the tendered honor.

The time of arrival, and other details, are subject to future arrangements.   Your obedient servant,

A. LINCOLN.

February 11, 1861.—FAREWELL ADDRESS AT SPRINGFIELD,
ILLINOIS.

My Friends: No one, not in my situation, can appreciate my feeling of sadness at this parting. To this place, and the kindness of
these people, I owe everything. Here I have lived a quarter of a
century, and have passed from a young to an old man. Here my
children have been born, and one is buried. I now leave, not knowing when or whether ever I may return, with a task before me
greater than that which rested upon Washington. Without the
assistance of that Divine Being who ever attended him, I cannot
succeed. With that assistance, I cannot fail. Trusting in Him
who can go with me, and remain with you, and be everywhere for
good, let us confidently hope that all will yet be well. To His care
commending you, as I hope in your prayers you will commend me,
I bid you an affectionate farewell.

February 11, 1861.—REPLY TO THE ADDRESS OF WELCOME AT
INDIANAPOLIS, INDIANA.

Governor Morton and Fellow-citizens of the State of Indiana: Most
heartily do I thank you for this magnificent reception; and while
I cannot take to myself any share of the compliment thus paid, more
than that which pertains to a mere instrument—an accidental instrument perhaps I should say—of a great cause, I yet must look
upon it as a magnificent reception, and as such most heartily do I
thank you for it. You have been pleased to address yourself to me
chiefly in behalf of this glorious Union in which we live, in all of
which you have my hearty sympathy, and, as far as may be within
my power, will have, one and inseparably, my hearty coöperation.
While I do not expect, upon this occasion, or until I get to Washington, to attempt any lengthy speech, I will only say that to the salvation of the Union there needs but one single thing, the hearts of a
people like yours. When the people rise in mass in behalf of the

Union and the liberties of this country, truly may it be said, "The gates of hell cannot prevail against them." In all trying positions in which I shall be placed, and doubtless I shall be placed in many such, my reliance will be upon you and the people of the United States; and I wish you to remember, now and forever, that it is your business, and not mine; that if the union of these States and the liberties of this people shall be lost, it is but little to any one man of fifty-two years of age, but a great deal to the thirty millions of people who inhabit these United States, and to their posterity in all coming time. It is your business to rise up and preserve the Union and liberty for yourselves, and not for me. I appeal to you again to constantly bear in mind that not with politicians, not with Presidents, not with office-seekers, but with you, is the question: Shall the Union and shall the liberties of this country be preserved to the latest generations?

February 12 1861.—ADDRESS TO THE LEGISLATURE OF INDIANA AT INDIANAPOLIS.

Fellow-citizens of the State of Indiana: I am here to thank you much for this magnificent welcome, and still more for the generous support given by your State to that political cause which I think is the true and just cause of the whole country and the whole world. Solomon says there is "a time to keep silence," and when men wrangle by the month with no certainty that they mean the same thing, while using the same word, it perhaps were as well if they would keep silence. The words "coercion" and "invasion" are much used in these days, and often with some temper and hot blood. Let us make sure, if we can, that we do not misunderstand the meaning of those who use them. Let us get exact definitions of these words, not from dictionaries, but from the men themselves, who certainly deprecate the things they would represent by the use of words. What, then, is "coercion"? What is "invasion"? Would the marching of an army into South Carolina without the consent of her people, and with hostile intent toward them, be "invasion"? I certainly think it would; and it would be "coercion" also if the South Carolinians were forced to submit. But if the United States should merely hold and retake its own forts and other property, and collect the duties on foreign importations, or even withhold the mails from places where they were habitually violated, would any or all of these things be "invasion" or "coercion"? Do our professed lovers of the Union, but who spitefully resolve that they will resist coercion and invasion, understand that such things as these on the part of the United States would be coercion or invasion of a State? If so, their idea of means to preserve the object of their great affection would seem to be exceedingly thin and airy. If sick, the little pills of the homeopathist would be much too large for them to swallow. In their view, the Union as a family relation would seem to be no regular marriage, but rather a sort of "free-love" arrangement, to be maintained only on "passional attraction." By

VOL. I.—43.

the way, in what consists the special sacredness of a State? I speak
not of the position assigned to a State in the Union by the Constitution; for that, by the bond, we all recognize. That position, however, a State cannot carry out of the Union with it. I speak of that
assumed primary right of a State to rule all which is less than itself,
and ruin all which is larger than itself. If a State and a county, in
a given case, should be equal in extent of territory, and equal in
number of inhabitants, in what, as a matter of principle, is the State
better than the county? Would an exchange of names be an exchange of rights upon principle? On what rightful principle may
a State, being not more than one fiftieth part of the nation in soil
and population, break up the nation and then coerce a proportion-
ally larger subdivision of itself in the most arbitrary way? What
mysterious right to play tyrant is conferred on a district of country
with its people, by merely calling it a State? Fellow-citizens, I am
not asserting anything; I am merely asking questions for you to
consider. And now allow me to bid you farewell.

February 12, 1861.— ADDRESS TO THE MAYOR AND CITIZENS OF CINCINNATI, OHIO.

Mr. Mayor, Ladies, and Gentlemen: Twenty-four hours ago, at the
capital of Indiana, I said to myself I have never seen so many people assembled together in winter weather. I am no longer able to
say that. But it is what might reasonably have been expected—
that this great city of Cincinnati would thus acquit herself on such
an occasion. My friends, I am entirely overwhelmed by the magnifi-
cence of the reception which has been given, I will not say to me, but
to the President-elect of the United States of America. Most heartily
do I thank you, one and all, for it.

I am reminded by the address of your worthy mayor that this
reception is given not by any one political party, and even if I had
not been so reminded by his Honor I could not have failed to know
the fact by the extent of the multitude I see before me now. I could
not look upon this vast assemblage without being made aware that
all parties were united in this reception. This is as it should be. It
is as it should have been if Senator Douglas had been elected. It is
as it should have been if Mr. Bell had been elected; as it should
have been if Mr. Breckinridge had been elected; as it should ever
be when any citizen of the United States is constitutionally elected
President of the United States. Allow me to say that I think what
has occurred here to-day could not have occurred in any other country on the face of the globe, without the influence of the free institutions which we have unceasingly enjoyed for three quarters of a
century.

There is no country where the people can turn out and enjoy this
day precisely as they please, save under the benign influence of the
free institutions of our land.

I hope that, although we have some threatening national difficulties now — I hope that while these free institutions shall continue to

be in the enjoyment of millions of free people of the United States, we will see repeated every four years what we now witness.

In a few short years I, and every other individual man who is now living, will pass away; I hope that our national difficulties will also pass away, and I hope we shall see in the streets of Cincinnati — good old Cincinnati — for centuries to come, once every four years, her people give such a reception as this to the constitutionally elected President of the whole United States. I hope you shall all join in that reception, and that you shall also welcome your brethren from across the river to participate in it. We will welcome them in every State of the Union, no matter where they are from. From away South we shall extend them a cordial good-will, when our present difficulties shall have been forgotten and blown to the winds forever.

I have spoken but once before this in Cincinnati. That was a year previous to the late presidential election. On that occasion, in a playful manner, but with sincere words, I addressed much of what I said to the Kentuckians. I gave my opinion that we as Republicans would ultimately beat them as Democrats, but that they could postpone that result longer by nominating Senator Douglas for the presidency than they could in any other way. They did not, in any true sense of the word, nominate Mr. Douglas, and the result has come certainly as soon as ever I expected. I also told them how I expected they would be treated after they should have been beaten; and I now wish to recall their attention to what I then said upon that subject. I then said, "When we do as we say,—beat you,— you perhaps want to know what we will do with you. I will tell you, so far as I am authorized to speak for the opposition, what we mean to do with you. We mean to treat you, as near as we possibly can, as Washington, Jefferson, and Madison treated you. We mean to leave you alone, and in no way to interfere with your institutions; to abide by all and every compromise of the Constitution; and, in a word, coming back to the original proposition, to treat you, so far as degenerate men — if we have degenerated — may, according to the examples of those noble fathers, Washington, Jefferson, and Madison. We mean to remember that you are as good as we; that there is no difference between us other than the difference of circumstances. We mean to recognize and bear in mind always that you have as good hearts in your bosoms as other people, or as we claim to have, and treat you accordingly."

Fellow-citizens of Kentucky!—friends!—brethren! may I call you in my new position? I see no occasion, and feel no inclination, to retract a word of this. If it shall not be made good, be assured the fault shall not be mine.

And now, fellow-citizens of Ohio, have you, who agree with him who now addresses you in political sentiment— have you ever entertained other sentiments toward our brethren of Kentucky than those I have expressed to you? If not, then why shall we not, as heretofore, be recognized and acknowledged as brethren again, living in peace and harmony again one with another? I take your response as the most reliable evidence that it may be so, trusting, through the good sense of the American people, on all sides of all rivers in

America, under the providence of God, who has never deserted us, that we shall again be brethren, forgetting all parties, ignoring all parties. My friends, I now bid you farewell.

February 12, 1861.— ADDRESS TO GERMANS AT CINCINNATI, OHIO.

Mr. Chairman: I thank you and those whom you represent for the compliment you have paid me by tendering me this address. In so far as there is an allusion to our present national difficulties, which expresses, as you have said, the views of the gentlemen present, I shall have to beg pardon for not entering fully upon the questions which the address you have now read suggests.

I deem it my duty — a duty which I owe to my constituents — to you, gentlemen, that I should wait until the last moment for a development of the present national difficulties before I express myself decidedly as to what course I shall pursue. I hope, then, not to be false to anything that you have to expect of me.

I agree with you, Mr. Chairman, that the working-men are the basis of all governments, for the plain reason that they are the more numerous, and as you added that those were the sentiments of the gentlemen present, representing not only the working-class, but citizens of other callings than those of the mechanic, I am happy to concur with you in these sentiments, not only of the native-born citizens, but also of the Germans and foreigners from other countries.

Mr. Chairman, I hold that while man exists it is his duty to improve not only his own condition, but to assist in ameliorating mankind; and therefore, without entering upon the details of the question, I will simply say that I am for those means which will give the greatest good to the greatest number.

In regard to the homestead law, I have to say that in so far as the government lands can be disposed of, I am in favor of cutting up the wild lands into parcels, so that every poor man may have a home.

In regard to the Germans and foreigners, I esteem them no better than other people, nor any worse. It is not my nature, when I see a people borne down by the weight of their shackles — the oppression of tyranny — to make their life more bitter by heaping upon them greater burdens; but rather would I do all in my power to raise the yoke than to add anything that would tend to crush them.

Inasmuch as our country is extensive and new, and the countries of Europe are densely populated, if there are any abroad who desire to make this the land of their adoption, it is not in my heart to throw aught in their way to prevent them from coming to the United States.

Mr. Chairman and gentlemen, I will bid you an affectionate farewell.

February 13, 1861.— ADDRESS TO THE LEGISLATURE OF OHIO AT COLUMBUS.

Mr. President and Mr. Speaker, and Gentlemen of the General Assembly of Ohio: It is true, as has been said by the president of the Senate, that very great responsibility rests upon me in the position to which the votes of the American people have called me. I am deeply sensible of that weighty responsibility. I cannot but know what you all know, that without a name, perhaps without a reason why I should have a name, there has fallen upon me a task such as did not rest even upon the Father of his Country; and so feeling, I can turn and look for that support without which it will be impossible for me to perform that great task. I turn, then, and look to the American people, and to that God who has never forsaken them. Allusion has been made to the interest felt in relation to the policy of the new administration. In this I have received from some a degree of credit for having kept silence, and from others some deprecation. I still think that I was right. . . .

In the varying and repeatedly shifting scenes of the present, and without a precedent which could enable me to judge by the past, it has seemed fitting that before speaking upon the difficulties of the country I should have gained a view of the whole field, being at liberty to modify and change the course of policy as future events may make a change necessary.

I have not maintained silence from any want of real anxiety. It is a good thing that there is no more than anxiety, for there is nothing going wrong. It is a consoling circumstance that when we look out there is nothing that really hurts anybody. We entertain different views upon political questions, but nobody is suffering anything. This is a most consoling circumstance, and from it we may conclude that all we want is time, patience, and a reliance on that God who has never forsaken this people.

Fellow-citizens, what I have said I have said altogether extemporaneously, and I will now come to a close.

February 14, 1861.—ADDRESS AT STEUBENVILLE, OHIO.

I fear that the great confidence placed in my ability is unfounded. Indeed, I am sure it is. Encompassed by vast difficulties as I am, nothing shall be wanting on my part, if sustained by God and the American people. I believe the devotion to the Constitution is equally great on both sides of the river. It is only the different understanding of that instrument that causes difficulty. The only dispute on both sides is, "What are their rights?" If the majority should not rule, who would be the judge? Where is such a judge to be found? We should all be bound by the majority of the American people; if not, then the minority must control. Would that be right? Would it be just or generous? Assuredly not. I reiterate that the majority should rule. If I adopt a wrong policy, the opportunity for condemnation will occur in four years' time. Then I can be turned out, and a better man with better views put in my place.

February 15, 1861.—ADDRESS AT PITTSBURG, PENNSYLVANIA.

I most cordially thank his Honor Mayor Wilson, and the citizens of Pittsburg generally, for their flattering reception. I am the more grateful because I know that it is not given to me alone, but to the cause I represent, which clearly proves to me their good-will, and that sincere feeling is at the bottom of it. And here I may remark that in every short address I have made to the people, in every crowd through which I have passed of late, some allusion has been made to the present distracted condition of the country. It is natural to expect that I should say something on this subject; but to touch upon it at all would involve an elaborate discussion of a great many questions and circumstances, requiring more time than I can at present command, and would, perhaps, unnecessarily commit me upon matters which have not yet fully developed themselves. The condition of the country is an extraordinary one, and fills the mind of every patriot with anxiety. It is my intention to give this subject all the consideration I possibly can before specially deciding in regard to it, so that when I do speak it may be as nearly right as possible. When I do speak I hope I may say nothing in opposition to the spirit of the Constitution, contrary to the integrity of the Union, or which will prove inimical to the liberties of the people, or to the peace of the whole country. And, furthermore, when the time arrives for me to speak on this great subject, I hope I may say nothing to disappoint the people generally throughout the country, especially if the expectation has been based upon anything which I may have heretofore said. Notwithstanding the troubles across the river [the speaker pointing southwardly across the Monongahela, and smiling], there is no crisis but an artificial one. What is there now to warrant the condition of affairs presented by our friends over the river? Take even their own view of the questions involved, and there is nothing to justify the course they are pursuing. I repeat, then, there is no crisis, excepting such a one as may be gotten up at any time by turbulent men aided by designing politicians. My advice to them, under such circumstances, is to keep cool. If the great American people only keep their temper on both sides of the line, the troubles will come to an end, and the question which now distracts the country will be settled, just as surely as all other difficulties of a like character which have originated in this government have been adjusted. Let the people on both sides keep their self-possession, and just as other clouds have cleared away in due time, so will this great nation continue to prosper as heretofore. But, fellow-citizens, I have spoken longer on this subject than I intended at the outset.

It is often said that the tariff is the specialty of Pennsylvania. Assuming that direct taxation is not to be adopted, the tariff question must be as durable as the government itself. It is a question of national housekeeping. It is to the government what replenishing the meal-tub is to the family. Ever-varying circumstances will require frequent modifications as to the amount needed and the sources of supply. So far there is little difference of opinion among the people. It is as to whether, and how far, duties on imports shall be adjusted to favor home production in the home market, that controversy begins. One party insists that such adjustment oppresses one class for the advantage of another; while the other party argues that, with all its incidents, in the long run all classes are benefited. In the Chicago platform there is a plank upon this subject which should be a general law to the incoming administration. We should do neither more nor less than we gave the people reason to believe we would when they gave us their votes. Permit me, fellow-citizens, to read the tariff plank of the Chicago platform, or rather have it read in your hearing by one who has younger eyes.

Mr. Lincoln's private secretary then read Section 12 of the Chicago platform, as follows:

That while providing revenue for the support of the General Government by duties upon imports, sound policy requires such an adjustment of these imposts as will encourage the development of the industrial interest of the whole country; and we commend that policy of national exchanges which secures to working-men liberal wages, to agriculture remunerating prices, to mechanics and manufacturers adequate reward for their skill, labor, and enterprise, and to the nation commercial prosperity and independence.

Mr. Lincoln resumed: As with all general propositions, doubtless there will be shades of difference in construing this. I have by no means a thoroughly matured judgment upon this subject, especially as to details; some general ideas are about all. I have long thought it would be to our advantage to produce any necessary article at home which can be made of as good quality and with as little labor at home as abroad, at least by the difference of the carrying from abroad. In such case the carrying is demonstrably a dead loss of labor. For instance, labor being the true standard of value, is it not plain that if equal labor get a bar of railroad iron out of a mine in England, and another out of a mine in Pennsylvania, each can be laid down in a track at home cheaper than they could exchange countries, at least by the carriage? If there be a present cause why one can be both made and carried cheaper in money price than the other can be made without carrying, that cause is an unnatural and injurious one, and ought gradually, if not rapidly, to be removed. The condition of the treasury at this time would seem to render an early revision of the tariff indispensable. The Morrill [tariff] bill, now pending before Congress, may or may not become a law. I am not posted as to its particular provisions, but if they are generally satisfactory, and the bill shall now pass, there will be an end for the present. If, however, it shall not pass, I suppose the whole subject will be one of the most pressing and important for the next Congress. By the Constitution, the executive may recommend measures which he may think proper, and he may veto those he thinks improper, and it is supposed that he may add to these certain indirect influences to affect the action of Congress. My political education strongly inclines me against a very free use of any of these means by the executive to control the legislation of the country. As a rule, I think it better that Congress should originate as well as perfect its measures without external bias. I therefore would rather recommend to every gentlemen who knows he is to be a member of the next Congress to take an enlarged view, and post himself thoroughly, so as to contribute his part to such an adjustment of the tariff as shall produce a sufficient revenue, and in its other bearings, so far as possible, be just and equal to all sections of the country and classes of the people.

February 15, 1861.— ADDRESS AT CLEVELAND, OHIO.

Fellow-citizens of Cleveland and Ohio: We have come here upon a very inclement afternoon. We have marched for two miles through the rain and the mud.

The large numbers that have turned out under these circumstances testify that you are in earnest about something, and what is that something? I would not have you suppose that I think this extreme earnestness is about me. I should be exceedingly sorry to see such devotion if that were the case. But I know it is paid to something worth more than any one man, or any thousand or ten thousand men. You have assembled to testify your devotion to the Constitution, to the Union, and the laws, to the perpetual liberty of the people of this country. It is, fellow-citizens, for the whole American people, and not for one single man alone, to advance the great cause of the Union and the Constitution. And in a country like this, where every man bears on his face the marks of intelligence, where every man's clothing, if I may so speak, shows signs of comfort, and every dwelling signs of happiness and contentment, where schools and churches abound on every side, the Union can never be in danger. I would, if I could, instil some degree of patriotism and confidence into the political mind in relation to this matter.

Frequent allusion is made to the excitement at present existing in our national politics, and it is as well that I should also allude to it here. I think that there is no occasion for any excitement. I think the crisis, as it is called, is altogether an artificial one. In all parts of the nation there are differences of opinion on politics; there are differences of opinion even here. You did not all vote for the person who now addresses you, although quite enough of you did for all practical purposes, to be sure.

What they do who seek to destroy the Union is altogether artificial. What is happening to hurt them? Have they not all their rights now as they ever have had? Do not they have their fugitive slaves returned now as ever? Have they not the same Constitution that they have lived under for seventy-odd years? Have they not a position as citizens of this common country, and have we any power to change that position? [Cries of "No!"] What then is the matter with them? Why all this excitement? Why all these complaints? As I said before, this crisis is altogether artificial. It has no foundation in fact. It can't be argued up, and it can't be argued down. Let it alone, and it will go down of itself.

I have not strength, fellow-citizens, to address you at great length, and I pray that you will excuse me; but rest assured that my thanks are as cordial and sincere for the efficient aid which you will give to the good cause in working for the good of the nation, as for the votes you gave me last fall.

There is one feature that causes me great pleasure, and that is to learn that this reception is given, not alone by those with whom I chance to agree politically, but by all parties. I think I am not selfish when I say this is as it should be. If Judge Douglas had

been chosen President of the United States, and had this evening
been passing through your city, the Republicans should have joined
his supporters in welcoming him just as his friends have joined with
mine to-night. If we do not make common cause to save the good
old ship of the Union on this voyage, nobody will have a chance to
pilot her on another voyage.

To all of you, then, who have done me the honor to participate in
this cordial welcome, I return most sincerely my thanks, not for myself, but for Liberty, the Constitution, and Union.

I bid you an affectionate farewell.

February 16, 1861.—ADDRESS AT BUFFALO, NEW YORK.

Mr. Mayor and Fellow-citizens of Buffalo and the State of New York:
I am here to thank you briefly for this grand reception given to me,
not personally, but as the representative of our great and beloved
country. Your worthy mayor has been pleased to mention, in his
address to me, the fortunate and agreeable journey which I have had
from home, on my rather circuitous route to the Federal capital. I
am very happy that he was enabled in truth to congratulate myself
and company on that fact. It is true we have had nothing thus far
to mar the pleasure of the trip. We have not been met alone by those
who assisted in giving the election to me—I say not alone by them,
but by the whole population of the country through which we have
passed. This is as it should be. Had the election fallen to any other
of the distinguished candidates instead of myself, under the peculiar
circumstances, to say the least, it would have been proper for all citizens to have greeted him as you now greet me. It is an evidence of
the devotion of the whole people to the Constitution, the Union, and
the perpetuity of the liberties of this country. I am unwilling on any
occasion that I should be so meanly thought of as to have it supposed
for a moment that these demonstrations are tendered to me personally. They are tendered to the country, to the institutions of the
country, and to the perpetuity of the liberties of the country, for
which these institutions were made and created.

Your worthy mayor has thought fit to express the hope that I
may be able to relieve the country from the present, or, I should say,
the threatened difficulties. I am sure I bring a heart true to the
work. For the ability to perform it, I must trust in that Supreme
Being who has never forsaken this favored land, through the instrumentality of this great and intelligent people. Without that assistance I shall surely fail; with it, I cannot fail. When we speak of
threatened difficulties to the country, it is natural that it should be
expected that something should be said by myself with regard to
particular measures. Upon more mature reflection, however, others
will agree with me that, when it is considered that these difficulties
are without precedent, and have never been acted upon by any individual situated as I am, it is most proper I should wait and see the
developments, and get all the light possible, so that when I do speak
authoritatively, I may be as near right as possible. When I shall

speak authoritatively, I hope to say nothing inconsistent with the
Constitution, the Union, the rights of all the States, of each State,
and of each section of the country, and not to disappoint the reasonable expectations of those who have confided to me their votes.
In this connection allow me to say that you, as a portion of the great
American people, need only to maintain your composure, stand up to
your sober convictions of right, to your obligations to the Constitution, and act in accordance with those sober convictions, and the
clouds now on the horizon will be dispelled, and we shall have a
bright and glorious future; and when this generation has passed
away, tens of thousands will inhabit this country where only thousands inhabit it now. I do not propose to address you at length;
I have no voice for it. Allow me again to thank you for this magnificent reception, and bid you farewell.

February 18, 1861.—ADDRESS AT ROCHESTER, NEW YORK.

I confess myself, after having seen many large audiences since
leaving home, overwhelmed with this vast number of faces at this
hour of the morning. I am not vain enough to believe that you are
here from any wish to see me as an individual, but because I am for
the time being the representative of the American people. I could
not, if I would, address you at any length. I have not the strength,
even if I had the time, for a speech at each of these many interviews
that are afforded me on my way to Washington. I appear merely to
see you, and to let you see me, and to bid you farewell. I hope it will
be understood that it is from no disinclination to oblige anybody that
I do not address you at greater length.

February 18, 1861.—ADDRESS AT SYRACUSE, NEW YORK.

Ladies and Gentlemen : I see you have erected a very fine and
handsome platform here for me, and I presume you expected me
to speak from it. If I should go upon it, you would imagine
that I was about to deliver you a much longer speech than I am.
I wish you to understand that I mean no discourtesy to you by thus
declining. I intend discourtesy to no one. But I wish you to
understand that though I am unwilling to go upon this platform,
you are not at liberty to draw any inferences concerning any other
platform with which my name has been or is connected. I wish you
long life and prosperity individually, and pray that with the perpetuity of those institutions under which we have all so long lived and
prospered, our happiness may be secured, our future made brilliant,
and the glorious destiny of our country established forever. I bid
you a kind farewell.

February 18, 1861.—ADDRESS AT UTICA, NEW YORK.

Ladies and Gentlemen : I have no speech to make to you, and no
time to speak in. I appear before you that I may see you, and that

you may see me; and I am willing to admit, that so far as the ladies are concerned, I have the best of the bargain, though I wish it to be understood that I do not make the same acknowledgment concerning the men.

February 18, 1861.—REPLY TO THE MAYOR OF ALBANY, NEW YORK.

Mr. Mayor: I can hardly appropriate to myself the flattering terms in which you communicate the tender of this reception, as personal to myself. I most gratefully accept the hospitalities tendered to me, and will not detain you or the audience with any extended remarks at this time. I presume that in the two or three courses through which I shall have to go, I shall have to repeat somewhat, and I will therefore only express to you my thanks for this kind reception.

February 18, 1861.— REPLY TO GOVERNOR MORGAN OF NEW YORK, AT ALBANY.

Governor Morgan: I was pleased to receive an invitation to visit the capital of the great Empire State of this nation while on my way to the Federal capital. I now thank you, Mr. Governor, and you, the people of the capital of the State of New York, for this most hearty and magnificent welcome. If I am not at fault, the great Empire State at this time contains a larger population than did the whole of the United States of America at the time they achieved their national independence, and I was proud to be invited to visit its capital, to meet its citizens, as I now have the honor to do. I am notified by your governor that this reception is tendered by citizens without distinction of party. Because of this I accept it the more gladly. In this country, and in any country where freedom of thought is tolerated, citizens attach themselves to political parties. It is but an ordinary degree of charity to attribute this act to the supposition that in thus attaching themselves to the various parties, each man in his own judgment supposes he thereby best advances the interests of the whole country. And when an election is past, it is altogether befitting a free people, as I suppose, that, until the next election, they should be one people. The reception you have extended me to-day is not given to me personally,—it should not be so,—but as the representative, for the time being, of the majority of the nation. If the election had fallen to any of the more distinguished citizens who received the support of the people, this same honor should have greeted him that greets me this day, in testimony of the universal, unanimous devotion of the whole people to the Constitution, the Union, and to the perpetual liberties of succeeding generations in this country.

I have neither the voice nor the strength to address you at any greater length. I beg you will therefore accept my most grateful thanks for this manifest devotion — not to me, but the institutions of this great and glorious country.

February 18, 1861.— ADDRESS TO THE LEGISLATURE OF NEW
YORK, AT ALBANY.

*Mr. President and Gentlemen of the General Assembly of the State
of New York :* It is with feelings of great diffidence, and, I may say,
with feelings of awe, perhaps greater than I have recently experienced, that I meet you here in this place. The history of this great
State, the renown of those great men who have stood here, and have
spoken here, and been heard here, all crowd around my fancy, and
incline me to shrink from any attempt to address you. Yet I have
some confidence given me by the generous manner in which you
have invited me, and by the still more generous manner in which
you have received me, to speak further. You have invited and received me without distinction of party. I cannot for a moment
suppose that this has been done in any considerable degree with
reference to my personal services, but that it is done, in so far
as I am regarded, at this time, as the representative of the majesty
of this great nation. I doubt not this is the truth, and the whole
truth, of the case, and this is as it should be. It is much more
gratifying to me that this reception has been given to me as the
elected representative of a free people, than it could possibly be if
tendered merely as an evidence of devotion to me, or to any one
man personally.

And now I think it were more fitting that I should close these
hasty remarks. It is true that, while I hold myself, without mock
modesty, the humblest of all individuals that have ever been elevated
to the presidency, I have a more difficult task to perform than any
one of them.

You have generously tendered me the support — the united support — of the great Empire State. For this, in behalf of the nation
— in behalf of the present and future of the nation — in behalf of
civil and religious liberty for all time to come, most gratefully do I
thank you. I do not propose to enter into an explanation of any
particular line of policy, as to our present difficulties, to be adopted
by the incoming administration. I deem it just to you, to myself,
to all, that I should see everything, that I should hear everything,
that I should have every light that can be brought within my reach,
in order that, when I do so speak, I shall have enjoyed every opportunity to take correct and true ground; and for this reason I do
not propose to speak at this time of the policy of the government.
But when the time comes, I shall speak, as well as I am able, for the
good of the present and future of this country — for the good both
of the North and of the South—for the good of the one and the
other, and of all sections of the country. In the mean time, if we
have patience, if we restrain ourselves, if we allow ourselves not
to run off in a passion, I still have confidence that the Almighty,
the Maker of the universe, will, through the instrumentality of this
great and intelligent people, bring us through this as he has through
all the other difficulties of our country. Relying on this, I again
thank you for this generous reception.

February 19, 1861.—ADDRESS AT TROY, NEW YORK.

Mr. Mayor and Citizens of Troy: I thank you very kindly for this great reception. Since I left my home it has not been my fortune to meet an assemblage more numerous and more orderly than this. I am the more gratified at this mark of your regard, since you assure me it is tendered, not to the individual, but to the high office you have called me to fill. I have neither strength nor time to make any extended remarks on this occasion, and I can only repeat to you my sincere thanks for the kind reception you have thought proper to extend to me.

February 19, 1861.—ADDRESS AT POUGHKEEPSIE, NEW YORK.

Fellow-citizens: It is altogether impossible I should make myself heard by any considerable portion of this vast assemblage; but, although I appear before you mainly for the purpose of seeing you, and to let you see rather than hear me, I cannot refrain from saying that I am highly gratified—as much here, indeed, under the circumstances, as I have been anywhere on my route—to witness this noble demonstration—made, not in honor of an individual, but of the man who at this time humbly, but earnestly, represents the majesty of the nation.

This reception, like all the others that have been tendered to me, doubtless emanates from all the political parties, and not from one alone. As such I accept it the more gratefully, since it indicates an earnest desire on the part of the whole people, without regard to political differences, to save—not the country, because the country will save itself—but to save the institutions of the country—those institutions under which, in the last three quarters of a century, we have grown to a great, an intelligent, and a happy people—the greatest, the most intelligent, and the happiest people in the world. These noble manifestations indicate, with unerring certainty, that the whole people are willing to make common cause for this object; that if, as it ever must be, some have been successful in the recent election, and some have been beaten—if some are satisfied, and some are dissatisfied, the defeated party are not in favor of sinking the ship, but are desirous of running it through the tempest in safety, and willing, if they think the people have committed an error in their verdict now, to wait in the hope of reversing it, and setting it right next time. I do not say that in the recent election the people did the wisest thing that could have been done; indeed, I do not think they did; but I do say that in accepting the great trust committed to me, which I do with a determination to endeavor to prove worthy of it, I must rely upon you, upon the people of the whole country, for support; and with their sustaining aid, even I, humble as I am, cannot fail to carry the ship of state safely through the storm.

I have now only to thank you warmly for your kind attendance, and bid you all an affectionate farewell.

February 19, 1861.—ADDRESS AT HUDSON, NEW YORK.

Fellow-citizens: I see that you have provided a platform, but I shall have to decline standing on it. The superintendent tells me I have not time during our brief stay to leave the train. I had to decline standing on some very handsome platforms prepared for me yesterday. But I say to you, as I said to them, you must not on this account draw the inference that I have any intention to desert any platform I have a legitimate right to stand on. I do not appear before you for the purpose of making a speech. I come only to see you, and to give you the opportunity to see me; and I say to you, as I have before said to crowds where there were so many handsome ladies as there are here, I think I have decidedly the best of the bargain. I have only, therefore, to thank you most cordially for this kind reception, and bid you all farewell.

February 19, 1861.—ADDRESS AT PEEKSKILL, NEW YORK.

Ladies and Gentlemen: I have but a moment to stand before you to listen to and return your kind greeting. I thank you for this reception, and for the pleasant manner in which it is tendered to me by our mutual friends. I will say in a single sentence, in regard to the difficulties that lie before me and our beloved country, that if I can only be as generously and unanimously sustained as the demonstrations I have witnessed indicate I shall be, I shall not fail; but without your sustaining hands I am sure that neither I nor any other man can hope to surmount these difficulties. I trust that in the course I shall pursue I shall be sustained not only by the party that elected me, but by the patriotic people of the whole country.

February 19, 1861.—ADDRESS AT NEW YORK CITY.

Mr. Chairman and Gentlemen: I am rather an old man to avail myself of such an excuse as I am now about to do. Yet the truth is so distinct, and presses itself so distinctly upon me, that I cannot well avoid it—and that is, that I did not understand when I was brought into this room that I was to be brought here to make a speech. It was not intimated to me that I was brought into the room where Daniel Webster and Henry Clay had made speeches, and where one in my position might be expected to do something like those men or say something worthy of myself or my audience. I therefore beg you to make allowance for the circumstances in which I have been by surprise brought before you. Now I have been in the habit of thinking and sometimes speaking upon political questions that have for some years past agitated the country; and, if I were disposed to do so, and we could take up some one of the issues, as the lawyers call them, and I were called upon to make an argument about it to the best of my ability, I could do so without much preparation. But that is not what you desire to have done here to-night.

I have been occupying a position, since the presidential election, of silence — of avoiding public speaking, of avoiding public writing. I have been doing so because I thought, upon full consideration, that was the proper course for me to take. I am brought before you now, and required to make a speech, when you all approve more than anything else of the fact that I have been keeping silence. And now it seems to me that the response you give to that remark ought to justify me in closing just here. I have not kept silence since the presidential election from any party wantonness, or from any indifference to the anxiety that pervades the minds of men about the aspect of the political affairs of this country. I have kept silence for the reason that I supposed it was peculiarly proper that I should do so until the time came when, according to the custom of the country, I could speak officially.

I still suppose that, while the political drama being enacted in this country, at this time, is rapidly shifting its scenes — forbidding an anticipation with any degree of certainty, to-day, of what we shall see to-morrow — it is peculiarly fitting that I should see it all, up to the last minute, before I should take ground that I might be disposed (by the shifting of the scenes afterward) also to shift. I have said several times upon this journey, and I now repeat it to you, that when the time does come, I shall then take the ground that I think is right — right for the North, for the South, for the East, for the West, for the whole country. And in doing so, I hope to feel no necessity pressing upon me to say anything in conflict with the Constitution; in conflict with the continued union of these States, in conflict with the perpetuation of the liberties of this people, or anything in conflict with anything whatever that I have ever given you reason to expect from me. And now, my friends, have I said enough? [Loud cries of "No, no!" and "Three cheers for Lincoln!"] Now, my friends, there appears to be a difference of opinion between you and me, and I really feel called upon to decide the question myself.

February 20, 1861.— REPLY TO THE MAYOR OF NEW YORK CITY.

Mr. Mayor: It is with feelings of deep gratitude that I make my acknowledgments for the reception that has been given me in the great commercial city of New York. I cannot but remember that it is done by the people who do not, by a large majority, agree with me in political sentiment. It is the more grateful to me because in this I see that for the great principles of our government the people are pretty nearly or quite unanimous. In regard to the difficulties that confront us at this time, and of which you have seen fit to speak so becomingly and so justly, I can only say I agree with the sentiments expressed. In my devotion to the Union I hope I am behind no man in the nation. As to my wisdom in conducting affairs so as to tend to the preservation of the Union, I fear too great confidence may have been placed in me. I am sure I bring a heart devoted to the work. There is nothing that could ever bring me to consent — willingly to consent — to the destruction of this Union (in which not only the great city of New York, but the whole country, has acquired its greatness), unless it would be that thing for which the Union itself was made. I understand that the ship is made for the carrying and preservation of the cargo; and so long as the ship is safe with the cargo, it shall not be abandoned. This Union shall never be abandoned, unless the possibility of its existence shall cease to exist without the necessity of throwing passengers and cargo overboard. So long, then, as it is possible that the prosperity and liberties of this people can be preserved within this Union, it shall be my purpose at all times to preserve it. And now, Mr. Mayor, renewing my thanks for this cordial reception, allow me to come to a close.

February 21, 1861.— ADDRESS TO THE SENATE OF NEW JERSEY.

Mr. President and Gentlemen of the Senate of the State of New Jersey: I am very grateful to you for the honorable reception of which I have been the object. I cannot but remember the place that New Jersey holds in our early history. In the Revolutionary struggle few of the States among the Old Thirteen had more of the battle-fields of the country within their limits than New Jersey. May I be pardoned if, upon this occasion, I mention that away back in my childhood, the earliest days of my being able to read, I got hold of a small book, such a one as few of the younger members have ever seen —Weems' "Life of Washington." I remember all the accounts there given of the battle-fields and struggles for the liberties of the country, and none fixed themselves upon my imagination so deeply as the struggle here at Trenton, New Jersey. The crossing of the river, the contest with the Hessians, the great hardships endured at that time, all fixed themselves on my memory more than any single Revolutionary event; and you all know, for you have all been boys, how these early impressions last longer than any others. I recollect thinking then, boy even though I was, that there must have been something more than common that these men struggled for. I am exceedingly anxious that that thing — that something even more than national independence; that something that held out a great promise to all the people of the world to all time to come — I am exceedingly anxious that this Union, the Constitution, and the liberties of the people shall be perpetuated in accordance with the original idea for which that struggle was made, and I shall be most happy indeed if I shall be a humble instrument in the hands of the Almighty, and of this, his almost chosen people, for perpetuating the object of that great struggle. You give me this reception, as I understand, without distinction of party. I learn that this body is composed of a majority of gentlemen who, in the exercise of their best judgment in the choice of a chief magistrate, did not think I was the man. I understand, nevertheless, that they come forward here to greet me as the constitutionally elected President of the United States—as citizens of the United States to meet the man who, for the time being, is the representative of the majesty of the nation — united by the single purpose to perpetuate the Constitution, the Union, and the liberties of the people. As such, I accept this reception more gratefully than I could do did I believe it were tendered to me as an individual.

February 21, 1861.—ADDRESS TO THE ASSEMBLY OF NEW JERSEY.

Mr. Speaker and Gentlemen : I have just enjoyed the honor of a reception by the other branch of this legislature, and I return to you and them my thanks for the reception which the people of New Jersey have given through their chosen representatives to me as the representative, for the time being, of the majesty of the people of the United States. I appropriate to myself very little of the demonstrations of respect with which I have been greeted. I think little should be given to any man, but that it should be a manifestation of adherence to the Union and the Constitution. I understand myself to be received here by the representatives of the people of New Jersey, a majority of whom differ in opinion from those with whom I have acted. This manifestation is therefore to be regarded by me as expressing their devotion to the Union, the Constitution, and the liberties of the people.

You, Mr. Speaker, have well said that this is a time when the bravest and wisest look with doubt and awe upon the aspect presented by our national affairs. Under these circumstances you will readily see why I should not speak in detail of the course I shall deem it best to pursue. It is proper that I should avail myself of all the information and all the time at my command, in order that when the time arrives in which I must speak officially, I shall be able to take the ground which I deem best and safest, and from which I may have no occasion to swerve. I shall endeavor to take the ground I deem most just to the North, the East, the West, the South, and the whole country. I take it, I hope, in good temper, certainly with no malice toward any section. I shall do all that may be in my power to promote a peaceful settlement of all our difficulties. The man does not live who is more devoted to peace than I am, none who would do more to preserve it, but it may be necessary to put the foot down firmly. [Here the audience broke out into cheers so loud and long that for some moments it was impossible to hear Mr. Lincoln's voice.] And if I do my duty and do right, you will sustain me, will you not? [Loud cheers, and cries of "Yes, yes; we will."] Received as I am by the members of a legislature the majority of whom do not agree with me in political sentiments, I trust that I may have their assistance in piloting the ship of state through this voyage, surrounded by perils as it is; for if it should suffer wreck now, there will be no pilot ever needed for another voyage.

Gentlemen, I have already spoken longer than I intended, and must beg leave to stop here.

February 21, 1861.—REPLY TO THE MAYOR OF PHILADELPHIA, PENNSYLVANIA.

Mr. Mayor and Fellow-citizens of Philadelphia : I appear before you to make no lengthy speech, but to thank you for this reception.

VOL. I.— 44.

The reception you have given me to-night is not to me, the man, the individual, but to the man who temporarily represents, or should represent, the majesty of the nation. It is true, as your worthy mayor has said, that there is great anxiety amongst the citizens of the United States at this time. I deem it a happy circumstance that this dissatisfied portion of our fellow-citizens does not point us to anything in which they are being injured or about to be injured; for which reason I have felt all the while justified in concluding that the crisis, the panic, the anxiety of the country at this time, is artificial. If there be those who differ with me upon this subject, they have not pointed out the substantial difficulty that exists. I do not mean to say that an artificial panic may not do considerable harm; that it has done such I do not deny. The hope that has been expressed by your mayor, that I may be able to restore peace, harmony, and prosperity to the country, is most worthy of him; and most happy, indeed, will I be if I shall be able to verify and fulfil that hope. I promise you that I bring to the work a sincere heart. Whether I will bring a head equal to that heart will be for future times to determine. It were useless for me to speak of details of plans now; I shall speak officially next Monday week, if ever. If I should not speak then, it were useless for me to do so now. If I do speak then, it is useless for me to do so now. When I do speak, I shall take such ground as I deem best calculated to restore peace, harmony, and prosperity to the country, and tend to the perpetuity of the nation and the liberty of these States and these people. Your worthy mayor has expressed the wish, in which I join with him, that it were convenient for me to remain in your city long enough to consult your merchants and manufacturers; or, as it were, to listen to those breathings rising within the consecrated walls wherein the Constitution of the United States, and, I will add, the Declaration of Independence, were originally framed and adopted. I assure you and your mayor that I had hoped on this occasion, and upon all occasions during my life, that I shall do nothing inconsistent with the teachings of these holy and most sacred walls. I have never asked anything that does not breathe from those walls. All my political warfare has been in favor of the teachings that come forth from these sacred walls. May my right hand forget its cunning and my tongue cleave to the roof of my mouth if ever I prove false to those teachings. Fellow-citizens, I have addressed you longer than I expected to do, and now allow me to bid you good-night.

February 22, 1861.—ADDRESS IN INDEPENDENCE HALL, PHILADELPHIA.

Mr. Cuyler: I am filled with deep emotion at finding myself standing in this place, where were collected together the wisdom, the patriotism, the devotion to principle, from which sprang the institutions under which we live. You have kindly suggested to me that in my hands is the task of restoring peace to our distracted country. I can say in return, sir, that all the political sentiments I entertain have been drawn, so far as I have been able to draw them, from the sentiments which originated in and were given to the world from this hall.   I have never had a feeling, politically, that did not spring from the sentiments embodied in the Declaration of Independence.   I have often pondered over the dangers which were incurred by the men who assembled here and framed and adopted that Declaration.   I have pondered over the toils that were endured by the officers and soldiers of the army who achieved that independence. I have often inquired of myself what great principle or idea it was that kept this Confederacy so long together.   It was not the mere matter of separation of the colonies from the motherland, but that sentiment in the Declaration of Independence which gave liberty not alone to the people of this country, but hope to all the world, for all future time.   It was that which gave promise that in due time the weights would be lifted from the shoulders of all men, and that all should have an equal chance.   This is the sentiment embodied in the Declaration of Independence.   Now, my friends, can this country be saved on that basis?   If it can, I will consider myself one of the happiest men in the world if I can help to save it.   If it cannot be saved upon that principle, it will be truly awful.   But if this country cannot be saved without giving up that principle, I was about to say I would rather be assassinated on this spot than surrender it. Now, in my view of the present aspect of affairs, there is no need of bloodshed and war.   There is no necessity for it.   I am not in favor of such a course; and I may say in advance that there will be no bloodshed unless it is forced upon the government.   The government will not use force, unless force is used against it.

My friends, this is wholly an unprepared speech.   I did not expect to be called on to say a word when I came here.   I supposed I was merely to do something toward raising a flag.   I may, therefore, have said something indiscreet.   [Cries of "No, no."]   But I have said nothing but what I am willing to live by, and, if it be the pleasure of Almighty God, to die by.

February 22, 1861.—ADDRESS ON RAISING A FLAG OVER INDEPENDENCE HALL, PHILADELPHIA.

Fellow-citizens: I am invited and called before you to participate in raising above Independence Hall the flag of our country, with an additional star upon it.[1]   I propose now, in advance of performing this very pleasant and complimentary duty, to say a few words.   I propose to say that when the flag was originally raised here, it had but thirteen stars.   I wish to call your attention to the fact that, under the blessing of God, each additional star added to that flag has given additional prosperity and happiness to this country, until it has advanced to its present condition; and its welfare in the future, as well as in the past, is in your hands.   Cultivating the spirit that animated our fathers, who gave renown and celebrity to this hall,

1 The State of Kansas, which was admitted into the Union January 29, 1861.

cherishing that fraternal feeling which has so long characterized us as a nation, excluding passion, ill temper, and precipitate action on all occasions, I think we may promise ourselves that not only the new star placed upon that flag shall be permitted to remain there to our permanent prosperity for years to come, but additional ones shall from time to time be placed there until we shall number, as it was anticipated by the great historian, five hundred millions of happy and prosperous people.

With these few remarks I proceed to the very agreeable duty assigned to me.

February 22, 1861.—REPLY TO GOVERNOR CURTIN OF PENNSYLVANIA, AT HARRISBURG.

Governor Curtin and Citizens of the State of Pennsylvania: Perhaps the best thing that I could do would be simply to indorse the patriotic and eloquent speech which your governor has just made in your hearing. I am quite sure that I am unable to address to you anything so appropriate as that which he has uttered.

Reference has been made by him to the distraction of the public mind at this time and to the great task that is before me in entering upon the administration of the General Government. With all the eloquence and ability that your governor brings to this theme, I am quite sure he does not — in his situation he cannot — appreciate as I do the weight of that great responsibility. I feel that, under God, in the strength of the arms and wisdom of the heads of these masses, after all, must be my support. As I have often had occasion to say, I repeat to you — I am quite sure I do not deceive myself when I tell you I bring to the work an honest heart; I dare not tell you that I bring a head sufficient for it. If my own strength should fail, I shall at least fall back upon these masses, who, I think, under any circumstances will not fail.

Allusion has been made to the peaceful principles upon which this great commonwealth was originally settled. Allow me to add my meed of praise to those peaceful principles. I hope no one of the Friends who originally settled here, or who lived here since that time, or who lives here now, has been or is a more devoted lover of peace, harmony, and concord than my humble self.

While I have been proud to see to-day the finest military array, I think, that I have ever seen, allow me to say, in regard to those men, that they give hope of what may be done when war is inevitable. But, at the same time, allow me to express the hope that in the shedding of blood their services may never be needed, especially in the shedding of fraternal blood. It shall be my endeavor to preserve the peace of this country so far as it can possibly be done consistently with the maintenance of the institutions of the country. With my consent, or without my great displeasure, this country shall never witness the shedding of one drop of blood in fraternal strife.

And now, my fellow-citizens, as I have made many speeches, will you allow me to bid you farewell?

February 22, 1861.—Address to the Legislature of
Pennsylvania, at Harrisburg.

*Mr. Speaker of the Senate, and also Mr. Speaker of the House of
Representatives, and Gentlemen of the General Assembly of the State
of Pennsylvania:* I appear before you only for a very few brief remarks in response to what has been said to me. I thank you most
sincerely for this reception, and the generous words in which support has been promised me upon this occasion. I thank your great
commonwealth for the overwhelming support it recently gave, not
me personally, but the cause which I think a just one, in the late
election.

Allusion has been made to the fact—the interesting fact perhaps
we should say—that I for the first time appear at the capital of the
great commonwealth of Pennsylvania upon the birthday of the
Father of his Country. In connection with that beloved anniversary connected with the history of this country, I have already gone
through one exceedingly interesting scene this morning in the ceremonies at Philadelphia. Under the kind conduct of gentlemen there,
I was for the first time allowed the privilege of standing in old Independence Hall to have a few words addressed to me there, and
opening up to me an opportunity of manifesting my deep regret
that I had not more time to express something of my own feelings
excited by the occasion, that had been really the feelings of my
whole life.

Besides this, our friends there had provided a magnificent flag of
the country. They had arranged it so that I was given the honor of
raising it to the head of its staff, and when it went up I was pleased
that it went to its place by the strength of my own feeble arm.
When, according to the arrangement, the cord was pulled, and it
floated gloriously to the wind, without an accident, in the bright,
glowing sunshine of the morning, I could not help hoping that there
was in the entire success of that beautiful ceremony at least something of an omen of what is to come. Nor could I help feeling then,
as I have often felt, that in the whole of that proceeding I was a very
humble instrument. I had not provided the flag; I had not made
the arrangements for elevating it to its place; I had applied but a
very small portion of even my feeble strength in raising it. In the
whole transaction I was in the hands of the people who had arranged
it, and if I can have the same generous coöperation of the people of
this nation, I think the flag of our country may yet be kept flaunt-
ing gloriously.

I recur for a moment but to repeat some words uttered at the
hotel in regard to what has been said about the military support
which the General Government may expect from the commonwealth
of Pennsylvania in a proper emergency. To guard against any possible mistake do I recur to this. It is not with any pleasure that I
contemplate the possibility that a necessity may arise in this country
for the use of the military arm. While I am exceedingly gratified to
see the manifestation upon your streets of your military force here,

and exceedingly gratified at your promise to use that force upon a proper emergency — while I make these acknowledgments I desire to repeat, in order to preclude any possible misconstruction, that I do most sincerely hope that we shall have no use for them; that it will never become their duty to shed blood, and most especially never to shed fraternal blood. I promise that so far as I may have wisdom to direct, if so painful a result shall in any wise be brought about, it shall be through no fault of mine.

Allusion has also been made by one of your honored speakers to some remarks recently made by myself at Pittsburg in regard to what is supposed to be the especial interest of this great commonwealth of Pennsylvania. I now wish only to say in regard to that matter, that the few remarks which I uttered on that occasion were rather carefully worded. I took pains that they should be so. I have seen no occasion since to add to them or subtract from them. I leave them precisely as they stand, adding only now that I am pleased to have an expression from you, gentlemen of Pennsylvania, signifying that they are satisfactory to you.

And now, gentlemen of the General Assembly of the Commonwealth of Pennsylvania, allow me again to return to you my most sincere thanks.

February 27, 1861.—REPLY TO THE MAYOR OF WASHINGTON, D. C.

Mr. Mayor: I thank you, and through you the municipal authorities of this city who accompany you, for this welcome. And as it is the first time in my life, since the present phase of politics has presented itself in this country, that I have said anything publicly within a region of country where the institution of slavery exists, I will take this occasion to say that I think very much of the ill feeling that has existed and still exists between the people in the section from which I came and the people here, is dependent upon a misunderstanding of one another. I therefore avail myself of this opportunity to assure you, Mr. Mayor, and all the gentlemen present, that I have not now, and never have had, any other than as kindly feelings toward you as to the people of my own section. I have not now, and never have had, any disposition to treat you in any respect otherwise than as my own neighbors. I have not now any purpose to withhold from you any of the benefits of the Constitution, under any circumstances, that I would not feel myself constrained to withhold from my own neighbors; and I hope, in a word, that when we shall become better acquainted — and I say it with great confidence — we shall like each other better. I thank you for the kindness of this reception.

February 28, 1861.— REPLY TO A SERENADE AT WASHINGTON, D. C.

My Friends : I suppose that I may take this as a compliment paid to me, and as such please accept my thanks for it. I have reached this city of Washington under circumstances considerably differing

CPSIA information can be obtained
at www.ICGtesting.com
Printed in the USA
BVHW041333281221
625055BV00004B/178